Lecture Notes in Computer Science 1098

Edited by G. Goos, J. Hartmanis and J. van Leeuwen

Advisory Board: W.

T0230279

Springer

Berlin
Heidelberg
New York
Barcelona
Budapest
Hong Kong
London
Milan
Paris
Santa Clara
Singapore
Tokyo

Pierre Cointe   (Ed.)

ECOOP '96 – Object-Oriented Programming

10th European Conference
Linz, Austria, July 8-12, 1996
Proceedings

Springer

Series Editors

Gerhard Goos, Karlsruhe University, Germany

Juris Hartmanis, Cornell University, NY, USA

Jan van Leeuwen, Utrecht University, The Netherlands

Volume Editor

Pierre Cointe
Ecole Nationale Supérieure des Techniques Industrielles
et des Mines de Nantes
La Chantrerie, 4, rue Alfred Kastler, F-44070 Nantes Cedex, France

Cataloging-in-Publication data applied for

Die Deutsche Bibliothek - CIP-Einheitsaufnahme

Object oriented programming : 10th European conference ;
proceedings / ECOOP '96, Linz, Austria, July 8 - 12, 1996.
Pierre Cointe (ed.). - Berlin ; Heidelberg ; New York ;
Barcelona ; Budapest ; Hong Kong ; London ; Milan ; Paris ;
Santa Clara ; Singapore ; Tokyo : Springer, 1996
   (Lecture notes in computer science ; Vol. 1098)
   ISBN 3-540-61439-7
NE: Cointe, Pierre [Hrsg.]; ECOOP <10, 1996, Linz>; GT

CR Subject Classification (1991): D.1-3, H.2, J.1

ISSN 0302-9743
ISBN 3-540-61439-7 Springer-Verlag Berlin Heidelberg New York

© Springer-Verlag Berlin Heidelberg 1996
Printed in Germany

Typesetting: Camera-ready by author
SPIN 10513259   06/3142 – 5 4 3 2 1 0   Printed on acid-free paper

Preface

This volume constitutes the proceedings of the tenth European Conference on Object-Oriented Programming, ECOOP96, in Linz, Austria, July 8-12 1996.

ECOOP was created in 1987 to structure object-oriented activities taking place in European countries by providing a European forum for theorists and practitioners interested in object-oriented programming. For a decade, ECOOP has established itself as an academic conference with a very high quality standard. In the same time, ECOOP has mainly contributed to the dissemination of object-oriented technology in the software industry. The ECOOP tradition is to move the conference location each year from one country to another. Previous ECOOP conferences were held in Paris (France-87), Oslo (Norway-88), Nottingham (England-89), Ottawa (Canada-90 jointly with OOPSLA), Geneva (Switzerland-91), Utrecht (the Netherlands-92), Kaiserlautern (Germany-93), Bologna (Italy-94) and Åarhus (Denmark-95).
ECOOP97 will be held in Jyväskylä (Finland) next year.

The ECOOP96 programme committee had the hard task of selecting 21 papers out of 173 submissions coming from all over the world. The selection of papers was carried out during a two-day meeting in Nantes. The only selection criteria were the quality and originality of the papers themselves. The papers published in these proceedings are of high quality and reflect the most advanced issues in the field of object-oriented programming. These papers cover a wide range of topics including applications, programming languages, implementation, specification, distribution, databases, and design.
Apart from the presentation of the selected papers, the technical conference also welcomes Adele Goldberg and François Bancilhon as two keynote speakers. ECOOP96 offers also 2 panels, 15 workshops, 17 tutorials, demonstrations, posters, and exhibits.

The success of such an international conference is due to the dedication of the members of various committees. We thank the authors for submitting such a large number of papers, and the reviewers and the program committee members for reviewing and selecting the papers contained herein. We thank I. Guyon for organizing the program committee and the student helpers: P. Mulet, F. Rivard and T. Ledoux. Special thanks to G. Kappel the organizing chair and to all other members of the Executive Committee and all local organizers.

AITO has continued to provide an essential support to the conference. The committee members also wish to thank their employers and sponsors for support of these conference activities. Finally, we thank the attendees and hope that you enjoy the conference and the proceedings.

April 1996   P. Cointe
                                                                ECOOP96 Programme Chair

Organization

ECOOP'96 is organized by the Institute of Computer Science of the Johannes Kepler University of Linz under the auspices of AITO (Association Internationale pour les Technologies Objets).

Executive Committee

Conference Co-Chairs: Oscar Nierstrasz (University of Berne, CH)
                         Peter Wegner (Brown University, USA)
Programme Chair: Pierre Cointe (École des Mines de Nantes & OTI Inc, F)
Organizing Chair: Gerti Kappel (University of Linz, A)
Tutorials: Hanspeter Mössenböck (University of Linz, A)
Workshops: Max Mühlhäeuser (University of Linz, A)
Panels: Markku Sakkinen (University of Jyväskylä, FIN)
Exhibits, Demos & Posters: Wolfgang Pree (University of Linz, A)

Program Committee

Mehmet Aksit (University of Twente, NL)
Giuseppe Attardi (University of Pisa, I)
François Bancilhon (O2 Technology, F)
Yves Caseau (Bouygues, F)
Pierre Cointe (Ecole des Mines de Nantes & OTI Inc, F, Chair)
James O. Coplien (OOPSLA'96 program chair)
Theo D'Hondt (Brussels Free University, B)
Erich Gamma (IFS Consulting, CH)
Rachid Guerraoui (École Polytechnique Fédérale de Lausanne, CH)
Ivar Jacobson (Rational, USA)
Mehdi Jazayeri (Technical University of Vienna, A)
Gregor Kiczales (Xerox PARC, USA)
Karl Lieberherr (Northeastern University, USA)
Ole Lehrmann Madsen (Aarhus University, DK)
Tom Maibaum (Imperial College, UK)
Boris Magnusson (Lund University, S)
Jacques Malenfant (University of Montreal, CDN)
José Meseguer (SRI, USA)
Bertrand Meyer (ISE, USA & F)
Max Mühlhäeuser (University of Linz, A)
Walter Olthoff (DFKI GmbH, D)
Jens Palsberg (MIT, USA)
Markku Sakkinen (University of Jyväskylä, FIN)
Dave Thomas (OTI Inc, CDN)
Mario Tokoro (Keio University/Sony CSL, J)
Akinori Yonezawa (Tokyo University, J)
Roberto Zicari (J.W.Goethe-University, D)

Referees

Bruno Achauer	Antonio Albano	Nicolas Anquetil
Didier Badouel	Jakob Bardram	Lodewijk Bergmans
Susanne Bødker	Jan Borchers	Isabelle Borne
Søren Brandt	Frank Buddrus	Henrik Bærbak Christensen
Laurent Dami	Marco Danelutto	Gerald Ehmayer
Erik Ernst	Christian Falkowski	Pascal Felber
Fabrizio Ferrandina	GianLuigi Ferrari	Harald Gall
Giorgio Ghelli	Görel Hedin	Roger Henriksson
Jean-Marc Jézéquel	Gerti Kappel	Kazuhiko Kato
Rudolf Keller	Markus Knasmüller	Piet Koopmans
Kevib Lano	Sven-Eric Lautemann	Jørgen Lindskov Knudsen
Rainer Lischka	Paolo Mancarella	Knut Manske
Hidehiko Masuhara	Satoshi Matsuoka	Rui Oliveira
Salvatore Orlando	Susanna Pelagatti	Stefan Rausch-Schott
Chrislain Razafimahefa	Siegfried Reich	Werner Retschitzegger
Annya Romanczuck	Rimbert Rudisch	Elmer Sandvad
Christoph Schommer	Michael Schwartzbach	Laura Semini
Maria Simi	Christoph Steindl	Thomas Strasser
Kenjiro Taura	Bedir Tekinerdogan	Josef Templ
Georg Trausmuth	Franco Turini	Alexandre Valente Sousa
Klaas van den Berg	Pim van den Broek	Maurice van Keulen
Marco Vanneschi	Mark Vermeer	Jan Vitek
Roland Wagner	Stéphane Wehrli	Rene Wenzel Schmidt

Cooperating Institutions of ECOOP'96

ACM/SIGPLAN (Association of Computing Machinery - Special Interest Group in Programming Languages)
IEEE Computer Society
AFCET (French Computer Society)
GI (Gesellschaft für Informatik)
SI (Schweizer Informatiker Gesellschaft)
OCG (Österreichische Computergesellschaft)
ÖGI (Österreichische Gesellschaft für Informatik)
ADV (Arbeitsgemeinschaft für Datenverarbeitung)
TMG (Upper-Austria Technology and Marketing Corporation)

Sponsoring Institutions

Johannes Kepler University of Linz
State Government of Upper Austria
Head Municipality of Linz

Christian Doppler Laboratory for Software Engineering, University of Linz
Department of Information Systems, University of Linz
Externa Salzburg GmbH
Wissenschaftshilfe der Wirtschaftskammer Oberösterreich
Elektro Bau AG, Linz
Fallmann & Bauernfeind, Linz-Puchenau
Focus Software Consult, Wien
GMO GmbH, Wien
IBM Österreich GmbH
KEBA GmbH & Co., Linz
Porsche Informatik, Salzburg
Raiffeisenlandesbank Oberösterreich
Siemens AG Austria
Siemens-Nixdorf Informationssysteme AG Austria
TakeFive Software, Salzburg
VOEST-Alpine Stahl Linz GmbH

Contents

Implementation/Dispatching

Specifications/Semantics/Inheritance2

Distribution

Databases

Language Design/OO Modelling

Keynote Address 1

Measurement Strategies
Adele Goldberg
ParcPlace-Digitalk Inc.

After ten years of attention to the development and use of object technology, how do we measure up? In software development projects, we measure for two reasons: to find out how we are doing relative to plan, and to determine whether we have reached our stated goals. We measure by counting those objective attributes of projects–products, processes, and resources–that provide useful information for managers, developers, and customers alike. But we only measure when we clearly understand how to objectively count and how what we count answers the questions we pose about our goals. A software code testing strategy is therefore only a part of an overall measurement program.

In this talk, I identify a technique for setting up an effective measurement program. The technique combines the ideas proposed in earlier publications about project management decision frameworks with basic quality assurance strategies. An application of this technique is used to measure whether we, as an industry, are meeting our goals for object technology.

Dr. Adele Goldberg serves as Chairman of the Board and a founder of ParcPlace-Digitalk, Inc. Prior to the creation of ParcPlace, Adele received a Ph.D. in Information Science from the University of Chicago and spent 14 years as researcher and laboratory manager of Xerox Palo Alto Research Center. From 1984-1986, Adele served as president of the ACM, the computer professional society. Solely and with others, Adele wrote the definitive books on the Smalltalk-80 system and has authored numerous papers on project management and analysis methodology using object-oriented technology. Dr. Goldberg edited "The History of Personal Workstations," published jointly by the ACM and Addison-Wesley in 1988 as part of the ACM Press Book Series of the History of Computing which she organized, and co-edited "Visual Object-Oriented Programming" with Margaret Burnett and Ted Lewis. In 1995, a new book on software engineering appeared entitled "Succeeding With Objects: Decision Frameworks for Project Management" with Kenneth S. Rubin. She was recipient of the ACM Systems Software Award in 1987 along with Dan Ignalls and Alan Kay, PC Magazine's 1990 Lifetime Achievement Award for her significant contributions to the personal computer industry, is a Fellow of the ACM, and was honored in 1995 with the Reed College Howard Vollum Award for contributions to science and technology. She is currently a member of the scientific advisory board of the German National Research Centers (GMD).

Keynote Address 2

Will Europe ever Produce and sell Objects?
François Bancilhon
O2 Technology

Europe has progressively dropped out of a number of hardware markets (microprocessors, workstations, PC, scientific computers, etc.). It has never been very active (despite a number of bright exceptions) on the software product market (languages, databases, operating systems, tools, etc.).

The quality and the success of this conference is a good demonstration of both the quality of European research and of the interest European users have in object technology. In the long run, however, the presence of this active community can only be justified by its participation in a global industrial effort to deliver object technology to users. Object technology, as an emerging market represent a tremendous opportunity and it is worth wondering whether Europe will seize it.

I will try to identify some of the reasons for the current state of the European software industry, study some of the success stories in this area and try to draw some conclusions on what could be done to change the current situation.

Born in 1948, Francois Bancilhon got his PhD from The University of Michigan in 1976, and the University of Paris XI in 1980. He was a researcher at INRIA from 1976 to 1980, doing theoretical work on relational databases. He was a professor at the University of Paris XI from 1981 to 1984 where he worked on database machines. He was a team Leader & chief architect at MCC, Austin, Texas, from 1984 to 1986 developping a deductive database systems. He managed the Altair R&D consortium in France from 1986 to 1991. This group designed and developed O2, an object database management system. In 1991, he founded O2 Technology, (Versailles and Palo Alto). O2 Technology is Number One on the European object database market.

Type-Safe Compilation of Covariant Specialization: A Practical Case

John Boyland[1]* and Giuseppe Castagna[2]

[1] University of California at Berkeley, Berkeley CA 94720-1776, USA
[2] CNRS, LIENS-DMI, École Normale Supérieure, 45 rue d'Ulm, 75005 Paris, France

Abstract. Despite its lack of type safety, some typed object-oriented languages use *covariant* specialization for methods. In this work, we show how one may modify the semantics of languages that use covariant specialization in order to improve their type safety. We demonstrate our technique using O_2, a strongly and statically typed object-oriented database programming language which uses covariant specialization. We propose a modification to the O_2 compiler that adds code to correct previously ill-typed computations that arise from the use of covariant specialization. The modification we propose does not affect the semantics of those computations without type errors. Furthermore, the new semantics of the previously ill-typed computations is defined in a very "natural" way and ensures the type safety (w.r.t. covariance) of the program. Since the solution consists of a conservative backward-compatible modification of the compiler, it does not require, unlike other solutions, any modification of existing O_2 code. Our solution is based solely on a type-theoretic analysis and thus is general. Therefore, although this paper applies it to a particular programming language, the same ideas could easily be applied to other languages that use covariant specialization.

1 Introduction

Strongly-typed object-oriented languages impose conditions in order to statically ensure type safety for method overriding. In particular, in the presence of subtyping, type safety requires that the type of the result of the overriding method be a subtype of the type of the result of the overridden one, and that the types of the parameters of the overridden method are subtypes of those of the corresponding parameters in the overriding one. In type theory, this rule is said to be *covariant* in the result type (since it preserves the sense of the subtype relation) and *contravariant* on the parameters' types (since it inverts the sense of the relation). Since the parameter behavior is taken as representative, one speaks in this case of *contravariant specialization*.

Although type-safe, contravariant specialization restricts the flexibility of a language considerably. For this reason, some object-oriented language designers put expressiveness above strict type safety and instead adopt the more flexible *covariant specialization* rule, which requires exactly the opposite subtyping relation for parameters, namely that

---

* The work of John Boyland was supported in part by Advanced Research Projects Agency grant MDA972-92-J-1028, and by NSF Infrastructure grant CDA-9401156. The content of this paper does not necessarily reflect the position or the policy of the U. S. Government, and no official endorsement should be inferred.

the type of the parameters in the overriding method are subtypes of those of the corresponding parameters in the overridden one. It would seem that one cannot combine covariant specialization and inheritanced-based subtyping in a type-safe manner.

In the last years, several solutions have been suggested to retain some of the flexibility of covariant specialization in a type-safe framework. These solutions propose new languages constructs (e.g. [Cas95a]), or new relations on types (e.g. [Bru94]), or the use of different typing techniques for the methods (e.g. [BHJL86]): see [BCC+96] for a wide review. However, none of them can be directly applied to programs written in languages that use covariant specialization. To use these solutions, one has to throw away the programs written with covariant specialization, and to rewrite them from scratch either in a different language or in a extended version of the old language. In many practical cases, such as in large databases, a complete rewrite of the existing code would be much too expensive, even if feasible. Such cases are not merely hypothetical, since the world's third most popular commercial object-oriented database system, O_2, uses covariant specialization.

Despite its great practical implications, nearly no work to our knowledge has tried to handle the problem of ensuring the type safety of existing code that uses covariant specialization. A notable exception to this is given by the work done for the language Eiffel [Mey91, Mey96]. Eiffel uses covariant redefinition, but uses an additional check, the "system validity" check to detect possible type errors admitted due to covariant specialization. Currently, the definition of Eiffel gives a link-time (i.e. global) data-flow analysis for this purpose, but Meyer has proposed a new check that can be done locally. Due to its complexity, the current definition is not incorporated into any widely available compiler. The new check is much less complex, but may possibly prove too strict. Either analysis guarantees type-safety but can only reject programs with potential type errors.

In this article we propose another solution, different from Eiffel's, but in the same spirit, since it can be directly applied to the existing code. What we show is that it is not necessary to rewrite or discard any programs, since by slightly changing the interpretation of the programs, we can ensure complete type safety. Furthermore, this change will affect only those computations that would otherwise have undefined semantics due to a type error.

In other words, type theoretic research so far addresses the question: *How should I have written my program to obtain type safety and also the flexibility of covariant specialization without using it?* The analysis for Eiffel answers the question: *Is my program type-safe even if I used covariant specialization?* The problem addressed by this article is substantially different. This work answers the question: *How can I change the semantics of my programs that use covariant specialization in order to ensure type safety?*

Of course, the new semantics must satisfy some minimal requirements:

1. The new semantics must be conservative over (dynamically) type-safe programs, in the sense that the programs that worked safely even with covariance must not be

affected by the change. In other words, programs that have no type problems must have, with the new semantics, the same meaning as with the old semantics.

2. The new semantics of ill-typed computations[3] must be somehow "natural", in the sense that the definition of the new semantics must take into account why an ill-typed situation has been reached and what could reasonably be its intended meaning. The new semantics must recover from the errors, not simply hide them.

We describe our solution which fulfils these requirements by applying it to O_2, a strongly-typed object-oriented database programming language [BDK92] that uses covariant specialization together with run-time checks to ensure type safety. The choice is not arbitrary since the question we address is acutely pertinent in the presence of persistent data. In particular, we sketch how to modify the standard O_2 compiler to make O_2's covariant specialization rule type-safe. Our solution does not require any source code to be changed, neither does it require the "bases" to be recompiled; a "schema" recompilation will suffice.[4]

Although in this paper, we apply our ideas to a particular programming language, our solution is general. Being based solely on type theoretic observations, it can be applied to other languages that uses covariant specialization, to yield a type-safe semantics, or it can be used to define a *new* type-safe object-oriented language that provides covariant specialization.

The work is organized as follows. Section 2 introduces O_2 and shows why covariant specialization is not type-safe. Section 3 reviews the work on multi-methods done in [Cas95a]. These ideas are used in Section 4 to illustrate the solution we propose here in the case of single inheritance. Section 5 shows that the naive extension of the previous solution to multiple inheritance doesn't work and uses this analysis to describe a more sophisticated solution that does work. We close our presentation by comparing our work with other solutions presented in the literature.

2 The Language O_2 and Covariance

O_2 is a strongly-typed, object-oriented database programming language. The most important aspect of O_2's type system, as with most typed object-oriented languages, is its *subtyping relation*. Subtyping allows a value of a *subtype* to be used anywhere a value of the *supertype* is expected. The use of this relation enhances the flexibility of the language since it allows the values of a given type to use operations originally defined for a different type.

However, the O_2 type discipline is not safe; type errors may occur at run-time, even if a program has successfully passed static type checking.[5] In particular, type errors

---

[3] By an *ill-typed computation* we mean a computation that includes at least one *ill-typed application*: an application of a function or a method to an argument whose type is not compatible with the parameter type (the domain) of the function/method.

[4] In O_2 jargon, the *schema* of a database is the description of the structure and the behavior of the data; it essentially consists of class and method definitions. A collection of data (objects and values) whose structure and behavior conforms to the definitions in a schema is called *base*. A schema may be created and modified without a reference to a particular base and it can be shared by several bases, while a base must always refer to a single schema.

[5] In classical languages, the definition of a type error is well-known. In addition, in object-oriented languages, sending a message to an object that cannot respond to it is considered a type error.

may arise due to the use of covariant specialization. We demonstrate the problem by an example:[6]

```
class Point
   type tuple (x:real,
               y:real)
   method equal(p:Point):boolean
end;

method body equal(p:Point):boolean in class Point
   return( self->x == p->x && self->y == p->y );;


class ColorPoint inherit Point
   type tuple(c:string)              /* x and y are inherited from Point */
   method equal(p:ColorPoint):boolean
end;

method body equal(p:ColorPoint):boolean in class ColorPoint
   return( self->x == p->x && self->y == p->y && self->c == p->c );
```

We have two classes that represent two-dimensional points and colored points respectively. The class Point has two instance variables x and y of type real and a method for the message equal that returns a boolean when applied to an argument of class Point. Its definition compares the instance variables of the receiver of the message (self) with the ones of the argument. The class ColorPoint is obtained by inheritance from Point. To represent the color, it adds the instance variable c to those inherited from Point. It redefines (or, *overrides*) the method for the message equal, in order to take into account the color of the point.

In O_2, an overriding method must satisfy the following covariant specialization rule:

1. It must have the same number of parameters as the method it overrides.
2. The type of each parameter must be a (possibly improper) subtype of the type of the corresponding parameter in the overridden method.
3. The type of the result must be smaller than or equal to the type of the result of the overridden method.

The classes Point and ColorPoint satisfy these conditions. The rule is quite intuitive, but it is not type-safe, as can be demonstrated by adding the following method to the class Point:

```
method break_it(p:Point) in class Point;
method body  break_it(p:Point) in class Point {p->equal(self);}
```

This method[7] sends the message equal to the parameter p and with self as argument. It is easy to verify that, although the command (new Point)->break_it(new

---

[6] We use version 4.0 of O_2 and we specify the methods in O_2C.

[7] In O_2, methods can be declared outside class definitions, as in the example above. This allows one to add new methods to an existing class or to redefine the old methods.

ColorPoint) is well typed according to the rules of O_2 (the command new creates a new instance of the specified class), it leads to a type error: its execution produces the ill-typed application of the equal method in ColorPoint to an argument of class Point.[8]

The problem arises from the covariance introduced in condition (2). Type theory states that a class C_2 is a subtype of another class C_1 (namely, that objects of C_2 can be type-safely used wherever an object of C_1 is expected) only if the methods defined in C_1 can be type-safely replaced by those of C_2 [Car88]. If a method for a message is inherited in C_2, then no typing issue is raised, since the method is the same for C_1 and C_2. If the method is redefined in C_2, type safety is ensured only if the new method can replace the method defined in C_1 *in every context*. In particular, the method in C_2 must be able to handle at least the same arguments that can be passed to the method in C_1. In our example with points, the method for equal in Point accepts arguments of type *Point* while the one in ColorPoint does not. The type error in the call of break_it is caused by the fact that the method for equal in ColorPoint is applied to an argument of type *Point*, a legal argument for the method it overrides.

More formally, the problem is that the type *ColorPoint* $\rightarrow$ *boolean* of the equal method in ColorPoint is not a subtype of *Point* $\rightarrow$ *boolean*.[9] Indeed recall that by definition of subtyping, $S \rightarrow T \leq S' \rightarrow T'$ holds only if every function f of type $S \rightarrow T$ can be used where a function g of type $S' \rightarrow T'$ is expected. This implies that the result of f (of type T) must be able to replace the result of g (of type T'), i.e. $T \leq T'$; and that f can handle any argument g can, i.e. $S' \leq S$. Thus the orientation of the inequality of the arrow is inverted on the domains: the subtyping rule is "contravariant" in the left component of the arrow.

In conclusion, to ensure type safety in an object-oriented language (such as used in O_2), one must require that the types of the parameters of an overriding method are *supertypes* of those of the parameters of the overridden method. Otherwise the subclass cannot be considered a subtype of its superclass, and thus objects of the subclass cannot be used where objects of the superclass are expected. This rule disallows a useful specialization of equal in ColorPoint, because there is no way to compute the color component of an argument known only to be a *Point*. Going ahead with the specialization would mean that the class ColorPoint would not be a subtype of the class Point, and thus that colored point could not be used where points are expected. Thus, it appears one is left with the choice between a useful subtype relation and a useful specialization.

The designers of O_2 have preferred to give up some type safety, and to adopt covariant specialization. In the next section, we show that there is way to allow covariant specialization without sacrificing type safety.

---

[8] Note that the kind of error produced by break_it is not so hard to generate. Every function that needs to test the equality of two parameters of type Point may generate a type error of this sort.

[9] According to the O_2's notation, the types of the methods for equal in ColorPoint and Point are, respectively, *ColorPoint* $\times$ *ColorPoint* $\rightarrow$ *boolean* and *Point* $\times$ *Point* $\rightarrow$ *boolean* since the type of the receiver (i.e. of self) is included among the parameters of the method. In order to simplify the exposition, we will omit the receiver's type from the type of the methods. This omission does not affect the core of our discussion. For more details on receiver types, see [Cas95a].

3 Multi-methods

Our solution for making covariant specialization type-safe uses multi-methods. Multi-methods appear in the CLOS language [DG87] and their typing issues have been studied in [ADL91, CGL95, Cas96, CL95]. However, none of these approaches can be directly applied to the case of O_2, since they do not retain the notion of method encapsulation: there is no privileged receiver —as in O_2— to which a message is sent. Thus in this article, we utilize a different kind of multi-methods, those studied in [Cas95a, MHH91] (and, implicitly, also in [Ing86]). These multi-methods allow the use of multiple dispatching (i.e., the possibility that the selection of a method is also based on other arguments of the message) even in presence of a privileged receiver. (A detailed comparison between the two kinds of multi-methods can be found in [BCC+96]).

In particular, it is possible to have type-safe covariant specialization when using this second kind of multi-method with late-binding [Cas95a]. We demonstrate the idea with the Point/ColorPoint example introduced in the previous section. The problem with the definition of equal in ColorPoint is that it cannot handle arguments of type *Point*. The intuition of our solution is that some code can be added to compensate for this deficiency. The original method definition is executed for arguments of type *ColorPoint* while the new code handles arguments of type *Point*. In practice, this corresponds to changing the definition of ColorPoint:

```
class ColorPoint inherit Point
    type tuple(c:string)
    method equal(p:Point):boolean,
           equal(p:ColorPoint):boolean
end;

method body equal(p:Point):boolean in class ColorPoint
  {return( self->x == p->x && self->y == p->y );};

method body equal(p:ColorPoint):boolean in class ColorPoint
  {return( self->x == p->x && self->y == p->y && self->c == p->c );};
```

There are now two different *method branches* (*branches* for short) for the message equal in ColorPoint. Both method branches together can be considered a single *multi-method*.[10] When the message equal is sent to an object of type *ColorPoint*, one of the two method branches is selected for execution according to the type of the argument. If the argument is of type *Point*, the first branch is used; if it is of type *ColorPoint*, or of a subtype, the the second method branch is used. The selection of the branch is performed at run-time after the argument of the message has been fully evaluated. This is a crucial feature that differentiates multi-methods from C++'s overloaded methods (where the selection is performed at compile time), and ensures the appropriate use of the covariant specialization. Consider the fragment p->equal(self) in the code of break_it in Point; self has static type *Point*, therefore if the selection of the method were performed at compile time, the first branch of equal would be always executed, even for

---

[10] These kinds of multi-methods are called *multivariant* in [MHH91] and *encapsulated multi-methods* in [BCC+96] in order to distinguish them from CLOS's multi-methods.

```
(new ColorPoint)->break_it(new ColorPoint)
```

Here, we would expect the two points to be compared also in their color component.

What then are the rules that ensure the type safety of this approach? Recall that type safety is guaranteed only if every overriding method possesses a subtype of the type of the method it overrides. The type of a multi-method is the set of the types of its various branches. The subtyping relation between sets of types (not to be confused with the type of sets) states that one set of types is smaller than another set of types only if for every type contained in the latter, there exists a type in the former smaller than it.[11] This fits the intuition that one multi-method can be replaced by another multi-method of different type, when for every method branch that can be selected in the former, there is one in the latter that can replace it (for subtyping, an ordinary method is considered to be a multi-method with just one branch: its type is a singleton).

In the new version of the point example, the type of the multi-method for equal in ColorPoint is $\{Point \to boolean, ColorPoint \to boolean\}$. By the rule above we have

$$\{Point \to boolean, ColorPoint \to boolean\} \leq \{Point \to boolean\}$$

Since $\{Point \to boolean\}$ is the type of the method associated with equal in Point, the subtyping condition is fulfilled and type safety ensured.

More generally, if one wishes to override a method[12] and covariantly specialize the type of its parameters, it is necessary also to add another branch to handle the arguments that could be passed to the overridden method.

Adding multi-method branches to achieve type safety does not require a large amount of programming: in case of single inheritance, the number of branches sufficient to override covariant methods is independent from both the size and the depth of the inheritance hierarchy; it is always equal to two. Indeed, when a multi-method of type $\{S_1 \to T_1, \ldots, S_n \to T_n\}$ is applied to an argument of type U, the branch executed is the one defined for the type $S_j = \min_{i=1..n}\{S_i \mid U \leq S_i\}$. Thus a single branch with a sufficiently high (in the inheritance hierarchy) type may handle all the remaining arguments that are not handled by the specializing code. For example, suppose that we further specialize our point hierarchy by adding dimensions, each with their own equal methods:

```
class Point3D inherit Point
      type tuple(z:real)
      method equal(p:Point3D) : boolean
end;
```

```
class Point4D inherit Point3D
      type tuple(w:real)
      method equal(p:Point4D) : boolean
end;
```

and so on, up to dimension n. The new classes form a chain in the inheritance hierarchy. Each class covariantly overrides the equal method inherited from its superclass. It may appear to be necessary to add $n - 2$ more branches to each class Point$n$D in order to

---

[11] The subtyping relation for function types is, of course, the contravariant rule defined before.

[12] We assume here that overriding a multi-method overrides all its branches.

guarantee safety; however, one additional branch with a parameter of type *Point* suffices. This branch will handle all other possible points. For example, in the case of $n = 4$, one could define

```
class Point4D inherit Point3D
    type tuple(w:real);
    method equal(p:Point4D) : boolean,
           equal(p:Point)  : boolean
end;

method body equal(p:Point4D):boolean in class Point4D
  {return( self->x == p->x && self->y == p->y
        && self->z == p->z && self->w == p->w );};

method body equal(p:Point):boolean in class Point4D
  {return( p->equal(self) ); }
```

Type safety stems from the fact that the subtyping condition is satisfied.[13]

In conclusion, if we extend the syntax of O_2 with multi-methods, we can have type safety and covariant specialization. Every time we perform a covariant specialization in a class with a single direct superclass, it will suffice to add one (and one only) branch to handle all the arguments "inherited" from the superclasses, although one may wish to add multiple branches for semantic reasons.

This still does not solve the problem we want to address with this work and which concerns existing O_2 code. In the rest of this paper, we show that a compiler can automatically add branches that make a program type-safe. Note that the type safety is obtained without any modification of the source code.

A more formal treatment of multi-methods can be found in [Cas95a]. For the formal type system and the proof of its type safety see [CGL95]. Examples of type safe use of multi-methods in programming languages with a privileged receiver are proposed in [MHH91], [Cas95b] and [Cas96].

4 Single inheritance

We first describe our solution as it applies when there is only single inheritance. We generalize this solution to multiple inheritance hierarchies in Section 5.

For this section, we use $\varsigma(C)$ to denote the unique *direct superclass* of C, i.e. the class that follows the inherit keyword in the definition of C. Besides this notation, we need to introduce some more O_2 syntax.

---

[13] In general, according to the subtyping rule for multi-methods, if $T_1 \geq T_2 \geq \ldots \geq T_n$ and $S_1 \geq S_2 \geq \ldots \geq S_n$ then we have the following type inequalities:

$$\{S_n \rightarrow T_n, S_1 \rightarrow T_{n-1}\} \leq \ldots \leq \{S_{i+1} \rightarrow T_{i+1}, S_1 \rightarrow T_i\} \leq \{S_i \rightarrow T_i, S_1 \rightarrow T_{i-1}\} \leq \ldots \leq \{S_1 \rightarrow T_1\}$$

The declarations of the classes for points are a special case of this, where $S_1 =$ *Point*, for $i \in [3..n]$ $S_{i-1} =$ *PointiD*, and for $i \in [1..n-1]$ $T_i =$ *boolean*.

4.1 The @ notation

In O_2, it is possible to invoke the method attached to a specific class by the following @-notation: r->C@m. This invokes the method attached to the message m in the class C instead of the one attached in the class of the receiver r, provided that the latter is a subclass of C. In particular, in this work we use the @-notation in commands of the form self->A@m which inside a proper subclass of A dispatches the message m to self but it starts the search for the method associated to m from the class A. This mechanism is different from the super mechanism of, say, Smalltalk: suppose that the class A defines a method for the message m, that the class B is defined by inheritance from A (i.e. $A = \varsigma(B)$) and that B inherits from A the method for m. Then self->A@m always begins the search for the method for m from the class A (thus, in this case it is equivalent to self->m), while super->m begins the search from the superclass of the class containing the method, namely from the superclass of A (therefore, in this example it is equivalent to self->$\varsigma(A)$@m). In other words, the @-notation expresses absolute addressing, whereas super is a relative addressing.

4.2 The solution

We start the presentation of our solution in the simplified case of methods with just one parameter. Suppose we have two classes C_0 and C_n in a chain $C_n < C_{n-1} < \ldots < C_0$, defined by the following program

```
class C₀
    type ...                        /* The type is not important */
    method m(x:S₀):T₀
end;

class Cₙ inherit Cₙ₋₁
    method m(x:Sₙ):Tₙ
end
```

where $S_n < S_0$ and $T_n \leq T_0$. Suppose also that the message m has not been redefined in the inheritance hierarchy between C_n and C_0. Our solution has the compiler add the following method branch to C_n:

```
method m(x:S₀):T₀ in class Cₙ;
method body m(x:S₀):T₀ in class Cₙ { return(self->Cₙ₋₁@m(x)); }
```

The program is now type-safe since by the subtyping rule of multi-methods $\{S_0 \rightarrow T_0, S_n \rightarrow T_n\} \leq \{S_0 \rightarrow T_0\}$, that is, the type of the (multi-)method in C_n is smaller than the type of the method in C_0 it overrides. Note also that since m has not been redefined between C_0 and C_n, the type of self->C_{n-1}@m(x) is the type of the result of the method in C_0 (that is, T_0) and that therefore the body of the new method branch conforms to its signature. This same branch must also be added to all subclasses of C_n which *invariantly override* m, by which we mean that the parameter type of m remains the same in the redefinition.

In the case in which m has been covariantly redefined multiple times in the hierarchy between C_0 and S_0, our solution has the compiler add multiple branches. For example, suppose that for a class C_i, $C_n < C_i < C_0$, the method for m has been redefined with signature $S_i \to T_i$, where $S_n < S_i < S_0$, but that it is not redefined elsewhere between C_0 and C_n. Then the compiler will add to the class C_i a method branch of type $S_0 \to T_0$, and will add two method branches to C_n: one of type $S_0 \to T_0$ and another of type $S_i \to T_i$.

```
method m(x:Sᵢ):Tᵢ in class Cₙ;
method body m(x:Sᵢ):Tᵢ in class Cₙ { return(self->Cₙ₋₁@m(x)); }
```

```
method m(x:S₀):T₀ in class Cₙ;
method body m(x:S₀):T₀ in class Cₙ { return(self->Cₙ₋₁@m(x)); }
```

By the multi-method subtyping rule we have

$$\underbrace{\{S_0 \to T_0, S_i \to T_i, S_n \to T_n\}}_{\text{type of } m \text{ in } C_n} \quad \leq \quad \underbrace{\{S_0 \to T_0, S_i \to T_i\}}_{\text{type of } m \text{ in } C_i} \quad \leq \quad \underbrace{\{S_0 \to T_0\}}_{\text{type of } m \text{ in } C_0}$$

The subtyping condition is fulfilled since the type of every overriding (multi-)method is a subtype of the type of the (multi-)method it overrides. This guarantees type safety.[14] Both added method branch bodies have the same code; each uses a different branch of the multi-method $\texttt{self->}C_{n-1}@m$. We will return to this fact after describing the algorithm more precisely.

Viewed as a top-down process over the inheritance hierarchy, our solution descends the inheritance hierarchy looking for the first class containing a covariant redefinition of a given message. When it finds one, it adds to the class a branch that points to the last definition of the message, and continues to descend the hierarchy looking for the next class where the message is redefined (either covariantly or invariantly). If the redefinition is invariant, it adds to the class all the branches that were added to the last definition; if the redefinition is covariant, it adds the same branches plus one branch that points to the last definition.

The general task of the compiler can be described as follows

Algorithm 1. For every class C, for every message m overridden in C with type $S \to T$, and for every superclass C_i (for which m has type $S_i \to T_i$) where m is covariantly redefined in the direct subclass C_{i+1} to $S_{i+1} \to T_{i+1}$ (that is $C \leq C_{i+1} < C_i$, $\varsigma(C_{i+1}) = C_i$, $S \leq S_{i+1} < S_i$), add the following method branch:

```
method m(x:Sᵢ):Tᵢ in class C;
method body m(x:Sᵢ):Tᵢ in class C { return(self->ς(C)@m(x)); }
```

∎

The intuition underlying this rule is that the compiler adds branches to handle all possible arguments that are not handled by the original redefinition. There is a one-to-one correspondence between the superclasses of a class (including itself) that covariantly redefine a method, and method branches one has to add to it.

---

[14] For those familiar with [Cas95a] note that O_2's covariance rule ensures that the overloaded types are well formed.

Note that the method body declarations are well typed (this can be proved by induction on the depth of the inheritance hierarchy). Note also that all the added branches perform the same thing: they search up in the inheritance hierarchy for the first definition of a method that can handle the argument. In practice, the compiler can collapse all the added branches into a single branch to be selected when the argument is of a supertype of that in the covariant method. This branch simply performs a lookup in the inheritance hierarchy. This observation is used in Section 4.5 to give an implementation of our solution. Since our methods already have multi-method type, with a little abuse of notation, we could use multi-method typed branches as well. For the second example with C_n, C_i and C_0, the addition would look like

```
method m:{S₀ → T₀, Sᵢ → Tᵢ} in class Cₙ
method body m(x) in class Cₙ { return(self->ς(Cₙ)@m(x)); }
```

Intuitively, such a (multi-)method is selected when the type of the argument is a subtype of S_i (in which case the result will be of type T_i), or is a type included between S_0 and S_i (in which case the result is of type T_0)[15].

More generally, when a message m has been covariantly overridden, the compiler adds a single branch of multi-method type to the class. The type of this branch is that of the superclass' definition of the method, except that we ignore any method type whose domain is the same as the one defined for this class. Intuitively, this branch handles all the cases handled by the superclass that are not handled in the overriding method. This understanding can be expressed by reformulating the previous algorithm in the following implementation-oriented way:

Algorithm 1 (Implementation-Oriented Version) For every class C, for every message m that is redefined in C whose type is not a subtype of the method defined in some superclass, add the following branch:

```
method m : typeof(ς(C)@m)/{S} in class C
method body m(x) in class C { return(self->ς(C)@m(x)); }
```

where S is the parameter type of m in C, $typeof(.)$ is a meta-operator that returns the type of a (multi-)method, and $T/\{S\}$ denotes the multi-method type T in which a possible arrow of domain S has been erased. ∎

It is not necessary that the syntax of the language being made safe actually allow these new multi-methods, since the method is added by the compiler as a part of the implementation, as shown in Section 4.5. This notation is only used to express implementation at the source level.

4.3 Naturalness

In the introduction, we state that our solution is natural. First of all, note that the semantics of well-typed programs is not modified: indeed all the (non-functional) expressions have, after the compiler's completion, the same type as before the completion. Thus in the

---

[15] Note that it is not necessary to restate the type of the branch in the body declaration since there will be only one such branch.

case of well-typed programs, the original method definitions are always selected. For example, if we compare a *ColorPoint* with another *ColorPoint*, after the completion, the method written by the programmer in the `ColorPoint` class is executed. We give a new semantics only to those computations that produce a run-time type error. Because of covariant specialization, it may happen that a method is applied to an argument that it cannot handle. In that case, an added method branch is executed: it ascends the inheritance hierarchy to look for the last definition of that method that can handle the argument (it knows that one exists). Thus, we have an intelligent compiler that inserts the code the programmer has forgotten to write, thus ensuring type safety for covariant specialization. The naturalness of our solution is given by the fact the method executed is always the most specialized one written by the programmer for the arguments in the call. Of course, no solution for adding multi-methods automatically can be as natural as one in which the multi-methods are hand-written, but our solution is the most natural fix that can be done automatically. Furthermore, the new semantics takes into account the reason for an ill-typed application, namely the application can be ill-typed only if the receiver is statically considered an object of a superclass of its actual class. Our solution has the method lookup mechanism ascend the inheritance hierarchy from the receiver's dynamic class (where it would otherwise stop) towards the static class, looking for a definition that supports the arguments given.

4.4 Multiple-argument methods

It is straightforward to extend this solution to covariant specialization of methods with multiple parameters. As before, the most specific method definition will be used:

Algorithm 2. For every class C, for every message m with k parameters overridden in C with type $(S^1 \times \cdots \times S^k) \to T$, and for every superclass C_i (for which m has type $(S_i^1 \times \cdots \times S_i^k) \to T_i$) where m is covariantly defined in the direct subclass C_{i+1} (that is, $C \leq C_{i+1} < C_i, C_i = \varsigma(C_{i+1}), (S_{i+1}^1 \times \cdots \times S_{i+1}^k) < (S_i^1 \times \cdots \times S_i^k))$, add the following method branch:

```
method m(x₁:Sᵢ¹,...,xₖ:Sᵢᵏ):Tᵢ in class C;
method body m(x₁:Sᵢ¹,...,xₖ:Sᵢᵏ):Tᵢ in class C {return(self->ς(C)@m(x₁,...,xₖ));}
```

∎

The implementation-oriented version of Algorithm 1 can be extended similarly so that the solution works by adding a single (multi-method) branch.

The formal justification of the type safety of this second algorithm is straightforwardly obtained by using cartesian products to type multi-argument methods.

4.5 Implementation

The solution admits at least two different implementation techniques.

One could change the compiler to use the observation that all the method branches added to a method definition have the same body, thus applying the implementation-oriented versions of Algorithms 1 and 2. The (new) compiler "marks" methods needing extra branches, and compiles these methods differently. Either extra code may be added which tests the argument types, or a description of the types may be used at run-time by the message dispatcher. In any case, if a marked method does not handle its arguments, the dispatch mechanism searches for a new method definition starting from the superclass. If this method is also marked then the argument types must be checked again and so on. Our solution ensures that as long as a method is marked, there is another method for the same message higher up in the inheritance hierarchy that can handle more argument types. It also ensures that if a method definition is not marked, then it can handle all arguments that the static type system permits. Effectively, a marked method overrides a previous definition for only *some* of its arguments.

A more conservative, but less efficient way to implement the algorithms is to simulate multi-methods in the source language, using the technique proposed by Ingalls [Ing86]. Ingalls' simulation, offered in the context of single-dispatching languages such as Smalltalk-80 [GR83], uses a second message dispatch to obtain the dynamic selection on an extra argument. Every multi-method can be simulated by several normal method dispatches. After the first dispatch, only the type of the receiver is known. After the second dispatch, the type of the first argument is known, and so on. The realization of this method for the example from Section 3 is presented in Appendix A. The reader can try to follow the execution of p->equal(q): for all the possible combinations of p and q (both arguments instances of Point, p instance of Point and q instance of ColorPoint, and so on) the code executed is always the same as that executed with the multi-methods defined in Section 3. Also, note that all the methods have the same types for Point and ColorPoint. This means that covariant specialization is not used and therefore, as expected, the class definitions are type-safe.

The advantage of using Ingalls' simulation is that it can be implemented by a pre-processor, rather than changing the core of the standard O_2 compiler. The preprocessor would transform the covariant specialization of a method with one argument into one dispatching method plus one more for the original method and one more for each additional branch determined by Algorithm 1 in any of its subclasses. This advantage, however, must be weighed against several disadvantages. The method-marking implementation is more efficient both in terms of space (there is no code duplication) and of time (the overhead to select the branch is much more prominent in Ingalls' simulation). Furthermore, Ingalls' simulation is neither modular nor incremental. If we compiled some classes using the marking implementation and later added some new subclasses, we do not need to recompile the first ones. With an implementation based on Ingalls' simulation, every new covariant redefinition would require the recompilation of every class that implements a method for the message. Another problem is that, as shown in [BCC+96], Ingalls' simulation does not work properly when the result types of overriding methods differ from the methods they override. This problem can be fixed using parametric polymorphism, but since O_2 does not provide this kind of polymorphism, it would be necessary to bypass the type-checking phase when compiling pre-processed code.

Finally, note that although marked methods require extra checking to implement the added method branches, the current O_2 compiler already generates code to perform these checks, in order to detect the run-time type-errors caused by covariant specialization.

5   Multiple inheritance

Multiple inheritance presents several obstacles to our solution as defined for single inheritance. The most pertinent is that we do not have a privileged superclass; therefore the notation $\varsigma(.)$ is undefined. To put it otherwise, there is no longer a standard place from where to start the search for a method definition for an ill-typed application.

A second problem concerns the application of multi-methods. In Section 3, we said that if a multi-method of type $\{S_1 \to T_1, \ldots, S_n \to T_n\}$ is applied to an argument of type U, the branch executed is the one defined for the type $S_j = \min_{i=1..n}\{S_i \mid U \le S_i\}$. With multiple inheritance, some conditions are needed to ensure that the set $\{S_i \mid U \le S_i\}$ has a least element.

These two problems are connected. Indeed, if we generalize the algorithm given for single inheritance in a straightforward way, we run into pathological cases that break naturalness and type safety.

In this section, we first study the cases in which the straightforward extension of the solution for single inheritance fails. Next, we define an extension of the multi-method syntax and behavior that allows us to generalize the single inheritance solution to multiple inheritance in a type-safe and natural way.

5.1   Pathological cases

Consider four classes A_1, A_2, B, and C, with C defined by inheritance from B and B defined by multiple inheritance from A_1 and A_2. This situation is graphically represented in the figure below. Consider now the following program, where $T \le T_1, T_2$ (as before, we omit the type declarations):

```
class E
    method m(x:A1):T1;
    method n(x:B):T1
end;

class F
    method m(x:A2):T2;
    method n(x:B):T2
end;

class G inherit E, F
    method m(x:C):T;
    method n(x:C):T
end;
```

The class G inherits from E and F. Since the message m is defined in both E and F, O_2 requires the programmer to redefine the message inside G (otherwise there would be a conflict in the choice of the method to inherit). In G, the method for m covariantly overrides the two previous methods. In order to make this redefinition type-safe, one must add new method branches to handle potential arguments of type A_1, A_2 and B. For the arguments of type A_1, our solution has the compiler use the method defined in E; it will add to G the following method branch:

method body m(x:A_1):T_1 in class G {return(self->E@m(x))}
Similarly for arguments of type A_2 it will add

method body m(x:A_2):T_2 in class G {return(self->F@m(x))}
Note also that the compiler *must* add a branch for B, otherwise the type of the multi-method in G would be $\{A_1 \rightarrow T_1, A_2 \rightarrow T_2, C \rightarrow T\}$ and for an argument of type B, there would be no branch with least parameter type. So the compiler also adds a branch for B. But what shall the compiler use as the body for this branch? There are only two possible choices: either it uses the method in E or it uses the method in F, but both choices are equally good (or bad). The return type for the method branch will reflect this choice, either T_1 or T_2. A similar problem arises when trying to add a method branch for n to handle arguments of type B. If one wants to use multi-methods as defined in Section 3 then the only way out is to perform arbitrary choices that break the type safety of our solution and, perhaps more seriously, its naturalness.

To see how arbitrary choices break type safety, consider again the example of m. Imagine that T_1 and T_2 are incomparable (as in the figure to the right), and that for the body of the code for B in G, the compiler has arbitrarily chosen the method in E. Let b be an object of class B and consider the expression o->m(b). If the static type of o is F, then the static type of this expression is T_2. But if the dynamic type of o is G (which

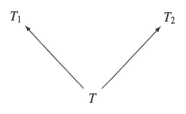

is feasible since $G \leq F$) then the method inserted for B in G is selected and, as a consequence of the arbitrary choice, the method in E is executed. Thus the dynamic type of the expression is T_1 which is incompatible with the static type T_2. This inconsistency may lead to a run-time type error. In this case, the natural method to call would be the one in F, but of course, choosing that method for the branch could also lead to a type error. No automatic addition of method branches (as defined so far) can give complete type safety.

All these pathological cases can only occur in the following situation: some class has two incomparable superclasses each defining a method for the same message and the domains of these two methods have a common subtype not handled by the redefinition in the class. For some particular configurations of the result types of the two methods there exists a type-safe and natural choice, but in the remaining cases one cannot avoid an arbitrary choice.

This arbitrary choice breaks the naturalness of the solution and, in particular, when it is necessary to make an arbitrary choice between methods with incomparable result types, a run time type error may occur.

In conclusion, the analysis performed for single inheritance is no longer sufficient to solve the problem with multiple inheritance.

5.2 The intuition of our solution

To give a solution for multiple inheritance we revisit the causes of type errors due to the covariant specialization.

Recall that covariant specialization can lead to ill-typed applications only in the case that an object has a (non-trivial) superclass of its true class as its static type. Consider the following fragment in the context of the example in the Section 5.1 (where t_1 is some message that can be sent only to objects of the T_1 class, and t_2 is legal only for T_2):

```
o2 B b = new B;          /* create an object of the B class */
o2 G g = new G;          /* create an object of the G class */
o2 E e = g;          /* treat g as an object of the E class */
o2 F f = g;          /* treat g as an object of the F class */
(e->n(b))->t₁;                        /* Application #1 */
(f->n(b))->t₂;                        /* Application #2 */
```

First, note that both applications are ill-typed in unmodified O_2, despite being legal under covariant specialization. Note also that the only way to avoid type errors in both applications is to select a different method for each, despite the fact that both applications have the same receiver and argument objects.

Our multi-method solution works for single inheritance by ascending the inheritance hierarchy starting from the dynamic class of the receiver object. If the method definition for the class can handle the parameters, it is used, otherwise the direct superclass is examined, and so on. This solution works because eventually the search will reach the static class of the receiver which must have a method definition that can handle the arguments. This solution does not work for multiple inheritance because when the search must continue from a class with multiple direct superclasses, it does not know which of the direct superclasses to try next since it does not know the static class of the receiver. The intuition behind our solution for multiple inheritance is to use the static class of the receiver to direct the ascension of the hierarchy.

So the first idea for a solution for multiple inheritance is to limit the search of the method to that part of the inheritance hierarchy that is included between the static and the dynamic type of the receiver. Applying this restriction in the fragment above, the method for the receiver e will not be looked for in F and the one for f will not be looked for in E.

This idea is enough to avoid type errors, but it does not remove the need for arbitrary choices. Arbitrary choices interfere with naturalness and, more seriously, with the predictabilty and understandability of the semantics.

Consider again the example at the beginning of Section 5.1 and suppose that both E and F are subclasses of some class D (as in the figure on the side) which has methods for both m and n. Consider further that we are sending the message m or n to a receiver with static type D and dynamic type G.

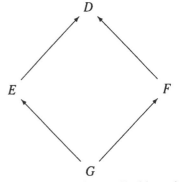

If the type of the argument is B, the methods of E and F are equally applicable and only an arbitrary choice can choose between them. Predictability can be restored in a type-safe manner by choosing the method defined for D, but at the expense of some naturalness, since the methods in E and F are not considered.[16]

The solution we present for multiple inheritance uses both these ideas to assure type-safety and (a certain degree of) naturalness, namely:

1. The search of the method is restricted to the portion of the inheritance hierarchy included between the static type and the dynamic type of the receiver.
2. If this portion of the inheritance hierarchy includes a zone in which a pathological case may happen, this zone is skipped by the search.

Note that the decision to skip a zone is based on the static type of the receiver. For example, for m or n messages, if the receiver's dynamic type is G then the class E must be skipped if the receiver's static type is D, but E must be searched if the static type of the receiver is E.

To see the solution in a different way, consider the inheritance hierarchy between the static and the dynamic class of the receiver. The hierarchy forms a directed acyclic graph. There are several paths that lead from the dynamic to the static class. Consider the set of nodes that belong to every such path. Because of the acyclicity of the graph, this set is totally ordered (w.r.t. the subtyping relation). Therefore if we consider only the classes of this set, we have a single-inheritance-like hierarchy going from the dynamic class to the static class of the receiver. Our solution applies the single inheritance solution from Section 4 to this hierarchy.

The multi-methods described in Section 3 do not suffice to implement this strategy. A further extension and semantics must be given that permit the selection to take into account the receivers' static type. Before defining this extension, some further notation is needed.

5.3 Notation

A *chain* from a class C to another class C_0 is a set of comparable classes $\{C_{n-1}, \ldots, C_0\}$, $n > 0$, where $C = C_n < C_{n-1} < \ldots < C_0$. If each C_i is the direct superclass of C_{i+1}, we call it a *path*. There are many chains in a multiple inheritance hierarchy. Thus, we pick a particular chain (denoted $\kappa(C, C_0)$), which is defined as the set of all classes that appear in every path from C to C_0, or more precisely:

$$\kappa(C, C_0) \equiv \{C' \mid C < C' \leq C_0, \forall T. (C < T \leq C_0 \Rightarrow T \leq C' \vee T \geq C')\}$$

We distinguish the least class in this chain, C_{n-1}, as $\varsigma_{C_0}(C)$, the *direct join superclass* of C for C_0, and the greatest class (other than the superclass itself), C_1, as $\varsigma'_C(C_0)$, the *direct join subclass* of C_0 for C:

$$\varsigma_{C_0}(C) \equiv \min \kappa(C, C_0)$$
$$\varsigma'_C(C_0) \equiv \max(\,(\{C\} \cup \kappa(C, C_0))\backslash\{C_0\}\,)$$

Intuitively, the direct join superclass of a class C for a class A is the next class up the inheritance hierarchy that is comparable with every other class between A and C. Note

---

[16] Of course, predictability could be also achieved by, say, searching from the first parent that is on a path to the static class of the receiver. Such a definition, however, makes the semantics dependent on the order of the parents in the inheritance clause which can be confusing and inelegant.

that the direct join superclass of C for A is not necessarily a direct superclass of C and the direct join subclass of A for C is not necessarily a direct subclass of A. Note also that in the case of single inheritance, the direct join superclasses are simply the direct superclasses (that is, $C_0 > C \Rightarrow \varsigma_{C_0}(C) = \varsigma(C)$)

The method branches added in the enhanced solution are restricted to calls depending on the static class of the receiver. The notation

```
method ... in class C < C'
```

is used to specify that this method branch should only be considered if C' is in the chain from C to the static class A of the receiver, that is, $C' \in \kappa(C, A)$. The intuition is that the body of this method has been defined in the class C' and therefore it should be executed (that is, C' can be searched) only if C' is on all paths going from the dynamic to the static class of the receiver.

Note that in the case of single inheritance, the branch is applicable when the receiver is of the class C' or any superclass of C'. Since the typing rules of O_2 ensure that branches added by our solution are only needed in such situations, a restriction of this form is vacuous.

5.4 The solution

Our solution works very similarly to the case of single inheritance, a method branch is added for each definition in a superclass which is covariantly redefined in a subclass. The difference is that the added branch is restricted to apply only to certain static classes of the receiver.

For the example in the Section 5, the compiler would add the following methods

```
method body m(x:A₁):T₁ in class G < E {return(self->E@m(x));}
method body m(x:A₂):T₂ in class G < F {return(self->F@m(x));}
method body n(x:B):T₁ in class G < E {return(self->E@n(x));}
method body n(x:B):T₂ in class G < F {return(self->F@n(x));}
```

Note that this completion avoids the arbitrary choices imposed by the pathological cases: if an object of class G receives the message m or n with an argument of class B then the method will be selected on the base of the static type of the receiver (if the static type is a superclass of D —see Section 5.2— then the algorithm will add other branches that handle it).

In general, the solution (for the single argument case) works as follows:

Algorithm 3. For every class C, for every message m overridden in C with type $S \to T$, and for every superclass C_i (for which m has type $S_i \to T_i$) where m is covariantly redefined in the direct join subclass C_{i+1} to $S_{i+1} \to T_{i+1}$ (that is, $C \leq C_{i+1} < C_i, C_{i+1} = \varsigma'_C(C_i), S \leq S_{i+1} < S_i$), add the following method branch:

```
method m(x:Sᵢ):Tᵢ in class C < Cᵢ;
method body m(x:Sᵢ):Tᵢ in class C < Cᵢ { return(self->ςCᵢ(C)@m(x)); }
```

■

Notes:

First note that in the case of single inheritance, this algorithm yields exactly the same method branches as Algorithm 1 aside from "$<$" restrictions, all of which are vacuous. More generally, if C has a single superclass, then despite any multiple inheritance among its ancestors, its direct superclass is always its direct join superclass.

Secondly, note that the type safety of the method branch bodies is proved by induction down the inheritance hierarchy. The class $\varsigma_{C'}(C)$ is the first in the chain to C', and if it is not equal to C', it will have a similar method branch added to it. In general, $\varsigma_{C'}(C)@m$ has multi-method type.

Lastly, and most importantly, for every receiver with static class A and dynamic class C, the set of applicable method branches includes only the original method definition in C and branches for classes along the chain $\kappa(C, A)$. By including the original definition, the solution ensures that well-typed applications have the same semantics as previously. The covariant specialization rules for O_2 guarantee that the domains of these branches will form a chain themselves, and a minimum applicable branch is ensured.

So what is the exact behavior of this new algorithm? Imagine that the message m has been sent to some object whose static type was C_0, but whose dynamic type was C_n. The systems looks for the method in class C_n but because of covariant specialization, the method for m cannot handle the actual argument of the method. Our algorithm adds the branches that make the system continue the search up in the inheritance hierarchy. This search continues from the direct join superclass of C_n for C_0 (C_{n-1} in the figure on the right). Note that in the inheritance hierarchy between C_n and C_{n-1} (darker in the figure) there may be some definitions for m able to handle the argument of the method. For precisely this reason, this particular part of the inheritance hierarchy is a place of potential indeterminacies, where an arbitrary choice might be required. Therefore the search skips this and other dangerous zones.

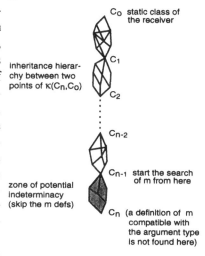

C_0 static class of the receiver

inheritance hierarchy between two points of $\kappa(C_n, C_0)$

C_1

C_2

C_{n-2}

C_{n-1} start the search of m from here

zone of potential indeterminacy (skip the m defs)

C_n (a definition of m compatible with the argument type is not found here)

Since the search goes up through subclasses of the static class of the receiver eventually reaching this class, there will always be a method that can handle the argument. Note that in the limit case, where $\varsigma_{C_0}(C_n) = C_0$, the algorithm simply executes the method that was statically predicted for the message, that is, the one defined for the static class of the receiver.

The solution given here does maintain a degree of naturalness: it may not perform the most specialized method for the argument (e.g. any method that is defined in the grey zone) but it never has to make an arbitrary choice. This property makes it behave predictably. In the case of single inheritance, the semantics of the multi-method solution is that each covariant specialization is only overriding part of the definition of its direct superclass. This concept is clear and natural. Here, we are overriding the definition of the direct join superclass, in order to avoid choosing between two direct superclasses. Note that we have done nothing but to expand the solution we gave for single inheritance; indeed the single inheritance solution is nothing but the special case in which all inheritance hierarchies between two classes of the chain are replaced by a single link (in single inheritance $\varsigma_{C_0}(C_n) = \varsigma(C_n)$).

Thus in summary, this solution is good, not merely because it avoids type errors, but more importantly because it makes a natural and predictable completion of the class.

As with the first algorithm, it is straightforward to extend Algorithm 3 to methods with multiple arguments by considering the arguments to be a single argument with cartesian product type.

5.5 Implementation

There are at least two possible implementation possibilities for the enhanced solution.

The first implementation possibility involves compiling all message sends to implicitly also send some indication of the static class of the receiver. As with the marking method for single inheritance, all methods that have additional branches added are marked. If the arguments are not handled by the method definition, then the method must compute the direct join superclass of the class which defined the method for the static class passed implicitly. This computation could involve a table lookup compiled into the marked method. Once a new class was determined, the method lookup mechanism could proceed from there. A compiled table lookup requires that every method in a class be recompiled if there is any change in the inheritance hierarchy above the class. Alternately, if the structure of the hierarchy was available at runtime, the computation of the direct join superclasses could be deferred to this point.

The second implementation possibility involves having a different method lookup table depending on the static class of the receiver. For example, if an object of class G were given static class F, it would be given a different set of method definitions. The compiler can detect these occurrences statically and arrange that the correct method definition table be used. The original definitions would not need to be marked, because the static typing rules of O_2 would prevent any type errors. A compiled method for a particular static non-trivial superclass would have to check its arguments and then if the defined method was unable to handle them, would defer to the appropriate method of the direct join superclass (known statically). The method tables for a class tailored for two different superclasses on the same $\kappa(.,.)$ chain could be identical, thus avoiding massive code duplication. This implementation possibility does not require method sends to implicitly send the static class of the receiver and thus should not impact the efficiency of the dispatch mechanism. However, this possibility would require a class to be recompiled if any class above it in the hierarchy was changed.

These two possibilities both share the advantage that they would not require the data to have a new representation, and thus large bases would not need to be recompiled.

6 Comparison with other works and conclusion

We want to stress, once more, that our main concern for this work is to define a technique that could be applied to the existing programs without requiring any modification of them. This is a crucial characteristic in the field of large databases, where the rewriting of the code would be much too expensive, even if feasible. Indeed, there already exist several solutions that handle the problem of covariant specialization: some very "ad hoc" like the run-time handling of exceptions [ABDS96], others much more elegant and formal such as a relation that replaces subtyping [Bru94], or the use of less precise types for the methods [BHJL86]. In the same spirit, we could have further developed Section 3 and defined an extension of O_2 to handle multi-methods. But all these solutions require at least the modification of the existing code, if not the use of a totally different paradigm. Therefore they cannot be strictly compared with the solution we propose.

The solutions proposed for Eiffel are the only other solutions that, like ours, does not require any modification of existing code. The former definition of system validity [Mey91] would use global data-flow analysis to ensure that arguments to procedures such as `break_it` in Section 3 can only be passed expressions of dynamic type *Point*. The newer definition [Mey96] would disallow routines like `break_it` outright. If a compiler using one of these rules detects a violation, it can only issue warnings (to little effect) or reject the program. It cannot fix the (potential) error.

Our solution takes a different tack. Rather than disallowing potentially ill-typed applications, our solution patches them so that they are well-typed. The patch is executed only upon an actual ill-typed application, and could optionally generate a warning message at this point as well. The added code uses the conditions under which application occurred to choose the most appropriate method definition. To use a medical metaphor, Eiffel performs a much more accurate screening process to search for type errors, while our solution addresses more the prophylaxis by vaccinating risky situations. It is important to stress that the solution affects only the definition of the methods. All the existing bases are unaffected and can be used as before.

Another important remark is that our solution does not merely fix existing code, it also provides a fix that works for possible evolutions of the system. Every use of covariant specialization is a potential time bomb that can explode a long time after the code has been written. This may happen, for example, because a new version of a library is released or merely because the run-time values of the data are different. Eiffel's solution blocks all possible explosive situations (thus the use of a new library version may occasion that an old program no longer type-checks). Our solution instead defuses the time bombs.

In other words, our solution gives a predictable and type-safe semantics for covariant specialization. Covariant specialization may be seen as *partial overriding* of a previous definition, contrasting with the *full overriding* by an invariant (or contravariant) specialization. Our solution could be incorporated into a new language that permits type-safe covariant specialization. As testimony to the practical interest of such an approach, a note envisaging a similar solution for C++ appeared while we were preparing the final version of this paper [BG96].

Incidentally, our paper also proposes extending O_2 with multi-methods. This idea deserves more extensive treatment, especially concerning modularity issues, which constitute a peculiar problem of multi-methods (see [Coo91]). The great advantage of multi-methods is that the programmer can choose the definition to be used in the case of failure of the covariant specialization, instead of delegating this choice to the compiler.

Last but not least, our analysis is founded on well-established type-theoretic bases, so that the correctness of our solution is formally proved and type-safety is guaranteed.

Acknowledgments

We are very grateful to Kim Bruce, Luca Cardelli, Gary Leavens, Scott Smith and Benjamin Pierce. The joint paper [BCC+96] and the several e-mails exchanges were crucial to the development of this work. In particular, Gary gave the pointer to Ingalls' simulation and Scott was the first who noticed that this simulation might be used to implement our ideas. Manuel Fähndrich, William Maddox and Tim A. Wagner read early drafts of this paper and provided useful criticism.

References

[ABDS96] E. Amiel, M.-J. Bellosta, E. Dujardin, and E. Simon. Type-safe relaxing of schema consistency rules for flexible modelling in OODBMS. *Very Large Databases Journal*, 5(2):108–119, April 1996.

[ADL91] R. Agrawal, L. DeMichiel, and B. Lindsay. Static type checking of multi-methods. *ACM SIGPLAN Notices*, 26(11):113–128, 1991. Proceedings of OOPSLA'91.

[BCC+96] K. Bruce, L. Cardelli, G. Castagna, The Hopkins Object Group, G. Leavens, and B. Pierce. On binary methods. *Theory and Practice of Object Systems*, 1(3), 1996.

[BDK92] F. Bancilhon, C. Delobel, and P. Kanellakis, editors. *Implementing an Object-Oriented Database System: The Story of O₂*. Morgan Kaufmann, 1992.

[BG96] M. F. Barrett and M. E. Giguere. A note on covariance and contravariance unification. *ACM SIGPLAN Notices*, 31(1):32–35, Jan. 1996.

[BHJL86] A. Black, N. Hutchinson, E. Jul, and H. Levy. Object structure in the Emerald system. In Norman Meyrowitz, editor, *OOPSLA '86 Conference Proceedings*, volume 21(11) of *SIGPLAN Notices*, pages 347–349, Nov. 1986.

[Bru94] K.B. Bruce. A paradigmatic object-oriented programming language: Design, static typing and semantics. *Journal of Functional Programming*, 4(2):127–206, 1994.

[Car88] L. Cardelli. A semantics of multiple inheritance. *Information and Computation*, 76:138–164, 1988. A previous version can be found in Semantics of Data Types, LNCS 173, 51-67, Springer-Verlag, 1984.

[Cas95a] G. Castagna. Covariance and contravariance: conflict without a cause. *ACM Transactions on Programming Languages and Systems*, 17(3):431–447, 1995.

[Cas95b] G. Castagna. A meta-language for typed object-oriented languages. *Theoretical Computer Science*, 151(2):297–352, Nov. 1995.

[Cas96] G. Castagna. *Object-Oriented Programming: A Unified Foundation*. Progress in Theoretical Computer Science. Birkäuser, Boston, 1996.

[CGL95] G. Castagna, G. Ghelli, and G. Longo. A calculus for overloaded functions with subtyping. *Information and Computation*, 117(1):115–135, 1995. A preliminary version was presented at the *1992 ACM Conference on LISP and Functional Programming*, San Francisco, June 1992.

[CL95] C. Chambers and G. Leavens. Typechecking and modules for multi-methods. *ACM Transactions on Programming Languages and Systems*, 17(6):805–843, Nov. 1995.

[Coo91] W. Cook. Object-oriented programming versus abstract data types. In J. W. de Bakker, W. P. de Roever, and G. Rozenberg, editors, *Foundations of Object-Oriented Languages, REX School/Workshop*, volume 489 of *LNCS*, pages 151–178. Springer-Verlag, 1991.

[DG87]   L.G. DeMichiel and R.P. Gabriel. Common Lisp Object System overview. In Bézivin, Hullot, Cointe, and Lieberman, editors, *ECOOP '87 Conference Proceedings*, volume 276 of *LNCS*, pages 151–170. Springer-Verlag, 1987.

[GR83]   A. Goldberg and D. Robson. *Smalltalk-80: The Language and Its Implementation*. Addison-Wesley, Reading, Mass., 1983.

[Ing86] D. H. H. Ingalls. A simple technique for handling multiple polymorphism. In Norman Meyrowitz, editor, *OOPSLA '86 Conference Proceedings*, volume 21(11) of *SIGPLAN Notices*, pages 347–349, Nov. 1986.

[Mey91] Bertrand Meyer. *Eiffel: The Language*. Prentice-Hall, 1991.

[Mey96] Bertrand Meyer. *Object-Oriented Software Construction*. Prentice-Hall, 2nd edition, to appear 1996.

[MHH91] W. B. Mugridge, J. G. Hosking, and J. Hamer. Multi-methods in a statically-typed programming language. In P. America, editor, *ECOOP '91 Conference Proceedings*, volume 512 of *LNCS*, pages 307–324. Springer-Verlag, 1991.

A   Ingalls' simulation for the Point/ColorPoint problem

```
class Point
   type tuple (x:real,
               y:real)
   method equal(p:Point):boolean,
   method equalPoint(p:Point):boolean,
   method equalColorPoint(p:ColorPoint):boolean
end;

method body equal(p:Point):boolean in class Point
   {return(p->equalPoint(self));};

method body equalPoint(p:Point):boolean in class Point
   {return( self->x == p->x && self->y == p->y );};

method body equalColorPoint(p:ColorPoint):boolean in class Point
   {return( self->equalPoint(p) );};



class ColorPoint inherit Point   /* x and y are inherited from Point */
   type tuple(c:string)          /* and the signature of the methods */
end;                             /* does not change                  */

method body equal(p:Point):boolean in class ColorPoint
   {return( p->equalColorPoint(self) );};

/* ColorPoint inherits equalPoint from Point */

method body equalColorPoint(p:ColorPoint):boolean in class ColorPoint
   {return( self->x == p->x && self->y == p->y && self->c == p->c );};
```

Integrating Subtyping, Matching and Type Quantification:
A Practical Perspective[*]

Andreas Gawecki   Florian Matthes

Universität Hamburg, Vogt-Kölln-Straße 30
D-22527 Hamburg, Germany
{gawecki,matthes}@informatik.uni-hamburg.de

Abstract. We report on our experience gained in designing, implementing and using a strongly-typed persistent programming language (TooL) which integrates object types, subtyping, type matching, and type quantification. Our work complements recent type-theoretical studies of subtyping and type matching by focusing on the issue of how to integrate both concepts into a practical, orthogonal programming language. We also shed some light on the subtle typing issues which we encountered during the construction of a substantial bulk data library where it was necessary to trade-off subtyping against type matching. Our practical experience suggests that the benefits of an integration of subtyping and type matching are achieved at the expense of a significant increase in modeling complexity.

[*] This research is supported by ESPRIT Basic Research, Project FIDE, #6309 and by a grant from the German Israeli Foundation for Research and Development (*bulk data classification*, I-183 060).

1 Introduction and Motivation

The purpose of this paper is to report on our practical experience gained in designing, implementing, and using **TooL**, a language integrating subtyping and type matching, which should be of value for anyone who plans to incorporate type matching into a fully-fledged programming language.

The TooL project started off with the observation that existing statically-typed polymorphic programming languages with subtyping only (Modula-3 [Nelson 1991], C++ [Ellis and Stroustrup 1990], Tycoon [Matthes and Schmidt 1992] or Fibonacci [Albano *et al.* 1994]) provide application programmers with rich re-usable generic class libraries organized into subtype hierarchies. However, the type system of these languages obstructs programmers who intend to maximize code sharing between library classes through implementation inheritance following the successful library design principles of Smalltalk and Eiffel. As discussed in the literature [Black and Hutchinson 1990; Bruce 1994; Bruce *et al.* 1995b; Abadi and Cardelli 1995] and illustrated in the rest of the paper, a more liberal notion of *type matching* is needed, for example, to support the type-safe inheritance of *binary methods* [Bruce *et al.* 1995a].

The design and implementation of TooL has been heavily influenced by experience gained with the **Tycoon** language [Matthes and Schmidt 1992] developed at the University of Hamburg in the framework of the European basic research project FIDE [Atkinson 1996] where six European database language research groups collaborated towards the goal of *Fully Integrated Data Environments* using state-of-the-art language technology.

The rationale behind the original Tycoon type system is to provide a set of unbiased, orthogonal primitives to support various database programming styles, including functional, imperative and different flavors of object-oriented modeling. Tycoon is based on function types, record types, and recursive types in a full higher-order type system where subtyping and unrestricted existential and universal quantification is provided over types, type operators and higher-order type operators, including a limited form of dependent types. Tycoon is therefore similar to Quest [Cardelli 1989; Cardelli and Longo 1991] and the type theoretic model of $F^\omega_{\leq}$ [Pierce and Turner 1993].

Based on our extensive experience using Tycoon for large-scale programming (for example, building and maintaining systems with several hundred modules) our motivation behind the design of TooL was to verify the following hypotheses: (1) A *purely* object-oriented language where objects and classes combine aggregation, encapsulation, recursion, parameterization and inheritance leads to program libraries which are more uniform and easier to understand since programmers do not have the freedom to choose between combinations of modules, records, tuples, functions, recursive declarations, etc. (2) Type matching increases code reuse within complex libraries.

To verify these hypotheses it was not only necessary to design and to implement

TooL, but also to *utilize* it for non-trivial library examples. In a nutshell, this experimental validation was carried out by augmenting the Tycoon type system by a notion of type matching, omitting existential type quantification and all higher-order type concepts like kinds, but otherwise adhering closely to the proven type and language concepts of Tycoon. We then used the functionality of the mature and highly-structured Eiffel collection library [Meyer 1990] as a yardstick for the construction of a type-safe TooL bulk type library.

This paper is organized as follows: In section 2 we provide insight into the rationale behind the TooL language design. Section 3 and section 4 as well as the appendix give an overview of the language and the libraries constructed with the language. Section 5 motivates and explains the TooL subtyping, matching and type quantification rules. The TooL inheritance rules and the non-trivial interaction of subtyping, matching and type quantification are discussed in section 6 and section 7, respectively. The impact of this interaction on the use of the TooL language for library programming is described in section 8. The paper ends with a comparison with related work and a summary of our research contributions.

2 TooL Design Goals

The key aspects of the TooL language design can be summarized as follows:

Purely object-oriented: TooL supports the classical object model where objects are viewed as abstract data types encapsulating both state and behavior. Similar to Smalltalk [Goldberg and Robson 1983] and Self [Ungar and Smith 1987], TooL is a *purely* object-oriented language in the sense that *every* language entity is viewed as an object and *all* kinds of computations are expressed uniformly as (typed) patterns of passing messages [Hewitt 1977]. Even low-level operations such as integer arithmetic, variable access, and array indexing are uniformly expressed by sending messages to objects.

It should be noted that modern compiler technology eliminates most of the run-time performance overhead traditionally associated with the purely object-oriented approach [Chambers and Ungar 1991; Hölzle 1994; Gawecki 1992]. For example, TooL uses dynamic optimization across abstraction barriers based on a persistent continuation passing style (CPS) program representation to "compile away" many message sends [Gawecki and Matthes 1996].

Higher-order functions as objects: Contrary to other statically-typed object-oriented languages [Goguen 1990], TooL provides statically-scoped higher-order functions which are viewed as first-class objects that understand messages. Thereby control structures like loops and conditionals do not have to be built into the language, but can be defined as add-ons using objects and dynamic binding. To improve code reusability, even instance and pool variables (which unify the concepts of global and class variables in

Smalltalk) are accessed by sending messages [Johnson and Foote 1988]. This unification at the value level leads to a significant complexity reduction at the type level where it is only necessary to define type and scoping rules for class signatures, message sends and inheritance clauses which we explore in the rest of the paper.

Strong and static typing: No operation will ever be invoked on an object which does not support it, i.e. errors like "message not understood" cannot occur at run time. Type rules are defined in a "natural-deduction" style based on the abstract TooL syntax similar to [Milner *et al.* 1990] and [Matthes and Schmidt 1992]. In the remainder of the paper we restrict ourselves to an informal discussion of the finer points of these type rules.

Structural type checking: Several conventional object models couple the implementation of an object with its type by identifying types with class names (e.g. C++, ObjectPascal, Eiffel). In these models, an object of a class named A can only be used in a context where an object of class A or one of its statically declared superclasses is expected. This implies that type compatibility is based on a single inheritance lattice which is difficult to be maintained in a persistent and distributed scenario.

Therefore, TooL has adopted a more expressive notion of type compatibility based on *structural subtyping*, called *conformance* in [Hutchinson 1987]. Intuitively, an object type A is a subtype of another object type B when it supports at least the operations supported by B. That is, TooL views types as (unordered) sets of method signatures, abstracting from class or type names during the structural subtype test. The additional flexibility of structural subtyping is especially useful if A and B have been defined independently, without reference to each other. Such situations occur in the integration of pre-existing external services, in the communication between sites in distributed systems [Birell *et al.* 1993], and on access to persistent data.

Modular type checking: During type checking of a given class only the interfaces of imported classes and of superclasses have to be accessed. In particular, it should be possible to type-check new subclasses without having to re-check method implementation code in superclasses again. Modular type checking speeds up the type-checking process significantly, thus supporting rapid prototyping within an incremental programming environment. It also has the advantage that class libraries – developed independently by different vendors – can be delivered in binary form without a representation of their source code with the option of type-safe subclassing at the customer side.

Modular type-checking requires the *contravariant* method specialization rule for soundness, which means that the types of method arguments are only permitted to be generalized when object types are specialized. The contravariant rule has been criticized of being counter-intuitive [Meyer 1989]. Accordingly, Eiffel has adopted a *covariant* method specialization rule which is in conflict with substitutability. Therefore, Eiffel requires some form of global data flow analysis at link-time to ensure type correctness. Such an analysis generally requires a representation of the source code of all classes and methods which constitute the whole program to be available to the type-checker at link-time which is not acceptable in our setting. TooL provides a partial solution to the covariance/contravariance problem without giving up modular type-checking by adopting the notion of *type matching* which allows the covariant specialization of method arguments in the important special case where the argument type is equal to the receiver type.

3 TooL Syntax Overview

TooL minimizes built-in language functionality in favor of flexible system add-ons, both at the level of values and at the level of types. This semantic simplicity and orthogonality is reflected by the abstract syntax of TooL depicted in figure 1 which provides a starting point for the definition of the static semantics of TooL and which constitutes the canonical internal representation used by the TooL language processors.

The definition of the abstract TooL syntax involves syntactic objects that are denoted by meta variables using the following naming conventions:

$X, Y, Self$	type and class identifiers
x, y	value identifiers
ψ	type relations
S	type and value signatures
D	type and value bindings
T	type expressions
A	named type expressions
v	values
m	method selectors
c	named class definitions
$slots$	instance variable declarations
$methods$	method declarations

Since most aspects of the abstract syntax are similar to other polymorphically-typed languages [Cardelli and Longo 1991; Cardelli 1993], we only highlight some of the productions.

A TooL program is a set of (mutually recursive) named class definitions $c_1, \ldots, c_n$.

A class definition defines the name of the *Self* type (see section 5.2), the name X of the class, the signatures S of the class type parameters, an ordered sequence of direct superclasses $A_1, .., A_n$, a metaclass declaration A (not treated in this paper), and a set of public and private slots and a suite of method declarations. Each method declaration specifies a method selector m_i, the signatures S_i of the method arguments, the method result type T_i, and a method body D_i given

$$\psi ::= \; <:$$ subtyping
$$\quad | \; <\!*\!: $$ type matching
$$\quad | \; = $$ type equivalence
$$S ::= \oslash $$ empty signature
$$\quad | \; S, x : T $$ value signature
$$\quad | \; S, X \psi T $$ type signature
$$D ::= \oslash $$ empty binding
$$\quad | \; D, x = v $$ value binding
$$\quad | \; D, x : T = v $$ constrained value binding
$$\quad | \; D, X = T $$ type binding
$$T ::= \mathbf{Nil} $$ bottom type constant
$$\quad | \; A $$ type identifier or type instantiation
$$\quad | \; \mathbf{Interface} \; X(S; Self) $$ named parameterized object type
$$\quad\quad \{m_1(S_1)T_1, .., m_n(S_n)T_n\}$$
$$A ::= X $$ type identifier
$$\quad | \; X(D) $$ type instantiation (type bindings only)
$$v ::= b $$ constants (integer, character, ... literals)
$$\quad | \; \mathbf{self} \; | \; \mathbf{super} $$ receiver object
$$\quad | \; x $$ value identifier
$$\quad | \; \mathbf{fun}(S)D $$ (polymorphic) function constructor
$$\quad | \; \mathbf{send}(m, v, D) $$ message send
$$c ::= Self \; \psi \; \mathbf{class} \; X(S; A_1, .., A_n; A) $$ named class definition
$$\quad\quad \mathbf{public} \; slots \; methods$$
$$\quad\quad \mathbf{private} \; slots \; methods$$
$$slots ::= x_1 : T_1 ..., x_n : T_n$$
$$methods ::= m_1(S_1)T_1 = D_1, ... m_n(S_n)T_n = D_n$$

Fig. 1. The TooL abstract syntax

by a list of bindings. The return value computed by a method is the value of its last value binding. A class declaration implicitly defines an object type **Interface** $X(S; Self)\{m_1(S_1)T_1, .., m_n(S_n)T_n\}$ with the same name.

A message send operation defines a message m which is sent to an object determined by evaluating the receiver expression v, passing a sequence D of type and value bindings as actual parameters.

Within bindings and signatures, a distinguished *anonymous* identifier '_' can be used to denote omitted identifiers. For example, the expression x.m(3) in the concrete syntax is mapped to the binding $\_ = \mathbf{send}(m, x, (\oslash, \_ = 3))$.

A function type (denoted as **Fun**(S):T in the concrete syntax of our examples) is represented as an object type with an apply method with signature S and result type T. A function abstraction $\mathbf{fun}(S)D$ evaluates to an instance of such an object type.

Each slot $x : T$ is mapped to a pair of an access method and an update method

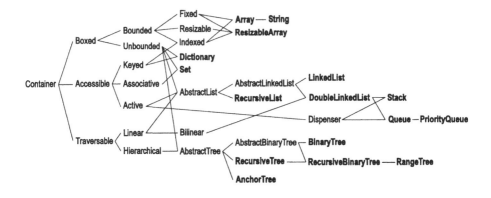

Fig. 2. Overview of the TooL bulk type library

with the signatures $x_{get}(\oslash) : T$ and $x_{set}(\oslash, _ : T) : $ **Void**, respectively.

TooL supports a separation of classes into a *public* and a *private* part. The only object which can legally apply private methods is the object itself. The expressions where these methods can be used are restricted to (statically determinable) messages to the pseudo-variables self and super.

Despite the semantic simplicity of TooL, a rich set of syntactic variants exists to write down message sends. This syntactic sugar helps to define compact yet easy to read message patterns, for example to capture control structures or arithmetic computations. In fact, the TooL language is based on extensible grammars [Cardelli *et al.* 1994] which give users full control over the concrete syntax of TooL, for example, to support domain-specific abstractions like query language notations or concurrency control schemes. The default concrete syntax used in this paper is similar to C++ and Java.

4   The TooL Bulk Type Library

Figure 2 shows the part of the TooL class library relevant for bulk data manipulation. A bold font indicates concrete (instantiable) classes, whereas a non-bold font indicates abstract classes, i.e., classes where some or all method bodies consist of empty bindings (cf. figure 1).

This class hierarchy is designed to maximize code sharing between library classes through implementation inheritance following the successful library design principles of Smalltalk and Eiffel [Meyer 1990]. For example, the abstract classes Boxed, Accessible, and Traversable provide code fragments which capture certain aspects of containers and which can be inherited, combined and refined in subclasses to implement concrete classes such as priority queues.

In the rest of the paper, we will utilize this library not only to explain some of the more subtle TooL language design decisions, but also to shed some light on the practical issues that arise if subtyping, type matching and type quantification interact.

5 Basic TooL Type Concepts

In this section we motivate and explain the TooL subtyping, matching and type quantification rules. Their impact on the TooL inheritance rules and their non-trivial interaction is discussed in later sections.

5.1 Structural Subtyping

The main motivation for subtyping is *subsumption* or *substitutability*: we may use an object of a subtype in situations where an object of some of its super-types is expected. Another application of subtyping in TooL is bounded type quantification as discussed in section 5.3.

As a practical example for substitutability in the TooL libraries, consider the printOn method defined in class Object to print any TooL object onto a stream of characters:

```
class Object
  printOn(aStream :WriteStream(Char))
```

For example, we may send a string literal object the message printOn to print itself onto the object stdout (standard output) which is an instance of the class File.

```
"a string".printOn(stdout)
```

In order to substitute a File in a context where a WriteStream of characters is expected, we have to show the subtype relationship File <: WriteStream(Char).

Note that in TooL it is not required that an explicit inheritance relationship between these two classes exists. The subtype relationship holds implicitly and can be deduced from the structure of the following class interfaces:

```
class WriteStream(E <: Object)
  put(e :E) :Void

class File
  get :Char
  put(ch :Char) :Void
  close :Void
```

The generic class WriteStream is parameterized with an element type E which is bounded by the type Object (cf. section 5.3) and exports a single method put to append an object e of type E to the stream. The (possibly independently defined) unparameterized class File also exports a put method, which only accepts characters, in addition to a get and close method.

Subtyping is transitive and reflexive and the TooL subtype lattice contains all closed object types which correspond to non-parameterized class interfaces. TooL class definitions implicitly define a corresponding object type and there is no extra syntax in TooL to define object types (e.g. as in PolyTOIL [Bruce *et al.* 1995b]).

The top element of the subtype lattice is called Void, which is an object type with an empty method suite. Currently, all TooL classes are descendants of a more specialized class Object which already provides some core methods (e.g. testing for object identity and printing).

The bottom element of our type lattice is the type constant Nil. The only subtype of Nil is Nil itself (due to reflexivity). The special object nil (the *undefined object*) is the single instance of this type. Conceptually, the type Nil consists of an infinite method suite, supporting any operation with any signature. At runtime, however, only the methods defined in class Nil and its single superclass Object (e.g. identity testing and printing) may be legally applied, sending any other message to nil triggers an exception. The value nil is used to initialize instance variables and to mark empty slots in hash tables. The type Nil is also used to type expressions which raise an exception.

5.2 Type Matching

As explained in the introduction, a key contribution of TooL is to provide a second relation between object types in addition to subtyping. This relation is called *matching* (denoted by A <*: B) and has been introduced in type-theory [Black and Hutchinson 1990; Bruce 1994] to overcome some well-known problems with subtyping [Canning *et al.* 1989]. In general, matching does not support subsumption (see section 7 for a relaxation of this statement), but it supports the inheritance and specialization of methods with negative (contravariant) occurrences of the recursion variable with binary methods as a special case.

Intuitively, the matching relation captures certain forms of self-referential similarity of object types. Similar to MyType in PolyTOIL [Bruce *et al.* 1995b] or like Current in Eiffel, a distinguished type identifier Self is used in TooL to indicate a self reference which is automatically updated during subclassing to refer to the new subclass.

Similar to the subtype relation, the matching relation is defined by structural induction on object types; it is reflexive and transitive and has Void and Nil as its top and bottom elements, respectively. An object type A matches another object type B (denoted by A <∗: B) if they are subtypes (A <: B) under the assumption that the corresponding Self types are equal. In the example below, the relationship Int <∗: Equality holds implicitly, again without any explicit declarations of relationships between these two classes.

In the following example, we define a class Equality supporting a single infix equality predicate ("="):

```
class Equality
  "="(x :Self) :Bool
```

Exploiting the notion of matching in TooL we can write a generic method "!=" which compares two objects for equality and returns the negated result. All that is required is to know that both objects are of some type T which matches Equality:

```
"!="(T <∗: Equality, x :T, y :T) { !(x = y) }
```

In this example, the method type parameter T can be instantiated by arbitrary types which *match* the type Equality, like the following class Int which exports two additional binary infix operators:

```
class Int
  "="(x :Self) :Bool
  "+"(x :Self) :Self
  "-"(x :Self) :Self
```

Note that the *contravariant* occurrence of the Self type in the method signature of "=" prevents a subtype relationship between Int and Equality. Therefore, we cannot use subtyping instead of matching in the signature of "!=" (e.g. T <: Equality) if we want to apply this polymorphic method to objects of type Int, instantiating T with Int.

As explained in section 6, the explicit type quantification in the definition of the method "!=" can be avoided by defining "!=" in class Equality utilizing the quantification of the Self type within classes during inheritance.

In class definitions, the TooL programmer has the choice between implicit recursion by class name (to promote subtyping) and explicit recursion with the keyword Self (to enable matching). For example, one could write

```
class Equality
  "="(x :Equality) :Bool
```

to decouple the receiver type of the infix message from its argument type in future subclasses. Similar design issues are discussed in section 6.1.

5.3 Type Quantification

Classes as discussed up to now introduce named type constants. Classes can be turned into *generic classes* by type parameterization. Type parameterization is important for the type-safe definition of generic container classes and polymorphic iteration abstractions. For example, virtually all subclasses of Container (see figure 2) have one or several formal type parameters.

In the following example, the element type of sets is parameterized, but constrained to be a subtype of Object in order to allow some basic messages to elements (e.g., comparisons for object identity and printing):

```
class Set(E <: Object)
    add(e :E) :Void
    includes(e :E) :Bool
    inject(F <: Object, unit :F, f :Fun(:F, :E):F) :F
    map(F <: Object, f :Fun(:E):F) :Set(F)
    printOn(aStream :WriteStream(Char))
```

This class interface shows that type parameterization is also available in individual method and function signatures, for instance in the higher-order inject method which iterates over all elements of type E within the set, accumulating the values computed by a binary user-specified function f on arguments of type F and E, given an initial value unit of type F.

In TooL, parameterized classes are not simple templates which can only be type-checked after instantiation as in C++ or in Trellis. Type parameters are *bounded* by a type, permitting local, modular type checking within the scope of the quantifier. For example, the element type of the set returned by the polymorphic map method depends on the argument type of the function f passed as a run-time argument to the map function.

As indicated by the example above, TooL incorporates the full power of bounded parametric polymorphism as found in $F_{<:}$ [Cardelli *et al.* 1991].

TooL provides type argument synthesis in message sends and function applications, thus intSet.inject(0, plus) is equivalent to intSet.inject(:Int, 0, plus). This is particularly useful in the typing of control structures modeled with message passing. We use a simple but incomplete inference algorithm similar to the one described in [Cardelli 1993] which works well in practice.

First-class functions do not introduce additional complexity at the type level since they are treated as objects supporting an apply method that captures the function signature. This also scales to polymorphic and higher-order functions.

6 Inheritance

In the preceding discussion, classes were introduced mainly as a mechanism to describe object types. In TooL, classes also serve as repositories of type and behavior specifications which can be reused and modified by multiple inheritance. This is one of the main differences between TooL and Tycoon.

Similar to CLOS [Bobrow *et al.* 1988], a TooL class definition may give an ordered specification of its direct superclasses, for example the container class Indexed with an element type E inherits from two superclasses (see figure 2):

class Indexed(E <∗: Equality)
super Bounded(E), Keyed(Int, E)

Possible inheritance conflicts (name clashes between inherited methods) are resolved by a linearization of the inheritance tree (i.e. a class precedence list) performed by a topological sort on the superclass lattice. Inheriting from the same class more than once has no effect: TooL has no repeated inheritance as in Eiffel [Meyer 1988] or C++ [Ellis and Stroustrup 1990]. More elaborated schemes of conflict resolution are possible, for example allocating different roles for objects as in Fibonacci [Albano *et al.* 1994]. We chose to omit such sophisticated features to keep our language simple and to focus on the typing issues discussed in the subsequent sections.

If a method specification m(S):T takes precedence during method lookup over another method specification m(S'):T', the result type T has to be a subtype of T' assuming that the signatures S' are subsignatures of the signatures S. The full type rules for inheritance in TooL are similar to those of PolyTOIL [Bruce *et al.* 1995b] and have to take parameterized classes and Self type specifications (see section 6.1) into account.

Type parameters of superclasses may be refined during inheritance. For example, a subclass PointSet can be defined which further constrains the element type of class Set to be a subtype of Point. This more specific type information enables us to access the coordinates of points stored within the set to compute the average value of all X coordinates:

class PointSet(E <: Point)
super Set(E)
    averageX() :Int {**self**.inject(0, **fun**(total :Int, e :E) total+e.x) / size}

In this example, a consistency check is performed by the TooL type-checker to verify that the specified actual type parameter conforms to the bound specified for the formal parameter, i.e Point has to be a subtype of Object.

6.1 Typing Self

During the type-checking of a given TooL class c, the method bodies have to be checked with a certain assumption about the type Self of the receiver object denoted by self. Due to subclassing, this assumption must take *all* possible extensions of c into account since we want to perform modular type-checking. As described in this section, a major contribution of TooL is to give the library programmer explicit control over this particular assumption.

In the most commonly used object-oriented languages (e.g. C++, ObjectPascal, Modula-3, Eiffel), subclassing means subtyping. In these languages, Self has to a subtype of the current class[2]. We say that Self is *subtype-bounded* by the type of the current class.

In some newer languages (e.g. TOOPLE [Bruce 1994], PolyTOIL [Bruce *et al.* 1995b]), the subtype hierarchy implicitly defined by the subtype relation '<:' does not have to be the same as the class hierarchy explicitly defined by inheritance declarations: class specialization by inheritance can lead to *incompatible* types which are not related by subtyping any more. In these languages, inheritance ensures *matching* of subclasses. This means that the only assumption that can be made during modular type-checking is that Self will always match the current class. This *match-bounded* Self typing provides more flexibility because the programmer is not constrained to produce subtypes during subclassing.

Finally, there are programming situations where library designers would like to express the constraint that all subclasses will have identical types and only differ in their method implementations. For example, the TooL leaf classes (Int, Char, ...) which provide builtin functionality for literal constants (numbers, characters, ...) require this constraint to allow literal constants to appear as return values in methods with return type Self.

Therefore, TooL offers three kinds of Self typing (subtype-bounded, match-bounded and equivalence), leaving the choice to the programmer to use one of the following notations:

class Equality ...
Self <*: **class** Equality ...
Self <: **class** Equality ...
Self = **class** Equality ...

The notation class Equality ... is a shorthand for Self <*: class Equality .... We now discuss the advantages and disadvantages of theses alternatives in turn.

In general, match-bounded Self typing is used in classes close to the root of the inheritance lattice to support inheritance of methods with contravariant occurrences of Self, e.g. binary methods. A switch to subtype-bounded Self typing can

---

[2] If the notion of a type Self is part of the language at all, which is not the case in C++, for example.

then be performed when going down the inheritance lattice to support subsumption.

For example, suppose we have modeled points in the usual way, with coordinates as slots and an equality operation. We would like to inherit the default implementation of inequality from class Equality, but we override the default implementation of equality which uses simple object identity:

```
Self  <*: class Equality
  super Object
  "="(x :Self) :Bool { self == x }
  "!="(x :Self) :Bool { !(self = x) }

Self  <: class Point
  super Equality
  x :Int
  y :Int
  "="(aPoint :Self) :Bool { x = aPoint.x & y = aPoint.y }
  paint(aPen :Pen) :Void  { aPen.dot(self) }

Self  <: class ColoredPoint
  super Point
  color :Color
  . . .
```

In the classes Point and ColoredPoint, we have explicitly specified which assumption the type-checker should make about Self, i.e. that subclasses will always be subtypes of Point. This specification allows us to exploit subsumption with the receiver object (denoted with the pseudo-variable self) by passing it as a parameter to an operation which expects a Point as an argument, e.g. the dot method of Pen.

6.2 Enforcing the Self Constraint

A Self constraint assumed during modular type checking is enforced when actual subclassing takes place:

1. Inheritance from a match-bounded class Self <*: class c is equivalent to copying the method signatures of c into the subclass.
   For example, the match-bounded Self in class Equality above makes it possible to overwrite the equality method with contravariant occurrences of Self in the subclass Point, producing a subclass which is not a subtype of Equality.
2. Inheritance from a subtype-bounded class Self <: class c is equivalent to copying the method signatures of c into the subclass and replacing all inherited occurrences of Self by c, turning all explicit self references into implicit ones. Therefore, subclasses do not have to match c any more. For example, ColoredPoint does not match Equality since the Self argument type of the equality

method defined in the superclass has been replaced by Point (the name of the superclass).

At first glance, it seems to suffice to replace the negative (contravariant) occurrences of Self only, as proposed in [Eifrig *et al.* 1994]. This would provide more accurate type information in subclasses for the positive occurrences of Self, since these would be specialized automatically in subclasses. However, this approach is unsound if we do not treat positive (covariant) and negative occurrences of Self as different types. From our practical experience we believe that the additional complexity of introducing two distinct Self type variables is not worth the relatively small gain in expressive power.

As a consequence of the subtype constraint, no further specializations of methods with contravariant occurrences of Self are allowed. For example, we may not overwrite the equality method in the subclass ColoredPoint in the following way, trying to take the color attribute into account during the comparison:

```
Self <: class BadColoredPoint
  super Point
  color :Color
  "="(aColoredPoint :Self) :Bool
    { super."="(aColoredPoint) & color = aColoredPoint.color }
```

This code fails to type-check correctly in TooL.[3]

Note that a match-bound Self specification for class Point would enable a further refinement of the equality method in class BadColoredPoint. But then subsumption on self would be lost and the paint method in class Point would fail to type-check.

More general, to support *both* subsumption and refinement in TooL, a dynamic type test in the equality method in BadColoredPoint is required to check whether the argument is colored or not. A restricted form of such a dynamic type test is performed in languages which support multi-methods (see section 9).

3. Inheritance from a class Self = **class** C is equivalent to (1) and requires a check that no additional methods are defined or refined in the subclass.

In all three cases inheritance implies code sharing.

7 Reconciling Subtyping, Matching and Quantification

Up to now, we have discussed the subtyping and matching relation in isolation. Since TooL makes heavy use of parameterized types, a given piece of TooL code

---

[3] If the paint method would be invoked on such an incorrectly defined colored point, the code in class Point could break since we pass an object (i.e. self) with an interface which does not conform to Point to the pen. The dot method of pen might compare the incorrectly defined colored point with some other ordinary point, which leads to a runtime error since the other point does not support colors.

typically refers to multiple types and type *variables*, some of which are bounded by matching, others by subtyping. It is therefore important to have expressive type rules which establish relationships between elements in the subtyping and matching lattice.

The following TooL type rule states that, within a static context S, a type variable X is a subtype of a given type T, if we know that, within the same static context, X matches an object type with method suite M, *and* we are able to prove that this object type is a subtype of T, whereby all occurrences of Self within the method suite have been replaced by X:

[Match vs. Subtype]

$$\frac{S \vdash X <\!\!*: ObjectType(Self)M \quad S, X <: T \vdash ObjectType(Self)M[X/Self] <: T}{S \vdash X <: T}$$

From the languages incorporating matching, only TooL and Emerald [Black and Hutchinson 1990] provide such a rule which is generalized to parameterized types in TooL. The rule can be viewed as a safe, conservative approximation of the proof steps taken by the type-checker if the exact type structure of X was known.

Intuitively, this rule is sound because matching requires that X must contain at least the methods present in the method suite M, and if ObjectType$(Self)M[X/Self]$ is a subtype of T, X must also contain at least the methods present in T (due to reflexivity of subtyping). This means that, by the definition of matching (see also [Abadi and Cardelli 1995; Bruce *et al.* 1995b]), X can only be not a subtype of T if M contains methods with negative (contravariant) occurrences of Self. But this case is covered since these have been replaced by X.

While it seems possible to map all other TooL type rules (not shown in this paper) in a rather straightforward way onto corresponding type rules of core languages developed for the formal study of type systems incorporating some form of matching, this particular rule indeed looks rather "ad-hoc" and suspicious to a type theoretician. Without this rule, many of TooL class definitions would not type-check successfully. From a type-theoretical point of view it should therefore be interesting to formally prove the soundness of this rule or to come up with an equivalent or a more general rule, which might be easier to prove.

This TooL type rule is utilized, for example, to prove the trivial relationship X <: Void for any type variable X which is known to match some object type. Otherwise, special inference rules involving the top type Void have to be added to the type system (as, for example, in PolyTOIL [Bruce *et al.* 1995b]).

Bounded type parameterization leads to other, more compelling practical examples where the type rule *[Match vs. Subtype]* is needed. For example, we might define a subclass of Set by inheritance which further constrains the set element types to match Equality, overriding the element constraint E <: Object (see section 5.3):

```
class EqualitySet(E <*: Equality) super Set(E)
  includes(x :E):Bool {elements.some(fun(e :E) {e = x})}
```

Here, the more specific constraint on the element type E enables us to use the equality test (rather than object identity) for the set membership test. The type rule *[Match vs. Subtype]* ensures that all types matching Equality will also be subtypes of Object. Without this rule we could not ensure type safety by checking the methods in EqualitySet in isolation, but we would have to type-check Set again in the context of the new subclass (where the element type is bounded differently), violating our design principle of modular type checking.

Unfortunately, the type rule above is one-way only and there is no symmetric rule to prove matching of type variables from known subtype relationships. In particular, we cannot know whether two types match (say, A <*: C) if the only thing we know about them is that the smaller one (A) is a subtype of some other type (say, A <: B). Even if this other type (B) is itself a subtype of the larger type (i.e. B <: C), the matching relation between these two types is unknown since the type Self might have been replaced with the name of the class without affecting subtyping.

For practical programming in TooL, the lack of a rule to deduce matching from subtyping is a major problem in library construction, since it is not "safe" to simply replace matching by the "stronger" subtyping constraint wherever it holds between any two classes.

8   Programming Experience

In this section we try to assess the impact of the increased type system expressiveness gained by the introduction of matching on the practical value of the TooL language.

First, subtyping and type matching both interact well with other TooL language concepts such as type quantification and Self type constraints. Moreover, students with some background in strongly-typed higher-order programming languages like Modula-3 or Tycoon grasp these concepts rather fast. However, as already discussed in section 2 and 7, problems arise as soon as programmers wish to combine the advantages of both partial orders on types.

For example, library designers typically prefer match-bounded quantification to maximize code reuse. This may conflict with the goal of library clients which like to exploit the subsumption property of subtyping to absorb later (unforseen) system extensions. As a concrete example, consider a method f in an application class with the following signature:

```
f(d :Dictionary ... ) ...
```

This method can be applied uniformly to all instances of classes D derived by subtyping from the class Dictionary. To achieve the same effect for all classes D matching Dictionary, a verbose explicit match-bounded quantification has to be used in all application methods which is unlikely to be carried out in practice:

f(D <#: Dictionary d :D ...) ...

A similar argument holds for type parameters of classes. For example, the constraint E <#: Equality for the class EqualitySet defined in the previous section works fine only if we refrain from deriving subclasses by subtyping. If we attempt to instantiate EqualitySet with type ColoredPoint, the type checker would fail to verify ColoredPoint <#: Equality since the type Self in class ColoredPoint is replaced by Point during subtype-bounded inheritance.

Again, a more elaborate parameterization would solve this problem:

```
class EqualitySet2(T <#: Equality, E <: T)
super Set(E)
  includes(x :E) :Bool { elements.some(fun(e :E) {e = x}) }
```

More complex parameterizations (such as alternating chains of subtype- and match-bounded type parameters) do not seem to be necessary. Up to now, we have found no compelling example where a subclass of a subtype-bounded class needs to be refined by match-bounded inheritance.

Since such investigations can only be carried out by implementing practical programming languages and by using them for application development, the TooL experiment constitutes a valid complement to ongoing type-theoretical research on the integration of type matching and subtyping.

9 Related Work

The common formal interpretation of matching is as a form of F-bounded subtyping [Canning *et al.* 1989]. Abadi and Cardelli [Abadi and Cardelli 1995] propose to interpret matching as higher-order subtyping, arguing that this interpretation leads to better properties of the matching relation, e.g. reflexivity and transitivity. The implementation of the matching relation in TooL conforms to this interpretation. An equivalent interpretation has been given in [Black and Hutchinson 1990], using a somewhat different terminology: Black and Hutchinson use the terms *namemaps* (object types) and *namemap generators* (type operators).

To our knowledge, Emerald [Black and Hutchinson 1990] was the first language incorporating both subtyping and matching, but it does not support classes and inheritance. No distinction between ordinary recursion and self-reference was made.

The languages TOOPLE [Bruce 1994] also integrates subtyping and matching but lacks type rules which relates one notion to the other (see section 7). Poly-TOIL is a recent successor to TOOPLE that adds polymorphism but is restricted to match-bounded quantification [Bruce *et al.* 1995b]. The parameterized classes of TooL could be modeled with type operators in PolyTOIL. However, the interaction between parameterization and inheritance is not addressed in [Bruce *et al.* 1995b].

Like TooL, Strongtalk [Bracha and Griswold 1993] aims to support strong typing in a purely object-oriented language. Universal type quantification is provided, but no form of (match or subtype-) bounded quantification is available. Contrary to TooL, Strongtalk relies on extra typing machinery to type-check metaclasses.

In LOOP [Eifrig *et al.* 1994], no distinction between subtyping and matching is made, attempting to merge the two relations into one, which seems to be the least common denominator of the two relations. The subtyping rules of LOOP are not as powerful as those of TooL and PolyTOIL. While LOOP does not provide bounded type quantification, correctness and decidability have been proved formally.

Multi-methods have been proposed as a solution to the binary method problem (covariance vs. contravariance) by several authors [Ghelli 1991; Castagna 1994; Chambers 1993]. Multi-methods circumvent the problem by choosing an appropriate method implementation on behalf of the dynamic class or type of *every* argument of a message, not merely the receiver alone. However, multi-methods expose other problems, of which the lack of encapsulation is the most serious one. Moreover, most current multi-method approaches identify classes with types again and therefore identify inheritance and subtyping. Even in Cecil [Chambers and Leavens 1994], where these problems are addressed (subtype and inheritance graphs are allowed to differ), an explicit declaration of subtyping is required. Therefore, all these models do not scale well into distributed, open environments where some form of structural subtyping (or matching) is needed [Black and Hutchinson 1990].

10   Conclusion

The main results of our work presented in this paper can be summarized as follows:

Type matching and subtyping can be integrated orthogonally and cleanly into a fully-fledged, practical programming language based on a rather small set of constructs at the type and at the value level. In particular, type matching interacts well with type quantification.

In a type system with subtyping and matching, modular type checking requires the programmer to specify how the receiver type Self is related to the type of the enclosing class. TooL offers three possibilities: (1) Self is a subtype of the enclosing class; (2) Self matches the enclosing class; (3) Self is identical to the enclosing class.

Existing type-theoretical models of languages incorporating subtyping and type matching lack type rules to derive relationships between elements in the subtype and the matching lattice which are important for library construction. We define and informally justify such a type rule for TooL. Together with the presentation of the TooL core syntax we thus provide useful input for further type-theoretical work in this area. In this context it is interesting to note that TooL inherits undecidability from $F_{<:}$ [Pierce 1994] since it employs the same powerful contravariant subtyping rule on polymorphic functions (i.e. methods). However, this contravariant rule could be replaced by a more rigid rule which avoids undecidability without invalidating any of the existing TooL library classes.

A comparison of the TooL class library with the Tycoon bulk type library supports both our hypotheses stated in the introduction of this paper: TooL as a purely object-oriented language with type matching leads to more uniform program libraries with an increased code reuse. However, we also observed some practical difficulties encountered by programmers designing large libraries involving both matching and subtyping.

References

Abadi and Cardelli 1995: Abadi, M. and Cardelli, L. On Subtyping and Matching. In *Proceedings ECOOP'95.* Springer-Verlag, 1995.

Albano et al. *1994:* Albano, A., Ghelli, G., and Orsini, R. Fibonacci reference manual: A preliminary version. FIDE Technical Report Series FIDE/94/102, FIDE Project Coordinator, Department of Computing Sciences, University of Glasgow, Glasgow G128QQ, 1994.

Atkinson 1996: Atkinson, M.P. *Fully Integrated Data Environments.* Springer-Verlag (to appear), 1996.

Birell et al. *1993:* Birell, A., Nelson, G., Owicki, S., and Wobber, E. Network objects. In *14th ACM Symposium on Operating System Principles*, pages 217–230, June 1993.

Black and Hutchinson 1990: Black, Andrew P. and Hutchinson, Norman C. Type-checking polymorphism in Emerald. Technical Report TR 90-34, Dept. of Computer Science, University of Arizona, December 1990.

Bobrow et al. *1988:* Bobrow, D.G., De Michiel, L.G., Gabriel, R.P., Keene, S.E., Kiczales, G., and Moon, D.A. Common lisp object system specification. *ACM SIGPLAN Notices*, 23, September 1988.

Bracha and Griswold 1993: Bracha, Gilad and Griswold, David. Strongtalk: type-checking Smalltalk in a production environment. In *Proceedings OOPSLA'93*, pages 215–230, October 1993.

Bruce et al. *1995a:* Bruce, K.B., Cardelli, L., Castagna, G., The Hopkins Object Group, Leavens, G.T., and Pierce, B. On binary methods. Technical report, DEC SRC Research Report, 1995.

Bruce et al. 1995b: Bruce, K.B., Schuett, A., and Gent, R. van. PolyTOIL: a type-safe polymorphic object-oriented language. In *Proceedings ECOOP'95*. Springer-Verlag, 1995.

Bruce 1994: Bruce, Kim B. A paradigmatic object-oriented programming language: Design, static typing and semantics. *Journal of Functional Programming*, 4(2), April 1994.

Canning et al. 1989: Canning, P.S., Cook, W.R., Hill, W.L., and Olthoff, W. F-bounded polymorphism for object-oriented programming. In *Proceedings of Conference on Functional Proramming Languages and Computer Architecture (FPCA'89)*, *Imperial College, London*, pages 273–280, September 1989.

Cardelli and Longo 1991: Cardelli, L. and Longo, G. A semantic basis for Quest. *Journal of Functional Programming*, 1(4):417–458, October 1991.

Cardelli et al. 1991: Cardelli, L., Martini, S., Mitchell, J.C., and Scedrov, A. An extension of system F with subtyping. In Ito, T. and Meyer, A.R., editors, *Theoretical Aspects of Computer Software, TACS'91*, Lecture Notes in Computer Science, pages 750–770. Springer-Verlag, 1991.

Cardelli et al. 1994: Cardelli, L., Matthes, F., and Abadi, M. Extensible grammars for language specialization. In Beeri, C., Ohori, A., and Shasha, D.E., editors, *Proceedings of the Fourth International Workshop on Database Programming Languages, Manhatten, New York*, Workshops in Computing, pages 11–31. Springer-Verlag, February 1994.

Cardelli 1989: Cardelli, L. Typeful programming. Technical Report 45, Digital Equipment Corporation, Systems Research Center, Palo Alto, California, May 1989.

Cardelli 1993: Cardelli, L. An implementation of F$_{<:}$. Technical Report 97, Digital Equipment Corporation, Systems Research Center, Palo Alto, California, February 1993.

Castagna 1994: Castagna, G. Covariance and contravariance: conflict without a cause. Technical Report liens-94-18, LIENS, October 1994.

Chambers and Leavens 1994: Chambers, Craig and Leavens, Gary T. Typechecking and modules for multi-methods. In *Proceedings OOPSLA '94*, volume 29, pages 1–15, October 1994.

Chambers and Ungar 1991: Chambers, C. and Ungar, D. Making pure object-oriented languages practical. In *Proceedings of the Object-Oriented Programming Systems, Languages and Applications Conference, Phoenix, Arizona*, pages 1–15, October 1991.

Chambers 1993: Chambers, C. Object-oriented multi-methods in Cecil. In *Proceedings of the ECOOP'92 Conference, Uetrecht, the Netherlands*, pages 33–56. Springer-Verlag, July 1993.

Eifrig et al. 1994: Eifrig, J., Smith, S., Trifonov, V., and Zwarico, A. Application of OOP type theory: State, decidability, integration. In *Proceedings OOPSLA'94*, pages 16–30, October 1994.

Ellis and Stroustrup 1990: Ellis, M.A. and Stroustrup, B. *The Annotated C++ Reference Manual*. Addison-Wesley Publishing Company, 1990.

Gawecki and Matthes 1996: Gawecki, A. and Matthes, F. Exploiting persistent intermediate code representations in open database environments. In *Proceedings of the 5th Conference on Extending Database Technology, EDBT'96*, Avignon, France, March 1996. (to appear).

Gawecki 1992: Gawecki, A. An optimizing compiler for Smalltalk. Bericht FBI-HH-B-152/92, Fachbereich Informatik, Universität Hamburg, Germany, September 1992. In German.

Ghelli 1991: Ghelli, G. A static type system for message passing. In *Proceedings of the Object-Oriented Programming Systems, Languages and Applications Conference, Phoenix, Arizona*, pages 129–145, 1991.

Goguen 1990: Goguen, J.A. Higher-order functions considered unnecessary for higher-order programming. In Turner, D., editor, *Research Topics in Functional Programming*, pages 309–351. Addison-Wesley Publishing Company, 1990.

Goldberg and Robson 1983: Goldberg, Adele and Robson, David. *Smalltalk 80: the Language and its Implementation.* Addison-Wesley, May 1983.

Hewitt 1977: Hewitt, C. Viewing control structures as patterns of passing messages. *Artificial Intelligence*, 8:323–364, 1977.

Hölzle 1994: Hölzle, U. *Adaptive Optimization for Self: Reconciling high performance with Exploratory Programming.* PhD thesis, Stanford University, August 1994.

Hutchinson 1987: Hutchinson, Norman C. *Emerald: An Object-Based Language for Distributed Programming.* PhD thesis, University of Washington, September 1987.

Johnson and Foote 1988: Johnson, Ralph E. and Foote, Brian. Designing reusable classes. *Journal of Object-Oriented Programming*, 1(2), 1988.

Matthes and Schmidt 1992: Matthes, F. and Schmidt, J.W. Definition of the Tycoon Language TL – a preliminary report. Informatik Fachbericht FBI-HH-B-160/92, Fachbereich Informatik, Universität Hamburg, Germany, November 1992.

Meyer 1988: Meyer, B. *Object-oriented Software Construction.* International Series in Computer Science. Prentice Hall, Englewood Cliffs, New Jersey, 1988.

Meyer 1989: Meyer, B. Static typing for Eiffel. (Technical report distributed with Eiffel Release 2), July 1989.

Meyer 1990: Meyer, B. Lessons from the design of the eiffel libraries. *Communications of the ACM*, 33(9):69–88, September 1990.

Milner et al. 1990: Milner, R., Tofte, M., and Harper, R. *The Definition of Standard ML.* MIT Press, Cambridge, Massachusetts, 1990.

Nelson 1991: Nelson, G., editor. *Systems programming with Modula-3.* Series in innovative technology. Prentice Hall, Englewood Cliffs, New Jersey, 1991.

Pierce and Turner 1993: Pierce, B.C. and Turner, D.N. Statically typed friendly functions via partially abstract types. Rapport de Recherche 1899, INRIA, Domaine de Voluceau Rocquencourt 78153 Le Chesnay Cedex - France, May 1993.

Pierce 1994: Pierce, B. C. Bounded quantification is undecidable. *Information and Computation*, 112(1):131–165, July 1994. Also in Carl A. Gunter and John C. Mitchell, editors, *Theoretical Aspects of Object-Oriented Programming: Types, Semantics, and Language Design* (MIT Press, 1994).

Ungar and Smith 1987: Ungar, D. and Smith, R.B. Self: The power of simplicity. In *Proceedings of the Object-Oriented Programming Systems, Languages and Applications Conference, Orlando, Florida*, pages 227–242, 1987.

Typed Object-Oriented Functional Programming with Late Binding[*]

Zhenyu Qian and Bernd Krieg-Brückner

FB3 Informatik, Universität Bremen, Postfach 330440, D-28334 Bremen, Germany

Abstract. Object-oriented programming languages are suitable for describing real-world objects, functional programming languages for algebraic values. In this paper we propose an *object-oriented functional* programming language, called TOFL, which combines many desired properties of the two paradigms. In particular, TOFL unifies object classes, inheritance, (method) redefinitions and late binding as in object-oriented languages, algebraic data types, higher-order functions, type classes and type inference (without type reconstruction in this paper) as in functional languages. We translate TOFL into a stratified and explicitly typed λ-calculus $\mathcal{T}$ with overloaded functions, where redefinitions and late binding become late binding of overloaded functions. The operational semantics of $\mathcal{T}$ gives a semantics and a simple prototyping implementation of TOFL.

1 Introduction

A programming language should provide constructs for coding real-world objects such as persons and cars, and algebraic values and operations such as integers, vectors and their operations. Object-oriented (programming) languages can naturally describe *objects* by giving their features, while functional (programming) languages can naturally construct algebraic values by terms of function symbols. This paper proposes an *object-oriented functional (programming) language*, called TOFL, which combines many desired properties of the object-oriented and the functional paradigm.

Note that algebraic values are supported in almost all object-oriented languages. Some object-oriented languages such as `Smalltalk` and `Eiffel` view algebraic values as objects. But the behaviors of these algebraic values are sometimes unusual in comparison with what is well known in mathematics. In other object-oriented languages such as `C++`, one may use conventional imperative constructs to define algebraic values and operations, but one needs also to struggle with many low-level constructs unnecessary for software design at a high level. We believe that the ways how algebraic values are supported in object-oriented programming could be greatly improved in an object-oriented functional language.

From a certain perspective, real-world objects can also be represented in a functional language such as `ML` or `Haskell` as terms of function symbols. However, the coding is much less natural than in object-oriented languages, since data of some fixed term structures do not enjoy many properties of data characterized by features.

[*] Research partially supported by ESPRIT Basic Research WG *COMPASS* 6112.

Both object-oriented and functional languages provide excellent support for writing reusable code. However, due to the fundamental difference in their data representations, the forms of code reuse they support are very different. The language TOFL combines some important mechanisms for code reuse in **Eiffel** [34] and **Haskell** [29].

The most important notions supporting code reuse in **Eiffel** are *inheritance, subtyping, (method) redefinition*, and *late (method) binding*. Syntactically an **Eiffel** program is a collection of *classes* and each class declares a set of *attribute names* and *methods*. Semantically an object can be created from a class and may be regarded as a record consisting of the name of the class, *attributes* for all attribute names of the class, and all methods of the class. The type of an object is the class from which the object has been created. Inheritance allows to define a *subclass* by reusing the code of *superclasses* and adding new attribute names and methods. A redefinition can bind a method name inherited from a superclass to a new type and body for a subclass. A subclass is a subtype of a superclass, and an object of a subclass can be used for a superclass. More concretely, a variable, an attribute name or a method parameter of a superclass can hold an object of a subclass. A method is a function or a procedure applied to a *privileged* object, called a *receiver*, and possible *additional arguments*. When a method application is executed, *late binding* decides, depending on the class of the receiver at run time, which body the method name should be really bound to.

The main features supporting code reuse in **Haskell** [29] are ML-polymorphism, a kind of overloaded functions [49] and higher-order functions. Note that ML-polymorphism usually means at least two things: (1) a type is an expression possibly containing type variables, which are all-quantified at the outermost position, and (2) a typable expression always has a *principal type* (i.e. a most general type), and if the type is not explicitly given then it can always be reconstructed automatically. An overloaded function is a function name of a certain type, where the function name is bound to different bodies for different instantiations of the type. Higher-order functions allow functions to take functions as arguments. Note that **Haskell** is statically type-safe in the sense that if a program is typable at compile time, then no type-errors will occur at run time.

Eiffel does not support ML-polymorphism nor higher-order functions, and is not statically type-safe [16]. **Haskell** does not support inheritance and late binding of **Eiffel**. In fact, **Haskell** requires that all elements of a list must strictly have the same type, (i.e. does not allow heterogeneous lists,) and does not need late binding.

The language TOFL unifies and extends inheritance, subtyping, redefinition, late binding as in **Eiffel**, the kind of overloaded functions and higher-order functions as in **Haskell**. In addition, TOFL will support a kind of ML-polymorphism extending that of **Haskell**, but the design of type reconstruction is still open. In fact, if an expression in TOFL contains no explicit types at all, then its type reconstruction may be problematic due to polymorphic recursive functions and subtyping. Although there is a first study on type reconstruction for restricted expressions with some explicit types [44], we have not yet found a solution, with which we are completely satisfied. For this paper, we assume that an expression in TOFL always contains explicit types where needed. Note that both **ML** and **Haskell** programs may need a few explicit types for type reconstruction.

The language TOFL is just a language core: it does not consider imperative features like pointers and assignments. However, TOFL could be easily extended with reference values and reference types in the style of SML [35].

Based on the type inference, we translate TOFL into a calculus denoted as $\mathcal{T}$. The calculus $\mathcal{T}$ is a stratified and explicitly typed λ-calculus with a notion of overloaded functions. The concepts of redefinition and late binding in TOFL are translated into the concept of late binding of overloaded functions in $\mathcal{T}$.

Technically, the calculus $\mathcal{T}$ will be built in two steps. The first step constructs a calculus denoted as $\mathcal{Q}$ by extending Core-XML by Harper and Mitchell [26] with subtyping and a kind of bounded quantification. The second step constructs $\mathcal{T}$ by introducing a notion of overloaded functions into $\mathcal{Q}$. It can be proved that the reduction of $\mathcal{T}$ satisfies the usual Subject Reduction property and Church-Rosser property. Thus $\mathcal{T}$ has a consistent semantics. A consistent semantics of TOFL can be derived from its translation into $\mathcal{T}$.

The rest of the paper is organized as follows: Section 2 discusses some related work. The language TOFL is introduced and justified in Sections 3 and 4. Section 5 defines the calculus $\mathcal{Q}$. Section 6 defines the calculus $\mathcal{T}$. The rules for typing TOFL and translating TOFL into the calculus $\mathcal{T}$ are given in Section 7. We conclude in Section 8. Due to lack of space we omit some standard inference rules and all proofs in the paper. The reader may refer to the long version [43] for details.

In the sequel we write $\tau_1 \to \tau_2 \to \tau_3$ for $\tau_1 \to (\tau_2 \to \tau_3)$, where τ_1, τ_2 and τ_3 are types, and $(s_1\ s_2\ s_3)$ for $((s_1\ s_2)\ s_3)$, where s_1, s_2 and s_3 are terms. Furthermore, we write $\overline{o_n}$ for the sequence $o_1, \cdots, o_n$, where o_i, $i = 1, \ldots, n$, are syntactic objects.

2 Related work

Strachey [47] distinguished between parametric and ad-hoc polymorphism. Cardelli and Wegner [12] refined Strachey's classification by distinguishing between parametric, inclusion, overloading and coercion polymorphism. In Cardelli and Wegner's terminology, TOFL supports some forms of parametric, inclusion and overloading polymorphism.

From a certain type-theoretical perspective, many languages and powerful type theories (see e.g. [6, 7, 12, 11, 41, 3, 2, 40, 8, 17, 21, 24] and the collections [25, 1]) have been successful in modeling many important concepts of object-oriented and functional programming. However, they did not pay enough attention to the combination of object classes, late binding and static polymorphic type inference.

Several authors, e.g. Cardelli [10], Castagna, Ghelli and Longo [15] and Curien and Ghelli [18], suggested encodings of operations on objects e.g. the creation, update and access operations, in their frameworks. Since our approach allows algebraic operations directly, we regard these operations directly as algebraic operations.

Läufer and Odersky [32, 33] combined existential types with ML-polymorphism for functional languages. In fact, an existential type is an *interface*, where the existentially quantified type variables model a *hidden* part [36, 12]. Thus an existential type can nicely formulate a special case of inheritance, namely the relationship between abstract and concrete classes. However, it is relatively difficult to use an existential type for other cases of inheritance such as refinement and extension.

The language Haskell++ [30] extends Haskell with object classes, instances of object classes, an instantiation relation between object classes and instances of object classes, an inheritance relation among object classes and an inheritance relation among instances of object classes. In addition, all these concepts can be combined with a form of existential types as in [32, 33]. But the relationship between these concepts appears to be involved.

Some object-oriented languages such as Eiffel and Smalltalk are called *single dispatching*, since their methods must have a receiver and late binding is based on the run-time type of the receiver. Other object-oriented languages such as CLOS are called *multiple dispatching*, since their methods can have more than one receiver and late binding is equally based on the (possibly different) types of all receivers at run time. The language TOFL is neither single dispatching nor multiple dispatching in the above sense. In fact, a method in TOFL belongs to a class, but can be applied to a composite argument, e.g. a tuple, which contains several "receivers". Furthermore, late binding selects a body for a method name based on one common type, i.e. the least type, of all receivers at run time. Note that binary methods[1] can be naturally supported.

Most object-oriented languages so far are heavily based on a concept of message-passing. Castagna, Ghelli and Longo [15] distinguished two forms of message-passing. One form is called *record-based*, where an object is a record containing a method for each message (see e.g. [9]). The other form is called *overloading-based*, where messages are names of (overloaded) functions and the selection of a body for a function name depends on the type of the object the message is passed to. The approaches of CLOS [5] and Dylan [4] are overloading-based. Ghelli was the first to introduce an overloading-based approach for typed languages [22].

Castagna, Ghelli and Longo [15] have studied an overloading-based simply typed λ-calculus with subtypes, called the $\lambda\&$ calculus. Roughly speaking, the $\lambda\&$ calculus extends the usual (simply typed) λ-terms with terms of the form $(t_1\&\cdots\&t_n)$, called *overloaded functions*. Each component t_i of an overloaded function is a term of type $\tau_i \to \tau_i'$, and the overloaded function $(t_1\&\cdots\&t_n)$ has the type $(\tau_1 \to \tau_1'\&\cdots\&\tau_n \to \tau_n')$. Applying an overloaded function to an argument s that is closed and in normal form[2] is equivalent to applying t_k to s, when the type τ_k is among $\overline{\tau_n}$, the least type of s. Note that the selection has to be made at run time, since the type of a term may be decreased when the term is reduced. This means that the $\lambda\&$ calculus does have late binding. However, the $\lambda\&$ calculus is still very restricted since its types do not contain type variables.

Recently, Castagna [14] added overloaded functions to the explicit polymorphism of $F_\le$ by Curien and Ghelli [18] and built a calculus denoted as $F_\le^\&$. In the calculus $F_\le^\&$, an overloaded function $(t_1\&\cdots\&t_n)$ must have the type $(\Lambda\alpha \le A_1.\sigma_1 \to \sigma_1'\&\cdots\&\Lambda\alpha \le A_n.\sigma_n \to \sigma_n')$ where each A_i is a base type[3]. If A_k is among $\overline{A_n}$, the

---

[1] Informally, a method is called *binary*, when its late binding depends on the common class of at least two arguments at run time. In Eiffel, these two arguments are in fact the receiver and one additional argument.

[2] A term is closed if it contains no free variables. A term is in normal form if it cannot be reduced any more.

[3] In reality the restriction is more subtle than explained here [14].

least supertype of a type σ, then applying $(\tau_1 \& \cdots \& t_n)$ to σ leads to the selection of t_k and yields $(t_k\ \sigma)$. However, the selection in the calculus $F_{\leq}^{\&}$ is essentially different from the one in the $\lambda\&$ calculus, since the type argument, on which the selection in the calculus $F_{\leq}^{\&}$ depends, is obtained by static type analysis[4].

The calculus $\mathcal{T}$ to be proposed in this paper can be obtained by extending a stratified fragment of $F_{\leq}$ with overloaded functions from the $\lambda\&$ calculus. In order to avoid the complication caused by types of the form $(\tau_1 \to \tau_1' \& \cdots \& \tau_n \to \tau_n')$, we require that all bodies $\overline{t_n}$ of an overloaded function $(t_1 \& \cdots \& t_n)$ have types that are only different on the quantifications of type variables, and one body has the type with a greatest quantification for each variable. This generalizes the situation in **Haskell**, where the class-instance relation is regarded as a subtyping relation $\leq$. Experiences with **Haskell** suggest that the above restriction on the types of bodies should not lead to any serious inconvenience in practical programming.

Let us summarize the relationship between the calculus $\mathcal{T}$ and the calculus $\lambda\&$ or $F_{\leq}^{\&}$ as follows. From one perspective, the calculus $\mathcal{T}$ is less general than the $\lambda\&$ calculus, since the former does not allow types formed by $\&$ and the latter does. From another perspective, the calculus $\mathcal{T}$ is more general than the $\lambda\&$ calculus, since the former allows type variables and the latter does not. In addition, the calculus $\mathcal{T}$ is different from the calculus $F_{\leq}^{\&}$, since the selection of bodies of an overloaded function in $\mathcal{T}$ is not comparable to that in $F_{\leq}^{\&}$, but rather to that in the $\lambda\&$ calculus, i.e. the selection in $\mathcal{T}$ is a run-time one.

3 Some ideas behind the design of the language TOFL

3.1 Values and types in TOFL

A *value* of TOFL is either like an *object* in **Eiffel** or a *functional value* in **Haskell**. Analogously, a *type* of TOFL is either like a *class* in **Eiffel** or a type (hereafter an *algebraic data type*) in **Haskell**.

Note that some other authors, e.g. [6, 7, 8, 17], considered the interface-implementation relationship in object-oriented programming and call an interface a type and an implementation a class. The language TOFL does not consider this relationship.

More precisely, a class in TOFL is a named collection of attribute names with types and methods. A method consists of a name, a type and a body. Since we do not consider the interface-implementation relationship, everything in a class is "public".

An *object* in TOFL can only be *created* from a class and is semantically a record with the name of the class as the tag and consisting of *attributes* and *methods*. The tag of an object can never be changed. An attribute is a value for an attribute name and can be updated at run time. An object contains one attribute for each attribute name of its class. All attributes of an object compose a mutable *internal state*. An object contains all methods of its class. The methods of an object cannot be changed at run time and thus all objects of the same class have the same methods.

A *subclass* of a *superclass inherits* all attribute names and methods of the super-class, may have new ones, and may *redefine* some inherited methods by new bodies.

---

[4] This should be possible in most practical cases according to the claim by Ghelli [23] that the undecidable cases [42] of type checking in $F_{\leq}$ are negligible for real programs.

An object of a subclass in TOFL can be used for a superclass. Different from `Eiffel`, a redefinition in TOFL cannot change the type of a method, except that the self-type, which corresponds to `like Current` in `Eiffel`, is implicitly adjusted to the subclass. (See below for more details.)

A functional value or an algebraic data type in TOFL is constructed by *value constructors* or *type constructors*, respectively, like in `Haskell`. Since objects and functional values are mixed in TOFL, a value constructor may be applied to objects. Since classes and algebraic data types are also mixed in TOFL, a type constructor may also be applied to classes. For example, if *Point* is a class, *pt* an object of *Point*, *List* a type constructor, *empty* and *cons* are constructors for *List*, then *List(Point)* is a type, and *(cons pt empty)* a value in TOFL.

3.2 Declaring subtyping in TOFL

In an object-oriented language allowing subtyping, a value of a subtype can be used for a supertype. Since this is also how a subclass in TOFL is intended to be used, a subtyping relation defined by a TOFL program always includes the subclass relation in the program.

Since objects need not be constructed as terms of function symbols, there is no guarantee that an object can be used for an algebraic data type. Thus TOFL does not allow a class to be a subtype of an algebraic data type.

A functional value can be regarded as an object, but it usually cannot have an internal state. Thus TOFL allows an algebraic data type to be a subtype of a class when the class has no attribute names.

In order to simulate the `Haskell` type-class system, TOFL allows a kind of conditionals similar to those in instance declarations in `Haskell`[5]. For example, let *Eq* be a class containing no attribute names, and *List* a type constructor declared as in a functional language. Then TOFL allows a declaration with the meaning that "if a type τ is a subtype of *Eq* then *List(τ)* is a subtype of *Eq*". According to this declaration, if a class *Point* (or an algebraic data type *Int*) is a subtype of *Eq* then the type *List(Point)* (or *List(Int)*, respectively) is a subtype of *Eq*.

One may still ask whether TOFL allows subtyping among algebraic data types. Although it is technically not impossible, TOFL chooses to avoid it at the moment for the sake of simplicity. Since no widespread functional languages allow subtyping, the decision does not affect our intention to combine widespread object-oriented and functional languages.

We may also justify the design decisions made above from a methodological point of view, where we view a class as an executable specification[6] and an algebraic data type as an implementation. The difference between a specification and an implementation is that a specification can be refined into another specification or an implementation, i.e. the latter is a subtype of the former, whereas an implementation cannot be refined any more. This view also coincides with that in `Haskell` [49], where a class represents a specification that may be nonexecutable, and an algebraic data type an implementation.

---

[5] Note that a class in `Haskell` has no notion of attributes as in object-oriented languages.

[6] In fact, TOFL would support this view more strongly if it were extended to have pre- and postconditions as `Eiffel`. But this topic is out of the scope of the current paper.

Note that the coexistence of some kinds of objects and functional values is not that unusual in existing object-oriented languages. For example, the language Sather [48] allows user-defined value classes for (functional) values without internal states. However, TOFL is more expressive than Sather in the sense that TOFL allows type constructors to be applied to algebraic data types and classes, whereas Sather does not.

3.3   The self-type, co- and contra-variance

The *self-type* (or *current type*) is a notation denoting the run-time class of the receiver, to which a method is applied. In Eiffel, the construct like Current is the self-type. For example, if we have the following method declaration in Eiffel:

```
equal (other: like Current): Boolean is ... end;
```

then the expression X.equal(Y) is type-correct at run time only when the run-time type of Y is the same as or a subclass of that of X.

Co- or *contra-variance* describes changes of types along subtyping. It may describe how a redefinition can modify the type of a method. We say that a part of the type of a method can be redefined *co-variantly* (or *contra-variantly*) when it can become a subtype (or supertype, respectively) in a redefinition. Note that even if a redefinition is made for a subclass without changing the type of the method, the self-type in the type induces a special kind of co-variantly redefined types, which we call *systematically co-variantly redefined types*, since the self-type in the redefinition represents the subclass.

Co- or contra-variance may also describe how a composite type changes when a component changes. We say that a subtyping relation is *co-variant* (or *contra-variant*) for a type constructor, e.g. *List* or $\rightarrow$, at an argument position when a type constructed by the type constructor, e.g. $List(\tau_1)$ or $\tau_1 \rightarrow \tau_2$, always becomes a subtype (or supertype, respectively) whenever the argument τ_1 or τ_2 becomes a subtype.

Different languages may emphasize different aspects of program development and thus have different approaches to changing types [15, 13]. In Eiffel, a redefinition should specialize a method, and thus all argument types of a method can be redefined co-variantly [34], even when this causes static type unsafety [16]. The language Sather [48] emphasizes static type safety, and thus supports only systematically co-variantly redefined types at the receiver position and contra-variantly redefined types at all other argument positions. Many type theories following the idea of Cardelli [9] emphasize static type safety, and thus require subtyping to be contra-variant for $\rightarrow$-types at the domain position, co-variant for $\rightarrow$-types at the range position and for all other types at all positions.

The language TOFL allows the self-type in method declarations and thus the systematically co-variant redefinition of types. However, TOFL does not allow the domain type of a method to be redefined co-variantly nor contra-variantly. The reason against the co-variance is that TOFL should be statically type-safe, the reason against the contra-variance is that it seems to be of little use in practice and would make the type system of TOFL very complicated. In fact, a redefinition in TOFL can never modify the type. Bruce reported similar experiences and came to a similar design decision in a different object-oriented language [6].

A subtyping relation $\leq$ in TOFL must be co-variant at all positions of all type constructors except $\to$. For $\to$-types the following condition must hold:

$$\tau_1 \to \tau_2 \leq \tau_1' \to \tau_2' \iff \tau_1 = \tau_1' \ \& \ \tau_2 \leq \tau_2'.$$

The requirement that the domain types of the $\to$-types should be equal is called *non-variance* at the domain position. Note that non-variance is simple and does not restrict the parts of TOFL that correspond to **Eiffel** and **Haskell**. If a subtyping relation in TOFL were contra-variant for $\to$-types at the domain position, then the type system would become more complicated. To see this, let us first mention that TOFL allows the programmer to write a set of types as a bound in a quantification of a type variable. Intuitively, a set of types means the greatest subtype of these types. If TOFL allowed contra-variance at the domain of an $\to$-type, then we would need a mechanism to construct the least supertype of two types, since the greatest subtype of two $\to$-types would intuitively have a domain that should be the least supertype of the domains of these two $\to$-types. A mechanism for constructing least supertypes in TOFL would make the type system very complicated.

4 The language TOFL

The syntax of TOFL is given in Figure 1, where α, β range over *type variables*, x, y, z over *identifiers*, κ ranges over *classes*, χ over *type constructors* and a over *attributes*.

Monomorphic types	τ =	$\alpha \ \mid \ \kappa \ \mid \ \chi(\overline{\tau_n})$ (for n-ary $\chi, n \geq 0$)
Type sets	T =	$\{\overline{\tau_n}\}$ $(n \geq 1)$
Polymorphic types	σ =	$\tau \ \mid \ \forall \alpha \leq T.\sigma$
Expressions	s, t =	$x \ \mid \ (s \ t) \ \mid \ \lambda x.s \ \mid \ \mathbf{let} \ x = s \ \mathbf{in} \ t \ \mid \ \mathbf{fix} \ x.t$
		$\mid \ new(\kappa) \ \mid \ update(s, a, t) \ \mid \ s.a \ \mid \ s{\uparrow}$
Declarations	d =	$\mathbf{class} \ \kappa \leq K \ \mathbf{attr} \ a :: \xi \ \mathbf{meth} \ x :: \sigma = s, y = t$
		$\mid \ \mathbf{datatype} \ \chi(\overline{\alpha_h}) \ \mathbf{constr} \ x :: \sigma$
		$\mid \ \mathbf{subtype} \ \overline{\alpha_h} \leq \overline{K_h} \Rightarrow \chi(\overline{\alpha_h}) \leq \kappa \ \mathbf{meth} \ y = t$
Programs	p =	$s \ \mid \ d; p$

Figure 1: The syntax of TOFL

4.1 Types

Intuitively, *classes* in TOFL combine object classes in **Eiffel** and type classes in **Haskell**. *Type constructors* construct agebraic data types in a similar way as in **Haskell**. *Monomorphic types* are constructed by type variables, classes and type constructors. We presume that the type constructors $\to$ and $(\_, \cdots, \_)$ are predefined so that $\to$-types $\tau_1 \to \tau_2$ and n-tuples $(\overline{\tau_n})$ with $n > 0$ always are defined. Classes and type constructors requiring no arguments are called *base types*. Monomorphic types containing no type variables are called *ground* types and ranged over by ξ.

A set T of monomorphic types is called a *type set*. Intuitively, if the semantics $[\![\tau]\!]$ of a monomorphic type τ is a set, then the semantics of a type set $\{\overline{\tau_n}\}$ is the intersection $\bigcap_{1 \leq i \leq n} [\![\tau_i]\!]$. A singleton type set $\{\tau\}$ is considered to be equal to the element τ. A type set consisting of only classes may also be called a *class set* and denoted by K.

Polymorphic types are obtained from monomorphic types by all-quantifying type variables at the outermost position using subtyping $\leq$ and type sets as bounds. The definition of $\leq$ will be given below.

The notion of type sets is inspired by that of sorts by Nipkow and Prehofer in a **Haskell** type class system [38]. The differences are that a quantification in TOFL uses a subtyping relation, whereas a quantification in **Haskell** uses a membership relation, and a type set in TOFL may contain monomorphic types, whereas a sort in [38] contains only names of type classes.

A polymorphic type is said to be *closed* if it contains no free type variables. A subexpression of a monomorphic type is called a *fragment* of the monomorphic type.

4.2 Declarations

A class declaration (cf. the syntax in Figure 1) declares a *class* κ, which is a *subclass* of each *superclass* in K and contains an *attribute name declaration* $a :: \xi$, a *method declaration* $x :: \sigma = s$ and a *redefinition* $y = t$. All classes in K must be declared beforehand. In general, a class may come with 0 or more declarations of attribute names and methods and redefinitions. We write the syntax with one piece of each for notational simplicity. A class can be declared at most once in the entire program. For convenience, we assume that an attribute name and a method name can be declared at most once in the entire program. We say that an attribute name or a method is *available* in a class when it is either declared in the class or available in a superclass. It is assumed that there are no mutually recursively defined methods available in the same class. This is not a restriction since such methods can be coded by *recursive functions* to be mentioned below [37].

An attribute name a can only be of a ground type ξ. This looks restrictive but is a consequence of several design decisions. First, as in many object-oriented languages, an object or a class in TOFL is global in the sense that it is visible everywhere in a program. Thus the type of an attribute should be closed. Furthermore, we decide that the type of an attribute in TOFL should not have any quantifications of type variables. If this was not the case, a more complex type system would be needed. For example, if an attribute a in a class declaration κ has a type $\forall \alpha \leq \kappa'.\alpha \to \alpha$, then the function $\lambda x.(x.a)$ would be of the type $\forall \beta \leq \kappa.\beta \to (\forall \alpha \leq \kappa'.\alpha \to \alpha)$, which is clearly not allowed in TOFL. Since attributes of an object have only ground types, TOFL does not need a type inference system as in [50, 45, 39].

A method declaration in a class declaration (cf. the syntax in Figure 1) declares a method with a name x, a closed polymorphic type σ and a *body* s. The type σ must be of the form $\overline{\forall \alpha_n \leq K_n}.\forall \alpha \leq \kappa.\tau_1 \to \tau_2$ for $n \geq 0$. It is clear that a method must be a function. The type variable α of the innermost quantification denotes the self-type, and thus its bound must be the class κ. In static type inference the self-type can be instantiated into a subtype of κ as a normal type variable.

A redefinition $y = t$ in a class declaration (cf. the syntax in Figure 1) redefines the method named y available in κ with a body t. A redefinition cannot include any type for y.

Note that there are no possibilities in TOFL to introduce the self-type for an attribute name, since an attribute name must have a ground type. This coincides with our requirement on static type safety. In fact, the self-type for an attribute name may easily cause static type unsafety at a place where its attribute value is updated. The reader may refer to [43] for an example.

A datatype declaration (cf. the syntax in Figure 1) declares a type constructor χ with a value constructor x as in functional languages such as Haskell. (Again our syntax includes only one value constructor for notational simplicity.) A type constructor can be declared at most once in the entire program. A value of a type $\chi(\overline{\tau_h})$ must be of the form $x(\overline{t_h})$ where each t_i is a value of the type τ_i. For example, an n-tuple type constructor $(\_, \cdots, \_))$ is assumed to be declared with a value constructor also written as $(\_, \cdots, \_)$ of the polymorphic type $\forall \overline{\alpha_2}.\alpha_1 \rightarrow \cdots \rightarrow \alpha_n \rightarrow (\overline{\alpha_n})$, and the type constructor $List$ can be declared with value constructors $empty$ and $cons$ of the polymorphic types $\forall \alpha.List(\alpha)$ and $\forall \alpha.\alpha \rightarrow List(\alpha) \rightarrow List(\alpha)$, respectively.

A subtype declaration (cf. the syntax in Figure 1) declares that a type $\chi(\overline{\tau_h})$ is a subtype of class κ whenever each τ_i is a subtype of K_i. (The definition of subtyping on all types will be given below.) As explained in Subsection 3, class κ cannot have any attribute names available. Note that a subtype declaration may only contain redefinitions, but no attribute name and method declarations. (Again the syntax includes only one redefinition for notational simplicity.)

A formula of the form $\kappa \leq K$ or $\forall \overline{\alpha_h \leq K_h} \Rightarrow \chi(\overline{\alpha_h}) \leq \kappa$, which occurs in a class or subtype declaration, is called a *subtyping declaration*. For notational simplicity, we use a (finite) set Ω to record all subtyping declarations in a program. Then the subtyping relation $\leq$ defined by the program is the smallest reflexive and transitive relation on ground types and sets of ground types satisfying the following conditions:

- If Ω contains $\overline{\kappa \leq K}$, then $\kappa \leq K$ holds.
- If Ω contains $\overline{\alpha_h \leq K_h} \Rightarrow \chi(\overline{\alpha_h}) \leq \kappa$ and $\xi_i \leq K_i$ hold for all $i = 1, \ldots, h$, then $\chi(\overline{\xi_h}) \leq \kappa$ holds.
- $\xi_1 \rightarrow \xi_2 \leq \xi_1' \rightarrow \xi_2'$ holds if and only if $\xi_1 = \xi_1'$ and $\xi_2 \leq \xi_2'$ hold.
- For every type constructor χ that is not $\rightarrow$, $\chi(\overline{\xi_n}) \leq \chi(\overline{\xi_n'})$ holds if and only if $\xi_i \leq \xi_i'$ hold for all $i = 1, \ldots, n$.
- For all sets T and T' of ground types, $T \leq T'$ holds if and only if for each $\xi' \in T'$ there is $\xi \in T$ such that $\xi \leq \xi'$ holds.

The last condition in the above coincides with the intuition that if the semantics of a type is a set then the semantics of a type set is the intersection of its types and the relation $\leq$ the subset relation. Note that for all sets T and T' of ground types, if $T \supseteq T'$ then $T \leq T'$. But the converse does not always hold. For example, if Ω contains $Circ \leq Fig$, then $\{Circ\} \leq \{Fig\}$ holds but $\{Circ\} \supseteq \{Fig\}$ does not.

We know when an attribute name or a method is available in a class. Now we define that a method is *available* in a non-class ground type ξ if it is available in some ground type ξ' with $\xi \leq \xi'$. Note that ξ' may be a class.

Now we formulate some restrictions on the declarations of a program, which have not been described in the above syntax.

1. Ω contains exactly one formula $\kappa \leq K$ for each κ.
2. $\kappa \leq Top$ holds for each κ.
3. Ω contains $\forall \overline{\alpha_h} \leq Top \Rightarrow \chi(\overline{\alpha_h}) \leq Top$ for each h-ary type constructor χ.
4. Ω contains at most one formula $\forall \overline{\alpha_h} \leq K_h \Rightarrow \chi(\overline{\alpha_h}) \leq \kappa$ for each χ and κ.
5. If Ω contains $\forall \overline{\alpha_h} \leq K_h \Rightarrow \chi(\overline{\alpha_h}) \leq \kappa$, then for each κ' with $\kappa \leq \kappa'$, Ω contains $\forall \overline{\alpha_h} \leq K'_h \Rightarrow \chi(\overline{\alpha_h}) \leq \kappa'$ such that $K_i \leq K'_i$ for all $i = 1, \ldots, h$.
6. For any two ground types ξ_1 and ξ_2, if a method x is available in both of them, then there must be a unique supertype ξ of ξ_1 and ξ_2 satisfying that the method x is (re)defined for ξ but not redefined for any type ξ' such that $\xi' \leq \xi$, $\xi' \neq \xi$, $\xi_1 \leq \xi'$ and $\xi_2 \leq \xi'$.

The restriction 1 is not a real restriction, since one can always write $\kappa \leq K \cup K'$ instead of separate $\kappa \leq K$ and $\kappa \leq K'$. The restrictions 2 and 3 say that a program in TOFL always presumes a class Top, which is the supertype of all ground types. A polymorphic type $\forall \alpha \leq Top.\sigma$ will sometimes be written as $\forall \alpha.\sigma$.

The restrictions 4 and 5 are translations of restrictions in Haskell [29]. (See also [38].) They are used to ensure the uniqueness of principal types and late binding. We need them in Subsection 6.3 when considering late binding.

The restriction 6 is also used to ensure the uniqueness of late binding. For example, consider the following declarations:

$$\textbf{class } Eq \; \textbf{meth } eq :: \forall \alpha \leq Eq.(\alpha, \alpha) \to Bool = s;$$
$$\textbf{class } A \leq Eq \; \textbf{meth } eq = t_1;$$
$$\textbf{class } B \leq Eq \; \textbf{meth } eq = t_2;$$

It is easy to see that the program satisfies the restriction. If a and b are objects of A and B, respectively, then the expression $eq(a, a)$ can uniquely select the body t_1 for eq, the expression $eq(b, b)$ the body t_2, and the expression $eq(a, b)$ the body s. Note that this treatment of $eq(a, b)$ is unusual in existing object-oriented languages. If we add an additional declaration

$$\textbf{class } C \leq \{A, B\};$$

then the program no longer satisfies the restriction. In this case, if c is an object of C, then the expression $eq(c, c)$ cannot uniquely select a body for eq since both t_1 and t_2 are available in C. If instead we add a declaration with a redefinition

$$\textbf{class } C \leq \{A, B\} \; \textbf{meth } eq = t_3;$$

then the program satisfies the restriction again. In this case, $eq(c, c)$ can uniquely select the body t_3 for eq.

Note that the restriction 6 generalizes a restriction in many existing object-oriented languages: if a method is (re)defined in two different classes then the method must be redefined in their common subclasses.

4.3 Expressions

The forms of expressions are divided into three groups. The first group consists of the usual expressions as in Core-ML [19], i.e. *function applications* $(s\ t)$, *function abstractions* $\lambda x.s$ and *let-constructs* let $x = s$ in t, and *recursive functions* **fix** $x.t$ as in [37]. It is assumed that in let $x = s$ in t, x does not occur in s, since this may be coded by a recursive function. The occurrence of x directly after let in let $x = s$ in t or directly after **fix** in **fix** $x.t$ is called the *binder*.

In order to deal with objects in TOFL, we need a second group of constructs $new(\kappa)$, $update(s, a, t)$ and $(s.a)$. Their meanings are as follows. First, $new(\kappa)$ creates a new object of class κ with arbitrary initial attributes. Assume that an object s has a value for an attribute name a and t is a value of the same type as a. Then $update(s, a, t)$ replaces the value for a in s by t. Finally, $s.a$ yields the value for a in s. Note that the approach here is direct and simple, compared with e.g. [10, 15, 18, 14].

The third group of expressions consists only of the form $s\uparrow$. The up-arrow *coerces* the static type of a value to a supertype and is only useful in static type inference: at run time $s\uparrow$ and s have the same meaning. In **Eiffel**, implicit coercion takes place at many places. However, implicit coercion in an ML-style type inference with subtyping may lead to a huge amount of subtyping constraints on type variables [28] (see also [20, 46]). The language TOFL chooses to annotate the coercion explicitly so that the amount of subtyping constraints may be controlled by the programmer. The advantage is that pure functional programs in TOFL can go through static type inference as they usually do in functional languages. Note that the notation of explicit coercion in TOFL does not necessarily mean that the programmer has to write all explicit coercions himself. A compiler for TOFL could automatically insert explicit coercions at many places. Where an explicit coercion should be inserted is not a subject of the current paper.

Note that expressions in TOFL contain no types. However, a TOFL programmer is allowed to annotate an expression s by a type σ, i.e. to write $s :: \sigma$. How an expression can be annotated will be formally determined by a type inference system in Section 7. Here we just mention that the binder x of a let-construct let $x = s$ in t and of a recursive function **fix** $x.t$ can be annotated with a polymorphic type $\forall \overline{\alpha_n}.\tau$ and an occurrence of x in t in both cases by a monomorphic type $\tau[\overline{\tau_n/\alpha_n}]$. Note that if the binder x of a recursive function **fix** $x.t$ can be annotated with a polymorphic type, then typing an expression containing no types is undecidable [27, 31]. Therefore, in many functional languages, e.g. **ML**, the binder x in **fix** $x.t$ can only be annotated by a monomorphic type τ, and all occurrences of x in t by the same monomorphic type τ. This is too restrictive for TOFL, since a redefinition of a method in a subclass may affect the type of a method in a superclass when they both are (mutually) recursive. Note that in order to avoid the undecidability of type inference, a TOFL program should really contain explicit types for the binders of recursive functions. In fact, this has been achieved for recursively defined methods, since, as we have seen, a method in TOFL always has an explicit type.

4.4 Programs

Figure 2 contains a simple program in TOFL. As in most functional languages, functions in the program are defined using *patterns*, and are recursively defined, instead of using recursive functions of the form **fix** $x.s$. Functions in this style can be transformed into the TOFL syntax in a standard way. Furthermore, we assume that the base types *Bool* and *Int* with the usual values and the operations &, *eqInt* and *plusInt* are predefined, and the type constructor *List* with the usual value constructors *empty* and *cons* has been defined via a datatype declaration as mentioned before. Finally, we write let $x_1 = s_1$ in (let $x_2 = s_2$ in t) as let $x_1 = s_1, x_2 = s_2$ in t and $update((update(s, a_1, t_1) \cdots), a_n, t_n)$ as $update(s, a_1 = t_1, \cdots, a_n = t_n)$. In order to make the program more interesting, we assume that a function $noMethodBody ::$ $\forall \alpha.Str \rightarrow \alpha$ for exception handling has been predefined at class *Top*, where *Str* is the type for strings. Note that a discussion about exception handling is beyond the scope of the current paper.

```
class Eq
    meth eq :: ∀α ≤ Eq.(α, α) → Bool
        eq (x, y) = noMethodBody('for eq at Eq')
class Point ≤ Eq  attr pos :: Int
    meth move :: ∀α ≤ Point.α → Int → α
        move x y = update(x, pos, y);
        eq (x, y) = eq (x.pos, y.pos);
class ColorPoint ≤ Point  attr color :: Int
    meth eq (x, y) = (eq (x.pos, y.pos))&(eq (x.color, y.color));
class Num ≤ Eq;
    meth plus :: ∀α ≤ Num.(α, α) → α
        plus (x, y) = noMethodBody('for plus at Num');
subtype Int ≤ Num
    meth eq (x, y) = eqInt (x, y);
        plus (x, y) = plusInt (x, y);
subtype  α ≤ Eq ⇒ List(α) ≤ Eq
    meth eq (empty, empty) = True
        eq (empty, (cons y ys)) = False
        eq (cons x xs), empty) = False
        eq ((cons x xs), (cons y ys)) = (eq (x, y))&(eq (xs, ys));
let x = update(new(Point), pos = 1), y = update(new(ColorPoint), pos = 2, color = 2),
    z = (cons x↑ (cons y↑ empty :: List(Point))) in eq (z, z)
```

Figure 2: A program in TOFL

Intuitively, the class *Eq* should be a superclass of all classes that contain a method *eq*, but no objects of *Eq* should be created. Accordingly, we define no real body for *eq* at *Eq*. Any call to a body of *eq* here will lead to an exception handling. In **Eiffel** such classes are called *deferred* classes [34]. Although the notion of deferred classes is important, we do not think that it should be included in the language core.

The class *Point* is a subclass of *Eq*. It contains an attribute name *pos* for positions and two methods *eq* and *move* for testing the equality of two objects and moving an object to a new position. The class *ColorPoint* is a subclass of *Point*, contains an additional attribute *color* and redefines the method *eq*.

For modeling different kinds of numbers, we define a subclass *Num* of *Eq*, which should be the superclass of all classes containing the methods *eq* and *plus*. The type *Int* is a subtype of *Num* containing redefinitions for *eq* and *plus*.

The subtype declaration for *List* relates infinitely many list types with *Eq*. The method *eq* for a list type has its own body, which contains calls of *eq* on list elements. The selection of a body of *eq* for list elements is made at run time.

The last expression creates objects *x* and *y* of *Point* and *ColorPoint*, respectively, builds a heterogeneous list (*cons x↑* (*cons y↑* *empty* :: *List*(*Point*))), and compares the list with itself by *eq*. The up-arrows lift the static types of *x* and *y* to *Point*. Note that the method name *eq* in the expression should be first bound to a body for lists. In executing this body at run time, the bodies of *eq* for *Point* and *ColorPoint* are selected for the calls on the list elements.

5   The target calculus without overloaded functions

The language TOFL should be translated into a calculus denoted as $\mathcal{T}$. In this section we begin with a simplified case of $\mathcal{T}$, denoted as $\mathcal{Q}$, which can be obtained from the calculus $F_{\leq}$ by stratifying the types into monomorphic and polymorphic types, and by adding type constructors, classes, attributes and type sets.

5.1   Types, terms and environments

The types in $\mathcal{Q}$ are those of TOFL. Since a monomorphic type can be regarded as a term, we can define *positions* in a monomorphic type as in a term. A position of a monomorphic type corresponds to a fragment of the monomorphic type. For example, the positions $1 \cdot 1$ and $2 \cdot 1$ of $List(Eq) \rightarrow List(Bool)$ correspond to the fragments Eq and $Bool$, respectively. Note that the type constructor $\rightarrow$ is always written in an infix way. We use ϵ to denote the *root position*, p and q to range over positions and P and Q over sets of positions. A singleton position set $\{p\}$ may be written as p. We define $\mathcal{P}os(\tau, \alpha)$ as the set of all positions of occurrences of α in τ. We use $\tau_{|p}$ to denote the fragment at the position p in τ and $\tau[\tau']_P$ the result obtained from τ by replacing all fragments at positions of P by τ'. For example, let $\tau = List(Eq) \rightarrow List(Bool)$ and $P = \{1 \cdot 1, 2 \cdot 1\}$. Then $\tau[Point]_P = List(Point) \rightarrow List(Point)$.

The terms of $\mathcal{Q}$ are given by the following syntax, where x, y, z range over *variables*, and a, b over *attributes*:

$$\text{Terms} \quad s, t = \lambda x :: \tau.s \mid (s\ t) \mid \varLambda \alpha \leq T.s \mid (s\ \tau)$$
$$\mid \ \mathbf{let}\ x :: \sigma = s\ \mathbf{in}\ t \mid \mathbf{fix}\ x :: \sigma.t$$
$$\mid \ new(\kappa) \mid update(s, a, t) \mid (s.a)$$

A term is said to be *closed* if it contains no free type and term variables.

The intuitive meaning of each term is either standard or similar to the corresponding expression in TOFL except that we would like to comment on two things. First, the role of the let-construct $\mathbf{let}\ x :: \sigma = s\ \mathbf{in}\ t$ is similar to that in Core-ML [19]: it cannot be considered as a short-hand for $((\lambda x :: \sigma.t)\ s)$, since its type inference rule cannot be derived from other rules. Second, the binder x in $\mathbf{fix}\ x :: \sigma.t$ can have a polymorphic type σ. The reason has been given in Subsection 4.3. This is in contrast to Core-XML, where only recursive functions **fix** $x :: \tau.s$ with monomorphic types τ are allowed.

We define Σ as the set consisting of the pairs $(\kappa, \{\overline{a_n :: \xi_n}\})$ for each class κ in a program, where $\overline{a_n :: \xi_n}$ are all attribute names with types available in class κ. If $(\kappa, \{\overline{a_n :: \xi_n}\}) \in \Sigma$ then we use $\Sigma(\kappa)$ to denote $\{\overline{a_n :: \xi_n}\}$.

We use Γ to denote a sequence of formulas of the forms $\alpha \leq T$ or $x :: \sigma$, where $\alpha \leq T$ *declares* a type variable α with a type set T as *bound*, and $x :: \sigma$ a term variable x of a polymorphic type σ. In the sequel, a sequence Γ may be written as $[d_1, \cdots, d_n]$, and $+$ denotes the sequence concatenation operation.

An *environment* is a triple of the sets Σ and Ω (as defined in Subsection 4.2) and a sequence Γ. Since Σ and Ω remain fixed in many cases, they will be omitted whenever possible, and Γ will sometimes be called an environment.

Enviroments and types are constructed by some standard formation rules as e.g. in [18]. In particular, if the environment $\Gamma + [\alpha \leq T]$ (or $\vdash \Gamma + [x :: \sigma]$) is well-formed, then α (or x, respectively) must not occur freely in Γ or T (or Γ, respectively). Furthermore, if a monomorphic type τ is well-formed under an environment Γ then all type variables in τ must be declared in Γ.

5.2 Subtyping

A set of inference rules for deriving $\Gamma \vdash \tau \leq T$ or $\Gamma \vdash \sigma \leq \sigma'$ can easily be obtained from the definition of $\leq$ in Subsection 4.2 by allowing type variables and adding environments in a direct way. Furthermore we have the following two additional inference rules

$$\frac{\alpha \leq T \text{ occurs in } \Gamma}{\Gamma \vdash \alpha \leq T} \qquad \frac{\Gamma + [\overline{\alpha_n \leq T_n}] \vdash \tau \leq \tau'}{\Gamma \vdash \forall \overline{\alpha_n \leq T_n}.\tau \leq \forall \overline{\alpha_n \leq T_n}.\tau'}$$

Then we can define a subtyping relation, denoted by $\Gamma \vdash \tau \leq T$ or $\Gamma \vdash \sigma \leq \sigma'$, as the least reflexive transitive relation closed under these rules.

Note that the last rule means that $\Gamma \vdash \forall \overline{\alpha_n \leq T_n}.\tau \leq \forall \overline{\alpha_n \leq T'_n}.\tau'$ holds if and only if $\Gamma + [\overline{\alpha_n \leq T_n}] \vdash \tau \leq \tau'$ and $T_i = T'_i$ for all $i = 1, \ldots, n$ hold. The relation $\leq$ relates only polymorphic types with the same quantification bounds.

Wes distinguish two kinds of positions in a monomorphic type τ. A position of τ is called *non-variant* if it is inside the left-hand side of an $\rightarrow$ in τ, *co-variant* otherwise.

Proposition 1. *Let Γ be an environment and τ and τ' arbitrary types defined under Γ. Then it is decidable whether $\Gamma \vdash \tau \leq \tau'$ holds.*

5.3 Typing terms

Let $\Gamma \vdash t :: \sigma$ denote that a term t has a type σ under an environment Γ. Then the relation can be defined as the least relation closed under a set of inference rules, consisting of six rules slightly extending the inference rules for Core-XML [26], three straightforward rules for dealing with creation, update and access of objects and the following rules for coercions and recursive functions:

$$\frac{\Gamma \vdash s :: \sigma \quad \Gamma \vdash \sigma \leq \sigma'}{\Gamma \vdash s :: \sigma'} \; (Sub) \qquad \frac{\Gamma + [x :: \sigma] \vdash t :: \sigma}{\Gamma \vdash \mathbf{fix}\; x :: \sigma.t :: \sigma} \; (Fix)$$

Theorem 2. *(The least type) If $\Gamma \vdash s :: \sigma$ then there is a unique least type σ' such that $\Gamma \vdash s :: \sigma'$.*

We use $\Gamma \models s : \sigma$ to denote that σ is the least type for Γ and s such that $\Gamma \vdash s :: \sigma$.

5.4 Reduction

The equational theory of the terms of $\mathcal{Q}$ is given by the reduction relation of the form $\Gamma \vdash s \triangleright t$ defined by some single-step reduction rules and context rules. The context rules are as usual. The single-step reduction rules are as follows:

- $\lambda\beta$-reduction: $\Gamma \vdash (\lambda x :: \tau.s \; t) \triangleright s[t/x]$.
- $\Lambda\beta$-reduction: $\Gamma \vdash (\Lambda\alpha \leq T.s \; \tau) \triangleright s[\tau/\alpha]$.
- (let)-reduction: $\Gamma \vdash \mathbf{let}\; x :: \sigma = s \; \mathbf{in}\; t \triangleright t[s/x]$.
- (fix)-reduction: $\Gamma \vdash \mathbf{fix}\; x :: \sigma.t \triangleright t[\mathbf{fix}\; x :: \sigma.t/x]$.
- (sel)-reduction:

$$\Gamma \vdash (update(s, b, t).a) \triangleright \begin{cases} t & \text{if } b = a \\ (s.a) & \text{if } b \neq a \end{cases}$$

Now we formulate some properties of the reductions of $\mathcal{Q}$.

Theorem 3. *(Subject reduction property) If $\Gamma \vdash s \triangleright t$ and $\Gamma \vdash s :: \sigma$ then $\Gamma \vdash t :: \sigma$.*

Corollary 4. *If $\Gamma \vdash s \triangleright t$, $\Gamma \models s :: \sigma$ and $\Gamma \models t :: \sigma'$ then $\Gamma \vdash \sigma' \leq \sigma$ holds.*

Theorem 5. *(Church-Rosser property) The reduction $\triangleright$ is Church-Rosser.*

6 The target calculus with overloaded functions

This section extends the calculus $\mathcal{Q}$ by a notion of overloaded functions. The extension is called the calculus $\mathcal{T}$. We will show that all important properties of $\mathcal{Q}$ hold also for $\mathcal{T}$.

6.1 Syntax and overloaded functions

The calculus $\mathcal{T}$ has the same types and subtyping relations as the calculus $\mathcal{Q}$. The terms of $\mathcal{T}$ are defined as follows:

$$s, t \; = \; \cdots \text{ as in } \mathcal{Q} \cdots \; | \; ((\alpha, \tau_0, \tau) \leq \langle \overline{\xi_n} \rangle \Rightarrow \langle \overline{s_n} \rangle) \; (n \geq 1)$$

The terms $((\alpha, \tau_0, \tau) \leq \langle \overline{\xi_n} \rangle \Rightarrow \langle \overline{s_n} \rangle)$, called *overloaded functions*, correspond to a method declaration together with all its redefinitions in a TOFL program. The type variable α is the self-type. The monomorphic type τ_0, called an *annotated type*, is the type of the overloaded function in static type inference, except that the instance of α is denoted by an additional monomorphic type τ, called a *self-type instance*. In other words, the monomorphic type $\tau_0[\tau/\alpha]$ denotes the monomorphic type of the overloaded function in static type inference. From the type inference point of view, an overloaded function as a whole behaves like a term, which has a type $\tau_0[\tau/\alpha]$. The annotated type τ_0 is always an $\rightarrow$-type. For convenience, the domain is denoted as $d(\tau_0)$ and the range as $r(\tau_0)$, i.e. $\tau_0 = d(\tau_0) \rightarrow r(\tau_0)$. The ground types ξ_i, called *guards*, correspond to the types for which the methods are (re)defined. The terms s_i denote the *bodies* of these redefined methods. For example, the following s_0 is an overloaded function:

$$s_0 = ((\alpha, List(\alpha) \rightarrow List(\alpha), \alpha) \leq \langle Eq, Point \rangle \Rightarrow \langle s_1, s_2 \rangle).$$

A substitution of the self-type at compile time may cause a type-error in a body of an overloaded function, since the subtype, for which a method is redefined, may be smaller than an instance of the self-type defined by the substitution. To avoid such type-errors, we just record, but do not execute, the substitution of the self-type at compile time. Therefore, we define

$$((\alpha, \tau_0, \tau) \leq \langle \overline{\xi_n} \rangle) \Rightarrow \langle \overline{s_n} \rangle)[\tau'/\beta]$$
$$= \begin{cases} ((\alpha, \tau_0, \tau[\tau'/\beta]) \leq \langle \overline{\xi_n} \rangle \Rightarrow \langle \overline{s_n} \rangle) & \text{if } \alpha = \beta \\ ((\alpha, \tau_0[\tau'/\beta], \tau[\tau'/\beta]) \leq \langle \overline{\xi_n} \rangle \Rightarrow \langle \overline{s_n[\tau'/\beta]} \rangle) & \text{if } \alpha \neq \beta \end{cases}$$

Only until run time will it be decided whether the recorded self-type instance or the run-time type of the receivers should really be used to replace the self-type.

Now we consider the body selection. Roughly speaking, in an application of an overloaded function as above, only when the guard ξ_k is the least type among $\overline{\xi_n}$ such that $d(\tau_0)[\xi_k/\alpha]$ is a type of the run-time argument, the body s_k is selected. Consider the previous overloaded function s_0 as an example. Then $d(\tau) = List(\alpha)$, $d(\tau)[Eq/\alpha] = List(Eq)$ and $d(\tau)[Point/\alpha] = List(Point)$. Assume that $Point \leq Eq$ holds. Let t be a term of the least type $List(Point)$. Then t is also of type $List(Eq)$. Since $Point$ is the smallest type in $\langle Eq, Point \rangle$ such that $d(\tau)[Point/\alpha]$ is a type of t, the second body s_2 should be selected. More precisely, if it is decided at run time that the self-type should be instantiated to type $Point$, then the application $(s\ t)$ should yield $(s_2[Point/\alpha]\ t)$.

In an object-oriented language, the selection of a body for a method usually depends on the type of the receiver. In TOFL, as shown above, the selection depends on some fragments of the type of the argument. The reason for this decision is that TOFL should include type classes in `Haskell` as a special case. These points will be made clearer in the rest of this and the next section.

The above discussion on the body selection of an overloaded function is rough, since it does not consider that the least type of the argument may change when its subterms are reduced or free (term or type) variables are instantiated. Therefore, one may still ask when the body selection should take place during execution. Indeed, the calculus $\mathcal{T}$ requires that the body selection is made only when it is known that no further reduction or instantiation of the term argument is possible or the body selection remains correct even when the term argument is further reduced or instantiated. The former case is when the term argument is closed and in normal form, and its least type is a ground type. The latter case is guaranteed when a guard can be selected based on the static type of the term argument and no other guard is a subtype of the selected guard, since, as we will see, the least type of a term in the calculus $\mathcal{T}$ either remains unchanged or decreases during execution.

The latter case in the above could be of practical significance. Suppose a practical implementation of TOFL has a call-by-value evaluation strategy and allows, however, function bodies to be evaluated only when they are applied (in the style of ML). If the set Ω contains the formula $\alpha \leq Eq, \beta \leq Top \Rightarrow (\alpha \rightarrow \beta) \leq Eq$, then an application of the overloaded function $((\alpha, \alpha \rightarrow Top, \alpha) \leq \langle Eq, Eq \rightarrow Top \rangle \Rightarrow \langle s_1, s_2 \rangle)$ to an argument $\lambda x :: Eq.t$ will select the body s_2 for the further computation, no matter whether t is terminating or not.

If $\overline{\tau_n}$ are well-formed monomorphic types under an environment Γ, then we use $min_\Gamma\{\overline{\tau_n}\}$ to denote the least τ_k among $\overline{\tau_n}$, i.e. $\Gamma \vdash \tau_k \leq \tau_i$ hold for all $i = 1, \ldots, n$. We can write $min\{\overline{\tau_n}\}$ when all $\overline{\tau_n}$ are ground.

An overloaded function $((\alpha, \tau_0, \tau) \leq \langle \overline{\xi_n} \rangle \Rightarrow \langle \overline{s_n} \rangle)$ should still satisfy the following restrictions.

1. The self-type α must occur in τ_0.
2. If α only occurs at co-variant positions in $d(\tau_0)$ then it only occurs at co-variant positions in $r(\tau_0)$.
3. $\xi_i \leq \xi_1$ hold for all $i = 1, \ldots, n$.
4. For any two ground types ξ_1' and ξ_2' such that $\xi_1' \leq \xi_1$ and $\xi_2' \leq \xi_1$, there exists a unique ground type $\xi_k = min\{\xi_i \mid \xi_1' \leq \xi_i, \xi_2' \leq \xi_i, 1 \leq i \leq n\}$, and for each ground type ξ, if $\xi_1' \leq \xi, \xi_2' \leq \xi$ and $\xi \leq \xi_1$ hold, then $\xi \leq \xi_k$ or $\xi_k \leq \xi$ holds.

The restriction 2 guarantees that at least one fragment of the run-time type of the argument can be obtained for the body selection. The restriction 2 is useful in ensuring the preservation of static types during execution. The restriction 3 is used to guarantee that at least one body can be selected during executing a statically well-typed application of an overloaded function, provided that the argument has been enough reduced and instantiated. The restriction 4 corresponds to the restriction 6 in Subsection 4.2. It ensures the uniqueness of the body selection and is also useful in ensuring the preservation of static types during execution. It can be proved that all these restrictions are implied by the syntax of and restrictions on TOFL in Subsection 4, when the overloaded function is obtained by the translation in Section 7.

6.2 Type inference

The inference rules of $\mathcal{T}$ are those of $\mathcal{Q}$ plus the following type inference rule.

$$\frac{\Gamma + [\alpha \leq \xi_i] \vdash s_i :: \tau_0 \ (i = 1, \ldots, n) \qquad \Gamma \vdash \tau \leq \xi_1}{\Gamma \vdash ((\alpha, \tau_0, \tau) \leq \langle \overline{\xi_n} \rangle \Rightarrow \langle \overline{s_n} \rangle) :: \tau_0[\tau/\alpha]} \quad \text{(Over)}$$

Rule (Over) is the only rule that derives a type for an overloaded function. After having been assigned a type, an overloaded function as a whole can be treated by other type inference rules just like a usual term. Many properties of the calculus $\mathcal{Q}$ can be extended to the calculus $\mathcal{T}$. One of them is the least type property.

Theorem 6. *(The least type) Theorem 2 also holds in the calculus $\mathcal{T}$.*

As an example, assume that Ω contains $ColorPoint \leq Point$, $Int \leq Num$, $Ord \leq Eq$, $Eq \leq Top$, $(\alpha_1 \leq Point, \alpha_2 \leq Num \Rightarrow Pair(\alpha_1, \alpha_2) \leq Ord)$, $(\alpha_1 \leq Eq, \alpha_2 \leq Num \Rightarrow Pair(\alpha_1, \alpha_2) \leq Eq)$ and $(\alpha_1 \leq Top, \alpha_2 \leq Top \Rightarrow Pair(\alpha_1, \alpha_2) \leq Top)$. Then we have

$$glb\{\{Top, Eq\}, Pair(ColorPoint, Int)\}$$
$$= Pair(glb\{Top, Eq, ColorPoint\}, glb\{Top, Num, Int\})$$
$$= Pair(\{Top, Eq, ColorPoint\}, \{Top, Num, Int\}).$$

The second function $upbd$ recursively replaces every free type variable in a monomorphic type τ by its upper bound in an environment Γ, where if the bound is a set of ground types then the greatest lower bound is computed. Assume that τ is well-formed under Γ. Then we define

$$upbd(\Gamma, \tau) = \tau[glb\{upbd(\Gamma, \tau') \mid \tau' \in T\}/\alpha \mid \alpha \in \mathcal{FV}(\tau), \alpha \leq T \in \Gamma]$$

For example, let $\Gamma = [\alpha_1 \leq Point, \alpha_2 \leq Eq, \alpha_3 \leq \{\alpha_1, \alpha_2\}]$ and $\tau = List(\alpha_3)$. Then $upbd(\Gamma, \tau) = List(\{Point, Eq\})$. Note that the termination of $upbd$ is guaranteed by the fact that if an environment is of the form $\Gamma_1 + [\alpha \leq T] + \Gamma_2$ then all free type variables in T must be declared in Γ_1.

At this stage we slightly extend the notion of overloaded functions such that an extended ground type is allowed to be a guard. In fact, all discussions made before and to be made later hold for both the original and the slightly extended version of overloaded functions. Therefore, we use the same notation as before also for the slightly extended version, i.e. as we have just done in the above, let ξ range over extended ground types.

Now the single-step reduction rule can be formulated as follows.

- $\langle\rangle\beta$-reduction: $\Gamma \vdash (((\alpha, \tau_0, \tau) \leq \langle\overline{\xi_n}\rangle \Rightarrow \langle\overline{s_n}\rangle)\, t) \triangleright (s_k[min_\Gamma\{\xi_k, \tau\}/\alpha]\, t)$
  where
  - $\Gamma \models t :: \tau'$,
  - if $\mathcal{P}os(d(\tau_0), \alpha) \neq \emptyset$ and all $\tau'_{|p}$ for $p \in \mathcal{P}os(d(\tau_0), \alpha)$ are defined and ground then let $\xi_k = min\{\xi_i \mid \forall p \in \mathcal{P}os(d(\tau_0), \alpha).(\tau'_{|p} \leq \xi_i), 1 \leq i \leq n\}$, otherwise let $\xi_k = min\{\xi_i \mid upbd(\Gamma, \tau) \leq \xi_i, 1 \leq i \leq n\}$,
  - if t is not closed or not in normal form or some $\tau'_{|q}$ for some $q \in \mathcal{P}os(d(\tau_0), \alpha)$ is not defined or not ground then ξ_k has no subtypes among $\overline{\xi_n}$.

Note that the unique existence of ξ_k in $\langle\rangle\beta$-reduction is ensured by the restrictions 3 and 4 in Subsection 6.1 and the second premise of rule (Over). The fragments in τ' at the positions, at which α occurs in $d(\tau_0)$, may be different, but they are each equal to or smaller than τ. They are the basis for the body selection when they are ground and $\mathcal{P}os(d(\tau_0), \alpha)$ is nonempty. The selection depends on the self-type instance τ, when $\mathcal{P}os(d(\tau_0), \alpha)$ is empty, or when some fragments in τ' at the positions, at which α occurs in $d(\tau_0)$, are not ground.

The motivation for considering the case that $\mathcal{P}os(d(\tau_0), \alpha)$ is empty is to allow the calculus $\mathcal{T}$ to code e.g. some quite useful functions such as the exception handling function $noMethodBody :: \forall\alpha.Str \to \alpha$ in Subsection 4.3.

The calculus $\mathcal{T}$ has the following important properties.

As an example, assume that Ω contains $ColorPoint \leq Point$, $Int \leq Num$, $Ord \leq Eq$, $Eq \leq Top$, $(\alpha_1 \leq Point, \alpha_2 \leq Num \Rightarrow Pair(\alpha_1, \alpha_2) \leq Ord)$, $(\alpha_1 \leq Eq, \alpha_2 \leq Num \Rightarrow Pair(\alpha_1, \alpha_2) \leq Eq)$ and $(\alpha_1 \leq Top, \alpha_2 \leq Top \Rightarrow Pair(\alpha_1, \alpha_2) \leq Top)$. Then we have

$$
\begin{aligned}
&glb\{\{Top, Eq\}, Pair(ColorPoint, Int)\} \\
&= Pair(glb\{Top, Eq, ColorPoint\}, glb\{Top, Num, Int\}) \\
&= Pair(\{Top, Eq, ColorPoint\}, \{Top, Num, Int\}).
\end{aligned}
$$

The second function $upbd$ recursively replaces every free type variable in a monomorphic type τ by its upper bound in an environment Γ, where if the bound is a set of ground types then the greatest lower bound is computed. Assume that τ is well-formed under Γ. Then we define

$$upbd(\Gamma, \tau) = \tau[glb\{upbd(\Gamma, \tau') \mid \tau' \in T\}/\alpha \mid \alpha \in \mathcal{FV}(\tau), \alpha \leq T \in \Gamma]$$

For example, let $\Gamma = [\alpha_1 \leq Point, \alpha_2 \leq Eq, \alpha_3 \leq \{\alpha_1, \alpha_2\}]$ and $\tau = List(\alpha_3)$. Then $upbd(\Gamma, \tau) = List(\{Point, Eq\})$. Note that the termination of $upbd$ is guaranteed by the fact that if an environment is of the form $\Gamma_1 + [\alpha \leq T] + \Gamma_2$ then all free type variables in T must be declared in Γ_1.

At this stage we slightly extend the notion of overloaded functions such that an extended ground type is allowed to be a guard. In fact, all discussions made before and to be made later hold for both the original and the slightly extended version of overloaded functions. Therefore, we use the same notation as before also for the slightly extended version, i.e. as we have just done in the above, let ξ range over extended ground types.

Now the single-step reduction rule can be formulated as follows.

- $\langle\rangle\beta$-reduction: $\Gamma \vdash (((\alpha, \tau_0, \tau) \leq \langle\overline{\xi_n}\rangle \Rightarrow \langle\overline{s_n}\rangle) \, t) \rhd (s_k[min_\Gamma\{\xi_k, \tau\}/\alpha] \, t)$
  where
  - $\Gamma \models t :: \tau'$,
  - if $\mathcal{P}os(d(\tau_0), \alpha) \neq \emptyset$ and all $\tau'_{|p}$ for $p \in \mathcal{P}os(d(\tau_0), \alpha)$ are defined and ground then let $\xi_k = min\{\xi_i \mid \forall p \in \mathcal{P}os(d(\tau_0), \alpha).(\tau'_{|p} \leq \xi_i), 1 \leq i \leq n\}$, otherwise let $\xi_k = min\{\xi_i \mid upbd(\Gamma, \tau) \leq \xi_i, 1 \leq i \leq n\}$,
  - if t is not closed or not in normal form or some $\tau'_{|q}$ for some $q \in \mathcal{P}os(d(\tau_0), \alpha)$ is not defined or not ground then ξ_k has no subtypes among $\overline{\xi_n}$.

Note that the unique existence of ξ_k in $\langle\rangle\beta$-reduction is ensured by the restrictions 3 and 4 in Subsection 6.1 and the second premise of rule (Over). The fragments in τ' at the positions, at which α occurs in $d(\tau_0)$, may be different, but they are each equal to or smaller than τ. They are the basis for the body selection when they are ground and $\mathcal{P}os(d(\tau_0), \alpha)$ is nonempty. The selection depends on the self-type instance τ, when $\mathcal{P}os(d(\tau_0), \alpha)$ is empty, or when some fragments in τ' at the positions, at which α occurs in $d(\tau_0)$, are not ground.

The motivation for considering the case that $\mathcal{P}os(d(\tau_0), \alpha)$ is empty is to allow the calculus $\mathcal{T}$ to code e.g. some quite useful functions such as the exception handling function $noMethodBody :: \forall \alpha.Str \rightarrow \alpha$ in Subsection 4.3.

The culculus $\mathcal{T}$ has the following important properties.

Lemma 7. Let $s = ((\alpha, \tau_0, \tau) \leq \langle\overline{\xi_n}\rangle \Rightarrow \langle\overline{s_n}\rangle)$. If $\Gamma \vdash (s\ t) \triangleright (s_k[min_\Gamma\{\tau, \xi_k\}/\alpha]\ t)$ then $\Gamma \vdash (s_k[min_\Gamma\{\tau, \xi_k\}/\alpha]\ t) :: \tau(\tau_0)[\tau/\alpha]$.

Theorem 8. *(Subject reduction property) Theorem 3 holds for the calculus $\mathcal{T}$.*

Corollary 9. *Corollary 4 holds for the calculus $\mathcal{T}$.*

Theorem 10. *(Church-Rosser property) Theorem 5 holds for the calculus $\mathcal{T}$.*

7 Type inference and translation

Due to the strong correspondence between TOFL and the calculus $\mathcal{T}$, it should not be surprising that the type inference for TOFL is similar to that of $\mathcal{T}$ and the translation of TOFL into $\mathcal{T}$ is rather straightforward in most cases.

Indeed, the well-formedness of environments and types, and subtyping in TOFL are defined in the same way as in $\mathcal{T}$. We use combined inference rules both for type inference and for translation. The type inference extends that of Core-XML [26] by considering classes, subtyping, overloaded functions and polymorphic recursive functions, and is related to that for Mini-Haskell [49, 38].

The rules are divided into three groups. The first group treats the expressions of TOFL and is given in Figure 3. A judgement of the form $\Gamma \vdash s :: \sigma \rightsquigarrow s'$ means that an expression s in TOFL has a polymorphic type σ under the environment Γ and can be translated into a term s' in $\mathcal{T}$.

$$\frac{\Gamma(x) = \sigma}{\Gamma \vdash x :: \sigma \rightsquigarrow x}\ (TAUT) \qquad \frac{\Gamma \vdash s :: \sigma \rightsquigarrow s' \quad \Gamma \vdash \sigma \leq \sigma'}{\Gamma \vdash s\uparrow :: \sigma' \rightsquigarrow s'}\ (TYP\uparrow)$$

$$\frac{\Gamma \vdash s :: \forall\alpha \leq T.\sigma \rightsquigarrow s' \quad \Gamma \vdash \tau \leq T}{\Gamma \vdash s :: \sigma[\tau/\alpha] \rightsquigarrow s'\ \tau}\ (SPEC) \qquad \frac{\Gamma + [\alpha \leq T] \vdash s :: \sigma \rightsquigarrow s'}{\Gamma \vdash s :: \forall\alpha \leq T.\sigma \rightsquigarrow \Lambda\alpha \leq T.s'}\ (GEN)$$

$$\frac{\Gamma \vdash s :: \tau' \rightarrow \tau \rightsquigarrow s' \quad \Gamma \vdash t :: \tau' \rightsquigarrow t'}{\Gamma \vdash (s\ t) :: \tau \rightsquigarrow (s'\ t')}\ (APP) \qquad \frac{\Gamma + [x :: \tau] \vdash s :: \tau' \rightsquigarrow s'}{\Gamma \vdash \lambda x.s :: \tau \rightarrow \tau' \rightsquigarrow \lambda x :: \tau.s'}\ (ABS)$$

$$\frac{\Gamma \vdash s :: \sigma \rightsquigarrow s' \quad \Gamma + [x :: \sigma] \vdash t :: \tau \rightsquigarrow t'}{\Gamma \vdash \mathbf{let}\ x = s\ \mathbf{in}\ t :: \tau \rightsquigarrow \mathbf{let}\ x :: \sigma = s'\ \mathbf{in}\ t'}\ (LET) \qquad \frac{\Gamma + [x :: \sigma] \vdash t :: \sigma \rightsquigarrow t'}{\Gamma \vdash \mathbf{fix}\ x.t :: \sigma \rightsquigarrow \mathbf{fix}\ x :: \sigma.t'}\ (FIX)$$

$$\frac{\kappa\ \text{occurs in } \Omega}{\Gamma \vdash new(\kappa) :: \kappa \rightsquigarrow new(\kappa)}\ (NEW) \qquad \frac{a :: \xi \in \Sigma(\kappa) \quad \Gamma \vdash s :: \kappa}{\Gamma \vdash s.a :: \xi \rightsquigarrow s.a}\ (ATT)$$

$$\frac{a :: \xi \in \Sigma(\kappa) \quad \Gamma \vdash s :: \kappa \rightsquigarrow s' \quad \Gamma \vdash t :: \xi \rightsquigarrow t'}{\Gamma \vdash update(s, a, t) :: \kappa \rightsquigarrow update(s', a, t')}\ (UPD)$$

Figure 3: Typing/translation rules for TOFL

Each of the rules in Figure 3 is either quite standard (see e.g. [26]) or straightforward. Note that rule (LET) is designed under the presumption that in **let** $x = s$ **in** t, x does not occur freely in s. Rule (TYP↑) reflects our intention that the run-time meaning of $s\uparrow$ is exactly that of s.

The second group of rules deals with declarations in TOFL. In order to formulate them, we use O to denote a set of pairs $x = s$, where x is a method name and s an overloaded function in $\mathcal{T}$. The set O is used to record all method declarations and redefinitions encountered during the inference process. We define an operation $+$ for inserting both a new method and a redefinition of an existing method. That is, if O contains no elements of the form $x = \cdots$, then

$$O + [x :: \overline{\forall \alpha_n \leq K_n}.\forall \alpha \leq \xi.\tau = \overline{\Lambda \alpha_n \leq K_n}.\Lambda \alpha \leq \xi.u)]$$
$$= O \cup \{x = \overline{\Lambda \alpha_n \leq K_n}.\Lambda \alpha \leq \xi.((\alpha, \tau, \alpha) \leq \langle \xi \rangle \Rightarrow \langle u \rangle)\};$$

if $O = O_1 \cup \{y = \overline{\Lambda \alpha_n \leq K_n}.\Lambda \alpha \leq \xi_1.((\alpha, \tau, \alpha) \leq \langle \overline{\xi_m} \rangle \Rightarrow \langle \overline{v_m} \rangle)\}$, then

$$O + [y = \overline{\Lambda \alpha_n \leq K_n}.\Lambda \alpha \leq \xi.v]$$
$$= O_1 \cup \{y = \overline{\Lambda \alpha_n \leq K_n}.\Lambda \alpha \leq \xi_1.((\alpha, \tau, \alpha) \leq \langle \overline{\xi_m}, \xi \rangle \Rightarrow \langle \overline{v_m}, v \rangle)\}.$$

Since from now on the sets Σ and Ω in environments in TOFL may change, we write them explicitly. A judgement of the form $\Sigma, \Omega, \Gamma, O \vdash d \rightsquigarrow \Sigma', \Omega', \Gamma', O'$ means that a declaration d changes the environment Σ, Ω, Γ with O into the $\Sigma', \Omega', \Gamma'$ with O'. The first rule deals with a class declaration. The formulation is straightforward. Remember that we presume that the methods available in a class are not mutually recursive. Note that the body of a method (re)defined in a class declaration can use the attribute names, the name of the class and the subtyping relation declared in the class declaration. Thus the environment for the bodies s and t is Σ', Ω', Γ.

$$\frac{\begin{array}{l}\Sigma', \Omega', \Gamma \vdash s :: \sigma \rightsquigarrow s' \\ y :: \overline{\forall \alpha_n \leq K_n}.\forall \alpha \leq \kappa'.\tau \in \Gamma \qquad\qquad \{\}, \Omega', [] \vdash \kappa \leq \kappa' \\ \Sigma', \Omega', \Gamma \vdash t :: \overline{\forall \alpha_n \leq K_n}.\forall \alpha \leq \kappa.\tau \rightsquigarrow t'\end{array}}{\Sigma, \Omega, \Gamma, O \vdash \mathbf{class}\, \kappa \leq K \,\mathbf{attr}\, a :: \xi\, \mathbf{meth}\, x :: \sigma = s, y = t \rightsquigarrow \Sigma', \Omega', \Gamma', O'} \quad \text{(CLS)}$$

where $\Sigma' = \Sigma \cup \{(\kappa, \bigcup_{\kappa'' \in K} \Sigma(\kappa'')) \cup \{a :: \xi\})\}$, $\Omega' = \Omega \cup \{\kappa \leq K\}$, $\Gamma' = \Gamma \cup \{x :: \sigma\}$ and $O' = O + [x :: \sigma = s'] + [y = t']$.

For example, if $\Sigma', \Omega', \Gamma' \vdash s :: \forall \alpha \leq Eq.(\alpha, \alpha) \rightarrow Bool \rightsquigarrow s'$ is derivable, then

$$\Sigma, \Omega, \Gamma, O \vdash \mathbf{class}\, Eq \leq Top\, \mathbf{meth}\, eq :: \forall \alpha \leq Eq.(\alpha, \alpha) \rightarrow Bool = s \rightsquigarrow \Sigma, \Omega', \Gamma', O'$$

is derivable, where $\Omega' = \Omega \cup \{Eq \leq Top\}$, $\Gamma' = \Gamma + [eq :: \forall \alpha \leq Eq.(\alpha, \alpha) \rightarrow Bool]$ and $O' = O \cup [\Lambda \alpha \leq Eq.((\alpha, (\alpha, \alpha) \rightarrow Bool, \alpha) \leq \langle Eq \rangle \Rightarrow \langle s' \rangle)]$.

The second rule deals with a datatype declaration. Note that this rule does not put the type constructor χ in the environment: this will be done by the next rule on the presumed subtype declaration $\mathbf{subtype}\, \overline{\alpha_h} \leq Top \Rightarrow \chi(\overline{\alpha_h}) \leq Top$.

$$\frac{}{\Sigma, \Omega, \Gamma, O \vdash \mathbf{datatype}\, \chi(\overline{\alpha_h})\, \mathbf{constr}\, x :: \sigma \rightsquigarrow \Sigma, \Omega, \Gamma \cup \{x :: \sigma\}, O} \quad \text{(DAT)}$$

The third rule deals with a subtype declaration. The key is the way to handle bounded quantifications of type variables. Since the subtypes of class κ declared here are all of the form $\chi(\overline{\tau_h})$, where each τ_i is a subtype of K_i, the least upper bound of these subtypes $\chi(\overline{\tau_h})$ is $\chi(\overline{K_h})$. We use the extended type $\chi(\overline{K_h})$ as the guard for selecting the body t for method y.

$$\frac{y :: \forall \overline{\alpha'_n \leq K'_n}.\forall \alpha \leq \kappa'.\tau \in \Gamma \qquad \{\}, \Omega', [] \vdash \kappa \leq \kappa'}{\Sigma, \Omega', \Gamma \vdash t :: \forall \overline{\alpha_h \leq K_h}.\forall \overline{\alpha'_n \leq K'_n}.\forall \alpha \leq \chi(\overline{\alpha_h}).\tau \rightsquigarrow \Lambda \overline{\alpha_h \leq K_h}.t'}{\Sigma, \Omega, \Gamma, O \vdash \mathbf{subtype}\ \overline{\alpha_h \leq K_h} \Rightarrow \chi(\overline{\alpha_h}) \leq \kappa\ \mathbf{meth}\ y = t \rightsquigarrow \Sigma, \Omega', \Gamma, O'} \quad \text{(SBT)}$$

where $\Omega' = \Omega \cup \{\overline{\alpha_h \leq K_h} \Rightarrow \chi(\overline{\alpha_h}) \leq \kappa\}$ and $O' = O + [y = t'[\overline{K_h/\alpha_h}]]$.

For example, if $\Gamma = \Gamma_1 \cup \{eq :: \forall \alpha \leq Eq.(\alpha, \alpha) \rightarrow Bool\}$, $O = O_1 \cup \{eq = \Lambda \alpha \leq Eq.((\alpha, (\alpha, \alpha) \rightarrow Bool), \alpha) \leq \langle Eq \rangle \Rightarrow \langle s \rangle)\}$ and $\Sigma, \Omega', \Gamma \vdash t :: \forall \alpha_1 \leq Eq.\forall \alpha \leq List(\alpha).\tau \rightsquigarrow \Lambda \alpha_1 \leq Eq.t'$ is derivable, then

$$\Sigma, \Omega, \Gamma, O \vdash \mathbf{subtype}\ \alpha \leq Eq \Rightarrow List(\alpha) \leq Eq\ \mathbf{meth}\ eq = t \rightsquigarrow \Sigma, \Omega', \Gamma, O',$$

is derivable, where $\Omega' = \Omega \cup \{\alpha \leq Eq \Rightarrow List(\alpha) \leq Eq\}$ and $O' = O_1 \cup \{eq = \Lambda \alpha \leq Eq.((\alpha, (\alpha, \alpha) \rightarrow Bool), \alpha) \leq \langle Eq, List(Eq) \rangle \Rightarrow \langle s, t'[Eq/\alpha_1] \rangle)\}$.

The final group consists of one straightforward rule for a program.

$$\frac{\Sigma_i, \Omega_i, \Gamma_i, O_i \vdash d_i \rightsquigarrow \Sigma_{i+1}, \Omega_{i+1}, \Gamma_{i+1}, O_{i+1}\ (i = 1, \ldots, n)}{\Sigma_{n+1}, \Omega_{n+1}, \Gamma_{n+1} \vdash s :: \sigma \rightsquigarrow s'}{\Sigma_1, \Omega_1, \Gamma_1 \vdash d_1; \cdots; d_n; s :: \sigma \rightsquigarrow \mathbf{let}\ \overline{x_m = t_m}\ \mathbf{in}\ s'} \quad \text{(PROG)}$$

where $O_{n+1} = \{\overline{x_m = t_m}\}$.

Now we are finished with the type inference and the translation. It is simple enough to see that a well-typed source program in TOFL can always be translated into a term with an environment in $\mathcal{T}$. In particular, it is straightforward to check that if the source program satisfies all restrictions for TOFL, then the term and environment satisfy the restrictions for $\mathcal{T}$.

Note that both TOFL and $\mathcal{T}$ have a type system. The final theorem shows that these two type systems and the translations fit together. The theorem can be proved by induction on the application of the typing/translation rules.

Theorem 11. If $\Sigma, \Omega, \Gamma \vdash s :: \sigma \rightsquigarrow s'$ is derivable by the above rules then $\Sigma, \Omega, \Gamma \vdash s' :: \sigma$ is derivable in $\mathcal{T}$.

8 Conclusion

We have presented an approach to combining the object-oriented and functional paradigms. The approach is formal, since it is based on a type theory with formally proved properties. Yet the approach is practical in the sense that it has succeeded in formulating many important features as they exist in the widespread programming languages **Eiffel**, **ML** and **Haskell**.

The language TOFL is going to be a core of a practical programming language. Indeed, the full language of TOFL will contain many **ML** and **Haskell** constructs so that many **ML** and **Haskell** programs can be easily adjusted and transformed into TOFL. Furthermore, the implementation of TOFL is going to combine the techniques for implementing functional and object-oriented languages. At the moment a prototyping implementation of TOFL based on the typing rules, the translation rules and the calculus $\mathcal{T}$ presented in this paper is under way.

Acknowledgement. Thanks are due to Giorgio Ghelli, Tobias Nipkow and Stefan Kahrs for explaining some related work.

References

1. Special issue on type systems for object-oriented programming. *J. Functional Programming*, 4(2), 1994.
2. M. Abadi and L. Cardelli. A theory of primitive objects: second-order systems. In *Proc. European Symp./ on Programming*. Springer LNCS, 1994.
3. M. Abadi and L. Cardelli. A theory of primitive objects: untyped and first-order systems. In *Proc. Theoretical Aspects of Computer Software*. Springer LNCS, 1994.
4. Apple Computer Inc., Eastern Research and Technology. Dylan: an object-oriented dynamic language. Technical report, 1992.
5. D. Bobrow, L. DeMichiel, R. Gabriel, S. Keene, G. Kiczales, and D. Moon. Common List Object System Specification. *SIGPLAN Notice*, 23, 1988.
6. K. Bruce. Typing in object-oriented languages: Achieving expressibility and safety. Technical report, Williams College, 1995. http://www.cs.williams.edu/~kim/.
7. K. Bruce, A. Schuett, and R. van Gent. PolyTOIL: A type-safe polymorphic object-oriented language (extended abstract). In *Proc. 9th ECOOP*. Springer LNCS, 1995.
8. P. Canning, W. Cook, W. Hill, and W. Olthoff. Interfaces for strongly-typed object-oriented programming. In *Proc. OOPSLA'89*, pages 457–467. 1989.
9. L. Cardelli. A semantics of multiple inheritance. *Information and Computation*, 76:130–164, 1988.
10. L. Cardelli. Extensible records in a pure calculus of subtyping. In C. Gunter and J. Mitchell, editors, *Theoretical Aspects of Object-Oriented Programming: Types, Semantics, and Language Design*. The MIT Press, 1994.
11. L. Cardelli and G. Longo. A semantics for Quest. *J. of Functional programming*, 1(4):417–458, 1991.
12. L. Cardelli and P. Wegner. On understanding types, data abstraction, and polymorphism. *Computing Surveys*, 17(4):471–522, 1985.
13. G. Castagna. Covariance and contravariance: Conflict without a cause. *Trans. on Prog. Lang. and Sys.*, 17(3), 1995.
14. G. Castagna. Integration of parametric and ad hoc second order polymorphism in a calculus with subtyping. *Formal Aspects of Computing*, 1995. To appear.
15. G. Castagna, G. Ghelli, and G. Longo. A calculus for overloaded functions with subtyping. *Information and Computation*, 1995. To appear.
16. W. Cook. A proposal for making eiffel type-safe. In *Proc. European Conf. on Object-oriented Programming*, 1989.
17. W. Cook, W. Hill, and P. Canning. Inheritance is not subtyping. In *Proc. 17th ACM Symp. Principles of Programming Languages*. 1990.
18. P.-L. Curien and G. Ghelli. Coherence of subsumption, minimum typing and the type checking in $F_\le$. *Mathematical Structiures in Computer Science*, 2(1), 1992.
19. L. Damas and R. Milner. Principal type schemes for functional programs. In *Proc. 9th ACM Symp. Principles of Programming Languages*, pages 207–212, 1982.
20. Y.-C. Fuh and P. Mishra. Type inference with subtypes. *Theoretical Computer Science*, 73:155–175, 1990.
21. K. Futatsugi, J. Goguen, J.-P. Jouannaud, and J. Meseguer. Principles of OBJ2. In *Proc. 12th ACM Symp. Principles of Programming Languages*, pages 52–66, 1985.
22. G. Ghelli. A static type system for message passing. In *Proc. of OOPSLA'91*. 1991.
23. G. Ghelli. Divergence of $F_\le$ type checking. Tech. Rep. 5/93, University of Pisa, 1993.
24. J. Goguen and J. Meseguer. Order-sorted algebra I: Equational deduction for multiple inheritance, polymorphism, and partial operations. Technical report, SRI, 1989.
25. C. Gunter and J. Mitchell (Eds.). *Theoretical Aspects of Object-Oriented Programming: Types, Semantics, and Language Design*. The MIT Press, 1994.

26. R. Harper and J. Mitchell. The essence of ML. In *Proc. 15th ACM Symp. Principles of Programming Languages*, pages 28–46, 1988.
27. F. Henglein. Type inference with polymrophic recursion. *ACM Trans. on Prog. Lang. and Sys.*, 15(2):253–289, 1993.
28. M. Hoang and J. Mitchell. Lower bounds on type inference with subtypes. In *Proc. 22nd ACM Symp. Principles of Programming Languages*, pages 176–185, 1995.
29. P. Hudak, S. Peyton Jones, and P. Wadler (Editors). Report on the programming language Haskell: A non-strict, purely functional language (version 1.2). *ACM SIGPLAN Notices*, 27(5), 1992.
30. J. Hughes and J. Sparud. Haskell++: An object-oriented extension of haskell. In *Proc. 1995 Workshop on Haskell*, 1995.
31. A. Kfoury, J. Tiuryn, and P. Urzyczyn. Type reconstruction in the presence of polymrophic recursion. *ACM Trans. on Prog. Lang. and Sys.*, 15(2):290–311, 1993.
32. K. Läufer. Combining type classes and existential types. In *Proc. Latin American Informatics Conference (PANEL)*. ITESM-CEM, Mexico, Sept. 1994.
33. K. Läufer and M. Odersky. Polymorphic type inference and abstract data types. *ACM Transactions on Programming Languages and Systems*, 1994.
34. B. Meyer. *Object-Oriented Software Construction*. Prentice Hall, 1988.
35. R. Milner, M. Tofte, and R. Harper. *The Definition of Standard ML*. MIT Press, 1990.
36. J. Mitchell and G. Plotkin. Abstract types have existential type. *ACM Trans. on Prog. Lang. and Sys*, 10(3):475–502, 1988.
37. A. Mycroft. Polymorphic type schemes and recursive definitions. In *Proc. Int. Symposium on Programming*, pages 217–228. Springer LNCS 167, 1984.
38. T. Nipkow and C. Prehofer. Type reconstruction for type classes. *Journal of Functional Programming*, 5(2):201–224, 1995.
39. A. Ohori. A compilation method for ML-style polymorphic record calculi. In *Proc. 19th ACM Symp. Principles of Programming Languages*, pages 154–165, 1992.
40. J. Palsberg. Efficient type inference of object types. In *Proc. IEEE Symposium on Logic in Computer Science*, pages 186–195, 1994.
41. B. Pierce and D. Turner. Simple type-theoretical foundations for object-oriented programming. *J. of Functional Programming*, 4(2):207–247, 1994.
42. B. C. Pierce. Bounded quantification is undecidable. *Information and Computation*, 112(1):131–165, 1994.
43. Z. Qian and B. Krieg-Brückner. TOFL: a typed object-oriented functional programming language with late binding. Technical report, FB Informatik, Universität Bremen, March 1996.
44. Z. Qian and B. Krieg-Brückner. Object-oriented functional programming and type reconstruction. Nov. 1995. Submitted for publication.
45. D. Rémy. Typechecking records and variants in a natural extension of ml. In *Proc. 16th ACM Symp. Principles of Programming Languages*, pages 77–87, 1989.
46. G. S. Smith. Polymorphic type inference with overloading and subtyping. In J.-P. J. M.-C. Gaudel, editor, *Proc. TAPSOFT'93*, pages 670–685. Springer LNCS 668, 1993.
47. C. Strachey. Fundamental concepts in programming languages. In *Lecture Notes for the Int. Summer School in Computer Programming, Copenhagen*, August 1967.
48. C. Szyperski, S. Omohundro, and S. Murer. Engineering a programming language: The type and class system for Sather. In *Programming Languages and System Architectures*, pages 208–227. Springer LNCS 782, 1994.
49. P. Wadler and S. Blott. How to make *ad-hoc* polymorphism less *ad hoc*. In *Proc. 16th ACM Symp. Principles of Programming Languages*, pages 60–76, 1989.
50. M. Wand. Complete type inference for simple objects. In *Proc. 2nd IEEE Symp. Logic in Comp. Sci.*, 1987. Corrigendum in Proc. 3rd IEEE Symp. Logic in Comp. Sci., 1988.

Large Scale Object-Oriented Software-Development in a Banking Environment

An Experience Report

Dirk Bäumer, Rolf Knoll
RWG GmbH

Räpplenstraße 17
D-70191 Stuttgart, Germany

Phone: +49-711-2012-587
Fax: +49-711-2012-502
E-mail: dirk_baeumer@rwg.e-mail.com

Guido Gryczan, Heinz Züllighoven
University of Hamburg
Arbeitsbereich Softwaretechnik
Vogt-Kölln-Str. 30
D-22527 Hamburg, Germany

Phone: +49-40-54715-413
Fax: +49-40-54715-303
E-mail: zuelligh@informatik.uni-hamburg.de

Abstract

While many books have been published on object-oriented programming and design, little has been said about the overall development process. In parallel, evolutionary and participatory strategies have been discussed and used for years with variing success. We claim that combining object-oriented development with an evolutionary strategy which we call an application-oriented approach, will yield synergetic effects leading to a higher level of software quality, usability and system acceptance. This paper describes the various ingredients of our approach which are unified under a common leitmotif with matching design metaphors. A series of major industrial software projects serves as example and practical proof of the approach. We report about documents that have been produced and used within these projects and about the technical construction of the applications.

Keywords

object-oriented design, evolutionary system development, design metaphors, interactive software systems.

1. Introduction

Looking at recent and successful software projects and trying to identify the "success factors", two tendencies come to mind:

- an increased usage of object-oriented technologies and
- a change away from traditional phase-oriented life cycle models towards more evolutionary strategies which put a stress on involving end users.

But, over all, it seems that both tendencies can be found relatively separated from each other. This is somewhat amazing since object-oriented software development can be based from analysis to implementation on terms and concepts of the respective application domain. So, this type of approach to object-oriented system design will yield development documents and prototypes with features, objects and characteristics of the professional environment and language, the users are familiar with. In turn, these documents and prototypes are the prerequisites of a real integration of users into the entire development process.

We claim, that combining object-oriented design and evolutionary system development strategies with user involvement to what we call "application-orientation" will show a synergy of positive effects. Application-orientation will lead to application systems of high quality with respect to usage and software technology and a high level of user acceptance.

In this paper we will present our experiences applying an object-oriented methodology, that we and others have developed (cf. (Budde, 1992), (Bürkle 1995)), in a series of industrial software projects. In order to characterize the methodology few ideas can be seen as fundamental:

- We regard software design in general as being primarily a *learning and development process* with a strong emphasis on communication and the use of the professional language of the application domain.

- Our approach to object-orientedness centers around the terms and the daily work within an application domain and not its structural properties.

- Developing a taxonomy of the professional language in use in the application domain is a sufficient basis from which the object-oriented system design can start. Once defined, this taxonomy helps to improve communication and interaction between developers and users.

- An intelligible guideline is needed for designing and constructing interactive software systems. This guideline comprises the underlying leitmotif of *a workplace for skilled human work* and the design metaphors *Tools and Materials*.

- If the professional language of an application domain and the mutual learning processes are of major importance, than there is a need for a set of application-oriented document types which can be understood and used by all parties involved.

This approach to object-oriented software development is illustrated by experiences gained from an ongoing series of complex industrial software projects employing these principles.

2. Failure of the Conventional Approach

2.1. The Project Context

The aim of the overall GEBOS[1] project is to develop and install an integrated office system to support all tasks and services in the banking sector. The project is being conducted by a service center, the RWG in Stuttgart, responsible for some 450 banks. The banks carry out all their financial transactions via the RWG, and also draw on the RWG's central databases for information about clients, accounts, and other institutions like news agencies. The RWG currently employs a total staff of 470, the majority of

---

[1] The acronym Gebos stands for **Ge**nossenschaftliches **B**ürokommunikations- und **O**rganisations**s**ystem, which translates to Office Communication and Organization System for Cooperatives.

them engaged in production, marketing, and development. Some 120 persons are employed in software development, most of whom have so far been working on mainframes using Cobol, PL/I, and Assembler.

The first GEBOS project was launched in December 1989 at the instigation of the banks. Computer support was already available for certain areas of their work, but an integrated, uniform system had yet to be developed. Customer advisors, for example, were obliged to repeatedly enter and process account numbers or clients' addresses. Complex, customer-related work processes could only be carried out using a variety of different tools. And such application systems as were already in use differed greatly with respect to their user interfaces.

It was this unsatisfactory situation that led the banks to call for an integrated processing system with a uniform user interface, which would allow universal use of the data available. In the initial project phase, these requirements were to be realized in a selected application area: support for customer advisors in the investments section.

2.2. The Conventional Development Strategy

The conventional phase of the project lasted from December 1989 until July 1990. It was conducted by the RWG along the lines of a specially tailored life-cycle model (cf. (Boehm 1976), (Bürkle 1995)). The use of this life-cycle model was explicitly stipulated and had actually constituted the prescriptive basis of numerous previous projects, although these did, in practice, deviate from it. The characteristics and problems of such process models have been widely discussed, e.g., by Budde and Züllighoven (1992), and are not given further consideration here.

Two teams formulated system requirements from their own particular perspectives. One team elaborating an application-specific concept, and producing initial interface designs, while the other team specified a data and function model. The main characteristics of this design process were:

- The central aim was to automate the major work steps or working routines in the application domain.

- In order to overcome the different work processes and organizational structures found in the various banks, a major reorganization effort during the organizational implementation of the system was envisioned.

- In order to represent the working processes, the system was designed as a sequence of selection menus and fill-in screen forms.

- The traditional separation of the data and function models during technical design could only insufficiently be related to the application concepts. With both models, the strong decomposition made it difficult to preserve the relations between model and application.

- In line with the separation of data and functions the underlying design metaphor was a "window on data". This means, that the user was presented with the impression of viewing application data through various windows (implemented as database views) and having the means of directly changing these data (implemented as access functions).

- The gap between the application domain and the computer modeling process was not only evident in the different models built; it was also rooted in the thoroughly conventional organization of the project team. One team contained system analysts, not software developers. This group also included user representatives and consultants. The other team, which was responsible for modeling process control, consisted mainly of software developers. No provision was made here for establishing and maintaining a communication process between the parties concerned.

- There was no continuous cooperation between the groups involved. The cooperative design process was restricted to the so-called requirements analysis. The main group consulted here were DP organizers from banks, as the developer team preferred total to this group of persons. Although their common communication basis was of a DP-related rather than of a professional nature, it proved practically impossible to continue this cooperation during the technical phases of the project.

- Although, there was a strong urge of integrating application domain knowledge into the design process, there were little means for cooperation. The design documents were mainly technical, understandable to the developers team only. There was no adequate type of design documents for cooperation.

In April 1990, a prototype of the system was presented at RWG's own annual in-house trade fair: a menu-driven interface prototype without functionality. Its presentation failed to meet the users' expectation. The following three months were taken up with efforts to eliminate the deficiencies described above. In July 1990, however, the project management decided to abandon the project in its conventional form.

3. The Application-Oriented Development Strategy

After abandoning the conventional project, the RWG management took stock and analyzed together with the project team the reasons for this failure. It was then decided to test object-oriented development combined with an evolutionary approach. During the initial resumption period of the project in October 1990, this method was discussed with the core team, and adapted to suit the application context. Since the method with its application-oriented model formed the explicit basis of the development process for all subsequent projects, we will introduce it below.

3.1. The Setting of the Problem Space

First of all, it is important to understand the difference in the design task at hand compared to what the RWG had been doing previously. Looking at the reasons why the conventional approach had failed, it seems obvious that the development task was far too complex for the team to handle it in a traditional way. The complexity lies in two areas: the tasks at hand which have to be supported and the requirements for handling the system.

What characterizes the tasks is that they are open or not fixed in their sequence of (inter-) actions. In addition, these tasks can be described as customer-centered, which means that the various services and information requests of the customers are the driving force of the work place in question. The actual choice or sequence of these requests cannot be foreseen but have to be answered at one workplace by one advisor using one integrated system. Finally, the handling of the system should allow for an advisor to utilize it in a non-obtrusive way while talking with a customer.

All these requirements add up to a system which cannot implement a fixed routinized series of work processes but has to provide support for the various tasks at a workplace in a most flexible and convenient way. In the literature from areas like work Computer–Supported Cooperative Work, psychology, sociology, or epistemology, this type of work, its cultural and social importance and our failing ability to formalize it has been widely discussed (cf. (Robinson, 1993), (Suchman, 1987), (Miller, Galanter, and Pribram 1960)).

So, the key concept of our method is "support for complex tasks". These tasks demand what is called expert work done by qualified and trained persons. This type of work is what we, in line with many current economical concepts and strategies, see as the key potential of an enterprise. Utilizing this potential, an enterprise will hold or improve its position in the market. As a consequence, expert work needs to be supported and not to be rationalized. In the following we will show how to reconcile this goal with our concept of object-oriented approach.

3.2. The Fundamentals of Our Object-Oriented Approach

Object-oriented development starts with analysis. There, the fundamental decisions are made and the groundworks for the design of the future system are laid. What is *principally* overlooked or misinterpreted in analysis will rarely be detected or compensated by the other development activities. This, of course, regards basic assumptions or viewpoints and not individual requirements for a system.

Typical components of a workplace in a bank are: blank forms, memos, manuals, cheques, currencies, interest rates, folders, pens, staplers. Most of these things will be obvious to the developers, because they are tangible, others, like interest rate, are not. Still, the non-tangible things are very important "things" or objects of work at a banker's workplace. All theses things need to be there for the banker to do his or her job of e.g. client consulting.

Application Domain	Object-Oriented Design
Thing, Item	Object
Ways of Handling	Operation
Concept, Term	Class
Specialization, Generalization	Inheritance
Taxonomy	Class Hierarchy

Fig. 1. Concepts of the Application Domain Related to the Object-Oriented Model

Looking at a simple folder, we can identify some basic ideas. To this concrete thing ("this folder") we relate a general concept ("a folder") and a specific way of handling. We have all this in mind when we use the term "folder" and we need to have this understanding in order to identify a thing as a folder. Thus, we do not characterize a folder by its inner structure, but by giving it a *name* and describing the ways we can *work with it*.

The concrete things of everyday work are the starting point of object-oriented analysis and design. In our models, they are represented by objects. In our approach, it is obvious that objects are modeling elements which encapsulate related ways of handling and information that are meaningful in the application domain. So, this is a behavioral approach (cf. (Monarchi and Puhr 1992)) with a strong application domain focus.

Consequently, we design classes for every relevant concept in the application domain. These classes are related to each other according to the conceptual hierarchy of terms we are modelling. In our model, we can express specializations or generalizations of terms by using the inheritance mechanism between classes. As a consequence, the main structural design criterium for our programs is the *taxonomy of terms of the application domain*.

Figure 1 gives an overview of the main terms used in our approach. On the left, it shows the terms relevant for analysing an application domain. For each term there is a corresponding one on the right, where the components of object-oriented design are listed. The figure indicates the close relation between application concepts and object-oriented modelling elements.

So far, we have presented our main design idea. This does not mean, however, that there is a schematic transformation of every item, found at a workplace, into its object-oriented simulation. In the following section, we present additional guidelines that are needed to balance the modeling of the well-known things at hand with new means and opportunities of a software system.

3.3.   Designing the Future System

Defining the main components of an object-oriented model is important. But in an actual software project, you will find too soon that this is not enough. The question arises, how to design the future system.

We have established a guideline for designing interactive software on graphic workstations, as this is the predominant platform for the systems, we build. This guideline has to go beyond the layout of a graphic interface, e.g. discussing the advantages of buttons over pull-down menus. It is of major importance that the developers can form a vision of the future system in use, thereby relating issues of form to the design of the system's functionality. The key to solving this problem has been recently discussed both in work psychology and in the Human Computer Interaction community (Maaß and Oberquelle 1992) and will be presented in the subsequent section.

3.3.1.   The Leitmotif

Characterizing the overall guideline for designing interactive application systems we use the term *leitmotif*. A leitmotif is an idea which underlies or permeates a piece of art, i.e. an artefact. Extending this notion of leitmotif, we use it in software design to characterize a basic but predominant idea that helps us to transform a model of the application domain into the design of the future system. This process deliberately pulls down the (temporal) separation between analysis and design, which other object-oriented methods still maintain: We use our growing insight into the application domain to design the software system, while the evolving vision of the future system focuses our analysis process.

Our *leitmotif* is the *well-equipped workplace for expert human work*. This could be a desk of a customer advisor in a bank or the workbench in a workshop of a craftsman. This leitmotif is detailed or illustrated by so-call design metaphors (cf. also: (Madsen, 1988); (Carroll, Mack, & Kellogg, 1988)). These design metaphors have to fit into the overall "picture". They help us to design the various components needed to equip and utilize a workplace (Budde and Züllighoven 1992).

3.3.2. Tools, Materials and Other Design Metaphors

We have chosen tools and materials as the main design metaphors. This distinction has shown to be useful beyond the realms of handcraft and is valuable for office work as well.

Frequently, we have found that people have little difficulties classifying the things they use in their office work as tools or materials. There may be discussions, whether an index card box is more like a tool or like a material, or it is noted that a pencil is a tool while we write but becomes material when we sharpen it. We will have a closer look at these problems. But in general, we can say that these design metaphors have proved conducive to systems that are both understandable and can be constructed efficiently (Budde, Christ-Neumann & Sylla, 1992).

On a software technical level, which will not be dealt with in this paper, we have elaborated a set of design patterns which can be used for technically specifying and implementing the design metaphors as software components (Riehle & Züllighoven 1995). As we have elaborated this basic conceptual distinction between tools and materials elsewhere (cf. (Bürkle, Gryczan and Züllighoven, 1995)), a short summary should be sufficient.

A *Material* is something, which in our work becomes eventually part of the result of our work. Working with materials means working with tools upon materials. Every material has its application-specific functionality and can be probed and transformed by adequate tools. Materials in a software system, however, are by no means mere passive components like the data in a database application. It is important to understand, that materials are always motivated by the work tasks of an application domain. They have an internal (hidden) structure and a state and they offer ways of handling that again strongly motivated by the application domain. Thus, an account should not have so-called generic operations like set_account_value and read_account_value, but deposit, withdraw or settle, which will change the value of the account when used.

We use *Tools* in our work to accomplish a task. They are the means of work for probing and transforming the materials at hand. Tools always show the materials worked upon and they give permanent feedback on both the way they are handled and of our progress of work. A tool thus both has a task-related functionality ("it is good for something") and a specific way of handling ("it must be easy to handle").

Tools and materials are not the only design metaphors we use. Obviously, tools and materials need a place to be put and stored. This is were the *environment* metaphor comes in. A familiar example of an environment for application software is the so-called electronic desktop of many workstation systems. There we spread our materials and tools ready for use or we store them according to our own principles and working habits.

It has also proved useful to introduce the design metaphor of an *automaton*. Automata encapsulate automatic processes which will run for a considerable time without human interaction. They realize programmable work routines or mechanical procedures which can be specified with a minimum of context information and external control. Once set, an automaton will run and produce a predefined result. In a bank office, examples of automata are print spoolers, mail routers, or an automaton for transferring banker's orders.

Our design goal is no simple simulation of the physical characteristics of tools, materials and automata as we find them in the "real" world. We try to identify the conceptual characteristics of these things and their contribution to the goals and intentions we try to achieve in working. In other words: an adequate collection of flexible reactive components will support a user in dealing with his or her tasks effectively and efficiently. So, as a result of an evolutionary process you will find on an electronic desktop tools and "small" automata which will offer new means and perspectives on materials.

This new or complementary software components will eventually change the work situation. But even if new and different workplaces evolve, these new software components should never be out of place or extraneous elements, but should become in time as familiar as the other objects and means of work.

3.4. The Evolutionary Process

So far, we have looked at the design of application-oriented product using the concepts of object-oriented software development. As said in the introduction, there is the further complimentary dimension encompassing the organization, execution, and management of the development process itself (Floyd, 1987).

We have said that understanding the work relations of a given application domain is central to the evolutionary design process. One major obstacle, we have identified, is the gap between the developers' and the users' worlds. The key to a solution is the complementarity of object-oriented design of the product and the evolutionary system design process. Key issues are the intertwining of analysis, design, and evaluation activities (Swartout and Balzer, 1978), and the explicit consideration of communication and learning processes (Floyd, 1992).

As a consequence, two essential elements of our evolutionary design process are:

- We base our development documents on the professional language of the application domain and continue to develop them further.

- We view the design of an application system as part of a continuous learning process between all the parties involved on the basis of prototypes.

What we hope to achieve thereby is the evolution of a common project language, based on the professional language of the application domain. All the design documents, discussed among the groups involved, use the terminology and forms of representation familiar to the application domain. This design process is driven by these application-oriented document types and prototyping (cf. Budde et al., 1992).

The original methodology comprised a small set of application-oriented documents (as described in (Bürkle, Gryczan and Züllighoven, 1995)), namely scenarios, system visions and glossaries (cf. (Rubin and Goldberg (1992)). In the subsequent experience report we will report on how and why we have refined these basic concepts.

4. The GEBOS Project

Having outlined so far the application-oriented development methodology adopted by the GEBOS project, we return to our experience report. In table 1 we summarize the main project stages of the first project and then we report on the development process.

End	Project Stage
Feb.1991	Development of a HyperCard presentation prototype. First sketch of the future system presented to management and project team. No end users involved.
Apr. 1991	First prototype combining handling and functionality presented at the RWG trade fair. It met broad acceptance by banking management and users. RWG management decided to continue project.
Aug. 1991	Working group of software team and end users of 15 banks established. Evaluation of extended prototype.
Mar. 1992	Redesign of the prototype in line with the increased technical competence of the team. Additional application-oriented requirements by the working group integrated. Pilot system installed at 2 banks.
Dec. 1992	Functional enhancement and partial redesign of prototype in close cooperation with future end users. More pilot installations at banks.
Jun. 1993	Official shipping of the system.
Jun. 1993 - now	Due to wide acceptance, RWG management decides to launch 4 more projects for counter services, bond trading, loans and self-services.

Tab. 1. The main project stages

4.1. Refining the Application-Oriented Document-Types

4.1.1. Scenarios

Our major document type for capturing the findings of the analysis was the scenario (cf. with different meanings (Rubin and Goldberg, 1992), (Rumbaugh et al.,1991), (Sharble and Cohen, 1993)). We use scenarios for describing the *current* situation at a workplace.

Based on interviews and discussions at various workplaces, developers have written short pieces of prose, covering work tasks, work routines and typical situations of everyday work. This has been done using the professional language of the application domain. It is crucial that these scenarios, once written by the developers, are then discussed with the experts of the application domain.

Very soon in the development process it became clear, that the load of scenarios had to be structured, in order to maintain the information captured. Thus, we developed a taxonomy of scenarios (needless to say, that this taxonomy makes use of object-oriented techniques). Figure 2 shows this taxonomy.

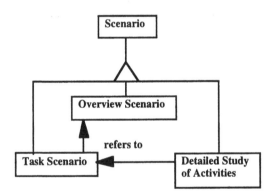

Fig. 2. Taxanomy of Scenarios

- Overview Scenarios provide (what´s in a name?) an overview of tasks at a specific workplace.

  What was needed was the overall "picture", i.e. an overview of which people (or better "roles") deal how often with what tasks at which work places. It proved to be essential that these descriptions focus on the task and its goal and not on a temporal sequence of work activities. So this type of scenario helps to provide an overall understanding of the kind of tasks related to a person or a workplace.

- A Task Scenario describes an individual task with respect to its nature and the way to cope with it.

  The style of this scenario types is that of a script or a little "episode". Alternatives at decision points are hinted at, but sparsely. Frequently we had to decide whether in a scenario alternatives ways of dealing with a specific situation had to be described, or, whether different ways of dealing with a task should be described in different scenarios. A rule of thumb is, that simple decisions can be understood in one scenario, whereas different levels of alternatives are unsuitable to be captured in one scenario.

- A Detailed Study of Activities describes – not surprisingly – in detail, how a specific task or activity is handled.

  Most often this level of description has to be encountered only for activities that occur frequently in very different tasks. As an example consider how a form is found in a folder. By describing this activity on a very detailed level it gets clear, what the concept of a folder, i.e. the specific way of dealing with it, means in the application domain. On the other hand, this activity needs not to be described in detail in each Task Scenario, where, among other activities a form has to be found in a folder.

In the context of the Projects these kinds of scenarios have not only proven to be a helpful means for developers to increase their understanding of the application domain, but also they serve for the user management incorporated in the process as job profiles. Figure 3 shows an excerpt from a task scenario.

The advisor then fetches his customer advice file, looks for the required product in the index , and opens the file at the desired point. In addition to the customer advice file, there is a form file in which standard forms (e.g., contracts with third parties) are deposited, and a specimen file in which completion guides for contracts and code sheets are deposited.

Fig. 3. Excerpt from a task scenario

4.1.2. System Visions

While scenarios are mainly used to document the work situation as is, we have used system visions to capture the design of the future system. They document the "vision" which evolves within the software team prior to the construction of prototypes. As was the case with scenarios, a single type of system visions proofed to be to coarse. System visions were written on different levels of details reaching from an overview of the future work situation in general to a detailed description of the anticipated system use for a specific work task. Basically, we distinguish between three different kinds of visions, that are further specialised (cf. Figure 4).

- General visions: They provide an overview of the systems functionality and how this functionality is embedded into its technical environment. More specific, an overview vision describes, to what extend tasks described in scenarios will be dealt with support of the future system.

- Procedural Visions: Whereas scenarios describe how tasks are performed actually, Procedural Visions describe how tasks should be performed in the future, with the aid of tools, automatons, and materials. Application Orentied PVs are written at an early stage of the visionary process. Their main task is to serve as a means of discussion to shape the ideas that are more specifically described in other visions, namely Technical PVs and Handling Visions. To start with the latter, Handling Visions describe how tasks (usually described in Task Scenarios) are performed in the future. Technical PVs use textual description as well as CRC Cards to envision a first idea of the class structure of system components. Here, first decisions are made, where and how functionality should be implemented, i.e. as support for qualified work (which needs tools) or as formalized routine, which is implemented using automatons. PVs refer to

- Component Visions, where functionality of components is decribed independant of tasks. Here first sketches of tool-interfaces are drawn, the functionality of automatons and materials are described.

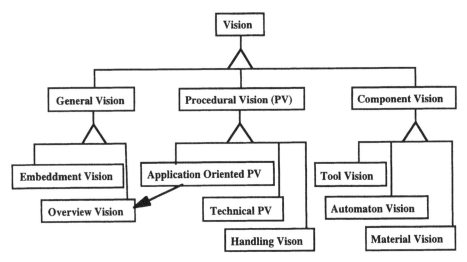

Fig. 4. Taxanomy of Visions

This taxanomy of Visions emerged from the needs of the projects we consulted. Having this taxonomy, it is not said, that each kind of vision has to be produced in every project. We stress, that these documents primarily serve as means of communication among developers. An example of a handling vision is given in Figure 5.

> The advisor then opens his customer advice file by double-clicking the mouse, selects first of all the product from a visible table of contents, then selects the desired variant from a second table of contents by double-clicking the mouse again, thus causing the corresponding sales help facility to be displayed as well.

Fig. 5. Excerpt from a system vision.

4.1.3.Prototypes

System visions are the basis for the development of *prototypes*. Prototypes are preliminary versions of the future system which represent selected features. They are the fundamental for discussing design decisions between all parties involved and they are the most effective vehicle for the various learning processes. Different kinds of prototypes are needed according to the problems at hand (cf. (Lichter et al. 94)), e.g. presentation prototypes that give a quick first sketch of the future handling, functional prototypes showing both the user interface and selected functionality or "breadboard" prototypes that implement important design alternatives which are then discussed within the software team.

Naturally, prototyping is not restricted to object-oriented design. But what makes prototyping so attractive for our application-oriented approach is first of all its strong support to evolutionary design. As the mutual understanding of the design task evolves, so do the different prototypes. They always maintain the strong link between the application-oriented design metaphors and the architecture of the underlying software. So, when the user speaks of handling a customer advice folder and a money order, the developer will find matching tools and materials classes of the software. Figure 6 shows a screen shot of a browser tool for folders.

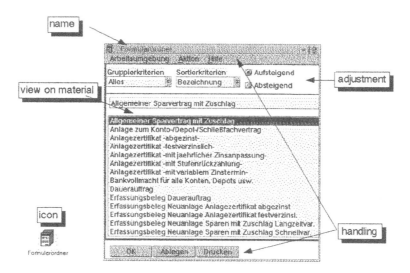

Fig. 6. A Browser Tool for Folders

4.2.   Using the Application-Oriented Document-Types

In this section we summarize the integration of the application-oriented document types into the object-oriented development process as meanwhile established at the RWG for the GEBOS project family.

Every project starts by establishing an integrated working group of the development team and representatives of about 15 banks. All bank representatives are application domain experts and potential end users of the future system. Within this working group (qualitative) interviews are conducted, leading to the documents, just mentioned. Usually, most efforts in the initial stages of a project are put into writing scenarios and glossary entries and evaluating them in feedback cycles. In this way, *233 scenarios* and more than *1800 glossary* entries have been developed so far. They provide the basis for the subsequent user manuals of the various system components.

The design of the future system evolves in parallel, based on this documents. The central document type of the early design stages being the system visions written by the software team. While these visions emphasize the functionality of the future tools and materials, the design of their handling is supported by presentation prototypes, constructed with the help of an interface builder. Both system visions and presentation prototypes are used for discussing the design of application features and the handling within the working group. Questions of interface layout are of minor concern. The GEBOS projects have built *406 system visions* so far. During further development, system vision relate functional requirements to technical design decisions.

When the mutual understanding within the working group has stabilized, then the first functional prototype is built. Functional prototypes are used to design and test the actual support of work tasks. Beyond a certain point of maturity, a functional prototype is developed evolutionary into the system version that is shipped to users.

On the organizational level the task of the software team is supported by a common architecture group (cf. also Jacobson, 1992). The members of this group work as consultants to the individual GEBOS projects. Their major group tasks, however, are to identify emerging general concepts and integrating them as new technical components of the various class libraries, and encouraging the regular use of these libraries in their projects. The long-term goal of this activity is to arrive at an application framework for the banking business.

4.3   The Technical Framework

Classes and frameworks developed in the Gebos-Projects are structured on different levels. On the lowest level a Kernel-Cluster was developed. Its responsobility is to

- encapsulate operating system specific services (including services of the graphics library),
- implement a Meta Object Prototcol, and
- implement commonly needed data structures like different kinds of containers.

The kernel cluster does not include bank-specific classes. Table 2 summarizes the classes of the Kernel-Cluster.

These classes are used by all projects, to be more specific, by classes of the Gebos-Framework. The Gebos-Framework comprises all classes, that can be shared among different projects, i.e. these classes contain domain specific, but not application specific concepts.

The Framework is divided into a horizontal and a vertical component. The horizontal component divides the framework into sub-frameworks, which are responsible for a specific functionality. Examples for this kind of sub-frameworks are: electronic forms, domain values, and classes for the construction of interactive tools.

Parts	Total
Meta Object Protocol	31
Containers	60
Interface to Operating System	17
Garbage Collection & Tracetool	4
Late Creation	42
Interface to Graphics Library(CommonView)	60
	214

Tab. 2. Classes of the Kernel-Cluster

Each horizontal component is divided vertically into a concept- and a basic implementation part. They are responsible for:

- abstract protocols offered by the sub-frameworks and implemented patterns (for example the observer pattern (Gamma, 1995). This part of the framework is the concept part;

- basic implementations of the abstract protocols. Projects can use these implementations as is, but are also allowed to redefine the basic implementations. It is not recommended to change the protocols. This part of the framework is the basic implementation part.

Table 3 summarizes the sub frameworks implemented so far.

Sub-Frameworks	Concept	Base	Total
Domain Values	18	67	85
Test Environment for Domain Values	11	40	51
Converter for Domain Values	4	14	18
Container	9	23	32
Database Interface	8	20	28
Tool construction	41	162	203
Aspect classes	43	0	43
Interface to bank specific hardware	24	39	63
Interface for the host-system	23	38	61
Special interfaces for host transactions	0	66	66
Global Tools	0	105	105
Electronic Forms (incl. Tools)	20	70	90
Customer, Account, Product (incl. Tools)	13	46	59
debits	7	29	36
Offline-Framework	0	6	6
Bank, Employee	0	20	20
Total	221	745	966

Tab. 3. Sub frameworks of the Gebos-Projects

The basic implementation part of the frameworks is used to construct application specific tools, materials and automatons in the projects. Table 4 provides an overview of these projects and how many classes of which kind have been implemented there.

Project	Materials	Tools	Automatons	Total
Administrators Workplace	17	10	0	27
Credit	72	36	27	135
Database (Administration)	40	0	25	65
Ejour (Over night clean up)	0	2	0	2
Sending of Offline-Transactions	0	2	0	2
Offline Data-Management	0	2	0	2
Investment	34	10	6	50
Self-Service	19	58	7	84
Shares	42	66	1	109
Teller-Banking	30	58	26	114
Total	254	244	92	590

Tab. 4. Project specific classes

There is a clear tendency, that the number of project specific classes to design is decreasing from project to project. On the other hand this "return on investment" has to be paid by an increased work effort in maintaining and enhancing the structure of the sub frameworks. For that purpose the RWG has installed an "architecture group" which is responsible for adapting sub frameworks to project needs (cf. paragraph 4.2).

5. Evaluation of the Object-Oriented Approach

After more than 4 years of GEBOS projects and various projects completed or under way at other institutions, it seems clear that major application systems can be developed using the application-oriented approach presented in this paper. The GEBOS system has been shipped so far to more than 130 banks and is successfully used at more than 1600 workplaces.

What is recognized by both management and the teams, is the high degree of user acceptance combined with a level of software quality way beyond standard.

The intense cooperation between developers and users has encouraged the RWG to reengineer their organization according to the increased demands for user involvement, feedback cycles and smaller but faster software projects.

The tools and materials design metaphors have proved constructive in the design of complex interactive systems with high flexibility and changeability. These metaphors are the key to seamlessly linking models and structures of professional languages of an application domain via class design to the actual program code.

The benefits of the design metaphors are twofold. The similarity between technical and application-oriented concepts allow the designers to relate technical components to the work tasks, which are supported thereby. On the other hand, metaphors provide a new abstract level of speaking about design – they enhance communication and are part of an evolving design language.

Thus we believe, that the right choice of design metaphors, in our case tools and materials among others, is a prerequisite for the design and continuous further development of large application systems. The projects, we are reporting on, can serve as an empirical basis for the systematic use of metaphors as demanded by (Madsen, 1995). But, unlike Madsen, we do not believe, that using metaphors is a benefit in itself. Not every metaphor (cf. his examples of "TV-broadcasting" and "a meeting place") seems fit for bridging the gap between application domain and technical models. This bridge, we feel, is the key to building high quality and highly accepted software systems.

Acknowledgement. The GEBOS projects would not have been successful without the work of Karl-Heinz Sylla and Reinhard Budde who cooperate in developing the methodology presented here and helped substantially in establishing the early stages of the application-oriented project phase.

References

Boehm, B. W. (1976). Software engineering. *IEEE Transactions on Computers.* 25(12), 1226–1241.

Budde, R., Christ-Neumann, M.-L. , & Sylla, K. H. (1992). Tools and materials, an analysis and design metaphor. *Proceedings of the TOOLS 7,* 135–148, Englewood Cliffs, NJ: Prentice-Hall.

Budde, R., Kautz, K., Kuhlenkamp, K., & Züllighoven, H. (1992) *Prototyping – An approach to evolutionary system development.* Berlin: Springer.

Budde, R., & Züllighoven, H. (1992). Software tools in a programming workshop. In C. Floyd, H. Züllighoven, R. Budde, & R. Keil-Slawik (Eds.), *Software development and reality construction* (pp. 252–268). Berlin: Springer.

Bürkle, U., Gryczan, G., & Züllighoven, H. (1995). Object-Oriented System Development in a Banking Project: Methodology, Experience, and Conclusions. Human Computer Interaction 10 (1995) 2 & 3, pp. 293 - 336

Carroll, J. M., Mack, R. L., & Kellogg, W. A. (1988). Interface metaphors and user interface design. In M. Helander (Ed.), *Handbook of Human-Computer Interaction,* 1 pp. 283–307.

Carroll, J. M., & Rosson, M. B. (1990). Human computer interaction scenarios as design representation. *Proceedings of the Hawaii International Conference on System Sciences,* 555-561. Los Alamitos, CA: IEEE Computer Society Press.

Floyd, C. (1987). Outline of a paradigm change in software engineering. In G. Bjerknes, P. Ehn, & M. Kyng (Eds.), *Computers and democracy – a Scandinavian challenge* (pp. 191–210). Aldershot, England: Avebury.

Floyd, C. (1992). Software development as reality construction. In C. Floyd, H. Züllighoven, R. Budde, & R. Keil-Slawik (Eds.), *Software development and reality construction.* (pp. 86–100). Berlin: Springer.

Gamma, E., Helm, R., Johnson, R., Vlissides, J. (1995): Design Patterns - Elements of Reusable Object-Oriented Software. Reading, Mass.: Addison-Wesley.

Jacobson, I. (1992). *Object-oriented software engineering – A use case driven approach.* Reading: Addison-Wesley.

Lichter, H., Schneider-Hufschmidt, M., & Züllighoven, H. (1995). Prototyping in industrial software projects. Bridging the Gap Between Theory and Practice. *IEEE Tranasactions on Software Engineering,* 20(11), (pp-825-832).

Maaß, S., & Oberquelle, H. (1992). Perspectives and Metaphors for Human-Computer-Interaction. In C. Floyd, H. Züllighoven, R. Budde, & R. Keil-Slawik (Eds.), *Software development and reality construction* (pp. 233–251). Berlin: Springer.

Madsen, K. H. (1988). Breakthrough by breakdown: Metaphors and structured domains. In H. K. Klein, & K. Kumar (Eds.), *Information systems development for human progress in organizations* . Amsterdam: North-Holland.

Madsen, K.-H. (1995). A Guide to Metaphorical Design. *Communications of the ACM,* 37(12), 57–62.

Miller, G., Galanter, E., and Pribram, K. (1960). Plans and the Structure of Behavior. New York, NY: Holt, Rinehart and Winston.

Monarchi, D. E.; Puhr:, G. I.: A research typology for object-oriented analysis and design. Communications of the ACM, 35 (1992) 9 S. 35 – 47.

Riehle, D., Züllighhoven, H(1995). A Pattern Language for Tool Construction and Integration Based on the Tools & Materials Metaphor. In: J.D. Coplien & D.C. Schmidt (EDS.), *Pattern Languages of Programs.* Addison-Wesley, to appear.

Robinson, M. (1993): *Design for unanticipated use.*In: G. de Michelis, C. Simone, K. Schmidt (Eds.) Proc. ECSCW '93. 187-202.

Rubin, K. S., & Goldberg, A. (1992). Object behavior analysis. *Communications of the ACM,* 35(9), 48–62.

Rumbaugh, J., Blaha, M., Premerlani, W., Eddy, F., & Lorensen, W. (1991). *Object-oriented modeling and design.* Englewood Cliffs, NJ: Prentice-Hall.

Sharble, R.C. & Cohen, S.S. (1993). The Object-Oriented Brewery. Software EWngineering Notes, 18(2), 60–73.

Suchman, L. (1987): Plans and Situated Actions; Cambridge University Press, 1987.

Swartout, W., & Balzer, R. (1978). On the inevitable intertwining of specification and implementation. *Communications of the ACM, 25*(7), 438-440.

An Application Framework for Module Composition Tools*

Guruduth Banavar[1] and Gary Lindstrom[2]

[1] IBM TJ Watson Research Center, 30 Saw Mill River Road, Hawthorne, NY 10532
USA. Email: banavar@watson.ibm.com
[2] Department of Computer Science, University of Utah, Salt Lake City, UT 84112
USA. Email: lindstrom@cs.utah.edu

Abstract. This paper shows that class inheritance, viewed as a mechanism for composing self-referential namespaces, is a broadly applicable concept. We show that several kinds of software artifacts can be modeled as self-referential namespaces, and software tools based on a model of composition of namespaces can effectively manage these artifacts. We describe four such tools: an interpreter for compositionally modular Scheme, a compositional linker for object files, a compositional interface definition language, and a compositional document processing tool. We show that these tools benefit significantly from incorporating inheritance-based reuse. Furthermore, the implementation of these tools share much in common since they are based on the same underlying model. We describe a reusable OO framework for efficiently constructing such tools. Three of the above tools were built by directly reusing the application framework, and the fourth evolved in parallel with it. We provide reuse statistics and experiences with the development of our framework and its completions.

1 Introduction

Inheritance of classes in object-oriented programming has been touted for enabling significant levels of implementation reuse. Inheritance is widely acknowledged to support reuse via incremental programming — one needs to only program how new classes differ from already existing ones.

One characterization of class-based inheritance is that it is the combination of self-referential namespaces [12]. By carefully designing operations to manipulate such namespaces, a wide spectrum of effects of single and multiple inheritance can be obtained. *Compositional modularity* [3, 6] is such an inheritance model, in which self-referential namespaces, known as modules, can be adapted and composed in various ways to achieve implementation reuse. Compositional modularity supports a stronger and more flexible reuse model than traditional class-based inheritance.

---

* This research was sponsored by the Defense Advanced Research Projects Agency under contract number DABT63-94-C-0058, and by the Office of Naval Research under grant number N00014-95-1-0737.

When class-based inheritance is distilled down to a notion of *operations on self-referential namespaces*, it becomes possible to explore the breadth of applicability of the concept of inheritance. There is indeed a wide range of software artifacts that can be modeled as self-referential namespaces. For instance, it is well known that interface types can be viewed as self-referential namespaces [8]. A traditional compiled object file can also be viewed as a self-referential namespace. Furthermore, structured document fragments can be modeled as self-referential namespaces. Even other artifacts, such as GUI components and file system directories can be regarded as self-referential namespaces.

There currently exists a range of tools that manage the range of artifacts mentioned above. However, many such tools are usually based on disparate, and often impoverished, underlying models. In this paper, we argue that it is advantageous to manage the above artifacts from the viewpoint of a well understood model such as compositional modularity, and design tools based on this viewpoint. The primary advantage of such an approach is that the underlying model of such tools can be significantly enriched, and reuse mechanisms akin to inheritance can be supported on the artifacts they manage. Moreover, the uniformity of the underlying model of such tools can be exploited to support better interactions between them.

The model of compositional modularity can be easily and effectively applied within tools that manipulate artifacts such as the ones given above. To demonstrate, we describe four such tools in this paper: (i) an interpreter for a compositional module system for the Scheme programming language, (ii) a linker that manipulates compiled object files as compositional modules, (iii) a compiler front-end for an interface definition language with compositional interfaces, and (iv) a document processing system that manipulates documents as compositional modules. We also discuss other tools that could be based on compositional modularity. We show that tools such as the above derive important benefits from incorporating compositional modularity.

Naturally, the implementations of these tools share much in common, since they are all based on compositional modularity. It is therefore beneficial to abstract their common aspects, and realize them as a reusable software architecture. We have designed an OO application framework known as ETYMA that encompasses the reusable architecture of tools based on compositional modularity. The primary utility of the ETYMA framework is that it enables one to easily and rapidly build module composition engines for tools that manipulate a variety of compositional modules. ETYMA consists of more than 40 reusable C++ classes. In this paper, we document the architecture of ETYMA using design patterns and describe the construction of three of the above four tools as direct completions of the framework. We report that significant design and code reuse (between 73 and 91%) was obtained in the construction of the above prototypes as completions of the framework. We also outline our experience with the iterative development of the framework.

The following section provides some background on the semantic foundations of compositional modularity (also referred to as CM for short). Subsections of

Section 3 describe each of the four compositional tools mentioned above. In particular, Subsection 3.1 describes the CM model via examples in a Scheme based language; this subsection is intended as an extended introduction to CM. Section 4 then presents the architecture, class design, and reuse statistics for the ETYMA framework and its completions.

2 Background and Related Work

Based on the notion of operations on records developed by Cardelli and others [9], Cook and Palsberg [12] modeled a class as a self-referential record generating function, also known as a *generator*. For example, the generator $g = \lambda s. \{a_1 = v_1, a_2 = v_2, \ldots, a_n = v_n\}$ has method names $a_1 \ldots a_n$ bound to method bodies $v_1 \ldots v_n$. The parameter s corresponds to the generator's notion of "self." References to names from within the method bodies are made via the s parameter, e.g., $s.a_1$, and hence are known as self-references. The fixpoint $Y(g)$ of such a generator, a record, corresponds to an *instance* of the class g. Taking the fixpoint of the generator binds the generator's self-references $s.a_x$.

The notion of class inheritance is modeled as combination of generators, via operators such as merge and override. For instance, the notion of method overriding for generators, override, is defined in terms of record overriding ($\leftarrow_r$ denotes the record override operator):

$$\text{override} = \lambda g_1. \lambda g_2. \lambda s. g_1(s) \leftarrow_r g_2(s)$$

The crucial aspect of inheritance is that of self-reference manipulation — while combining classes during inheritance, a superclass' notion of self must be properly modified to include that of the subclass. This is captured by the above definition.

Based on Cook's work, Bracha and Lindstrom [6] developed a uniform and comprehensive suite of linguistic operations on a simple notion of classes known as *modules*, also modeled as generators. These operations individually achieve effects of rebinding, sharing, encapsulation, and static binding. In addition to making previously existing operators explicit linguistic constructs, they define three new operators: hide, freeze, and copy-as. For example, a method of a generator can be copied under another name in order to achieve access to overridden methods, as follows ($\|_r$ denotes the record merge operation):

$$\text{copy-as } a \ b = \lambda g. \lambda s. \ let \ super = g(s) \ in \ super \ \|_r \ \{b = super._r a\}$$

In [3], we further augment the above model to include a notion of hierarchical nesting as a composition operation, arguing that module nestability and separate development must co-exist in a modularity framework without compromising each other. This requires abstracting the environment of a generator, resulting in what we call a *closed* generator, e.g., $g_c = \lambda e. \lambda s. \{a_1 = v_1, a_2 = v_2, \ldots, a_n = v_n\}$. Environmental references from within method bodies are made via a separate e parameter. With this, separately developed modules can be *retroactively* nested into conforming modules via a composition operator named nest, defined as follows:

$$\text{nest } n = \lambda g_{c_{in}}.\ \lambda g_{c_{out}}.\ \lambda e.\ \lambda s.\ \{n = \lambda d.\ g_{c_{in}}(e \leftarrow_r s)\}\ \|_r\ g_{c_{out}}(e)(s)$$

Compositional Modularity. The above concept of closed generators, along with eight primary operations on them, merge, override, rename, copy-as, restrict, freeze, hide, and nest, within an imperative store-based framework with appropriate static typing rules comprise the model of compositional modularity [3]. The term *composition* is used here to mean implementation composition to achieve reuse akin to inheritance. The goal of CM is to get maximal reuse out of small, composable components. The composition constructs given above provide a powerful framework for building larger modules from smaller ones. These constructs can be used in combination to emulate various composite inheritance idioms in existing OO languages. As a result, CM supports a stronger (by virtue of compositional nesting) as well as a more flexible (by virtue of "unbundled," composable operators) notion of reuse than traditional inheritance models.

3   Systems based on Compositional Modularity

To provide a better understanding of how one can apply CM within various tools, we describe four systems based on CM in this section. As mentioned earlier, CM can be layered on top of systems that have a notion of self-referential namespaces and some benefit to be derived from composing them. For systems that have these characteristics, a software tool that manipulates namespaces using operations of CM can be constructed. However, it must be pointed out that not all eight of the CM operations may be useful or even possible within every system. Nevertheless, we will show in the following sections that enriching a system by incorporating CM gives rise to specific benefits relating to the system's expressive power, flexibility, and/or scope.

3.1   CMS

The first obvious choice for applying compositional modularity is within a modular programming language. In this section, we describe via examples a module system based on CM for the programming language Scheme [10], which we call Compositionally Modular Scheme, or *CMS* for short.

A module is generally understood to be an independent namespace. A Scheme module may be modeled as a self-referential namespace, as follows. A Scheme module may be regarded as a set of symbols (identifiers) bound either to locations (variables) or to any of the various Scheme values, including procedures. Procedures may contain self-references to other names defined within the module, or to unbound names within the module which correspond to "abstract methods." (In more traditional module systems, unbound names might correspond to the notion of imported names, with the actual importation performed via module combination, described below.)

Several module systems for Scheme have been proposed previously [13, 26, 24], but these systems mainly provide a facility for structuring programs via decomposition. However, the ability to *recompose* first-class modules can additionally support design and implementation reuse akin to inheritance in OO programming. Furthermore, the notion of first-class modules and their operations in CM is consistent with the uniform use of first-class values and the expression-oriented nature of Scheme. Consequently, we argue that the incorporation of CM into a module system for Scheme can be very beneficial. (There is previous work on Scheme module systems based on reflective operations on first-class environments [18]; however, the CMS module system is different in its approach and scope, please see [3].)

Module definition and encapsulation. A module in *CMS* is a Scheme value that is created with the mk-module primitive. It consists of a set of attributes (symbol-binding pairs) with no order significance. Attributes that are bound to procedures are referred to as *methods*, borrowing from OO programming. Modules may be manipulated, but their attributes cannot be accessed or evaluated until they are instantiated via the mk-instance primitive. The attributes of a module instance can be accessed via the attr-ref primitive, and assigned to via the attr-set! primitive. A method can access other attributes within its own instance via analogous primitives: self-ref and self-set!.

Figure 1 (a) shows a simple module with three attributes bound to a Scheme variable fueled-vehicle. Note that the fill method refers to an attribute capacity that is not defined within the module, but is expected to be the fuel capacity of the vehicle in gallons.

The primitive hide retroactively encapsulates its argument attribute. In Figure 1 (b), the hide expression returns a new module with an encapsulated fuel attribute that has an internal, inaccessible name, shown by the describe primitive as <priv-attr>.

Module combination. The module capacity-module given in Figure 1 (c) exports two symbols, including one named capacity. Thus, the module encap-fueled-vehicle can be combined with capacity-module to satisfy the former's "import" requirement, via the primitive merge. The new merged module vehicle in 1 (c) contains four public attributes: empty?, fill, capacity, and greater-capacity?.

The primitive merge does not permit combining modules with conflicting defined attributes, i.e., attributes that are defined to have the same name. In the presence of conflicting attributes, one can use override, which creates a new module by choosing the right operand's binding over the left operand's in the resulting module. For example, the module new-capacity in Figure 1 (d) cannot be merged with vehicle since the two modules have a conflicting attribute capacity. However, new-capacity can override vehicle, as shown.

Module adaptation. Besides hide, there are four other primitives which can be used to create new modules by adapting some aspect of the attributes of existing modules. The primitive restrict simply removes the definition of the given

```
      (define fueled-vehicle (mk-module
                     ((fuel 0)
(a)                   (empty?  (lambda () (= (self-ref fuel) 0)))
                     (fill (lambda () (self-set! fuel (self-ref capacity)))))))))
```

```
      (define encap-fueled-vehicle (hide fueled-vehicle 'fuel))
(b)   (describe encap-fueled-vehicle)
      ⟹
      ((empty? (lambda () (= (self-ref <priv-attr>) 0))) (fill ... ))
```

```
      (define capacity-module
         (mk-module ((capacity 10)
(c)                    (greater-capacity? (lambda (in)
                                    (> (self-ref capacity) (attr-ref in capacity)))))))
      (define vehicle (merge encap-fueled-vehicle capacity-module))
```

```
(d)   (define new-capacity (mk-module ((capacity 25))))
      (define new-vehicle (override vehicle new-capacity))
```

Fig. 1. Basic module operations. (a) Definition via mk-module, (b) Encapsulation via hide, (c) Combination via merge, and (d) Rebinding via override.

(defined) attribute from the module, i.e., makes it undefined (see Figure 2 (a)). The primitive rename changes the name of the definition of, *and* self-references to, the attribute in its second argument to the one in the third argument. An undefined attribute, i.e., an attribute that is not defined but is self-referenced, can also be renamed. An example is shown in Figure 2 (b).

The primitive copy-as copies the binding of the attribute in its second argument (which must be defined) with the name in its third argument. An example is shown in Figure 2 (c). The primitive freeze statically binds self-references to the given attribute, provided it is defined in the module. Freezing the attribute capacity in the module vehicle causes self-references to capacity to be statically bound, but the attribute capacity itself is available in the public interface for further manipulation, e.g., rebinding by combination. As shown in Figure 2 (d), frozen self-references to capacity are transformed to refer to a private version of the attribute.

Module nesting. In CMS, modules may be nested within other modules by binding them to attributes, as in modules type1 and type2 within vehicle-category in Figure 3 (a). Nested modules may refer to name bindings in their surrounding module via the env-ref primitive. Additionally, a seperately developed module may be retroactively nested within another module via the operator nest. An example is shown in Figure 3 (b). The nest expression in the example produces a module that contains the attribute type3 bound to the nested module veh-type just as if it was directly lexically nested.

(a)	(describe (restrict vehicle 'capacity)) $\Longrightarrow$ ((fill ...) (empty? ...) (greater-capacity? ...))
(b)	(describe (rename vehicle 'capacity 'fuel-capacity)) $\Longrightarrow$ ((fuel-capacity 10)(fill ... (self-ref fuel-capacity))...)
(c)	(describe (copy-as vehicle 'capacity 'default-capacity)) $\Longrightarrow$ ((capacity 10)(default-capacity 10)(fill ...(self-ref capacity))...)
(d)	(describe (freeze vehicle 'capacity)) $\Longrightarrow$ ((capacity 10)(fill ...(self-ref \<priv-attr\>)) ...)

Fig. 2. Adaptation. (a) Removing an attribute via restrict (b) Renaming an attribute and self-references to it via rename (c) Copying an attribute via copy-as, and (d) Statically binding self-references to an attribute via freeze.

(a)	(define vehicle-category
	   (mk-module
	      ((capacity 10)
	      (type1 (mk-module ((fill (lambda... (env-ref capacity)...)))))
	      (type2 (mk-module ((fill (lambda... (env-ref capacity)...))))))))
	(define mycategory (mk-instance vehicle-category))
	(define v1 (mk-instance (attr-ref mycategory type1)))

(b)	(define veh-type (mk-module ((fill (lambda ... (env-ref capacity) ...))))) (define new-vehicle-category (nest 'type3 veh-type vehicle-category))

Fig. 3. Nested Modules. (a) Lexical nesting, and (b) Retroactive nesting via the nest operator.

Composite Inheritance. With the above suite of primitives, several composite inheritance idioms including super-based and prefix-based single inheritance, as well as mixin-based and general forms of multiple inheritance with various types of conflict resolution and sharing strategies can be emulated; please see [3] for a detailed description. To give some insight, Figure 4 pictorially shows how super-based and prefix-based single inheritance can be emulated using CM primitives. Figure 4 (a) shows a "superclass" super with a method meth and self-references to it. An increment delta has a redefinition of meth in terms of the previous definition, referred to as old, as well as some self-references to meth. The classes

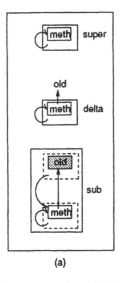 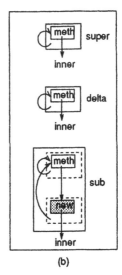

(a)   (b)

Fig. 4. Pictorial representation of subclassing with single inheritance. Expressions for obtaining sub are: (a) Super-based: (hide (override (copy-as super 'meth 'old) delta) 'old), and (b) Prefix-based: (hide (override (copy-as delta 'meth 'new) (rename super 'inner 'new)) 'new).

super and delta can be combined to form the "subclass" sub by using the sequence of operators copy-override-hide shown in the figure caption. Similarly, the BETA-style [20] prefixes super and delta in Figure 4(b) can be combined into sub using a similar sequence of operations. The difference is that (an adapted version of) the superclass overrides the increment in the case of prefix-based inheritance, as opposed to the reverse for super-based inheritance. Indeed, that is the difference between the two forms of single inheritance.

Two idiomatic sequences of operations in CM have proven to be very useful: copy-override-hide, and rename-merge-hide. These and other idioms of CM will be shown as we proceed.

3.2 Compositional Linking

In this section, we describe the second of the four tools based on CM: a programmable linker.

The physical notion of a separately compiled object file may be modeled logically as a self-referential namespace. An object file essentially consists of a set of symbols, each associated with data or code. This set of symbols is represented as a symbol table within the object module. Furthermore, there are internal self-references to these symbols which are represented as relocation information within the object module.

The traditional notion of linking object files essentially corresponds to the merge operation in CM. However, the full power of CM made available via a programmable linker can significantly enhance the ability to manage and bind ob-

```
(open-module ⟨path-string-expr⟩)
(merge ⟨module-expr1⟩ ⟨module-expr2⟩ ...)
(override ⟨module-expr1⟩ ⟨module-expr2⟩ ...)
(copy-as ⟨module-expr⟩ ⟨from-name-expr⟩ ⟨to-name-expr⟩)
(rename ⟨module-expr⟩ ⟨from-name-expr⟩ ⟨to-name-expr⟩)
(hide ⟨module-expr⟩ ⟨sym-name-expr⟩)
(restrict ⟨module-expr⟩ ⟨sym-name-expr⟩)
(fix ⟨section-locn-list⟩ ⟨module-expr⟩)
```

Fig. 5. Syntax of some OMOS module primitives.

ject modules. In particular, facilities such as function interposition, management of incremental additions of functionality to compiled libraries, and namespace management can be made more principled and flexible, as shown below. Consequently, there is much to gain from incorporating CM into a programmable linking tool.

A programmable linker. OMOS [23, 5] is a programmable linker that supports CM for C language object files. OMOS is programmed using a Scheme based scripting language similar to *CMS* above, except that the modules manipulated in this language are compiled object files (dot-o files) as opposed to Scheme modules. A dot-o can be converted into a first-class compositional module via a primitive open-module, manipulated using the CM primitives, and instantiated into executable programs (bound to particular points in a process' address space) using the primitive fix. The syntax of some OMOS module primitives is shown in Figure 5.

Implementationally, most module operations transform the symbol table of the object file. For instance, the restrict operation essentially modifies a symbol table entry to indicate that the symbol is only declared (extern) and not defined. The hide operation removes a definition from the external interface of the object file, i.e. makes the definition static. Similarly, the rename and copy-as operations modify symbol table entries. The primitive nest is not supported by OMOS, since the notion of nesting is not supported by the base language, C.

Wrapping. To illustrate the use of the above primitives, this section describes how to achieve several variations of a facility generally referred to as "wrapping." Figure 6 shows a C language service providing module LIB with a function f(), and its client module CLIENT that calls f(). (Although OMOS really operates on compiled dot-o files, the C source for modules is shown in the figure for illustration purposes.) Three varieties of wrapping can be illustrated with the modules shown in the figure.

(1) A version of LIB that is wrapped with the module LWRAP so that all accesses to f() are indirected through LWRAP's f() can be produced with the expression:

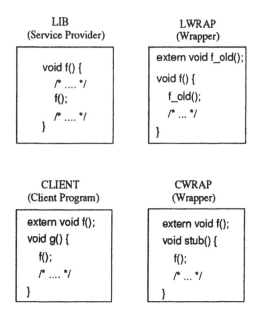

Fig. 6. Module definitions for wrapping examples in OMOS.

```
(hide (override (copy-as LIB 'f 'f_old) LWRAP) 'f_old)
```

By using copy-as instead of rename, this expression ensures that self-references to f() within LIB continue to refer to (the overridden) f() in the resultant, and are not renamed to f_old.

(2) Alternatively, a wrapped version of LIB in which the definition of and self-references to f() are renamed can be produced using the expression:

```
(hide (merge (rename LIB 'f 'f_old) LWRAP) 'f_old)
```

This might be useful, for example, if we want to wrap LIB with a wrapper which counts only the number of external calls to LIB's f(), but does not count internal calls.

(3) If we want to wrap all calls to f() from CLIENT so that they are mediated via the stub() function of module CWRAP, we can use the following expression:

```
(hide (merge (rename CLIENT 'f 'stub) CWRAP) 'stub)
```

Note that in this last case, only a particular client module is wrapped, without wrapping the service provider. In the example, renaming the client module's calls to f() produces the desired effect, since the declaration of f() as well as all self-references to it must be renamed.

The idioms given above are in fact the basis of inheritance in OO programming. Scheme macros that perform various kinds of single and multiple inheritance can be used within OMOS just as in *CMS*. In [5], we describe an architecture for OO application development via programmed linkage using OMOS. Specifically, we show how to manage extensions to libraries, how to generate static constructors and destructors, and how to manage the problem of flat namespaces with dot-o files generated from the C langauge.

3.3 Interface Composition

In this section, we describe the third of the four tools based on CM: a compositional interface definition language.

An interface is essentially a naming scope, with labels bound to types. In the case of recursive interfaces, type constituents of the interface may recursively refer back to the interface itself [8]. Thus, an interface can be modeled as a self-referential namespace.

Explicit specification and composition of interfaces is becoming widespread in modern programming languages and distributed systems [22, 2, 19], particularly in interface definition languages (IDLs). It is useful to specify an interface by *reusing*, i.e., inheriting from, existing interfaces. Reuse facilitates the evolution of interfaces [17] by ensuring that inheriting interfaces evolve in step with the inherited interfaces. It also simplifies maintenance by reducing redundant code. Most importantly, an IDL should be able to express the types of components generated via implementation inheritance in module implementation languages. In fact, it has been shown that inheritance of interfaces generates exactly those types, known as *inherited types*, that correspond to the types of inherited objects [11]. These reasons point to the need for flexible interface inheritance (or composition) mechanisms in IDLs.

A compositional IDL. We have developed a compositional IDL to demonstrate the concepts of compositionality of interfaces. The base type domain of the language consists of primitive types, function types, and record types. Interfaces in this language follow a structural type discipline. Interfaces can be recursive, in that a type constituent can use the keyword selftype to refer to its own interface. Furthermore, we take the analogy between interface type constituents and methods of objects so far as to allow interface type constituents to refer to sibling type constituents by selecting on selftype [9]. For example, consider a Point module that contains attributes corresponding to rectangular coordinates x and y, a method move for changing the position of the point, and an equality predicate equal. Its interface may be expressed as follows, where recursion is expressed using the selftype keyword. (As a convenience, selftype.x is abbreviated to x.)

```
interface FloatPointType {
  float x, y;
  selftype move (x, y);
  boolean equal (selftype);
}
```

Inheritance is an operation on self-referential structures, thus it can be applied to interfaces as well. For instance, the interface FloatPointType above can be extended to have a color attribute using the merge operation, as follows:

```
interface ColorType {
  color_type color;
};
interface ColorPointType = FloatPointType merge ColorType;
```

Although it inherits from FloatPointType, the ColorPointType interface is not a subtype of FloatPointType, due to the contravariance of the equal method. However, ColorPointType shares the same structure as FloatPointType, hence it is known as an *inherited type* of FloatPointType [8, 7].

An important point to note here is that the merge operation on interfaces generates types that correspond to the types of inherited module implementations generated via both the merge *and* override operations on module implementations. An override operation is defined on interfaces as well, by which type constituents of interfaces may be arbitrarily rebound. The primary motivation for including such an operator is to support a high degree of reuse of existing interface specifications. In the following example, the x and y constituents of FloatPointType are rebound to complex_type; note that this will automatically result in the proper type for the move constituent, due to self-reference.

```
interface ComplexPointType =
  FloatPointType override
    interface {
      complex_type x, y;
    };
```

Type constituents may be rename'd, which results in self-references to get renamed as well. This is useful for resolving name conflicts while performing operations equivalent to multiple inheritance. Furthermore, particular interface constituents may be project'ed. This operation is analogous to the one in relational algebra, and is the dual of the restrict operator presented earlier.

The operator copy-as does not seem very useful in the context of interfaces. Also, the operators freeze and hide do not apply, since interfaces by definition represent the public types of modules. An operation corresponding to nest may be supported, but we are doubtful as to whether that level of expressiveness is useful in IDLs.

3.4 Compositional Document Processing

In this section, we describe the fourth of the four tools based on CM: a compositional document processing system.

A structured document may be viewed as a compositional module. Sections within the document correspond to module attributes, with each section comprising a label, associated section heading, and some textual body. Cross references within text to other section labels correspond to self-references. Thus, the document can be regarded as a self-referential namespace.

A large and complex document is often broken down into and composed from smaller pieces. In such scenarios, there are many cases where documents developed for one purpose can be reused for other purposes. For example, a report, such as a user manual, can be composed from several document fragments, such as design documents. A specific scenario of modular document processing that motivated the document processing application of CM was document generation and consumption in the activity of building construction such as that described in [25]. Building architects routinely extract and maintain large bases of document fragments that they reuse, edit, and compose into architectural specifications for delivery to particular clients. As another example, in a document centered industrial process, document fragments are generated at all phases of the process with the objective of producing a number of reports such as inventory statement, parts catalog, assembly reports, process monitoring and quality control documents, etc. Thus, effective document composition tools can be useful in enterprises where several documents are generated, edited, composed, maintained, and delivered in various ways. In such environments, the model of compositional modularity can be used to enhance the composability and reusability of documents.

A tool for composing document modules. We have developed a programmable document processing system based on CM named MT$_E$X which can help a document preparer to adapt and compose documents effectively. It is built on top of a restricted version of the LaT$_E$X document preparation system [21]. An MT$_E$X program is a script based on Scheme (as in *CMS*) that describes how LaT$_E$X document modules should be constructed and composed.

An MT$_E$X module is modeled as a generator of an *ordered* set of sections, each of which is a label bound either to a section body, or to a nested module. The section label is a symbolic name that can be referenced from other sections (defined using LaT$_E$X's \label command). The section body is a tuple (H, B) where H is text corresponding to the section heading, and B corresponds to the actual text body, which consists of textual segments interspersed with self-references to labels. Given this model of document modules, consider the meaning of the operations of compositional modularity.

The binary operator merge produces a new document module with the sections of its right module operand concatenated to its left module operand, if there are no conflicting labels between the two module operands. Since the order of sections is significant, merge is associative, but not commutative. The binary operator override concatenates two modules in the presence of conflicting section labels. Conflicting sections in the right operand replace corresponding ones in the left operand. Non-conflicting sections in the right operand are appended to the left operand in the same order that they occur in the right operand.

The restrict operator has the usual meaning of removing sections. However, its dual operator project (analogous to relational algebra) is potentially more useful in the context of document composition. The operators rename and copy-as have the usual meaning. We have chosen not to support encapsulation, i.e., the hide operator, and static binding, i.e., freeze, although it could conceivably have some natural meanings for some applications of document processing.

Hierarchical nesting is a very important and useful notion in document struc-

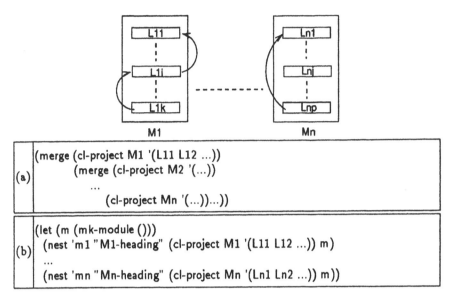

Fig. 7. Example of report generation.

turing. The nest operator supports retroactive nesting of document modules. However, in keeping with the generator semantics of CM, an environmental reference within a nested module is resolved to a definition of the name in the innermost enclosing module. While this semantics does not permit references from a section to non-enclosing modules, it has the potential to produce highly structured documents. Finally, the notion of instantiating document modules interestingly corresponds to running the LATEX document processing system on them.

Report Generation. To illustrate some of the above notions, consider the example in Figure 7. At the top of the figure is shown a set of document fragments labeled M1 through Mn. Each of these fragments has several sections, where section Lij is the jth section in fragment Mi. Sections contain cross references to other defined or undefined sections within the document fragment.

Considering each document fragment as an MTEX compositional module, two ways in which they can be usefully put together are described in the figure using the MTEX scripting language. The examples use a function named cl-project which projects sections corresponding to the closure of self-references within a module. This function can be written using the module primitive project and an introspective primitive self-refs-in, which returns the self-referenced names within a section. The expression in Figure 7(a) merges (closures of) particular sections projected from each of the modules, producing a document containing several sections at the same level. The expression in Figure 7(b) creates a new document module and nests within it one subsection per original module that contains (closures of) particular sections projected from each of the original modules.

4 The ETYMA Framework and its Completions

Earlier, it was mentioned that tools for systems based on CM can be constructed from a common architecture that encompasses the concepts of CM. In this section, we describe a simple software architecture, an OO framework named ETYMA[3], that can be effectively *reused* to build tools for a wide variety of systems based on CM such as the ones described in the previous section. Tools constructed from this framework benefit not only from the power and flexibility that the underlying model offers, but also from significant design and code reuse. Thus, ETYMA could significantly reduce the resources spent in developing tools, as well as increase their reliability. Furthermore, ETYMA represents a good model for studying the domain of systems based on CM.

A tool for a system based on CM can be said to consist of a front-end that reads in command and data input, a processing engine that performs CM operations on an internal representation (IR), and an optional back-end that transforms the IR into some external representation. The ETYMA framework is intended for constructing the processing engine along with the IR, rather than for building the front- and back-ends to such systems.

ETYMA is implemented in the C++ language[14]. It is continually evolving, but currently consists of about 45 reusable classes, and approximately 7,000 lines of C++ code. The C++ realization of the ETYMA framework has undergone several iterations over almost two years. In Section 4.3, we outline the major evolutionary stages of the framework.

4.1 Structure of Abstractions

Compositional modularity deals with modules, their instances, the attributes they are composed of, and the types of all the above. Thus, the primary concepts that must be captured by a reusable architecture for CM such as ETYMA are those of *modules, instances, names, values, methods, variables*, and their corresponding types. However, ETYMA is also a linguistic framework, i.e., a framework from which language processing tools will be designed. Thus, while modeling the above concepts, we must not inadvertently limit their generality. For example, a *method* is a specialization of the general concept of a *function*. Similarly, the concept of a *record* is closely related to that of a *module* and an *instance*. We must also be careful in determining the precise relationships between concepts. For example, a module is a record generator whereas an instance is itself a record; thus, the concept of an instance is a subtype of the concept of a record, but neither of these concepts is subtype-related to the concept of a module.

The abstractions of ETYMA form two layers. An abstract layer consists of abstract class realizations (partial implementations) of the concepts given above. These classes may be used as a "white box" framework (via inheritance) by completions. A concrete layer provides full implementations of the abstract classes

---

[3] et.y.mon (pl. et.y.ma also etymons) [L, fr. Gk] ... 2: a word or morpheme from which words are formed by composition or derivation. — Webster Dictionary

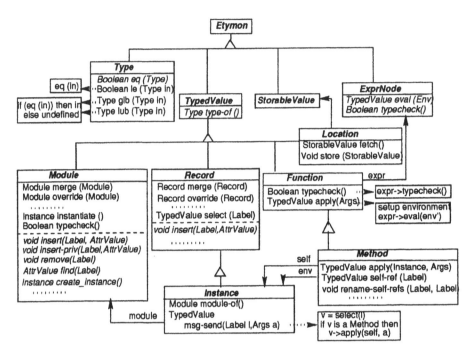

Fig. 8. An overview of the abstract classes of ETYMA.

that can be directly used as a "black box" framework (via instantiation) by completions. This layer, as customary, is meant to increase the reusability of the framework. Only, the important classes in both layers, i.e., those corresponding to modules, instances, and methods, are described in more detail below. (For brevity, we omit classes corresponding to the type system.) We utilize the notion of design patterns [16] to elucidate the structure of the ETYMA framework.

Abstract classes. Figure 8 shows an overview of the abstract classes of ETYMA diagrammed using the OO notation in [16] extended to show protected methods. Class *Etymon* is the abstract base class of all classes in ETYMA, and classes *TypedValue* and *Type* represent the domains of values and their types respectively.

The abstract class *Module* captures the notion of a compositional module in its broadest conception. Its public methods correspond to the module operators introduced earlier. Within this class, no concrete representation for module attributes is assumed. Instead, the public module operations are implemented as template method patterns in terms of a set of protected abstract methods such as *insert, remove,* etc. which manage module attributes. Concrete subclasses of *Module* are expected to provide implementations for these abstract protected methods. Two of these are abstract factory method patterns: create_instance, which is expected to return an instance of a concrete subclass of class *Instance* (below), and create_iter, which is expected to return an instance of a concrete subclass of class *AttrIter,* an iterator pattern for module attributes. Thus, the generality of class *Module* results from its use of a combination of the following patterns: template method, abstract factory method, and iterator.

Class *Instance* is a subclass of *Record*; hence it supports record operations, implemented in a manner similar to those of class *Module*. In addition, it models the traditional OO notion of sending a message (dispatch) to an object as *select*'ing a method-valued attribute followed by invoking *apply* on it. This functionality is encapsulated by a template method pattern msg-send(Label,Args). Furthermore, class *Instance* has access to its generating module via its module data member.

The concept of a method is modeled as a specialization of the concept of a function. Class Function supports an apply method that evaluates the function body. Although class Function is a concrete class, the function body is represented by an abstract class *ExprNode*, a composite pattern. Since a method "belongs to" a class, class Method requires that the first argument to its apply method is an instance of class *Instance*, corresponding to its notion of self.

Concrete classes. Some abstract classes in Figure 8 are subclassed into concrete classes to facilitate immediate reuse. Class StdModule is a concrete subclass of *Module* that represents its attributes as a map. An attribute map (object of class AttrMap) is a collection of individual attributes, each of which maps a name (object of class Label) to a binding (object of class AttrValue). A binding encapsulates an object of any subclass of *TypedValue*. This structure corresponds to a variation of the bridge pattern, which makes it possible for completions to reuse much of the implementation of class *Module* by simply implementing classes corresponding to attribute bindings as subclasses of *TypedValue*.

Each of StdModule's attribute management functions is implemented as the corresponding operations on the map. Furthermore, the factory method pattern create_iter of StdModule returns an object of a concrete subclass of class *AttrIter*, class StdAttrIter. Similarly, the factory method pattern create_instance returns an object of the concrete subclass of class *Instance*, class StdInstance. Class StdInstance itself is also implemented using attribute maps.

4.2 Completion Construction

As mentioned earlier, ETYMA can be used to construct the processing engines of tools for compositionally modular systems. In practice, one must first identify the various kinds of name bindings comprising namespaces in the system. One can then identify generalizations of these concepts specified as classes in the ETYMA framework. For each such general ETYMA class, one must then subclass it to implement the more specific concept in the system. Once this is done, concrete classes in the framework corresponding to modules, instances, and interfaces can usually be almost completely reused, due to the bridge pattern mentioned above.

Architecturally, tools constructed as completions of ETYMA have the basic structure given in Figure 9. The command input component reads in module manipulation programs that direct the composition engine. The data input component creates the internal representation (IR) of compositional modules

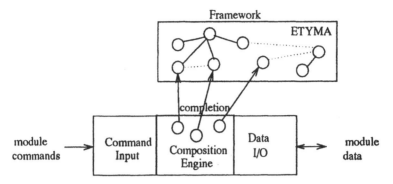

Fig. 9. Architecture of completions.

by parsing module source data and instantiating appropriate framework and completion classes. The optional data output component transforms IR into a suitable output format. The composition engine itself is derived from the ETYMA framework, and comprises classes (data and composition behavior) corresponding to module related entities. In the following subsections, three tools derived from the ETYMA framework in this manner are described.

An Interpreter for CMS The *CMS* interpreter consists of two parts: a basic Scheme interpreter written in the C language, and the module system, implemented as a completion of ETYMA. The basic Scheme interpreter itself was extracted from a publicly available scriptable windowing toolkit called *STk* [15]. The interpreter implementation exports many of the functions implementing Scheme semantics, thus making it easy to access its internals. Furthermore, the interpreter was originally designed to be extensible, i.e., new Scheme primitives can be implemented in C/C++ and easily incorporated into the interpreter. ' Thus, in order to implement *CMS*, Scheme primitives implementing concepts of compositional modularity such as mk-module, mk-instance, self-ref, merge, etc. were implemented in C++ and incorporated into the interpreter.

The class design for the *CMS* module system completion is as follows. Attribute bindings within *CMS* modules can be Scheme values, variables, or methods. These can be modeled as subclasses of framework classes PrimValue (not shown in Figure 8), Location, and Method respectively. The method subclass need not store the method body as a subclass of *ExprNode*; instead, it can simply store the internal representation of the Scheme expression as exported by the interpreter implementation. Additionally, the method subclass must define methods corresponding to the *CMS* primitives self-ref, self-set!, etc. which call similar methods on the stored self object.

With the classes mentioned above, the implementation of class StdModule can be almost completely reused for implementing *CMS* modules. However, methods to handle *CMS* primitives mk-module, mk-instance, etc. must be added. The only modification required is to redefine the method create_instance of class StdModule to return an object of an appropriate subclass of class StdInstance. This subclass

Reuse parameter		New	Reused	% reuse
Module	Classes	7	25	78
system	Methods	67	275	80.4
only	Lines of Code	1550	5000	76.3
Entire interpreter	Lines of Code	1800	20000	91.7

Table 1. Reuse of framework design and code for *CMS* interpreter.

needs to implement code for *CMS* primitives such as attr-ref and attr-set!.

Table 1 shows several measures of reuse for the *CMS* module system implemented as a completion of ETYMA. The percentages for class and method reuse give an indication of *design* reuse, since classes and their methods represent the functional decomposition and interface design of the framework. On the other hand, the percentages for lines of code give a measure of *code* reuse.

A Compiler Front-end for Compositional IDL Although we have not described the classes in ETYMA that relate to types, there is a comprehensive set of reusable classes that correspond to the notions of interfaces, record types, function types, etc. All type classes are subclasses of the abstract superclass *Type* in Figure 8 which defines abstract methods for type equality, subtyping, and for finding bounds of type pairs in a type lattice. Interfaces correspond to the types of modules, and support predicate methods that implement the typechecking rules for each of the module operators. Furthermore, abstract class *Interface* and its concrete subclass StdInterface are implemented in a manner similar to classes *Module* and StdModule.

Briefly, the class design for the compositional IDL front-end completion are as follows. Attribute bindings within interfaces can be base types, function types, or record types, designed as subclasses of the corresponding generic classes in the framework. Define class IDLInterface as a subclass of class StdInterface, and define methods merge (IDLInterface), rename (Label,Label), etc. to return new interface objects after performing the appropriate operations. Furthermore, the notion of the recursive type selftype is implemented as the special framework class SelfType (a singleton pattern). Recursive type equality and subtyping methods of StdInterface, which implement the algorithms given in [1] can be reused directly in the IDLInterface class. Design and code reuse numbers for this completion prototype are given in Table 2.

An Interpreter for MTEX The STk-derived Scheme interpreter was used for MTEX in a manner similar to *CMS*. The subclasses of ETYMA created to construct the MTEX module engine are: TexLabel of Label, Section of Method, TexModule of StdModule, SecMap of AttrMap, and TexInterface of StdInterface. Also, a new class Segment that represents a segment of text between self-references

Reuse parameter	New	Reused	% reuse
Classes	5	22	81.5
Methods	20	155	88.6
Lines of Code	1300	3600	73.5

Table 2. Reuse of framework design and code for IDL front-end.

Reuse parameter		New	Reused	% reuse
Module	Classes	6	20	77
system	Methods	36	231	86.5
only	Lines of Code	1600	4400	73.3
Entire system	Lines of Code	1800	19400	91.5

Table 3. Reuse of framework design and code for building MTEX.

was created. Approximate design and code reuse numbers for the MTEX implementation are shown in Table 3.

4.3 Framework Evolution

The very first version of ETYMA was almost fully concrete, and was designed to experiment with a module extension to the C language. It consisted only of the notions of modules, instances, primitive values, and locations, along with a few support classes. No front and back ends were constructed. The next incarnation of ETYMA was used to build a typechecking mechanism for C language object modules, described in [4]. This experiment solidified many of the type classes of ETYMA. However, at this point, ETYMA was still primarily a set of concrete classes. The third incarnation was used to *direct* the reengineering of the programmable linker/loader OMOS described earlier. In this iteration, the framework was not directly used in the construction of OMOS (due to practical, not technical constraints), but it evolved in parallel with the actual class hierarchy of OMOS. The design of OMOS classes follow that of ETYMA closely. Also, much of the framework, including the abstract and concrete layers, developed during this iteration.

The fourth iteration over ETYMA was the construction of *CMS* completion. There were few changes to the framework classes in this iteration; these were mostly to fix implementation bugs. However, some new methods for retroactive nesting were added. Nonetheless, the *CMS* interpreter was constructed within a very short period of time, and resulted in a high degree of reuse. The next iteration was to design and implement an IDL compiler front-end. There were almost no modifications to the framework; additions included selftype related code. The sixth, and most recent, iteration over ETYMA has been to build the MTEX document composition system. There were no changes to the framework.

The first three iterations essentially evolved the framework from a set of concrete classes to a reusable set of abstract and concrete classes, thus crystallizing the reusable functionality of the framework. From the fourth iteration onwards, the framework was mostly reused, with some additions, but very few modifications. As the observed reusability of the framework increased, measurements were taken to record the reuse achieved, as shown in the tables earlier.

5 Conclusions and Future Work

We have shown in this paper that OO class inheritance viewed as operations on self-referential namespaces is a broadly applicable concept. Specifically, we have shown how to apply compositional modularity (CM), a model that defines a comprehensive suite of operations on modules viewed as self-referential namespaces, to a variety of software artifacts such as Scheme language modules, compiled object files, interfaces, and document fragments.

We have described four tools that can help effectively manage these software artifacts. These are: (i) an interpreter for the programming language Scheme extended with the notion of compositional modules, (ii) a linker that manipulates compiled object files as compositional modules, (iii) a compiler front-end for a language with compositional interfaces, and (iv) a document processing system that manipulates documents as compositional modules. Furthermore, we show that these systems benefit significantly by incorporating concepts of module composition (i.e., class inheritance).

The implementation of tools for systems based on CM share a lot in common. Hence, we argue that a reusable software architecture for such tools is beneficial. We describe a reusable OO framework named ETYMA from which tools such as the above can be efficiently constructed. ETYMA currently comprises about 45 reusable C++ classes in 7000 lines that evolved over six iterations. Three of the above tools were built by directly reusing ETYMA, resulting in significant levels (between 73 and 91%) of design and code reuse.

Many other tools can be based on CM and can be built by completing ETYMA. Naturally, CM can be applied within other programming language processors: compiler and interpreters for modular and non-modular languages. There is also an abundance of software artifacts that can be viewed as self-referential namespaces, and that have a useful notion of composition. For example, tools that manage GUI components viewed as compositional entities are conceivable. File systems that view directories as self-referential namespaces (i.e., filenames bound to file contents that refer back to other filenames) could also be useful. We also speculate that the commonality of the underlying models of such tools can be exploited for supporting interoperability among them.

Acknowledgements. We gratefully acknowledge support and several useful comments on this work from Jay Lepreau, Bjorn Freeman-Benson, Gilad Bracha, Bryan Ford, Doug Orr, Robert Mecklenburg, and Nevenka Dimitrova.

References

1. Roberto M. Amadio and Luca Cardelli. Subtyping recursive types. *ACM Transactions on Programming Languages and Systems*, 15(4), September 1993.
2. Joshua Auerbach and James Russell. The Concert signature representation: IDL as intermediate language. In Jeanette Wing, editor, *Proc. of Workshop on Interface Definition Languages*, pages 1 – 12, January 1994. Also available as ACM SIGPLAN Notices 29 (8), August 1994.
3. Guruduth Banavar. *An Application Framework for Compositional Modularity*. PhD thesis, University of Utah, Salt Lake City, Utah, 1995. Available as report CSTD-95-011.
4. Guruduth Banavar, Gary Lindstrom, and Douglas Orr. Type-safe composition of object modules. In *Computer Systems and Education*, pages 188–200. Tata McGraw Hill Publishing Company, Limited, New Delhi, India, June 22-25, 1994. ISBN 0-07-462044-4. Also available as University of Utah Technical Report UUCS-94-001.
5. Guruduth Banavar, Douglas Orr, and Gary Lindstrom. Layered, server-based support for object-oriented application development. In Luis-Felipe Cabrera and Marvin Theimer, editors, *Proceedings of the Fourth International Workshop on Object Orientation in Operating Systems*, pages 2–11, Lund, Sweden, August 14 – 15 1995. IEEE Computer Society. Also available as University of Utah TR UUCS-95-007.
6. Gilad Bracha and Gary Lindstrom. Modularity meets inheritance. In *Proc. International Conference on Computer Languages*, pages 282–290, San Francisco, CA, April 20–23, 1992. IEEE Computer Society. Also available as University of Utah Technical Report UUCS-91-017.
7. Kim B. Bruce. A paradigmatic object-oriented programming language: Design, static typing and semantics. *J. Functional Programming*, 4(2):127–206, 1994.
8. P. Canning, W. Cook, W. Hill, and W. Olthoff. Interfaces for strongly-typed object-oriented programming. In Norman Meyrowitz, editor, *Proceedings of the ACM Conference on Object-Oriented Programming, Systems, Languages, and Applications*, pages 457–467, 1989.
9. Luca Cardelli and John C. Mitchell. Operations on records. Technical Report 48, Digital Equipment Corporation Systems Research Center, August 1989.
10. William Clinger and Jonathan Rees. Revised[4] report on the algorithmic language Scheme. *ACM Lisp Pointers*, 4(3), 1991.
11. William Cook, Walter Hill, and Peter Canning. Inheritance is not subtyping. In Carl Gunter and John Mitchell, editors, *Theoretical Aspects of Object-Oriented Programming*, pages 497 – 517. MIT Press, 1994.
12. William Cook and Jen Palsberg. A denotational semantics of inheritance and its correctness. In *Proc. ACM Conf. on Object-Oriented Programming: Systems, Languages and Applications*, pages 433–444, 1989.
13. Pavel Curtis and James Rauen. A module system for Scheme. In *Conference Record of the ACM Lisp and Functional Programming*. ACM, 1990.
14. Margaret A. Ellis and Bjarne Stroustrup. *The Annotated C++ Reference Manual*. Addison-Wesley, Reading, MA, 1990.
15. Erick Gallesio. STk reference manual. Version 2.1, 1993/94.
16. Erich Gamma, Richard Helm, Ralph Johnson, and John Vlissides. *Design Patterns: Elements of Reusable Object-Oriented Software*. Professional Computing Series. Addison-Wesley Publishing Company, Reading, Massachusetts, 1995.

17. Graham Hamilton and Sanjan Radia. Using interface inheritance to address problems in system software evolution. In Jeanette Wing, editor, *Proc. of Workshop on Interface Definition Languages*, pages 119 – 128, January 1994. Available as August 1994 issue of ACM SIGPLAN Notices.

18. Suresh Jagannathan. Metalevel building blocks for modular systems. *ACM Transactions on Programming Languages and Systems*, 16(3):456–492, May 1994.

19. Dinesh Katiyar, David Luckham, and John Mitchell. A type system for prototyping languages. In *Proc. of the ACM Symp. on Principles of Programming Languages*, pages 138–150, Portland, OR, January 1994. ACM.

20. Bent Bruun Kristensen, Ole Lehrmann Madsen, Birger Moller-Pedersen, and Kristen Nygaard. The BETA programming language. In *Research Directions in Object-Oriented Programming*, pages 7 – 48. MIT Press, 1987.

21. Leslie Lamport. LaTeX, *a Document Processing System*. Addison Wesley Publishing Company, Reading, MA, 1986.

22. Object Management Group. *The Common Object Request Broker: Architecture and Specification*, December 1991. Revision 1.1.

23. Douglas B. Orr and Robert W. Mecklenburg. OMOS — An object server for program execution. In *Proc. International Workshop on Object Oriented Operating Systems*, pages 200–209, Paris, September 1992. IEEE Computer Society. Also available as technical report UUCS-92-033.

24. Jonathan Rees. Another module system for Scheme. Included in the Scheme 48 distribution, 1993.

25. Wayne Rossberg, Edward Smith, and Angelica Matinkhah. Structured text system. US Patent Number 5,341,469, August 1994.

26. Sho-Huan Simon Tung. Interactive modular programming in Scheme. In *Proceedings of the ACM Lisp and Functional Programming Conference*, pages pages 86 – 95. ACM, 1992.

University of Utah Technical Reports are available from the Department of Computer Science WWW page http://www.cs.utah.edu/.

Automatic Generation of User Interfaces from Data Structure Specifications and Object-Oriented Application Models

Vadim Engelson[1], Dag Fritzson[2] and Peter Fritzson[1]

[1] Dept. of Computing and Information Science, Linköping University, S-58183, Linköping, Sweden, {vaden,petfr}@ida.liu.se
[2] SKF ERC B.V., Postbus 2350, 3430 DT Nieuwegein, The Netherlands, adsdtf@skferc.nl

Abstract. Applications in scientific computing operate with data of complex structure and graphical tools for data editing, browsing and visualization are necessary.

Most approaches to generating user interfaces provide some interactive layout facility together with a specialized language for describing user interaction. Realistic automated generation approaches are largely lacking, especially for applications in the area of scientific computing.

This paper presents two approaches to automatically generating user interfaces (that include forms, pull-down menus and pop-up windows) from specifications.

The first is a semi-automatic approach, that uses information from object-oriented mathematical models, together with a set of predefined elementary types and manually supplied layout and grouping information. This system is currently in industrial use. A disadvantage is that some manual changes need to be made after each update of the model.

Within the second approach we have designed a tool, PDGen (Persistence and Display Generator) that automatically creates a graphical user interface and persistence routines from the declarations of data structures used in the application (e.g., C++ class declarations). This largely eliminates the manual update problem. The attributes of the generated graphical user interface can be altered.

Now structuring and grouping information is automatically extracted from the object-oriented mathematical model and transferred to PDGen. This is one of very few existing practical systems for automatically generating user interfaces from type declarations and related object-oriented structure information.

1   Introduction

Almost all applications include some kind of user interface. Graphical user interfaces (GUI) provide the opportunity to control an application's execution, to modify the input data and to inspect the results of computations.

Application programs have different data structures. Each application domain puts special requirements on visual presentation of data. Therefore, graphical interfaces are traditionally designed individually for each application.

The following properties are expected from applications with graphical user interfaces:

- The data must be presented to the user in a well-structured way. The graphical user interface should be consistent with the computational part of the application (for example, elements of the graphical user interface for data input should correspond to components of the application data).
- The user interface should satisfy style guidelines, conventions and standards. The compromise between large amounts of information and limited screen space can be achieved if the graphical user interface allows the user to choose only interesting information and ignore all else.
- The user interface software should be portable and not be dependent on a specific operating system or compiler.
- Entered data should be persistent: it should be possible to store entered data outside the program memory and reload it again later.

For realistic applications the design and implementation of a graphical user interface often become rather laborious, expensive and error-prone. Currently available toolkits are very powerful. Unfortunately, they are also very complicated and not user-friendly enough. In order to obtain some result the programmer often has to take too many implementation details into account. The high cost of implementing user interfaces can be partly reduced by the use of *user interface generation tools*. Such tools usually include a WYSIWYG layout definition tool that helps the programmer to design the layout of windows, menus, buttons and other user interface items. The graphical user interface code is generated automatically.

However, every time the application code is updated or the layout is changed, the interface code between them has to be updated manually.

1.1   User interface generation based on data declarations

In this paper we propose a different approach, based on the automated generation of user interfaces from data structure information. As a preliminary we present some terminology.

Data structures in traditional languages (such as Pascal or C) are described by variable and type declarations. In object-oriented languages (e.g. C++) data structures are defined using classes, objects and relations (inheritance, part-of) between objects.

The *structure of a graphical user interface* can be described in terms of graphical elements such as windows, menus, dialog boxes, frames, text editing boxes, help texts etc., and layouts that define how these elements are placed on the screen.

In which *context* the interface is used ? The main purpose of a graphical user interface is to let the user inspect and modify some data. The input data can be edited by a stand-alone graphical tool, saved in file and then loaded by the computing application. The output data can be saved by the application and inspected by a separate tool. The application may suspend computations, initiate graphical interface in order to allow data editing, and then resume the computations again. *We consider graphical interfaces that can be used in all these cases.*

The data have some structure and it is used to control the application functionality. Therefore the structure of the graphical user interface should be similar to the structure of the application data.

Typically there is an implicit or explicit correspondence between the structure of a program and the structure of data. On the other hand, there is a correspondence between the structure of the interface and data structures of the program. This means that the way the programmer perceives the structure of the implementation is close enough to the way the end-user perceives the structure of the application area.

The basic idea of our approach is to *generate the graphical user interface automatically from the application data structures.*

The similarity between the data structures and the structure of the graphical user interface is characteristic for a wide spectrum of applications, including simulation tools and information systems.

Data persistence is a generic property that includes saving data structures on permanent storage such as a file system and being able to restore these data next time the application is executed. To implement persistence, we need routines that can save or load all the application data (or some part of the data). *Such persistence routines can be generated automatically from the application data structures.*

Automatic support for data persistence as well as generation of graphical user interfaces will allow designers to concentrate on the main goals of the applications rather than on mundane tasks such as implementing a graphical user interface and input/output.

We applied the method of generating user interfaces from data structure declarations to two object-oriented languages: ObjectMath (an object-oriented extension of Mathematica [Wolfram91]) and C++.

In Section 1.1 we have discussed some reasons and motivation for the design of a user interface generator according to these principles.

The rest of the paper is organized as follows:

First we describe relevant features of ObjectMath, an environment for scientific computing (Sect. 2.1) and consider a *semi-automatic* approach to the creation of user interfaces from application data structures, which also has been tested in industrial applications. A new *automatic* graphical user interface generation is based on our PDGen tool (Sect. 3) that automatically generates persistence and graphical user interface code from given data-type declarations. This tool is applied to ObjectMath models.

In Sect. 4 we describe how the PDGen tool can be applied to ObjectMath models.

Sect. 5 discusses related work on persistence and display generation and we conclude with proposals for future work. More details can be found in [PDGen96, E96].

2 The Semi-automatic GUI Generating System

2.1 The ObjectMath Environment

Applications in scientific computing are often characterized by heavy numerical computations, as well as large amounts of numerical data for input and output.

The data often have a complicated structure including objects with fields of various types, vectors and multidimensional arrays. This structure often changes during the course of program design.

An important application area in scientific computing is the simulation of various mechanical, chemical and electrical systems. These applications can be described by mathematical models of the physical systems to be simulated. Additionally, routines for numerical solution systems of equations are needed, as well as routines for input/output and routines and tools for user interfaces.

The process of manually translating mathematical models to numerical simulation programs in C or Fortran is both time-consuming and error prone. Therefore, a high level programming environment for scientific computing, Object-Math [Fritzson95, Viklund95, Fritzson93] , has been developed that supports the semi-automatic generation of application code from object-oriented mathematical models.

The ObjectMath programming environment has been applied to realistic problems in mechanical analysis. ObjectMath class libraries describing coordinate transformations and contact forces have been developed. They are used for mathematical modeling of rolling bearings by our industrial partner, SKF Engineering and Research Center.

In ObjectMath formulae and equations can be written in notation that is very similar to conventional mathematics. The ObjectMath language is an object-oriented extension of the Mathematica computer algebra language, in a similar way as C++ is an extension to C.

The ObjectMath language includes object-oriented structuring facilities such as *classes*, *instances*, single and multiple *inheritance* (for reuse), and the *part-of* relation (to compose new classes from existing ones).

2.2 The simulation environment for ObjectMath models

First, an *ObjectMath model* is specified with the help of a class relationship editor and class text editor. The *ObjectMath code generator* generates parallel or sequential programs for systems of equations expressed in ObjectMath. Typically a system of ordinary differential equations is considered.

The generated code is linked with model-independent run-time libraries. The *executable code* requires a large number of input values (such as start values, limitations, model geometry and conditions, solver parameters) in order to start a simulation.

The *input data editor* is designed for input data inspection and update. It has a window-based graphical interface for ObjectMath variable editing and can load and save a file with variable values. In this paper we present two graphical user interface generation systems that can create an input data editor from model specifications. The first system is described here, the second in Sect. 4.

The simulation program reads the data prepared by the input data editor and computes a large amount of output data for every simulated time step.

This data can be explored with the help of an *output data browser* . This browser can create graphs that illustrate how the variables change during the simulation.

The *animation tool* reads the output data step by step and shows the model geometry in motion.

2.3 An ObjectMath example: a Bike model

In this section we present an ObjectMath model example, a mechanical model of bicycle (Fig. 1) in order to explain the relations between classes and instances in ObjectMath[3].

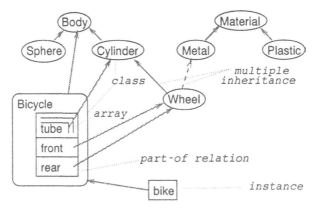

Fig. 1. *An ObjectMath class diagram for a bike model. Arrows denote single or multiple inheritance. The* **bike** *instance contains the parts* **tube** *(array of tubes),* **front** *and* **rear,** *which inherit from the classes* **Cylinder** *and* **Wheel,** *respectively. Such diagrams are editable with graphical class relationship editor.*

---

[3] We discuss the constructs relevant for graphical user interface generation only.

Every model specification consists of *classes* and *instances*. The textual part of classes and instances contain variable declarations, formulae and equations. This is the way the formulae and equations related to the same phenomenon are grouped. Classes and instances inherit variables, formulae and equations from one or several (multiple inheritance) classes. The classes serve as templates for instances.

The class Bicycle on Fig. 1 inherits all variables, equations and formulae from the class Body. The instance bike inherits everything from the class Bicycle. An instance or a class can also contain its *own* variable declarations and formulae. Every instance is created *statically* and its variables (both its own and inherited ones) can be referenced in formulae and equations of other classes and instances.

A Bicycle consists of three *parts* in this model: the front wheel, the rear wheel and the frame consisting of several tubes. The number of tubes is equal to the value of some variable, in our example it is framesize (this is not shown in the picture).

2.4 Variables and built-in data types

Let us assume that there are several ObjectMath variables[4] declared in the class definitions:

```
In Body:     Declare [angle, "doubleVec3", "rad", uII]
In Cylinder: Declare [radius, "double", "m", uII]
In Wheel:    Declare [pressure, "double", "H/m^2",uII]
In Bicycle:  Declare [framesize," int", "-", uII]
```

In the general form variable name, type, physical unit and persistence status are specified:

```
Declare[name, type-name, "unit",(uII|uOO|uL)].
```

Types. In ObjectMath there is a fixed set of twenty primitive data types that can be used for variables in the model. Some of the types have complex structure and may contain up to 100 double precision real numbers, integers and strings.

A variable of type double has a double precision floating value. The type doubleVec3 is a 3-element vector of double.

Units. A string such as "H/m^2" contains the name of the physical unit of the value this variable represents. This unit name is used as part of the prompting information for the relevant input field in the input data editor that is generated from the declarations above.

---

[4] This declaration syntax is for ObjectMath version 3.0. The latest version 4.0, fall 1995, has a different declaration syntax.

Persistence status. The variable declarations provide the persistence information: whether a variable should be initialized by the input data editor, should be output and stored as a computed result, or is simply a local variable for intermediate results.

Here uII means "to input from the input file", uOO means "to output to the output file", and uL means "local variable, neither input, nor output".

From this information a window with text input boxes (Fig. 2) is generated. The variable instance identifier, text input area for value editing and "units" are shown for each variable component.

2.5 Generation of input data editor

The *basic idea* of this approach is that part of the code necessary for graphical user interface creation is *automatically* generated from ObjectMath variable declarations. Then the *layout* information is manually inserted into this code.

In order to create the input data editor we have to create the hierarchy of windows and variables; this hierarchy is created half-automatically and combines display routines provided that create widgets for every ObjectMath variable type.

When model specification code is analyzed, the names of variables such as angle, radius and pressure, are converted to unique names (within the model) by adding prefixes (part and object names). This is the list of *all* the variables available in this model, where notation *name*[n] denotes an array with *n* elements:

```
bike'front'radius        bike'front'angle        bike'front'pressure
bike'rear'radius         bike'rear'angle         bike'rear'pressure
bike'tube'radius[bike'framesize]
bike'tube'angle[bike'framesize]                   bike'framesize
```

A specially designed filter reads the model specification and generates a comma-separated list of function calls:

```
var_double_array("bike'tube'radius","m"),
var_doubleVec3_array("bike'tube'angle","rad"),
var_double("bike'front'radius","m"),
    ... ...
```

The calls of var_....() functions above register the variables as members of the list of relevant variables and return a frame handle which is used for constructing corresponding windows. The rest of the code needed in order to display these variables in a separate window (see Fig. 2) is inserted *manually* (manual part is shown in *italic* font):

```
make_dialog(
    layout_vertical(
      layout_horizontal(
        layout_vertical(
          var_double("bike'front'radius","m"),
          var_doubleVec3("bike'front'angle","rad"),
          var_double("bike'front'pressure","H/m^2")),
        layout_vertical(
          var_double("bike'rear'radius","m"),
          var_doubleVec3("bike'rear'angle","rad"),
          var_double("bike'rear'pressure","H/m^2"))
        )
      layout_frame(
        layout_vertical(
          var_int("framesize","-"),
          array("framesize",
            layout_vertical(
              var_doubleVec3_array("bike'tube'angle","rad"),
              var_double_array("bike'tube'radius","m")
))))));
```

Fig. 2. *Example of variable display in the input data editor.*

2.6 Presentation of arrays.

Two variables (bike'tube'angle and bike'tube'radius) represented in the example (see Fig. 2) are arrays of doubleVec3 and double. They have the same length; therefore they may be grouped together. These arrays share common control buttons (Vert, Hor, Copy to all etc.) in the upper part of their frame. (It is also possible to build displays where every array has a separate control panel.)

As shown in Fig. 2 only one element (currently the 2nd element) of each array is visible, as indicated by the label "2" in the upper left corner. This is the compact presentation of the array. The buttons with the triangles ("Up" and "Down") switch the current element to the previous or the next, respectively. Then the label may change to "3" ("Up") or "1" ("Down"). The button "Copy to all" copies all the values from the visible element of the arrays to all other elements.

The buttons "Vert" and "Hor" change the presentation of the array: they spread its elements vertically or horizontally, respectively. Then the button "Collapse" appears that changes the presentation back to compact form.

2.7 Frame hierarchy definition functions

Every application window contains a hierarchy of *frames*. Each frame is a rectangular area that contains graphical user interface elements (widgets) such as labels, text input boxes, buttons, as well as compositions of other frames in the vertical or horizontal direction. A number of functions are needed in order to specify this hierarchy of frames:

- The function make_dialog(*frame*) specifies the top frame of the window.
- The function *frame*=layout_vertical($frame_1, frame_2, \ldots, frame_n$) specifies that the frames $frame_1, frame_2, ..., frame_n$ are allocated in the vertical direction.
- The function layout_horizontal allocates them in the horizontal direction.
- The function *frame*=array("*bound-variable*", $frame_1$) specifies that length of all arrays within $frame_1$ is equal to the current value of the variable *bound-variable* and they are controlled all together by the buttons in the upper part of the frame. The control buttons for array variables can change the index of the currently displayed element (see Figure 2).

There are several functions for additional help texts and decorations.

- The function *frame*=layout_frame($frame_1$) draws a rectangle around $frame_1$;
- The function *frame*=layout_label("*text*") specifies a label containing the *text* string.

The description this hierarchy is stored as a tree. When necessary, the tree is traversed, relevant Motif API functions are invoked, and the windows are displayed on the screen.

2.8 Description of variables

For every displayed variable a function for a corresponding data type should be called. These calls are automatically generated from the list of model variables. There is a separate function for each data type used in the ObjectMath language: var_double, var_int, var_doubleVec3 and all others (totally, twenty) ObjectMath basic data types.

For example, *frame=*var_double("bike'front'radius","m") specifies that a text input box is constructed for the variable bike'front'radius of type double and that the physical unit is "m".

Every such call registers a variable and arranges for the value of this variable to be displayed at an appropriate place in the layout. For every type a certain specific layout has been designed and hard-coded. For example, for the type doubleVec3 (a structure with three double values) the layout is three vertically aligned text input boxes. Arbitrary double values can be entered here. For integer, double and string variables the layout is a single input box with the variable name to the left and the unit to the right (see Fig. 2). Arbitrary integer, double and string expressions can be entered into the input boxes respectively.

Persistence. When the button Save is pressed, the persistence function is called and all the registered variables are written to the input data file. When the button Load is pressed all the variables in the list receive their values from the input data file. Both the input data editor and the application program should register the variables with the same name and type.

2.9 Evaluation of the first generation system

If the ObjectMath model changes, the graphical user interface programmer has two ways to solve the update problem. If many changes are introduced, the graphical user interface code should be generated again and the programmer has to insert the layout functions manually. If the changes are small and local (such as renaming some variables), the variable registration function calls (var_...(...)) should be manually updated.

The first generation system described so far in this paper has several *disadvantages*:

The update problem. If the model is changed, the new code that is automatically generated from the variable list must be manually merged with the layout description. Every small change in the list of variables from the ObjectMath model may lead to inconsistency between the generated application and the input data editor. Therefore the inherent flexibility of the ObjectMath environment cannot be used to full advantage.

Insufficiency of the basic type set. Only a limited number of basic data types are supported. These data types are either primitive ones or are specially designed for a particular application domain. There is no way to specify other types than these and there are no new type declaration constructs. The persistence routines and the layout routines are designed for the fixed set of types only.

Variable grouping. There is no automatic graphical user interface generation for distributing variables between different windows. Moreover, there is no automatic generation of the menu structure. However the structure of the model (i.e. the names of classes, objects and parts) can be used for this purpose.

Practical application of the system has also shown its *positive* features.

The first generation system has proved quite effective in producing practical user interfaces for specialized application domains such as bearing simulation. Recently SKF ERC researchers used the system to produce user interfaces for 6 new variants of similar bearing models using only 3-4 days of work. The difference between the variable sets in these models were rather limited and all the adjustments of the graphical interface for the input data editor were done manually.

3 The Persistence and Display Generating tool (PDGen)

The basic idea of PDGen is that display layout for every data item exactly corresponds (by default) to the type structure of this item.

Through the *display* for a given variable the user can inspect and update all the data items that can be reached from the variable by recursively traversing its structure. In the same way, the *persistence* routines save and load all the data items that can be reached from a given variable by recursively traversing its structure.

Traversing all of a complex data structure is a non-trivial task if we want to provide this automatically. Special complications arise in languages with pointers and dynamic data structures. Code necessary for this purpose can be automatically generated from data type declarations of the variables we are going to traverse.

We primarily orient PDGen to handling C++ data types. This tool can analyze almost any C++ data type and class declarations and add graphical user interface and persistence routines to an *arbitrary* C++ program. The manual efforts necessary for this are minimal.

The creation of the PDGen tool has been inspired by the PGen (see Section 5.1) approach from which we cite Walter Tichy et al.:

> *The class and type declarations can be used to generate browsers and editors. For instance, a class variable can be presented as a dialog box that contains sub-windows for all members to be inspected or edited. Pointers could be drawn as arrows to other variables. [...] The browsers and*

editors could be used to inspect or modify persistent data on files. More importantly, they could become the default graphical interfaces for all applications. The difference with other interface construction tools is that they require absolutely no programming. Debuggers are another application area. [Tichy94]

In Sect. 3.1 a graphical user interface generation example is given and in Sect. 3.2 display generation for every C++ data type is presented . In Sect. 3.4 we discuss window display issues; the generation process is analyzed step by step in Sect. 3.5 and the use of the generated code is discussed in Sects. 3.6 and 3.7.

The tool is based on the C++ language (Section 5.3) and the Tcl/Tk toolkit [Ou94].

3.1 Example of graphical user interface generation

Let us consider some type declarations that can appear in a header file (see Fig. 3(a)) of some application.

The PDGen tool analyzes these data type declarations, recognizes the C++ class hierarchy, and generates necessary code for creation of a graphical interface. If the application calls the function show(bike) (see Fig. 3(b)) then the dialog window shown in Fig. 3(c) appears on the screen. The specification of physical units (rad, H/m^2, m) is performed with the help of an attribute specification script (see Section 3.10).

All the data items that belong to bike are shown and they are available for editing. This example illustrates the display for *classes* and *arrays*. and elementary data items of types int and double.

The array tube is shown at the bottom part of the window. The user can press the buttons "+" and "-" in order to change the index of the currently displayed element of the array bike.tube. In the window shown in the picture the index is equal to 2, i.e. bike.tube[2] is displayed.

3.2 Graphical presentation of variables

Every window may contain one or several variables. The graphical presentation of every variable depends on its type and it is combined from graphical presentations of its components.

Types char, char* *and* char[n]. The types char* and char[n] are typically used for 0-terminated strings. A text input box is constructed for such variables and the string can be edited. Scrolling of the text is always provided so that character strings longer than the text box can be inspected and edited.

The display for variables of type char is similar to char[1].

Types integer, float *and* double. Variables of these types are displayed as text editing boxes (see Fig. 3(c)). Only numbers or expressions (consisting of numbers and arithmetical operations) can be entered. The range of permitted values can be specified (see Section 3.10).

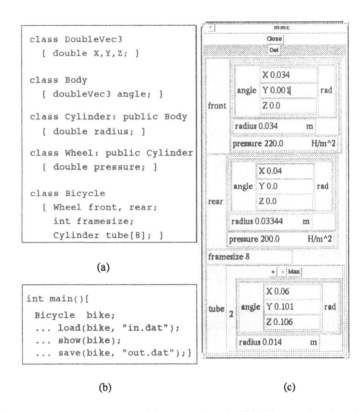

```
class DoubleVec3
   { double X,Y,Z; }

class Body
   { doubleVec3 angle; }

class Cylinder: public Body
   { double radius; }

class Wheel: public Cylinder
   { double pressure; }

class Bicycle
   { Wheel front, rear;
     int framesize;
     Cylinder tube[8]; }
```

(a)

```
int main(){
   Bicycle bike;
   ... load(bike, "in.dat");
   ... show(bike);
   ... save(bike, "out.dat");}
```

(b)   (c)

Fig. 3. *(a) Data type declarations. (b) Function call. (c) The window for editing the variable* **bike**.

Structures and classes. They are represented as horizontal or vertical[5] combinations of the components. The names of the data members of a structure or class are used as labels that appear to the left of corresponding components (see Fig. 3(c)).

Pointers. In our initial approach a pointer variable is represented by the referenced variable if the address is not NULL. There is a button **Delete** that deallocates the memory and sets the pointer to NULL. If the address is NULL, then there is a **New** button that creates a new variable in the dynamic memory, initializes it if it is an object and sets the correct value for the pointer variable.

Let us specify the class **Tree**:

```
class Tree
   { Tree * right;
```

---

[5] In order to choose between horizontal and vertical combinations we use some heuristics. For example, we choose one that makes the resulting frame more similar to a square i.e. the ratio between the height and the width of the frame is closer to 1. With the help of customization options this default layout can be altered.

```
    int elem;
    Tree * left;
};
```

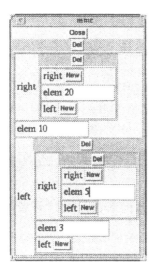 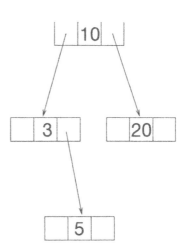

Fig. 4. *The window for editing the pointer structure of type* Tree* *and memory diagram of this structure.*

A variable of class Tree is displayed as a structure with three components (right, elem and left). We can also display a variable that contains a pointer to Tree. A variable of type Tree* is visualized as shown in Fig. 4.

This is a simple and quite straightforward approach if we are not concerned about the cases when two or more pointers refer to the same address.

In the *alternative* representation every dynamically allocated object (that has two or more references) is shown as a separate sub-window and arrows are drawn from the pointers to these objects in order to indicate the references.

Enumeration. The enumerations are represented as a group of radio buttons (or, as an alternative, as a pop-up menu). Enumerator names are written beside the buttons and only one of them may be selected at a time.

An object of class Foo is shown in Fig. 5(a).

```
enum weekday
    { Mon, Tue, Wed, Thu, Fri, Sat, Sun } ;
enum colors
    { Red, Orange, Yellow, Green, Blue, DarkBlue, Violet };
class Foo
    { weekday Days;
      colors  Colors;};
```

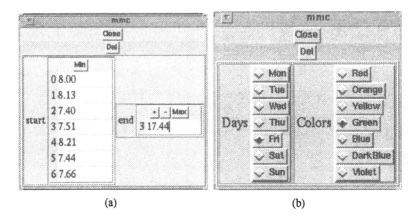

Fig. 5. *The windows for editing variable with (a) enumerators and (b) arrays.*

One-dimensional array. Fig. 5(b) shows how an object of class Foo is visualized.

```
class Foo
{ double start [7];
  double end[7];
};
```

The elements of Foo::**start** are shown in the *complete presentation,* i.e. all of them are available for browsing. In the *compact presentation* of the array Foo::**end** only one element (currently it is the element **end[3]**) is shown at a time. By using the buttons + and - we can increase or decrease the index of the currently visible element. The button **Max** switches the display to the *complete presentation*; the **Min** button changes the display back to the compact presentation.

An array of dimension larger than one is represented as a combination of one-dimensional arrays. This is not very convenient for browsing. A special browser [FWHSS96] is designed for two-dimensional arrays. We are working on an universal array browser for an unlimited number of dimensions.

A special interface is provided for dynamically allocated arrays. These can grow and shrink dynamically. For this purpose the buttons **Insert** (insert new element after the current one) and **Remove** (remove the current element) are added above the presentation of the array values. This option has some limitations and requires some additions in the description of data structures: the dynamic array (A) must belong to some class and an additional integer variable (A_length) should store its length:

```
class Test
 { Element * array_foo;
   int      array_foo_length; }
```

3.3 PDGen restrictions

There are some restrictions in the PDGen system that are partly caused by the restrictions of the PGen tool.

- References, constants, bit fields, unions, pointers to functions, pointers to members, void* pointers are skipped and ignored, because they cannot be persistent or are compiler-dependent, or there is no sense in keeping them persistent.
- Virtual base classes are supported for persistence only.
- Pointers to memory inside an object are supported for persistence only.

3.4 Hiding and detaching windows

The number of data items that can be displayed on the screen simultaneously is limited. Normally we cannot show a hierarchical layout of more than approximately one hundred text editing fields. We propose a window handling scheme where every displayed data item can be in three states (see Fig. 6):

- **hidden**: only a button with the data item identifier is shown in its default place;
- **normal**: the data item is displayed as usual in its default place;
- **detached**: the button with data item identifier is shown in its default place; the item is shown in a separate (top-level) window.

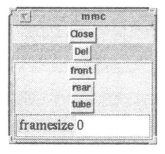

Fig. 6. *The variables* front, rear *and* tube *are hidden in the window for editing the variable* bike.

Switching between normal, hidden and detached state is performed by the mouse buttons. In each case the user has to click on the name of the item.

The *default* status is "hidden" for all non-elementary data elements and "normal" for elementary ones. The user can specify the default status with the help of attributes discussed in Section 3.10.

The buttons have the same function as pull-down menu items. The end-user has complete control over the information layout on the screen and there is no problem with the windows occupying all the display space. This way the user can hide unnecessary information and select interesting data for display in separate windows. Since the buttons have almost the same behaviour as pull-down menu, this approach is rather close to graphical user interface standards and conventions.

3.5 Data type analysis and code generation.

This section discusses the generation process in detail, phase by phase.

The stages of graphical user interface generation are shown in Fig 7.

The PDGen tool reuses some ideas and essential code fragments from the PGen tool [Tichy94, PGen94, Paulisch90].

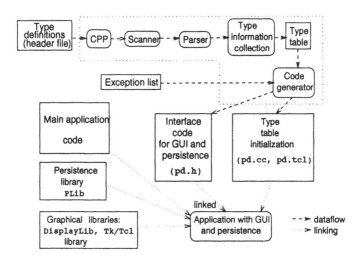

Fig. 7. *Phases of graphical user interface generation from C++ code and generation results.*

The basic source of the graphical user interface generation is a file with data type declarations. In C++ applications it involves one (or several) *header* files.

Parsing. The file is preprocessed by standard C preprocessor cpp and analyzed by the C++ scanner and parser.

Together with the PGen analyzer (see Section 5.1) we reuse the C++ grammar parser with semantic actions for syntax tree construction.

The syntax tree contains nodes of different kinds and references between them. The collection phase traverses all the nodes   describing typedef, enum, struct and class declarations and produces the data-type table.

The syntax tree contains all the syntactical elements that appear in the input file. For our purposes we use typedef, enum, struct and class declarations only. In the class declarations we are interested in data members and constructors only.

Data type table. This table contains the names of all types, the names and types of class data members, inheritance information, the element type and the length of arrays, as well as information on elementary data types.

The analyzer assigns a unique type number (used for references); the numbers are assigned in increasing order: the first several numbers are reserved for fundamental types such as int and double.

The exception list. This list is optional and helps to prevent inclusion of unnecessary classes and data members to the type table.

Generation. The generation phase creates **type information** and **overloaded access routines**. All the generated code belongs to the class PD (**P**ersistence and **D**isplay) defined the header file pd.h , with member functions defined in the file pd.cc

Generation of data type information. The PDGen code generator writes to pd.cc a code fragment that initializes the data type table.

For the example given above (Fig. 3(a)) a fragment of relevant code is:

```
initSimpleType(3,"int",sizeof(int));
....
initClassType(33,"Wheel",sizeof(Wheel),0);
initBaseClass(33,32,0, "Cylinder");
initMember(33,12,offsetof(Wheel,pressure),   "pressure");

initClassType(34,"Bicycle",sizeof(Bicycle),0);
initMember(34,33,offsetof(Bicycle,front),    "front");
initMember(34,33,offsetof(Bicycle,rear),     "rear");
initMember(34, 3,offsetof(Bicycle,framesize),"framesize");
initMember(34,35,offsetof(Bicycle,tube),     "tube");

initArrayType(35,"Cylinder[8]",sizeof(Cylinder[8]),0,8);
```

The standard C macro offsetof(Bicycle,rear) calculates the offset (position) of data member rear within objects of class Bicycle[6].

This code fragment is later compiled and linked with the application. When the application starts, the data type table is initialized. This table is available to the persistence and display routines at the run time. When the data are saved, loaded, or shown, appropriate routines use this table in order to recursively traverse the data structures.

Generation of overloaded access routines. For every data type or class T that is defined in the header file the appropriate instances of the overloaded functions PD::show(T&p), PD::load(T&p), PD::store(T&p) are constructed.

These functions can take the variable of type T as an argument.

---

[6] This approach is more portable and safe than to sum up the sizes of every data member.

3.6 Input and output procedures

When the functions load and store are called , a variable of the corresponding data type is passed as a parameter.

The function load reads the variable value from the file and restores it in the memory. The function store saves the value on disk.

These functions traverse the application data that can be reached from the passed argument variable by recursively following data members, including pointer references. Every step of this process is controlled by the data type table. When data items of an elementary type are reached, the functions load/store the data in some format (textual or binary); see Section 3.8 where formats are discussed.

When the data is *loaded*, memory is dynamically allocated if a pointer variable is visited and its value is not *NULL*. When memory is allocated for class instances, the class constructor is called without parameters. It is assumed that every class has a constructor without parameters.

3.7 Data display procedure

The function show activated from the application program displays the required variable.

For data display we have designed a universal data browser which can show and edit the data when the data-type table is given. We use the Tcl/Tk graphical library [Ou94]. First, the C++ variables are associated with Tcl variables. It produces the following effect: if a Tcl variable changes, the C++ data change automatically. If a Tcl variable value is requested, then it is taken from the C++ variable.

We recursively traverse all data members, including pointer references. The algorithm that builds the window as a hierarchy of frames recursively traverses Tcl variables with the help of the data type table (Tcl script pd.tcl) which is generated automatically.

When some value is *updated* by the user, the corresponding Tcl and C++ variables are automatically updated; when it is updated by the application, its text presentation is changed, too.

If necessary (i.e. when the New button is pressed in the display of a pointer variable), memory is allocated and a class instance is initialized by the constructor.

3.8 Data storage formats

Complex data items are traversed recursively when loaded or stored. The original PLib library includes load and store routines for two machine-independent formats, ASCII and XDR [SUN90]. XDR is a data representation format used in remote procedure call. These formats are not self-describing formats, i.e., there is no possibility of discovering mismatches between the loaded data and the program data structures.

In the PDGen tool we extend this format by simply adding the type table information. When the **store** procedure writes some data, it also writes the type table. When the **load** procedure reads data from file, it also reads the type table and verifies that it is identical to the original one (for all data types that actually appear in the loaded file).

Difficulties can arise if old data are **loaded** by a program with new data structure. In our approach some basic data scheme correction is provided. If the old data contain classes with permuted order of data members, the correction works automatically. Extra members in the old data are ignored, the missing ones are not initialized. Finally, the user can explicitly specify the old and the new name for *renamed* class data members and renamed class names in the exception list.

3.9 Universal browser design

Since the data table is stored together with data (i.e. in a self-describing data format), a stand-alone universal browser can easily be designed. This is one of directions of our future work.

This browser automatically adapts the interface to the structure of loaded data. It works independently on underlying C++ data type declaration files and can browse and edit a file with arbitrary data structures if it is prepared by the PDGen persistence routines or by the universal browser.

It should be noted that there will be limitations for dynamic memory allocation during editing, because the C++ code (where necessary constructors without parameters are defined) is not available to the universal browser.

A semi-universal browser may contain some application-specific C++ classes and adapt itself to data structures constructed from these classes and elementary types.

3.10 Attributes

Attributes are used for additional control over class instances, type components and single data items in such cases when we want to alter the default behaviour of the PDGen tool when traversing the data elements.

The attribute information is *orthogonal* to the type structure declaration. Therefore it should normally be described outside the code containing the data types.

The graphical user interface designer (or generator) writes the attributes in a separate script file (the attribute definition file) which can be unspecified until the application program starts. It allows altering many preference settings and options without recompilation and even during the runtime.

Each attribute specification has syntax:

set_attr { *component1, component2, ...* } { *attribute1, attribute2, ...* }

Component is specified as *path* or *Class-name*::*path* where the *path* has the same syntax as C++ qualified names. This means that the data members are selected with dot (.), and array elements are specified in square brackets [*index*].

The use of patterns and regular expressions (within pair of "-s) is allowed instead of standard C++ path syntax. In this case the attribute specification applies to all paths that match the pattern.

The attributes are specified as *attribute=value*.

Example: The attribute specification script

```
set_attr { Bicycle::front.pressure  Bicycle::rear.pressure }
          { postfix = "H/m^2" }
```

states that for these variables the postfix (area normally used for physical units) should have the value H/m^2. The script is checked for correctness of the syntax; e.g. the system verifies that **pressure** is defined as a member of the class **Wheel**.

The same effect can be achieved by specifying a pattern:

```
set_attrp { "*pressure" } { postfix="H/m^2" }
```

The complete attribute specification necessary for the window in the Fig. 3(c) is:

```
set_attrp { "*angle" }  { postfix = "rad" }
set_attrp { "*radius*" } { postfix = "m" }
set_attrp { "*pressure*" } { postfix = "H/m^2" }
```

We just mention several other available attributes:

- **validate** specifies a Tcl function   that will be called each time when the input text area is altered.
- **hidden** specifies how and whether the item value is shown at the beginning. It can be shown, hidden or detached (Sect. 3.4).
- **load** and **save** specify whether the value is loaded from disk file and saved. By default it is both loaded and saved. **required** specifies that the user *must* enter some value; **read-only** specifies that the user cannot update it.
- **layout** specifies whether the array or structure should be displayed in vertical or horizontal layout. By default a heuristic is applied.
- Finally, **hook** gives the designer "free hands"; it specifies a Tk/Tcl function that is responsible for complete graphical representation of the value. A Tcl variable name with the value and Tk window name is given. The function is written by the designer and it has to create a window with the given name.

4   Automatic Generation of GUI from ObjectMath Models

The basic idea behind the second generation system is to generate all components of the graphical user interface from the application model, and to avoid manual editing when the model is updated and the user interface code is re-generated.

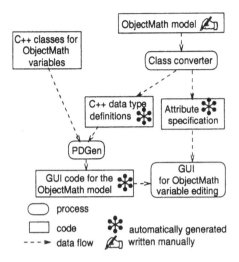

Fig. 8. *Second generation graphical user interface generating system.*

The phases of the generation process are depicted in Fig. 8. First the ObjectMath model is analyzed by the *class converter*. All the data necessary for the class converter are contained in the class hierarchy diagram and the ObjectMath variable declarations. The class converter translates the ObjectMath class hierarchy to the relevant C++ class hierarchy.

The ObjectMath variables can be of twenty different predefined types which are implemented as C++ classes. For example, the ObjectMath type DoubleVec3 (contains three double precision real numbers and can serve as operand in various ObjectMath arithmetic expressions) corresponds (in the simulation code) to the C++ class DoubleVec3. The data members of these C++ classes can represent the corresponding ObjectMath variables in the graphical interface. For example, the class DoubleVec3 is defined as

```
class DoubleVec3
{ double X,Y,Z; // data members
  ....           // member functions, friend functions etc.
}
```

and the DoubleVec3 type in ObjectMath can be presented in graphical user interface as three text input boxes marked with X, Y and Z.

The C++ class hierarchy (generated from the model) and C++ classes (that correspond to ObjectMath variable data types) are merged together and passed as the input for the PDGen tool. This tool generates code for graphical user interface for the corresponding ObjectMath model.

Attribute specifications are necessary for the application with graphical interface at run-time. They contain some information absent in the C++ class declarations, such as physical units and persistence status. These attribute specifications are generated separately for the members of every class by the class converter.

4.1 Translation of an ObjectMath model to a C++ class hierarchy

Every single ObjectMath class gives rise to a C++ class. The ObjectMath inheritance means that all variables are inherited by the subclass. The same happens in the C++ class inheritance.

ObjectMath instances correspond to C++ classes, too. Such ObjectMath instances inherit all variables and formulae from the superclasses, and, in addition, they may declare their own variables. ObjectMath *parts* serve for aggregation of class instantiations. They cannot specify their own variables. The parts can be modeled by C++ class data members.

ObjectMath variables become C++ data members.

The ObjectMath model (as a whole) corresponds to a single C++ class that includes one data member for every instance in the model.

4.2 Translation example

For the purpose of illustration we take our basic example (Fig. 1), a bicycle model. When the conversion described above is applied, the C++ type declarations shown in Fig. 3(a) are generated.

The attribute information is generated from the parameters in `Declare` statements. The attribute information is created according to the syntax rules described in the Section 3.10:

```
set_attr {Body::angle       } {postfix="rad"}
set_attr {Cylinder::radius  } {postfix="m"}
set_attr {Wheel::pressure   } {postfix="H/m^2"}
set_attr {Bicycle::framesize} {postfix="int"}
```

The graphical interface generated for this example is identical to the Fig. 3(c).

4.3 Advantages of the second generation approach.

The new approach successfully solves the problems arising in the first generation approach (Section 2.9). There are no *update problems* because the application and its graphical user interface are generated simultaneously. The set of supported types can include arbitrarily complex types because we analyze all type declarations and derive the graphical user interface from them. The *variable grouping* and menu structure are automatically derived from the class structure of the ObjectMath model.

An additional advantage of the new approach is the automatic generation of persistence routines for arbitrarily complex data types.

5 Related work

5.1 Persistence generation systems

There exist various ways to make objects persistent in object-oriented database management systems. In [BB88] such objects must be instances of special classes. In [Deux91] and [LLOW91] objects are assigned to "persistent variables" or "placed into persistent sets". In the *OBST* system [OBST94, CRSTZ92, AC-SST94] application developers can program in an object-oriented extension of C. There are no pointers; unique object identifiers are used for references instead. The language includes an option to create objects as persistent data. Primitive data components are not lightweight, therefore high performance necessary for scientific computations and fitting memory constraints is hard to achieve.

Typically OODBMS provide automatically persistence for specific language with the help of OODB language compiler.

The *PGen* system [Tichy94, PGen94, Paulisch90] analyses C++ header files and generates C++ code for reading and writing variables of arbitrary types and classes defined there. This way persistence of data can be easily achieved. Traditionally, to make C++ objects persistent the user has to write the Store() and Load() functions for every class in the application. The PGen tool generates appropriate functions automatically. In most cases almost no modifications are needed in the C++ header files.

One of the difficult problems with persistent data is how the data should be converted if the type declarations change. It is difficult to do automatically with C++ header files. A special type declaration editor can be designed to trace down all the changes in the type definitions. Then a conversion program can be generated.

Our system reuses the ideas and the code of PGen and extends it for variable display generation.

5.2 Display generation systems

In the *OBST* system a graphic shell visualizes the OBST objects and is used for debugging the data.

The systems *DOST* and *SUITE* [Dewan87, Dewan91, Dewan90, Suite91] generate variable displays from C header files. The translator analyzes specially annotated header files and generates C code that controls message-based communication between the application and a universal display manager. The generated code is linked with the original application. A variable of arbitrarily complex type can be displayed. The display manager can show various C data structures (including pointers and dynamic arrays coded as pointers). The layout can be customized by a large number of attributes (such as colors, help texts, constraints and validation functions) that can be adjusted interactively (with the help of special preference setting dialog) or in the code. In these systems a single description of data types can specify the internal data, the data used for communication between the processes and the data for structure displays. Despite the large number of attributes associated with every type, variable or variable element, there is no possibility for the programmer to construct new graphical elements when necessary. Persistence can be implemented outside the system.

The *SmallTalk visualization system* [Dewan90A] uses the fact that all the objects in the program have an ultimate ancestor, Object that has access to meta-information about the objects, e.g. description of its structure. The display of any object is based on this meta-information. The user can change the attributes of object display by adding some extra SmallTalk code. Persistence can be supported by other SmallTalk methods and it is not part of the visualization system.

Some modern *debuggers* [Debug92] show displays with selected C, C++ or Pascal data structures for data inspection. They are based on symbol tables and dynamically change during program execution. The displays appear automatically in a manner similar to our approach, but they *cannot* be customized by the designer. The user can modify the values, but the validation procedures cannot be specified.

5.3 The C++ language and access to meta-information

C++ is a high level object-oriented language. Nowadays it is widely used in industry for scientific software design, including scientific computing.

C++ supports many ways to simplify the work of the application programmer and to avoid writing unnecessary code. Macro definitions, templates, operator overloading, class inheritance and standard class libraries cover almost all typical needs of application designers. They allow code to be written at a very high level and its size is close to the minimal possible if accurate design is applied. Therefore C++ code analysis and generation is not applied very often. One case where this is necessary is automatic code generation for persistence and displaying data for arbitrary C++ data types.

C++ is a hybrid language in the sense that it operates both with objects and non-objects. This creates difficulties when applying a uniform approach to all values. C++ is a strongly typed language. Therefore when we create code for universal operations that could be applied to many types, code for every type should be written.

It is possible to design persistence and display routines for C++ manually. The problem is that *for every data type* separate routines should be written. Unlike a SmallTalk object, a C++ object cannot automatically provide (or inherit) meta-information about its structure (declarations of types, component names, sizes and types) during run-time. Therefore it does not know how to read, write or display itself.

Unlike SmallTalk, in C++ we cannot tell simply that the variable foo should be stored, loaded or shown. For this purpose a relevant function must be declared and defined. The argument type for this function must be the same as foo has, and this function must access the internal structure of foo. Obviously, the code and control information for such a function should be created in advance. Such information can be extracted from C++ data type declarations. This is what the PDGen tool does.

6 Conclusions and Future Work

There is a substantial need of automatic generation of graphical user interfaces for many applications. The first generation system for generating user interfaces described in this paper has been in industrial use during more than two years. Experience shows that the model changes tend to require a number of manual changes to the user interface. We have provided a more flexible system that can automatically cope with model changes. Therefore, the more universal second generation system has been designed. The user interface constructed in a partly manual way using the first generation tool can now be generated completely automatically.

The PDGen tool is applied to ObjectMath, C and C++ programs, but it can also be adapted to other languages. Type definitions can be extracted in several ways:

- the source code is parsed and analyzed (in our tool we reuse the analyzer from PGen (see Section 5.1) and apply it to the C++ code),
- analysis of the symbol tables generated by some standard compiler (this is the approach implemented in Suite, see Section 5.2),
- extracting type definitions from the model description, if the application is generated from this model (we apply this to the ObjectMath models),
- creation of the type table with the help of a special data-type definition editor.

The last approach can be combined with the customization tool. In this way both data-type definitions and information about interface details (attribute values) will be integrated under the strict control of one tool. This reduces the possibility of data type mismatches and update problems.

In some languages the type information can be available at run-time with the help of built-in functions; in this case there is no need in code analysis and generation at all.

We are currently working on several extensions to the basic idea implemented in the automatic graphical user interface generator. Some interesting questions that could be considered include:

- the application of the PDGen tool to programs in other languages;
- integration of the tool with (extensible) symbolic debuggers;
- automatic generation of graphical user interface for member functions (not only for data members). For example, if a member function has no arguments it is displayed as a button. When the button is pressed, the function is invoked.
- a more general array browser implementation;

- integration of ObjectMath with tools for data visualization, as it is implemented in the output data browser;
- implementation of the universal browser (Section 3.9) that adapts the graphical user interface according to the type tables given together with the input data;
- the design of a meta-editor that can edit data type definitions.

Remote data editing with the help of widely distributed WWW browsers is another application area. The data resides on the server and can be updated by the clients with the help of HTML interactive forms. One of our future research topics is automatic generation of HTML-based editing tools from data structure specifications.

Finally we would like to mention that a WWW site devoted to the PDGen tool has been organized [PDGen96]. More details about the systems discussed in this paper are available in [E96].

Acknowledgments

Lars Viklund and other members of PELAB group contributed to the design of the ObjectMath language and its implementation. Ivan Rankin improved the English in this paper.

This project is supported by the Swedish Board for Industrial and Technical Development, the Swedish Board for Technical Research and SKF Engineering and Research Centre and the PREPARE Esprit-3 project.

References

[ACSST94] J.Alt, E. Casais, B. Schiefer, S. Sirdeshpande, D. Theobald. *The OBST Tutorial*, Forschungszentrum Informatik (FZI), Karlsruhe, Germany, FZI.049.2, 15nd December, 1994

[BB88] A. Björnerstedt, S. Britts, "AVANCE: An Object Management System", *SIGPLAN Notices*, vol. 23, pp. 206-221. Nov. 1988. In *Proceedings of the OOPSLA'88 Conference*, San Diego, CA, 25-30 September 1988.

[CRSTZ92] E. Casais, M. Ranft, B. Schiefer, D. Theobald, W. Zimmer. *OBST - An Overview*, Forschungszentrum Informatik (FZI), Karlsruhe, Germany, FZI.039.1, June 1992

[Debug92] Debugging a Program. *SparcWorks documentation*. SunPro, October 1992

[Deux91] O. Deux et al., "The O2 System", *Communications of the ACM*, vol. 34, pp.34-48, Oct. 1991

[Dewan87] P.Dewan, M.Solomon. "Dost: An Environment to Support Automatic Generation of User Interfaces". In *Proceeding of the ACM SIGSOFT/SIGPLAN Software Engineering Symposium on Practical Software Development Environments*, *SIGPLAN Notices* Vol. 22, No. 1, January 1987, pp. 150-159.

[Dewan90] P. Dewan, M. Solomon. "An Approach to Support Automatic Generation of User Interfaces". *ACM TOPLAS*, Vol. 12, No. 4, pp. 566–609 (October 1990)

[Dewan90A] P. Dewan. "Object-Oriented Editor Generation". *Journal of Object-Oriented Programming*, vol. 3, 2 (July/Aug 1990), pp. 35-49

[Dewan91] P. Dewan. "An Inheritance Model for Supporting Flexible Displays of Data Structures". *Software - Practice and Experience*, vol. 21(7), 719-738 (July 1991)

[Dewan91A] P. Dewan. *A Tour of the Suite User Interface Software*. Included in [Suite91]

[E96] V. Engelson. *An Approach to Automatic Construction of Graphical User Interfaces for Applications in Scientific Computing*. Linköping Studies in Science and Technology. Licentiate thesis No 545. Department of Computer and Information Science, Linköping University, 1996.

[Fritzson93] P.Fritzson, V. Engelson, L.Viklund. "Variant Handling, Inheritance and Composition in the ObjectMath Computer Algebra Environment". In *Proc. Of DISCO'93 - Conference On Design and Implementation of Symbolic Computation Systems*, LNCS 722, Sept. 1993

[Fritzson95] P. Fritzson, L. Viklund, J. Herber and D. Fritzson. "High-level Mathematical Modeling and Programming". *IEEE Software*, July 1995, pp. 77-86.

[FWHSS96] P. Fritzson, R. Wismüller, Olav Hansen, Jonas Sala, Peter Skov. "A Parallel Debugger with Support for Distributed Arrays, Multiple Executables and Dynamic Processes". In *Proceedings of International Conference on Compiler Construction*, Linköping University, Linköping, Sweden, 22-26 April, 1996, LNCS 1061, Springer Verlag.

[LLOW91] Ch. Lambs, G. Landis, J. Orenstein, D. Weinreb, "The ObjectStore Database System", *Communications of the ACM*, vol. 34, pp. 50-63, Oct. 1991

[OBST94] OBST, a persistent object management system. Available as ftp://ftp.ask.uni-karlsruhe.de/pub/education/computer_science/OBST, see also http://www.fzi.de/divisions/dbs/projects/OBST.html

[Ou94] John K. Ousterhout. *Tcl and the Tk Toolkit*. Addison-Wesley, 1994

[Paulisch90] F.N.Paulisch, S. Manke, W.F.Tichy. "Persistence for Arbitrary C++ Data Structures". In *Proc. of Int. Workshop on Computer Architectures to Support Security and Persistence of Information*, Bremen, FRG, May 1990, pp. 378-391.

[PDGen96] V. Engelson. *The PDGen tool*. Information available as http://www.ida.liu.se/~vaden/pdgen.

[PGen94] *PGen, a persistence facility*. This software is available as ftp://ftp.ira.uka.de/systems/general.

[Tichy94] W.F.Tichy, J.Heilig, F.N.Paulisch. "A Generative and Generic Approach to Persistence". *C++ report*, January 1994. Also included in [PGen94].

[Wolfram91] S. Wolfram, *Mathematica - A System for Doing Mathematics by Computer* (second edition), Addison-Wesley, Reading, Mass., 1991.

[Viklund95] L. Viklund and P.Fritzson, "ObjectMath: An Object-Oriented Language for Symbolic and Numeric Processing in Scientific Computing", *Scientific Programming*, Vol. 4, pp. 229-250, 1995.

[Suite91] SUITE, user interface software. This software is available as ftp://ftp.cs.unc.edu/pub/users/dewan/suite. Some information available as http://www.cs.unc.edu/~dewan/

[SUN90] SUN Microsystems Inc. *Network Programming Guide (Ch. 5,6)*, 1990

Eliminating Virtual Function Calls in C++ Programs

Gerald Aigner
Urs Hölzle[1]

Abstract. We have designed and implemented an optimizing source-to-source C++ compiler that reduces the frequency of virtual function calls. Our prototype implementation demonstrates the value of OO-specific optimization for C++. Despite some limitations of our system, and despite the low frequency of virtual function calls in some of the programs, optimization improves the performance of a suite of large C++ applications totalling over 90,000 lines of code by a median of 18% over the original programs and reduces the number of virtual function calls by a median factor of five. For more call-intensive versions of the same programs, performance improved by a median of 26% and the number of virtual calls dropped by a factor of 17.5. Our measurements indicate that inlining barely increases code size, and that for most programs, the instruction cache miss ratio does not increase significantly.

1 Introduction

Object-oriented programming languages confer many benefits, including abstraction, which lets the programmer hide the details of an object's implementation from the object's clients. Unfortunately, object-oriented programs are harder to optimize than programs written in languages like C or Fortran. There are two main reasons for this. First, object-oriented programming encourages code factoring and differential programming [Deu83]; as a result, procedures are smaller and procedure calls more frequent. Second, it is hard to optimize calls in object-oriented programs because they use *dynamic dispatch*: the procedure invoked by the call is not known until run-time since it depends on the dynamic type of the receiver. Therefore, a compiler usually cannot apply standard optimizations such as inline substitution or interprocedural analysis to these calls.

Consider the following example (written in pidgin C++):

```
class Point {
        virtual float get_x();          // get x coordinate
        virtual float get_y();          // ditto for y
        virtual float distance(Point p); // compute distance between receiver and p
}
```

When the compiler encounters the expression p->get_x(), where p's declared type is Point, it cannot optimize the call because it does not know p's exact run-time type. For example, there could be two subclasses of Point, one for Cartesian points and one for polar points:

---

[1] Authors' addresses: Computer Science Department, University of California, Santa Barbara, CA 93106; {urs, gerald}@cs.ucsb.edu; http://www.cs.ucsb.edu/oocsb.

```
class CartesianPoint : Point {
    float x, y;
    virtual float get_x() { return x; }
    (other methods omitted)
}
class PolarPoint : Point {
    float rho, theta;
    virtual float get_x() { return rho * cos(theta); }
    (other methods omitted)
}
```

Since p could refer to either a CartesianPoint or a PolarPoint instance at run-time, the compiler's type information is not precise enough to optimize the call: the compiler knows p's *declared type* (i.e., the set of operations that can be invoked, and their signatures) but not its *actual type* (i.e., the object's exact size, format, and the implementation of operations).

Since dynamic dispatch is frequent, object-oriented languages need optimizations targeted at reducing the cost of dynamic dispatch in order to improve performance. So far, much of the research on such optimizations has concentrated on pure object-oriented languages because the frequency of dynamic dispatch is especially high in such languages. Several studies (e.g., [CUL89, HU94a, G+95]) have demonstrated that optimization can greatly reduce the frequency of dynamic dispatch in pure object-oriented languages and significantly improve performance. However, so far no study has shown that these optimizations also apply to a hybrid language like C++ where the programmer can choose between dispatched and non-dispatched functions, and where programs typically exhibit much lower call frequencies.

We have developed a proof-of-concept optimizing compiler for C++ that demonstrates that optimization can reduce the frequency of virtual function calls in C++, and that programs execute significantly faster as a result. On a suite of large, realistic C++ applications totalling over 90,000 lines of code, optimization improves performance by up to 40% and reduces the number of virtual function calls by up to 50 times.

2 Background

Since our main goal was to demonstrate the value of OO-specific optimizations for C++, we chose to implement and evaluate two relatively simple optimizations that have demonstrated high payoffs in implementations of pure object-oriented languages like SELF or Cecil. In this section, we briefly review these optimizations before describing our C++-specific implementation in the next section.

2.1 Profile-Based Optimization: Type Feedback

Type feedback [HU94a] is an optimization technique originally developed for the SELF language. Its main idea is to use profile information gathered at run-time to eliminate dynamic dispatches. Thus, type feedback monitors the execution characteristics of individual call sites of a program and records the set of receiver classes encountered at each call site, together with their execution frequencies. Using this information, the compiler can optimize any dynamically-dispatched call by *predicting* likely receiver types and inlining the call for these types. Typically, the compiler will perform this optimization only if the execution frequency of a call site is high enough and if one receiver class dominates the distribution of the call site. For example, assume that p points to a CartesianPoint most of the time in the expression x = p->get_x(). Then, the expression could be compiled as

```
if (p->class == CartesianPoint) {
        // inline CartesianPoint case (most likely case)
        x = p->x;
} else {
        // don't inline PolarPoint case because method is too big
        // this branch also covers all other receiver types
        x = p->get_x(); // dynamically-dispatched call
}
```

For CartesianPoint receivers, the above code sequence will execute significantly faster since the original virtual function call is reduced to a comparison and an assignment. Inlining not only eliminates the calling overhead but also enables the compiler to optimize the inlined code using dataflow information particular to this call site.

In the SELF-93 system, the system collects receiver type information on-line, i.e., during the actual program run, and uses dynamic compilation to optimize code accordingly. In contrast, a system using static compilation (like the present C++ compiler) gathers profile information off-line during a separate program run.

2.2 Static Optimization: Class Hierarchy Analysis

We also implemented a static optimization technique, class hierarchy analysis (CHA) [App88, DGC95, Fer95], which can statically bind some virtual function calls given the application's complete class hierarchy. The optimization is based on a simple observation: if a is an instance of class A (or any subclass), the call a->f() can be statically bound if none of A's subclasses overrides f. CHA is simple to implement and has been shown to be effective for other systems [DGC95, Fer95], and thus we included it in our prototype compiler.

Another benefit of combining a static optimization like CHA with a profile-based optimization like type feedback is that they are complementary optimizations [AH95]: each of them may improve performance over the other. CHA may provide better performance because it can inline or statically bind sends with zero overhead. Since CHA can prove that a call can invoke only a single target method in all possible executions, any dispatch overhead is completely eliminated. In contrast, a profile-based technique like type feedback can inline the same send only by using a type test; even if the profile shows that the send always invoked the same target method, a test must remain since other target methods may be reached in different executions of the program. Thus, while the send can still be inlined, some dispatch overhead remains. On the other hand, type feedback can optimize any function call, not just monomorphic sends. Furthermore, being profile-based, it can also better determine whether the send is actually worth optimizing (i.e., executed often enough).

3 Related Work

Profile information has been used for optimization in many systems; as usual, Knuth [Knu70] was the first to suggest profile-based optimization, and today it is part of many research systems (e.g., [CM+92, Höl94, G+95]) as well as production compilers. Studies of inlining for procedural languages like C or Fortran have found that it often does not significantly increase execution speed but tends to significantly increase code size (e.g., [DH88, HwC89, CHT91, CM+92, Hall91]). Our results indicate that these previous results do not apply to C++ programs.

In implementations of dynamic or object-oriented languages, profiling information has often been used to identify (and optimize for) common cases. For example, Lisp systems usually inline the integer case of generic arithmetic and handle all other type combinations with a call to a routine in the run-time system. The Deutsch-Schiffman Smalltalk compiler was the first object-oriented system to predict integer receivers for common message names such as "+" [DS84]. All these systems do not use application-specific profiles.

The SELF system pioneered the use of profile information for optimizing object-oriented languages. An experimental proof-of-concept system [HCU91] was the first one to use type feedback (then called "PIC-based inlining") for optimization purposes. The SELF-93 system [HU94a] used on-line profile information to select frequently executed methods for optimization and to determine receiver types via type feedback. Similarly, the Cecil compiler [G+95] uses off-line profiling for optimization and inlining. Grove et al. [G+95] also examined the cross-input stability of receiver class profiled in C++ and Cecil and found it good enough to be used for optimization.

Until now, few profile-based techniques have been applied to hybrid, statically-typed languages like Modula-3 or C++. Based on measurements of C++ programs, Calder and Grunwald [CG94] argued that type feedback would be beneficial for C++ and proposed (but did not implement) a weaker form of class hierarchy analysis to improve efficiency. Their estimate of the performance benefits of this optimization (2-24% improvements, excluding benefits from inlining) exceeds the improvements measured in our system, partially because they assume a more aggressively pipelined CPU (DEC Alpha) which benefits more from reduced pipeline stalls than the SuperSPARC system we used. Fernandez [Fer95] applied link-time optimization to Modula-3 programs and found that class hierarchy analysis eliminated between 2% and 79% of the virtual calls in the Modula-3 applications measured, reducing the number of instructions executed by 3-11%. Profile-driven customization (procedure cloning) resulted in an additional improvement of 1-5%.

Several systems use whole-program or link-time analysis to optimize object-oriented programs, starting with the Apple Object Pascal linker [App88] which turned dynamically-dispatched calls into statically-bound calls if a type had exactly one implementation (e.g., the system contained only a CartesianPoint class and no PolarPoint class). To our knowledge, this system was the first to statically bind dynamically-dispatched calls, although it did not perform any inlining. As mentioned above, Fernandez [Fer95] used class hierarchy analysis for Modula-3, and Dean et al.

[DGC95] describe its use for Cecil. In both studies, the analysis' impact on virtual call frequency was significantly higher than in our system, as discussed in section 6.1. Srivastava and Wall [SW92] perform more extensive link-time optimization but do not optimize calls.

Bernstein et al. [B+96] describe a C++ compiler (apparently developed concurrently with ours) that also inlines virtual function calls using class hierarchy analysis and type feedback. Unlike the compiler described here, this system cannot perform cross-file inlining, always predicts the most frequent receiver class, inlines no more than one case per call, and always optimizes all call sites (even if they were executed only once). Furthermore, the compiler does not specialize inlined virtual functions (so that nested calls to this cannot be inlined), and cannot optimize calls involving virtual base classes. Although the experimental data presented in [B+96] is sketchy and mostly based on microbenchmarks, it appears that the system's limitations significantly impact performance. For lcom (the only large benchmark measured) Bernstein et al. report a speedup of 4% whereas our system improves performance by 24% over the original program and by 9% over the baseline (see section 6).

More ambitious analyses such as concrete type inference systems (e.g., [Age95, PR94, PC94]) can determine the concrete receiver types of message sends. Compared to type feedback, a type inferencer may provide more precise information since it may be able to prove that only a single receiver type is possible at a given call site. However, its information may also be less precise since it may include types that could occur in theory but never happen in practice. (In other words, the information lacks frequency data.) For SELF, concrete type inference removed more dispatches than type feedback for most programs [AH95]. Like link-time optimizations, the main problem with type inference is that it requires knowledge of the entire program, thus precluding dynamic linking.

4 Implementation

This section describes the implementation of our optimizing source-to-source C++ compiler as well as the motivations for its design decisions.

4.1 Overview

The implementation consists of several parts (Figure 1). First, a pre-pass combines the original sources into a single baseline program to simplify the work of later phases (section 4.2). Then, the program is compiled with a modified version of GNU C++ to produce an instrumented executable which serves to collect receiver class profile information (section 4.4). The centerpiece of the system, the optimizing compiler, then uses this profile to transform the baseline source program into an optimized source

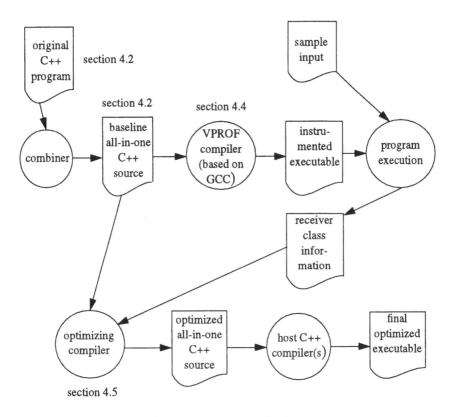

Figure 1. Overview of optimization process

program (section 4.5) which is subsequently compiled and optimized by the native host C++ compiler. The rest of this section describes these steps in more detail.

4.2 Program Preparation

Before any optimization begins, a pre-pass merges the source files of the original C++ program into a single C++ source file that contains all the declarations, global variables, and functions of the original program. The various program parts are arranged in a suitable order so that all declarations precede any use (see Table 1). Within the "inline" and "function" parts, function definitions are sorted topologically to improve

Source Section	Description
declarations	all declarations normally found in C/C++ header files, like prototypes, typedefs, class declarations, and external declarations; contains no function definitions
global	all global variables
inline	all inline functions
function	all non-inline functions

Table 1. The sections of a baseline C++ program

subsequent inlining by the host compiler (some C++ compilers do not inline functions unless the definition of an inlinable function precedes its use).

In later sections, we will refer to programs compiled from the original source as "original" programs and those compiled from the all-in-one equivalent as "baseline" programs. Combining the entire program's code into a single baseline file simplifies the subsequent optimization process. In particular, the compiler does not need to handle cross-module (cross-file) inlining, i.e., obtaining the body of a function to be inlined is much simpler than if the program were divided into separate compilation units.

To implement this pre-pass, and for the actual optimizing compiler, we used a commercial tool, the CCAuditor C++ parser from Declarative Systems [Dec95]. CCAuditor contains an empty attribute grammar for C++ which can be extended to implement arbitrary analyses or transformations. We used CCAuditor to build a simplified parse tree of the program which is then traversed and transformed by a C++ program. CCAuditor proved to be an invaluable tool since it handles the semantic analysis of the C++ code (i.e., resolution of overloaded functions, copy constructors, etc.), thus relieving us from dealing with C++'s difficulties.

4.3 Source-To-Source Transformation

We chose to implement our compiler using source-to-source transformation for several reasons:

- It is simpler to implement and test; in particular, the generated (source) code is much easier to debug than assembly code. In essence, the back-end C++ compiler serves as an output verification tool.
- Source-to-source compilation allows experimenting with several back-end compilers to determine how much the quality of back-end code generation affects performance. Also, using well-tested back-end compilers provides more reliable results (and usually better performance) by ensuring that performance isn't affected or obscured by unknown back-end deficiencies.
- Similarly, it simplifies porting the compiler to new architectures to compare optimization effects on different hardware platforms and to estimate the impact of architectural features on performance.

The main alternative, changing an existing compiler, implied using the GNU C++ compiler, as it is the only C++ compiler for which source code is readily available. Unfortunately, the GNU compiler does not build complete parse trees for functions; instead, it builds parse trees only as far as necessary to perform its task. Without parse trees, the high-level transformations performed by the optimizing compiler are hard to implement. (For example, it is hard to duplicate or modify the body of a function later.) This deficiency, coupled with the problems of understanding a compiler of gcc's size and the advantages of source-to-source transformation, tilted the scales towards the current solution.

On the other hand, source-to-source transformation is not without problems. In particular, it restricts the extent to which high-level information can be transmitted to the back end. For example, the optimizer may have a very good idea of which execution paths are more likely, but this information cannot easily be encoded in C++, and thus the back end does not benefit from this information. In general, the source-to-source compiler has less control over the final generated code; for example, it cannot force the back end compiler to inline a function since the inline modifier is only a hint, not an order (although gcc appears to always follow such hints). Finally, some constructs cannot be portably expressed in source form. In particular, type tests are back-end-dependent since different back end compilers may use different vtable allocation strategies. In spite of these potential problems, we felt that the advantages of source-to-source optimization outweighed the disadvantages in a research setting.

4.4 Collecting Receiver Class Profiles

Before actual optimization starts, the baseline file is compiled with VPROF, a modified version of the GNU C++ compiler. VPROF inserts a non-virtual call to a run-time routine before each virtual call, passing in all information needed to identify the call site (e.g., file name, line number, and call number within the line). Additionally, the run-time routine receives a pointer to the receiver's dispatch table (vtable [ES90]) and the index of the vtable entry being used to dispatch the call. In order to obtain the class name of receiver and the method name, the compiler enhances the vtable with one extra element per entry containing the necessary information.

The resulting executable is then used to collect the receiver class profiling information for each call site. At the end of the program run, a small run-time library collects and outputs the data collected; this output is later used by the optimizing compiler. In Grove's terminology [G+95], VPROF collects 1-CCP information, i.e., individual receiver class distributions for each call site.

4.5 The Optimizing Compiler

The main optimization step in our system consists of a source-to-source optimizing compiler that eliminates virtual function calls using either the profile information, knowledge of the complete class hierarchy, or both. This section describes the main implementation difficulties we faced as well as their solutions (summarized in Table 2). The next section then describes the optimization policies used.

4.5.1 Type Tests

One of the central transformations of the optimizing compiler is to replace virtual function calls with more efficient equivalents. Many of these transformations involve a type test that tests for a predicted class. So far, we sketched this test as a simple comparison, e.g., p->_class == CartesianPoint. Unfortunately, this isn't legal C++ code: neither do objects contain a _class field, nor can a class be used as a run-time constant. So, how can such type tests be implemented? We considered three alternatives.

First, the compiler could add a new virtual function __class to each class, and have each of them return a unique type identifier (class number). Then, the type test could be written portably as p—>__class() == CartesianPointID. Unfortunately, this approach isn't very attractive since in trying to eliminate a virtual function call the compiler introduces another virtual function call.

Problem	Solution
complexity of changing an existing C++ compiler	source-to-source optimization
body of methods to be inlined must be known during the optimization phase	transform the whole program into one file
implementation of a fast type check	use the address of a vtable to determine the class type
virtual function to be inlined may not be accessible (declared protected or private)	add dispatch_function to target class
get back-end C++ compiler to inline a virtual function while leaving the original function for other callers	duplicate the original virtual function , change name, remove virtual attribute, add inline attribute
cast receiver pointer down from virtual base class	create a helper application computing the offsets for all possible class combinations
static functions or variables with the same name	move to global scope and rename

Table 2. Problems and Solutions for the source-to-source approach

Alternatively, the compiler could add an additional instance variable to each object containing virtual functions and change the class' constructors to initialize this field to the class' ID. This approach provides fast type tests (a load and a comparison) but leads to two major problems. First, the size of each object grows by one word; if multiple inheritance is used, the object even contains multiple extra fields, one for each base class that uses virtual functions. The additional type field not only uses more space but will also impose a run-time penalty since the additional field has to be initialized; also, the extra words may increase the data cache miss ratio. Second, subclasses cannot easily access the type field if they inherit base classes privately (so that the type field is hidden). To solve this problem, the code could directly access the type field using casts, as in *((int*)(BaseClass*)this). However, this solution is non-portable since different C++ compilers may use different object layouts.

The third approach, which is the one we are currently using, is an extension of the method described above. Instead of adding a new variable and initializing it to a unique value, it uses a variable already added by the compiler, the vtable pointer. Although there are some difficulties with this approach, they can all be solved:

- *A class may have multiple vtables.* C++ does not guarantee anything about vtables, and thus a compiler may generate multiple vtables for a single class (e.g., one per .c file where the class definition was included). Although this was a problem in early C++ implementations, today's compilers try hard to avoid multiple vtables in order to produce smaller executables, and thus multiple vtables have not been a problem in practice. Furthermore, their presence would only reduce the efficiency of the optimized programs, not their correctness.

- *A class may share the vtable of one of its superclasses* since the superclass vtable is a prefix of (or identical to) the subclass vtable. This sharing isn't problematic since the compiler uses the type information only for dispatching methods. If two classes share the same vtable, then they will behave identically with respect to all functions called through this vtable, and thus can share inlined code as well. In fact, such sharing is beneficial for type feedback as it allows instances of several classes to share the same piece of inlined code.

- *The vtable isn't a C++ entity, so that a source program cannot name it.* This problem is caused by source-to-source optimization, and we circumvent it by using a dummy "vtable address" constant in the comparison and post-editing the assembly file generated by the back-end compiler.

- *The position of the vtable field is unknown.* This is the most serious problem, again caused by using source-to-source optimization. One solution is to introduce an additional superclass for every class in the program which has a superclass with virtual functions. The sole purpose of this superclass is to contain a virtual function definition, forcing the compiler to place the vtable at the beginning of the object. This solution works well for single-inheritance hierarchies but breaks down for multiple inheritance since it doesn't force the placement of multiple vtable pointers in an object.

  Therefore, our system uses a helper application (automatically generated during the initial pre-pass over the original program) to compute the offsets of all subobjects within an object and assumes that each subobject's vtable is at offset 0. (If this assumption were false, the helper program could create a zeroed-out instance of each class in the original program and find then the positions of embedded vtable pointers.) The offset information is needed to perform casts to virtual base classes.

To summarize, source-to-source optimization poses some difficulties that are caused by the need to access implementation-dependent information at the source level. However, none of these difficulties are insurmountable. In practice, they mainly impact the portability of the generated optimized source code since different back-end compilers may require different vtable manipulation code.

4.5.2 Optimization Example

Figure 2 shows a program fragment optimized with type feedback. The left column shows unoptimized code, and the right column the code created after optimizing the call a->foo() in function bar. In order to optimize this call, the compiler creates the dispatch function A::dispatch_B_foo which has the same signature as A::foo but is declared inline and non-virtual. Using this dispatch method minimizes the syntactic transformation needed at the call site, even with nested function calls. In case the dynamic receiver class is B, the dispatch method calls B::inline_B_foo(); in all other cases, a normal virtual method call is performed. The inline_B_foo() method serves two purposes. First, it ensures that the called method is declared inline; some C++ compilers only inline functions explicitly declared inline. Second, the inline function may be specialized since its receiver type is precisely known to be a B (and only a B). Thus, implicit self calls within the method can be statically bound [CUL89].

4.6 Inlining Strategies

Some calls should not be inlined; for example, if a call has 20 different receiver types, each of which occurs 5% of the time, inlining is unlikely to improve performance: inlining just one case improves only 5% of the call site's executions but slows down the

original program	optimized program
```class A { virtual int foo(); }; class B : public A { private: virtual int foo(); }; int bar(A *a) { // a contains an instance // of class B for 90% of // all invocations a->foo(); ... }```	```class A { ... inline int dispatch_B_foo(); }; class B : public A { ... inline int inline_B_foo(); }; inline int B::inline_B_foo() { // modified copy of the source // of B::foo() } inline int A::dispatch_B_foo() { if (this->_class == class_B) return ((B*)this-> B::inline_B_foo()); else return foo(); } int bar(A *a) { a->A::dispatch_B_foo(); }```

Figure 2. Source-to-source optimization example

other 95%. Thus, for each call site, the compiler must decide whether to optimize it or not. Currently, the compiler considers two factors in its inlining decisions. First, it exploits peaked receiver class distributions by inlining only classes whose relative frequency exceeds a certain threshold. The compiler can inline multiple cases per send, although for all measurements in this paper the compiler was limited to inlining at most one case per send. The compiler's default inlining threshold is 40%, and thus a call site won't be optimized unless the most frequent class represents more than 40% of all receivers at that call site. (Section 4.6 will show the performance impact of varying the threshold value.) With lower thresholds, more calls will be inlined, but chances are lower that the inlined code is actually executed, and thus actual performance may degrade because of the overhead of testing for the inlined case.

Second, the compiler restricts optimization to the "hot spots" of an application by considering the call site's contribution to the total number of calls in the application. For example, with the default threshold of 0.1%, the compiler will not optimize call sites responsible for less than 0.1% of the (virtual) calls executed during the profile run. By inlining only the important calls, the compiler reduces the potential code growth; often, relatively few call sites account for most of the calls, and thus good performance can be achieved with only moderate amounts of inlining.

Finally, our optimizer relies on the inlining strategies of the back-end compiler to some extent since the inline keyword is only a suggestion to that compiler; if the function is too large, the back end may decide not to inline it. Consequently, our compiler currently does not take function size into account when deciding whether to optimize a call or not. If the back end does not actually inline a call, the only benefit of optimization is the elimination of the dispatch (in the case of class hierarchy analysis) or the replacement of a virtual function call with a somewhat faster comparison-and-direct-call sequence (for type feedback). However, our current back-end compiler (gcc) always inlines inline functions.

5 Experimental Setup

To evaluate the performance of our optimizer, we used a suite of eight C++ applications totalling over 90,000 lines of code. In general, we tried to obtain large, realistic applications rather than small, artificial benchmarks. Unfortunately, the choice of publicly available C++ programs which compile with current C++ compilers on current operating system versions (Solaris 2.5 and AIX 4.1) is still limited. Two of the benchmarks (deltablue and richards) are much smaller than the others; they are included for comparison with earlier studies (e.g., [HU94a, G+95]). Richards is the only artificial benchmark in our suite (i.e., the program was never used to solve any real problem). Table 3 lists the benchmarks and their sizes.

program		lines of code	
name	description	original	baseline
deltablue	incremental dataflow constraint solver	1,000	1,400
eqn	type-setting program for mathematical equations	8,300	10,800
idl	SunSoft's IDL compiler (version 1.3) using the demonstration back end which exercises the front end but produces no translated output.	13,900	25,900
ixx	IDL parser generating C++ stubs, distributed as part of the Fresco library (which is part of X11R6). Although it performs a function similar to IDL, the program was developed independently and is structured differently.	11,600	11,900
lcom	optimizing compiler for a hardware description language developed at the University of Guelph.	14,100	16,200
porky	back-end optimizer that is part of the Stanford SUIF compiler system	22,900	41,100
richards	simple operating system simulator	500	1,100
troff	GNU groff version 1.09, a batch-style text formatting program	19,200	21,500

Table 3. Benchmark programs

Recall that "original" refers to programs compiled from the original sources, and "baseline" refers to the same programs compiled from the all-in-one source file without any inlining of virtual function calls. The latter versions are longer since they also contain system include files (/usr/include/...) and since the combiner pre-pass splits some constructs into multiple lines. For both versions, the line counts exclude empty lines, preprocessor commands, and comments.

In addition to measuring the unchanged programs, we also ran "all-virtual" versions of the benchmark programs where every function (with the exception of some operators and destructors, which currently cannot be optimized by our compiler) is declared as virtual. We chose to include these program versions in order to simulate programming styles that extensively use abstract base classes defining virtual functions only (C++'s way of defining interfaces). For example, the Taligent CommonPoint frameworks provide all functionality through virtual functions, and thus programs using CommonPoint (or similar frameworks) will exhibit much higher virtual function call frequencies [Ser95]. Lacking real, large, freely available examples of this programming style, we created the "all virtual" programs to provide some indication of how optimization would impact such programs.

program	classes	unmodified programs				"all-virtuals" programs			
		functions		virtual call sites		functions		virtual call sites	
		virtuals	nonvirt.	all	used	virtuals	nonvirt.[a]	all	used
deltablue	10	7	74	3	3	73	8	213	145
eqn	56	169	102	174	100	252	19	248	138
idl	82	374	450	1,248	578	675	149	2,095	786
ixx	90	445	582	596	147	994	33	3,026	824
lcom	72	314	508	460	309	594	228	1,214	825
porky	118	274	995	836	163	724	545	4,248	930
richards	12	5	61	1	1	66	0	105	100
troff	122	484	403	405	98	834	53	1172	351

Table 4. Basic characteristics of benchmark programs

[a] The compiler currently cannot optimize all operators and destructors, and thus they are kept nonvirtual. Furthermore, constructors are always nonvirtual.

For each program, Table 4 shows some basic program characteristics such as the number of classes, C++ functions (excluding constructors and non-member functions), and virtual function call sites. For the latter, "all" refers to the total number of virtual function call sites in the program, and "used" to those executed at least once during the test runs. The numbers given for the virtual call sites exclude the call sites that the GNU C++ 2.6.3 compiler can optimize away. All benchmarks were compiled with GNU C++ 2.6.3 with optimization flags "-O4 -msupersparc" and linked statically. The "all-virtual" versions of ixx, porky, and troff were compiled with the optimization flags "-O2 - msupersparc" since "-O4" compilation ran out of virtual memory. To measure execution performance, we ran each benchmark in single-user mode on an idle SPARCstation-10 workstation with a 40 MHz SuperSPARC processor and used the best of five runs. In addition to measuring actual execution time, we also simulated the programs with an instruction-level simulator to obtain precise instruction counts and cache miss data (simulating the SPARCstation-10 cache configuration[2]).

---

[2] 16Kbyte 4-way primary instruction cache, 20Kbyte 5-way data cache, and 1Mbyte unified direct-mapped secondary cache.

6 Results

This section presents the results of the empirical evaluation of our optimizing compiler. Unless mentioned otherwise, all numbers are dynamic, i.e., based on run-time frequencies.

6.1 Virtual Function Calls

Figure 3 shows that the optimizing compiler successfully removes many virtual function calls. Not surprisingly, the baseline programs execute the same number of virtual calls as the original programs: even though the back-end compiler has the entire program available at compile time, it cannot optimize virtual function calls. In contrast, type feedback is quite successful: on the large programs, it reduces the number of virtual calls by a factor of five (for idl, by a factor of 25). On some programs, however, type

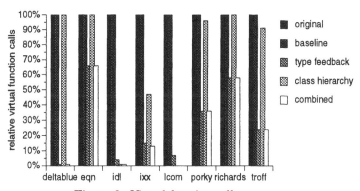

Figure 3. Virtual function calls

feedback performs relatively poorly. For richards, the reason is simple: this program contains only a single virtual function call whose receivers are fairly evenly spread over four classes. On eqn, type feedback removes less than half of the virtual function calls because some of the most frequently executed call sites are megamorphic, i.e., have many receiver classes (up to 17). Since no receiver class dominates these call sites, type feedback cannot eliminate the calls.

Class hierarchy analysis is much less successful: for many of the large programs, it fails to reduce the number of virtual calls appreciably, removing only a median of 4% of the calls (mean: 23%).[3] This poor performance surprised us since others have reported very good results for CHA [DGC95, Fer95]; at first, we suspected an implementation bug. However, many of our programs simply do not have enough monomorphic calls that could be optimized. For example, only 3% of the virtual function calls in eqn are from (dynamically) monomorphic call sites, and class hierarchy analysis can optimize only a single call site (a call to font::handle_unknown_font_command which is never executed). Before concluding that class hierarchy analysis is ineffective, the reader

---

[3] lcom cannot be optimized with class hierarchy analysis because it is not type-safe. The program contains assignments where the actual class is a superclass of the static type of the variable being assigned (i.e., a Base object is cast to Sub*). As a result, CHA incorrectly binds some virtual function calls whose receiver is incorrectly typed.

should keep in mind that its effectiveness depends on programming style. In particular, CHA performs better with programs using "interfaces" expressed as abstract classes containing only virtual functions (such as idl) because these programs contain many virtual functions with only a single implementation.

The combined system generally performs as well as type feedback. Currently, the combined system chooses class hierarchy analysis over type feedback when optimizing a call site: if the call can be statically bound, the compiler will not type-predict it. Though it may seem that this system should always perform at least as well as type feedback, this is not necessarily true. The reason is somewhat subtle: even though class hierarchy analysis can statically bind (and inline) a call, the inlined version cannot be specialized to a particular receiver class if several classes are possible (all of which inherit the same target method). In contrast, type feedback produces a specialized version of the method, possibly removing additional calls (with this as the receiver) within that method. However, this effect appears to be negligible—the combined system usually removes more calls than any other system.

Figure 4 shows the number of virtual function calls performed by the "all virtual" versions of the benchmark programs. As expected, all programs perform significantly more virtual function calls (a median of 5 times more). However, optimization still removes most of them, bringing the number of virtual calls to less than that of the original programs for all benchmarks except richards. Relative to the baseline, type feedback reduces virtual calls by a median factor of 8.5, and class hierarchy analysis reduces them by a factor of 12.6. We will discuss this result further in section 7.

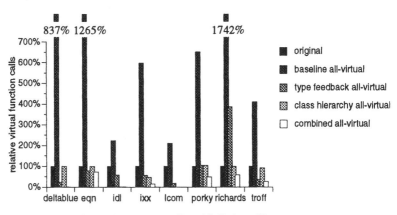

Figure 4. Virtual function calls of "allvirtual" programs

As a final remark, our implementations of both type feedback and class hierarchy analysis currently do not handle all virtual operators and virtual destructors, so that some calls are not optimized. Thus, our results are conservative estimates (lower bounds) on the achievable performance.

6.2 Performance

Ultimately, the main goal of optimization is to increase performance. Figure 5 shows the execution time of the various program versions relative to the execution time of the

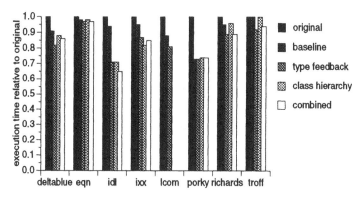

Figure 5. Execution time of optimized programs

original program. Overall, performance improves considerably relative to the original programs, with a median speedup of 18%. For all programs, type feedback or combined optimization produces the fastest executables whereas class hierarchy analysis does not significantly improve performance, which is not surprising given its ineffectiveness in removing virtual function calls. More surprisingly, about 40% of the speedup comes from combining all source files into a single file: the baseline programs run a median 6% faster than the original programs. Why?

The main reason for this speedup is the proper inlining of non-virtual inline functions in the baseline versions. Many C++ compilers (including GNU C++) do not inline function calls unless the inline function's definition is encountered before the call. In the original programs, function definitions often are not encountered in the correct order, and thus many calls to inline functions are not inlined. In contrast, our compiler topologically sorts all functions in the baseline versions so that all definitions precede their uses if possible (i.e., if there is no recursion).

We believe that our results are only a lower bound on the performance that could be achieved by a full-fledged optimizing compiler. Four factors contribute to our belief: the back-end compiler, hardware architecture, the set of optimizations our compiler performs, and our choice of benchmarks.

First, the current back-end compiler (GNU C++) does not take advantage of optimization opportunities exposed by inlining. In particular, it does not perform alias analysis, and thus it cannot remove redundant loads of instance variables and thus misses other opportunities for common subexpression elimination (including opportunities to CSE dispatch tests). We are planning to port our optimizer to other back-end compilers (Sun and IBM C++) to investigate the magnitude of this effect.

Second, our results may underestimate the performance impact on CPU architectures more advanced than the 3-year-old SuperSPARC chip used for our measurements. In particular, more aggressively pipelined superscalar CPUs are likely to benefit more from virtual call elimination since the cost of indirect calls tends to increase on such architectures [DHV95]. In fact, this trend is already visible on the SuperSPARC: whereas type feedback reduces the number of instructions executed by a median of only

5%, it reduces execution time by 16%. Clearly, optimization improves the effectiveness of superscalar issue and pipelining. Although further research is needed to resolve this question, we expect the speedups achieved by our system to increase on more recent processors like the UltraSPARC or the Intel P6 (Pentium Pro).

Third, type feedback could be complemented with additional optimizations to improve performance further. In particular, profile-based customization and some form of splitting [CU90] are attractive candidates, although the latter might not be needed if the back-end C++ compiler did a better job of alias analysis.

Finally, some of our benchmarks just don't execute that many virtual function calls to start with. Figure 6 shows that, as expected, speedups correlate well with call frequency: the more frequently a program uses virtual function calls, the better it is optimized. Several of our benchmark programs have a low virtual call frequency; for example, on average eqn executes 972 instructions between virtual function calls. We believe that such infrequent use of virtual calls is atypical of current and future C++ programs. In particular, the use of abstract classes as interfaces in application frameworks is becoming increasingly common and will drive up virtual function call frequencies. Unfortunately, we have been unable to find many publicly available programs exhibiting this programming style; the idl benchmark probably comes closest.

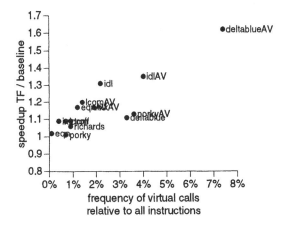

Figure 6. Correlation between call frequency and speedup

Figure 7 shows the performance of the "all-virtual" versions. In one group of programs (deltablue, idl, richards, troff), virtual function calls become much more frequent, and as a result the optimized programs achieve higher speedups. In the other group, the call frequency does not change significantly, and thus program behavior remains unchanged. Overall, the speedup of type feedback increases to 26%.

To summarize, despite the relatively low frequency of virtual calls in the benchmarks, our optimizing compiler demonstrates the value of OO-specific optimization for C++ programs, speeding up a set of realistic applications by a median of 18%. Moreover, with a better back-end compiler or on more recent processors, this speedup is likely to increase even further.

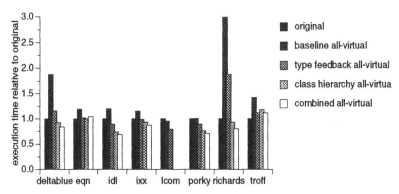

Figure 7. Execution time of "allvirtual" programs

6.3 Program Size

Inlining duplicates some code for better performance; Figure 8 shows the size of the programs before and after optimization. Program size was measured as the size of the text segment (i.e., instructions only, no data) of the dynamically-linked executables, excluding library code. Overall, code size barely increases with optimization; programs optimized with type feedback are a median 8% larger than the original programs and 3% larger than the baseline programs.

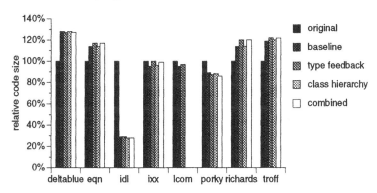

Figure 8. Code size

One program, idl, clearly sticks out: in its unoptimized form (baseline), it is three times smaller than the original program. The reason is simple: in the original program, the compiler generates multiple copies of inline functions, one per .C file that uses them. As a result, many inline functions are replicated 20 or more times. This problem still is a common problem with C++ compilers. Typically, compilers use a heuristic to decide when to generate a copy; since idl was written using a different compiler, it does not match GNU's heuristics. In the baseline version, of course, no duplication can occur since a single file contains the entire program.

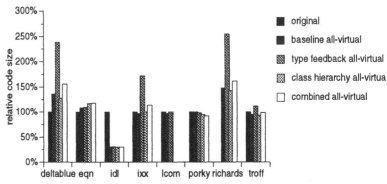

Figure 9. Code size of "allvirtual" programs

In the "all virtual" programs, code size increases more strongly (Figure 9), especially with type feedback in the small programs (richards and deltablue). However, the median increase for type feedback is only 11%.

Why doesn't inlining lead to larger code size increases? Recall that the compiler only optimizes call sites contributing more than 0.1% of the total calls in the program (section 4.6). This heuristic is responsible for keeping the code size small; without it, executables would have increased by a median of 23% (for the standard benchmarks) and 144% (all-virtual versions), respectively.

6.4 Instruction Cache Misses

The main time cost of larger executables lies in the increased instruction cache misses that larger programs can cause. Figure 10 shows the instruction cache misses incurred by the optimized programs on a SPARCstation-10. Overall, differences are small; for some programs, cache misses actually decrease slightly compared to the original programs (richards' miss ratio is virtually zero because it fits entirely into the cache). The major exception is troff, where misses increase by 35% over the original program when using type feedback. However, cache misses increase much less (10%) relative to the baseline program, indicating that the additional misses may be caused by different relative code placement (i.e., conflict misses) rather than by a systematic effect (i.e.,

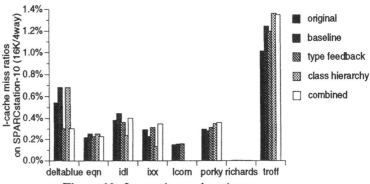

Figure 10. Instruction cache misses

capacity misses). deltablue experiences a significant drop in its miss ratios from 0.68% in the baseline to 0.31% with type feedback even though its size doesn't change much (see Figure 8). A separate simulation (modelling a 32-way associative cache of the same size as the standard 4-way associative cache) showed little variation between the various systems, confirming that indeed the differences in cache performance are caused by different code placement, i.e., are unrelated to the actual optimizations. Thus, our data show little significant difference in cache behavior between the optimized and original programs.[4]

6.5 Influence of Inlining Strategies

Figure 11 shows the average of the four performance characteristics (time, virtual calls, size, and cache misses) as a function of the inlining threshold. Recall from section 4.6 that the compiler inlines a virtual call only if the most frequent case exceeds a certain

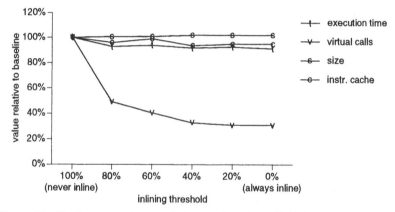

Figure 11. Performance characteristics as a function of inlining threshold (averages over all programs)

threshold. For example, the data points at x = 40% in Figure 11 represent the average performance of programs compiled with a threshold of 40%. In general, the lower the threshold, the more inlining the compiler performs, and the larger the optimized executables become. For the programs in our benchmark suite, the "sweet spot" appears to be near a threshold value of 40%; below that, there is little improvement in performance. For that reason, we chose 40% as the default threshold in our compiler even though a lower value could have improved performance slightly.

7 Discussion

One of the unintended effects of language implementations is that they can shape programming style. If a certain language construct is implemented inefficiently, programmers will tend to avoid it. Optimization of virtual function calls effectively lowers their average cost, and thus might change the way typical C++ programs are written. Figure 12 compares the original programs against the best optimized version

---

[4] We omit the cache data for the "all virtual" programs since they show similar effects.

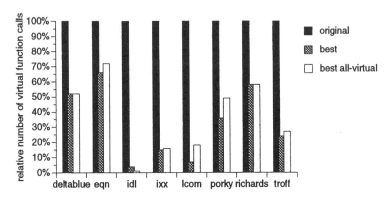

Figure 12. Virtual function calls

(usually compiled by the "combined" system) and shows that optimization indeed enables the programmer to use virtual function calls more liberally: for each of the benchmarks, optimization significantly lowers the number of virtual function calls actually executed at run time. Even the "all virtual" programs, which in their unoptimized form execute five times *more* virtual function calls than the original programs, perform a median of four times *fewer* calls when optimized. Similarly, almost all optimized programs, even the "all virtual" versions, execute faster than the original programs compiled with conventional optimization (Figure 13).

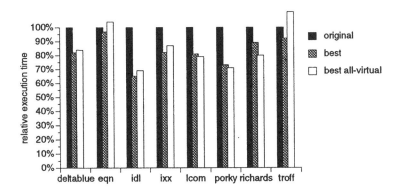

Figure 13. Execution time

In other words, even if the authors of these programs used virtual functions much more liberally (e.g., in order to make their programs more flexible and extensible), they would not have been penalized by inferior performance.

8   Future Work

Several areas for future work remain. First, we would like to investigate the impact of back-end optimizer quality by porting our compiler to another back-end C++ compiler that performs more optimizations. As mentioned above, we believe that a stronger back end would increase the performance gap between the original and optimized programs, but further measurements are needed to substantiate this hypothesis.

The compiler's inlining strategies could also be improved. Inlining should probably take into account the size of the inlinee [Höl94], and the compiler should estimate how much the inlinee's code can be simplified (i.e., because of constant arguments [DC94]). Furthermore, type feedback could be extended with profile-driven customization to further improve performance [DCG95]. Profiling could be extended to use k-CCP profiles (i.e., take call chains into account), although the improvement from the additional precision may be small [G+95].

Also, a more detailed investigation of the interaction of optimization with superscalar architectures is needed. Modern processors are increasingly deeply pipelined, contain multiple execution units, and can execute instructions out-of-order or speculatively. All of these features can significantly impact performance, and further study is needed to determine their impact on the performance of object-oriented programs.

Finally, we will continue to look for other C++ applications that can be used for benchmarking. Although we are already using large programs totalling over 90,000 lines of code, we feel that currently available benchmarks (including those used in other studies [CGZ94]) do not represent the entire spectrum of program characteristics. In particular, programs using large class libraries and frameworks are underrepresented. Fortunately, these programs are very likely to benefit even more from optimization (as discussed in section 6.2), and thus this underrepresentation does not invalidate the results of our study.

9   Conclusions

We have designed and implemented an optimizing source-to-source C++ compiler. To the best of our knowledge, this compiler is the first C++ compiler that can reduce the frequency of virtual function calls. Our prototype implementation demonstrates the value of profile-driven optimization for statically-typed, hybrid object-oriented languages like C++. Using a suite of large C++ applications totalling over 90,000 lines of code, we have evaluated the compiler's effectiveness. Despite some limitations of our system, and despite the low frequency of virtual function calls in some of the programs, optimization improves the performance of these C++ applications by up to 40% over the original programs (median: 18%) and reduces the number of virtual function calls by a median factor of five. For "all-virtuals" versions of the same programs, performance improved by a median of 26% and the number of virtual calls dropped by a factor of more than 17.

Our measurements produced some surprising results:

- On the original programs (but not on the "all-virtuals" programs, we found that class hierarchy analysis was ineffective in removing virtual function calls (removing a median of 4% and an average of 23% of the calls), contrary to the results previously published for Modula-2 programs [Fer95] or the pure object-oriented language Cecil [DGC95].

- Inlining does not significantly increase code size. On average, optimized programs only expand by 9%. Moreover, this code expansion does not impact performance much; for most programs, the instruction cache miss ratio does not increase significantly, and for some programs it even decreases.

We believe that our results underestimate the performance gains that could be obtained with a production-quality compiler. In other words, we believe that typical C++ programs can be sped up by more than the 18% improvement seen here. Several reasons lead us to this conviction:

- Our compiler uses source-to-source optimization for simplicity, which to some extent negatively impacts the quality of the generated code since the front-end cannot communicate all its information to the back end. Furthermore, our current back end (GNU C++) does not remove some of the redundancies exposed by inlining. In particular, better alias analysis could help remove redundant loads and type tests.
- The hardware platform used in our measurements (a SuperSPARC processor) probably benefits less from optimization than more recent aggressively pipelined processors. (This question remains an area for future study, however.)
- Several of our benchmark programs have a low virtual function call frequency and thus benefit less from optimization. Programs using abstract base classes may be significantly more amenable to optimization since they will use virtual function calls more frequently.

If these optimizations are integrated into production compilers, programmers therefore can hope to see even better speedups on typical programs.

Finally (and perhaps most importantly), our results show that programmers may use virtual functions much more liberally in order to make their programs more flexible and extensible without being penalized by inferior performance.

Acknowledgments: This work was supported in part by MICRO Grant 95-077, IBM Corporation, and Sun Microsystems. The first author was partially supported by a Kurt Gödel Fellowship. We would like to thank Jerry Schwarz for making the CCAuditor parser available to us and for answering our many questions. Finally, thanks to Ole Agesen, Lars Bak, Karel Driesen, Robert Griesemer, David F. Bacon, Jeff Dean, and Dave Grove for their comments on earlier versions of this paper.

References

[Age95]   Ole Agesen. The Cartesian Product Algorithm: Simple and Precise Type Inference of Parametric Polymorphism. In *ECOOP'95, Ninth European Conference on Object-Oriented Programming*, p. 2-26, Århus, Denmark, August 1995. Springer-Verlag LNCS 952.

[AH95]   Ole Agesen and Urs Hölzle. Type Feedback vs. Concrete Type Inference: A Comparison of Optimization Techniques for Object-Oriented Languages. In *OOPSLA'95, Object-Oriented Programming Systems, Languages and Applications*, p. 91-107, Austin, TX, October 1995.

[App88]   Apple Computer, Inc. *Object Pascal User's Manual*. Cupertino, 1988.

[B+96]   David Bernstein, Yaroslav Fedorov, Sara Porat, Joseph Rodrigue, and Eran Yahav. Compiler Optimization of C++ Virtual Function Calls. *2nd Conference on Object-Oriented Technologies and Systems*, Toronto, Canada, June 1996.

[CGZ94]   Brad Calder, Dirk Grunwald, and Benjamin Zorn. Quantifying Behavioral Differences Between C and C++ Programs. *Journal of Programming Languages* 2:313-351, 1994.

[CG94]   Brad Calder and Dirk Grunwald. Reducing Indirect Function Call Overhead in C++ Programs. In *21st Annual ACM Symposium on Principles of Programming Languages*, p. 397-408, January 1994.

[CUL89]   Craig Chambers, David Ungar, and Elgin Lee. An Efficient Implementation of SELF, a Dynamically-Typed Object-Oriented Language Based on Prototypes. In *OOPSLA '89, Object-Oriented Programming Systems, Languages and Applications*, p. 49-70, New Orleans, LA, October 1989. Published as *SIGPLAN Notices 24(10)*, October 1989.

[CU90]   Craig Chambers and David Ungar. Iterative Type Analysis and Extended Message Splitting: Optimizing Dynamically-Typed Object-Oriented Programs. In *Proceedings of the SIGPLAN '90 Conference on Programming Language Design and Implementation*, p. 150-164, White Plains, NY, June 1990. Published as *SIGPLAN Notices 25(6)*, June 1990.

[CM+92]   Pohua P. Chang, Scott A. Mahlke, William Y. Chen, and Wen-Mei W. Hwu. Profile-guided automatic inline expansion for C programs. *Software—Practice and Experience* 22 (5): 349-369, May 1992.

[CHT91]   K. D. Cooper, M. W. Hall, and L. Torczon. An experiment with inline substitution. *Software—Practice and Experience* 21 (6): 581-601, June 1991.

[DH88]   Jack W. Davidson and Anne M. Holler. A study of a C function inliner. *Software—Practice and Experience* 18(8): 775-90, August 1988.

[DC94]   Jeffrey Dean and Craig Chambers. Towards Better Inlining Decisions using Inlining Trials. In *Proceedings of the ACM Symposium on Lisp and Functional Programming Languages (LFP '94)*, Orlando, FL, June 1994.

[DCG95]   Jeffrey Dean, Craig Chambers, and David Grove. Identifying Profitable Specialization in Object-Oriented Languages. In *Proceedings of the SIGPLAN '95 Conference on Programming Language Design and Implementation*, La Jolla, CA June 1995.

[DGC95]   Jeffrey Dean, David Grove, and Craig Chambers. *Optimization of Object-Oriented Programs Using Static Class Hierarchy Analysis*. In *ECOOP '95, Ninth European Conference on Object-Oriented Programming*, Århus, 1995. Springer-Verlag LNCS 952.

[Dea95]   Jeffrey Dean. Corrected Cecil performance numbers. Private communication, May 1995.

[Dec95]   Declarative Systems. The C++ Auditor. Palo Alto, 1995. (auditor@declarative.com)

[DHV95]   Karel Driesen, Urs Hölzle, and Jan Vitek. Message Dispatch On Pipelined Processors. *ECOOP '95 Conference Proceedings*, Aarhus, Denmark, August 1995. Published as *Springer Verlag Lecture Notes in Computer Science 952*, Springer Verlag, Berlin, 1995.

[DS84]   L. Peter Deutsch and Alan Schiffman. Efficient Implementation of the Smalltalk-80 System. In *Conference Record of the Eleventh Annual ACM Symposium on Principles of Programming Languages*, p. 297-302, Salt Lake City, UT, January 1984.

[Deu83]   L. Peter Deutsch. Reusability in the Smalltalk-80 system. *Workshop On Reusability In Programming*, Newport, RI, 1983.

[ES90]   Margaret A. Ellis and Bjarne Stroustrup. *The Annotated C++ Reference Manual.* Addison-Wesley, Reading, MA, 1990.

[Fer95]   M. F. Fernandez. Simple and effective link-time optimization of Modula-3 programs. In *Proceedings of the SIGPLAN '95 Conference on Programming Language Design and Implementation*, p. 103-115, La Jolla, CA, June 1995. Published as *SIGPLAN Notices 30(6)*, June 1995.

[G+95]   David Grove, Jeffrey Dean, Charles D. Garrett, and Craig Chambers. Profile-Guided Receiver Class Prediction. In *OOPSLA '95, Object-Oriented Programming Systems, Languages and Applications*, p. 108-123, Austin, TX, October 1995.

[Hall91]   Mary Wolcott Hall. *Managing Interprocedural Optimization.* Technical Report COMP TR91-157 (Ph.D. Thesis), Computer Science Department, Rice University, April 1991.

[HCU91]   Urs Hölzle, Craig Chambers, and David Ungar. Optimizing Dynamically-Typed Object-Oriented Languages with Polymorphic Inline Caches. In *ECOOP '91, Fourth European Conference on Object-Oriented Programming*, p. 21-38, Geneva, July 1991. Springer-Verlag LNCS 512.

[Höl94]   Urs Hölzle. *Adaptive Optimization for SELF: Reconciling High Performance with Exploratory Programming.* Ph.D. Thesis, Department of Computer Science, Stanford University, August 1994. (Available via http://www.cs.ucsb.edu/~urs.)

[HU94a]   Urs Hölzle and David Ungar. Optimizing Dynamically-Dispatched Calls with Run-Time Type Feedback. In *Proceedings of the SIGPLAN '94 Conference on Programming Language Design and Implementation*, p. 326-336. Published as *SIGPLAN Notices 29(6)*, June 1994.

[HwC89]   W. W. Hwu and P. P. Chang. Inline function expansion for compiling C programs. In *Proceedings of the SIGPLAN '89 Conference on Programming Language Design and Implementation*, p. 246-57, Portland, OR, June 1989. Published as *SIGPLAN Notices 24(7)*, July 1989.

[Knu70]   Donald Knuth. *An empirical study of FORTRAN programs.* Technical Report CS-186, Department of Computer Science, Stanford University, 1970.

[Lea90]   Douglas Lea. Customization in C++. In *Proceedings of the 1990 Usenix C++ Conference*, p. 301-314, San Francisco, CA, April, 1990.

[PR94]   Hemant D. Pande and Barbara G. Ryder. *Static Type Determination and Aliasing for C++.* Technical Report LCSR-TR-236, Rutgers University, December 1994.

[PC94]   John B. Plevyak and Andrew A. Chien. Precise Concrete Type Inference for Object-Oriented Languages. *OOPSLA '94, Object-Oriented Programming Systems, Languages and Applications*, p. 324-340, Portland, OR, October 1994. Published as *SIGPLAN Notices 29(10)*, October 1994.

[Ser95]   Mauricio Serrano. *Virtual function call frequencies in C++ programs.* Private communication, 1995.

[SW92]   Amitabh Srivastava and David Wall. *A Practical System for Intermodule Code Optimization at Link-Time.* DEC WRL Research Report 92/6, December 1992.

[US87]   David Ungar and Randall B. Smith. SELF: The Power of Simplicity. In *OOPSLA '87, Object-Oriented Programming Systems, Languages and Applications*, p. 227-241, Orlando, FL, October 1987. Published as *SIGPLAN Notices 22(12)*, December 1987. Also published in *Lisp and Symbolic Computation 4(3)*, Kluwer Academic Publishers, June 1991.

[Wall91]   David Wall. Predicting Program Behavior Using Real or Estimated Profiles. In *Proceedings of the SIGPLAN '91 Conference on Programming Language Design and Implementation*, p. 59-70, Toronto, Canada, June 1991. Published as *SIGPLAN Notices 26(6)*, June 1991.

Supporting Explicit Disambiguation of Multi-methods

Eric Amiel[1] and Eric Dujardin[2]

[1] NatSoft, Air Center,
1214 Genève, Suisse
E-mail:amiel@rodin.inria.fr
[2] INRIA, Projet RODIN, BP 105,
78153 Le Chesnay Cedex, France
E-mail:eric.dujardin@inria.fr

Abstract. Multiple inheritance and multiple dispatching are two sources of ambiguities in object-oriented languages. Solving ambiguities can be performed automatically, using techniques such as totally ordering the supertypes of each type or taking the order of the methods' arguments into account. Such implicit disambiguation has the drawback of being difficult to understand by the programmer and hiding programming errors. Conversely, solving ambiguities can be left up to the explicit intervention of the programmer. The most common explicit disambiguation technique in existing systems consists in defining new methods for ambiguous invocations. However, finding ambiguities and adding as few methods as possible is a difficult task, especially in multi-method systems. In this paper, we propose a tool to help the programmer solve multi-methods ambiguities. We show that there always exists a unique minimal set of method redefinitions that explicitly disambiguate a set of multi-methods. The tool offers two modes: batch, directly yielding the disambiguation set, or interactive, one signature of the disambiguation set at a time, allowing the programmer to either accept the method redefinition or to solve the ambiguity in any other way, which restarts the disambiguation algorithm. In both modes, for each method that is to be added, the programmer is given the set of methods that caused the ambiguity as an explanation.

Keywords: method dispatch, multi-methods, multiple inheritance, ambiguities.

1   Introduction

Ambiguities are a well-known problem of any classification system supporting multiple inheritance. They plague semantic networks in artificial intelligence as well as class hierarchies in many object-oriented languages. Multiple inheritance ambiguities occur when it is impossible to decide from which superclass to inherit a property, i.e. an instance variable or a method. Consider a class hierarchy where class *TeachingAssistant (TA)* is a subtype[3] of two superclasses *Student* and *Employee* and has one subclass *ForeignTA*. Assume that both

---

[3] In this paper, we indifferently use *subtyping* and *inheritance*, *class* and *type*, although we are primarily interested in the *typing* aspects.

Student and *Employee* define a method *vacation*[4] which computes the number of days of vacation. Then, any invocation of *vacation* on a *TA* or *ForeignTA* is ambiguous, as it is impossible to know which method must be called, *Student*'s or *Employee*'s *vacation*.

Multi-methods add another kind of ambiguity. Indeed, run-time method selection looks for the method whose arguments most closely match those of the invocation. Ambiguities may arise if two methods most closely match different subsets of an invocation's arguments. Consider the above class hierarchy with two multi-methods $m_1(TA, Student)$ and $m_2(Student, TA)$ and invocation $m(aTA, aTA)$. With respect to the first argument, m_1 is a closer match than m_2, while the reverse holds for the second argument. Thus, the invocation $m(aTA, aTA)$ is ambiguous, as are all invocations whose arguments are of class *TA* or *ForeignTA*.

There are two ways to eliminate ambiguities: *implicit* and *explicit* disambiguation. Implicit disambiguation consists in *automatically* solving ambiguities *in the place* of the programmer. For example, CLOS defines a total order on all the superclasses of each class to eliminate multiple inheritance ambiguities [BDG+88]. In the above example, if *Student* precedes *Employee* in *TA*'s definition, then invoking *vacation* on a *TA* results in the invocation of the *vacation* method of *Student*. Implicit disambiguation of multi-methods ambiguities is based on taking the order of the arguments into account: in this way, $m_1(TA, Student)$ is a closer match than $m_2(Student, TA)$, because its first argument is more specific than m_2's.

Explicit disambiguation, used in languages like C++ [ES92], Eiffel [Mey92] and Cecil [Cha93], consists in requiring *the programmer* to solve ambiguities. One way of achieving this consists in *redefining* the method for ambiguous invocations. For example, if the programmer redefines *vacation* for *TA*, invoking *vacation* on a *TA* is no longer ambiguous. Note that this redefinition also solves ambiguities for *ForeignTA*. In the same way, defining a method $m_3(TA, TA)$ solves the multiple dispatching ambiguity between m_1 and m_2 for all invocations with arguments of class *TA* or *ForeignTA*.

Implicit disambiguation is increasingly being criticized for mainly two reasons: first, the way it solves ambiguities can be difficult to understand and counter-intuitive in some cases. This is particularly obvious for multiple dispatching ambiguities where the order of the arguments is taken into account. Second, ambiguities can actually reveal programming errors, which implicit disambiguation hides.

On the other hand, explicit disambiguation imposes some burden on the programmer who faces two problems: first, (s)he must find which methods are ambiguous and with respect to which class(es) of argument(s). Second, (s)he must determine which methods must be added. Indeed, if carefully chosen, very few method redefinitions can solve all ambiguities at the same time. However, adding a method to solve an ambiguity may sometimes result

---

[4] For the rest of the paper we consider ambiguous methods as they capture the case of instance variables through encapsulation.

in the creation of a new ambiguity. Unfortunately, to our knowledge, no system assists the programmer in the task of explicit disambiguation. Such help is especially needed for multi-method systems, notably because multi-methods are more complex to master than mono-methods and suffer from two kinds of ambiguities, increasing the potential number of ambiguities.

In this paper, we address this need by proposing a tool to help the programmer solve multi-methods ambiguities. We show that there always exists a unique minimal set of method redefinitions that explicitly disambiguate a set of multi-methods. The tool offers two modes: batch, directly yielding the disambiguation set, or interactive, one signature of the disambiguation set at a time, allowing the programmer to either accept the method redefinition or to solve the ambiguity in any other way, which restarts the disambiguation algorithm. In both modes, for each method that is to be added, the programmer is given the set of methods that caused the ambiguity as an explanation. In our example, the tool outputs *vacation(TA)*[5] as the method that must be added and { *vacation(Student)*, *vacation(Employee)* } as the explanation.

The paper is organized as follows. Section 2 surveys previous work on ambiguities. Section 3 defines the problem we address and gives an overview of our solution. Section 4 presents our disambiguation algorithm. Section 5 deals with implementation issues, notably optimization and complexity. We conclude with future work in section 6.

2 Background on Disambiguation

2.1 Basic Definitions

In traditional object-oriented systems, methods have a single specially designated argument – called the *receiver* or *target* – whose run-time type is used to select the method to execute at run-time. Such methods are called *mono-methods*. *Multi-methods*, first introduced in CommonLoops [BKK+86] and CLOS [BDG+88], generalize mono-methods by considering that all arguments are targets. Multi-methods are now a key feature of several systems such as Kea [MHH91], Cecil [Cha92], Polyglot [DCL+93], and Dylan [App95]. Following [ADL91], we denote *subtyping* by $\preceq$. Given two types T_1 and T_2, if $T_1 \preceq T_2$, we say that T_1 is a subtype of T_2 and T_2 is a supertype of T_1.

A generic function is defined by its name and its arity (in Smalltalk parlance, a generic function is called a *selector*). To each generic function m of arity n corresponds a set of methods $m_k(T_k^1, \ldots, T_k^n) \to R_k$, where T_k^i is the type of the ith formal argument, and where R_k is the type of the result. We call the list of argument types $(T_k^1, \ldots, T_k^n)$ of method m_k the *signature* of m_k[6]. An invocation of a generic function m is denoted $m(T^1, ..., T^n)$,

---

[5] For the rest of the paper, we use the functional notation as we consider multi-method systems.

[6] For our purposes, we do not include the return type in the signature.

where $(T^1, \ldots, T^n)$ is the signature of the invocation, and the T^i's represent the types of the expressions passed as arguments. Finally, we call *MSA method* for *Most Specific Applicable* method, the method selected at run-time for some invocation.

2.2 Method Ordering and Ambiguity

The basis of method specificity is a precedence relationship called *argument subtype precedence* in [ADL91]: a method m_i is more specific than a method m_j, noted $m_i \prec m_j$, if all the arguments of m_i are subtypes of the arguments of m_j. However, in the presence of multiple inheritance or multiple dispatching, argument subtype precedence may be unable to totally order applicable methods for some invocations, yielding several *conflicting* MSA methods. Such invocations are then *ambiguous*.

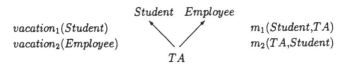

$vacation_1(Student)$ $m_1(Student, TA)$
$vacation_2(Employee)$ $m_2(TA, Student)$

Multiple Inheritance Ambiguity Multiple Dispatching Ambiguity

Fig. 1.: Ambiguities

Example 1. Consider the type hierarchy and methods of Figure 1. Argument subtype precedence can order neither $vacation_2$ w.r.t. $vacation_1$ (multiple inheritance ambiguity), nor m_2 w.r.t. m_1 (multiple dispatching ambiguity). Thus, invocations $vacation(aTA, aTA)$ and $m(aTA, aTA)$ are ambiguous.

2.3 Disambiguation Techniques

As noted in [Cha92], "the key distinguishing characteristic of method lookup (...) is how exactly ambiguities are resolved". Techniques to solve ambiguities can be classified in two categories: *implicit* and *explicit* disambiguation.

Implicit Disambiguation Implicit disambiguation consists in augmenting the power of argument subtype precedence to automatically resolve ambiguities. To solve multiple inheritance ambiguities, the subtype relationship, $\preceq$, is complemented by a precedence relationship, α, that strictly orders all the supertypes of a type. The supertypes ordering is generally local to each type (local supertypes precedence) as in Loops [SB86], CommonLoops [BKK+86], Flavors [Moo86], Orion [BKKK87] and CLOS [BDG+88]. To solve multiple dispatching ambiguities, the formal arguments of the rival methods are examined in some given order, e.g. left-to-right, and the comparison stops as soon as an argument of one method strictly precedes the corresponding argument of the other method. [ADL91] extensively covers the different ways to augment argument subtype precedence to avoid ambiguities.

Example 2. Assume local supertype precedence establishes that *Student α Employee* and left-to-right argument examination is chosen. Then, the ambiguities of Figure 1 are resolved and $vacation_1$ has precedence over $vacation_2$ and m_2 has precedence over m_1.

Note that dispatch based on a local supertypes precedence ordering of methods may select a method in an counter-intuitive way. Indeed, CLOS, Loops and Dylan do not support *monotonicity* [DHHM92]. Monotonicity captures the intuitive property that, if a method is applicable to, but is not the most specific applicable method for some signature, it cannot be the MSA of a more specific signature. To address the anomalies created by local supertypes precedence, [DHHM94] proposes a *monotonous* supertypes linearization algorithm. However, in some inheritance hierarchies there are classes for which no monotonous linearization exist.

C++ [ES92] implicitly solves some multiple inheritance ambiguities by using the static type of the receiver object: the inheritance path between the corresponding class, and the class of the receiver at run-time, takes precedence.

Example 3. Consider the example in Figure 2 and a C++ invocation b->$m()$, where b is a variable of type $B*$. If b points to an instance of class E at run-time, then m_2 takes precedence. However, invocation e->$m()$, where e is of type $E*$, is still ambiguous.

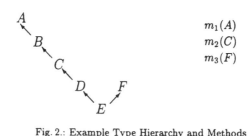

Fig. 2.: Example Type Hierarchy and Methods

This disambiguation scheme also appears in [CG90] with the *points of view*, in Fibonacci [ABGO93] with its *roles*, in O_2 [O₂92] and in Self 2.0 with its *sender path tiebraker rule* [CUCH91]. However, these techniques cannot resolve all ambiguities (e.g. the invocation e->$m()$ above), and they go against the need to "ensure that the same function is called for an object independently of the expression used to access the object", as stated in [ES92].

As argued in [LR89], [Sny86b], [DH89] and [Cha92], implicitly solving ambiguities raises several serious problems. First, ambiguities may be the result of programming errors. Implicit disambiguation prevents the detection of such errors. Second, it makes programs hard to understand, maintain and evolve. This is particularly obvious for multiple dispatching ambiguities where the order of the arguments is taken into account. Third, they cannot resolve all ambiguities, except the algorithms of Loops and CLOS, which trade this for counter-intuitive selections. Finally, there are ambiguities that implicit disambiguation cannot resolve according to the programmer's wish, because it is not fine enough.

Example 4. Consider the type hierarchy and methods of Figure 3. Assume the programmer would like *vacation₁(Student)* to be the MSA method for ambiguous invocation *vacation* *(aTA)* and *taxes₂(Employee)* to be the MSA method for ambiguous invocation *taxes(aTA)*. Such disambiguation cannot be automatically performed by ordering supertypes *Student* and *Employee*.

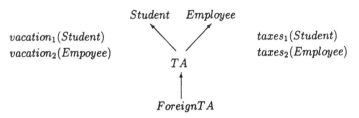

Fig. 3.: Example Type Hierarchy and Methods

Explicit Disambiguation The second way of solving ambiguities is *explicit disambiguation*. In this approach, the programmer him/herself solves ambiguities at the level of either *invocations* or *methods*.

Explicit Disambiguation at the Invocation Level

In C++, multiple inheritance ambiguities can be resolved on a per invocation basis and in two different ways. First, the programmer can explicitly force a particular method to be the MSA method for some invocation by prefixing the invocation by the name of a class followed by the *scoping* operator "::". The MSA method for the invocation is then *statically* determined to be the MSA method for that class, bypassing late binding.

Example 5. Consider the type hierarchy of Figure 2. The C++ invocation e->$m()$, where e is of type $E*$, is ambiguous. The programmer can resolve the ambiguity by writing e->$B :: m()$. This statically binds the invocation to the method applicable to class B, namely the method defined in class A.

Type casting, i.e. type coercion, is the second way of explicitly resolving ambiguities at the invocation level in C++. Contrary to the scoping operator, type casting preserves late binding.

Example 6. Consider again the type hierarchy of Figure 2. The programmer can resolve the ambiguous invocation e->$m()$ by writing $((B*)e)$->$m()$, making use of the implicit disambiguation rule described above. This forces e to be considered as referring to the B part of an E object. Late binding is preserved: the method that actually gets executed is the one defined in class C.

Explicit disambiguation at the invocation level provides the finest control over ambiguities. However, it imposes a heavy burden on the programmer who must disambiguate every ambiguous invocation. Moreover, the scoping operator suspends late binding. This can be dangerous when the type hierarchy or the methods evolve:

Example 7. Consider again the type hierarchy of Figure 2. If the programmer disambiguates invocation $e->m()$ by writing $e->C :: m()$ and then, a new method is defined in class D, then the disambiguation must be rewritten $e->D :: m()$.

Explicit Disambiguation at the Method Level

A programmer can perform explicit disambiguation of methods by either *selecting* or *adding* methods. Method selection consists in explicitly declaring which of the conflicting methods takes precedence *for all invocations*. It is supported in Traits [CBLL82], Trellis [SCB+86] and CommonObject [Sny86a]. Eiffel [Mey92] performs method selection by either *renaming* all conflicting methods but one and using a "select" statement or *undefining* all conflicting methods but one. O_2 [$O_2$92] automatically performs renaming of conflicting methods by prefixing them with the name of the class.

The second way of performing explicit disambiguation at the method level consists in *adding* new methods so that argument subtype precedence is sufficient to totally order applicable methods for any invocation. The augmented set of methods then satisfies a condition, described in [LR89], and called *regularity* in [MGS89] and Zelig [DS92], and *consistency* in Cecil [Cha93]. This disambiguation policy is used in Extended Smalltalk [BI82], Zelig [DS92], Self 3.0 [ABC+93], Laure [CP93] and Cecil [Cha93].

Example 8. Consider again the type hierarchy and methods of Figure 1. To eliminate ambiguities, it is enough to define two new methods: $vacation_3(TA)$ and $m_3(TA, TA)$.

The new methods may perform specific code written by the programer or deduced from the code of the conflicting methods as in Laure [CP93]. These new methods may also just serve the purpose of resolving an ambiguity, by explicitly calling another method of the same generic function using a scoping operator like Cecil's "@@" or C++'s "::", or a special construct like "*call-method*" in CommonObject.

Example 9. Cecil [Cha92] has the *resend* construct to explicitly call another method of the same generic function. Given the type hierarchy and methods of Figure 1, $vacation_3(TA)$ can resolve the ambiguity in favor of $vacation_1(Student)$ as follows:

```
method vacation(c1@@TA) { resend(c1@@Student) }
```

As shown in Example 7, it is dangerous to suspend late binding like that. It would not be suspended if the semantics of the declaration above was to invoke the MSA method of the invocation $vacation(Student)$.

Methods selection declarations must be taken into account in the late binding mechanism, making it more complex. Explicit disambiguation by addition of methods encompasses the functionality of explicit disambiguation by selection without making it necessary to incorporate the selection declarations in the late binding mechanism.

2.4 Conclusion

From some recent language updates, it appears that language designers increasingly favor explicit disambiguation, because of the problems associated with implicit disambiguation. For example, Self 3.0 [Se393] has abandoned *prioritized inheritance*, a kind of local supertypes precedence, together with the sender path tiebraker implicit disambiguation rule. The priority mechanism is described as being "of limited use, and had the potential for obscure errors". Cecil does not include implicit disambiguation either. In Dylan, the linear ordering of supertypes is similar to CLOS's, but Dylan does not assume any order on the multi-method's arguments, leaving room for multiple dispatching ambiguities and requiring explicit disambiguation.

Besides, even in languages with implicit disambiguation, solving ambiguities explicitly is useful in cases where implicit disambiguation leads to violate monotonicity.

3 Problem Statement and Overview of the Solution

The problem with explicit disambiguation is the burden it imposes on the programmer who faces two problems: first, (s)he must find which methods are ambiguous for which signature(s). Second, (s)he must determine which methods must be added to solve the ambiguities. An obvious solution is to define a method for each and every ambiguous signature. However, this results in the creation of a potentially huge number of disambiguating methods, whereas carefully choosing for which signatures to redefine methods can solve several or even all ambiguities at the same time. Consider the type hierarchy and methods of Figure 4. Signatures $(D,G),(D,I),(K,G),(K,I)$ are ambiguous because of methods $m_1(A,G)$ and $m_2(B,F)$. However, defining a method $m_4(D,G)$ is enough to solve these four ambiguities.

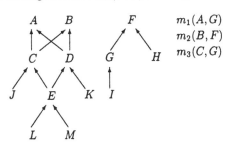

Fig. 4.: Reference Type Hierarchy and Methods

Finding the minimal set of disambiguating methods is further complicated by the fact that adding a method to solve some ambiguity can actually result in the creation of a new ambiguity. Indeed, in the type hierarchy of Figure 4, invocation $m(E,G)$ is initially not ambiguous, with $m_3(C,G)$ as its most specific applicable method. However, the addition of method $m_4(D,G)$ to solve the $m(D,G)$ ambiguity makes $m(E,G)$ ambiguous, as m_3 now conflicts with m_4.

Unfortunately, to our knowledge, no system assists the programmer in the task of explicit disambiguation by method addition. Such help is especially needed for multi-methods systems, notably because multi-methods are more complex to master than mono-methods and suffer from two kinds of ambiguities, increasing the potential number of ambiguities.

To help explicitly disambiguate multi-method systems, we propose to provide the programmer with a disambiguation tool that can be integrated into the interpreter, compiler or programming environment. This tool takes as input the signatures of a generic function's methods. In batch mode, its output is the minimal set of signatures of the methods that must be added in order to eliminate ambiguities. The programmer must then provide bodies to the methods of the disambiguation set, be they just resend clauses. In interactive mode, it yields one signature of the disambiguation set at a time, in a specific order: the programmer can either accept to solve the ambiguity by the addition of a method with that signature, or stop the disambiguation algorithm and solve the ambiguity in another way (e.g. by deleting methods or changing the type hierarchy). The algorithm is then restarted from the beginning. The interactive mode gives the programmer finer control over the disambiguation process, as (s)he is not forced to solve all ambiguities through method addition. In both modes, for each new method's signature, the tool presents the set of methods that created the ambiguity as an explanation to the programmer. In this paper, we focus on the batch mode for space reason.

Our results apply to all languages in which the precedence ordering of multi-methods conforms to argument subtype precedence and monotonicity. This includes Cecil and Dylan, as well as CLOS and SQL3 provided the latter two slightly change their precedence order to adopt a monotonic order, as proposed in [DHHM94][7]. Our results also apply to languages with mono-methods, such as C++, Self or Laure.

Our disambiguation algorithm is based on two results: (i) the minimal disambiguation set is unique and (ii) it is included in a set of signatures called the *pole signatures*. The algorithm is composed of two steps. The first step consists in computing the pole signatures, using the signatures of the initial set of methods as follows. Multiple inheritance ambiguities are explicitly solved for each argument position, i.e. the set of types appearing at a given position is augmented with the minimal set of types needed to eliminate multiple inheritance ambiguities. This process yields a set of *pole types* or *poles* for each argument position. The set of pole signatures is the Cartesian product of the sets of poles at each argument position.

Example 10. Given the methods of Figure 4, the set of poles on the first argument position is the union of $\{A, B, C\}$ and $\{D, E\}$. $\{A, B, C\}$ is the set of types appearing in the first argument position, and $\{D, E\}$ is the minimal disambiguation set. The poles of the second argument position are only the types appearing in the second argument position, $\{F, G\}$, as this

---

[7] Such a change was recently adopted for Dylan

set is not ambiguous. The pole signatures are then $\{(A, F), (B, F), (C, F), (D, F), (E, F), (A, G), (B, G), (C, G), (D, G), (E, G)\}$.

The second step of the disambiguation algorithm is the following: for each pole signature, the algorithm computes the MSA method of the corresponding invocation. If there are more than one MSA method, then the invocation is ambiguous and a method with that signature must be added to the initial set of methods with the signatures of the conflicting MSA methods for explanation. In order to minimize the number of methods to add and to detect ambiguities created by the addition of a method, the algorithm processes the pole signatures in a total order that is compatible with argument subtype precedence, from the most general to the most specific signatures.

Example 11. The pole signatures given above are already ordered in a way that is compatible with argument subtype precedence from the most general to the most specific signature. The first pole signature for which there is more than one MSA is (D, G) with $m_1(A, G)$ and $m_2(B, F)$ as conflicting MSA methods. A first method $m_4(D, G)$ is thus added to the disambiguation set with $m_1(A, G)$ and $m_2(B, F)$ as explanation. The next and last signature, (E, G), also has more than one MSA method, namely $m_3(C, G)$ and the newly added $m_4(D, G)$. Hence, method $m_5(E, G)$ is added to the disambiguation set with $m_3(C, G)$ and $m_4(D, G)$ as explanation and the algorithm ends.

Notice that the algorithm tests for ambiguity a number of signatures that is much smaller than the total number of well-typed invocations. In the example of Figure 4, there are 34 different well-typed invocations and the algorithm only needs to test 7 signatures (the signatures of the three methods m_1, m_2, and m_3 can be skipped as they are obviously not ambiguous).

4   Disambiguation Algorithm

Before presenting the disambiguation algorithm, we first give some definitions and the theoretical result on which the algorithm is based.

4.1   Definitions

For the rest of this paper, we call Θ the set of existing types, and we consider a generic function m of arity n, whose methods are $m_1, \ldots, m_p$. We also consider a set $S = \{s_1, \ldots, s_p\}$ such that for all k, s_k is the signature of m_k, i.e. $s_k = (T_k^1, \ldots, T_k^n)$.

We first review some notations and results introduced in [AGS94]. Here is the formal definition of a *pole* type that is used to solve multiple inheritance ambiguities at each argument position:

I-Pole. A type $T \in \Theta$ is an i-pole of generic function m, $i \in \{1, \ldots, n\}$, denoted $is\_pole_m^i(T)$, iff:

$$\exists k \in \{1, \ldots, p\} \text{ s.t. } T = T_k^i$$
$$\text{or} \quad |min_{\preceq} \{T' \in \Theta \mid is\_pole_m^i(T') \text{ and } T' \succ T\}| > 1$$

The first part of the conjunction corresponds to the types appearing at the i-th argument position (*primary poles*), while the second part defines which types must be added to solve multiple inheritance ambiguities (*secondary poles*). The set of i-poles of m is denoted $Pole_m^i = \{T \mid is\_pole_m^i(T)\}$. The set of *pole signatures* is denoted $Poles_m = \prod_{i=1}^{n} Pole_m^i$.

Example 12. Going back to Figure 4, D is a 1-pole because of the ambiguity created by the 1-poles A and B. In the same way, E is a 1-pole because of C and D.

Signature Specificity. A signature $s = (T^1, \ldots, T^n) \in \Theta^n$ is more specific than a signature $s' = (T'^1, \ldots, T'^n) \in \Theta^n$, noted $s \preceq s'$, iff for all i in $\{1, \ldots, n\}$, $T^i \preceq T'^i$.

By analogy with methods, if $s \preceq s'$, s' is said to be applicable to s.

Method Precedence Order. We note by α_s the precedence order of method signatures with respect to signature s: $s_1 \alpha_s s_2$ means that s_1 and s_2 are the signatures of two methods applicable to s (i.e., $s \preceq s_1$ and $s \preceq s_2$), and s_1 is more specific than s_2 for s. This order is used to determine the MSA method. We assume that α conforms to argument subtype precedence, and that it is monotonic:

$$s_1 \preceq s_2 \text{ and } s \preceq s_1, \ s \preceq s_2 \ \Rightarrow \ s_1 \ \alpha_s \ s_2 \ \text{(argument subtype precedence)}$$
$$s_1 \ \alpha_s \ s_2 \text{ and } s' \prec s \ \Rightarrow \ s_1 \ \alpha_{s'} \ s_2 \quad \text{(monotonicity)}$$

Conflicting Signatures. Given a set of signatures $S' \subseteq \Theta^n$, the set of conflicting signatures of S' w.r.t. a signature $s \in \Theta$, noted $conflicting(s, S')$, is defined as follows:

$$conflicting(s, S') = min_{\alpha_s} \{s' \in S' \mid s' \succeq s\}$$

If S' is a set of method signatures and s the signature of an invocation, then $conflicting(s, S')$ represents the signatures of the most specific applicable methods for the invocation. This is a generalization of the notion of MSA method that takes ambiguities into account. It is used both to test a signature for ambiguity and to determine the origin of the ambiguity as an explanation.

Ambiguity of a Signature Set, Ambiguous Signature. A set of signatures $S' \subseteq \Theta^n$ is ambiguous iff there exists a signature $s \in \Theta$ such that $|conflicting(s, S')| > 1$. s is then said to be an ambiguous signature w.r.t. S'.

Disambiguation Set. Given a set of signatures $S' \subseteq \Theta^n$, $\Delta \subseteq \Theta^n$ is a disambiguation set of S' iff $S' \cup \Delta$ is not ambiguous.

4.2 Main Theorem

We assume the existence of a total order on the pole signatures $Poles_m$, denoted by $\leq$, and compatible with argument subtype precedence, i.e. $\forall s, s' \in Poles_m, (s \preceq s' \Rightarrow s \leq s')$. Such an order always exists and can be found using a topological sort [Knu73].

We then define a sequence of signatures $(s_k)_{k>p}$ in the following way:

- $s_{p+1} = max_{\leq}\{s \in Poles_m \mid |conflicting(s, \{s_1, \ldots, s_p\})| > 1\}$.
- $\forall k > p, s_{k+1} = max_{\leq}\{s \in Poles_m \mid s_k > s \text{ and } |conflicting(s, \{s_1, \ldots, s_k\})| > 1\}$.

As each signature s_k is found by applying $max_{\leq}$, building $(s_k)_{k>p}$ from this definition is achieved by going over $Poles_m$ in the order of $\leq$, starting from the most generic signatures. Note that testing the ambiguity of a signature at stage $k + 1$ is done using *all* preceding signatures, not just the first p ones.

Theorem 1. $\Delta^S_{min} = \{s_k \mid p < k\}$ *is finite, and is the minimal disambiguation set of S.*

Proof: see Appendix.

Example 13. Consider again the types and methods in Figure 4. The original signature set is $S = \{(A, G), (B, F), (C, G)\}$, and $\Delta^S_{min} = \{(D, G), (E, G)\}$.

4.3 Main Algorithm

As explained in Section 3, the disambiguation algorithm takes place in two steps: first, the poles of every argument position are computed to yield the pole signatures in an order compatible with argument subtype precedence, then the minimal disambiguation set is computed by iterating over the set of pole signatures. The algorithm in Figure 5 invokes a subroutine that builds the ordered list of pole signatures, and then performs the second step of this process. We describe the ordering of pole signatures in the next section, and pole computation is isomorphic to the second step of the disambiguation algorithm. Indeed, computing the poles amounts to determining the minimal disambiguation set of the types appearing as arguments: the types of the hierarchy are iterated over in an order compatible with argument subtype precedence; for each type, the most specific applicable poles are computed. If there are more than one most specific applicable pole, then the type becomes a secondary pole. Note that, as for the second step of the main algorithm, the order in which types are considered guarantees the *minimality* of the disambiguation set.

From the definition of (s_k), it is straightforward to build an algorithm that produces Δ^S_{min} by going over $Poles_m$ in the order of $\leq$ and adding ambiguous signatures to the original set of signatures to test following signatures. Moreover, the set of conflicting signatures is associated with each ambiguous signatures as an explanation.

```
Disambiguation algorithm
input:     a set of methods M, a boolean interactive
output:    a list result of 2-tuples (disambiguation signature,conflicting signatures)
```

Step 1: Computation of the Ordered Pole Signatures
$S \leftarrow$ signatures(M) ;   // method signatures
$P \leftarrow$ OrderedPoleSignatures(S) ;

Step 2: Computation of Δ^S_{min} with explanations
$\Delta \leftarrow \emptyset$;   // disambiguation signatures
$result \leftarrow \emptyset$;

for s in P do
   $CONF \leftarrow conflicting(s, S \cup \Delta)$;
   if $|CONF| > 1$ then   // s is ambiguous in $S \cup \Delta$
     if $interactive$ then
       if $user\text{-}refuse(s, CONF)$ then // ask the user if (s)he wants to stop
         exit   // stop execution
     insert s into Δ ;
     add $(s, CONF)$ to $result$;

return($result$) ;

Fig. 5.: Disambiguation Algorithm

The algorithm assumes the existence of two subroutines: `OrderedPoleSignatures`(S) returns the list of pole signatures in an order that is compatible with argument subtype precedence and $conflicting(s, S)$ returns the signatures in S that conflict as most specific applicable to s.

Example 14. Back to Figure 4, let us assume that $OrderedPoleSignatures(S)$ returns ((A, F), (B, F), (C, F), (D, F), (E, F), (A, G), (B, G), (C, G), (D, G), (E, G)). First, (D, G) is found to be ambiguous as it has (A, G) and (B, F) as conflicting signatures. (D, G) is thus added to Δ and ((D, G), {(A, G), (B, F)}) to $result$. Then, (E, G) is found to be ambiguous, with (C, G) and (D, G) as conflicting signatures. (E, G) is thus added to Δ and ((E, G), {(C, G), (D, G)}) to $result$, which is then returned as the minimal disambiguation set with associated explanations.

Finally, in testing pole signatures for ambiguity, the disambiguation algorithm can also fill the dispatch table of the generic function, presented in [AGS94]. Indeed, the dispatch table stores the MSA method of all pole signatures: if $conflicting$ yields a singleton set, then the single element is the signature of the MSA method.

5 Implementation And Complexity

This section describes the ordering of poles in $OrderedPoleSignature$, and the computation of conflicting signatures in $conflicting$.

5.1   Ordering the Pole Signatures

Ordering the pole signatures in an order that is compatible with argument subtype precedence comes down to turning a partially ordered set into a linear list. A classical algorithm
is given in [Knu73]. The basic idea is to pick as first element one that has no predecessor,
remove this element from the original set to append it to the originally empty list, and start
over until no elements are left. In the case of pole signatures, it is necessary to scan the set
of pole signatures to find that a given signature has no predecessor. Hence, ordering the pole
signatures has a complexity of $O(|Poles_m|^2)$.

However, it is possible to obtain a complexity of $O(|Poles_m|)$ if the poles of each argu-
ment position, $Pole^i_m$, are themselves sorted in an order compatible with argument subtype
precedence. Indeed, it is easy to show that it suffices to produce the signatures in the lexicographic ordering generated by the total orders on the poles[8].

Example 15. The table in Figure 6 represents the pole signatures of the methods and types
of Figure 4. The order on 1-poles (resp. 2-poles) in lines (resp. columns) is compatible with
argument subtype precedence. A total order of $Poles_m$ is a path through this table. Such a
path is compatible with argument subtype precedence, if it traverses each signature s before
the signatures on the right and below s. The path given by a lexicographic ordering, as
shown in Figure 6 satisfies the condition. For example, the signatures that are more specific
than (C, F) are all included in the grayed area.

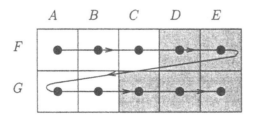

Fig. 6.: Order of Pole Signatures

5.2   Computing the Conflicting Signatures

The computation of the conflicting signatures consists in finding the most specific applicable
signatures. In the case of a totally ordered set, there is a single smallest element, and the cost
to find it is linear in the number of elements of the set, if the comparison of two elements is
done in a constant time. Unfortunately, signatures are only partially ordered, increasing the
complexity to the square of the number of signatures to compare. As $S \cup \Delta^S_{min}$ is a superset

---

[8] This ordering of poles is not expensive as poles are produced in this order, from an ordering of
types that is done once for all pole computations.

of the set of applicable signatures, the worst-case complexity of *conflicting* is $O(|S \cup \Delta|^2)$ signature comparisons[9]. However, this complexity can be lowered when there is no ambiguity, i.e. there is a single most specific applicable signature.

The basic idea of our optimization is to store $S \cup \Delta$ in the total order of $\leq$. To compute $conflicting(s, S \cup \Delta)$, the signatures in $S \cup \Delta$ are examined in the order $\leq$ starting from the smallest, i.e. most specific signatures. If there is a single MSA s_k, then it is the first signature s_k applicable to s. Moreover, a single loop over the ordered $S \cup \Delta$ is enough to prove it, bringing the complexity down to $O(|S \cup \Delta|)$. Indeed, if there is a single MSA method s_k, we have:

$$\forall s_{k'} \in S \cup \Delta, \; s_{k'} \succeq s \Rightarrow s_{k'} \succeq s_k \Rightarrow s_{k'} \geq s_k.$$

On the other hand, if the iteration finds another applicable signature that is not more generic than s_k, then s is ambiguous and the complexity is $O(|S \cup \Delta|^2)$. Hence the complexity of disambiguating m is $O(|S \cup \Delta|^2 \times |\Delta| + |S \cup \Delta| \times (|Poles_m - \Delta|))$ comparisons of signatures.

Example 16. Assume a new method $m_4(C, I)$ is added to the schema of Figure 4, so that I is now a 2-pole. Assume that (D, G) and (E, G) have already been found to be ambiguous and added to Δ. Signature (D, I) must now be tested for ambiguity. Using the lexicographic order represented in Figure 6 to sort $S \cup \Delta$ yields $((C, I), (E, G), (D, G), (C, G), (A, G), (B, F))$. The first signature applicable to (D, I) is (D, G) and no following signatures is more generic than it. Hence (D, G) is not ambiguous. On the other hand, when (E, I) is tested for ambiguity, (C, I), then (E, G) are found to be applicable to (E, I), and $(E, G) \not\succ (C, I)$. Hence (E, I) is ambiguous $(conflicting((E, I)) = \{(E, G), (C, I)\})$.

6 Future Work

Three issues are worth future investigation: impossible signatures, mixing method addition with method selection and incremental disambiguation.

Impossible signatures We call *impossible signatures*, signatures that can never occur as invocation signatures of a given generic function. They may be signatures containing an abstract class, that is, a class that cannot have instances, or they may be forbidden signatures as described in [ABDS94]. These signatures are user-defined and their use as invocation signatures are type errors.

In case an impossible signature appears in a disambiguation set, defining the body of a method with this signature may have no sense. Hence for some impossible signatures, the

---

[9] This comparison is done in constant time, if n is constant and the technique of [Cas93] is used to keep the transitive closure of the subtyping relationship. The latter computation is done once for all generic functions.

programmer may want to define methods for the signatures that are directly more specific, and not impossible. Our algorithm should be extended to ignore those signatures and rather examine the signatures that are directly more specific.

Mixing Method Addition and Method Selection Another interesting research direction consists in studying how disambiguation by method selection can be mixed with disambiguation by method addition. Indeed, whenever the disambiguation algorithm finds the first ambiguous signature s, it could pause and ask the programmer to choose between two alternatives: add a new method with signature s or add a method selection clause, saying "select method m_i for signature s", where m_i is one of the conflicting methods. This is especially relevant in the case where the new method only serves as a forwarder to one of the conflicting methods. The algorithm would then look for the next ambiguous signature. Interestingly, choosing method selection instead of method addition is not indifferent: adding a method selection clause can actually solve more ambiguities and lead to a smaller set of ambiguous signatures *depending on which conflicting method is chosen*.

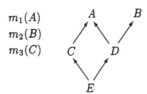

Fig. 7.: Conflicting Method Selection

Example 17. Consider the schema in Figure 7. In the case of disambiguation by method addition, two disambiguation methods $m(D)$ and $m(E)$ must be added. The conflicting signatures for (E) are (C) and (D). Assume that instead, a selection clause is added when finding ambiguous signature (D). If the user selects $m_1(A)$ for (D), $m_2(B)$ cannot be selected for $m(E)$ because of the monotonicity property [DHHM92]. The applicable methods for $m(E)$ are then $m_1(A)$ and $m_3(C)$, and the latter being more specific than the former, $m(E)$ is not ambiguous as in the case of method addition. Note that (E) is ambiguous if the programmer selects $m_2(B)$ for (D).

Incremental Disambiguation As the type hierarchy and the methods may evolve, especially during application development, it is interesting to investigate if it is possible to compute the minimal disambiguation set based on the evolution operations performed on the type hierarchy and methods.

7 Conclusion

In this paper, we addressed the problem of supporting programmers in the task of explicitly disambiguating multi-methods by method addition. This process involves finding a set of disambiguating methods as small as possible. We proved that there always exists a single minimal disambiguation set, and proposed an algorithm to compute it. This algorithm is efficient in that it avoids testing all possible invocations for ambiguity, examining instead a much smaller set of signatures, the *pole signatures*. Moreover, this algorithm associates to each disambiguating method the set of conflicting signatures that caused the ambiguity. This provides explanations and allows implementation of a disambiguating method as a forwarder to one of the conflicting methods.

Future work involves taking impossible signatures into account. Moreover, the algorithm can be extended to allow explicit disambiguation by mixing method addition with method selection. Finally, we are interested in studying the relationship between the minimal disambiguation set and evolution operations on the type hierarchy and methods.

Acknowledgments: We would like to thank Eric Simon and Marie-Jo Bellosta for their insightful comments on earlier versions of this paper, and Anthony Tomasic whose helpful suggestions greatly improved the quality of this paper.

8 Appendix : Proof of Theorem 1

We first introduce the following definition:

Well-typed signatures. $Well\text{-}Typed(m) = \{s \in \Theta^n \mid \exists k \in \{1, \ldots, p\} \text{ s.t. } s \preceq s_k\}$

To prove Theorem 1, we start from a slightly different definition of the sequence (s_k), as follows:

- $s_{p+1} = max_{\leq}\{s \in Well\text{-}Typed_m \mid |conflicting(s, \{s_1, \ldots, s_p\})| > 1\}$
- $\forall k > p, s_{k+1} = max_{\leq}\{s \in Well\text{-}Typed_m \mid s_k > s \text{ and } |conflicting(s, \{s_1, \ldots, s_k\})| > 1\}$

In this definition, we take $\{s_k \mid p < k\}$ in $Well\text{-}Typed_m$ instead of $Poles_m$. We use this definition to prove that (s_k) is finite and that it is the smallest disambiguation set. Then we prove that it is included in $Poles_m$, which shows that both definitions of (s_k) are equivalent.

A Finiteness

To prove that $\{s_k \mid k \in \mathbb{N}\}$ is finite, it suffices to remark that it is included in Θ^n, which is finite. For the rest of the paper, q the index of the last element of the sequence (s_k).

B Lemma

This lemma basically expresses that the way Δ_{min}^S is built "does not leave ambiguous signatures behind":

Lemma 2. $\forall k \in \{p + 1, \ldots, q\}, \nexists s \in Well\text{-}Typed_m \text{ s.t. } s \text{ is ambiguous w.r.t. } \{s_1, \ldots, s_k\}$ and $s \geq s_k$.

Proof: Let $k > p$ and $s \in Well\text{-}Typed_m$. We assume that s is ambiguous w.r.t. $\{s_1, \ldots, s_k\}$ and $s \geq s_k$. In the following, we prove that $s \in \{s_1, \ldots, s_k\}$, to conclude that the assumption is false.

We have $|conflicting(s, \{s_1, \ldots, s_k\})| > 1$, i.e. $|min_\alpha \{s_j \mid j \leq k$ and $s_j \succeq s\}| > 1$. Obviously the members of this minimum are strictly more generic than s, hence $|min_\alpha \{s_j \mid j \leq k$ and $s_j \succ s\}| > 1$. Let us consider $\{s_j \mid p < j \leq k$ and $s_j > s\}$. Two cases may occur:

- $\{s_j \mid p < j \leq k$ and $s_j > s\} = \emptyset$, which implies that $s \geq s_{p+1}$.

  We show that s is ambiguous w.r.t. S. $\leq$ being compatible with $\preceq$, $\nexists j$ s.t. $p < j \leq k$ and $s_j \succ s$. Hence the members of $conflicting(s, \{s_1, \ldots, s_k\})$ are in S, i.e. s is ambiguous w.r.t. S.

  From $s \geq s_{p+1}$ and the construction of s_{p+1}, it follows that $s = s_{p+1}$.

- $\{s_j \mid p < j \leq k$ and $s_j > s\} \neq \emptyset$: let $k' = max_\leq \{j \mid p < j \leq k$ and $s_j > s\}$. $k' \neq q$ since $s_{k'} > s \geq s_k \geq s_q$. Thus $s_{k'+1}$ exists, and $s_{k'} > s \geq s_{k'+1}$.

  We show that s is ambiguous w.r.t. $\{s_1, \ldots, s_{k'}\}$. $\leq$ being compatible with $\preceq$, $\nexists j$ s.t. $k' < j$ and $s_j \succ s$. Hence the members of $conflicting(s, \{s_1, \ldots, s_k\})$ are in $\{s_1, \ldots, s_{k'}\}$, i.e. s is ambiguous w.r.t. $\{s_1, \ldots, s_{k'}\}$.

  By construction of $s_{k'+1}$, it follows that $s = s_{k'+1}$.

Hence $s \in \{s_1, \ldots, s_k\}$, which implies that s in not ambiguous w.r.t. this set, in contradiction with the assumption. This concludes the proof of Lemma 2.

C Δ_{min}^S is a Disambiguation Set

To prove that Δ_{min}^S is a disambiguation set, let us assume the existence of $s \in Well\text{-}Typed_m$ ambiguous w.r.t. $S \cup \Delta_{min}^S$. We show that $s \leq s_q$, and then we apply Lemma 2 to conclude that the assumption is false.

If $s_q > s$ we have $\{s' \in Well\text{-}Typed_m \mid s_q > s'$ and $|conflicting(s', \{s_1, \ldots, s_q\})| > 1\} \neq \emptyset$, i.e. s_{q+1} exists, in contradiction with the construction of q. Thus $s \geq s_q$.

As a consequence, s is ambiguous w.r.t. $\{s_1, \ldots, s_q\}$ and $s \geq s_q$, in contradiction with Lemma 2. Hence $S \cup \Delta_{min}^S$ is not ambiguous, and Δ_{min}^S is a disambiguation set.

D Δ_{min}^S is the Smallest Disambiguation Set

We prove that Δ_{min}^S is included in every disambiguation set.

Let $\{s_{p+1}^d, \ldots, s_r^d\}$ be a disambiguation set. For convenience, we note that for all k, $k \leq p$, $s_k^d = s_k$. Thus, $\{s_1^d, \ldots, s_r^d\}$ is not ambiguous. We prove by induction on k, that $\forall k \in \{p+1, \ldots, q\}$, $\{s_1, \ldots, s_k\} \subset \{s_1^d, \ldots, s_r^d\}$. This induction hypothesis obviously holds for $k = 1, \ldots, p$ by construction of $(s_k^d)_{k \in \{1, \ldots, r\}}$.

Assuming it is true for some k such that $p \leq k < q$, we take j such that $\{s_j^d\} = conflicting(s_{k+1}, \{s_1^d, \ldots, s_r^d\})$. s_j^d is unique because $\{s_1^d, \ldots, s_r^d\}$ is not ambiguous. Let us show that $s_j^d = s_{k+1}$. We first show that $s_j^d \neq s_{k+1} \Rightarrow s_j^d$ is ambiguous w.r.t. $\{s_1, \ldots, s_{k+1}\}$, then we apply Lemma 2.

Let $A = \{s_i \mid i \leq k \text{ and } s_i \succeq s_{k+1}\}$. We have $min_{\alpha_{s_{k+1}}} A = conflicting(s_{k+1}, \{s_j \mid j \leq k\})$. From the induction hypothesis, $A \subset \{s_1^d, \ldots, s_r^d\}$, hence the elements of this set are more generic than s_j^d. This means that $A \subset \{s_i \mid i \leq k \text{ and } s_i \succeq s_j^d\}$. Reciprocally, $s_i \succeq s_j^d \Rightarrow s_i \succeq s_{k+1}$, thus $A = \{s_i \mid i \leq k \text{ and } s_i \succeq s_j^d\}$.

Assuming s_j^d were not ambiguous w.r.t. $\{s_1, \ldots, s_k\}$, let $\{s_a\} = conflicting(s_j^d, \{s_1, \ldots, s_k\}) = min_{\alpha_{s_j^d}} A$. As α is monotonous, for s_{k+1} also s_a would be more specific than the other elements of A, i.e. we would have $\{s_a\} = conflicting(s_{k+1}, \{s_1, \ldots, s_k\})$, which is impossible by construction of s_{k+1}. Hence s_j^d is ambiguous w.r.t. $\{s_1, \ldots, s_k\}$.

Let us assume that $s_j^d \succ s_{k+1}$: s_{k+1} is not applicable to s_j^d, hence s_j^d is ambiguous w.r.t. $\{s_1, \ldots, s_{k+1}\}$. As $s_j^d \geq s_{k+1}$, we apply Lemma 2 to show that this assumption is false.

Finally $s_j^d \succeq s_{k+1}$ and $s_j^d \not\succ s_{k+1}$ implies $s_j^d = s_{k+1}$, thus $\{s_1, \ldots, s_{k+1}\} \subset \{s_1^d, \ldots, s_r^d\}$, which concludes our proof.

E Δ_{min}^S is Made of Poles

We first recall some results mainly introduced in [AGS94].

Influence of a Pole. For all i in $\{1, \ldots, n\}$, and all T_π in $Pole_m^i$,

$$Influence_m^i(T_\pi) = \{T \in \Theta \mid T \preceq T_\pi \text{ and } \forall T_\pi' \in Pole_m^i, T \not\preceq T_\pi' \text{ or } T_\pi \preceq T_\pi'\}.$$

Ith Dynamic Argument. $Dynamic_m^i = \{T \in \Theta \mid \exists k \in \{1, \ldots, p\} \text{ s.t. } T \preceq T_k^i\}$

Note that $\forall(T^1, \ldots, T^n) \in Well\text{-}Typed_m, \forall i \in \{1, \ldots, n\}, T^i \in Dynamic_m^i$.

Theorem 3. Let $\{T_\pi^1, \ldots, T_\pi^l\}$ be $Pole_m^i$. Then $\{Influence_m^i(T_\pi^1), \ldots, Influence_m^i(T_\pi^l)\}$ is a partition of $Dynamic_m^i$.

The latter theorem allows to define the following functions:

Pole of a Type, Poles of a Signature. For all i in $\{1, \ldots, n\}$, all T in $Dynamic_m^i$, and all $(T^1, \ldots, T^n)$ in $Well\text{-}Typed_m$, we define:

$$pole_m^i(T) = T_\pi, \text{ s.t. } T_\pi \in Pole_m^i \text{ and } T \in influence_m^i(T_\pi)$$
$$pole_m((T^1, \ldots, T^n)) = (pole_m^1(T^1), \ldots, pole_m^n(T^n))$$

We also introduce the following lemma:

Lemma 4. $\forall s \in Well\text{-}Typed_m, \forall s' \in Poles_m, s' \succeq s \Rightarrow s' \succeq pole_m(s)$.

186

Proof: Let $s = (U^1, \ldots, U^n) \in \textit{Well-Typed}_m$, $s_\pi = \textit{pole}_m(s) = (U^1_\pi, \ldots, U^n_\pi)$, and $s' \in \textit{Poles}_m$, $s' = (T^1, \ldots, T^n)$. Let us show that $\forall i \in \{1, \ldots, n\}$, $T^i \succeq \textit{pole}^i_m(U_i)$.

Let $i \in \{1, \ldots, n\}$. We have $T^i \succeq U^i$ because $s' \succeq s$.

From the definition of $\textit{Influence}^i_m$, as $U^i \in \textit{Influence}^i_m(U^i_\pi)$, $T^i \in \textit{Pole}^i_m$, and $U^i \preceq T^i$, we have $U_\pi \preceq T^i$. Thus $s_\pi \preceq s'$, which concludes the proof of Lemma 4.

To show that $\Delta^S_{min} \subset \textit{Poles}_m$, we prove by induction that $\forall k \geq p, \{s_1, \ldots, s_k\} \subset \textit{Poles}_m$. This is true for $k = p$ from the definitions of an i-pole and of $\textit{Poles}_m$, because $s_1, \ldots, s_p$ are the signatures of $m_1, \ldots, m_p$.

Assuming the induction hypothesis holds for some k such that $p \leq k < q$, we show that $s_{k+1} \in \textit{Poles}_m$, by proving that $s_{k+1} = \textit{pole}_m(s_{k+1})$.

Let s'_{k+1} be $\textit{pole}_m(s_{k+1})$. We show that $s'_{k+1} \succ s_{k+1} \Rightarrow s'_{k+1}$ is ambiguous w.r.t. $\{s_1, \ldots, s_{k+1}\}$), then we apply Lemma 2.

Let $A = \{s_i \mid i \leq k \text{ and } s_i \succeq s_{k+1}\}$. We have $min_{\alpha_{s_{k+1}}} A = \textit{conflicting}(s_{k+1}, \{s_j \mid j \leq k\})$. From the induction hypothesis, $A \subset \textit{Poles}_m$, hence the elements of this set are more generic than s'_{k+1}. This means that $A \subset \{s_i \mid i \leq k \text{ and } s_i \succeq s'_{k+1}\}$. Reciprocally, $s_i \succeq s'_{k+1} \Rightarrow s_i \succeq s_{k+1}$, thus $A = \{s_i \mid i \leq k \text{ and } s_i \succeq s'_{k+1}\}$.

Assuming s'_{k+1} were not ambiguous w.r.t. $\{s_1, \ldots, s_k\}$, let $\{s_a\} = \textit{conflicting}(s'_{k+1}, \{s_1, \ldots, s_k\}) = min_{\alpha_{s'_{k+1}}} A$. As α is monotonous, for s_{k+1} also s_a would be more specific than the other elements of A, i.e. we would have $\{s_a\} = \textit{conflicting}(s_{k+1}, \{s_1, \ldots, s_k\})$, which is impossible by construction of s_{k+1}. Hence s'_{k+1} is ambiguous w.r.t. $\{s_1, \ldots, s_k\}$.

Let us assume that $s'_{k+1} \succ s_{k+1}$: s_{k+1} is not applicable to s'_{k+1}, hence s'_{k+1} is ambiguous w.r.t. $\{s_1, \ldots, s_{k+1}\}$. Moreover $s'_{k+1} \geq s_{k+1}$, hence we can apply Lemma 2 to show that this assumption is false.

From $s'_{k+1} \succeq s_{k+1}$ and $s'_{k+1} \not\succ s_{k+1}$, it follows that $s'_{k+1} = s_{k+1}$, thus $\{s_1, \ldots, s_{k+1}\} \subset \textit{Poles}_m$. This concludes our proof.

References

[ABC+93] O. Agesen, L. Bak, C. Chambers, B.-W. Chang, U. Hölzle, J. Maloney, R. B. Smith, D. Ungar, and M. Wolcsko. *The Self 3.0 Programmer's Reference Manual.* Sun Microsystems and Stanford University, 1993. Available by ftp from self.stanford.edu as /pub/Self-3.0/manuals/progRef.ps.gz.

[ABDS94] E. Amiel, M.-J. Bellosta, E. Dujardin, and E. Simon. Supporting exceptions to schema consistency to ease schema evolution. In *Proc. Intl. Conf. on VLDB*, 1994.

[ABGO93] A. Albano, R. Bergamini, G. Ghelli, and R. Orsini. An object data model with roles. In *Proc. Intl. Conf. on Very Large Data Bases*, 1993.

[ADL91]   R. Agrawal, L. G. DeMichiel, and B. G. Lindsay. Static type checking of multi-methods. In *Proc. OOPSLA*, 1991.

[AGS94]   E. Amiel, O. Gruber, and E. Simon. Optimizing multi-methods dispatch using compressed dispatch tables. In *Proc. OOPSLA*, 1994.

[App95]   Apple Computer. *Dylan Reference Manual, draft* , September 1995. Available from the Dylan Home Page on the World-Wide Web at address http://www.cambridge.apple.com/dylan/dylan.html.

[BDG+88] D. G. Bobrow, L. G. DeMichiel, R. P. Gabriel, S. Keene, G. Kiczales, and D. A. Moon. Common Lisp Object System specification. *SIGPLAN Notices*, 23, Sept. 1988.

[BI82]   A. H. Borning and D. H. H. Ingalls. Multiple inheritance in Smalltalk-80. In *Proc. AAAI*, 1982.

[BKK+86] D. G. Bobrow, K. Kahn, G. Kiczales, L. Masinter, M. Stefik, and F. Zdybel. Common-Loops: Merging Lisp and object-oriented programming. In *Proc. OOPSLA*, 1986.

[BKKK87] J. Banerjee, W. Kim, H.J. Kim, and H. F. Korth. Semantics and implementation of schema evolution in object-oriented databases. In *Proc. ACM SIGMOD Intl. Conf. on Management Of Data*, 1987.

[Cas93]   Yves Caseau. Efficient handling of multiple inheritance hierarchies. In *Proc. OOPSLA*, 1993.

[CBLL82] G. Curry, L. Baer, D. Lipkie, and B. Lee. Traits : An approach to multiple-inheritance subclassing. In *Proc. ACM SIGOA Conference on Office Automation Systems*, 1982.

[CG90]   B. Carré and J.-M. Geib. The point of view notion for multiple inheritance. In *Proc. ECOOP/OOPSLA*, 1990.

[Cha92]   C. Chambers. Object-oriented multi-methods in Cecil. In *Proc. ECOOP*, 1992.

[Cha93]   C. Chambers. The Cecil language, specification and rationale. Technical Report 93-03-05, Dept of Computer Science and Engineering, FR-35, University of Washington, March 1993.

[CP93]   Yves Caseau and Laurent Perron. Attaching second-order types to methods in an object-oriented language. In *Proc. ECOOP*, 1993.

[CUCH91] C. Chambers, D. Ungar, B.-W. Chang, and U. Hoelzle. Parents are shared parts of objects : inheritance and encapsulation in SELF. *Lisp and Symbolic Computation*, 4(3), 1991.

[DCL+93] L. G. DeMichiel, D. D. Chamberlin, B. G. Lindsay, R. Agrawal, and M. Arya. Polyglot: Extensions to relational databases for sharable types and functions in a multi-language environment. In *Proc. Intl. Conf. on Data Engineering*, 1993.

[DH89]   R. Ducournau and M. Habib. La multiplicité de l'héritage dans les langages à objets. *Technique et Science Informatiques*, January 1989.

[DHHM92] R. Ducournau, M. Habib, M. Huchard, and M.L. Mugnier. Monotonic conflict resolution mechanisms for inheritance. In *Proc. OOPSLA*, 1992.

[DHHM94] R. Ducournau, M. Habib, M. Huchard, and M.L. Mugnier. Proposal for a monotonic multiple inheritance linearization. In *Proc. OOPSLA*, 1994.

[DS92]   S. Danforth and E. Simon. *The Next Generation of Information Systems - from Data to Knowledge*, chapter A Data and Operation Model for Advanced Database Systems. Springer Verlag, 1992.

[ES92]   M. A. Ellis and B. Stroustrup. *The annotated C++ reference manual*. Addison-Wesley, Reading, Mass., 1992.

[Knu73]   D. Knuth. *The Art of Computer Programming, Fundamental Algorithms, Second Edition*. Addison-Wesley, 1973.

[LR89]   C. Lecluse and P. Richard. Manipulation of structured values in object-oriented databases. In *Proc. Intl. Workshop on Database Programming Languages*, 1989.

[Mey92]   B. Meyer. *EIFFEL : The Language*. Prentice Hall Intl., 1992.

[MGS89]   José Meseguer, Joseph Goguen, and Gert Smolka. Order-sorted unification. *Journal of Symbolic Computation*, 8:383–413, 1989.

[MHH91]   W. B. Mugridge, J. Hamer, and J. G. Hosking. Multi-methods in a statically-typed programming language. In *Proc. ECOOP*, 1991.

[Moo86]   D. A. Moon. Object-oriented programming with Flavors. In *Proc. OOPSLA*, 1986.

[O₂92]   O$_2$ Technology. *The O$_2$ User's Manual*, 1992.

[SB86]   M. Stefik and D. G. Bobrow. Object-oriented programming: Themes and variations. *The AI Magazine*, 6(4), 1986.

[SCB+86]   C. Schaffert, T. Cooper, B. Bullis, M. Kilian, and C. Wilpot. An introduction to Trellis/Owl. In *Proc. OOPSLA*, 1986.

[Se393]   Self 3.0 - about this release. Available by ftp from self.stanford.edu as /pub/Self3.0/manuals/aboutThisRelease.ps.gz, 1993.

[Sny86a]   A. Snyder. CommonObjects : An overview. *Sigplan Notices*, 21(10), 1986.

[Sny86b]   A. Snyder. Encapsulation and inheritance in object-oriented programming languages. In *Proc. OOPSLA*, 1986.

Towards Alias-Free Pointers

Naftaly H. Minsky*

Rutgers University, New Brusnwick NJ 08903 USA

Tel: (908) 445-2085; e-mail: minsky@cs.rutgers.edu

Abstract. This paper argues that pointer-induced aliasing can be avoided in many cases by means of a concept of *unique pointer*. The use of such pointers is expected to fortify the concept of encapsulation, to make systems easier to reason about, to provide better control over the interaction between threads, and to make storage management safer and more efficient. We show that unique pointers can be implemented by means of few minor and virtually costless modifications in conventional OO languages, such as Eiffel or C++; and that they can be used conveniently in a broad range of algorithms and data structures.

Key Words and Phrases: pointer-induced aliasing, hiding, encapsulation, programming with threads, storage management.

---

* Work supported by NSF grant No. CCR-9308773.

1 Introduction

Dynamic objects, i.e., objects allocated on the heap and addressed by means of pointers, are widely considered a mixed blessing in imperative programming. A blessing, because dynamic objects have some very useful properties, such as *indefinite lifetime, indefinite scope, efficient transferability*, and the ability to be *shared* by multiple pointers to a single object. But the shareability of dynamic objects via pointers dispersed throughout a system is very problematic. It allows for aliases to exist for a given dynamic object, anywhere in the system, making it hard to to reason about this object; and it undermines the principles of *hiding*, and of *encapsulation*, the very foundations of object-oriented programming. The virtually uncontrollable dispersal of pointers also makes storage management more hazardous and costly.

In this paper we argue that pointer-induced aliasing is largely a self inflicted wound, caused by the almost universal practice in programming to transfer information *by copy*. As a remedy for this defect we introduce a concept *unshareable objects*, and the companion concept of *unique pointers*, which can be *moved* from one place to another, but which cannot be copied. We argue that unshareable objects can be employed conveniently in many, if not most, situations where dynamic objects are being used, and without incurring their pitfalls. And we show that it takes no more than minor, and virtually costless, modifications to a typical imperative programming language to support such objects.

For the sake of specificity we couch our discussion in terms of the object-oriented language Eiffel [7]. But we believe that the essence of our conclusions is valid for many other object-oriented languages, and, in a broader sense, is applicable to imperative languages in general. (A close approximation to unique pointers under C++ has been constructed.) The rest of this paper is organized as follows: The pitfalls of conventional pointers are discussed in Section 2; in Section 3 we describe a simple variant of Eiffel that supports unique pointers; the use and applications of such pointers are discussed in Section 4; and some related works are discussed in Section 5.

2 The Pitfalls of Dynamic Objects

Under conventional programming languages, dynamic objects have several pitfalls, some are better known than others. We start by showing that dynamic objects are very difficult to hide in any specific locale, due to the virtually uncontrollable dispersal of pointers to such objects. We then briefly discuss the difficulties caused by conventional dynamic objects to *storage management*, to *encapsulation*, and to programming with *threads*.

2.1 The Difficulty in Hiding Dynamic Objects

Although the concept of hiding in software is well known [9] — and is widely considered the bedrock of modularization and of encapsulation — it is a somewhat slippery concept, that may have several definitions reflecting different concerns. The following is one such definition, whose full significance will become clear in due course.

Definition 1 (a concept of hiding) *A component c of object x is considered hidden in x only if it is not accessible (from anywhere) while x does not have control. (x is said to have control between the invocation of one of its methods, and the return from this method.)*

Note that although this definition of hiding is strictly stronger than hiding by scope rules, it allows for a component c of an object x to be accessed by other objects, *as long as control is in* x. For example, x may invoke operation y.p(c), thus having procedure p of object y operate on c. (This is one sense in which the concept of hiding is slippery.)

Now, if a component c of an object x is physically *contained* in it, as illustrated in part (a) of Figure 1, then the condition of Definition 1 can be readily established by the scope rules of the language.[2] But if c is a dynamic object, addressed via a reference variable p_c contained in x then, the scope rules are not

---

[2] Actually, even the hiding of such components is rarely, if ever, *completely* ensured, because of the *unsafe* features [2] that most languages have, such as the ability to use naked C-code in C++, or in procedures of Eiffel. We ignore the effect of such unsafe features in this paper.

sufficient to hide it. Indeed, even if variable p_c is not visible from the outside, the object c itself is quite exposed to any object that may have a pointer to it, as illustrated by part (b) of Figure 1. Any such object may operate on c even when x does not have control, in direct contradiction to the above definition of hiding.

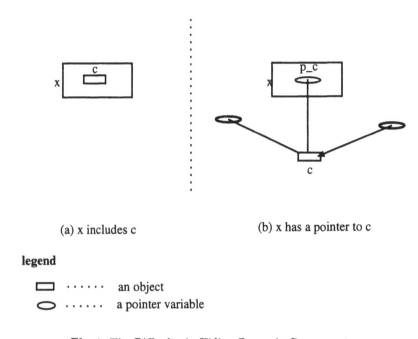

(a) x includes c   (b) x has a pointer to c

legend

☐ · · · · · · an object
◯ · · · · · · a pointer variable

Fig. 1. The Difficulty in Hiding Dynamic Components

Moreover, under conventional languages, it is virtually impossible to control the dispersal of pointers for a given object throughout a system, or to figure out the extent of such dispersal [5]. This is due to the fact that information is generally transferred from one place in a system to another *by copy* — the copy of pointers when dealing with dynamic objects. This, in particular, is the case in Eiffel for the *assignment statement*

```
u := v;
```

which (when v is a *reference variable*) copies the pointer in v into u, leaving v intact — thus creating a duplicate of this pointer. Therefore, if object x obtained its component c (that is, the pointer to it) from some other object, then x cannot tell if there are any pointers to c left elsewhere in the system. Moreover, even if x itself is the original creator of c, there is very little it can do to prevent the leakage of pointers to c into other objects in the system. This, because almost anything that x does with p_c would provide other objects with the opportunity to acquire a duplicate pointer to c. For example, a call y.f(p_c) carried out by x, allows procedure f to save a pointer for c permanently in some attribute of object y.

2.2   The Adverse effects of Dynamic Objects on Storage Management

In a language without garbage collection, where dynamic objects need to be deallocated explicitly, the uncontrollable dispersal of pointers causes two kinds of dire phenomena. First, when an object is deallocated, any surviving pointer to it, left anywhere is the system, becomes a *dangling reference*, which may cause serious errors that are notoriously difficult to debug. Second, partially due to the fear from dangling reference one is often reluctant to deallocate an object even when there is no apparent need for it. This contributes to *memory leaks*, which depletes the memory available to the program.

It is because of the specter of dangling reference that languages with garbage collection do not provide for explicit deallocation of objects. But, as we shall see later, if such deallocation can be made safe it can be very useful in such languages, by reducing the amount of garbage collection needed.

2.3   The Conflict Between Encapsulation and Pointers

Encapsulation is based on the *hiding* of the constituent parts of the state of an object from anything but its own program. Such hiding is supposed to have two distinct consequences, which are critical for large systems: First, it should provide objects with *implementation transparency*; i.e., the ability to change the internal representation of the state of an object (together with its program) without having to change anything in the rest of the system. Second, encapsulation is supposed to enable us to endow an object with what is sometimes called *invariants* (or *class invariants*). These are properties that *"hold whenever control is not in the object"* (Sethi ([10]), and which are completely independent of the rest of the system.

Now, while implementation transparency can be achieved by "weak hiding," via scope rules, invariant properties require the stronger kind of hiding of Definition 1. Indeed, our ability to establish properties of an object which are independent of the rest of the system, is clearly undermined if this object has dynamic components, which may be accessible to any number of other objects.

This is a serious problem because invariant properties are essential for meaningful encapsulation, and for abstract data types. Yet, although this problem with encapsulation is not unknown (see [6] page 159, in particular) it is rarely discussed in the literature, and has not been satisfactorily resolved so far.

2.4 A Difficulty with Threads

The dispersal of pointers also has an adverse effect on *programming with threads* [11]. Suppose that x is built as a *monitor*, meaning that only one thread can gain access to the internals of x at any given moment in time. This is supposed to prevent *race conditions* between processes when they manipulate x.

Unfortunately, if the components of x are dynamic objects, then the mutual exclusion with respect to x does not prevent race conditions. This is illustrated in Figure 2, where the component c of x is accessed concurrently by two threads: T1, which gained exclusive access to x, and T2, which operates concurrently outside of x, but which may operate on component c of x through one of the pointers to it dispersed in the system.

3 Unshareable Objects & Unique Pointers

For situations where the dispersal of pointers is undesirable, we introduce the following concepts:

Definition 2 *A dynamic object is called **unshareable**, or a u-object, if there can be only one pointer in the system leading to it. A pointer to a u-object is called a* u-pointer, *in part because it is guaranteed to be **unique**.*

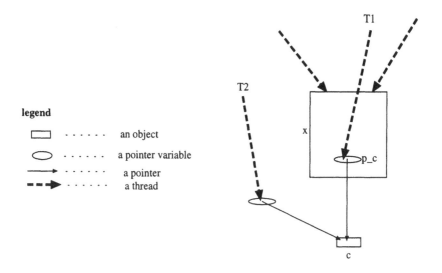

Fig. 2. Race Condition Between Threads

We show in this section how these concepts can be supported, and made usable, under the object-oriented language Eiffel. Technically, we describe a variant of Eiffel, obtained by a small set of minor modifications (defined by a set of rules) of the semantics of this language. We refer to this variant as Eiffel*, but what we really advocate here is that the Eiffel language itself be changed to meet these rules, and that analogous changes be made in other object-oriented languages, if necessary. (In certain languages, such as C++, some of these rules can be established without any changes in the language itself.)

The implementation proposed here for u-objects rests, in part, on a departure from the almost universal use of *copying* (the copying of pointers, in the case of dynamic objects) as the means for transferring information from one place in the system to another. Generally speaking, we propose that objects designated as unshareable be transferred *by move* rather than *by copy*. In addition, some constraints are required on the treatment of formal parameters of procedures. The compile-time cost and the run-time overhead required to establish the rules advocated here for Eiffel* turn out to be quite negligible. Moreover, these rules impose no constraint on anything not involving u-objects.

A disclaimer is in order here: The assurance provided by Eiffel* that pointers claimed to be u-pointers are in fact unique is not absolute. It provides about the same level of the certainty that Eiffel provides for type correctness and for its scope rules. All such integrity conditions are not absolute because Eiffel, like practically all other languages, has some *unsafe features* which if used carelessly may violate the semantics of the language itself, as already mentioned in Footnote 3.

The rest of this section is organized as follows: We start with a concept of u-variables. These are variables declared as unique, each of which contains either a u-pointer or void. This is followed by rules that define the treatment of u-variables by the assignment statements, by parameter passing, and by some other constructs of Eiffel. Finally, in Section 3.5 we introduce means for safe and efficient recycling of u-objects.

Two comments about terminology, before we start: First, we use the term "variable" for what is called an "entity" in Eiffel, which is a name used in the program text to refer to values, which may, at run time, be associated with objects. Second, Our term "unique" in this paper should not be confused with an integer entity declared as "unique" in Eiffel.

3.1 u-variables

Eiffel* allows variables of any class to be declared as *unique*, subject only to a restriction imposed by Rule 4, introduced later. Such variables, which are guarantees to contain either u-pointers or void, may be used to represent *attributes* of an object, *parameters* and *local variables* of a procedure, or the implicitly defined result variable of a function; we will refer to such variables as u-attributes, u-parameters, etc. We also provide for a class to be declared as unique, which means that all variable declared to be of this class are u-variables. The first rule of Eiffel* is as follows:

Rule 1 *No transfer of pointers from regular variables into u-variables is allowed.*

In particular, this rule prohibits the assignment of a regular variable into a u-variable, and the passing of a regular actual parameter into a formal parameter declared as unique. The reason for this prohibition is, of course, that a regular variable may contain a non-unique pointer.

3.2 Assignment of u-variables

The assignment statement in Eiffel has *reference semantics*, when applied to reference variables; i.e., it is a pointer which is copied by an assignment, not the object being pointed to. The following rule causes pointers to u-objects to be *moved* by an assignment, instead of being copied.

Rule 2 *An assignments statement* v := u, *where* u *is a u-variable, is carried out as follows: first, the value of* u *is copied into* v, *then* u *is nullified; i.e., the value* void *(the null pointer of Eiffel) is stored in it.*

In other words, if u is a u-variable then its pointer *moves* into v, leaving void in its wake. Note that if the right hand side of an assignment is a function call that returns a u-pointer, then the variable that contains the value of this function disappears automatically along with its activation record, and is of no concern to us here. (The assignment statement is also subject to the optional Rule 9, which deals with the deallocation of unusable u-objects.)

Note that instead of changing the semantics of the conventional assignment operator, one may prefer to prohibit its use on u-variables, adding a new *move* operator to replace it. This is largely a matter of taste.

3.3 The Treatment of Formal Unshareable Parameters

If parameter passing is done *by reference*, as is the case in Eiffel, it causes no duplication of pointers. But it presents another kind of difficulty: a u-variable u used in a call p(u) may be *nullified* by this call. This would happen, in particular, if the corresponding formal parameter v is assigned to any other variable. By Rule 2, this would be a move-assignment that nullifies v, as well as u. In a sense, procedure p *consumes* the u-pointer given to it in u.

Although such consumption of an actual argument is sometimes required, it is generally undesirable. It is required, for example, in the following situation: Let object x have a u-component u, and suppose that x performs the operation

    s.push(u),

where s is a stack. The pointer in u *must* be consumed by this operation, so that it can be stored in the stack, since it points to a u-object. Object x should "expect" u to be nullified by this call. On the other hand, suppose, that x performs the operation

```
t.display(u),
```

which is supposed to display u on the user-terminal t. It would be quite unreasonable for this call to consume u, yet this is precisely what would happen if procedure display assigns its formal parameter to anything.

The very concept of unshareable objects would be quite untenable without the means for ensuring that an actual parameter cannot be consumed, when consumption is not intended. We, therefore, require a formal u-parameter to be declared as either consumable or non-consumable (we take the latter, which is likely to be the more common one, as the default). The treatment of non-consumable formal parameters is subject to the following constraints:

Rule 3 *The value of a formal u-parameter* v *declared as* non-consumable *cannot be changed. This entails the following constraints on the treatment of such parameters:*

1. *No assignment into* v *is allowed. (Actually, in Eiffel this constraint is already imposed on* all *formal parameters).*
2. v *cannot be assigned to any variable.*
3. v *cannot be used as an actual argument in a procedure call if the corresponding formal parameter is declared as consumable.*

There is an important special case of parameter passing in OO programming which requires special attention here. This is an operation of the form

```
u.m(...),
```

where u is a u-variable of some class C, and m is one of the methods of C. The problem here is that u itself might be nullified by this operation — quite a disconcerting prospect. The reason for this is that u must be considered a parameter to its own method m. In Eiffel, in particular, it is bound to the implicitly defined local variable Current[3] of method m. Now, if m happens to assign Current

---

[3] The equivalents in other languages have names such as "self" or "this".

to some other variable, then u will be consumed by this operation. Such consumption would not occur if m satisfies the constraints of Rule 3 with respect to variable Current. This is ensured by the following rule[4], (which, like all the rules of Eiffel*, can be checked at compile time):

Rule 4 *Variables of a given class* C *can be declared as u-variable only if all the methods defined for this class treat their implicitly defined local variable* Current *as non-consumable formal parameter, satisfying the constraints of Rule 3.*

This constraint on the the classes whose variables can be declared as unshareable is not as restrictive as it may seem, for two reasons: First, the conditions imposed by this rule on the use of variable Current are almost always satisfied in normal use. For example, an analysis of the official Eiffel library of ISE (their EiffelBase) indicates that less than 2% of its classes violate this rule, and an analysis of three (fairly randomly chosen) applications programs revealed *no* such violations. Second, even if some method of a given class C does not satisfy Rule 4, it is often possible to define a class C1 that inherits from C, redefining the offending methods in it, so that C1 would satisfy our rule and can thus be used as a basis for u-variables.

3.4 Miscellaneous Rules

We describe here the rest of the rules that support unshareable objects in Eiffel*. These rules tend to be more specific to the Eiffel language, and of a somewhat lesser general import than those considered above. The statement of each rule is preceded by its motivation.

First, most languages provide some means for copying entire objects. (In Eiffel this can be done by means of explicit copy routines such as copy and clone, and by the assignment of *expanded* objects, which are used infrequently in this language.) Such a copy is problematic if an object being copied contains u-

---

[4] We point out, in response to a question by Bertrand Meyer, that the call u.m(u), where u is a u-variable and the argument of m is consumable, would cause u to be consumed, after the call is carried out. We dot not find this consequence, of this rare construct, to be particularly distressing.

attributes. The copying of objects must, therefore, be subjected to the following rule (stated in very general terms):

Rule 5 *The copying of a complete object must not be allowed to copy any u-attributes of it. Such attributes must be either moved, according to Rule 2, or not transferred at all by the copy routine. (Another possibility is to completely disallow any copying of objects with unshareable attributes.)*

Second, we confront the following problem[5]: if an object **x** has an *exported* u-attribute u, then due to Rule 2, the assignment statement

```
v := x.u;
```

would consume the u attribute of **x**. But this would violate one of the basic properties of encapsulation in Eiffel, namely that it is not possible to change the value of an attribute of an object directly from the outside. To prevent this violation we impose the following rule:

Rule 6 *A u-attribute of a class cannot be exported.*

Of course, this does not prevent an object from "voluntarily" giving up one of its private u-attributes, returning it as a result of one of its methods.

Finally, we must impose the following constraint on *once functions*, which is an unusual Eiffel device designed to support globally accessible objects:

Rule 7 *The result of a* once function *cannot be declared as unshareable.*

The reason for this rule is that a once function in Eiffel returns the same result every time it is called. This result, then, is not unique, and thus cannot be unshareable.

3.5 Recycling of Unshareable Objects

The Eiffel language provides no explicit means for the deallocation of dynamic objects. This is, because such means would be unsafe due to possible *dangling reference*, and because they are considered unnecessary in a language with garbage

---

[5] This problem has been pointed out by Partha Pal

collection. The deallocation of u-objects, however, is quite safe, and, as we shall see, can be very helpful even in the presence of garbage collection. The following rule introduces an appropriate deallocation method, `recycle`, for u-objects[6].

Rule 8 (the `recycle` method) *Let there be a method* `recycle` *that can be applied to any u-variable* u *which is not an unconsumable argument of a procedure. Method* `recycle` *does nothing when* u *is void, and operates as follows, otherwise:*

1. *It applies* `recycle` *(recursively) to all u-attributes of* u*;*
2. *It deallocates the object addressed by* u*, and nullifies variable* u *itself.*

Note that `recycle` terminates because pointers to u-objects cannot form a cycle.

Recycling of u-objects can be done in two ways: *manually*, whenever one decides that an object is not needed, or *automatically*, whenever it is evident that an object *cannot be used* anymore. Such automatic recycling is established by the following rule.

Rule 9 (automatic recycling) *The* `recycle` *method introduced in Rule 8 is applied automatically, as follows:*

1. *Before a procedure exits all u-objects addressed by its local variables are recycled (i.e., the method* `recycle` *is applied to them.)*
2. *When an object is collected, during garbage collections, all its unshareable components are recycled.*
3. *Before an assignment* u := v *is carried out,* u *is recycled.*

(Note that automatic deallocation can be established easily in C++, but it would not be generally safe unless it is applied to u-variables.) The implications of recycling for storage management are discussed briefly in Section 4.4.

4   On the Use and Applications of Unshareable Objects

Being used, as we are, to the traditional transfer-by-copy in programming, the use of u-objects requires a change of viewpoint — one should think about them

---

[6] This rule and the following one are not required for the support of unshareable objects, but they can help making the most of them.

as things that *move* from one place to another, just like the physical objects we manipulate in daily life. As an example of this difference, note that a stack designed to maintain u-objects cannot have the traditional top method, which returns a pointer to the top of the stack, without removing it. This is inherently impossible when this top is unshareable.[7] In spite of such unfamiliar aspects of unshareable objects, we will show in this section that they can be used quite conveniently in many applications, and can even be shared via intermediate "handle" objects, when such sharing is required.

We start this section with a very simple programming example, introducing regular handle-objects that can be used to effectively share u-objects. In Section 4.2 we discuss applications for which u-objects are naturally suitable. In Section 4.3 we show that u-objects can be maintained in arbitrary data-structure, which makes them usable in a broad range of applications. Finally, in Section 4.4 we discuss the implication of u-objects to storage management.

4.1 Shareable Handles for U-Objects

Suppose that the instances of a given class C are meant to be sometimes hidden in some other objects, and be sometimes easily accessible to many parts of the system. These seemingly contradictory usages can be supported by (a) making all instances of C unshareable, so they can be truly hidden, when hiding is called for; and (b) making them accessible through *shareable handles*, when wider accessibility is called for.

To see in detail how this can be done, consider the class HANDLE defined in Figure 3 (assuming, for simplicity, that class C itself is declared as unshareable). Every handle has an u-attribute of class C, called body; and there are two methods applicable to it: the method install(b), which installs b as the body of the handle, and remove, which removes the body of the handle, returning it as its value.

Consider, now, a regular (i.e., shareable) handle h that has an object p as its body. Although p itself is unsahreable, it can be accesses through h by anybody

---

[7] But one can approximate the conventional top method, if such is desired, by producing a copy of the top of the stack and returning a pointer for this copy.

```
class HANDLE
  feature
    body:C            -- This is a u-variable, because class C is unshareable
    install(b:C consumable) is    -- b is a consumable argument
      do body := b    -- this is a move that consumes the actual argument
      end;
    remove:C is       -- the result of this function is unshareable
      do result := body          the body is consumed by this method
      end;
end -- class NODE
```

Fig. 3. A handle for an u-object

that has a pointer to it, like object **x** in Figure 4. In particular, if m is one of the methods of p then **x** can perform the operation

    h.body.m,

thus applying m to p; and so can other objects that have access to h. This arrangement allows p to be shared, in spite of its unshareable status; but it also allows one to hide p at will. In particular, a statement

    v:=h1.remove

carried out by **x** (see Figure 4), *moves* p from h into v, thus hiding this object inside **x**, regardless of who shared it before via the handle h. Finally, **x** may at any time return p to handle h by means of operation

    h1.install(v)

which moves p back into h, making p widely accessible again.

4.2 Natural Applications of Unshareable Objects

Perhaps the most natural and important application of u-objects is as a means for fortifying encapsulation. Such fortification is called for when: (a) an object

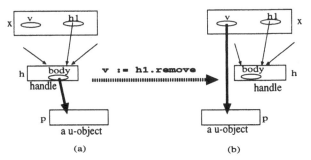

State (a) is transformed into state (b) by an operation
v := h1.remove
carried out by object x

Legend

▢ · · · · · an object
⬯ · · · · · a pointer variable
⟶ · · · · · regular pointer
⟹ · · · · u-pointer

Fig. 4. The sharing of a u-object via a handle

has a varying number of components, or (b) the components of an object have an indefinite lifetime, or (c) when components are being moved dynamically from one object to another. If any of these conditions are satisfied one needs to have the components of an object allocated on the heap, which, as argued in Section 2, makes them hard to hide effectively, unless they are made unshareable. Making the component parts of an object unshareable would facilitate, in particular, the construction of reliable class invariants, and the prevention of race conditions between threads.

Another natural application of u-objects is discussed in [8], where we show how such objects can be used to implement *tokens* — objects that, like the *capabilities* of operating systems, represent certain authority. Such unshareable tokens can be utilized, in particular, for the control of sharing in software systems such as object-oriented databases.

4.3 General Programming with Unshareable Objects

Besides the above natural applications of u-objects, such objects can be used effectively in a broad range of applications where the ability to prevent aliasing is important. Indeed, there is no serious limitation to the applicability of u-objects. We already saw that u-objects can be effectively shared via handle objects. One can, therefore, build arbitrary data structure involving u-objects, although such objects cannot be used *directly* as nodes in many kinds of list structures, such as in doubly linked lists. Indeed, employing a simple generalization of the handles of the previous section, u-objects can be stored in any graph, with one level of indirection, as is illustrated in Figure 5 for doubly linked lists. Although such indirection involves a certain amount of overhead, it is very common in data structures anyway, and should not be seen as a serious limitation on the use of u-objects.

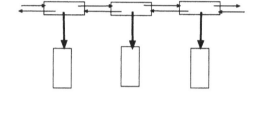

legend

⊏⊐   regular object
▯   u-object
⟶   regular pointer
➤   u-pointer

Fig. 5. A doubly linked list of u-objects

Of course, not all dynamic objects can be made unshareable. At the very least, we need regular objects to serve as handles for unshareable ones, allowing for controlled sharing of u-objects, and for their incorporation in complex data structures.

Finally, it should also be pointed out that u-objects can contain pointers to regular objects, and that regular objects can point to u-objects (which is the case with handles, for example). The one thing that should not be allowed is to have a pointer into an internal component of a u-object. No such pointers are possible in Eiffel, but they can be generated in C++ by means of the & operator, which should be prohibited in any implementation of u-objects in this language.

4.4   The Effect of Unshareability on Storage Management

Unshareable objects should have a significant beneficial impact on the safety and efficiency of storage management, particularly if they are used massively. This is due to the fact that u-objects can be *recycled* safely, as described in Section 3.5. The precise nature of this impact depends on whether or not the language in question provides garbage collection.

In a language without garbage collection (like C++) the use of u-objects should have two beneficial effects: First, the conventional unsafe deallocation of dynamic objects would be replaced by the safe explicit recycling. Second[8], the automatic recycling of manifestly unreachable u-objects, as defined by Rule 9, should reduce the amount of *memory leakage* in the system, i.e., the number of allocated objects that have *no* pointers leading to them, and are therefore lost to the program.

In a language with garbage collection (like Eiffel) the manual and automatic recycling of u-objects should reduce the frequency of invocation of the expensive garbage collection procedure, thus making storage management more efficient. This effect would be particularly strong if u-objects are used for all but the handle-objects required for complex data structure. This is because in this case mostly the handle objects would be subject to garbage collection, and since such objects are likely to have several standard small sizes, which are easier to manage.

5   Related Work

This work bears significant similarities to two recent efforts. Both support objects that satisfy our Definition 2 and for some of the same reasons that motivated this work. But there are deficiencies in both of these proposals, particularly for object-oriented programming (which, in fairness, was not the context in which these proposal were made.)

One of these efforts is by Harms and Weide [4], who may have been the first to challenge the conventional use of copying as the primary mechanism for transferring data in programming. They proposed to replace all such transfers (i.e.,

---

[8] I owe the last observation to Yaron Minsky.

assignment and parameter passing) with *swaps*, which would make *all* dynamic objects unshareable.

One problem with this proposal is that swapping, as a mechanism for the transfer of data, is inconsistent with the polymorphic, strongly typed, object oriented languages. This is because in such languages the type constraints on assignments are *antisymmetric*, and thus incompatible with the symmetric swap. This problem can be demonstrated as follows: Let class C1 be a proper superclass of C2, and let v1 and v2 be variables of classes C1 and C2, respectively. Now consider the assignment statement

```
v1 := v2;
```

Such statements are allowed in Eiffel, and are very important to OO languages in general, because they provide for polymorphism. But the swapping paradigm would replace this statement with a swap of values which, in particular, will place the value of v1 into v2, violating the requirement that a variable should not hold instances of its superclasses [6]. Another problem with the scheme proposed by Harms and Weide is that it fails to protect u-parameters from being consumed by the procedure they are submitted to. This particular difficulty is even more serious in Baker's proposal discussed next.

The second work has been recently reported in a paper[9] by Baker [1]. Baker introduces a concept of *use-once* variable, which point to what he calls *linear object*. His concept of linear object, which was inspired by Girard's *linear logic* [3], is equivalent to our u-object. But we find the manner these objects are handled, via use-once variables, problematic. The term "use-once" variables, indicates that *every* use of such a variable consumes its value. That is, if u is a use-once variable, then every procedure call p(...,u,...), and every operation u.m, nullifies it. This is a serious drawback, which would make programming with u-object very difficult and very unsafe, particularly in the context of an object oriented language. Baker himself states that *"The acceptance by a function of a linear argument object places a great responsibility on the function..."*. Because, if the argument of a function is to be retained by the caller, it must be returned to him as a value of this function. Baker admits that this would make writing

---

[9] This paper also contains a fairly extensive review of previous related works

programs syntactically complex, because functions may have to have several return values; and he proposes a graphical language as a solution. But what is perhaps worse about this scheme is that the failure of a function to return some of its linear (unshareable) arguments may cause very grave consequences to the internal state of its caller, by having some of its private components consumed.

6 Conclusion

We have argued in this paper that the serious problem of pointer-induced aliasing is largely a self inflicted wound, caused by the almost universal practice in programming to transfer information *by copy*. We have shown that it takes only few minor, and virtually costless, modifications of a typical programming language (involving, in part, the transfer of pointers) to ensure that certain variables contain unique pointers. And we have argued that the use of such variables are likely to have a salutary effect on our ability to reason about large systems, and on the safety and efficiency of storage management.

Although the complete implementation of u-pointers and u-objects generally requires some changes to the definition of a language, of the kind described here for Eiffel, we have constructed a good approximation for u-objects in C++, which requires no changes in the language itself. This construction, which has been carried out by Yu-min Liang from Rutgers University, only approximates u-objects in that it relies on a program to satisfy certain simple constraints, such as that the & operator is never applied to objects designated as unshareable. This construction will be described elsewhere.

Acknowledgment: I would like to thank Alex Borgida, Rock Howard, Yaron Minsky, Partha Pal and Yossi Stein for many useful conversation during the writing of this paper. I am also indebted to Bertrand Meyer for his many useful comments when reviewing this paper.

References

1. H.G. Baker. Use-once variables and linear objects — storage management, reflection and multi-threading. *ACM SIGPLAN Notices*, January 1995.

2. L. Cardelli, J. Donahue, L. Glassman, M. Jordan, and G. Nelson. Modula-3 report (revised). Technical Report 52, Digital System Research Center, November 1989.

3. J. Y. Girard. Linear logic. *Theoretical Computer Science*, pages 1–102, 1987.

4. Dougles E. Harms and Bruce W. Weide. Copying and swapping: Influences on the design of reusable software components. *IEEE Transactions on Software Engineering*, pages 424–434, May 1991.

5. W Landi. Undecidebility of static analysis. *Lett. Program. Lang. Syst.*, 1(4), December 1992.

6. B. Meyer. *Object-Oriented Software Construction*. Prentice-Hall, 1987.

7. B. Meyer. *Eiffel: The Language*. Prentice-Hall, 1992.

8. N.H. Minsky. On the use of tokens in programming. Technical report, Rutgers University, LCSR, October 1995.

9. D.L. Parnas. On the criteria to be used in decomposing systems into modules. *Communications of the ACM*, 15(12), December 1972.

10. R. Sethi. *Programming Languages, Concepts and Constructions*. Addison Wesley, 1989.

11. A. Tanenbaum. *Modern Operating Systems*. Prentice Hall, 1992.

Inheritance and Cofree Constructions

Bart Jacobs

CWI, Kruislaan 413, 1098 SJ Amsterdam, The Netherlands.

Email: bjacobs@cwi.nl

Abstract. *The coalgebraic view on classes and objects is elaborated to include inheritance. Inheritance in coalgebraic specification (of classes) will be understood dually to parametrization in algebraic specification. That is, inheritance involves restriction (specialization), where parametrization involves extension. And cofree constructions are "best" restrictions, like free constructions are "best" extensions. To make this view on inheritance precise we need a suitable notion of behaviour preserving morphism between classes, which will be defined as a "coalgebra map up-to-bisimulation".*

1 Introduction

Two basic relations in object-oriented languages are: object o belongs to class C, and: class C inherits from class C' (see e.g. [23]). Class membership yields what is sometimes called a "first order" classification of objects by classes, whereas inheritance provides a "second order" classification of classes by their superclasses (ancestors). According to Cardelli [2, p. 139]: "... a theory of object-oriented programming should first of all focus on the meaning of inheritance". The first of these relations (class membership) is interpreted in [12] (following [19], and also [10, 11]): briefly, a class is a coalgebra, and an object belonging to a class is an element of the underlying state space of the class, as a coalgebra. This will be used as a basis for an interpretation of the second (inheritance) relation in the present paper: inheritance will involve a behaviour preserving coercion function between classes.

Inheritance in object-oriented programming is used primarily for two purposes: reuse and conceptual modeling (i.e. classification). In the first case inheritance is useful in implementation, and in the second case its advantages come up mainly in design: it allows suitable representations of the data domain, giving the "is-a" relation between classes (see e.g. [22] for an elaborate discussion). We think that inheritance is intuitively a clear and useful notion: for example, it is convenient to have a class of students inheriting from a class of humans, so that all operations acting on humans can directly be applied to students, without reimplementation. And because inheritance is intuitively clear, it should admit a simple set-theoretic semantics (without complicated fixed points, like for example in [23, 3]).

In our approach the aspect of conceptual modeling gets more attention than the aspect of reuse. We make a clear separation between class specifications (also called "abstract" classes) and class implementations (or, "concrete" classes), where the latter are models of the former. We shall put more emphasis on specification, than on actual implementation. Class implementations are (non-deferred) classes as used in object-oriented languages. They will be interpreted as so-called coalgebras, consisting of a state space (the interpretation of the class as a type), together with a collection of functions (the interpretation of the methods) acting on the state space. Coalgebras may be understood as general dynamical systems, consisting of a state space with a transition function. Objects belonging to such a class are elements of the state space (i.e. of the carrier of the coalgebra), see [12]. A class implementation gives the method interpretations on a state space, and an object belonging to that class contains specific data values. A class specification gives a behavioural description of classes. The format of class specifications is "coalgebraic", as opposed to the more traditional "algebraic" format (see below).

Two ideas in particular are elaborated in this paper.

(1) In a class specification we distinguish a "core" part and a "definition" part. The definition part may contain definitions of functions (possibly non-unary), in terms of unary methods in the core part. Models of the specification are models of the core part, in which the defined functions receive their interpretation via their definitions and the interpretations of the core part. The definition part does not contribute to the semantics. It may be altered freely in descendants. But the core part may only become more specific in descendants, ensuring monotony. Thus we essentially model what is sometimes called "strict" inheritance, but we do have some flexibility in the definition part.

In fact, the distinction between core and definition part provides a criterion for when it is appropriate to redefine in descendant classes.

(2) Inheritance in coalgebraic specification is similar, but dual, to parametrization in algebraic specification. Both are mechanisms for the stepwise construction of data-structures, but the paradigm for algebraic specification is *extension* (with "unit" morphism as "extension" map), and in coalgebraic specification the paradigm is *restriction* (with "counit" morphism as "restriction" or "coercion" map). Accordingly, one has *free* constructions in algebraic specification where one has *cofree* constructions in coalgebraic specification. We shall use some elementary category theory—involving categories and functors only—to make this duality explicit.

We illustrate this duality between parametrization and inheritance in a simple example, using some ad hoc notation. Consider an algebraic specification NELIST of non-empty lists (of elements of some fixed data set A), as below. It is imported (or, used as a parameter) in a subsequent parametrized specification LIST of possibly empty lists. Coalgebraically we first specify an elementary bank account BANK, and then describe the inheriting specification NBANK with an additional name attribute. The crucial difference between the algebraic and the coalgebraic specification techniques is that in the first case we only have "constructors" pointing into the unknown type X that we are specifying, whereas in the second coalgebraic case we have "destructors" or "observers" pointing out of X (see also the difference between abstract data types and procedural abstraction in [4], and between functional modules and object modules in [9] going back to [8]; the unknown X is a (single) hidden sort in the latter approach). Our use of the terminology of constructors and destructors comes from data type theory, and is different from their use in C++, see [21]. A typical constructor has the form $A \times X \times \cdots \times X \longrightarrow X$ where A is a constant set, whereas typical destructors are $X \longrightarrow A$ and $X \longrightarrow X^B$. The latter can equivalently be written as $X \times B \longrightarrow X$, so that it is also a constructor. Hence constructors and destructors form non-disjoint sets of function symbols.

Here, then, are the specifications: the algebraic ones on the left, and the coalgebraic ones on the right.

Alg spec: NELIST
  operations:
    el: $A \longrightarrow X$
    conc: $X \times X \longrightarrow X$
  assertions:
    $\mathrm{conc}(x, \mathrm{conc}(y, z))$
      $= \mathrm{conc}(\mathrm{conc}(x, y), z))$

Coalg spec: BANK
  operations:
    bal: $X \longrightarrow \mathbf{Z}$
    ch_bal: $X \times \mathbf{Z} \longrightarrow X$
  assertions:
    $\mathrm{bal}(\mathrm{ch\_bal}(s, x)) = \mathrm{bal}(s) + x$

Alg spec: LIST
  imports:
    NELIST
  operations:
    empty: $1 \longrightarrow X$
  assertions:
    $\mathrm{conc}(x, \mathrm{empty}) = x$
    $\mathrm{conc}(\mathrm{empty}, x) = x$

Coalg spec: NBANK
  imports:
    BANK
  operations:
    name: $X \longrightarrow$ String
  assertions:
    $\mathrm{name}(\mathrm{ch\_bal}(s, x)) = \mathrm{name}(s)$

A model of such a (algebraic or coalgebraic) specification consists of a "carrier" set $U = [\![X]\!]$ interpreting the type X, together with interpretations of the specified operations (as suitable functions) satisfying the assertions. (In the algebraic case these functions form an *algebra* $T(U) \to U$ on U, and in the coalgebraic case they form a *coalgebra* $U \to S(U)$ on U, for suitable functors T, S: **Sets** $\rightrightarrows$ **Sets** describing the signatures.)

The import clause in the LIST and NBANK specifications tells us that all the operations and assertions are copied from the imported specification. This means that every model of the LIST specification is also a model of the NELIST specification, and every model of the NBANK specification is also a model of the BANK specification: we have "forget" operations $\mathcal{U}$: **Models**(LIST) $\to$ **Models**(NELIST) and $\mathcal{V}$: **Models**(NBANK) $\to$ **Models**(BANK), which respectively, forget the interpretations of the empty operation, and of the name operation (but keep the carrier sets unaltered). At this point the difference in interpretation of the import clause starts: algebraically one thinks of every non-empty list as a list, whereas coalgebraically every bank account with name is seen as a bank account. Notice the reversal of direction. Thus, (algebraic) parametrization is about *extension*, whereas (coalgebraic) inheritance is about *restriction* (or *specialization*). For example, we can take as model of NELIST the set A^+ of non-empty finite sequences of A's, and as model of LIST the set A^* of finite sequences of A's, including the empty one. There is then an obvious "extension" map $\eta: A^+ \to \mathcal{U}(A^*)$, commuting with the interpretations of the NELIST-operations. For the coalgebraic specifications we can take as bank account model the set $\mathbf{Z}$ of integers (with identity as interpretation for bal and addition for ch_bal). And as model of a bank account with name we can take the set $\mathbf{Z} \times$ String, with obvious interpretations of the operations. There is then a "restriction" or "coercion" map $\varepsilon: \mathcal{V}(\mathbf{Z} \times$ String$) \to \mathbf{Z}$ given by first projection, which commutes with the interpretations of the BANK-operations.

This difference between parametrization and inheritance results from the difference between the use of constructors in algebraic specification and of destructors in coalgebraic specification. All the constructors of the imported (algebraic) specification also construct elements of the importing specification, so that we have extension. And all destructors (or observers) of the imported (coalgebraic) specification also act on the importing specification, but in this case we have restriction. This difference is crucial.

In the preliminary Sections 2, 3 and 4 we explain the essentials of coalgebraic specification, of free and cofree constructions, and of bisimilarity on classes. The latter means indistinguishability of objects via attributes, and plays an important role for our notion of morphism between classes, involving "coalgebra maps up-to-bisimulation". The rest of this paper is essentially devoted to examples, explaining the coalgebraic view on classes and inheritance. Examples will be given of single inheritance, of multiple inheritance (both with and without common ancestor) and of repeated inheritance. We are not so concerned about specific syntactic details of the language that we use, because we start from a clear semantics, and see language as derived.

2   Class specifications and implementations

In this section we recall the essentials from [12], which forms the basis for what follows. We distinguish between class specifications and class implementations. These class implementations are what are usually simply called classes in object-oriented languages. Class specifications are linguistic entities consisting of three parts describing (1) the methods (operations), (2) the logical assertions which these methods should satisfy, and (3) the conditions which should hold for newly created objects. A class specification may be understood as a class in Eiffel (see [15]) in which all methods (or, features, in Eiffel-speak) are deferred (i.e. not yet interpreted) and in which pre- and post-conditions and invariants specify[1] the behaviour of the methods. In C++ one can also have classes with deferred methods (or, virtual data/member functions, in C++-speak), but assertions do not form part of the language.

As mathematical model of class implementations we use *coalgebras*. These are the formal duals of algebras. They consist of a carrier set (or local state space) U together with a (transition) function $U \to T(U)$ acting on this set U, with as codomain $T(U)$ an expression, possibly containing U, denoting a set. Formally, T is a functor **Sets** $\to$ **Sets**; it describes the signature of function symbols. The state space U gives an interpretation $U = [\![X]\!]$ of the type X occurring in class specifications, and the function $U \to T(U)$ interprets the methods. Objects belonging to a class with operations $U \to T(U)$ are elements $u \in U$ of this state space. An object evaluates a method via function application (to itself). Especially, we require that each class comes with a distinguished element (or initial state) $u_0 \in U$ serving as interpretation of newly created objects. Below we shall use class specifications with methods having one of the following two forms (like in [19]):

$$\text{at:} X \longrightarrow A \qquad \text{or} \qquad \text{proc:} X \times B \longrightarrow X$$

where A and B are constant sets, not depending on the "unknown" type X (of self). In the first case we have an *attribute* giving for a "local state" $s \in X$ an (observable) attribute value s.at = at(s) $\in A$. One can only observe the state space X via such attributes. In the second case we have a *procedure* proc which has an effect on the local state space X: it yields for a local state $s \in X$ and a parameter value $b \in B$ a new state s.proc(b) = proc(s, b) $\in X$. The effect of such a procedure call may be visible via the attributes. Attributes are like instance variables in object-oriented languages; procedures may be used to change the values of these instance variables, see the example below. When the parameter set B is a singleton set $1 = \{*\}$, then we write $X \to X$ instead of $X \times 1 \to X$. Also, B may consist of a product $B_1 \times \cdots \times B_n$. For simplicity we here restrict ourselves to these two forms of methods. Functions $X \times A \to B$ are seen as special instances of attributes using function spaces, in $X \to B^A$. In [12] a more general form of method $X \times A \to B + C \times X$ is used, giving additional expressive power. But this is not needed to describe inheritance, and only distracts from the essentials.

---

[1] Assertions in Eiffel are used not only for specification but also for run-time monitoring.

Two methods $X \to A$ and $X \times B \to X$ may be combined into a single "destructor" map $X \to A \times X^B$, giving us a coalgebra on X, pointing *out of* X. Dually, algebras are "constructor" maps of the form $T(X) \to X$ pointing *into* X. Algebraically, one constructs where coalgebraically one observes (or, destructs). See [12] for more details. Multiple attributes $X \longrightarrow A_1$, ..., $X \longrightarrow A_n$ may be combined into a single attribute $X \longrightarrow A_1 \times \cdots \times A_n$. And multiple procedures $X \times B_1 \longrightarrow X$, ..., $X \times B_m \longrightarrow X$ may be combined into a single one $X \times (B_1 + \cdots + B_m) \longrightarrow X$, where $+$ is disjoint union.

A typical example of a class specification is as follows. It describes an unknown type X behaving like a set of locations in a plane.

> **class spec: LOC**
>   **methods:**
>   fst: $X \longrightarrow \mathbb{R}$
>   snd: $X \longrightarrow \mathbb{R}$
>   move: $X \times \mathbb{R} \times \mathbb{R} \longrightarrow X$
>   **assertions:**
>   s.move(dx, dy).fst = s.fst + dx
>   s.move(dx, dy).snd = s.snd + dy
>   **creation:**
>   new.fst = 0
>   new.snd = 0
> **end class spec**

Here we specify classes of locations with first and second coordinate attributes fst and snd yielding real numbers, and with a move procedure yielding a new state. In the assertion clause we have the obvious conditions that after a move with change parameters dx and dy the first coordinate is incremented by dx and the second one by dy. In such specifications we use 's' for 'self' or 'state' as pseudovariable describing an arbitrary inhabitant of X. We shall use the object-oriented dot (.) notation, instead of the functional notation, so that we write s.move(dx, dy).fst for what would functionally be written as fst(move(s, dx, dy)). Finally in the creation clause we stipulate that newly created objects must have first and second coordinate equal to $0 \in \mathbb{R}$. This is coalgebraic (behavioural) specification since we prescribe nothing about what should be inside the local state space X or about how the methods should be implemented, but only what the observable behaviour should be. Typically, one cannot construct inhabitants of X via methods. This X is best seen as a black box to which we have limited access via the specified methods. In fact, we do not really care about what is inside X as long as X comes with operations as specified. Proper implementation is a local responsibility.

A class (implementation) satisfying such a specification is a (coalgebraic) model of the specification. In the example it consists of an interpretation $U = [\![X]\!]$ of the local state space X, together with interpretations $[\![\text{fst}]\!]: U \to \mathbb{R}$, $[\![\text{snd}]\!]: U \to \mathbb{R}$, $[\![\text{move}]\!]: U \times \mathbb{R} \times \mathbb{R} \to U$ of the methods in such a way that the equations are satisfied. Also a class should contain a distinguished element $u_0 \in U$ satisfying the creation conditions: $[\![\text{fst}]\!](u_0) = 0 = [\![\text{snd}]\!](u_0)$. These interpretations of the methods correspond to a single function $U \to \mathbb{R} \times \mathbb{R} \times U^{(\mathbb{R} \times \mathbb{R})}$ forming a coalgebra of the functor $X \mapsto \mathbb{R} \times \mathbb{R} \times X^{(\mathbb{R} \times \mathbb{R})}$.

Formally, a class (implementation) is a 3-tuple $\langle U, U \to T(U), u_0 \in U \rangle$, consisting of a state space U, a coalgebra $U \to T(U)$ on this set, and an initial state $u_0 \in U$. When part of this structure is understood from the context, we often refer to a class simply by mentioning its state space U.

An obvious example of a class implementation is obtained by taking Cartesian coordinates $[\![X]\!] = \mathbb{R}^2$ as local states, with operations:

$[\![\, \mathsf{fst} \,]\!] = \pi \colon \mathbb{R}^2 \longrightarrow \mathbb{R}, \quad$ i.e. $(x, y) \mapsto x, \qquad [\![\, \mathsf{snd} \,]\!] = \pi' \colon \mathbb{R}^2 \longrightarrow \mathbb{R}$ i.e. $(x, y) \mapsto y.$

And

$$[\![\, \mathsf{move} \,]\!] \colon \mathbb{R}^2 \times \mathbb{R} \times \mathbb{R} \longrightarrow \mathbb{R}^2 \qquad \text{is} \qquad (x, y, dx, dy) \mapsto (x + dx, y + dy).$$

Obviously, the assertions in the specification hold for this interpretation. As initial state we take the element $(0,0) \in \mathbb{R}^2$. Another class can be obtained with polar coordinates $[\![\, X \,]\!] = [0, \infty) \times [0, 2\pi)$, but this complicates the definition of the (interpretations of the) methods. A totally different class implementation has as state space the set $(\mathbb{R}^2)^\star$ of finite sequences of Cartesian coordinates. Such a sequence as object may be seen as the sequence of consecutive changes in the lifetime of the object. We can interpret the operations as:

$$
\begin{aligned}
[\![\, \mathsf{fst} \,]\!] \colon (\mathbb{R}^2)^\star &\longrightarrow \mathbb{R} \\
((x_1, y_1), \ldots, (x_n, y_n)) &\longmapsto x_1 + \cdots + x_n \\
[\![\, \mathsf{snd} \,]\!] \colon (\mathbb{R}^2)^\star &\longrightarrow \mathbb{R} \\
((x_1, y_1), \ldots, (x_n, y_n)) &\longmapsto y_1 + \cdots + y_n \\
[\![\, \mathsf{move} \,]\!] \colon (\mathbb{R}^2)^\star \times \mathbb{R} \times \mathbb{R} &\longrightarrow (\mathbb{R}^2)^\star \\
\langle ((x_1, y_1), \ldots, (x_n, y_n)), dx, dy \rangle &\longmapsto ((x_1, y_1), \ldots, (x_n, y_n), (dx, dy)).
\end{aligned}
$$

where the latter involves concatenation of the parameter (dx, dy). It is not hard to see that the equations hold in this model. The empty sequence $() \in (\mathbb{R}^2)^\star$ can serve as initial state. But one can also take the singleton sequence $(0,0) \in (\mathbb{R}^2)^\star$ as initial state, or $((0,0),(0,0))$ etcetera. (These are all "bisimilar" (or indistinguishable), see Section 3 below.) Thus we have another example of a class (implementation). Notice that although these three examples give quite different interpretations, a client cannot see these differences, since a client can only use the specified methods. Implementation is not a client's concern. We achieve this encapsulation by separating specification (including the interface) from implementation.

In the remainder of this text we shall omit the interpretation braces $[\![\, - \,]\!]$. When we write a method, the context should make clear whether it is meant as a function symbol in some specification, or as an interpretation thereof in some model.

2.1 Class specifications with definitions

We now extend our class specification format with an extra clause for definable functions. This extension does not yet occur in [12]. It will help us avoid some of the anomalies usually associated with inheritance, see [1] for a discussion. Such an extended class specification may contain, besides a "core" part as described above, an additional part describing some function definitions. These functions may have types of the form $X^n \to A$ or $X^n \times B \to X$, for $n \geq 1$, where X is the local state space (the type of self). Notice that these definable functions may thus be binary (or ternary etcetera). But the function definitions may only use the unary methods described in the core specification. This core will determine the meaning of the specification, and within a particular model the definable functions will receive their meaning via their definitions. Thus, in every specific model, we have specific interpretations of the definable functions. For example, we may write a variation LOC+ on the above specification LOC as:

class spec: LOC+
    (methods, assertions and creation as for LOC)
    definitions:
        dist: $X \longrightarrow \mathbb{R}$
            $\text{dist}(s) = \text{sqrt}((s.\text{fst})^2 + (s.\text{snd})^2)$
        eq: $X \times X \longrightarrow$ Bool
            $\text{eq}(s_1, s_2) = (s_1.\text{fst} = s_2.\text{fst}) \wedge (s_1.\text{snd} = s_2.\text{snd})$
end class spec

Hence by dist we mean distance to the origin. These defined functions dist and eq do not contribute to the meaning of the specification. Thus any model of the LOC specification is also a model of the LOC+ specification. But in different models the interpretations of dist and eq will be different, as a result of the different interpretations of the fst and snd attributes. For example, in the above LOC model with state space $\mathbb{R}^2$ we have

$$\text{dist}(x, y) = \sqrt{x^2 + y^2}$$

whereas in the LOC model with state space $(\mathbb{R}^2)^\star$ it will be

$$\text{dist}((x_1, y_1), \ldots, (x_n, y_n)) = \sqrt{(x_1 + \cdots + x_n)^2 + (y_1 + \cdots + y_n)^2}.$$

There are similarly different interpretations of the equality function eq, determined by the different interpretations of fst and snd. We shall use the function notation for these definable functions, since for multiple state arguments there is in general no preferred component which should be mentioned first: it seems more natural to write $\text{eq}(s_1, s_2)$ than $s_1.\text{eq}(s_2)$ or $s_2.\text{eq}(s_1)$. For unary methods in the core part, the dot-notation s.method does make sense.

Since these definable functions do not contribute to the meaning of specifications, we may freely alter them in descendants without affecting monotonicity (or "strictness") for the interpretations of the core part. This is the main point of separating the core part and the definition part. The alterations that we allow are removal of definitions and overriding of definitions, for which we shall use ad hoc syntax. An example will be presented in the next section, consisting of a specification of circles inheriting from locations by extension with an extra radius attribute, in the core part. For circles we shall redefine the equality function eq, in the definition part.

Definability is a language dependent notion, but what definability means in a specific programming language will be unproblematic. We shall use elementary language constructs only, meant as illustration.

Within this framework one must choose in advance which methods of a class specifications are essential and belong to the core part, and which to the definition part. But (good) class design is the hardest part of object-oriented programming anyway.

3   Bisimulation and morphisms of classes

Consider the class specification LOC of locations from the previous section, with the implementation (class) on the set $(\mathbb{R}^2)^\star$ of finite sequences of pairs of reals. A client of this class cannot distinguish between the locations $((2,3),(1,1)) \in (\mathbb{R}^2)^\star$ and $((3,0),(0,4)) \in (\mathbb{R}^2)^\star$: in both cases the first coordinate is equal to 3, and the second to 4, and by moving these points around we cannot create a difference between them. These locations (or states) are indistinguishable by the methods in the LOC-specification, and are called **bisimilar**. Here is the general notion. (We can restrict ourselves to class specifications with a single attribute and procedure only, by combination of attributes and methods, as mentioned in Section 2.)

3.1. Definition. Consider a functor $X \mapsto A \times X^B$ and a coalgebra $\varphi = \langle \varphi_1, \varphi_2 \rangle : U \to A \times U^B$ of this functor, giving us interpretations of an attribute φ_1 and a procedure φ_2 acting on a set U.

(i) A **bisimulation** on φ is a relation $R \subseteq U \times U$ on its state space which satisfies for each pair $x, y \in U$:

$$R(x, y) \Rightarrow \left[\varphi_1(x) = \varphi_1(y) \quad \text{and} \quad \text{for all } b \in B, \ R(\varphi_2(x)(b), \varphi_2(y)(b)) \right].$$

(ii) Two elements $x, y \in U$ are called **bisimilar** (with respect to the coalgebra structure φ) if there is a bisimulation $R \subseteq U \times U$ with $R(x, y)$. We then write $x \leftrightarrow y$.

It is not hard to see that bisimilarity $\leftrightarrow$ is itself a bisimulation: it is the greatest bisimulation. And it is an equivalence relation, since the identity relation, the opposite $\leftrightarrow^{\mathrm{op}}$ and the composite $\leftrightarrow \circ \leftrightarrow$ are bisimulations, and are thus contained in $\leftrightarrow$. Bisimilarity $\leftrightarrow$ formalizes behavioural indistinguishability. It is a standard notion in process theory (see e.g. [17]) and in coalgebra.

Bisimilarity on the above LOC-class $(\mathbb{R}^2)^*$ is given by

$$((x_1, y_1), \ldots, (x_n, y_n)) \leftrightarrow ((x_1', y_1'), \ldots, (x_m', y_m'))$$
$$\Leftrightarrow$$
$$x_1 + \cdots + x_n = x_1' + \cdots + x_m' \quad \text{and} \quad y_1 + \cdots + y_n = y_1' + \cdots + y_m'.$$

States in this relation $\leftrightarrow$ are indeed indistinguishable by the LOC-methods. Bisimilarity on the LOC-class $\mathbb{R}^2$ is simply the identity relation. This is because states are simply given by their first and second coordinate. (The class is based on a terminal coalgebra, see [12].)

A client of a class can only see objects (inhabitants of a state space) up-to-bisimulation. This will be reflected in the notion of morphism of classes that we introduce below.

3.2. Definition. Consider a class specification S with its signature of methods described by the functor $S(X) = A \times X^B$. We define a category **Class**(S) of classes satisfying this specification in the following manner.

objects   pairs $\langle U \xrightarrow{\varphi} S(U), u_0 \in U \rangle$ consisting of a coalgebra $\varphi = \langle \varphi_1, \varphi_2 \rangle$ with local state space U, giving an interpretation of the methods in S which satisfies the assertions in S, together with an initial state $u_0 \in U$ satisfying the creation conditions in S.

morphisms $\langle U \xrightarrow{\varphi} S(U), u_0 \in U \rangle \longrightarrow \langle V \xrightarrow{\psi} S(V), v_0 \in V \rangle$ consist of a function $f : U \to V$ between the underlying state spaces satisfying the requirements:

         (i) f preserves bisimilarity: $u \leftrightarrow u'$ implies $f(u) \leftrightarrow f(u')$;
         (ii) $\psi_1 \circ f = \varphi_1 : U \to A$;
         (iii) for each $u \in U$ and $b \in B$ one has $\psi_2(f(u))(b) \leftrightarrow f(\varphi_2(u)(b))$;
         (iv) $f(u_0) \leftrightarrow v_0$.

The first condition (i) is actually derivable from (ii) and (iii)—see the lemma below— but is convenient to have explicit in the definition, for example to see that these maps are closed under composition.

What is traditionally called a "morphism of coalgebras" from $U \xrightarrow{\varphi} \mathcal{S}(U)$ to $V \xrightarrow{\psi} \mathcal{S}(V)$ is a function $f \colon U \to V$ satisfying (ii) as above but (iii) with bisimilarity $\leftrightarrow$ replaced by equality $=$. The conditions (ii) and (iii) in this definition describe what may be called a "morphism of coalgebras up-to-bisimulation" (like one has "bisimilarity up-to-bisimulation", see [17]). Since bisimilarity on terminal coalgebras is equality, changing the notion of morphism between coalgebras in this way does not affect terminality.

For example, in the category $\mathbf{Class}(\mathrm{LOC})$ of classes of the LOC-specification we have morphisms

$$(\mathbb{R}^2)^* \xrightarrow{\quad f \quad} \mathbb{R}^2 \qquad \text{and} \qquad \mathbb{R}^2 \xrightarrow{\quad g \quad} (\mathbb{R}^2)^*$$

given by

$$f((x_1, y_1), \ldots, (x_n, y_n)) = (x_1 + \cdots + x_n, y_1 + \cdots + y_n) \quad \text{and} \quad g(x, y) = ((x, 0), (0, y)).$$

We show that g commutes up-to-bisimulation with the move-interpretations:

$$
\begin{aligned}
\mathrm{move}(g((x, y), dx, dy)) &= \mathrm{move}(((x, 0), (0, y)), dx, dy) \\
&= ((x, 0), (0, y), (dx, dy)) \\
&\leftrightarrow ((x + dx, 0), (y + dy, 0)) \\
&= g(x + dx, y + dy) \\
&= g(\mathrm{move}((x, y), dx, xy)).
\end{aligned}
$$

3.3. Lemma. *The first condition (i) for morphisms in* $\mathbf{Class}(S)$ *in Definition 3.2 is derivable from conditions (ii) and (iii).*

Proof. Assume coalgebras φ, ψ as in the definition, and a function $f \colon U \to V$ between their state spaces, satisfying conditions (ii) and (iii). For an element $u \in U$ and a sequence $\beta \in B^*$, define $u_\beta \in U$ by induction on the length of β as:

$$u_{\langle\rangle} = u \qquad \text{and} \qquad u_{\beta.b} = \varphi_2(u_\beta)(b).$$

We claim that for $u, u' \in U$ with $u \leftrightarrow u'$ and for $\beta \in B^*$ the following holds.
   (a) $u_\beta \leftrightarrow u'_\beta$;
   (b) $f(u_\beta) \leftrightarrow f(u'_\beta)$.
Notice that (b) gives the required result, for $\beta = \langle\rangle$. Statement (a) follows directly by induction on β from the fact that $\leftrightarrow$ is itself a bisimulation. For (b) we have to do some work. Define relations $R, S \subseteq V \times V$ by

$$R = \{\langle f(u_\beta), f(u'_\beta)\rangle \mid u, u' \in U \text{ with } u \leftrightarrow u', \text{ and } \beta \in B^*\} \qquad \text{and} \qquad S = \leftrightarrow \circ R \circ \leftrightarrow.$$

Our aim is to show that S is a bisimulation. This yields that R is also a bisimulation (since $\leftrightarrow$ is reflexive), and thus that $R \subseteq \leftrightarrow$, as required.

Assume therefore $\langle v, v'\rangle \in S$, say with $v \leftrightarrow f(u_\beta) R f(u'_\beta) \leftrightarrow v'$, where $u \leftrightarrow u'$ and $\beta \in B^*$. Then

• $\psi_1(v) = \psi_1(f(u_\beta)) \overset{(ii)}{=} \varphi_1(u_\beta) \overset{(a)}{=} \varphi_1(u'_\beta) \overset{(ii)}{=} \psi_1(f(u'_\beta)) = \psi_1(v')$.

• $\psi_2(v)(b) \leftrightarrow \psi_2(f(u_\beta))(b) \overset{(iii)}{\leftrightarrow} f(\varphi_2(u_\beta)(b)) = f(u_{\beta.b}) R f(u'_{\beta.b}) = f(\varphi_2(u'_\beta)(b)) \overset{(iii)}{\leftrightarrow}$
  $\psi_2(f(u'_\beta))(b) \leftrightarrow \psi_2(v')(b)$. Hence $\langle \psi_2(v)(b), \psi_2(v')(b)\rangle \in S$.   □

The relation R used in this proof is what Milner [17] calls a "bisimulation up-to-bisimilarity", since $\leftrightarrow \circ R \circ \leftrightarrow$ is a bisimulation.

4 Cofree constructions

"Cofree" constructions are the formal duals of "free" constructions. These free constructions are well-known in mathematics, and also in computer science in the theory of algebraic specifications. The starting point consists of two notions where one naturally gives rise to the other by forgetting part of the structure. As paradigmatic example we take monoids and sets. A monoid consists of a set with a unary and binary operation satisfying some equations. Every monoid gives us a set, simply by forgetting its operations. In this situation we can say that the **free monoid** on a given set A consists of a monoid $(M, u, \cdot)$ together with a "unit" function $\eta \colon A \to M$ such that for every monoid $(N, v, \bullet)$ with a function $f \colon A \to N$ there is a unique homomorphism $g \colon (M, u, \cdot) \to (N, v, \bullet)$ of monoids[2] with $f = g \circ \eta$. This monoid $(M, e, \cdot)$ is called the "free" monoid on A. It can intuitively be understood as the "smallest" monoid which "contains" the set A via $\eta \colon A \to M$. It is the "best possible" monoid into which one can map A. Free monoids on a set exist: it is not hard to see that the set A^* of finite sequences of elements of A with the empty sequence and concatenation as unary and binary operation, is the free monoid on A. The required unit map $\eta \colon A \to A^*$ sends an element $a \in A$ to the singleton sequence $\langle a \rangle \in A^*$.

Free constructions are used in algebraic specification to give meaning to parametrized specifications, see e.g. [5]. For example, consider a specification ABMON of Abelian monoids, with signature $e \colon 1 \longrightarrow X$, $m \colon X \times X \longrightarrow X$ and equations $m(x, e) = x$, $m(x, y) = m(y, x)$, $m(m(x, y), z) = m(x, m(y, z))$. If we now wish to write a specification ABGR of Abelian groups, we can extend the specification of monoids with an extra function symbol $i \colon X \longrightarrow X$ for inverse with equation $m(x, i(x)) = e$. One says that the specification ABGR is parametrized by ABMON. And one thinks of ABGR as an extension of ABMON, which can be expressed formally via an inclusion ABMON $\hookrightarrow$ ABGR of specifications. Semantically, every Abelian group yields an Abelian monoid by forgetting the inverse operation. This gives us a forget operation **Models**(ABGR) $\to$ **Models**(ABMON) induced by the inclusion ABMON $\hookrightarrow$ ABGR. And if we have a model of the ABMON specification, consisting of an Abelian monoid $(M, u, \cdot)$. then the **free Abelian group** on this monoid gives us a canonical model for the specification ABGR. Also this free construction exists, and can be described via a quotient of the free Abelian group on the underlying set, see the "Grothendieck group" example in [14]. One can think of this free construction as adding to the given Abelian monoid as little as necessary to obtain an Abelian group. One does not build an Abelian group from scratch, but one starts from an already given Abelian monoid. Such mechanisms are important in the stepwise construction of (algebraic) data-structures.

The general situation is the following. Suppose we have two categories $\mathbb{C}$ and $\mathbb{D}$ and a forgetful functor $\mathcal{U} \colon \mathbb{C} \to \mathbb{D}$. One can think of $\mathcal{U}$ as the forgetful functor from monoids to sets, or from Abelian groups to Abelian monoids. A **free construction** (also called **universal arrow**) on an object $A \in \mathbb{D}$ (with respect to this functor $\mathcal{U}$) consists of an object $B \in \mathbb{C}$ together with an arrow $\eta \colon A \to \mathcal{U}(B)$ in $\mathbb{D}$ which is universal in the following sense: for each object $B' \in \mathbb{C}$ with a map $f \colon A \to \mathcal{U}(B')$ in $\mathbb{D}$ there is a unique map $g \colon B \to B'$ in $\mathbb{C}$ such that $f = \mathcal{U}(g) \circ \eta$. In a diagram:

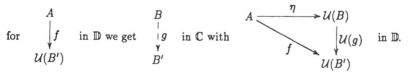

----

[2]This means that g is a function $g \colon M \to N$ between the underlying sets with $g(u) = v$ and $g(x \cdot y) = g(x) \bullet g(y)$.

Such a free construction, if it exists, is determined up-to isomorphism. And if a free construction exists for each object $A \in \mathbb{D}$, then we can define a functor $\mathcal{F}: \mathbb{D} \to \mathbb{C}$, *left* adjoint to the forgetful functor $\mathcal{U}$, see [13, IV] for details.

A **cofree construction** with respect to a functor $\mathcal{U}: \mathbb{C} \to \mathbb{D}$ can now simply be defined by duality as a free construction with respect to the associated functor $\mathcal{U}^{\mathrm{op}}: \mathbb{C}^{\mathrm{op}} \to \mathbb{D}^{\mathrm{op}}$ between opposite categories (with arrows reversed). Explicitly, a cofree construction on an object $A \in \mathbb{D}$ consists of an object $B \in \mathbb{C}$ together with a "counit" arrow $\varepsilon: \mathcal{U}(B) \to A$ in $\mathbb{D}$ which is universal: for every $B' \in \mathbb{C}$ and map $f: \mathcal{U}(B') \to A$ in $\mathbb{D}$ there is a unique map $g: B' \to B$ in $\mathbb{C}$ with $\varepsilon \circ \mathcal{U}(g) = f$, like in:

$$
\text{for} \quad
\begin{array}{c} A \\ \uparrow {\scriptstyle f} \\ \mathcal{U}(B') \end{array}
\quad \text{in } \mathbb{D} \text{ there is} \quad
\begin{array}{c} B \\ \uparrow {\scriptstyle g} \\ B' \end{array}
\quad \text{in } \mathbb{C} \text{ with} \quad
\begin{array}{c} \mathcal{U}(B) \xrightarrow{\ \varepsilon\ } A \\ {\scriptstyle \mathcal{U}(g)} \uparrow \quad \nearrow {\scriptstyle f} \\ \mathcal{U}(B') \end{array}
\quad \text{in } \mathbb{D}.
$$

Thus every map into A out of an object coming from $\mathbb{C}$ must factor uniquely through the counit ε. If we have such a cofree construction for each object $A \in \mathbb{D}$, then we get a *right* adjoint to the forgetful functor $\mathcal{U}$.

Cofree constructions (right adjoints to forgetful functors) are more rare in mathematics. Here is a simple example. Consider the forgetful functor $\mathcal{U}: \mathbf{PreOrd} \to \mathbf{Sets}$ from the category of preorders (with monotone functions) to sets. The cofree construction on a set A yields the "indiscrete" preorder $\langle A, A \times A \rangle$ on A, where $A \times A$ is the order relation on A relating all elements. The identity function $\mathcal{U}(A, A \times A) \to A$ is then the universal map ε. As an aside, the *free* construction with respect to this functor assigns to the set A the "discrete" preorder $\langle A, = \rangle$ in which only equal elements are related. Similarly, with respect to the forgetful functor $\mathbf{Top} \to \mathbf{Sets}$ from topological spaces to sets, the free construction puts the discrete topology on a set (everything open), and the cofree construction imposes the indiscrete topology (only $\emptyset$ and the set itself are open).

The main point of this paper is that cofree constructions arise naturally in the semantics of inheritance of object-oriented languages. The paradigm underlying inheritance is restriction, instead of extension: groups extend monoids and lorries inherit from vehicles (i.e. form a restricted class of vehicles). This is because the (algebraic) operations for constructing elements of a monoid also yield elements of a group, and dually, the (coalgebraic) operations which act on (or, destruct) vehicles also act on lorries. Free constructions are minimal extensions, and similarly, cofree constructions are minimal restrictions. This minimality of restriction is called "minimal realization", see e.g. [6, 8], but also [7, 5.3].

5 Main definitions, and examples

Class specifications have been introduced above as a means of describing the methods and behaviour of classes (their models, or implementations). We shall now describe inheritance both between class specifications and between class implementations (so that we get "specification and implementation hierarchies", as discussed in [22, 1.1]). A class specification S **inherits from** a class specification T if the text of S mentions "inherits from: T" (instead of the more neutral "imports: T" as used in the introduction). Then it is understood that all the methods, assertions, creation conditions and definitions of T form part of S. But S may contain more, namely:

(1) S may have additional methods.

(2) S may have additional assertions; moreover, the assertions of T may be strengthened.

(3) S may have additional creation conditions; moreover, the creation conditions of T may be strengthened.

(4) The output type A of an attribute $X \longrightarrow A$ in T may be restricted to a subtype $A' \hookrightarrow A$. And the input type B of a procedure $X \times B \longrightarrow X$ in T may be extended to a supertype $B' \hookleftarrow B$.

(5) In the definition section of S, function definitions from T may be removed or redefined, and new function definitions may be added.

These five points ensure that models of the child specification S are also models of the parent specification T. Formally, they ensure that there is a forgetful functor

$$\text{Class}(S) \xrightarrow{\quad \mathcal{F} \quad} \text{Class}(T)$$

between the corresponding categories of classes. This expresses the monotonicity (or strictness) of inheritance.

(We sketch some details of this forgetful functor $\mathcal{F}$. Suppose the specification T has an attribute $X \longrightarrow A_1$ and a procedure $X \times B_1 \longrightarrow X$, so that a model of these methods is a coalgebra $U \to A_1 \times U^{B_1}$ of the functor $T(X) = A_1 \times X^{B_1}$. Assume the inheriting specification S adds a new attribute $X \longrightarrow A_2$ and procedure $X \times B_2 \longrightarrow X$, and further restricts the attribute of T to $i: A_1' \hookrightarrow A_1$, and extends the input of the procedure of T to $j: B_1 \hookrightarrow B_1'$. The functor associated with S is then $S(X) = (A_1' \times A_2) \times X^{(B_1' + B_2)}$. It is not hard to see that an S-coalgebra $\varphi = \langle \varphi_1, \varphi_2 \rangle: U \to (A_1' \times A_2) \times U^{(B_1' + B_2)}$ can be mapped to a T-coalgebra, namely to the composite $\mathcal{F}(\varphi) = (i \circ \pi) \times U^{(\text{in} \circ j)} \circ \varphi = \lambda u \in U. \langle i(\pi \varphi_1(u)), \varphi_2(u)(j(\text{inl } b)) \rangle: U \to A_1 \times U^{B_1}$. In going from φ to $\mathcal{F}(\varphi)$ the interpretations of the additional attribute and procedure in S are forgotten, and the input and output types are restored. This operation $\varphi \mapsto \mathcal{F}(\varphi)$ yields a functor $\text{Class}(S) \to \text{Class}(T)$ between categories of classes since the assertion and creation conditions in S imply those of T. On morphisms $\mathcal{F}$ is simply the identity.)

Two further remarks are in order. First, the monotonicity mentioned above exists because the function definitions do not contribute to the meaning of classes. Hence one can modify these definitions as one wishes. In fact, from a semantical perspective, the above point (5) is totally irrelevant. We shall see an example in Subsection 5.2. Secondly, in the examples below we shall not see instances of the fourth point. Therefore we can describe inheritance in these examples as an inclusion $T \hookrightarrow S$ of specifications, giving rise to the forgetful functor $\mathcal{F}: \text{Class}(S) \to \text{Class}(T)$.

We have described inheritance between class specifications as a syntactic notation for incremental specification. We now turn to inheritance between class implementations. This will be semantic in nature.

5.1. Definition. Consider a class specification S inheriting from a class specification T as above, together with the resulting forgetful functor

$$\text{Class}(S) \xrightarrow{\quad \mathcal{F} \quad} \text{Class}(T)$$

(i) In this situation we say that a class $B \in \text{Class}(S)$ **inherits from** a class $A \in \text{Class}(T)$ if there is a morphism of classes $f: \mathcal{F}(B) \to A$ in the category $\text{Class}(T)$. This means that the local states of B are mapped by f to the local states of A in such a way that f commutes (up-to-bisimulation) with the interpretations of the methods in T, and preserves the initial state (again, up-to-bisimulation).

We shall then call B a **subclass** of A, and $f: \mathcal{F}(B) \to A$ a **coercion map** (from B to A). This coercion map turns objects of B into objects of A, in such a way that T-behaviour is preserved.

(ii) The **cofree subclass** on $A \in \mathbf{Class}(T)$ is the cofree construction on A with respect to the forgetful functor $\mathcal{F}$. It consists of a subclass B with a universal coercion $\varepsilon: \mathcal{F}(B) \to A$: for each subclass B' with coercion $f: \mathcal{F}(B') \to A$ there is a unique map $g: B' \dashrightarrow B$ of classes with $\varepsilon \circ \mathcal{F}(g) = f$.

The intuition is that the cofree subclass on A is the "best possible" implementation of S, starting from the already given implementation A of the parent T.

The following result asserts that if class a B inherits from a class A, then, elements of B with the same B-behaviour, have, in A, the same A-behaviour. Thus, objects with are indistinguishable in a subclass are also indistinguishable in the parent. This is because morphisms of classes preserve behaviour.

5.2. Lemma. *Let $B \in \mathbf{Class}(S)$ inherit from $A \in \mathbf{Class}(T)$, say via $f: \mathcal{F}(B) \to A$ as above. Then*

$$x \leftrightarrow_B y \;\Rightarrow\; f(x) \leftrightarrow_A f(y).$$

Proof. It is not hard to see that the composite relation

$$R = \leftrightarrow_A \circ \; \{\langle f(x), f(y)\rangle \mid x \leftrightarrow_B y\} \circ \leftrightarrow_A$$

is a bisimulation on A. Hence $R \subseteq \leftrightarrow_A$, and thus $\{\langle f(x), f(y)\rangle \mid x \leftrightarrow_B y\} \subseteq \leftrightarrow_A$, as required. □

The rest of this paper is devoted to examples illustrating these concepts for toy class specifications. With multiple and repeated inheritance one does not have one class (specification) inheriting from another, so a slightly different functor $\mathcal{F}$ will be used. But the main points of the definition remain the same.

5.1 Single inheritance, without definitions

We shall elaborate the bank account example from the introduction. We first specify classes of elementary bank accounts with a balance attribute, and a change procedure (using the object-oriented dot notation, instead of the functional notation as in the introduction). Then we extend this specification with a name attribute, together with an associated procedure for setting the name (of the holder of the bank account; note that such a name may change—e.g. through marriage).

```
                              class spec: NBANK
                                inherits from:
class spec: BANK                  BANK
  methods:                        methods:
    bal: X ⟶ Z                      name: X ⟶ String
    ch_bal: X × Z ⟶ X               ch_name: X × String ⟶ X
  assertions:                     assertions:
    s.ch_bal(x).bal = s.bal + x      s.ch_bal(x).name = s.name
  creation:                          s.ch_name(y).bal = s.bal
    new.bal = 0                      s.ch_name(y).name = y
end class spec                    creation:
                                    new.name = ""
                              end class spec
```

where "" is the empty string. The idea is that the specification BANK is extended with an additional attribute name and procedure ch_name for telling and changing the name. Thus NBANK contains all the methods of BANK. Also the specification NBANK is extended with some extra assertions and conditions at creation. The first two assertions tell us that by changing the balance the name does not change, and by changing the name the balance remains the same. These assertions make sure that after a change of name we still have a balance, and that after changing the balance we still have a name. This corresponds to what is called "capture" in [18].

Let us now assume that we have a class implementation $A \in$ **Class**(BANK) of this specification BANK with as state space the set $\mathbf{Z}^*$ of finite sequences of integers. The "balance" and "change-balance" operations of A are interpreted as:

$$\begin{cases} \mathsf{bal} \colon \mathbf{Z}^* \longrightarrow \mathbf{Z} & \text{is} \quad (x_1, \ldots, x_n) \mapsto x_1 + \cdots + x_n \\ \mathsf{ch\_bal} \colon \mathbf{Z}^* \times \mathbf{Z} \longrightarrow \mathbf{Z}^* & \text{is} \quad \langle (x_1, \ldots, x_n), x \rangle \mapsto (x_1, \ldots, x_n, x). \end{cases}$$

As initial state of A we take the empty sequence $() \in \mathbf{Z}^*$.

The cofree subclass B on A gives the most efficient implementation of the extended specification NBANK, given the implementation A of the parent BANK. Its state space simply has an extra string field with respect to A, to accomodate for the extra name information. That is, the state space of B is $\mathbf{Z}^* \times$ String with operations

$$\mathsf{bal}((x_1, \ldots, x_n), \alpha) = x_1 + \cdots + x_n, \quad \mathsf{ch\_bal}((x_1, \ldots, x_n), \alpha, x) = ((x_1, \ldots, x_n, x), \alpha),$$
$$\mathsf{name}((x_1, \ldots, x_n), \alpha) = \alpha, \quad \mathsf{ch\_name}((x_1, \ldots, x_n), \alpha, \beta) = ((x_1, \ldots, x_n), \beta)$$

The initial state of B is $(\langle \rangle, \text{""}) \in \mathbf{Z}^* \times$ String. The first projection $\pi \colon \mathbf{Z}^* \times$ String $\to \mathbf{Z}^*$ is the appropriate universal coercion map from B to A. This will be shown in some detail.

First, we have that bisimilarity on $\mathbf{Z}^*$ is given by

$$\begin{aligned} (x_1, \ldots, x_n) \mathrel{\underline{\leftrightarrow}} (y_1, \ldots, y_m) \quad &\Leftrightarrow \quad \mathsf{bal}(x_1, \ldots, x_n) = \mathsf{bal}(y_1, \ldots, y_m) \\ &\Leftrightarrow \quad x_1 + \cdots + x_n = y_1 + \cdots + y_m. \end{aligned}$$

And similarly bisimilarity on $\mathbf{Z}^* \times$ String is

$$\langle (x_1, \ldots, x_n), \alpha \rangle \mathrel{\underline{\leftrightarrow}} \langle (y_1, \ldots, y_m), \beta \rangle \quad \Leftrightarrow \quad (x_1 + \cdots + x_n = y_1 + \cdots + y_m) \wedge (\alpha = \beta).$$

It is then not hard to check that the first projection $\pi \colon \mathbf{Z}^* \times$ String $\to \mathbf{Z}^*$ is a morphism $\mathcal{F}(B) \to A$ in the category **Class**(BANK). That is, $\mathsf{bal} \circ \pi = \mathsf{bal}$, $\mathsf{ch\_bal} \circ \pi \times id \mathrel{\underline{\leftrightarrow}} \pi \circ \mathsf{ch\_bal}$ (pointwise), and $\pi(\langle \rangle, \text{""}) \mathrel{\underline{\leftrightarrow}} \langle \rangle$.

If we assume another class $C \in$ **Class**(NBANK) implementing a bank account with name, together with a morphism $f \colon \mathcal{F}(C) \to A$ in **Class**(BANK), then we get a map $g = \langle f, \mathsf{name} \rangle \colon C \to \mathbf{Z}^* \times$ String. We shall show that g is a morphism of classes $C \to B$ in **Class**(NBANK) by checking conditions (ii)–(iv) in Definition 3.2.

(ii) We have $(\mathsf{bal} \circ g)(c) = \mathsf{bal}(f(c), \mathsf{name}(c)) = \mathsf{bal}(f(c)) = \mathsf{bal}(c)$ since f commutes with the BANK-operations. And $(\mathsf{name} \circ g)(c) = \mathsf{name}(f(c), \mathsf{name}(c)) = \mathsf{name}(c)$. Hence g commutes with the NBANK-attributes.

(iii) With respect to the procedures, we compute:

$$\begin{aligned} (\mathsf{ch\_bal} \circ g \times id)(c, x) &= \mathsf{ch\_bal}(f(c), \mathsf{name}(c), x) \\ &= (\mathsf{ch\_bal}(f(c), x), \mathsf{name}(c)) \\ &\mathrel{\underline{\leftrightarrow}} (f(\mathsf{ch\_bal}(c, x)), \mathsf{name}(\mathsf{ch\_bal}(c, x))) \\ &= (g \circ \mathsf{ch\_bal})(c, x). \end{aligned}$$

For commutation of the function g with the "change-name" procedure we first have to establish that $f(\text{ch\_name}(c, \beta)) \leftrightarrow f(c)$ in $\mathbf{Z}^\star$. This follows from

$$\text{bal}(f(\text{ch\_name}(c, \beta))) = \text{bal}(\text{ch\_name}(c, \beta)) = \text{bal}(c) = \text{bal}(f(c)).$$

Now we get

$$
\begin{aligned}
(\text{ch\_name} \circ g \times id)(c, \beta) \;&=\; \text{ch\_name}(f(c), \text{name}(c), \beta) \\
&=\; (f(c), \beta) \\
&\leftrightarrow\; (f(\text{ch\_name}(c, \beta)), \text{name}(\text{ch\_name}(c, \beta))) \\
&=\; (g \circ \text{ch\_name})(c, \beta).
\end{aligned}
$$

(iv) Finally, the initial state is preserved: $g(c_0) = (f(c_0), \text{name}(c_0)) \leftrightarrow (\langle\rangle, \text{""})$, since $f(c_0) \leftrightarrow \langle\rangle$.

Obviously $\pi \circ g = f$. And if there is another morphism of classes $h : C \to \mathbf{Z}^\star \times \text{String}$ with $\pi \circ h = f$, then $\pi' \circ h = \text{name} \circ h = \text{name}$, so that $h = \langle \pi \circ h, \pi' \circ h \rangle = \langle f, \text{name} \rangle = g$. This concludes the argument.

At the end of this subsection we notice how code is reused under inheritance: the implementations of the operations in the base class A are wrapped inside the descendant class B, where one has an extra field. In this way there is no coercion necessary when one calls a method from the parent class for an object of the child class.

5.2 Single inheritance, with definitions

We shall describe an example of inheritance between class specifications with definitions (see Subsection 2.1). We will start from the class specification LOC+ of locations with defined functions dist and eq, and extend the specification with an extra radius attribute so that we can describe circles (like in [3]). We keep the dist definition as it is, so that the distance of a circle to the origin is the distance of its center to the origin, and redefine the equality function; further, we add two new function definitions perim and surf for the perimeter and surface of a circle.

> **class spec:** CIRC
>   **inherits from:**
>   LOC+
>   **methods:**
>   rad: $X \longrightarrow \mathbb{R}_{\geq 0}$
>   magn: $X \times \mathbb{R}_{\geq 0} \longrightarrow X$
>   **assertions:**
>   s.move(dx, dy).rad = s.rad
>   s.magn(a).fst = s.fst
>   s.magn(a).snd = s.snd
>   s.magn(a).rad = $a \cdot$ (s.rad)
>   **creation:**
>   new.rad = 1
>   **definitions:**
>   perim: $X \longrightarrow \mathbb{R}_{\geq 0}$
>   perim$(s) = 2 \cdot \pi \cdot$ (s.rad)
>   surf: $X \longrightarrow \mathbb{R}_{\geq 0}$
>   surf$(s) = \pi \cdot$ (s.rad)^2

redefine:
eq: $X \times X \longrightarrow$ Bool
$eq(s_1, s_2) = (s_1.fst = s_2.fst) \wedge (s_1.snd = s_2.snd) \wedge (s_1.rad = s_2.rad)$
end class spec

Hence the magn procedure magnifies the radius of the circle by a certain factor, which is given as parameter. A class implementation (model) of this specification CIRC is an implementation of the core part of the specification (the part without the definitions). It consists of a model of the LOC-specification for which we have additional radius and magnification operations satisfying the above assertions. We thus have a forgetful functor

$$\mathbf{Class}(\text{CIRC}) \xrightarrow{\quad \mathcal{F} \quad} \mathbf{Class}(\text{LOC+}) = \mathbf{Class}(\text{LOC})$$

so that a class $B \in \mathbf{Class}(\text{CIRC})$ inherits from $A \in \mathbf{Class}(\text{LOC})$ if there is a map of classes $\mathcal{F}(B) \to A$. For example, taking A to be the class of locations on $\mathbb{R}^2$, the cofree subclass of circles on A has $\mathbb{R}^2 \times \mathbb{R}_{\geq 0}$ as state space with operations

$$fst(x, y, z) = x, \qquad snd(x, y, z) = y, \qquad rad(x, y, z) = z,$$
$$move(x, y, z, dx, dy) = (x + dx, y + dy, z), \qquad magn(x, y, z, a) = (x, y, a \cdot z),$$

and $(0, 0, 1) \in \mathbb{R}^2 \times \mathbb{R}_{\geq 0}$ as initial state. In this class the defined functions of CIRC take the form

$$dist(x, y, z) = \sqrt{x^2 + y^2}, \qquad perim(x, y, z) = 2 \cdot \pi \cdot z$$
$$surf(x, y, z) = \pi \cdot z^2, \qquad eq((x, y, z), (x', y', z')) = (x = x') \wedge (y = y') \wedge (z = z').$$

There is an obvious coercion map $\varepsilon: \mathbb{R}^2 \times \mathbb{R}_{\geq 0} \to \mathbb{R}^2$, namely $\varepsilon(x, y, z) = (x, y)$. It commutes with the (core) LOC-methods, but not with the defined functions, since we have separate equality functions for locations and for circles. We further stipulate (operationally) that for a location s and a circle t the expressions $eq(s, t)$ and $eq(t, s)$ will result in calling the equality function for locations. Thus, in the mixed case a coercion to the ancestor class takes place. Denotationally, this requires the composite functions

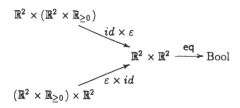

Due to our restriction that redefinition can only be applied to functions in the definition clause of a specification, certain inappropriate (non-monotonic) uses of inheritance are excluded under this coalgebraic interpretation. For example, if the core part of a specification contains certain methods which are characteristic for fish, then we can never get a subclass of birds by redefinition.

Since these definable functions are peripheral and present no complications in our description of inheritance, they will be omitted from the examples below.

5.3 Multiple inheritance, without common ancestor

Multiple inheritance means inheritance with multiple ancestors. It exists in Eiffel and in C++, but not in Smalltalk. We shall present an example in which we combine a class specification of flip-flops with the earlier class specification of locations in a class specification of flip-flops on location:

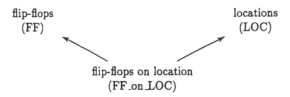

flip-flops
(FF)

locations
(LOC)

flip-flops on location
(FF_on_LOC)

Such "flip-flops on location" may be used as movable pixels on a black-and-white screen.

The class specification LOC of locations is as in Section 2. The specifications FF of flip-flops and FF_on_LOC of flip-flops on locations will be given below:

class spec: FF	**class spec: FF_on_LOC**
methods:	**inherits from:**
val: $X \longrightarrow \{0,1\}$	FF
on: $X \longrightarrow X$	LOC
off: $X \longrightarrow X$	**assertions:**
assertions:	s.move(dx, dy).val $=$ s.val
s.on.val $= 1$	s.on.fst $=$ s.fst
s.off.val $= 0$	s.on.snd $=$ s.snd
creation:	s.off.fst $=$ s.fst
new.val $= 0$	s.off.snd $=$ s.snd
end class spec	**end class spec**

In the class specification FF_on_LOC we do not add any new methods: we only inherit the methods from both the two parent classes FF and LOC, and specify how the attributes of the one act on the procedures of the other. There is no need to further specify the initial state. This gives us an example of multiple inheritance without common ancestors, because the class specifications FF and LOC do not have a specification from which they both inherit.

The idea is that a class implementing the FF_on_LOC specification implements both the specifications FF and LOC and additionally satisfies the conditions mentioned in FF_on_LOC. In this situation we have two forgetful functors $\mathcal{F}_1$: **Class**(FF_on_LOC) $\rightarrow$ **Class**(FF) and $\mathcal{F}_2$: **Class**(FF_on_LOC) $\rightarrow$ **Class**(LOC). They can be combined into a single functor

$$\textbf{Class}(\text{FF\_on\_LOC}) \xrightarrow{\quad \mathcal{F} = \langle \mathcal{F}_1, \mathcal{F}_2 \rangle \quad} \textbf{Class}(\text{FF}) \times \textbf{Class}(\text{LOC})$$

Inheritance and cofreeness will be described with respect to this forgetful functor $\mathcal{F} = \langle \mathcal{F}_1, \mathcal{F}_2 \rangle$. We can say that a class $B \in$ **Class**(FF_on_LOC) inherits from $A_1 \in$ **Class**(FF) and $A_2 \in$ **Class**(LOC) if there are maps of classes $\mathcal{F}_1(B) \rightarrow A_1$ and $\mathcal{F}_2(B) \rightarrow A_2$—or equivalently, if there is a single map $\mathcal{F}(B) \rightarrow (A_1, A_2)$.

An obvious class implementation A_1 of the flip-flop specification FF is obtained by taking the set $\{0,1\}$ of attribute values as state space. The val attribute $\{0,1\} \rightarrow \{0,1\}$ is then simply the identity functor. The on and off procedures are interpreted as the functions $\{0,1\} \rightrightarrows \{0,1\}$ given by $\mathsf{on}(x) = 1$ and $\mathsf{off}(x) = 0$. As initial state we take of course $0 \in \{0,1\}$. (Instead of $\{0,1\}$ one can take any set with at least two elements as state space.)

As class implementation A_2 of the locations specification LOC we choose the one from Section 2 with $(\mathbb{R}^2)^*$ as state space. This gives us a pair of classes $(A_1, A_2) \in \mathbf{Class}(\mathrm{FF}) \times \mathbf{Class}(\mathrm{LOC})$. We claim that the cofree construction on (A_1, A_2) gives us a class with state space $\{0,1\} \times (\mathbb{R}^2)^*$ and with operations:

$$
\begin{aligned}
\mathsf{val}(z, \alpha) &= z & \mathsf{move}(z, \alpha, dx, dy) &= (z, \alpha \cdot (dx, dy)) \\
\mathsf{on}(z, \alpha) &= (1, \alpha) & \mathsf{fst}(z, ((x_1, y_1), \ldots, (x_n, y_n))) &= x_1 + \cdots + x_n \\
\mathsf{off}(z, \alpha) &= (0, \alpha) & \mathsf{snd}(z, ((x_1, y_1), \ldots, (x_n, y_n))) &= y_1 + \cdots + y_n.
\end{aligned}
$$

where $\alpha \in (\mathbb{R}^2)^*$ and $\alpha \cdot (dx, dy)$ is the result of concatenating (dx, dy) at the end of α. There are obvious coercion maps $\{0,1\} \times (\mathbb{R}^2)^* \to \{0,1\}$ and $\{0,1\} \times (\mathbb{R}^2)^* \to (\mathbb{R}^2)^*$ given by first and second projection. For any class $B \in \mathbf{Class}(\mathrm{FF\_on\_LOC})$ with coercion maps $f_1 \colon \mathcal{F}_1(B) \to A_1$ and $f_2 \colon \mathcal{F}_2(B) \to A_2$ we get a unique map of classes $B \dashrightarrow \{0,1\} \times (\mathbb{R}^2)^*$, namely the tuple $\langle f_1, f_2 \rangle$.

5.4 Multiple inheritance, with common ancestor

We slightly modify the flip-flops on location from the previous subsection to flip-flops on circles in a situation:

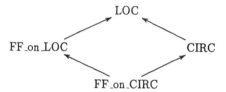

The extra $0/1$ information on circles may be used to indicate whether a circle is filled (i.e. a disk) or open (e.g. when displayed).

The specification FF_on_LOC for flip-flops on circles is as follows.

```
class spec: FF_on_CIRC
    inherits from:
        FF_on_LOC
        CIRC
    assertions:
        s.on.rad = s.rad
        s.off.rad = s.rad
        s.magn(a).val = s.val
end class spec
```

The set of methods in this specification FF_on_CIRC is the (ordinary, non-disjoint) union of the sets of methods in FF_on_LOC and in CIRC. A model (class implementation) of flip-flops on circles is thus at the same time a model of flip-flops on locations and of circles, and the underlying model of locations is the same. This means that we have the following commuting diagram of forgetful functors between the categories of classes of these specifications.

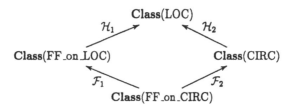

where $\mathcal{H}_1 \circ \mathcal{F}_1 = \mathcal{H}_2 \circ \mathcal{F}_2 = \mathcal{K}$, say. Then we can form the comma category $(\mathcal{H}_1 \times \mathcal{H}_2 \downarrow \Delta)$ of the two functors

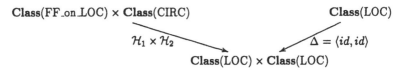

(see [13]), and define a functor

$$\mathbf{Class(FF\_on\_CIRC)} \xrightarrow{\quad \mathcal{F} \quad} (\mathcal{H}_1 \times \mathcal{H}_2 \downarrow \Delta)$$

which send a class $B \in \mathbf{Class(FF\_on\_CIRC)}$ to the pair of identities

$$\mathcal{H}_1(\mathcal{F}_1(B)) \qquad \mathcal{H}_2(\mathcal{F}_2(B))$$
$$\mathcal{K}(B)$$

We shall describe inheritance and cofreeness with respect to this functor $\mathcal{F}$.

Assume classes $A_1 \in \mathbf{Class(FF\_on\_LOC)}$ and $A_2 \in \mathbf{Class(CIRC)}$ with a common ancestor class $A \in \mathbf{Class(LOC)}$ via coercions $f_1 : \mathcal{H}_1(A_1) \to A$ and $f_2 : \mathcal{H}_2(A_2) \to A$. We say that $B \in \mathbf{Class(FF\_on\_CIRC)}$ inherits from $\mathcal{H}_1(A_1) \xrightarrow{f_1} A \xleftarrow{f_2} \mathcal{H}_2(A_2)$ if there is a morphism

$$\mathcal{F}(B) \longrightarrow \begin{pmatrix} \mathcal{H}_1(A_1) & & \mathcal{H}_2(A_2) \\ & f_1 \searrow \quad \swarrow f_2 & \\ & A & \end{pmatrix} \qquad \text{in the category } (\mathcal{H}_1 \times \mathcal{H}_2 \downarrow \Delta)$$

consisting of coercion maps $g_1 : \mathcal{F}_1(B) \to A_1$ and $g_2 : \mathcal{F}_2(B) \to A_2$ with $f_1 \circ \mathcal{H}_1(g_1) = f_2 \circ \mathcal{H}_2(g_2)$. And this B is the cofree subclass inheriting from $\mathcal{H}_1(A_1) \to A \leftarrow \mathcal{H}_2(A_2)$ if every such subclass $B' \in \mathbf{Class(FF\_on\_CIRC)}$ is a subclass of B via a unique morphism $B' \dashrightarrow B$ making appropriate diagrams commute.

We present one example. Assume we have implementations of FF_on_LOC on $\{0,1\} \times \mathbb{R}^2$, and of CIRC on $\mathbb{R}^2 \times \mathbb{R}_{\geq 0}$, with $\mathbb{R}^2$ as common implementation of the specification LOC of locations, via projection morphisms

$$\{0,1\} \times \mathbb{R}^2 \xrightarrow{\quad \pi' \quad} \mathbb{R}^2 \xleftarrow{\quad \pi \quad} \mathbb{R}^2 \times \mathbb{R}_{\geq 0}$$

Then the cofree subclass on these data has as state space the set $\{0,1\} \times \mathbb{R}^2 \times \mathbb{R}_{\geq 0}$. The definition of the operations on this state space is left to the reader. We only mention that there is an obvious commuting square of coercion maps:

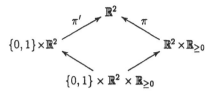

In the end, notice that multiple inheritance without common ancestor in the previous subsection may be fitted in the present framework, by taking the empty specification as common ancestor. The above comma category then becomes the cartesian product of categories of classes, as used in the previous subsection.

5.5 Repeated inheritance

Repeated inheritance occurs when a class (specification) inherits from the same ancestor more than once (via different inclusions). Naively this leads to name clashes. But these clashes can be avoided by appropriate renameings of methods (like in Eiffel, see [16, 20]). As an example, suppose we wish to specify two coupled flip-flops (CFFs), which can be switched on independently, but can only be switched off simultaneously.

```
class spec: CFF
    inherits from:
        FF   rename:
                    val   as   left_val
                    on    as   left_on
                    off   as   left_off
        FF   rename:
                    val   as   right_val
                    on    as   right_on
                    off   as   right_off
    assertions:
        s.left_on.right_val = s.right_val
        s.left_off.right_val = 0
        s.right_on.left_val = s.left_val
        s.right_off.left_val = 0
end class spec
```

The point of this renameing is that the specification FF of flip-flops is incorporated twice. The set of methods of the specification CFF of coupled flip-flops is the disjoint union with itself of the set of methods of the specification FF. Disjointness is achieved via this renaming. Thus we have two inclusions of specifications FF $\rightrightarrows$ CFF, and correspondingly two forgetful functors

$$\mathbf{Class(CFF)} \xrightarrow[\mathcal{R}]{\mathcal{L}} \mathbf{Class(FF)}$$

mapping a class $B \in \mathbf{Class(CFF)}$ to its interpretations of the "left" and "right" part of the specification.

There is something more going on in our understanding of repeated inheritance, which is not expressed by the pair of functors $\mathcal{L}, \mathcal{R}$. In constructing models of the specification CFF of coupled flip-flops from a model B of flip-flops we wish to use this same model B

twice; we do not seek to construct a CFF-model from two arbitrary models B, B' of flip-flops. This idea of using the same interpretation for an ancestor occurring twice occurs also for multiple inheritance in the previous subsection. The approach that we propose here to understand repeated inheritance is similar, except that we now use a comma category as a domain. We restrict ourselves to those models $B \in \textbf{Class}(\text{CFF})$ which inherit twice from a single FF-class, i.e. to those B with maps $\ell: \mathcal{L}(B) \to A$, $r: \mathcal{R}(B) \to A$ to a class $A \in \textbf{Class}(\text{FF})$. Such B's occur in the comma category $(\langle \mathcal{L}, \mathcal{R} \rangle \downarrow \Delta)$ of the functors

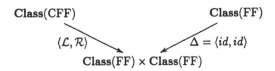

There is an associated "second projection" functor

$$(\langle \mathcal{L}, \mathcal{R} \rangle \downarrow \Delta) \xrightarrow{\quad \mathcal{F} \quad} \textbf{Class}(\text{FF})$$

which we use to describe inheritance and cofreeness in this situation. Explicitly, $B \in$ $\textbf{Class}(\text{CFF})$ together with $\mathcal{L}(B) \xrightarrow{\ell} A \xleftarrow{r} \mathcal{R}(B)$ inherits from $C \in \textbf{Class}(\text{FF})$ if there is a coercion $f: A \to C$. And this $\mathcal{L}(B) \xrightarrow{\ell} A \xleftarrow{r} \mathcal{R}(B)$ is the cofree subclass inheriting from $C \in \textbf{Class}(\text{FF})$ if for every B' with maps $\mathcal{L}(B') \xrightarrow{\ell'} A' \xleftarrow{r'} \mathcal{R}(B')$ there is a unique pair of maps $g: B' \dashrightarrow B$, $h: A' \dashrightarrow A$ making the following diagrams commute.

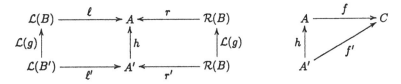

In our example, if $C \in \textbf{Class}(\text{FF})$ is the implementation of flip-flops with $\{0,1\}$ as state space, then the cofree subclass on C has $\{0,1\} \times \{0,1\}$ as state space, and operations

$$
\begin{array}{llll}
\textsf{left\_val}(x,y) & = & x, & \textsf{left\_on}(x,y) & = & (1,y), & \textsf{left\_off}(x,y) & = & (0,0), \\
\textsf{right\_val}(x,y) & = & x, & \textsf{right\_on}(x,y) & = & (x,1), & \textsf{right\_off}(x,y) & = & (0,0).
\end{array}
$$

Obviously there are coercion maps $\{0,1\} \times \{0,1\} \rightrightarrows \{0,1\}$, namely first and second projection. They commute with the flip-flop operations. And the above map $f: A \to C$ is simply the identity $\{0,1\} \to \{0,1\}$. If we have another subclass implementation $\mathcal{L}(B') \xrightarrow{\ell'} A' \xleftarrow{r'} \mathcal{R}(B')$ with common ancestor class A', then the required unique maps are $\langle \textsf{left\_val}, \textsf{right\_val} \rangle$ $: B' \dashrightarrow \{0,1\} \times \{0,1\}$, $\textsf{val}: A' \dashrightarrow \{0,1\}$.

6 Conclusions and further work

We have presented some paradigmatic examples of inheritance within the framework of coalgebraic specification and implementation. Of course, these example do not cover all possibilities. For instance, one can have multiple bank accounts on the same name via maps of specifications NBBANK $\rightrightarrows$ NBANK where the "balance" and "change-balance" methods are renamed, but the "name" and "change-name" methods are shared. This may be described by a combination of the above techniques.

In later work we shall have more to say about the existence of cofree constructions (of the kind used above). The logical aspects (completeness, conservativity) still have to be investigated. In the end we should emphasize that we have described examples of inheritance without genericity. The latter would require suitably indexed versions (via free type variables) of the above descriptions.

Acknowledgement

Thanks are due to Jan Rutten for helpful discussions.

References

1. K. Bruce, L. Cardelli, G. Castagna, The Hopkins Objects Group, G. Leavens, and B. Pierce. On binary methods. Manuscript, May 1995.
2. L. Cardelli. A semantics of multiple inheritance. *Inf. & Comp.*, 76(2/3):138–164, 1988.
3. W. Cook and J. Palsberg. A denotational semantics of inheritance and its correctness. *Inf. & Comp.*, 114(2):329–350, 1995.
4. W.R. Cook. Object-oriented programming versus abstract data types. In J.W. de Bakker, W.P. de Roever, and G. Rozenberg, editors, *Foundations of Object-Oriented Languages*, number 489 in Lect. Notes Comp. Sci., pages 151–178. Springer, Berlin, 1990.
5. H. Ehrig and B. Mahr. *Fundamentals of Algebraic Specification I: Equations and Initial Semantics*. Number 6 in EATCS Monographs. Springer, Berlin, 1985.
6. J.A. Goguen. Realization is universal. *Math. Syst. Theor.*, 6(4):359–374, 1973.
7. J.A. Goguen. A categorical manifesto. *Math. Struct. Comp. Sci.*, 1(1):49–67, 1991.
8. J.A Goguen and J. Meseguer. Universal realization, persistent interconnection and implementation of abstract modules. In M. Nielsen and E.M. Schmidt, editors, *Automata, Languages and Programming (ICALP'82)*, number 140 in Lect. Notes Comp. Sci., pages 263–281. Springer, Berlin, 1982.
9. J.A Goguen and J. Meseguer. Unifying functional, object-oriented and relational programming with logical semantics. In B. Shriver and P. Wegner, editors, *Research Directions in Object-Oriented Programming*, pages 417–477. The MIT Press series in computer systems, 1987.
10. B. Jacobs. Mongruences and cofree coalgebras. In V.S. Alagar and M. Nivat, editors, *Algebraic Methods and Software Technology*, number 936 in Lect. Notes Comp. Sci., pages 245–260. Springer, Berlin, 1995.
11. B. Jacobs. Coalgebraic specifications and models of deterministic hybrid systems. In M. Wirsing, editor, *Algebraic Methods and Software Technology*, Lect. Notes Comp. Sci. Springer, Berlin, 1996, to appear.
12. B. Jacobs. Objects and classes, coalgebraically. In B. Freitag, C.B. Jones, and C. Lengauer, editors, *Object-Orientation with Parallelism and Persistence*. Kluwer, 1996, to appear.
13. S. Mac Lane. *Categories for the Working Mathematician*. Springer, Berlin, 1971.
14. S. Lang. *Algebra*. Addison Wesley, 2nd rev. edition, 1984.
15. B. Meyer. *Object-Oriented Software Construction*. Prentice Hall, 1988.
16. B. Meyer. *Eiffel: The Language*. Prentice Hall, 1992.
17. R. Milner. *Communication and Concurrency*. Prentice Hall, 1989.
18. J. Palsberg and M.I. Schwartzbach. *Object-Oriented Type Systems*. Wiley, 1994.
19. H. Reichel. An approach to object semantics based on terminal co-algebras. *Math. Struct. Comp. Sci.*, 5:129–152, 1995.
20. R. Rist and R. Terwilliger. *Object-Oriented Programming in Eiffel*. Prentice Hall, 1995.
21. B. Stroustrup. *The C++ Programming Language*. Addison-Wesley, 2nd rev. edition, 1994.
22. P. Wegner. The object-oriented classification paradigm. In B. Shriver and P. Wegner, editors, *Research Directions in Object-Oriented Programming*, pages 479–560. The MIT Press series in computer systems, 1987.
23. P. Wegner. Concepts and paradigms of object-oriented programming. *OOPS Messenger*, 1(1):7–87, 1990.

(Objects + Concurrency) & Reusability – A Proposal to Circumvent the Inheritance Anomaly

Ulrike Lechner[1], Christian Lengauer[1], Friederike Nickl[2] and Martin Wirsing[3]

[1] Fakultät für Mathematik und Informatik
Universität Passau, D–94030 Passau, Germany
email: {lechner,lengauer}@fmi.uni-passau.de
[2] sd&m GmbH & Co. KG
Thomas-Dehler-Str. 27, D–81737 München, Germany
email: Friederike.Nickl@sdm.de
[3] Institut für Informatik
Ludwig-Maximilians-Universität, D–80538 München, Germany
email: wirsing@informatik.uni-muenchen.de

Abstract. We enrich the *object-oriented + concurrent* specification language Maude with language constructs for *reuse* and gain a high degree of code reusability. We consider three reuse constructs: (1) Maude's inheritance relation, (2) an algebra of messages and (3) the construct of a subconfiguration. By employing these constructs for different kinds of reuse, we show for all examples of the seminal paper on the inheritance anomaly [11] how to circumvent the inheritance anomaly. Our running example is the bounded buffer.

Keywords: Concurrent rewriting, inheritance anomaly, Maude, parallelism, reusability.

1 Introduction

Inheritance and concurrency are two paradigms which are difficult to combine in a satisfactory way. In [11] the necessity of reprogramming a high proportion of reused code when using inheritance is called the *inheritance anomaly.* In [13] it is claimed that the main reason for the inheritance anomaly is the presence of *synchronization code*, the code which determines which method calls can be accepted in dependence of the state of the object. The classical example for the use and the necessity of synchronization code is the bounded buffer which allows its get method to be invoked only if it is not empty [5, 11, 13].

The language Maude claims to overcome the inheritance anomaly: in [13] Meseguer, the developer of Maude, demonstrates how to use Maude's inheritance mechanism and modules with various ways of reuse to specify concurrent systems in a structured and modular way.

We agree with [13] in that the inheritance anomaly is caused by the *presence of synchronization code*, not by the way the program is structured and implemented. But, in resolving the inheritance anomaly, we develop a new idea:

Maude's inheritance mechanism, which allows only to add new attributes and new possibilities of state changes, is not sufficient. We present constructs in a language with *object-oriented concepts + concurrency* and gain a high degree of *reusability* of code. For us, reusability means not necessarily only inheritance. We introduce two new concepts: a *subconfiguration* and an *algebra of messages*. They allow us to reuse code not only by enhancing the set of possible state transitions but also by restricting them and by composing actions from basic actions in an object-oriented way.

Throughout, we use the bounded buffer as our example since it has been investigated in several languages with different inheritance and reuse mechanisms and different kinds of synchronization code [1, 5, 11, 13, 15].

2 Our specification language

This section provides a brief introduction to our specification language, which is based on Maude as defined in [14]. We adopt some notational ideas from OOSpectrum [16] and add the concept of a subconfiguration and a message algebra to Maude.

2.1 Basic Concepts

Maude [14] has two parts: one which is functional and another which specifies states (so-called *configurations*) and state changes. The functional part is OBJ3 [6]; it forms the subset of the language used to specify the properties of data types in a purely algebraic way.

In the state-dependent part of Maude one writes object-oriented specifications consisting of an import list, a number of class declarations, message declarations, equations and rewrite rules. An object of a class is represented by a term –more precisely, by a tuple– comprising a unique object identifier (of sort OId), a class identifier and a set of attributes with their values; e.g., the term < B:BdBuffer | cont:C, in:I, out:O, max:M > represents an object of class BdBuffer with identifier B and attributes cont, in, out, and max with values C, I, O and M, respectively. A message is a term of sort Msg (in mixfix notation) that consists of the message's name, the identifiers of the objects the message is addressed to and, possibly, parameters; e.g., the term (put E into B) is a message addressed to the bounded buffer B with a parameter E. A configuration is a multiset of objects and messages. Multiset union is denoted by juxtaposition; the term (put E into B) < B:BdBuffer | cont:C, in:I, out:O, max:M > denotes the union of the buffer and the message of above.

State changes are specified by transition rules on configurations as defined by the rewriting calculus given below.

As an example of a specification let us give the specification of buffers and bounded buffers and explain it subsequently. A similar Maude specification of bounded buffers can be found in [13]. The specification CONFIGURATION specifies the basic data types of objects, messages and configurations (for a formal definition see [12]). The specification OIDLIST (see App. A) specifies the sort OIdList of finite sequences of object identifiers together with a juxtaposition operation, where adding an element E to a list C on the left is written E C and adding it on the right is written C E.

Our syntax differs from Maude as follows. BD_BUFFER = { ... } corresponds to omod Buffer is ... endo. In Maude, each rewrite rule is preceded by eq or rl; we collect equations and transitions rules under the keywords equations and transitions. Our subclass declarations are part of a class declaration; in Maude class and subclass declarations are independent. Other than Maude, we collect variable declarations by universal quantification.

```
BD_BUFFER = {
enriches CONFIGURATION OIDLIST ;
classes Buffer attr cont: OIdList ;
        BdBuffer subclass of Buffer ;
            attr in: Nat, out: Nat, max: Nat ;
messages (new BdBuffer with _replyto _) : Nat OId -> Msg ;
   (to _ the new BdBuffer is _), (put _ into _),
   (get _ replyto _), (to _ answer to get is _) : OId OId -> Msg ;
transitions ∀ B,U,E:OId , C:OIdList, I,O:Nat in
[P](put E into B)
   < B:BdBuffer | cont:C, in:I, out:O, max:M >
   => < B:BdBuffer | cont:E C, in:I+1 >
            if (I - O < M) ;
[G](get B replyto U)
   < B:BdBuffer | cont:C E, in:I, out:O, max:M >
   => < B:BdBuffer | cont:C, out:O+1 >
      (to U answer to get is E) ;
[N](new BdBuffer with M replyto U)
   < P:Proto | class:BdBuffer, next:B >
   => < P:Proto | class:BdBuffer, next:inc(B) >
      < B:BdBuffer | cont:eps, in:0, out:0, max:M >
      (to U the new BdBuffer is B)
endtransitions }
```

In general, specifications have the following structure: $Sp = \{\text{enriches } R; \text{ functions } F; \text{ classes } C; \text{ messages } M; \text{ equations } E; \text{ transitions } T\}$. The operator enriches imports specifications: each component of Sp consists of the union of the components of the imported specifications and of Sp. We may omit empty parts of the specifications as, e.g., functions and equations in the example above.

Class Buffer has only one attribute, cont, which is used to store object identifiers. Class BdBuffer inherits the attribute via the inheritance relation from class Buffer, as stated by the declaration BdBuffer subclass of Buffer. Subclasses inherit all attributes and all rewrite rules (equations and transition rules) from their superclasses.

A bounded buffer may react to two messages: put and get. Put stores an element in the buffer, get removes the first element being stored in the buffer and sends it to a "user". The transition rule with rule label P says that an object of class BdBuffer can react to a put message only if the actual number of objects being stored, I-O, is smaller than the upper bound max. Sending a get message not only triggers a state change of buffer B but also initiates an answer message to a "user" U which contains the result (an object identifier).

While rules P and G are standard, rule N is particular to Maude. To create a new buffer, a message new is sent to a proto-object (of class Proto) which is responsible for creating new objects. The message new triggers a new object to be created with default values for the attributes in, out and cont. The value of max is determined by a parameter of the message. The proto-object changes (increases) the value of the parameter next by inc, and we assume that this is done in such a way that the same object identifier is never created twice.

Generally speaking, transition rules specify *explicit, asynchronous communication* via message passing: if a message is part of a configuration, a state transition may happen and new (answer) messages waiting to be processed in subsequent state transitions may be created as part of the resulting configuration (in the specification given above only one new message is generated). The transition rules specify not only the behavior but also the equivalent of the synchronization code of other languages: the pattern given at the left-hand side involves not only the presence of objects and messages but also certain properties like the equality of object identifiers, values of attributes and parameters of the messages. (We could also specify more than one object at the left-hand side of a transition rule and specify a synchronous state transition of several objects.)

Let us introduce some notation. A *specification* $Sp = (\Sigma, E, T)$ consists of a *signature* Σ, a set of *equations* E and a set of *transition rules* T. A signature $\Sigma = (S, C, \leq, F, M)$ consists of a set of (ordinary) sort names S, a set of class names C, a subclass relation $\leq$, a set of function symbols F and a set of messages M. $T(\Sigma, X)$ denotes the terms of signature Σ with variables from X. We use Cf as an abbreviation for Configuration, the sort of the states.

The *rewriting calculus*, given below in three rules, defines Maude's semantics in the form of a *transition system*.[4] In the following, let m, m' denote messages, a_i attribute names, v_i and w_i values, o_i object identifiers, C_i, C'_i, D_i and D'_i class identifiers, $atts_i$ sets of pairs of attributes together with their variables, and σ a substitution. An expression e und a double arrow, $\overleftrightarrow{e}$, stands for a set whose elements are of the form e (with the exception that $\overleftrightarrow{m}$ is a multiset of messages).

---

[4] In contrast to [12] we do neither have a reflexivity nor a transitivity rule in the calculus. The rule (Emb) is weaker than the replacement rule in the original calculus; the replacement rule could be obtained by (Emb), (Equ), and a transitivity rule. If subconfigurations may occur we need also the rule (Sub), see Sect. 2.2.

A transition

$$
\begin{array}{c}
\overleftrightarrow{m}[\sigma] \\
\overrightarrow{<\ \sigma(o_i) : D_i\ \mid\ \overleftrightarrow{a_i : v_i}[\sigma],\ atts_i\ >} \\
\rightarrow\overrightarrow{<\ \sigma(o_i) : D_i'\ \mid\ \overleftrightarrow{a_i : w_i}[\sigma],\ atts_i\ >} \\
\overleftrightarrow{m'}[\sigma]
\end{array}
\tag{Inst}
$$

is possible if T contains a transition rule (in which all attributes of classes C_i together with their values are stated)

$$
\begin{array}{c}
[R]\ \overleftrightarrow{m} \\
\overrightarrow{<\ o_i : C_i\ \mid\ \overleftrightarrow{a_i : v_i}\ >} \\
=> \overrightarrow{<\ o_i : C_i'\ \mid\ \overleftrightarrow{a_i : w_i}\ >} \\
\overleftrightarrow{m'}
\end{array}
$$

and there is a substitution $\sigma : Vars \rightarrow T(\Sigma, X)$, where $D_i \leq C_i$ and

$$
D_i' = \begin{cases} D_i, \text{ if } C_i = C_i' \\ C_i' \text{ else} \end{cases}
$$

Let us explain this rule. A transition rule in T is instantiated such that all variables of the rule are substituted according to σ. The classes of the objects of the configuration to which the rule is applied are subclasses of the objects of the rule. Since an object of a subclass may have more attributes than the object of the superclass, we introduce $atts_i$ to match the additional attributes of the subclass. The values of those attributes are not changed in the transition. The values v_i are changed to w_i according to the rule. For simplicity we assume that no objects are created or deleted by the transition rule. We make two simplifying assumptions for the case that objects change their class: the class of the object at the right-hand side of the rule becomes the class of the (instance) object, and classes between which class changes are possible have the same attributes.

As a notational convention we may omit at the left- and right-hand side of a rule attributes whose values are not needed in the transition and, additionally, at the right-hand side attributes whose values are not changed.

In the case of a conditional transition rule of the form:

$$m_1' o_{i_1}' \ldots o_{i_n}' => o_{j_1}' \ldots o_{j_m}' m_2' \ldots m_n' \text{ if } p_1 \wedge \ldots \wedge p_k$$

(with equations or transitions $p_1, \ldots, p_k$) we require additionally that all $p_i[\sigma]$ are derivable. We need two more rules: (Emb) embeds the left-hand and the right-hand side of a transition into a configuration containing objects and messages not changed by the transition and (Equ) makes the transition relation compatible with equations. Let c, d, c', d' and h be configurations and let $=_E$ denote equality modulo equations in the set E:

$$c\,h \rightarrow d\,h \text{ if } c \rightarrow d \tag{Emb}$$
$$c' \rightarrow d' \text{ if } c \rightarrow d \text{ and } c =_E c', d =_E d' \tag{Equ}$$

2.2 Subconfigurations

With subconfigurations we can structure our configuration by permitting an object to contain configurations. This enables us to restrict the choice of classes to which the objects in a subconfiguration may belong. A subconfiguration, as defined below, must contain only objects belonging to a non-empty set of class names but it may contain arbitrary messages.

    Subconfiguration of {classnames}⁺

Since we specify explicitly which messages may pass from a configuration into a subconfiguration or vice versa, we impose no restriction on the messages in the subconfiguration construct.

An example of a class declaration using the subconfiguration construct is:

    class HBuffer | conf: Subconfiguration of BdBuffer Flag .

Objects of class HBuffer have an attribute conf containing only objects belonging to class BdBuffer or class Flag.

In the presence of subconfigurations, we have to introduce one more rule, (Sub), to the rewriting calculus which specifies the application of transition rules to subconfigurations. Let $< o : C \mid a : S, atts >$ be an object containing a subconfiguration S stored under the attribute name a, and let $atts$ denote all other attributes with their values of o apart from a:

$$< o : C \mid a : S, atts > \to < o : C \mid a : S', atts > \text{ if } S \to S' \qquad \text{(Sub)}$$

2.3 The message algebra

We introduce an algebra of messages which permits the formation of *composed messages*, much like process terms in process algebras, from basic messages as defined in Maude specifications. This provides us with a new way of reusing code: it is possible to specify messages which trigger more than one single computation step and to have some sort of control flow within these computation steps.

```
MSG_ALGEBRA = {
   enriches CONFIGURATION
      _+_, _;_, _;;_, _|_, _||_ : Msg Msg -> Msg;
   transitions ∀ m1,m2,n1,n2:Msg, c,d,c1,c2,d1,d2,h:Cf in
   [C] (m1 + m2) c => d
             if   m1 c => d   ∨   m2 c => d ;
   [S1](m1 ; m2) c1 c2 => d1 d2
             if   m1 c1 => d1 h   ∧   m2 c2 h => d2 ;
   [S2](m1 ;; m2) c1 c2 => d1 d2 (n1 ;; n2)
             if   m1 c1 => d1 n1 h   ∧   m2 c2 h => d2 n2 ;
   [P1](m1 | m2) c1 c2 => d1 d2
             if   m1 c1 => d1   ∧   m2 c2 => d2 ;
   [P2](m1 || m2) c1 c2 => d1 d2 (n1 || n2)
             if   m1 c1 => n1 d1   ∧   m2 c2 => n2 d2)
   endtransitions }
```

Specification MSG_ALGEBRA contains three message combinators: choice (+), sequential (; and ;;) and parallel (| and ||) composition. In sequential composition there can be a dependence between the left and the right message, in parallel composition there must be no dependence. We have two versions of sequential and parallel composition: one composes the answer messages following the structure of the input message (; ; and ||) and one which does not pass this structure on to the next configuration (; and |). All combinators form atomic state transitions.

Generally, we have the freedom to specify any kind of sequential or parallel composition or choice in a message algebra. We have chosen the combinators given above only because we need them for the specifications in the next section.

3 Bounded Buffers and the inheritance anomaly

In this section, we extend the specification of the bounded buffer given in Sect. 2 with additional messages as originally suggested in [11] and partly also in [13]. With these extensions we demonstrate that Maude's inheritance relation, the message algebra and the concept of subconfiguration are powerful enough to overcome the inheritance anomaly. The first extension (by a message last) uses only Maude's inheritance mechanism, the second (by a message get2) the message algebra and for the third extension (by a message gget) we need the message algebra and subconfigurations. The class and module hierarchy we present in this section are depicted in Fig. 1.

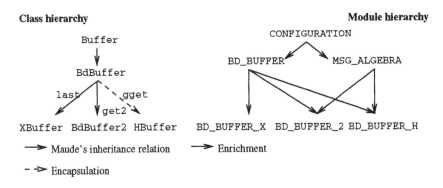

Fig. 1. Extensions of class BdBuffer and module BD_BUFFER

3.1 Message: last

One extension used in [11] to demonstrate how synchronization code requires the redefinition of existing code is the addition of a method last which returns the most recent element put into the buffer.

```
BD_BUFFER_X = {
    enriches BD_BUFFER ;
    class XBdBuffer subclass of BdBuffer ;
    messages (last _ replyto _),
            (to _ answer to last is _): OId OId -> Msg ;
transitions ∀ B,E,U:OId, C:OIdList, I,O:Nat in
[L] (last B replyto U)
    < B:XBdBuffer | cont:E C, out:O >
    => < B:XBdBuffer | cont:C, out:O+1 >
       (to U answer to last is E)
endtransitions }
```

Since XBdBuffer is a subclass of BdBuffer, an XBdBuffer inherits all attributes and all transition rules from BdBuffer. Thus an object of class XBdBuffer is capable of all state transitions an object of class BdBuffer is capable of in the same context. The transition rule L defines the behavior of a XBdBuffer when accepting a message last. When adding this new behavior to an existing specification we do not have to redefine or alter any piece of existing code and, thus, the inheritance anomaly does not apply.

3.2 Message: get2

Say we would like to extend the specification of class BdBuffer such that a buffer accepts an additional message, (get2 B replyto U), which sends two elements of buffer B to an object U. The specification given in [13] is:

```
subclass BdBuffer2 < BdBuffer
rl (get2 B replyto U)
   < B:BdBuffer2 | cont:C E' E, in:I, out:O, max:M >
  => < B:BdBuffer2 | cont:C, out:O+2 >
      (to U answer to get2  is E' and E) .
```

This solution is not "suffering" from the inheritance anomaly but has one drawback: it does not reuse the specification of the message get. Our solution uses MSG_ALGEBRA to derive a composed message get2 from the implementation of get:

```
BD_BUFFER_2 = {
    enriches BD_BUFFER MSG_ALGEBRA ;
    class BdBuffer2 subclass of BdBuffer ;
    messages (get2 _ replyto _) : OId OId -> Msg ;
        (to _ answer to get2 is _ and _) : OId OId OId -> Msg
equations ∀ B,U,E,E':OId, I,O,M:Nat in
[E1](get2 B replyto U)
    < B:BdBuffer2 >
    =  < B:BdBuffer2 >
       ((get B replyto U);;(get B replyto U)) ;
```

```
[E2]((to U answer to get is E);;(to U answer to get is E'))
    = (to U answer to get2 is E' and E)
endequations }
```

We allow the "transformation" of a get2 message to two get messages in sequence only if get2 is addressed to a buffer of class BdBuffer2 and, thus, we do not extend the set of messages a BdBuffer object accepts. The rewriting calculus and the algebra of messages allow us to process a get2 message in one step, since we have an equational "transformation" of get2 to get messages which does not require a computation step and since the algebra of messages allows us to build an atomic state transition get2.

Assume that we would like to implement get2 in a more conventional language, with methods encapsulated in objects and guards for the methods such as in [1, 5, 7, 11]. This implementation of get2 would apply get twice and its guard would have to make sure that get2 is only invoked if the buffer contains (at least) two elements. The synchronization code of get2 would have to be either derived from the synchronization code of the get method invoked twice by get2 or written "by hand". Both might be hard, although in our example both is rather trivial. In our approach the message algebra ensures that a get2 method may only be invoked if both invocations of get can be executed in sequence. This replaces the synchronization code of the message get2 and facilitates the reuse of methods.

3.3 Message: gget

Our last modification is to make bounded buffer history-sensitive: a new message, gget, is only accepted if the latest message was a put message. Adding a message with a history-sensitive behavior involves a change of the behavior of all messages: put has to set a flag, all other messages have to reset it.

```
BD_BUFFER_H = {
enriches BD_BUFFER MSG_ALGEBRA ;
classes
    Flag atts buffer : OId ;
    FSet subclass of Flag ;
    FUnset subclass of Flag ;
    HBuffer atts conf: Subconfiguration of BdBuffer Flag
messages (set _), (unset _), (reset _) : OId → Msg ;
    (gget _ replyto _) : OId OId -> Msg
equations ∀ B,U,F:OId, C:Subconfiguration of BdBuffer Flag in:
[E1](gget B replyto U)
    < B:HBuffer | conf:<B:BdBuffer> <F:Flag|buffer:B> C >
    = < B:HBuffer | conf:((get B replyto U)|(reset F))
                            <B:BdBuffer> <F:Flag> C > ;
[E2]< B:HBuffer | conf:(to U answer to get is E) C >
    = (to U answer to get is E) < B:HBuffer | conf:C > ;
```

```
[E3] (put E into B)
     < B:HBuffer | conf:<B:BdBuffer> <F:Flag|buffer:B> C >
     = < B:HBuffer | conf:((put E into B)|(set F))
                               <B:BdBuffer> <F:Flag> C > ;
[E4] (get B replyto U)
     < B:HBuffer | conf:<B:BdBuffer> <F:Flag|buffer:B> C >
     = < B:HBuffer | conf:((get B replyto U)|(unset F))
                               <B:BdBuffer> <F:Flag> C >
endequations
transitions ∀ F:OId in
[S]  (set F)  <F:Flag> => <F:FSet> ;
[U]  (unset F)  <F:Flag> => <F:FUnset> ;
[R]  (reset F)  <F:FSet> => <F:FUnset>
endtransitions }
```

A history-sensitive buffer HBuffer encapsulates, in a subconfiguration, a buffer and a flag which indicates whether the last message accepted was a put.

We model the state of the flag, according to the states-as-classes approach [10], as classes and not, as usual, as attributes. In doing so we are able to refine the state of class Flag and, thus, its ability to process messages by introducing more subclasses. A flag accepts three messages and, while the state (and class) is irrelevant for a set and unset message to be accepted, a reset message is only accepted if the actual state of the flag is FSet.

The messages addressed to an object HBuffer are transformed by equations to a composed message inside the subconfiguration. This composed message consists of a message addressed to the BdBuffer and one message addressed to the Flag. The combinator | ensures that the message responsible for the manipulation of the buffer and the message triggering the state change of the flag are processed in parallel. In equation E1 a message gget can be transformed into a parallel combination of a get and a reset message at any time. The state of the flag is only relevant for processing of the composed message consisting of a reset and a get message.

The two messages put and get migrate –like the message gget– into a sub-configuration and are transformed into a put, respectively a get message, and a message addressed to the flag. A put message is transformed into a composed message, consisting of a put and a set message, a get into a get and an unset message. The migration of answer messages from a subconfiguration into a configuration is also modeled by an equation.

The variable C of type subconfiguration in the equation matches messages which have already passed from the overall configuration into the subconfiguration. The use of configuration variables enhances also the reusability of the specification BD_BUFFER_H: if in a reusing specification more than two objects are contained in an HBuffer then the variable C can match these objects in the application of the transition rules by the rewriting calculus.

3.4 Analysis

In [11] several kinds of synchronization code are investigated. The inheritance anomaly occurs because no kind of synchronization code supports all types of modification when reusing a class declaration which contains synchronization code. Maude's equivalent to "synchronization code" is the pattern to be matched at the left-hand side of a transition rule. It consists of one or more messages, their parameters and the internal state of the object(s). Thus, each transition rule specifies a "synchronization constraint", more precisely an "enabled set", i.e., a condition under which a message may be accepted, individually for each message. Since each rule specifies such a pattern, adding new "enabled conditions" by adding new rules is the kind of modification of existing code which can be expressed straight-forwardly by Maude's inheritance relation (like get2 and last).

For other kinds of modification of the behavior of reused code, we provide different mechanisms. With encapsulation in subconfigurations we are able to restrict the ability of objects to react to messages. The algebra of messages supports the specification of complex systems with a large number of objects and a complex control flow in the reuse of specifications with "simple" transition rules.

The reason why we are able to reuse code in many ways is that we provide different kinds of synchronization or control code: for each particular type of modification there is one particular construct for reuse.

One of the advantages of using equations to model the migration of messages into and out of subconfigurations is that we do not add additional state transitions or actions to a rewrite system. The migration would be some special kind of state transition and could be modeled by an internal action (like τ in CCS), but this would cause the same problems in compositionality and verification as it does in CCS.

4 Another buffer

In the previous sections we have given methods and language constructs for the reuse of specifications. Each method covers a particular situation in reuse. But it remains to demonstrate that these three techniques of reuse fit and can be used together.

We specify a bounded buffer, PBuffer, which is capable of processing all the three messages last, get2 and gget.

```
BD_BUFFER_P = {
enriches BD_BUFFER_X BD_BUFFER_H BD_BUFFER2 ;
classes PBufferI subclass of XBdBuffer BdBuffer2 ;
        PBuffer subclass of HBuffer ;
messages (new PBuffer with _ replyto _): Nat OId -> Msg;
    (to _ the new PBuffer is _): OId OId -> Msg
equations ∀ B,E,U: OId, C:Cf in
```

```
[E1](last B replyto U)
    < B:PBuffer | conf:C >
    = < B:PBuffer | conf:C ((last B replyto U)|(reset B)) > ;
[E2]< B:PBuffer | conf:C (to U answer to last is E) >
    = < B:PBuffer | conf:C >
        (to U answer to last is E) ;
[E3](get2 B replyto U)
    < B:PBuffer | conf:C >
    = < B:PBuffer | conf:C ((get2 B replyto U)|(reset B))) > ;
[E4]< B:PBuffer | conf:C (to U answer to get2 is E' and E) >
    = < B:PBuffer | conf:C >
        (to U answer to get2 is E' and E) >
endequations
transitions ∀ P,B,U,F:OId, M:Nat in
[N] (new PBuffer with M replyto U)
    < P:Proto | class:PBuffer, next:(B,F) >
    => < P:Proto | class:PBuffer, next:(inc(B),inc(F)) >
        < B:PBuffer | conf:<B:PBufferI|cont:eps,in:0,out:0,max:M>
                            <F:FUnset|buffer:B> >
        (to U the new PBuffer is B)
endtransitions }
```

We have two subclass relations which inherit behavior from ancestor classes. The subclass definition of PBufferI ensures that put, get and last can be processed by PBufferI. Furthermore, it ensures that a get2 method can actually be converted to a sequence of two get messages. The subclass definition of PBuffer ensures that all messages which may migrate into an HBuffer, namely put, get and gget, may migrate into a PBuffer as well. Equations E1 to E4 specify the migration of the messages last and get2 and the answer message into and out of the subconfiguration. Rule N ensures that the buffer contained in the subconfiguration of PBuffer is of class PBufferI.

Note that again no changes of the reused specification are necessary. In fact, this specification demonstrates that our three concepts of reuse can be used together.

5 Buffers with synchronous communication

The transition rules of Maude offer a very powerful communication mechanism which we have not used up to now in our model of bounded buffers: a rewrite rule can employ more than one object and one message at its left-hand and right-hand side. Such a rule specifies joint atomic state transitions by all the objects involved. As an example we give a rule specifying a synchronous get message.

A message (sget by B and U) triggers a joint state transition of a buffer and a user. In it, the element which is retrieved from the buffer is stored in the attribute elem of the user; sget replaces the answer message used in the previous sections. We call this a synchronous implicit communication.

```
[SG] (sget by B and U)
     < U:User | buffer:B, elem:X >
     < B:BdBuffer | cont:C E, in:I, out:O, max:M >
     => < U:User | buffer:B, elem:E >
        < B:BdBuffer | cont:C, out:O+1 > ;
```

But is this kind of rule really appropriate for reuse? Of course, this depends on the kind of reuse, but a rule like this cannot be inherited easily when encapsulating one of the participants, say, the buffer in a subconfiguration. The rule relies very much on the structure of the configuration –namely, that both user and buffer are part of the same configuration– and on the shape of the objects.

We propose a specification, which uses the message algebra to specify a joint atomic state transition:

```
[H]  (h(U))
     (to U answer to get is E)
     < U:User | buffer:B, elem:X >
     => < U:User | buffer:B, elem:E > ;
```

```
[SE] (sget by B and U) = ((get B replyto U);h(U)) ;
```

Transition rule H specifies that a user requires two messages, an **answer** message and a help message h, to store an element retrieved from the buffer. Equation SE specifies that a synchronous **get** is a sequential composition of a **get** and an h message. The sequential composition ensures that the h message is always processed after the **get** message and, since the h and the **answer** message can only be processed in one joint synchronous transition, the **answer** message is also processed.

One can imagine that the other messages of the various buffers can be specified in a synchronous version using this technique. Moreover this specification of a synchronous communication can also be inherited to heirs which are encapsulated in a subconfiguration.

6 Related work

The SMoLCS approach [3, 4] combines algebraic specifications of data types and labeled state transition relations for the specification of behavior. Particular to this approach is a hierarchy of layers of specification with algebraic data types at the lowest layer and communication, parallel composition, abstraction and monitoring at successive higher layers. Algebras of actions allow to define the semantics of composed actions, modularized in the various layers.

The concept of subconfiguration also exists in several other object-oriented languages as, e.g., in Actor languages [1, 2] and Troll [7]. Particular to our approach is that we model the migration of messages into and out of subconfigurations by equations, not by transitions. This keeps the number of transitions reasonably small.

7 Conclusions

Maude's inheritance relation together with the concept of subconfiguration and an algebra of messages make it possible to reuse specifications. Our work on a verification technique for Maude specifications [9] demonstrates also that asynchronous message passing is better than synchronous message passing with respect to the inheritability of properties of specifications, a necessity for modular verification. The use of equations in modeling the migration of messages into and out of configurations keeps the number of transitions small. This helps to make the verification of properties of the behavior of single objects or configurations feasible. The use of equations contributes to a very abstract level of specification, where the structure of the state is of less importance, the focus of the specification lies on synchronization and communication of the objects, and one has few but powerful messages.

The degree of reusability of our specifications is far higher than one would expect for such a simple language in the presence of the inheritance anomaly [11]. This suggests that the basic design concepts of Maude, especially the object model, the communication mechanism and the transition rules for the specification of the behavior, are more appropriate for a structured design of specifications than the design concepts of more conventional languages with synchronous communication, explicit synchronization code and code of methods encapsulated in objects.

Together with our work on verification techniques for specifications in Maude [16], our picture of a sensible object-oriented specification language for the design of complex, concurrent systems is becoming more and more precise: Maude's object model, Maude's communication mechanism, a message algebra, subconfigurations and, maybe, also a module concept for programming in the large. In this paper we use Maude and made some small enhancements of its syntax. But, of course, our reuse mechanisms could be part of any object-oriented specification or programming language independent of the object model.

8 Acknowledgement

We wish to thank the anonymous referees for their valuable comments.

This work is part of the DFG project OSIDRIS and received travel support from the ARC program of the DAAD. The work of F. Nickl was carried out while she was a member of the Institut für Informatik, Ludwig-Maximilians-Universität München.

References

1. G. Agha, S. Frølund, W.Y. Kim, R. Panwar, A. Patterson, and D. Sturman. Abstraction and modularity mechanisms for concurrent computing. In G. Agha, P. Wegner, and A. Yonezawa, editors, *Research Directions in Concurrent Object-Oriented Programming*, pages 3–21. MIT Press, 1993.

2. M. Aksit, K. Wakita, J. Bosch, L. Bergmans, and A. Yonezawa. Abstracting object interactions using composition filters. In R. Guerraoui, I. Nierstrasz, and M. Riveill, editors, *Object-based Distributed Programming*, Lecture Notes in Computer Science 791, pages 152–183. Springer-Verlag, 1993.

3. E. Astesiano, G.F. Mascari, G. Reggio, and M. Wirsing. On the parameterized algebraic specification of concurrent systems. In H. Ehrig, C. Floyd, M. Nivat, and M. Thatcher, editors, *Mathematical Foundations of Software Development*, Lecture Notes in Computer Science 185, pages 342–358. Springer-Verlag, 1985.

4. E. Astesiano and M. Wirsing. Bisimulation in algebraic specifications. In H. Ait-Kaci and M. Nivat, editors, *Resolution of Equations in Algebraic Structures*, Algebraic Techniques, Vol. 1, pages 1–32. Academic Press, London, 1989.

5. S. Frølund. Inheritance of synchronisation constraints in concurrent object-oriented programming languages. In O. Lehrmann Madsen, editor, *European Conf. on Object-Oriented Programming (ECOOP'92)*, Lecture Notes in Computer Science 615, pages 185–196. Springer-Verlag, 1992.

6. J.A. Goguen, C. Kirchner, H. Kirchner, A. Megrélis, J. Meseguer, and T. Winkler. An introduction to OBJ3. In J.-P. Jouannaud and S. Kaplan, editors, *Proc. First Int. Workshop on Conditional Term Rewriting Systems*, Lecture Notes in Computer Science 308, pages 258–263. Springer-Verlag, 1988.

7. T. Hartmann, G. Saake, R. Jungclaus, P. Hartel, and J. Kusch. Revised version of the modelling language TROLL (Version 2.0). Technical Report Informatik-Bericht 94–03, TU Braunschweig, 1994.

8. A.E. Haxthausen and F. Nickl. Pushouts of order-sorted algebraic specifications. In *AMAST'96*, Lecture Notes in Computer Science. Springer-Verlag, 1996. To appear.

9. U. Lechner and C. Lengauer. Modal-μ-Maude — properties and specification of concurrent objects. In B. Freitag, C. B. Jones, C. Lengauer, and H.-J. Schek, editors, *Object Orientation with Parallelism and Persistence*. Kluwer, 1996. To appear.

10. U. Lechner, C. Lengauer, and M. Wirsing. An Object-Oriented Airport: Specification and Refinement in Maude. In E. Astesiano, G. Reggio, and A. Tarlecki, editors, *10th Workshop on Specification of Abstract Data Types Joint with the 5th COMPASS Workshop, Selected papers*, Lecture Notes in Computer Science 906, pages 351–367. Springer-Verlag, 1995.

11. S. Matsuoka and A. Yonezawa. Analysis of inheritance anomaly in concurrent object-oriented languages. In G. Agha, P. Wegner, and A. Yonezawa, editors, *Research Directions in Concurrent Object-Oriented Programming*, pages 107–150. MIT Press, 1993.

12. J. Meseguer. A logical theory of concurrenty objects and its realization in the Maude language. In G. Agha, P. Wegner, and A. Yonezawa, editors, *Research Directions in Concurrent Object-Oriented Programming*, pages 314–390. MIT Press, 1993.

13. J. Meseguer. Solving the inheritance anomaly in concurrent object-oriented programming. In O. Nierstrasz, editor, *ECOOP '93 – Object-Oriented Programming*, Lecture Notes in Computer Science 707, pages 220–246. Springer-Verlag, 1993.

14. J. Meseguer and T. Winkler. Parallel programming in Maude. In J.-P. Banâtre and D. Le Métayer, editors, *Research Directions in High-Level Parallel Programming Languages*, Lecture Notes in Computer Science 574, pages 253–293. Springer-Verlag, 1992.

15. O. Nierstrasz and M. Papathomas. Towards a type theory for active objects. *ACM OOPS Messenger*, 2(2):89–93, April 1991. (*Proceedings OOPSLA/ECOOP 90 Workshop on Object-Based Concurrent Systems*).

16. M. Wirsing, F. Nickl, and U. Lechner. Concurrent Object-Oriented Design Specification in Spectrum. In P.-Y. Schobbens, editor, *MeDiCis'94: Methodology for the Development of Computer System Specifications, Working Notes of a Workshop held in the Chateau de Namur 1994*, pages 163–179, 1994. Full version: Concurrent Object-Oriented Design Specification in SPECTRUM, Technical Report 9418, Institut für Informatik, Ludwig-Maximilians-Universität München, December 1994.

A Specification of OIDLIST

```
OIDLIST = {
   enriches OID ;
   sort OIdList ;
   functions
      eps : → OIdList ;
      _ _ : OId OIdList → OIdList ;     (* left append *)
      _ _ : OIdList OId → OIdList       (* right append *)
   equations ∀ E1,E2:OId, L:OIdList in
      E2 eps = eps E2 ;
      E1 (L E2) = (E1 L) E2
   endequations }
```

Note that we do not use subsorting to implement lists. The reason is that, in the presence of subsorting, the union operation, in general, does not preserve the coherence of signatures.

Coherence is a central property of order sorted signatures: in a coherent signature two connected subsorts have a common supersort (locally upward filteredness) and there is always a unique least sort for each term (regularity) [8]. This problem is illustrated by the following example: Assume we have signatures

$\Sigma_1 = $ Nat, NatList; subsorts Nat < NatList;

$\Sigma_2 = $ sorts Nat, Int; subsorts Nat < Int;

sharing the common subsignature

$\Sigma_0 = $ sorts Nat;

Then the union of Σ_1 and Σ_2 (more precisely, the pushout of the inclusions $\sigma_1 : \Sigma_0 \hookrightarrow \Sigma_1$ and $\sigma_2 : \Sigma_0 \hookrightarrow \Sigma_2$) is

$\Sigma = $ sorts Nat, Int, NatList; subsorts Nat < Int, Nat < NatList;

Σ is not locally upwards filtered. Hence, in the above specification OIDLIST, problems w.r.t. the coherence of its signature arise if OId is declared as a subsort of OIdList and OId is also declared as a subsort in the specification OID. Since we use overloading, we avoid this problem.

Modeling Subobject-Based Inheritance

Jonathan G. Rossie Jr.[1][*][†] Daniel P. Friedman[1][*] Mitchell Wand[2][‡]

[1] Department of Computer Science, Indiana University
Bloomington, IN 47405, USA
{jrossie,dfried}@cs.indiana.edu
[2] College of Computer Science, Northeastern University
Boston, MA 02115, USA
wand@ccs.neu.edu

Abstract. A model of subobjects and subobject selection gives us a concise expression of key semantic relationships in a variety of inheritance-based languages. Subobjects and their selection have been difficult to reason about explicitly because they are not explicit in the languages that support them. The goal of this paper is to present a relatively simple calculus to describe subobjects and subobject selection explicitly. Rather than present any deep theorems here, we develop a general calculus that can be used to explore the design of inheritance systems.

1 Introduction

In a system with inheritance, a class **P** (Point) represents a collection of members, the methods and instance variables that are shared by instances of **P**. When a class **CP** (ColorPoint) inherits from **P**, the language may be designed to do one of two things. It may attempt to merge the members of **P** with those of **CP**, usually by collapsing same-named members into single definitions. Alternatively, it may allow the members of **P** to be inherited as an indivisible collection. This collection, when instantiated, is known as a subobject. Each object of class **CP** has a distinct subobject **CP/P**, which we call the **P** subobject of **CP**, as well as a subobject **CP/CP**, which we call the primary subobject of **CP**. Subobjects are meant to support subclass polymorphism: each subobject represents a different view of the object, allowing it to be viewed as an instance of any of its ancestor classes. The notion of subobjects is necessary to model the behavior of a variety of complex multiple-inheritance systems such as in C++.

Since an instance no longer can be seen as a record with member names as field names, member references become more complicated. In this model, it is the subobjects that are seen as records, and an object is just a collection of subobjects. Member references are made by selecting a subobject that defines

---

[*]Research partially supported by NSF grant CCR–9302114.
[†]Current address: Department of Computer Science, North Carolina State University, Raleigh, NC 27695, USA
[‡]Received support from NSF grants CCR–9304144 and CCR–9404646.

the member, and referencing the appropriate field of that subobject. Since the field reference is unremarkable, we focus on the semantics of subobject selection.

In multiple-inheritance systems, it becomes complicated even to determine the set of subobjects for instances of a given class. In some systems, the methods and instance variables of **P** may in fact be *replicated* many times in **CP** depending on the different paths through which **P** may be inherited by **CP**. In other systems, there may be only one subobject for each ancestor, despite multiple paths to the same ancestor. Yet other systems may allow both kinds of inheritance to coexist, as in C++ [10, 26].

Subobject selection is complicated by the multiple views supported by an object. When a **CP** instance is viewed through its **CP/P** subobject, should it still be possible to access the members defined in the **CP/CP** subobject as well? What about the converse? And if both are accessible, which should be preferred if a member is defined in both subobjects? Moreover, how are these decisions affected by the presence of both late-binding (dynamic) and early-binding (static) references? These are the questions our semantics is designed to answer. We develop a core semantics, and extend it to express both single and multiple inheritance. Our goal is to present a general calculus that can be used to explore the design of inheritance systems.

Each of our systems is presented as a language in which an inheritance hierarchy is built and a query is made with respect to the hierarchy. Each query first identifies a primary subobject of some class in the hierarchy, and then asks which subobject of that class is selected when a certain member (or sequence of members) is referenced. An expression in one of these languages is seen as expressing the subobject that is ultimately selected as a result of a sequence of member references. Importantly, we are not concerned with the value of a member reference; we model only static properties of inheritance hierarchies.

For example, suppose we have a new object of class **CP**, and we select (statically) the **f** method, and then from inside that method we select (dynamically) the **g** method. What subobject of **CP** should the **g** method access? This may be expressed as $\mathbf{inh(P; ; f, g)}$ in $\mathbf{inh(CP; P; g)}$ in $\mathbf{CP.stat(f).dyn(g)}$, which is a term in our single-inheritance system. Call this term t. The semantics of our system allows us to show that $\vdash t \triangleright \mathbf{CP/CP}$, which says that this term selects the primary subobject of **CP**.

Our presentation is expressed in terms of an abstract syntax and an operational semantics for each member of a family of inheritance systems. Since our goal is modeling, we prove no deep theorems about these systems, but we do state some of their rudimentary properties. We begin with a common core in Sect. 2, and extend it to arrive at a single-inheritance system in Sect. 3. Section 4 extends the core in a different direction, arriving at a core system for multiple inheritance. Sections 5 and 6 extend this multiple-inheritance core in two directions, giving us replicating inheritance in one case, and shared inheritance in the other. Finally, Sect. 7 combines the replicating and shared systems into a single system, which closely models the C++ multiple-inheritance system.

2 Class-System Core

We begin with a core system, which we call CSC. Although this is not a powerful system itself, it is the common basis for all the systems that follow. Classes may be defined in CSC, but there is no inheritance, and therefore all subobjects are primary. Thus, subobject selection always yields the primary subobject. Nevertheless, the study of CSC lays important groundwork for the inheritance systems that follow.

2.1 CSC Syntax

A term T makes queries about subobject selection, but may first contribute to the construction of a class context, the inheritance hierarchy in which the queries are resolved. Environments encode the class context, including information about the classes that are defined and the members defined by those classes. The **class** form introduces new classes, but there is no notion of inheritance. The only query in CSC is the trivial a, which simply selects the primary subobject of the named class. Throughout, we let a–d range over class names, while every m is a member name.

CSC Syntax

$T ::=$		CSC term
	$\mathbf{class}(a; m_1, \ldots, m_n)\ \mathbf{in}\ T$	$(n \geq 0)$ class definition
	Q	query
$Q ::=$		CSC query
	a	primary subobject of a

For now, a subobject is identified by two classes, although this is extended in the multiple-inheritance systems in later sections. The first class is called the *actual* class of the subobject: In an instance of class a, every subobject's actual class is a. The second class is called the *effective* class of the subobject: Each subobject corresponds to an ancestor of the actual class, possibly the class itself. This ancestor is the effective class of the subobject. Subobjects are annotated as a/b, where a is the actual class and b is the effective class.

Judgments in CSC and the subsequent systems are categorized by the role they play in the proof system. Each of the categories *environments*, *well-formed subobjects*, and *subobject selection* has only one form of judgment. The *access* category comprises all judgments that de-construct environments, while *subobject relations* is a catch-all for the remaining judgment forms, each of which expresses some kind of relationship among subobjects with respect to a given environment.

CSC Judgments

environments

$\vdash E\ env$ E is a well-formed environment

access

$E \vdash a\ class$ a is a defined class

$E \vdash a \ni m$ a defines the member m

wf subobjects

$E \vdash a/b\ wf$ a/b is a well-formed subobject

subobject selection

$E \vdash T \rhd a/b$ the term T selects a/b

Environments contain information about the class names and member names defined in an inheritance hierarchy.

Environment Syntax

$E ::=$ Environment

$\emptyset$ the empty environment

E, a definition of class a

$E, a \ni m$ a defines the member m

$E, a \prec b$ a inherits directly from b (SI only)

$E, a \prec_r b$ replicating direct inheritance (RMI, SRMI)

$E, a \prec_s b$ shared direct inheritance (SMI, SRMI)

Sometimes it is useful to view an environment E as a set.

$$\mathrm{dom}(E) = \{a \mid (a \in E) \vee (a \prec b \in E) \vee (a \prec_r b \in E) \vee (a \prec_s b \in E)\}$$
$$\mathrm{codom}(E) = \{b \mid (a \prec b \in E) \vee (a \prec_r b \in E) \vee (a \prec_s b \in E)\}$$

2.2 CSC Rules

The rules for CSC are listed below. This system is intended primarily as a starting point in our derivation of inheritance systems. As such, it includes the (*Acc* ∋) and (*Wf base*) rules, which are never required for any proofs in the current system. Otherwise, the subobject-selection judgments can be seen as motivating the other rules.

The (*Sel class*) rule evaluates the subterm T in an environment extended to include a and $a \ni m_1, \ldots, a \ni m_n$. The well-formedness of environments ensures that a is not already defined in E. The member names $m_1, \ldots, m_n$ are assumed to be a set.

To select the primary subobject of a using (*Sel pri*), we have only to show that a is a class in E. This is shown by application of (*Acc a*), which in turn forces E to be well-formed.

Environments

(Env ∅)

$$\frac{}{\vdash \emptyset \; env}$$

(Env a)

$$\frac{\vdash E \; env \quad a \notin \text{dom}(E)}{\vdash E, a \; env}$$

(Env ∋)

$$\frac{E \vdash a \; class}{\vdash E, a \ni m \; env}$$

Access

(Acc a)

$$\frac{\vdash E, a, E' \; env}{E, a, E' \vdash a \; class}$$

(Acc ∋)

$$\frac{\vdash E, a \ni m, E' \; env}{E, a \ni m, E' \vdash a \ni m}$$

Well-formed Subobjects

(Wf base)

$$\frac{E \vdash a \; class}{E \vdash a/a \; wf}$$

Subobject Selection

(Sel pri)

$$\frac{E \vdash a \; class}{E \vdash a \triangleright a/a}$$

(Sel class)

$$\frac{E, a, a \ni m_1, \ldots, a \ni m_n \vdash T \triangleright a/c}{E \vdash \mathbf{class}(a; m_1, \ldots, m_n) \; \mathbf{in} \; T \triangleright a/c} \quad (n \geq 0)$$

2.3 CSC Basic Properties

With the CSC system we can prove such assertions as

$$\vdash \mathbf{class}(A;) \; \mathbf{in} \; A \triangleright A/A$$
$$\vdash \mathbf{class}(A; x, y) \; \mathbf{in} \; \mathbf{class}(B; z) \; \mathbf{in} \; A \triangleright A/A$$
$$\vdash \mathbf{class}(A; x, y) \; \mathbf{in} \; \mathbf{class}(B; z) \; \mathbf{in} \; B \triangleright B/B$$

We can state some easy properties of CSC.

Proposition 2.1 (CSC Properties)
Given an E, a term T, and a query Q:

(i) If $E \vdash Q \triangleright a/b$ then $E \vdash a/b$ wf.

(ii) There is at most one a/b such that $E \vdash T \triangleright a/b$.

Since (*Sel pri*) is the only selector, and since primary subobjects are well-formed by (*Wf base*), both (i) and (ii) follow.

3 Single Inheritance

The single inheritance system SI is now defined as an extension of the CSC system. The rules and judgment forms of SI extend those of CSC. The result is a model of a single-inheritance system much like Simula [8] or single-inheritance C++.

We consider both late-binding (dynamic) and early-binding (static) methods as well as instance-variables, which are static in the same sense as static methods. An unusual aspect of our formalism is that, rather than annotate each member as either static or dynamic in the class declarations, we annotate the reference sites, where the information is immediately useful. We assume that these annotations are consistent with a system in which the annotations at the reference sites are inferred from some information in the class declarations. Moreover, we do not distinguish between instance variables and static methods.

3.1 SI Syntax

To complement CSC's **class**, we introduce **inh** for class definitions with inheritance. We also add three new queries: **dyn** for dynamic references, **stat** for static references, and **super** for superclass references, which are also static.

SI Syntax

$T ::=$		SI term
	$\mathbf{class}(a; m_1, \ldots, m_n) \mathbf{\ in\ } T$	$(n \geq 0)$ class definition
	$\mathbf{inh}(a; b; m_1, \ldots, m_n) \mathbf{\ in\ } T$	$(n \geq 0)$ inheriting class definition
	Q	query
$Q ::=$		SI query
	a	primary subobject of a
	$Q.\mathbf{dyn}(m)$	dynamic subobject selection
	$Q.\mathbf{stat}(m)$	static subobject selection
	$Q.\mathbf{super}(m)$	superclass subobject selection

The new SI judgments extend the CSC judgments in order to express the effects of inheritance. First, $E \vdash a \prec b$ asserts that a inherits directly from b. For subobject selection, however, we must be able to compare subobjects, as in $E \vdash a/b \leq a/c$. Finally, we need a way to express the effects of subobject ordering on the search for a subobject that defines a member m; this is given by $E \vdash \text{selects}(a, m, c)$, which says that the a/c subobject of a is selected by m.

SI Judgments (extending CSC judgments)

access
$$E \vdash a \prec b \qquad a \text{ inherits directly from } b$$
subobject relations
$$E \vdash a/b \leq a/c \qquad a/b \text{ is more defined than } a/c$$
$$E \vdash \text{selects}(a, m, c) \qquad m \text{ selects } a\text{'s } a/c \text{ subobject}$$

3.2 SI Rules

The SI rules, listed below, are driven by the syntax-based rules. The new inheritance rule (*Sel inh sing*) now extends E with $a \prec b$, motivating (*Env* $\prec$); the condition in (*Env* $\prec$) that $a \notin \text{codom}(E)$ ensures that inheritance is acyclic in well-formed environments. The remaining syntax-based rules, (*Sel dyn*), (*Sel stat*), and (*Sel sup*), are all defined in terms of the *selects* relation, (*Rel sel*). This rule is the key to the entire system. We paraphrase (*Rel sel*) as follows:

> Subobject selection for a method m in a class a is a two-step process. First we determine the set S of candidates—the set of all subobjects of a in which m is defined. Then we select a/c, which is the least element of S.

This rule fails when m is undefined in every ancestor of a (including a). It also fails when S has incomparable minima, which indicates an ambiguous reference.

Of particular interest are the different ways in which *selects* is used by (*Sel dyn*), (*Sel stat*), and (*Sel sup*). In dynamic selection, the current static context of the reference is ignored; only the actual class of the object is considered. This is reflected in (*Sel dyn*) by ignoring b, which represents the current view of an a object. Only the actual class a is used in subobject selection, yielding a/c, another subobject of a.

In contrast, static selection is calculated with respect to the current static context, disregarding the actual class of the object. Thus, (*Sel stat*) uses b for its subobject selection. This yields a subobject b/c of b. Since b is an ancestor of a, it must be that c is also. The static selection therefore yields a/c. The case of (*Sel sup*) is nearly identical to (*Sel stat*), except that the immediate base class of the current static context is used to resolve the reference. Thus, super-method invocations are also static references.

The (*Rel sel*) rule motivates the rest of the system. The notion of a well-formed subobject is explicitly called for, as is the need for (*Acc* $\ni$), which was defined in CSC. Subobjects are compared using $\leq$, which is defined by (*Rel* $\leq$ *refl*), (*Rel* $\leq$ *arc*), and (*Rel* $\leq$ *trans*). Finally, (*Acc* $\prec$) is required by (*Sel sup*), (*Rel* $\leq$ *arc*), and (*Wf ind*).

The well-formed subobject rules for SI implement the notion that a class a has one subobject a/b for each ancestor class b. The term *ancestor* is taken to denote the transitive and reflexive closure of the $\prec$ relation. A very similar thing happens in the $\leq$ rules. The $\leq$ relation is the reflexive and transitive closure of $\prec$ as if it applied to subobjects. That is, $a/b \leq a/c$ if and only if c is an ancestor of b.

Environments

(*Env* $\prec$)

$$\frac{E \vdash a \ class \quad E \vdash b \ class \quad a \neq b \quad a \notin \text{codom}(E)}{\vdash E, a \prec b \ env}$$

Access

(Acc $\prec$)

$$\frac{\vdash E, a \prec b, E' \text{ env}}{E, a \prec b, E' \vdash a \prec b}$$

Well-formed Subobjects

(Wf ind)

$$\frac{E \vdash a/b \text{ wf} \quad E \vdash b \prec c}{E \vdash a/c \text{ wf}}$$

Subobject Relations

(Rel $\leq$ refl)

$$\frac{E \vdash a/b \text{ wf}}{E \vdash a/b \leq a/b}$$

(Rel $\leq$ arc)

$$\frac{E \vdash a/b \text{ wf} \quad E \vdash a/c \text{ wf} \quad E \vdash b \prec c}{E \vdash a/b \leq a/c}$$

(Rel $\leq$ trans)

$$\frac{E \vdash a/b \leq a/c \quad E \vdash a/c \leq a/d}{E \vdash a/b \leq a/d}$$

(Rel sel)

$$\frac{S = \{a/b \mid E \vdash a/b \text{ wf} \quad E \vdash b \ni m\} \quad a/c \in S \quad \forall (a/d \in S)[E \vdash a/c \leq a/d]}{E \vdash \text{selects}(a, m, c)}$$

Subobject Selection

(Sel inh sing)

$$\frac{E, a, a \prec b, a \ni m_1, \ldots, a \ni m_n \vdash T \triangleright a/c}{E \vdash \mathbf{inh}(a; b; m_1, \ldots, m_n) \text{ in } T \triangleright a/c} \quad (n \geq 0)$$

(Sel dyn)

$$\frac{E \vdash Q \triangleright a/b \quad E \vdash \text{selects}(a, m, c)}{E \vdash Q.\mathbf{dyn}(m) \triangleright a/c}$$

(Sel stat)

$$\frac{E \vdash Q \triangleright a/b \quad E \vdash \text{selects}(b, m, c)}{E \vdash Q.\mathbf{stat}(m) \triangleright a/c}$$

(Sel sup)

$$\frac{E \vdash Q \triangleright a/b \quad E \vdash b \prec c \quad E \vdash \text{selects}(c, m, d)}{E \vdash Q.\mathbf{super}(m) \triangleright a/d}$$

3.3 SI Basic Properties

As a demonstration of some of the important properties of SI, let Z abbreviate the string **class(A; x, y)** in **inh(B; A; y)**. Then we can obtain the following theorems in SI:

$$\vdash Z \text{ in } \mathbf{B} \qquad\qquad\qquad\qquad \triangleright \mathbf{B}/\mathbf{B}$$
$$\vdash Z \text{ in } \mathbf{B}.\mathbf{dyn}(\mathbf{x}) \qquad\qquad\quad \triangleright \mathbf{B}/\mathbf{A}$$
$$\vdash Z \text{ in } \mathbf{B}.\mathbf{stat}(\mathbf{x}) \qquad\qquad\quad \triangleright \mathbf{B}/\mathbf{A}$$
$$\vdash Z \text{ in } \mathbf{B}.\mathbf{stat}(\mathbf{x}).\mathbf{stat}(\mathbf{y}) \qquad \triangleright \mathbf{B}/\mathbf{A}$$
$$\vdash Z \text{ in } \mathbf{B}.\mathbf{stat}(\mathbf{x}).\mathbf{dyn}(\mathbf{y}) \qquad \triangleright \mathbf{B}/\mathbf{B}$$
$$\vdash Z \text{ in } \mathbf{B}.\mathbf{stat}(\mathbf{x}).\mathbf{dyn}(\mathbf{y}).\mathbf{super}(\mathbf{y}) \quad \triangleright \mathbf{B}/\mathbf{A}$$

Proposition 3.1 (SI Properties)
Given an environment E, a term T, and a query Q:

(i) If $E \vdash Q \triangleright a/b$ then $E \vdash a/b$ wf.

(ii) There is at most one a/b such that $E \vdash T \triangleright a/b$.

(iii) If $E \vdash Q \triangleright a/b$ and if Q' is a subterm of Q then there exists c such that $E \vdash Q' \triangleright a/c$.

(iv) Suppose $E \vdash Q \triangleright a/b$ and $E \vdash Q' \triangleright a/c$. If $E \vdash Q.\mathbf{dyn}(m) \triangleright a/d$ then $E \vdash Q'.\mathbf{dyn}(m) \triangleright a/d$.

(v) Suppose $E \vdash Q \triangleright a/b$ and $E \vdash Q' \triangleright a/b$. If $E \vdash Q.\mathbf{stat}(m) \triangleright a/c$ then $E \vdash Q'.\mathbf{stat}(m) \triangleright a/c$.

These are trivial except (ii). Certainly (*Sel pri*) selects at most one subobject. The other selectors, (*Sel dyn*), (*Sel stat*) and (*Sel sup*), select as many subobjects as can be proven by (*Rel sel*) with a and m fixed. Fixing a and m also fixes S, so the only question is whether there is more than one a/c such that $\forall (a/d \in S)[E \vdash a/c \leq a/d]$. Clearly, if $a/e \in S$ and $\forall (a/e \in S)[E \vdash a/e \leq a/d]$ then $E \vdash a/e \leq a/c$. But $E \vdash a/c \leq a/e$ since $a/e \in S$. Thus $a/c = a/e$ if $\leq$ is a partial order over S. Reflexivity and transitivity of $\leq$ follow from (*Rel $\leq$ refl*) and (*Rel $\leq$ trans*), respectively. Antisymmetry is proved by the following series of lemmas.

Lemma 3.2 ($\prec$ is acyclic)
There is no E, $a_1, \ldots, a_n$ ($n > 1$) such that

(i) $\vdash E$ env,

(ii) for $1 \leq i < n$, $E \vdash a_i \prec a_{i+1}$, and

(iii) $E \vdash a_n \prec a_1$.

Proof. For (i)–(iii) to hold, it must be that $a_i \prec a_{i+1}$, $a_n \prec a_1$ must all occur in E. Consider the one of these that occurs rightmost in E. It cannot be $a_i \prec a_{i+1}$ because (since it is last) a_i must already occur in the codomain of E, either as $a_{i-1} \prec a_i$ (if $i > 1$), or $a_n \prec a_i$ (if $i = 1$). Similarly, it cannot be $a_n \prec a_1$, because a_n already is in codom(E), as $a_{n-1} \prec a_n$.

```
class A {
  public:
    int x() { return( 10 + this->y() ); }
    virtual int y() { return( 0 ); } };
class B : public A {
  public:
    int y() { return( 1 ); } };

int main(void) {
    B *bp = new(B);
    printf("bp->x() ==> %d\n", bp->x());
}
```

Fig. 1. C++ single-inheritance example.

Lemma 3.3
If $E \vdash a/b \leq a/c$ then $E \vdash b \prec^* c$, where $\prec^*$ is the reflexive, transitive closure of $\prec$.

Proof. By induction on the derivation of $E \vdash a/b \leq a/c$. If the last step is (*Rel* $\leq$ *refl*) or (*Rel* $\leq$ *arc*) then the conclusion is true, and the hypothesis is clearly preserved by (*Rel* $\leq$ *trans*).

Lemma 3.4
If $E \vdash a/b \leq a/c$ and $E \vdash a/c \leq a/b$ then $b = c$.

Proof. Assume b and c are distinct. By Lemma 3.3, we deduce that $E \vdash b \prec^* c$ and $E \vdash c \prec^* b$. But this contradicts Lemma 3.2.

3.4 SI Example

To demonstrate the relationship between our subobject selection calculi and the semantics of an object-oriented language, consider the following translation from C++ into a hypothetical intermediate language that is similar in syntax to SI. From there, we show how SI relates to the semantics of the resulting code fragment.

We begin with a single-inheritance C++ program, shown in Fig. 1, which prints "bp->x() ==> 11". We translate this code into a more suitable intermediate language, without describing the language in detail. In the following code, class definitions are nested, as in SI, to construct a class context. An instance is created within the scope of this context, and the x member is referenced. This reference to x uses **stat** because x is a non-virtual method in the C++ version. The y reference, on the other hand, uses **dyn** because y is virtual in the original.

```
class(A; x=fun(self) 10 + self.dyn(y),
         y=fun(self) 0 ) in
  inh(B; A; y=fun(self) 1 ) in
    let bp = new(B) in
      bp.stat(x)
```

We are not concerned with the run-time system implied by this code fragment. Rather, we focus on the subobject-selection issues. The subobjects of **B** in this system are $\{\mathbf{B/B}, \mathbf{B/A}\}$. There are three sites in the code that call for subobject selection: **new(B)**, **bp.stat(x)**, and **self.dyn(y)**. The behavior at each site is determined by the following theorems of SI, where Z abbreviates **class(A; x, y) in inh(B; A; y)**:

$$
\begin{aligned}
&\vdash Z \text{ in } \mathbf{B} & &\rhd \mathbf{B/B} \\
&\vdash Z \text{ in } \mathbf{B}.\text{stat(x)} & &\rhd \mathbf{B/A} \\
&\vdash Z \text{ in } \mathbf{B}.\text{stat(x)}.\text{dyn(y)} & &\rhd \mathbf{B/B}
\end{aligned}
$$

The first of these says that, in a class context that defines the class **A** with members **x** and **y**, that also defines the class **B**, inheriting from **A** and defining the member **y**, the primary subobject of **B** is **B/B**, which represents a new instance of **B**. The second says that, in this same context, if we start with a fresh instance of **B** and make a static reference to **x**, the **B/A** subobject of **B** is selected. Finally, if we start with a new instance of **B**, make a static reference to **x**, and then—from the resulting **B/A** context—make a dynamic reference to **y**, the **B/B** subobject is selected.

4 Multiple-inheritance Core

We now define a core system for multiple inheritance as an extension of CSC. Significantly, MIC does not extend SI. Although SI shares many similarities with the multiple-inheritance systems, only the CSC subset of SI can be shared without modifications.

Like CSC, MIC is meant only as a foundation for the systems that follow. It comprises the rules that are common to those systems, but is not coherent on its own. (For example, it has no syntax for class definitions.) Nevertheless, we take this opportunity to look closely at these common rules, and to deal with some of the complications that arise in the move to multiple inheritance.

The most obvious change from SI is an extended subobject notation. In multiple inheritance, it is sometimes necessary to distinguish the two versions of a subobject a/c that arise when there are two inheritance paths between a and c. Subobject notation is therefore extended to allow sequences of classnames, as in a/α. We use α, β and γ to denote (possibly empty) sequences of class names. We freely use concatenation of sequences and individual classes, as in $a/\alpha b\beta$.

Consider the subobject $a/\alpha b$. Here, a is the actual class, b is the effective class, and α is a sequence of class names. In RMI (Sect. 5), α is a full inheritance path from a to b. In SMI (Sect. 6), α is empty. In SRMI (Sect. 7), α is a subpath satisfying certain properties to be described later.

4.1 MIC Syntax

Since each of the ensuing multiple-inheritance systems defines its own **inh** syntax, MIC does not provide one. It does provide **dyn** and **stat**, which are analogous to those in SI, but there is no obvious multiple-inheritance analog for SI's **super**, since there is no longer an obvious total order among the subobjects. (The question of whether to impose a total order, and what total order to use, is still a source of discussion [9, 12], especially for the CLOS [25] and Dylan [22] communities.)

MIC Syntax

$T ::=$		MIC term
	Q	query
$Q ::=$		MIC query
	a	primary subobject of a
	$Q.\mathbf{dyn}(m)$	dynamic subobject selection
	$Q.\mathbf{stat}(m)$	static subobject selection

Judgments in MIC include those in CSC, and some new forms. The $\leq$ judgment here is familiar from SI, as is the explicit subobject selection relation. These simply have been extended to the multiple-inheritance notation for subobjects. An additional judgment specifies the result of an injection from c's subobjects into a's. This requires a subobject of a to disambiguate the different images of c's subobjects in a.

MIC Judgments (extending CSC judgments)

subobject relations

$E \vdash a/\alpha \leq a/\beta$	a/α is more defined than a/β
$E \vdash \text{selects}(a, m, \alpha)$	m selects a's a/α subobject
$E \vdash \text{inj}(a/\alpha, c/\beta, a/\gamma)$	a/γ is the image of c's c/β in a, wrt a/α

4.2 MIC Rules

A number of the MIC rules are nearly copies of the corresponding rules in SI, using the extended subobject notation. These include (*Sel dyn*), (*Rel sel*), and (*Rel $\leq$ refl*). The remaining rules require further explanation.

In (*Sel stat*), subobject selection yields b/β, which we might expect to correspond to a/β, as in SI. But in SI this is an implicit injection from the space of subobjects of b to the space of subobjects of a: Suppose $a \prec b$. If b's subobjects are $\{b/c_0, \ldots, b/c_n\}$, the subobjects of a would be $\{a/a, a/c_0, \ldots, a/c_n\}$, so every b/c_i has exactly one image a/c_i in a's subobjects.

With multiple inheritance, however, it may be the case that a has two ancestors, b and c, with subobjects b/d and c/d respectively. If we use the same injection as in SI, both of these subobjects inject to the same a/d subobject of a; this is what we call *shared* inheritance of d, which is discussed in Sect. 6. If we want the two subobjects to map to different subobjects of a, we need a more elaborate injection. In Sect. 5, where we introduce *replicating* inheritance, the injection maps b/d to a/bd and c/d to a/cd. For now, we have only the (*Rel inj id*) rule, which is simply an identity map.

MIC is also incomplete because the notion of well-formed subobjects is incomplete, as is the notion of a more-defined subobject. The rules (*Rel $\leq$ repl*) and (*Rel $\leq$ shar*) are used in later sections to tie the $\leq$ relation to the arcs in E, much like (*Rel $\leq$ arc*) in SI.

Subobject Relations

(*Rel inj id*)

$$E \vdash \text{inj}(a/\alpha, a/\beta, a/\beta)$$

(*Rel $\leq$ trans*)

$$\frac{E \vdash a/\alpha \leq a/\beta \quad E \vdash a/\beta \leq a/\gamma}{E \vdash a/\alpha \leq a/\gamma}$$

(*Rel $\leq$ refl*)

$$\frac{E \vdash a/\alpha \; wf}{E \vdash a/\alpha \leq a/\alpha}$$

(*Rel sel*)

$$\frac{S = \{a/\alpha b \mid E \vdash a/\alpha b \; wf \quad E \vdash b \ni m\}}{a/\beta \in S \quad \forall (a/\gamma \in S)[E \vdash a/\beta \leq a/\gamma]}{E \vdash \text{selects}(a, m, \beta)}$$

Subobject Selection

(*Sel dyn*)

$$\frac{E \vdash Q \rhd a/\alpha \quad E \vdash \text{selects}(a, m, \beta)}{E \vdash Q.\mathbf{dyn}(m) \rhd a/\beta}$$

(*Sel stat*)

$$\frac{E \vdash Q \rhd a/\alpha b \quad E \vdash \text{selects}(b, m, \beta) \quad E \vdash \text{inj}(a/\alpha b, b/\beta, a/\gamma)}{E \vdash Q.\mathbf{stat}(m) \rhd a/\gamma}$$

5 Replicating Multiple Inheritance

We are now ready to present our first complete multiple-inheritance system, RMI. The defining assumption in RMI is that a class has one subobject for each inheritance path to each ancestor. Subobjects in RMI encode the complete path from the actual class of the object to one of its ancestors. If that ancestor is reached by different paths, these different paths will cause the subobjects to be annotated differently, resulting in distinct subobjects. Thus, if a class **C** inherits directly from **A** and **B**, where **B** also inherits directly from **A**, objects of **C** will have two subobjects for **A**. These are annotated **C/CA** and **C/CBA**. In RMI, each subobject is actually of the form $a/a\alpha$; that is, each encoded path begins with the actual class of the object. This will not be the case in the other systems we study.

5.1 RMI Syntax

The only new syntax introduced by RMI is the **inh** form. Here, $b_1, \ldots, b_k$ are multiple immediate base classes, which we may assume to be a set. The **class** syntax from CSC is dropped; we can now use an empty series of base classes to model the equivalent behavior.

RMI Syntax

$T ::=$	RMI term
$\quad \textbf{inh}(a; b_1, \ldots, b_k; m_1, \ldots, m_n) \textbf{ in } T$	$(k, n \geq 0)$ class def.
$\quad Q$	query
$Q ::=$	RMI query
$\quad a$	primary subobject of a
$\quad Q.\textbf{dyn}(m)$	dynamic selection
$\quad Q.\textbf{stat}(m)$	static selection

Judgments in RMI extend those in MIC with one new form: $E \vdash a \prec_r b$. The $\prec_r$ relation is analogous to the $\prec$ relation in SI, except that now we are identifying this as a replicating arc.

5.2 RMI Rules

The RMI rules are surprisingly similar to their counterparts in SI. The (*Sel inh repl*) rule is a simple extension of (*Sel inh sing*), and the $\prec_r$ relation is essentially identical to SI's $\prec$. The remaining rules are defined largely in terms of concatenation of paths, which deserves some discussion.

The (*Wf repl*) rule says that a subobject is well formed if it extends a well-formed subobject's inheritance path by one class, where that class is an immediate base class of the effective class of the original subobject. Similarly, (*Rel $\leq$ repl*) says that one subobject is immediately more defined than another if the other's effective class is an immediate base class of the effective class of the original subobject.

Finally, the injection rule (*Rel inj repl*) is more subtle than it might appear. It says that injection is only well defined if the actual class of the subobject that is being injected is the effective class of the current static context (as represented by b in the rule). Given this circumstance, the injection is formed by splicing the paths αb and $b\beta$ to arrive at $\alpha b\beta$. The motivation is that αb tells how to get from

a to a particular b, and $b\beta$ tells how to get from any b to a particular ancestor of b. The spliced path uses the first path to pin down the second.

Environments

$(Env \prec_r)$

$$\frac{E \vdash a\ class \quad E \vdash b\ class \quad a \neq b \quad a \notin \mathrm{codom}(E)}{\vdash E, a \prec_r b\ env}$$

Access

$(Acc \prec_r)$

$$\frac{\vdash E, a \prec_r b, E'\ env}{E, a \prec_r b, E' \vdash a \prec_r b}$$

Well-formed Subobjects

$(Wf\ repl)$

$$\frac{E \vdash a/\alpha b\ wf \quad E \vdash b \prec_r c}{E \vdash a/\alpha bc\ wf}$$

Subobject Relations

$(Rel\ inj\ repl)$

$$\frac{}{E \vdash \mathrm{inj}(a/\alpha b, b/b\beta, a/\alpha b\beta)}$$

$(Rel \leq repl)$

$$\frac{E \vdash a/\alpha\ wf \quad E \vdash a/\alpha b\ wf}{E \vdash a/\alpha \leq a/\alpha b}$$

Subobject Selection

$(Sel\ inh\ repl)$

$$\frac{E, a, a \prec_r b_1, \ldots, a \prec_r b_k, a \ni m_1, \ldots, a \ni m_n \vdash T \triangleright a/\alpha}{E \vdash \mathrm{inh}(a; b_1, \ldots, b_k; m_1, \ldots, m_n)\ in\ T \triangleright a/\alpha} \quad (k, n \geq 0)$$

5.3   RMI Basic Properties

As a demonstration of some of the important properties of RMI, let Z abbreviate the string $\mathrm{inh}(A; ; x, y)$ in $\mathrm{inh}(B; A; w, z)$ in $\mathrm{inh}(C; A, B; y, z)$. Then we can obtain the following theorems in RMI:

$$
\begin{array}{ll}
\vdash Z\ in\ C & \triangleright C/C \\
\vdash Z\ in\ C.\mathrm{stat}(w) & \triangleright C/CB \\
\vdash Z\ in\ C.\mathrm{stat}(w).\mathrm{stat}(y) & \triangleright C/CBA \\
\vdash Z\ in\ C.\mathrm{stat}(w).\mathrm{stat}(y).\mathrm{dyn}(y) & \triangleright C/C \\
\vdash Z\ in\ C.\mathrm{stat}(w).\mathrm{stat}(y).\mathrm{dyn}(z) & \triangleright C/C
\end{array}
$$

There is no a/α, however, such that $\vdash Z$ **in** $\mathbf{C}.\mathbf{stat}(\mathbf{x}) \rhd a/\alpha$, even though
x is defined in an ancestor of **C**. This is because the set S in (*Rel sel*) is
$\{\mathbf{C/CA}, \mathbf{C/CBA}\}$, and these two subobjects are incomparable by $\leq$. Such a
reference is said to be *ambiguous*.

Proposition 5.1 (RMI Properties)
Given an environment E, a term T, and a query Q:

(i) *If $E \vdash Q \rhd a/\alpha$ then $E \vdash a/\alpha$ wf.*

(ii) *There is at most one a/α such that $E \vdash T \rhd a/\alpha$.*

(iii) *If $E \vdash Q \rhd a/\alpha$ and if Q' is a subterm of Q then there exists β such that*
$E \vdash Q' \rhd a/\beta$.

(iv) *Suppose $E \vdash Q \rhd a/\alpha$ and $E \vdash Q' \rhd a/\beta$. If $E \vdash Q.\mathbf{dyn}(m) \rhd a/\gamma$ then*
$E \vdash Q'.\mathbf{dyn}(m) \rhd a/\gamma$.

(v) *Suppose $E \vdash Q \rhd a/\alpha$ and $E \vdash Q' \rhd a/\alpha$. If $E \vdash Q.\mathbf{stat}(m) \rhd a/\beta$ then*
$E \vdash Q'.\mathbf{stat}(m) \rhd a/\beta$.

Again, (ii) is the only non-trivial point. The proof of (ii) is essentially
identical to the proof for Proposition 3.1. Antisymmetry of $\leq$ follows from (*Rel
$\leq$ repl*), which relies on the well-formedness of subobjects (*Wf repl*) to tie the
subobject orderings to the order $\prec_r$ of the class hierarchy.

6   Shared Multiple Inheritance

Our second complete multiple-inheritance system, SMI, closely parallels RMI,
but differs in most details. The defining assumption of SMI is that each ancestor class leads to exactly one subobject in an inheriting class, regardless of
the number of paths by which it is inherited. This is, in fact, very similar to the
situation in SI, where a subobject is uniquely named by the actual class and the
effective class. It might be surprising, then, to find sequences and concatenation
in the semantics of SMI. The reason is that we define SMI with extra generality
so that later it can be merged with RMI without redefinition. For the present, it
is consistent to interpret every subobject of the form a/ab as equivalent to a/b.

6.1   SMI Syntax

The syntax of SMI is identical to that of RMI.

SMI Syntax

$$T ::=$$ SMI term

$T ::=$	SMI term
$\mathbf{inh}(a; b_1, \ldots, b_k; m_1, \ldots, m_n)$ **in** T	$(k, n \geq 0)$ class def.
Q	query
$Q ::=$	SMI query
a	primary subobject of a
$Q.\mathbf{dyn}(m)$	dynamic selection
$Q.\mathbf{stat}(m)$	static selection

As in RMI, judgments in SMI extend those of MIC with one new form: $E \vdash a \prec_s b$, in this case. The only difference from RMI is that $\prec_s$ is introduced in place of $\prec_r$, indicating a shared inheritance arc.

6.2   SMI Rules

The only significant differences between RMI and SMI lie in the (*Wf shar*), (*Sel inh shar*), and (*Rel $\leq$ shar*) rules. A subobject a/c is well formed in SMI if either $a = b$ (*Wf base*), or there exists another well-formed subobject such that c is an immediate base class of its effective class. The only reason the (*Wf shar*) rule uses $a/\alpha b$ rather than simply a/b is so that it still applies when this system is combined with RMI; in SMI, α is always empty, so only b is significant. This establishes that every well-formed subobject in SMI has only a singleton sequence in its notation. If we simplify (*Rel $\leq$ shar*) similarly, it is clearly the same ordering we described for SI. Finally, (*Rel inj shar*) is exactly the injection that is implicit in SI's (*Rel inj sing*).

Environments

   (*Env $\prec_s$*)

$$\frac{E \vdash a \; class \quad E \vdash b \; class \quad a \neq b \quad a \notin \operatorname{codom}(E)}{\vdash E, a \prec_s b \; env}$$

Access

   (*Acc $\prec_s$*)

$$\frac{\vdash E, a \prec_s b, E' \; env}{E, a \prec_s b, E' \vdash a \prec_s b}$$

Well-formed Subobjects

   (*Wf shar*)

$$\frac{E \vdash a/\alpha b \; wf \quad E \vdash b \prec_s c}{E \vdash a/c \; wf}$$

Subobject Relations

$$(Rel\ inj\ shar)$$

$$\frac{}{E \vdash \mathrm{inj}(a/\alpha b, b/c, a/c)}$$

$$(Rel \leq shar)$$

$$\frac{E \vdash a/\alpha b\ wf \quad E \vdash a/c\ wf \quad E \vdash b \prec_s c}{E \vdash a/\alpha b \leq a/c}$$

Subobject Selection

$$(Sel\ inh\ shar)$$

$$\frac{E, a, a \prec_s b_1, \ldots, a \prec_s b_k, a \ni m_1, \ldots, a \ni m_n \vdash T \triangleright a/\beta}{E \vdash \mathrm{inh}(a; b_1, \ldots, b_k; m_1, \ldots, m_n)\ \mathrm{in}\ T \triangleright a/\beta} \qquad (k, n \geq 0)$$

6.3 SMI Basic Properties

As a demonstration of some of the important properties of SMI, let Z abbreviate the string $\mathbf{inh(A;\,;x,y)}$ in $\mathbf{inh(B;A;x,z)}$ in $\mathbf{inh(C;A;y,z)}$ in $\mathbf{inh(D;B,C;\,)}$. Then we can obtain the following theorems in SMI:

$$\begin{array}{ll}
\vdash Z \ \mathbf{in}\ \mathbf{D} & \triangleright \mathbf{D/D} \\
\vdash Z \ \mathbf{in}\ \mathbf{D.stat(x)} & \triangleright \mathbf{D/B} \\
\vdash Z \ \mathbf{in}\ \mathbf{D.stat(x).stat(z)} & \triangleright \mathbf{D/B} \\
\vdash Z \ \mathbf{in}\ \mathbf{D.stat(x).stat(y)} & \triangleright \mathbf{D/A} \\
\vdash Z \ \mathbf{in}\ \mathbf{D.stat(x).dyn(y)} & \triangleright \mathbf{D/C} \\
\vdash Z \ \mathbf{in}\ \mathbf{D.stat(y)} & \triangleright \mathbf{D/C} \\
\vdash Z \ \mathbf{in}\ \mathbf{D.stat(y).stat(z)} & \triangleright \mathbf{D/C} \\
\vdash Z \ \mathbf{in}\ \mathbf{D.stat(y).stat(x)} & \triangleright \mathbf{D/A} \\
\vdash Z \ \mathbf{in}\ \mathbf{D.stat(y).dyn(x)} & \triangleright \mathbf{D/B}
\end{array}$$

There is no a/α, however, such that $\vdash Z$ **in** $\mathbf{D.stat(y).dyn(z)} \triangleright a/\alpha$, even though **z** is defined in two ancestors of **D**. The reference is ambiguous because the set $\{\mathbf{D/B}, \mathbf{D/C}\}$, which is the set S in $(Rel\ sel)$, has no least element.

Proposition 6.1 (SMI Properties)
The properties listed in Proposition 5.1 hold for SMI also.

As in SI, antisymmetry follows directly from $(Rel \leq shar)$, which bases subobject orderings on the acyclic order $\prec_s$ over class names.

7 Combined Shared and Replicating Multiple Inheritance

Finally, we may now develop the complete, merged multiple-inheritance system, SRMI. As with the other multiple-inheritance systems, SRMI uses the extended notation for subobjects. The semantics is almost entirely defined by the two systems RMI and SMI, with only two new rules added for SRMI. This merged system is essentially the same system we have previously defined with a less-formal semantics [17]. There, we demonstrated that this system captures the key semantic issues that arise in the C++ multiple-inheritance model.

7.1 SRMI Syntax

One new syntactic form is introduced—a variation on the **inh** form in which two sequences of base classes may be specified. The first sequence is interpreted as shared base classes, the second as replicating bases.

SRMI Syntax

$T ::=$	SRMI term
$\quad$ **inh**$(a; b_1, \ldots, b_k; c_1, \ldots, c_l; m_1, \ldots, m_n)$ **in** T	$(k, l, n \geq 0)$
$\quad Q$	query
$Q ::=$	SRMI query
$\quad a$	primary
$\quad Q.$**dyn**(m)	dynamic
$\quad Q.$**stat**(m)	static

Judgments in SRMI are simply the combined judgments of RMI and SMI.

7.2 SRMI Rules

Only two rules are added to form SRMI, but three rules are also removed. The new (*Sel inh comb*) rule is a simple extension of the analogous rules in RMI and SMI. The new (*Rel inj comb*) rule is very similar to SMI's (*Rel inj shar*), but includes a new condition. This condition, that $b \neq c$, ensures that c is a shared base class of b; the same condition would have meant something quite different (and undesirable) if it were included in the SMI rule. In fact, many of the interactions between the RMI and SMI versions of related rules deserve special attention.

Take, for example, the specification of well-formed subobjects. A well-formed subobject in SRMI is a subobject $a/c_1, \ldots, c_n$, $(n \geq 1)$ in which either $c_1 = a$ or there exists an ancestor b of a such that $b \prec_s c_1$. Moreover, $c_i \prec_r c_{i+1}$, for $0 \leq i < n$. In SRMI, this relationship is given a concise, formal definition in the three rules (*Wf base*), (*Wf repl*), and (*Wf shar*). Thus, the aggregation of rules in SRMI leads to a rich interaction of the two systems on which it is based.

Proposition 7.1
The properties listed in Proposition 5.1 hold for SRMI also.

Again, antisymmetry for $\leq$ is the only difficult point. By the use of *codom* in (*Env* $\prec_r$) and (*Env* $\prec_s$), the combined class hierarchy is still acyclic. It is therefore not possible for the combination of (*Rel* $\leq$ *repl*) and (*Rel* $\leq$ *shar*) to violate antisymmetry.

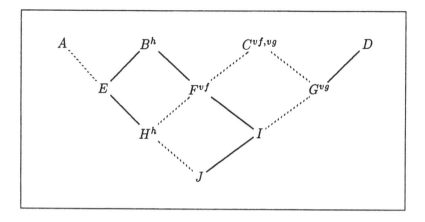

Fig. 2. A sample multiple-inheritance hierarchy. Dotted lines are shared arcs, solid lines are replicating arcs. Superscripts denote member functions of the class.

SRMI: Shared and Replicating Multiple Inheritance
(extends SMI, excluding (Sel inh shar) and (Rel inj shar))
(extends RMI, excluding (Sel inh repl))

Subobject Relations

(Rel inj comb)

$$\frac{b \neq c}{E \vdash \text{inj}(a/\alpha b, b/c\beta, a/c\beta)}$$

Subobject Selection

(Sel inh comb)

$$\frac{E, a, a \prec_s b_1, \ldots, a \prec_s b_k,}{a \prec_r c_1, \ldots, a \prec_r c_l,}$$
$$\frac{a \ni m_1, \ldots, a \ni m_n}{E \vdash \textbf{inh}(a; b_1, \ldots, b_k; c_1, \ldots, c_l; m_1, \ldots, m_n)} \quad (k, l, n \geq 0)$$
$$\text{in } T \triangleright a/\alpha$$

7.3 SRMI Example

In C++, members—rather than references—are divided into virtual and non-virtual. This is modeled in SRMI by agreeing that virtual members should only

```
inh(A;; ax=fun(self) 10 ) in
 inh(B;; bx=fun(self) 11,
          h=fun(self y) y + self.stat(bx)) in
  inh(C;; cx=fun(self) 12,
          vf=fun(self) fun(y) y + self.stat(cx),
          vg=fun(self)
               fun(y) self.dyn(vf)(y + self.stat(cx))) in
   inh(D;; dx=fun(self) 13 ) in
    inh(E; A; B; ex=fun(self) 100 ) in
     inh(F; C; B; fx=fun(self) 200,
                  vf=fun(self)
                       fun(y) self.stat(h)(y + self.stat(fx))) in
      inh(G; C; D; gx=fun(self) 300,
                   vg=fun(self)
                       fun(y)
                        self.dyn(vf)(y + self.stat(gx))) in
       inh(H; F; E; hx=fun(self) 1000,
                    h=fun(self)
                        fun(y) y + self.stat(hx)) in
        inh(I; G; F; ix=fun(self) 2000 ) in
         inh(J; H; I; jx=fun(self) 5000 ) in
          let ip = new(I),
              jp = new(J) in
            list(jp.dyn(vf), jp.dyn(vg), ip.dyn(vg))
```

Fig. 3. Translation of Fig. 4 into pseudo-code.

be used in **dyn** forms, with all others used only in **stat** forms. In SRMI and in C++, a virtual member function **vf** may be ambiguously referenced by an instance of class **J**, given the hierarchy in Fig. 2. In SRMI, instances of such a class will always find **vf** to be ambiguous, regardless of the static context of the dynamic reference. Unfortunately, only in the most recent semantics of C++ [1] can any similar requirement be found. This change in the C++ specification deserves further discussion.

The problem with the original C++ specification [10, 26] is that ambiguity was not considered a problem with the class definition, but rather a problem with the specific reference. Classes were allowed to inherit members ambiguously; only a flagrant reference to the ambiguous member could cause a compile-time error. Suppose, as in Fig. 2, that **J** inherits **vf** ambiguously. A reference jp->vf() would be clearly ambiguous, where jp is a pointer to an instance of **J**. This kind of reference is easily detected at compile time, and leads to the expected error message. What the original specification seems to have overlooked, however, is that the instance may be used in a static context of one of its base classes in which **vf** was not ambiguous, such as in **G**. That context was compiled without error; it assumed tacitly that any derived class would have an unambiguous definition of **vf**. We see that this was not a safe assumption. The result of this design flaw

```
class A { public: int ax; A(): ax(10) {} };
class B {
  public:
    int bx;
    B(): bx(11) {}
    int h(int y){ return( bx + y ); } };
class C {
  public:
    int cx;
    C(): cx(12) {}
    virtual int vf(int y){ return( cx + y ); }
    virtual int vg(int y){ return( this->vf( cx + y ) ); } };
class D { public: int dx; D(): dx(13) {} };
class E: public virtual A, public B {
  public: int ex; E(): ex(100) {} };
class F: public B, public virtual C {
  public:
    int fx;
    F(): fx(200) {}
    virtual int vf(int y){ return( this->h( fx + y ) ); } };
class G: public virtual C, public D {
  public:
    int gx;
    G(): gx(300) {}
    virtual int vg(int y){ return( this->vf( gx + y ) ); } };
class H: public E, public virtual F {
  public:
    int hx;
    H(): hx(1000) {}
    int h(int y){ return( hx + y ); } };
class I: public F, public virtual G {
  public: int ix; I(): ix(1000) {} };
class J: public virtual H, public I {
  public: int jx; J(): jx(50000) {} };

int main(){
  G *gp = new(G);
  I *ip = new(I);
  J *jp = new(J);
//   printf("jp->vf(0) = %d\n", jp->vf(0)); // obvious vf ambiguity
  printf("jp->vg(0) = %d\n", jp->vg(0));  // vf not ambiguous?! prints 511
  printf("ip->vg(0) = %d\n", ip->vg(0));  // prints 511
  printf("gp->vg(0) = %d\n", gp->vg(0));  // prints 312
}
```

Fig. 4. C++ multiple-inheritance example.

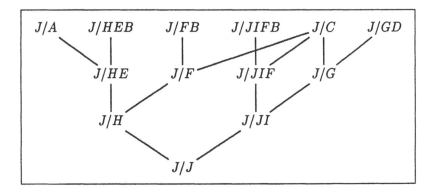

Fig. 5. The subobject poset for J in the class hierarchy shown in Fig. 2.

is that the reference that occurs in **G**'s static context actually chooses, by some hidden algorithm, one of the inherited definitions of **vf** and calls that code. Thus, **J.dyn(vf)** is not necessarily the same as **J.stat(vg).dyn(vf)**, and the semantics of the latter case is underspecified.

In the recent drafts of the proposed standard for C++ [1], this problem is remedied by forcing a class to provide its own definition of any such ambiguously inherited member function. The error is now associated with the class definition rather than the references. This leads to the behavior specified in SRMI, in which a virtual member leads to the same result whatever the static context of the reference. The irony of this result is that SRMI detects ambiguity on a reference-by-reference basis, much as in the original C++ specification. In fact, C++ implementors have always had enough information to know they were getting into trouble with virtuals in base-class contexts, but their hands were tied by the earlier specification. Because they could not be certain that an instance of **J** would make its way to an inherited context that referenced **vf**, they could not give an error. The new specification allows (in fact, requires) the implementor to make the more conservative choice.

Figure 3 shows a program in a hypothetical language, much as we used in the SI example. This program corresponds to the C++ code in Fig. 4, and implements the hierarchy in Fig. 2.

SRMI agrees, with both the old and the new C++ specifications, in that jp.dyn(vf) is ambiguous. We notice that jp.dyn(vg) is also ambiguous, since it leads to self.dyn(vf), where self is the J instance. As shown in Fig. 5, which contains the subobjects for J and their ordering, the subobjects J/F and J/JIF are unrelated. The new C++ specification says that the J definition should not compile at all, due to the ambiguity of **vf**. We simply show that a dynamic reference to the **vf** member of a J instance is equally ambiguous in any context. Finally, SRMI agrees with both the old and new specifications in that ip.dyn(vg) yields 312. This is the result of calling, in turn, G::vg, F::vf, and B::h.

Formally, we show these three results by the proofs of the following assertions. Let Z be the appropriate string $\textbf{inh}(\textbf{A}; ; \textbf{ax})$ $\textbf{in}$ ... $\textbf{inh}(\textbf{J}; \textbf{H}; \textbf{I}; \textbf{jx})$, encoding the class hierarchy above.

There is no a/α such that

$$\vdash Z \text{ in } \textbf{J.dyn(vf)} \qquad \rhd a/\alpha$$
$$\text{or } \vdash Z \text{ in } \textbf{J.stat(vg).dyn(vf)} \quad \rhd a/\alpha$$

however,

$$\vdash Z \text{ inI.dyn(vg)} \qquad\qquad\qquad \rhd \text{I/G}$$
$$\vdash Z \text{ inI.dyn(vg).dyn(vf))} \qquad \rhd \text{I/IF}$$
$$\vdash Z \text{ inI.dyn(vg).dyn(vf).stat(h)} \quad \rhd \text{I/IFB}$$

8 Related Work

The models of inheritance developed by Kamin [11], Reddy [16], and Cook and Palsberg [7, 6] laid the foundations for formal models of inheritance. While some of these mention the desire to model multiple inheritance, there is no comprehensive model proposed. Multiple inheritance introduces many design issues that have not been given a fully satisfactory taxonomy, although Carnese [3], Snyder [23] and Knudsen [13], for example, have made progress in this direction. Sakkinen [18] gives a comprehensive, informal introduction to the design issues surrounding subobjects in inheritance systems. Carré and Geib's point-of-view notion for multiple inheritance [4] is also aimed at understanding subobjects.

The C++ multiple-inheritance system [26] is a combination of design ideas, originating with Krogdahl's multiple-inheritance design [14]. The resulting system, as Sakkinen notes [19, 20], is best understood in terms of the subobjects of each kind of object. Snyder's informal model [24] of the C++ system, however, intentionally simplifies some of the complicating features of the multiple-inheritance system. Although Wallace [27] and Seligman [21] have developed formal models of C++, the former sheds little light on issues such as subobjects, subobject selection, and ambiguity analysis, while the latter models only single inheritance.

Unlike these models, our formalisms are not full language semantics. We develop instead a framework for resolving crucial static issues, which correspond to essential tasks that take place at compile time. Given the information obtained at this stage, a member reference in the run-time system is resolved with only a small run-time cost. We have previously presented a subobject-based algebra [17] for resolving similar issues in a system that is essentially the same as the system SRMI developed here. The current treatment, in terms of a logic system, allows us to make detailed comparisons of the semantics of a family of related inheritance systems.

Despite our interest in static issues, we do not develop a type theory for our object models. Some semantics have dealt chiefly with the type-safety vs.

expressiveness issues that arise in object-oriented languages, including those that support multiple inheritance [2, 15, 5]. The kind of multiple inheritance modeled in these systems does not resemble SRMI as much as it does SMI, which is simpler in many respects. In fact, a provably-safe static type system for a system such as SRMI is an open problem.

9 Conclusions

Expanding on our algebraic semantics of subobjects, we have presented a relatively simple calculus to describe subobjects and subobject selection explicitly. This gives us a framework for resolving crucial static issues in a formal proof system. The generality of this new methodology allows us to express a number of important design choices in inheritance-based languages, such as the distinction between a replicating and shared inheritance. This is demonstrated by the incremental development of several related inheritance systems,· culminating in the system SRMI, whose semantics is a subtle combination of the preceding systems. This last system is of particular interest, due to its correspondence to the C++ inheritance model, which has no satisfactory formal characterization.

A complete picture of multiple inheritance must deal with a number of runtime issues we have omitted here, as well as an analysis of the type-safety issues, among other things. We have chosen here to focus on a simple descriptive account of the issues relating to subobject selection. Although this is a static characterization based on class names, there is no reason it cannot be applied to dynamic classes, as long as each class is somehow uniquely identified. This enriched exposition of subobjects can be seen as the foundation for a broad formal theory of multiple inheritance.

10 Acknowledgments

We would like to thank Michael Ashley, Markku Sakkinen, and the anonymous reviewers for their comments on drafts of this paper.

References

1. Information Processing Systems Accredited Standards Committee X3. Working paper for draft proposed international standard for information systems—programming language C++. Draft of 28 April 1995.

2. Luca Cardelli and Peter Wegner. On understanding types, data abstraction, and polymorphism. *Computing Surveys*, 17(4):471–522, 1985.

3. Daniel J. Carnese. Multiple inheritance in contemporary programming languages. Technical Report MIT/LCS/TR-328, M.I.T., Sept. 1984.

4. Bernard Carré and Jean-Marc Geib. The point of view notion for multiple inheritance. In *Proceedings OOPSLA-ECOOP '90, ACM SIGPLAN Notices*, pages 312–321, 1990.

5. Adriana B. Compagnoni and Benjamin C. Pierce. Multiple inheritance via intersection types. Technical Report ECS-LFCS-93-275, University of Edinburgh, 1993. Also Technical Report 93-18, C.S. Department, Catholic University Nijmegen.

6. William R. Cook. *A Denotational Semantics of Inheritance*. PhD thesis, Brown University, 1989. Technical Report CS-89-33.

7. William R. Cook and Jens Palsberg. A denotational semantics of inheritance and its correctness. In *Proceedings OOPSLA '89, ACM SIGPLAN Notices*, pages 433–443, 1989.

8. Ole-Johan Dahl and Kristen Nygaard. Simula—an Algol-based simulation language. *CACM*, 9(9):671–678, September 1966.

9. Roland Ducournau, Michel Habib, Marianne Huchard, and Marie-Laure Mugnier. Proposal for a monotonic multiple inheritance linearization. In *Proceedings OOPSLA '94, ACM SIGPLAN Notices*, pages 164–175, 1994.

10. Margaret A. Ellis and Bjarne Stroustrup. *The Annotated C++ Reference Manual*. Addison-Wesley, 1990.

11. Samuel Kamin. Inheritance in SMALLTALK-80: A denotational definition. In *Proceedings POPL '88*, pages 80–87, 1988.

12. Gregor Kiczales, Jim des Rivières, and Daniel G. Bobrow. *The Art of the Metaobject Protocol*. The MIT Press, 1991.

13. Jørgen Lindskov Knudsen. Name collision in multiple classification hierarchies. In *Proceedings ECOOP '88*, LNCS 322, pages 93–108. Springer-Verlag, 1988.

14. Stein Krogdahl. Multiple inheritance in Simula-like languages. *BIT*, 25:318–326, 1984.

15. Benjamin C. Pierce. *Programming with Intersection Types and Bounded Polymorphism*. PhD thesis, Carnegie-Mellon University, Pittsburgh, PA, December 1991.

16. Uday Reddy. Objects as closures: Abstract semantics of object-oriented languages. In *Conf. on LISP and Functional Programming*, 1988.

17. Jonathan G. Rossie Jr. and Daniel P. Friedman. An algebraic semantics of subobjects. In *Proceedings OOPSLA '95, ACM SIGPLAN Notices*, pages 187–199, 1995. Published as Proceedings OOPSLA '95, ACM SIGPLAN Notices, volume 30, number 10.

18. Markku Sakkinen. Disciplined inheritance. In *Proceedings ECOOP '89*, The British Computer Society Workshop Series, pages 39–56. Cambridge University Press, 1989.

19. Markku Sakkinen. A critique of the inheritance principles of C++. *Computing Systems*, 5(1):69–110, 1992.

20. Markku Sakkinen. A critique of the inheritance principles of C++: Corrigendum. *Computing Systems*, 5(3), 1992.

21. Adam Seligman. FACTS: A formal analysis of C++: Type rules and semantics. B.A. Honors Thesis, Williams College, May 1995.

22. Andrew Shalit, Orca Starbuck, and David Moon. *Dylan Reference Manual.* Apple Computer, Inc., 1995. Draft of September 29, 1995.

23. Alan Snyder. Inheritance and the development of encapsulated software components. In B. Shriver and P. Wegner, editors, *Research Directions in Object-Oriented Programming*, pages 165–188. MIT Press, 1987.

24. Alan Snyder. Modeling the C++ object model, an application of an abstract object model. In *Proceedings ECOOP '91*, LNCS 512, pages 1–20. Springer-Verlag, 1991.

25. Guy L. Steele Jr. *Common Lisp: The Language.* Digital Press, 2nd edition, 1990.

26. Bjarne Stroustrup. Multiple inheritance for C++. *Computing Systems*, 2(4), 1989.

27. Charles Wallace. The semantics of the C++ programming language. In Egon Boerger, editor, *Specification and Validation Methods for Programming Languages*, pages 131–163. Clarendon Press, Oxford, 1995.

Parallel Operators

Jean-Marc Jézéquel*, Jean-Lin Pacherie**

I.R.I.S.A. Campus de Beaulieu
F-35042 Rennes Cedex, FRANCE
Tel: +33–99.84.71.92 — Fax: +33–99.84.71.71
E-mail: jezequel@irisa.fr

Abstract. Encapsulating parallelism and synchronization code within object-oriented software components is a promising avenue towards mastering the complexity of the distributed memory supercomputer programming. However, in trying to give application programmers benefit of supercomputer power, the library designer generally resorts to low level parallel constructs, a time consuming and error prone process. To solve this problem we introduce a new abstraction called *Parallel Operators*. A Parallel Operator exists simultaneously on all processors involved in a distributed computation: it acts as a single ubiquitous entity capable of processing shared or distributed data in parallel. In this paper we reify this concept in our Eiffel Parallel Execution Environment (EPEE) context, and we show that it is both natural and efficient to express computations over large shared or distributed data structures using Parallel Operators. We illustrate our approach with a Parallel Operator based solution for the well-known N-body problem.

Keywords: Distribution, Data Parallelism, Operators, Components and Frameworks

1 Introduction

Many programmers are eager to take advantage of the computational power offered by Distributed Computing Systems (DCSs) but are generally reluctant to undertake the porting of their application programs onto such machines. Indeed, it is widely believed that the DCSs commercially available today are difficult to use, which is not surprising since they are traditionally programmed with software tools dating back to the days of punch cards and paper tape.

It is now well established that an object-oriented approach can greatly alleviate the pain of programming such supercomputers [7, 9]. One of the most successful approaches relies on the Single Program Multiple Data (SPMD) programming model and is based on the idea that tricky parallel codes can be encapsulated in object-oriented software components presenting their clients with a familiar, more or less sequential-like interface [17, 12, 2, 5]. In EPEE for instance, the modularity and encapsulation properties available through the class concept are used to abstract the data representation that can then be either replicated, distributed, or virtually

---

* IRISA/CNRS, currently visiting Dept. of Info. Science, Tokyo University, Japan, under
   a JSPS grant
** IRISA/INRIA

shared (provided a Distributed Shared Memory (DSM) is available) among the processors of a DCS [4]. In this context, sequential code can safely be reused through inheritance in a distributed environment.

In order to give application programmers the benefit of DCS computational power, the library programmer still has to redefine and reprogram some features using explicit parallelism, which is both time consuming and error prone. Even if some very basic parallel patterns can be reused in new applications, they usually require syntactic contortions [6] or language extensions [10]. To solve this problem we introduce a new abstraction called *Parallel Operators*. A Parallel Operator exists simultaneously on all processors involved in a distributed computation: it acts as a single ubiquitous entity capable of processing distributed (or shared) data in parallel. In this paper we reify this concept in the EPEE framework, and we show that it is both natural and efficient to express computations over large shared or distributed data structures using Parallel Operators. Section 2 defines more precisely the notion of operator, and discuss how computations over large data structures can naturally be structured with operators. Section 3 shows how the concept of a Parallel Operator is used to go from a sequential application to an efficient parallel one. Throughout this paper, we illustrate our approach with a Parallel Operator based solution for the well-known N-body problem.

2 Using Operators in Computation Structuring

2.1 What is an Operator?

The concept of operator developed in this paper is inspired from both the G. Booch's classification of object relationships, and a reflection on the various design patterns involved in the processing of large collections of data.

We first planned to use the name agent for this design pattern, following the G. Booch [1] and the Harrap's Dictionary definitions. But the term agent is widely and increasingly used in the computer science community although not everyone agrees on the meaning.

Booch's definition of agents refers to a classification of object relationships that divides objects into *Actors*, *Servers* and *Agents*. Booch defines an agent as : "*An object that can both operate upon other objects and be operated upon by other objects; an agent is usually created to do some work on behalf of an actor or another agent*". The main concept of Booch's definition is based on the notion of a service provider. An agent is an object that *does* something on a second object and on behalf of a third one, even if the target and the client of the service can be the same object.

In the Artificial Intelligence (AI) community, the notion of agent has another, roughly similar, definition to the one given above. An AI agent is an autonomous entity that progresses in an environment where other agents exist. A system is then modeled by the interactions between several agents, each of them performing a limited set of actions. The common point between the object-oriented definition of agent and the AI definition lies in the notion of autonomy of agents, which is interpreted here as a loosely coupled design pattern. Furthermore, in both cases, an agent is only designed to perform a very specific operation.

To avoid confusion, we will use the term of *operator* in place of agent. The idea of operator is better known to object–oriented computer scientists and does not interfere with the AI world for which the definition of agent is the most famous at this time.

2.2 Beyond the Encapsulation Principle

One of the purposes of the operator design pattern is to better separate the responsibilities of each object in the modeling of a problem. A widely used approach to design classes is to follow the line of the encapsulation principle, which states that all methods manipulating data must be encapsulated along with these data. Taking for example a container class holding several items to be updated, the encapsulation principle would lead us to encapsulate the update method within the container class.

On second thoughts, this approach might not always be the best one. A container class is not necessarily an abstraction that provides operations intended to modify the state of the items holden in its structure. The only operations a class container should provide are related to the management of the data structure used to hold these items (accessing, adding and removing items, etc.). The update process is better modeled with an operator that performs the update operation on the elements stored in the container.

The main interest of such an approach in problem modeling is its ability to express the separation between classes related to the problem domain from those related to a specific implementation of the solution. Following this precept, it becomes easier to build an application in an incremental way, first providing a non optimal release to check whether the model described in the semantic classes is correctly designed. Having achieved a correct problem modeling, the programmer can think of optimizing time and space trade–offs just by modifying the implementation classes that are independent of the problem domain classes.

2.3 Modeling Computations over Large Data Structures

This section provides a definition of the patterns of collaboration between the few key abstractions used in designing operator–oriented applications. This design pattern is based on the relationships of four key abstractions, divided into *(i)* problem domain abstractions: *Operator, Element* and *(ii)* implementation abstractions: *Container, Element Provider*.

- Problem Domain Abstractions:
  Operator: An *operator* as considered here is the key abstraction suitable to model a regular operation to be performed over a collection of elements.
  Element: The *element* abstraction embodies the data manipulated by the application. Elements are the targets of operator computations.
- Implementation Abstractions:
  Container: A *container* stores elements using a specific data structure. The function of a container is also to retrieve, to access, to delete, etc, stored elements

Element Provider: The *element provider* is in charge of traversing a set of elements to be processed by an operator and generally stored in a container. Some element providers of the EPEE toolbox are also capable of generating themselves the elements they provide. Furthermore, this abstraction implements a traversal policy and do not access elements directly when associated with a container.

Thus an *operator* uses an *element provider* to reach the *elements* it has to process, these *elements* being stored in a *container* known to the *element provider*. It is possible for an operator, using the polymorphism of its element provider attribute both to traverse a container in various ways and to access elements independently of the container internal representation. These last two properties will be widely exploited in the design of parallel operators working in a distributed environment.

We can also note that we have only addressed the context of operators dealing with a collection of elements, regardless of the internal representation of the data structure used to stored these elements. But another kind of operator is also useful: those dealing with the mere organization of a data structure (*e.g.*, a sorting operation). This family of operators will not be addressed in this paper because their parallelization needs a different approach. Yet the general method we describe here is still applicable, even if its explanation would need too much space to be presented here.

2.4 Implementing the Model in Eiffel

We describe the implementation of this operator–based model in Eiffel [13], because this language features all the concepts we need (*i.e.* strong encapsulation, static typing allowing efficient code generation, multiple inheritance, dynamic binding and genericity), and has clearly defined syntax and semantics. However any other statically typed OO language could have been used instead (*e.g.*, Modula-3, Ada 95, or C++).

The implementation presented here is based on a four–part hierarchy reflecting the four key abstractions previously defined.

An Operator is implemented as a deferred class[3], where only the specific operation to be performed on each element is left deferred (see Example 2.1). In the same way, the class ELEM_PROVIDER is also a deferred class because we do not know how to access the items of a container, but we must be able to start a traversing, to detect the end of the traversing, and to go through the next item in the traversal (see Example 2.2). We must point out that the specification of the ELEM_PROVIDER class does not specify any order on the traversed elements.

The elements are referenced in this implementation through the generic formal parameter E because no assumption on instances of this class is necessary. Finally, the top of the class hierarchy of this implementation is shown in Figure 1 where possible effective classes are also mentioned for the Element Provider and Container hierarchies. The deferred features of the deferred classes are in italic.

---

[3] Also called an *abstract* class, that is a class where at least one method has no implementation: it is a deferred feature in Eiffel or a pure virtual function in C++.

```
deferred class OPERATOR[E]                        do_all is
feature                                               -- do itemaction on all
    run is do do_all end -- run                       -- provided elements
    attach ( prov : ELEM_PROVIDER[E] ) is             do
        require valid_prov: prov /= void                 from provider.start
        do provider := clone(prov) end                   until provider.exhausted        20
    item_action (element : E) is                         loop
        -- action to perform on provided elements            item_action(provider.item)
        require                                              provider.next
            element_exist: element /= void    10         end -- loop
        deferred                                      end -- doall
        end -- itemaction                        invariant
feature {NONE}                                       provider_exist: provider /= void
    provider : ELEM_PROVIDER[E]                   end -- OPERATOR
```

Example 2.1

```
deferred class ELEM_PROVIDER[E]                       deferred
feature                                               end -- item
    start is                                      exhausted : BOOLEAN is
        -- go to the traversal starting position         -- have all elements been seen*
        deferred                                      deferred
        end -- start                                  end -- exhausted
    next is                                      feature {NONE}
        -- advance to the next element                container : CONTAINER[E]              20
        deferred                                              -- Optionnal
        end -- next                       10     invariant
    item : E is                                      container_exist: container /= Void
        -- element under the provider            end -- ELEMPROVIDER
```

Example 2.2

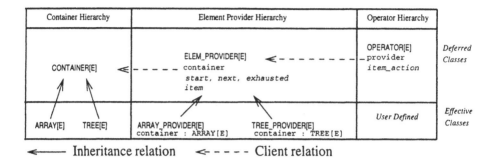

	← ——— Inheritance relation	← - - - - Client relation

Fig. 1. Top class hierarchy

2.5   Example: N-Body Simulation

We present an actual use of the ideas developed in this paper through the modeling and implementation of the well known N-Body problem. A large amount of literature has already been devoted to this subject. It is mainly related to the optimization of the naive algorithm, the accuracy trade–off in the optimized version [15], or the parallel implementation of N-Body algorithms [14].

We consider a set of masses located in a three dimensional space, in which each mass interacts with all the others. A body is a mass with an additional speed and acceleration. The purpose of the application is to compute the time–related evolution of the system. It relies on a two-step algorithm based on time slicing. First, we compute the contribution of each mass in the (Newtonian) flow exerted on each body, and then we update the speed and the position of the bodies, taking into account all the contributions. The container used to store the bodies is called a UNIVERSE, which is basically an array of bodies.

Updating the Bodies. The operator in charge of updating the bodies of a universe is called UPDATOR and is very simple to build (see Example 2.3). Since the regular operation to be performed on each body is to call its *update* method, the UPDATOR operator only needs to designate it as *item_action*, provided its provider attribute is initialized to be a relevant element provider, i.e. an instance of an AR-RAY_PROVIDER[BODY] able to reach the whole set of bodies of the Universe if this class inherits from ARRAY[BODY].

Computation of the Contributions. To compute the contributions, we first use a naive algorithm whose complexity is in $o(n^2)$. While not the best one, it allows us to introduce our methodology to design an evolutive application that can easily migrate to a distributed environment. It will be shown below that the optimal $o(n \log(n))$ algorithm is a direct consequence of choosing a tree based data structure mapped over the universe container for the computation of the contributions.

```
class UPDATOR
inherit
    OPERATOR[BODY]
creation make
feature
    make ( prov : ELEM_PROVIDER[BODY] ) is
        do
            attach(prov)
        end

    item_operation (b : BODY) is
        do
            b.update
        end
end -- UPDATOR
```

Example 2.3

The computation of the contributions is performed in a two-stage approach. First we consider the contribution of a set of masses over a single body. This is the first stage of the computation that leads to the first operator in our application, called BODY_CONTRIBUTOR. The purpose of this operator is to add the contribution of all the masses it receives from its element provider to a given body. This is done via the *add_contribution_of(b:MASS)* method provided in the BODY class.

The second stage of the computation of the contributions is to consider the contributions of one set of masses to a second set. This computation is performed by another operator, UNIV_CONTRIBUTOR, that computes the contributions of each masses it receives from its element provider to each body included in the universe it is in charge of. To achieve this, the operator UNIV_CONTRIBUTOR uses a BODY_CONTRIBUTOR in its *item_action* method, as represented in Figure 2.

N–Body Simulation with Operators. All the components needed to build an N-body simulation have been described: we now have to assemble and initialize them. This is the purpose of the class N_BODY_SIMULATION presented in Example 2.4.

For instance, in order to use the universe contributor operator the programmer must specify the element providers for both the UNIV_CONTRIBUTOR and the BODY_CONTRIBUTOR operators at instantiation time. This is done when initializing the operator:

!!contributor.make (univ_prov, body_prov)

Where both *univ_pro* and *body_prov* are instance of ELEM_PROVIDER[BODY] subclass and initialized to provide bodies holden in the universe container. Their name are recall that *univ_pro* will works with the *Univ_Contributor* operator and the *body_prov* will works with the *Body_Contributor* operator.

Optimization. The basic optimization principle used in the N-body problem is based on two ideas:

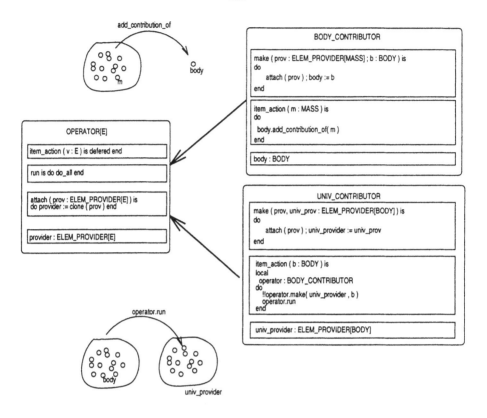

Fig. 2. Operators for contribution computations

- Spatially dividing the universe into nested regions, so as to get a tree structure.
- Using the dipole approximation that basically consists in identifying the set of bodies inside a region with their center of gravity, provided the region is far away enough from the considered target body.

Implementing this kind of optimization in our Operator Model is achieved through the design of a new container based on a tree of masses (representing the centers of gravity of each region) and whose leaves are filled with the references to the bodies contained in the universe. A new element provider is also designed to traverse the tree and provides either all its sub-trees or (if the dipole approximation applies) their center of gravity, thus transparently allowing a $o(n \log(n))$ complexity for the BODY_CONTRIBUTOR operator computation.

```
class N_BODY_SIMULATION                        —— stored in a data file; and        20
creation make                                  —— simulate its evolution over time
feature                                         do
    universe : UNIVERSE                             !!universe.read_from("input_data.dat")
        —— an array of bodies                       from
    contributor : UNIV_CONTRIBUTOR                      —— Initialize the element providers
        —— an operator computing the                    !!univ_prov.make(universe)
        —— contributions from one                       !!body_prov.make(universe)
        —— universe to another                          —— Initialize the operators
    updator : UPDATOR                    10             !!contributor.make(univ_prov,body_prov)
        —— an operator updating body states            !!updator.make(univ_prov)              30
    univ_prov : ARRAY_PROVIDER[BODY]                until universe.end_of_times
        —— provider for the contributor             loop
        —— and updator operator                         contributor.run
    body_prov : ARRAY_PROVIDER[BODY]                    updator.run
        —— for the BODYCONTRIBUTOR operator            universe.advance_time
feature —— entry point of the simulation            end —— loop
    make is                                     end —— make
        —— Create a universe with bodies        end —— NBODYSIMULATION
```

Example 2.4

3 From Sequential to Parallel with Parallel Operators

3.1 The EPEE Parallel Programming Model

The kind of parallelism we consider takes inspiration from Valiant's Block Synchronous Parallel (BSP) model [16]. A computation that fits the BSP model can be seen as a succession of parallel phases separated by synchronizations and sequential phases.

In EPEE [5], Valiant's model is implemented based on the Single Program Multiple Data (SPMD) programming model. Data can either be distributed across the processors, or virtually shared if a Distributed Shared Memory is available on the target architecture. EPEE provides a design framework where data representations are totally encapsulated in regular Eiffel classes [4], without any extension to the language nor modification of its semantics. In both cases, the user still views his program as a sequential one and the parallelism is derived from the data representation: each processor runs a subset of the original execution flow (based on the Owner Write Rule, that is, a processor may only write its data partition). The SPMD model preserves the conceptual simplicity of the sequential instruction flow, while exploiting the fact that most of the problems running on high-performance parallel computers are data-oriented and involve large amounts of data in order to generate scalable parallelism.

From the application programmer's point of view, the distributed execution of some part of his code is hidden through the use of software components that are responsible for the correct management of the parallel phases of the application. All it is needed to benefit from a parallelized execution would be to pick up the suited reusable components in the EPEE toolbox that match the global behavior expected during the parallel phases. Thus, the programmer manipulates concepts and abstractions whereas the matching components of the EPEE toolbox are designed to implement the details and to cooperate smoothly with each other.

The EPEE toolbox also includes cross-compilation tools that mainly consist of script files that deal with compiler flags and options correctly. Any application designed with EPEE thus can be compiled for any target mono–processor or multiprocessor (provided an Eiffel run-time system exists for this processor). EPEE also includes two highly portable communication libraries intended to deal with the two communication paradigms used in EPEE: the message passing and the shared memory. The Parallel Observable Machine (POM), which provides sophisticated facilities for tracing a distributed execution [3] is used to implement message passing communications. The Shared Virtual Memory Library (SVM Lib) is used to allow to allocation of objects in shared memory. These libraries are available for several platforms (*e.g.*, Intel iPSC/2, Paragon XP/S, Silicon Graphics Power Challenge and networks of UNIX workstations) using various communication kernels or operating systems (*e.g.*, PVM, BSD sockets, NX/2, SunMos, IRIX, etc.).

3.2 The Parallel Operator Model

The Parallel Operator Model is designed as an extension of the Operator Model to be used within the EPEE framework. Here are the new meanings of its key abstractions.

Shared Element. A shared element is an object allocated in a shared memory space using the facilities offered by the EPEE toolbox. The EPEE support for shared objects is based on a shared memory mechanism, called a Distributed Shared Memory (DSM) when it is provided at the operating system level on the target architecture. A DSM provides a virtual address space that is shared by the processes of different processors on distributed systems. More details on the mechanisms developed to make shared objects available in the EPEE framework can be found in [8]. The only thing the reader must keep in mind is that the shared objects are fully compatible with normal ones. This property is exploited to reuse the sequential containers that may now hold references to shared objects in the distributed version of an application.

Distributed Element Container. A distributed element container is an abstraction that is able to manage both local and non local items transparently. Basically, a distributed element container is implemented as a container for which the data structure is spread over all the processors. When a client object requests a reference to an item, the distributed element container is able to detect whether the requested item is local, and can thus reply with the local reference of the item. Or if the container detects that the requested item is allocated on another processor and then it asks the owner of the real item for a copy.

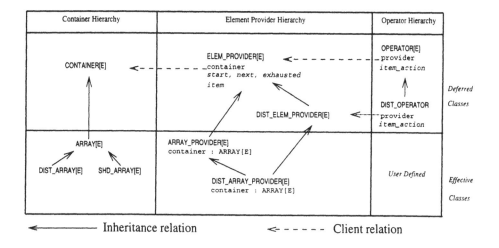

Container Hierarchy	Element Provider Hierarchy	Operator Hierarchy	

Inheritance relation   Client relation

Fig. 3. Top class hierarchy in the parallel operator model

Element Distributed Provider. The distribution of control over the processes of a data parallel program is achieved by a domain decomposition of the iterations used over the (large) data structure. Following this idea, when a sequential iteration accesses N variables, the data parallel iteration on each processor accesses $\frac{N}{p}$ variables only (if p processors are available).

The choice of the $\frac{N}{p}$ variables to be accessed on a given processor is made using the *owner write rule.* This rule states that only the items owned by the processor can be accessed for modification [5].

When the data are actually distributed across the memory of each process, the ownership exactly matches the distribution. When the data are allocated in shared memory, the ownership is translated to a virtual ownership. The virtual ownership states that even if all the processes might potentially modify all the data, only one process per shared datum can actually modify it. In our model design the control distribution is implemented with an Element Distributed Provider (EDP). Thus the same EDP can be used for shared and distributed data to reach the elements to be processed in a distributed iteration.

Parallel Operator. A Parallel Operator is the entry point of a parallel phase from the application programmer's point of view. Its role is basically to run the computation on each processor for the data made available through its EDP. The blocking semantics to be preserved in a distributed environment states that the execution flow goes out of the method call only when the execution is terminated. In a distributed environment a routine call execution is considered to be terminated when each execution flow in each processor has reach the end of the routine. As a consequence, the faster processors need to wait for the other ones to preserve the routine call semantics. It is the Parallel Operator that implements such a mechanism through the use of appropriate synchronizations. This is done using the Sync–Exec–Sync scheme as formally described in [11]. We can briefly recall the purposes of the synchronizations before and after the distributed execution of a computation:

- The first synchronization ensures that the values of the data read during the *Exec* stage are updated, i.e. are the same as they would have been under a sequential execution.
- The second synchronization ensures that the data read during the parallel phase will not be overwritten until global completion of the operator execution.

The actual implementation of the synchronizations depends on the memory model used in the container class holding the elements processed by a parallel operator. Thus, an parallel operator triggers the synchronization through an EDP which itself asks the container for the actual implementation of the synchronizations.

Summary of the Responsibilities. The patterns of collaboration among these four abstractions may be summarized as follows. A Parallel Operator manages the synchronizations ensuring a correct execution according to a SPMD programming model along with the Sync–Exec–Sync scheme. The EDP associated with the Parallel Operator implements a specific access policy on the subset of the whole data set using a data domain decomposition scheme. For a Parallel Operator the access to each element is made transparently from the container data structure through its EDP. Finally, the actual retrieval of an element, given a position in the structure, is performed by the container associated with the EDP. This last abstraction is in charge of dealing with the problem of data allocation that can either be shared or distributed.

3.3 Using Parallel Operators

To use parallel operators in an actual distributed application, the programmer first has to choose a memory model for his application. A distributed memory model or a shared memory model is available through EPEE library classes for basic data structures (DIST_ARRAY, SHD_ARRAY, etc.) used for containers. For each container class there is an EDP implementing a domain decomposition policy. These EDPs are independent of the memory model encapsulated in the container class but not of the data structure implemented by these containers.

The parallelization of the operator–based sequential application can then be easily done using the multiple inheritance mechanism. The main idea is to build specialized parallel operators by inheriting from both:

- the sequential operators to reuse the code for the local processing
- and the parallel operator class to achieve the distributed processing.

It should be noted that the programmer who uses operators must be aware of certain problems that can arise when one operator is used within another. Since there is no ordering specified on the elements provided by an ELEMENT_PROVIDER instance, a programmer can use nested operators only if no data dependencies exist between the data processed by the various operators. Processing the data in parallel therefore does not bring new problems, provided only one parallel operator runs at a given time. This constraint is motivated by both the semantics of a parallel phase in the BSP model (one parallel phase cannot launch a second one) and by the implementation of the parallel operators (the synchronizations of parallel operators would not work correctly). This constraint could be described as a class invariant in the parallel operator class, and forced upon the programmer through typing, because a user-defined parallel operator inherits from the general parallel operator class, and thus from its invariant.

3.4 Parallel N-Body Simulation

Using the method presented in the previous sections, we now describe the parallelization of the N–body application. We start with the modifications of the data allowing distributed computation and then we discuss the parallelization of the two main operators. We conclude with the main code of the distributed version of the N–body simulation program.

The parallel implementation of the N–body application is based on the use of shared bodies, that is BODY objects allocated in shared memory. To do so, we build a SHD_BODY class by inheriting from both the BODY and the SHD_OBJECT[4] classes.

The container used to store the bodies and to implement the UNIVERSE class can still be the same. This is possible because the class SHD_BODY conforms to the class BODY. Thus, no change is needed in the UNIVERSE class excepting for the method creating the bodies stored in the container.

Figure 4 shows how two processes can access the same shared bodies through the use of a local container. In this figure, each circle represents an instance of the class SHD_BODY. Shared bodies can be accessed for read purposes by the p processes of the parallel application using sequential element providers. However, when using an EDP with a local container, only a sub–set of the bodies are accessed, as represented by the dashed arrows starting from the DIST_UNIV_PROVIDER objects.

Parallelization of the Update Computations. To obtain a parallel operator which updates the bodies in parallel, we inherit from both the UPDATOR operator to get the definition of the ITEM_OPERATION and from the DIST_OPERATOR of the EPEE toolbox (see Figure 5). At initialization time, the parallel operator DIST_UPDATOR has to be provided with an EDP matching the container chosen during the UNIVERSE implementation. This is done using the class constructor: *updator.make(dist_provider)*, where *dist_provider* is an instance of DIST_ARRAY_PROVIDER and is initialized to work with the UNIVERSE container.

Parallelization of the Computation of the Contributions. In the computation of the contributions, only the UNIV_CONTRIBUTOR operator is parallelized. The

---

[4] Provided in the EPEE toolbox

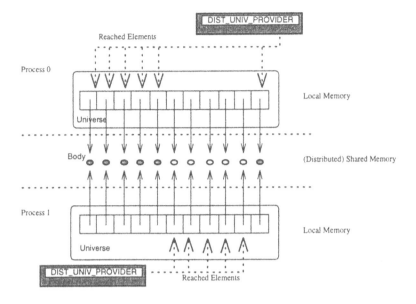

Fig. 4. Distributed access to shared bodies.

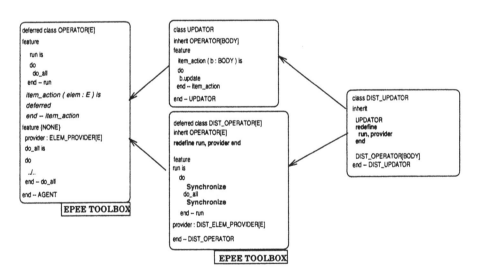

Fig. 5. The parallel updator operator

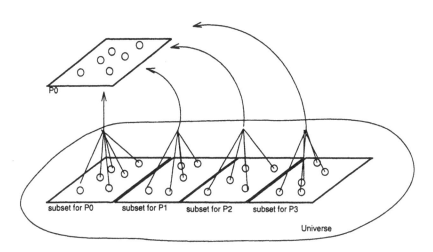

Fig. 6. Parallelization scheme for the contribution

parallel version of this operator still uses the sequential operator BODY_CONTRIBUTOR (itself working either with a container structured as an array or a tree).

For each processor, the parallel UNIV_CONTRIBUTOR operator works on one subset of the universe only. For each body of its sub-universe it computes the contribution of the whole universe using the sequential operator BODY_CONTRIBUTOR as defined previously. In this design, the parallelism comes from the fact that each sub-universe computation is run concurrently on each processor using the parallel operator. Figure 6 shows the behavior on the process 0 of the parallel operator DIST_UNIV_CONTRIBUTOR: for each body of the subset assigned to this process, the operator computes the contribution of all the bodies in the universe (itself either an array or a tree).

To implement this design we must point out that the notion of subset of the universe is purely virtual because no object in the system represents this abstraction. A subset of the whole universe can only be viewed through a specific element provider that reaches the bodies attached to this virtual subset of the universe only. The choice of the bodies assigned to one or another subset is effected using an EDP. The actual code of the DIST_UNIV_CONTRIBUTOR is described in Figure 7.

Parallel Version of the N–Body Simulation. Once both the universe container has been redefined to hold shared bodies and parallel operators have been defined, only limited modifications need to be applied to the sequential version of the code of the N–body simulation program. Indeed, in Example 3.1, we just redefine the type of the universe and that of the parallel operators, while reusing all the sequential code through inheritance.

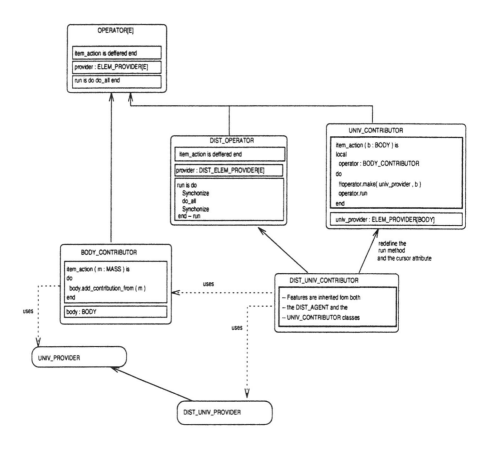

Fig. 7. The parallel contributor operator

3.5 About the Efficiency of Parallel Operators

Since we use rather advanced features of Eiffel (*e.g.*, multiple and repeated inheritance) to implement Parallel Operators, the question of their runtime efficiency arises. This in fact is a crucial point, since the main rationale for using distributed parallel computers lies in their potential computing power. If we were to end up with a parallelized code running slower than the (best) sequential one, we would have completely missed the point. Fortunately, this is not the case.

The design model we have presented in this paper allows the programmer to build applications which can easily migrate to distributed environments. Furthermore, thanks to the dynamic biding of the attributes in the operator and element provider classes, operators can dynamically change their behaviors at runtime. The drawback of this approach is that a sub-optimal code may be generated, because this generality and dynamism have a price. However, generality can be easily traded

```
class DIST_N_BODY_SIMULATION
inherit
    N_BODY_SIMULATION
        redefine
            universe, universe_provider, contributor, updator
        end
creation make
feature
    universe : SHD_UNIVERSE
            -- Now an array of shared bodies                              10
    contributor : UBIK_UNIV_CONTRIBUTOR
            -- redefined to a parallel operator
    updator : UBIK_UPDATOR
            -- redefined to a parallel operator
    universe_provider : DIST_ARRAY_PROVIDER
            -- Distributed provider for the parallel operators
end -- DISTNBODYSIMULATION
```

Example 3.1

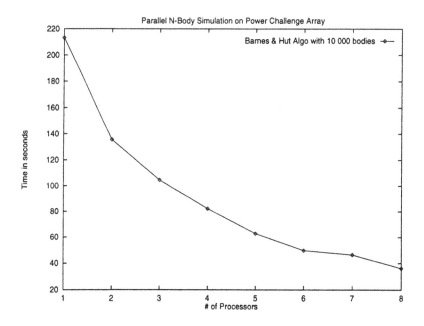

Fig. 8.

for performances if this is a critical key point in the application, as is the case for our N-body simulation. Indeed the programmer can specialize his operators and element providers using the redefinition of their attributes to match their known effective type (*e.g.*, provider can be redefined to be a DIST_ARRAY_PROVIDER[SHD_BODY] in the DIST_UPDATOR), thus allowing a compile-time binding of features (since most of the feature name resolutions can now be done at compile time).

For example, the call for the *run* method from the Parallel Operator DIST_UPDATOR can be statically bound, as well as for the inner call for the feature *update* on a SHD_BODY object (though the latter needs a simple data flow analysis). In these cases, the general dynamic binding mechanism can be discarded and replaced with a mere procedure call. Furthermore, since the feature size of the various operator classes is very small (typically a single line), it is possible to avoid the overhead of procedure calls through in-line expansions which most Eiffel compilers do automatically whenever the methods are small enough.

The generated code can then look exactly the same as if it had seen coded by hand by a proficient parallel programmer. A trivial example is the call for *updator.run* method, which is optimal because it involves absolutely no (machine level) message exchange: the best FORTRAN handwritten version would have exactly the same behavior and performance.

We have made some experiments of the N-Body simulation with the EPEE environment on the Power Challenge parallel computer. The results are shown in Figure 8 and are obtained using one to the eight processors available on this computer.

4   Conclusion and Future Work

In this paper, we have introduced a new abstraction called *Parallel Operator*. A Parallel Operator exists simultaneously on all processors involved in a distributed computation: it acts as a single ubiquitous entity able to process data in parallel. Parallel Operators help application programmers to make the most of the distributed memory supercomputers computational power, because they no more need to get involved in the tricky details of loop parallelization.

We have described an approach allowing an easy parallelization of object-oriented computations structured around operators acting as a design pattern for the programming of distributed systems. We have shown that it is both natural and efficient to express computations over large shared or distributed data structures using Parallel Operators. We have illustrated our approach with a Parallel Operator based solution for the well-known N-body problem.

While structuring object-oriented computations with operators slightly departs from established principles, it should be noted that it is often the most natural way to express solutions within a statically typed object-oriented language. For example, if block closures (as in Smalltalk) are not first class objects, the use of operators is one of the most elegant solutions to model a problem where data must be sorted according to various criteria. Thus it should not come as a surprise that some popular data structure libraries (such as Booch's components for Eiffel or C++) use the concept of operator extensively. This opens a very promising perspective: the parallelization of Booch's components using Parallel Operators within EPEE.

Another domain where we plan to apply the concept of Parallel Operator concerns distributed linear algebra over large sparse matrix computations. Indeed these computations can be modeled with Parallel Operators operating over large sparse distributed data structures. Since a Parallel Operator is decoupled from actual sparse matrix representations, it is much easier for the application programmer to benefit from internal representations using sophisticated data structures on shared or distributed memory.

References

1. Grady Booch. *Object-Oriented Analysis and Design with Applications*. Benjamin Cummings, 2nd edition, 1994.
2. J. Dongarra and al. An Object-Oriented Design for High-Performance Linear Algebra on Distributed Memory Architectures. In *Proceedings of the Object-Oriented Numerics Conference (OON-SKI'93)*, 1993.
3. F. Guidec and Y. Mahéo. POM: a Virtual Parallel Machine Featuring Observation Mechanisms. PI 902, IRISA, January 1995.
4. F. Hamelin, J.-M. Jézéquel, and T. Priol. A Multi-paradigm Object Oriented Parallel Environment. In H. J. Siegel, editor, *Int. Parallel Processing Symposium IPPS'94 proceedings*, pages 182–186. IEEE Computer Society Press, April 1994.
5. J.-M. Jézéquel. EPEE: an Eiffel Environment to Program Distributed Memory Parallel Computers. In *ECOOP'92 proceedings*, number 611. Lecture Notes in Computer Science, Springer Verlag, (also published in the Journal of Object Oriented Programming, 1993), July 1992.
6. J.-M. Jézéquel. Transparent Parallelisation Through Reuse: Between a Compiler and a Library Approach. In O. M. Nierstrasz, editor, *ECOOP'93 proceedings*, number 707, pages 384–405. Lecture Notes in Computer Science, Springer Verlag, July 1993.
7. J.-M. Jézéquel. *Object Oriented Software Engineering with Eiffel*. Addison-Wesley, March 1996. ISBN 1-201-63381-7.
8. J.-M. Jézéquel and J.-L. Pacherie. Shared Objects in KOOPE. Technical Report 2.3, Irisa-Intel ERDP, June 1995.
9. Michael F. Kilian. Object-oriented programming for massively parallel machines. In *1991 International Conference on Parallel Processing*, 1991.
10. H. Konaka, T. Tomokiyo, M. Maeda, Y. Ishikawa, and A. Hori. Data parallel programming in the parallel object-oriented language OCore. In *Proc. of the Workshop on Object-Based Parallel and Distributed Computation (OBPDC'95)*, Tokyo, June 1995. Springer-Verlag, LNCS, to be published.
11. Y. Mahéo. *Environnements pour la compilation dirigée par les données : supports d'exécution et expérimentations*. PhD thesis, IFSIC / Université de Rennes I, juillet 1995.
12. M. Makpangou, Y. Gourhant, J. Le Narzul, and M. Shapiro. Fragmented objects for distributed abstractions. *IEEE Software*, May 1991.
13. B. Meyer. *Object-Oriented Software Construction*. Prentice-Hall, 1988.
14. John W. Romein and Henri E. Bal. Parallel n-body simulation on a large-scale homegeneous distributed system. In Peter Magnusson Seif Haridi, Khayri Ali, editor, *EURO-PAR'95 Parallel Processing*, volume 966 of *Lecture Notes in Computer Science*, pages 473–484. Springer, August 1995.
15. John K. Salmon and Michael S. Warren. Skeletons from the treecode closet. *Journal of Computational Physics*, page 24, July 1993.

16. Leslie G. Valiant. A bridging model for parallel computation. *CACM*, 33(8), Aug 1990.
17. Youfeng Wu. Parallelism encapsulation in C++. In *International Conference on Parallel Processing*, 1990.

An Implementation Method of Migratable Distributed Objects Using an RPC Technique Integrated with Virtual Memory Management

Kenji KONO[1]* and Kazuhiko KATO[2] and Takashi MASUDA[1]

[1] Department of Information Science, Graduate School of Science,
University of Tokyo
7-3-1 Hongo, Bunkyo-ku, Tokyo 113, Japan
Email: {kono,masuda}@is.s.u-tokyo.ac.jp
[2] Institute of Information Sciences and Electronics, University of Tsukuba
Tsukuba, Ibaraki 305, Japan
Email: kato@is.tsukuba.ac.jp

Abstract. Object abstraction is indispensable to construction of distributed applications to encapsulate the details of execution entities. By applying an RPC technology integrated with virtual memory management, this paper presents a novel approach to implementing migratable distributed objects. The novelties of the approach are transparency achieved at the instruction code level, distributed dynamic methods, and applicability to heterogeneous environments. The instruction code level transparency naturally accomplishes object migration and enables efficient manipulation of migrated objects. The distributed dynamic methods provide the programmers with flexible control of activities.

1 Introduction

Construction of distributed application, which consists of autonomous execution entities running on loosely coupled machines, is hindered by the lack of knowledge on remote execution entities. Thus, it is essential to abstract these entities as the interacting modules with well-defined interfaces and encapsulate their details from the others. This observation naturally leads us to building an application as a collection of *distributed objects*, which are the direct embodiment of those modules. Research efforts in this past decade have invented various implementation mechanisms for object distribution. The mechanisms proposed so far can be classified into three approaches: 1) the virtual machine approach, 2) the proxy-object approach, and 3) the distributed shared memory (DSM) approach.

The virtual machine approach prepares a virtual machine [11, 18, 9, 22], often implemented as a byte-code interpreter, that provides a transparent mechanism for passing messages among distributed objects. Since the virtual machine encapsulates the underlying hardware and operating systems, this approach provides

---

* Research Fellow of the Japan Society for the Promotion of Science.

a platform on top of which we can design and implement distributed object-oriented programming languages with a high degree of distribution transparency. In addition, *object migration* is achieved with relative ease because of the encapsulation by the virtual machine. Using object migration, application programmers might improve the execution performance by gathering the objects on one address space among which messages are frequently exchanged. However, the virtual machine approach pays a high price for these advantages; it gives up the effective program execution in native machine code.

In the proxy-object approach, a remote object is invoked indirectly through invocation of the *proxy object* [19] that is a counterpart of the *stub* routine in a remote procedure call (RPC) [3]. A proxy encapsulates communication details from application programmers. In this approach, a language preprocessor emits the code of the necessary proxies and replaces remote object invocations with the corresponding local proxy calls, thereby accomplishing the literal level transparency. Given a language preprocessor, we can use the conventional native code compilers *not* designed for the distribution purpose. The most attractive feature of the proxy approach is flexibility; various mechanisms can be encapsulated in proxies. For example, proxy-based systems become applicable to heterogeneous environments if the code of data conversion is embedded in proxies. Object migration can be achieved with some restrictions on the optimizations by compilers. This issue is discussed later in Section 3.5.

The DSM approach is to build object systems on top of DSMs implemented by either hardware [15] or software [16]. Once DSM is provided, distributed object systems are not difficult to implement, since the DSM layer provides a single logical address space shared among distributed sites. Clouds [6] takes this approach. Most DSM implementations use the memory management unit (MMU) hardware to trap an access to absent pages, and cache the accessed pages on the local memory. Object systems built on those implementations bring about an effect similar to object migration and achieve transparency at the instruction code level. Thus, existing compilers can be used with few modifications. Generally, DSMs assume homogeneous environments because it is fairly difficult to implement them in heterogeneous environments. Even if implemented in heterogeneous environments, these systems are subject to many restrictions [23].

To summarize, the virtual machine approach provides a platform suitable for object migration, but precludes execution of application programs in native machine code. The proxy-object and the DSM approaches allow efficient execution in native machine code. The former is applicable to heterogeneous environments, but restricts compiler optimizations if object migration is achieved. Although the latter is not applicable to heterogeneous environments, it automatically achieves object caching similar to object migration.

Recently, a new RPC technology has been proposed [14, 13] that enables quite transparent treatment of remote pointers by integrating the RPC and virtual memory management techniques without sacrificing the virtues of RPCs, such as their applicability to heterogeneous environments. In this paper we describe an approach to implementing a system for migratable distributed objects by applying the proposed RPC technology. The implemented system has been named TRAP-DO. The notable feature of TRAP-DO is to put together the two advantageous points of the above-mentioned conventional approaches that enable native code execution: one advantageous point is transparency at the instruction code level in the DSM approach and the other is flexibility in the proxy-object approach.

In the TRAP-DO system, object references have a uniform representation; that is, remote objects are referenced by virtual addresses directly accessible by ordinary CPUs in the same manner as a local object reference. An attempt to access an absent (remote) object is detected by the hardware for virtual memory management. Thereafter, the accessed object migrates to the local address space. After the migration, the access to the migrated object is completely the same as the access to local objects. Thus, application programs can execute in native machine code, and no restrictions are imposed on compiler optimizations. This mechanism seems similar to the DSM approach; both the DSM approach and the TRAP-DO approach accomplish the instruction code level transparency and allows remote objects to be referenced by virtual addresses. However, the TRAP-DO approach is quite different from the DSM approach. Unlike the DSM approach, TRAP-DO does *not* share a single logical address space. Each address space manages its own local memory and reconstructs memory image of the migrated object independently of other address spaces. Thus, the TRAP-DO approach is applicable to heterogeneous environments if the internal representation of the migrating object is converted according to the target machine architecture to preserve the logical type of the migrated object. In addition, TRAP-DO is applicable to a variety of existing programming languages. This property contrasts with typical systems in which either original languages [11, 1] are developed or a single language is extended for distribution [20, 2, 12].

Generally, it is a difficult task to migrate objects in existing systems as pointed out in Douglis and Ousterhout [8]. In brief, this is because the entire state of an object may be scattered in the operating system data structures. TRAP-DO provides the *distributed dynamic methods* that utilizes the aspect that RPC can be applied to dynamic linking, as discussed in Hayes *et al* [10]. This mechanism bypasses the difficulties of migration. For example, consider the case where an object has a pointer to the data structure held by the operating system, and a method of the object interacts with the operating system using the pointer. If this object migrates to another address space and that method is executed there, the result would be an unexpected one. With a distributed dynamic method, the programmer can specify an address space on which a method is executed. Using this mechanism, in the above example, the programmer has only to direct the runtime system to execute the method in question at the appropriate address space. This mechanism also allows the programmers to utilize diverse architectures in a heterogeneous environment. For instance, they can specify a particular implementation to be executed on the machine with special equipment.

The rest of the paper is organized as follows. Section 2 overviews the entire system. The implementation is described in Section 3. Section 4 reports the experimental results. Section 5 concludes the paper.

2 System Overview

2.1 Basic Concepts

TRAP-DO supports from fine to medium-grain objects; a single address space can hold many objects at once. A *class* is a template from which objects are created, and every object is an instance of some class. TRAP-DO provides *passive objects* wherein the threads and objects are completely separate entities; a thread is not bound to a single object. We refer to a chain of nested invocations of methods as an *action*, and a distributed thread of control as an *activity*. In the passive object model, a single activity executes all the methods associated with an action, migrating from one object to another.

TRAP-DO provides two kinds of objects: *global* and *local* objects. The references to global objects can be passed beyond the address space boundaries. Thus, global objects can be invoked from outer address spaces, and may migrate to other address spaces. On the other hand, the references to local objects can not be transferred to remote address spaces. If an attempt is made to pass a reference to a local object to a remote address space, TRAP-DO automatically detects it and raises an exception. The programmers specify global or local for each object at the instantiation time.

In TRAP-DO, when an activity invokes a method, the target object migrates to the address space where the invoking activity is running, and the method is executed at that address space. This mechanism is completely hidden from the programmers; they need not to be aware of the location of objects. In this execution model, an activity is always bound to one address space. To allow the programmers to flexibly control the location of *activities*, TRAP-DO provides the mechanism called the *distributed dynamic methods*. When invoking a method, the programmers can *dynamically* specify the address space on which the method should be executed, regardless of the location of the target object. Using this mechanism, the programmers can incorporate various strategies into their applications; for example, they can distribute the computation for load sharing, or can exploit the heterogeneity of the distributed environment by executing a specific method on a machine with special equipment. Of course, location-dependent methods can be executed at the appropriate address space.

The current implementation of TRAP-DO employs a string composed of the host name and the service name as a logical name of an address space. For instance, a string "*Mozart:address-book*" specifies an address space that provides the service *address-book* on the host *Mozart*. The host name can be omitted so that the programmers can simply specify the service name. In this case, one host that provides the specified service is selected by the runtime system. The logical name string can be generated by programmers at runtime. From a logical name, the runtime system determines the actual address space and makes the

```
 1: //class definition
 2: class X {
 3:     //instance variables
 4: public:
 5:     void foo(void);
 6:     void bar(void)@"host:service";
 7: };
 8:
 9: ...
10: {
11:     TransactionalSession(hos, hls){
12:         X* o = new (global)X;    //instantiate a global object
13:
14:         //methods are executed on the default address spaces
15:         o->foo();        //executed locally
16:         o->bar();        //executed at "host:service"
17:
18:         //changing the executing address space
19:         o->foo()@"host:service"; //executed at "host:service"
20:         o->bar()@"local";        //executed locally
21:
22:         //an example of load sharing
23:             //dynamically select an address space
24:         const char* address_space = LoadSharing();
25:             //then execute foo() at the address space
26:         o->foo()@address_space;
27:     }
28: }
```

Fig. 1. An Example Code of TRAP-DOC.

activity migrate to the specified address space. The format of a logical name string and how it is interpreted are the problem of naming and beyond the range of this paper. TRAP-DO does not preclude more elaborate logical names; as a future extension, we are planning to employ a variant of URL (uniform resource location).

2.2 Language and Example

As a user programming language, TRAP-DO currently provides TRAP-DOC that extends ANSI C and provides C++-like notation to deal with distributed objects. In order to concentrate on the distribution issues, the current TRAP-DOC does not support inheritance.

Figure 1 shows an example of a class definition. This example defines a class X that provides two methods foo() and bar(). While the declaration of foo() is the same as that in C++, the declaration of bar() is annotated with "host:service". This annotation defines the default address space on which this method is executed. In this example, bar() is executed by default on the address space specified by host:service. If this annotation is omitted like the declaration of foo(), the default address space is the local address space. At the lines 15 and 16 in Fig. 1, the methods are executed at the default address spaces. The default address spaces can be dynamically changed as shown in the

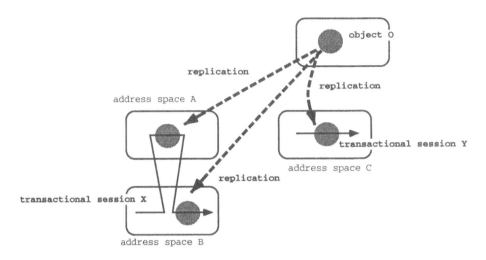

Fig. 2. Transactional session. Two transactional sessions X and Y are operating on the object O. The transactional session X operates on two replicas of the object O.

lines 19 and 20. The string "local" is an abbreviation of the logical name of the local address space. At the line 26, the executing address space is dynamically changed for load sharing. The function LoadSharing() returns the logical name of the host whose load is the lightest, and then the foo() is executed there. Note that TRAP-DOC accepts C++ programs without modifying the semantics of method calls, except that TRAP-DOC does not support inheritance.

2.3 Transactional Session

Since TRAP-DO allows multiple activities to execute concurrently and to perform update operations on objects, some problems must be dealt with, including maintaining the coherent state between replicas and synchronizing multiple activities of actions. To attack these problems we introduce *transactional session* into the system. A transactional session serves as a *transaction* that serializes the operations performed by multiple activities, and also serves as a *session* that determines the period during which the references to remote objects are valid. The references to remote objects are not valid beyond the transactional session; the programmers must split their programs into several transactional sessions among which remote object references are not shared. A programmer declares the beginning and the end of a transactional session. In Fig. 1 a transactional session is declared at the line 11. The role of the parameters "hos" and "hls" is explained in Section 3.2.

A set of operations performed within a transactional session is guaranteed to be atomic, serializable and isolated from the others by the *inter-session* protocol. In Figure 2, two activities within transactional sessions X and Y are simultaneously performing update operations on the replicas of the object O. The inter-session protocol serializes the transactional sessions X and Y. As shown in this figure, there may exist multiple replicas of a single object within a transactional session. Thus, the coherency between these replicas must be maintained. In this figure, the object O is replicated on the address spaces A and B within the transactional session X. The protocol named *intra-session* protocol maintains the coherency between these replicas. This protocol guarantees one-copy semantics within a transactional session. In other words, the activity always observes the results of the latest update within a transactional session. In TRAP-DO, the one-copy semantics is relatively easy to implement, since the synchronous property of method invocations assures that there is a single activity in each transactional session. This property simplifies the protocol and makes it efficient.

Management of replicas causes the problem of when to release them in addition to the problem of the coherency between them. We adopt the *per-session replication* policy for isolation of transactional sessions; replicas are not shared between transactional sessions. By using the per-session replication policy, we can dispense with distributed garbage collection to reclaim the replicas. Since object migration may occur only during a transactional session, replicas of objects are in use only within the transactional session. The system can simply dispose of the replicas created during a transactional session when it reaches the end of the transactional session, since the replicas are not shared by other transactional sessions.

3 Implementation

Our migration mechanism consists of three parts. Section 3.1 explains the integration of virtual memory management and object migration. Section 3.2 describes the intra-session protocol for replica coherency. Section 3.3 describes the inter-session protocol for synchronization. Section 3.4 describes the support from the programming language layer, and explains the mechanism of the distributed dynamic methods and stub generation. Section 3.5 discusses some aspects of TRAP-DO.

3.1 Integrating Virtual Memory Management with Object Migration

To provide transparent and efficient references to objects, TRAP-DO enables objects to be referenced by virtual addresses regardless of the location of the objects. Since a virtual address becomes meaningless outside the address space where it is defined, some mechanism must be provided to preserve the logical links between objects even when virtual addresses are transferred to remote address spaces. TRAP-DO introduces *universal object identifiers (UIDs)* valid in the entire distributed system. The UID of an object consists of three parts: 1) the address space identifier of the object's birthplace (typically a pair of the site ID and the process ID in the site), 2) the address of the object in the birthplace, and 3) the specifier of the class to which the object belongs. We assume that the

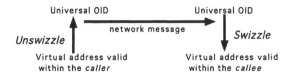

Fig. 3. Swizzling and unswizzling of a UID.

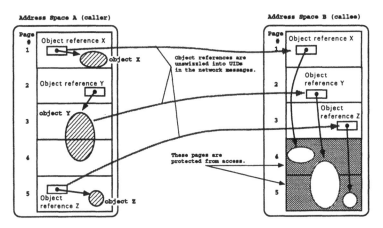

Fig. 4. Just after three object references are swizzled in the address space Y.

system can obtain an actual data structure from a class specifier by querying a database that serves as a network name server.

When an attempt is made to pass a reference (virtual address) to a remote address space as an input or output argument of a remote method, it is translated into the UID at the caller, and the UID is translated into a virtual address at the callee side. The translation from UID into a virtual address is called *pointer swizzling* and the reverse translation is called *pointer unswizzling* (see Fig. 3). When the callee receives the UID, it is not straightforward to swizzle the UID into a virtual address, since the object referenced by the UID exists only at the remote address space at this time. To swizzle the UID into a virtual address, the callee allocates a *protected* area in a memory page or pages that MMU protects from read and write access. The size of the allocated area is the same as the object referenced by the UID, the size of which is obtained from the class specifier embedded in the UID. The transferred UID is swizzled into the address of the allocated area. Note that the allocated area is empty at this time. The actual object *will* be copied to the location later when necessary. Figure 4 illustrates this situation. Three object references X, Y and Z are transferred from the caller to the callee. On the callee side, three empty areas are allocated respectively for each object in the two protected pages. As shown in the figure, one protected page can contain a set of remote objects, and an object can cross page boundaries.

MMU detects the first attempt to access an object allocated in a protected

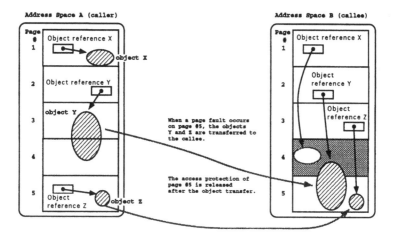

Fig. 5. When a protected page is accessed, all objects in the page are transferred.

page, and raises an access-violation exception. The operating system kernel is informed *a priori* that the runtime system handles this exception. When an exception is raised, the exception handler determines at which location this exception was raised. At this point, the accessed object is transferred from the caller to the callee. All objects allocated in the same page must be transferred at this time, because the access to the page can not be detected after the release of the page protection. When the objects are transferred, their internal representations are encoded and decoded to preserve their types in a heterogeneous environment. We can use the standard methods except in the case of references. They must be unswizzled and swizzled if embedded in the transferred objects. After the objects are transferred, the operating system kernel is directed to release the access protection of the page. Then, the faulting activity is resumed. At this time, only the read access is permitted to detect write access afterwards.

When an object migrates to a remote address space, TRAP-DO replicates the object and caches the replica to the remote address space. Since only one activity exists within a session, there is an "up-to-date" replica. We call the up-to-date replica *hot object*, and *hot location* the identifier of the address space from which the hot object is available. The runtime system maintains an *object allocation table*, the entries of which are the page number, the offset within the page, the UID, and the hot location. The hot location indicates the address space from which the hot object is available. The intra-session protocol manages the hot locations to maintain the replica coherency. The runtime system refers to this table at the page fault time to determine which object is to be transferred from which address space. This table also serves to preserve logical links between objects when remote invocations are nested. Whenever required, a reference can be translated into and from a UID by this table. In the example shown in Fig. 4, the object allocation table would be like Table 1. Figure 5 shows the transfer of objects in the example shown in Fig. 4. In Fig. 5 a page fault is detected on page

#5. By looking up the object allocation table, the runtime system decides the object Y crosses the page boundary, since the offset$_Y$ plus the size of the object Y is greater than the page size. Then the objects Y and Z are transferred from the address space A.

page #	offset	UID	Hot location
4	offset$_X$	X	A
4	offset$_Y$	Y	A
5	offset$_Z$	Z	A

Table 1. Object allocation table.

In the description above, an object is transferred on demand. If objects are traversed following the references, a terrible situation arises. The number of page faults and network communications are both increased. If fine-grain objects are transferred, network bandwidth is not utilized well. To avoid this situation, when passing a reference or fetching an object, TRAP-DO transfers a set of objects: a certain depth of the *transitive closure* of the passed object. There are many alternative algorithms to take a certain depth of transitive closure. By default, TRAP-DO uses the breadth-first traversal algorithm, and the programmers can explicitly specify the *closure size* parameter, the maximum amount of the transferred objects. At the traversal time, the system detects cycles, and prevents page faults by examining the page protection mode before accessing a page.

3.2 Replica Coherency Protocol

Generally, all replication techniques inherently require a protocol for replica coherency. TRAP-DO guarantees one-copy semantics of replicas within a transactional session by the *intra-session* protocol. Since each transactional session is completely isolated from the others by the per-session replication policy described in Section 3.3, we can assume there is a single activity in the system when discussing the intra-session protocol. Thus, it is sufficient to provide the activated address space with the up-to-date state of objects. The basic strategy of the protocol is to transfer a *hot location set* to the activated address space, together with the arguments of the method. As mentioned in Section 3.1, the intra-session protocol manages the hot location column of the object allocation table. The hot location set is a collection of a pair of the UID and the hot location of the modified object, and keeps track of the hot locations of the modified objects. When the activity attempts to access an out-of-date object, MMU detects it and the runtime system performs an RPC to obtain the hot object from the hot location. If hot objects are directly transferred to the activated address space instead of hot locations, we can expect better performance if there is locality of reference. In the intra-session protocol, the *hot object set*, a collection

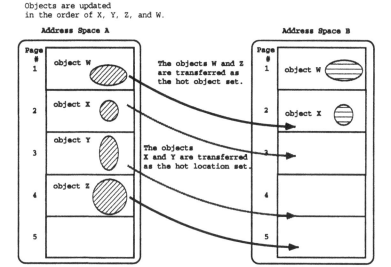

Fig. 6. Transfer of the hot object and location sets. The objects W and Z are transferred as the hot object set, and the others are transferred as the hot location set.

of the hot objects, is directly transferred to the activated address space for the *recently* modified objects. For the *less recently* modified objects, the hot location set is transferred. The programmer can specify the *HOS* and *HLS* parameters, which limit the sizes of the hot object set and the hot location set, respectively.

TRAP-DO implements the protocol described above in the following way. The runtime system maintains a link of dirty (modified) pages. When MMU detects an update on a page, the runtime system determines the page to which the update is applied, and links the entry of the page to the dirty page link in LIFO order. We can use this link to approximately determine the order of modifications; a recently modified page comes first in the link. When the activity attempts to migrate to another address space, the dirty page link is traversed to create a hot object set. Traversing the link, the objects on the modified pages are marshalled into the hot object set, until the size of the hot object set reaches the HOS parameter. After the creation of the hot object set, the hot location set is created for the modified objects not marshalled into the hot object set. Then the hot object and location sets are transferred, together with the arguments of the remote method. Figure 6 shows this situation. On the address space A, four objects W, X, Y, and Z are updated in the sequence of X, Y, Z, and W. Thus, the pages #1, #4, #3, #2 are linked to the dirty page link in this order. In this example, the objects W and Z are marshalled into the hot object set, and the others are transferred as the hot location set. On the address space B, the objects W and X already exist; they are out-of-date now.

The hot object and location sets are properly reflected to the objects on the receiving side. The objects in the hot object set are replicated into the receiving address space in the same way as described in Section 3.1, since this replication

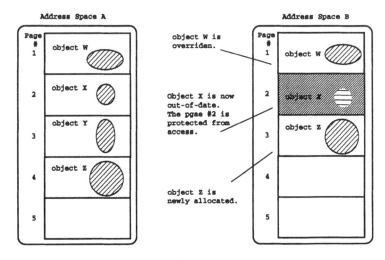

Fig. 7. Reflecting the hot object and location sets to the address space B.

can be regarded as object migration. The object whose UID is in the hot location set is out-of-date. The runtime system looks up the object allocation table for each UID in the hot location set, and closes all access permissions of the pages on which the out-of-date objects reside. The hot location column of the object allocation table is also updated to the new hot locations. When an attempt is made to access an out-of-date object, a page fault occurs, and the hot objects can be migrated as described in Section 3.1. Figure 7 illustrates this situation. The objects W and Z in the hot object set are replicated into the address space B. The transferred W overrides the object W on B, and the object Z is newly allocated. The runtime system determines the object X is out-of-date from the hot location set, and invalidates the page on which it resides.

When the size of the hot location set exceeds the HLS parameter, all hot objects are written back to their original locations, and the replicas created during the transactional session are invalidated. Thereafter, the hot location and object sets are reset to zero in size. We can always obtain the hot objects from their original locations until the activity moves beyond the address space boundary. The intra-session protocol works properly even when remote invocations are nested. While activated, the runtime system maintains the hot location set and the UIDs of the objects in the hot object set, in order to keep track of all the modifications during the session. The memory area for keeping them does not suppress the application programs, since the HOS and HLS parameters limit the sizes of the hot object and location sets.

3.3 Concurrency Control Protocol

Since multiple transactional sessions execute concurrently, concurrency must be controlled by the system. In TRAP-DO, the *inter-session* protocol guarantees serializable execution of transactional sessions. The inter-session protocol employs an optimistic approach. Generally, optimistic approaches have the following attractive features as against pessimistic approaches. The pessimistic approaches require additional network communications to acquire and release locks or to operate on distributed semaphores while the transaction is being executed. In addition, the problem of distributed deadlock must be dealt with. As our system assumes fine-to-medium grain objects, deadlocks are expected to be caused frequently. On the other hand, optimistic approaches enhance the effect of object caching, because they require no additional communications during the execution of a transactional session. Moreover, they do not cause deadlocks. The major drawback of the optimistic approaches is that they may cause cascading roll backs. Our current protocol avoids them by complete isolation of transactional sessions.

TRAP-DO manages a heap area based on the *per-session replication* policy to isolate a transactional session from the others. This section outlines the mechanism of the per-session replication and the inter-session protocol. The details are presented in our paper in preparation [13]. TRAP-DO divides a heap into three distinct parts: pages for replicas, global objects, and local objects. Since global and replicated objects may be shared among multiple activities, TRAP-DO maintains the coherent state of those objects. The programmers can avoid concurrency control cost by allocating objects in local objects' pages. Since local objects are not referenced from outer address spaces, TRAP-DO need not control the concurrency. TRAP-DO can detect an attempt to pass a reference to a local object to a remote address space, because a reference to a local object cannot be unswizzled into the UID by the object allocation table mentioned in Section 3.1; the entry is not found. Each transactional session prepares its own object allocation table. Thus, replicas are not shared among transactional sessions; transient states of replicas are automatically isolated from the other transactional sessions. To isolate updates on the global object pages, TRAP-DO creates a session-local image of the global pages on a copy-on-write basis. When an activity attempts an update on a global object page, the coherent image of the page is preserved, and then the update is applied directly to the global object page. When the activity switches, the transient image is preserved for each session, and the consistent image is reloaded. Consequently, TRAP-DO prevents each transactional session from observing the transient state of the objects in other transactional sessions.

In the optimistic concurrency controls, the updates performed during a transactional session are checked at the validation phase to ensure that the transactional session does not violate the serializability. In the current inter-session protocol, the transactional session that reaches its end fastest is successfully validated. If a transactional session is validated successfully, the hot objects are written back to their original global pages, and the replicas are disposed of simply by releasing the replica pages of the transactional session. If a transactional session fails to be validated, it is rolled back. The roll back is done by releasing the replica pages and transient images of the global pages.

3.4 Distributed Dynamic Methods and Stub Generation

The runtime system of TRAP-DO described in previous sections cooperates with the programming language layer. This language layer performs three tasks: attaining distributed dynamic methods, stub emission, and generation of closure traversal routines. The current user language, TRAP-DOC, is a preprocessor from TRAP-DOC to C.

Generally, distributed dynamic methods are invoked through proxies within which the target address space is determined by interpreting the specified logical name of the address space. However, in TRAP-DOC, most method invocations can be statically determined to be local calls. For example, invocations of methods, both the declaration and the invocation of which are annotated with nothing, are local calls and can be expanded into ordinary procedure calls by the preprocessor. If the target address space is not determined statically, the preprocessor emits proxies, or stubs, for the remote method invocation. This proxy interprets the logical name of the address space and performs an RPC to the target address space. As pointed out in Section 2.1, the mechanism of naming is independent of the TRAP-DO's runtime mechanism described in previous sections and various naming policies can be implemented on top of TRAP-DO. The proxy generation technique used in TRAP-DO allows higher order functions to be passed among distinct heterogeneous address spaces. This stub generation technique is based on the one described in Ohori and Kato [17].

As described in Section 3.1, when passing a reference to an object to a remote address space, a certain depth of the transitive closure of the reference is transferred. The language preprocessor generates a *traversal routine* that creates this closure of the passed reference. By default, TRAP-DOC emits the traversal routine for breadth-first traversal. Although the traversal mechanism is hidden from the programmers, they can incorporate their own algorithms into the system. TRAP-DO provides the interface between the runtime system and the programmers. If the programmers' traversal routines conform to this interface, the system detects the cycles and prevents page-faults at the traversing time. This interface and example codes are shown in another paper [13].

3.5 Discussion

To highlight some aspects of TRAP-DO, we contrast the object migration mechanism based on proxy objects with that of TRAP-DO. The proxy object approach is applicable to object migration by encapsulating the mechanism of migration within proxies. Many systems using proxies for migration examine with software whether the target object is present or not, each time before using a reference. In this mechanism, each access to an object requires additional software overhead. Amadeus [4] proposed a mechanism to avoid this additional overhead. It uses a proxy object called "O proxy" to trap attempts to access absent objects. O proxy contains no data but is the same size as the object it represents. The code bound to the proxy implements the same interface as the absent object. When a method of the O proxy is invoked, it notifies the Amadeus runtime system of the attempted invocation. Then the runtime system overlays the O proxy with the real object, and forwards the invocation to the real object. This approach does not work properly unless all method invocations are implemented as procedure calls even at the instruction code level. Hence, in the Amadeus approach, compilers can not use some sorts of optimization techniques [7, 5] such as inline-expansion that compilers of object-oriented programming languages use. On the other hand, TRAP-DO does not impose any restrictions on the code generation by compilers, because it accomplishes transparency at the instruction code level. Thus, in TRAP-DO, compilers can optimize frequent message exchanges among inter-related objects, and application programs can run as efficiently as possible after object migration.

The runtime behavior of TRAP-DO is adjustable to the access pattern of applications. In TRAP-DO, the programmers can explicitly specify the granularity of migration by the closure size parameter, which limits the size of the transferred transitive closures. For example, suppose that the reference which designates the head of a linked list is passed, and the linked list is traversed on the local address space. If the closure size parameter is set to zero, the linked objects are transferred on demand. Hence, the number of page faults and network communications increase, but the amount of the transferred data is minimized, since just the accessed portion of the linked list is transferred. If the closure size parameter is set to infinity, no page fault is incurred and the network communication is required only once. However, since all the linked objects are transferred at once, unnecessary objects are also transferred that are not accessed in the local address space. According to the access pattern of the applications, the programmers can specify the closure size parameter to tailor the runtime behavior of the system to the applications.

4 Experimental Results

In this section, we measure the basic performance of TRAP-DO and validate the discussion in Section 3.5. The prototype TRAP-DO is implemented on SunOS 4.1.3 running on SUN Sparc workstations (SuperSPARC, 60MHz, SPECint92 98.2, SPECfp92 107.2). They have 96 Mbytes of main memory and are connected by a 10 Mbps Ethernet network. The current implementation uses the TCP/IP network protocol and specifies the TCP_NODELAY option in the socket system call so that small packets are sent without buffering. As a canonical data representation, TRAP-DO uses the XDR (eXternal Data Representation) [21] that guarantees the transformation of basic data types such as integers, floating point numbers, and strings between CPUs with different architectures. Although the current system consists of only a few SPARC stations, the system is carefully designed to deal with heterogeneity. Therefore, the experimental results reflect heterogeneity overheads such as the data representation overhead.

4.1 Basic Performance

As described in Section 3.1, the TRAP-DO runtime system handles a page fault before migrating an object. The experimental results in this section show that the cost of page fault handling is small compared with the cost of network communication. In this experiment, objects each of which is 64 bytes in size are migrated from a remote address space to the local address space. This migration is executed in the following steps. First, a page fault is detected. Second, the exception handler requests the remote address space to transfer the objects. After the object migration, activity is resumed. Varying the number of migrated objects, we measured the total time of the migration and the cost of the page fault handling. Table 2 shows the result. In this result, the proportion of the cost of page fault handling to the total cost is from 2% to 21%. However, since the TRAP-DO runtime system transfers all objects allocated in a page at once, the size of transferred objects may be in the order of 4 Kbytes or 8 Kbytes. Thus, the proportion of the cost of page fault handling is considered to be from 2% to 4%.

Total size of objects (bytes)	64	256	1024	4096	8192
Cost of migration (ms)	1.4	1.7	3.2	7.3	12.7
Cost of page fault handling (ms)	0.3	0.3	0.3	0.3	0.3
page fault handling / migration (%)	21	18	9	4	2

Table 2. Proportion of the cost of page fault handling to the cost of network communication.

4.2 Closure Size

The closure size parameter plays an important role in TRAP-DO as discussed in Section 3.5. This section examines the effect of the closure size parameter. The experimental subject was a traversal of a complete binary tree. Each node of the tree is an object 16 bytes in size (two 4-byte references and 8-byte data). Initially, a complete binary tree of 32,767 nodes was instantiated in the *caller* address space. Then a reference to the root object of the tree is passed to a remote method on a *remote* address space. The remote method traverses the tree in a *depth-first* manner, following the references. We measured the average time required to process one remote method call that retrieves the tree, varying the number of the nodes visited in the remote method. In this experiment we compared three cases, changing the closure size parameter in each case.

- **Case (A)** Closure size parameter is set to zero. The objects migrate to the callee on demand.

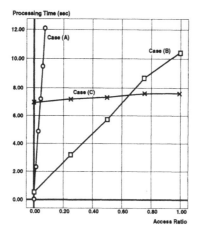

Fig. 8. Relationship between the Closure Size and Processing Time

- **Case (B)** Closure size parameter is set to 8 Kbytes. When an attempt is made to access an absent object, the 8 Kbytes transitive closure of the accessed object migrates to the callee. This transitive closure is retrieved in a *breadth-first* manner in the caller.
- **Case (C)** Closure size parameter is set to infinity. The entire tree (524,272 bytes) migrates to the callee at once.

Figure 8 shows the experimental result. The X-axis shows the ratios of the number of visited nodes to the total number of the nodes. The Y-axis shows the average processing time.

In case (A), the processing time is obviously bad. Since each object is 16 bytes in size in this experiment, the granularity of object migration is too fine to utilize the network bandwidth. The increased number of network communications degrades the execution performance. In case (C), the processing time is almost constant because the entire tree migrates to the callee at once. Case (B) shows the best processing time of the three for access ratios between 0.0 and 0.6. The improved performance of case (B) over case (C) is obtained because a relatively small number of objects are replicated. When the access ratio is larger than 0.6, case (B) becomes worse because of the increased number of communications. By adjusting the closure size parameter properly, the application programmers might improve the execution performance of their applications. In this experiment, the programmers should set the parameter to 8 Kbytes or so when the access ratio is less than 0.6. When the access ratio is larger than 0.6, the programmers should set the parameter larger.

4.3 Update

Finally we examine the effect of the HOS and HLS parameters described in Section 3.2. The HOS and HLS parameters limit the size of the hot object sets

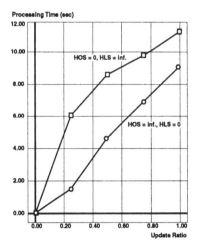

Fig. 9. Update Performance — In the case where locality of reference exists.

and the hot location sets, respectively. In this experiment, we use the same binary tree as in the previous section. To increase the effects of the HOS and HLS parameters, we set up the situation in which the entire tree is replicated on two address spaces A and B. In other words, each address space has its own replica of the identical tree. We can create this situation with the closure size parameter set to infinity, if the activity on the address space A passes a reference to the root object to the address space B; the entire tree migrates to the address space B with the migration of the activity.

We first examine the case where locality of reference exists. In this case, the activity on the address space A visits the nodes of the tree updating each visited node in the depth-first manner. Then the activity migrates to the address space B, traverses all the nodes of the replicated tree there, and returns to the address space A. We measured the processing time required from the activity migration to the address space B until it returns to the address space A, changing the ratios of the number of the updated nodes to the total number of the nodes. As shown in Fig. 9, the execution performance is better when the HOS parameter is set to infinity, since the objects modified in the address space A are accessed in the address space B. To examine the case where there is no locality, we carried out the same experiment as described above except that the activity does not traverse the tree at all on the address space B. The result is shown in Fig. 10. In this case, the execution performance is worse when the HOS parameter is set to infinity, since the hot object set transfers the objects that are not accessed in the address space B. The experimental results in this section validate our heuristics described in Section 3.2.

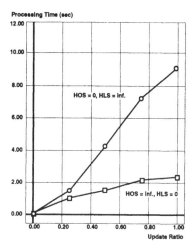

Fig. 10. Update Performance — In the case where there is no locality of reference.

5 Conclusion

We have described the design and implementation of the TRAP-DO distributed object system. TRAP-DO provides migratable distributed objects by applying the novel RPC technology integrated with virtual memory management. Compared with traditional distributed object systems, this integration brings about both the flexibility of proxy approaches and the instruction code level transparency of distributed shared memory (DSM) approaches. As a result, TRAP-DO naturally achieves object migration as DSM approaches, and is applicable to a heterogeneous environment as proxy approaches. The instruction code level transparency enhances the effect of object caching since it does not prevent compiler optimizations, and migrated objects are accessed without any additional overhead. The flexibility of proxies enables dynamic method binding in a distributed environment. To provide a natural and consistent view of distributed objects, TRAP-DO maintains the coherency of replicas and controls concurrency among multiple activities. The replica coherency protocol that provides one-copy semantics is simple and efficient because it makes use of the synchronous property of method invocations. The protocol for concurrency control takes an optimistic approach to avoid distributed deadlocks and additional network communications for distributed locks or semaphores. These protocols release the programmers from complex management of replicas.

Some interesting research issues still remain. The current protocol for concurrency control is a simple one. The primary drawbacks of the protocol is that it does not allow concurrency within a transactional session and that the programmers cannot make a decision what to do when a transactional session aborts. In principle, more elaborate protocols can be incorporated into TRAP-DO without sacrificing other features of TRAP-DO. We are currently designing a new protocol that allows a transactional session to create child transactions like nested transactions. In this new protocol, child sessions can execute concurrently, and the parent session can determine what to do when one of the child sessions aborts.

Another issue is to develop an optimal algorithm for taking the subset of the transitive closure of an object when the object migrates to a remote address space. If the access pattern of applications were precisely estimated, we could minimize the cost of network communication, but it requires predetermination of the access patterns of applications. One promising solution is to use hints provided by the programmers.

References

1. H. E. Bal, M. F. Kaashoek, and A. S. Tanenbaum. Orca: A language for parallel programming of distributed systems. *IEEE Transactions on Software Engineering*, Vol. 18, No. 3,, March 1992.
2. John K. Bennett. The design and implementation of distributed smalltalk. In *ACM OOPSLA '87*, pp. 318–330, 1987.
3. A. D. Birrell and B. J. Nelson. Implementing remote procedure calls. *ACM Transactions on Computer Systems*, Vol. 2, No. 1, pp. 39–59, February 1984.
4. Vinny Cahill, Sean Baker, Chris Horn, and Gradimir Starovic. The Amadeus GRT - generic runtime support for distributed persistent programming. In *OOPSLA Proceedings 1993*, pp. 144–161. ACM, 1993.
5. Craig Chambers and David Ungar. Making pure object-oriented languages practical. In *ACM OOPSLA '91*, pp. 1–15, 1991.
6. P. Dasgupta, R. LeBlanc Jr., M. Ahamad, and U. Ramachandran. The Clouds distributed operating system. *IEEE Computer*, Vol. 24, No. 11, pp. 34–44, Nov. 1991.
7. J. Dean, D. Grove, and C. Chambers. Optimization of object-oriented programs using static class hierarchy analysis. In *European Conf. on Object-Oriented Programming (ECOOP)*, pp. 77–101, 1995.
8. Fred Douglis and John Ousterhout. Transparent process migration: Design alternatives and the Sprite implementation. *Software Practice and Experience*, Vol. 21, No. 8, pp. 757–785, August 1991.
9. J. Gosling and H. McGilton. The Java language environments: A White Paper. Technical report, Sun Microsystems, 1995.
10. Roger Hayes and Richard D. Schlichting. Faciliating mixed language programming in distributed systems. *IEEE Transactions on Software Engineering*, Vol. SE-13, No. 12, pp. 1254–1264, December 1987.
11. E. Jul, H. Levy, N. Hutchinson, and A. Black. Fine-grained mobility in the Emerald system. *ACM Transactions on Computer Systems*, Vol. 6, No. 1, pp. 109–133, February 1988.
12. K. Kato, A. Ohori, T. Murakami, and T. Masuda. Distributed C language based on a higher-order remote procedure call technique. In *Advances in Software Science and Technology*, volume 5, pp. pp. 119–143. Academic Press, 1993.
13. K. Kono, K. Kato, and T. Masuda. Transparent pointers in remote procedure calls. In preparation for submission.
14. K. Kono, K. Kato, and T. Masuda. Smart remote procedure calls: Transparent treatment of remote pointers. In *Proc. IEEE 14th Int. Conf. on Distributed Computing Systems*, pp. 142–151, 1994.

15. D. Lenoski, J. Laudon, K. Gharachorloo, W. Weber, A. Gupta, J. Hennessy, M. Horowitz, and M. S. Lan. The stanford dash multiprocessor. *IEEE Computer*, pp. 63–79, March 1992.

16. K. Li and P. Hudak. Memory coherence in shared virtual memory systems. *ACM Transactions on Computer Systems*, Vol. 7, No. 4, pp. 321–359, November 1989.

17. A. Ohori and K. Kato. Semantics for communication primitives in a polymorphic language. In *Proc. 20th ACM Symp. on Principles of Programming Languages*, pp. 99–112, January 1993.

18. H. Okamura and Y. Ishikawa. Object location control using meta-level programming. In *European Conf. on Object-Oriented Programing (ECOOP)*, pp. 299–319, 1994.

19. Marc Shapiro. Structure and encapsulation in distributed systems: the Proxy Principle. In *Proc. IEEE Int. Conf. on Distributed Computing Systems*, pp. 198–204, 1986.

20. Marc Shapiro, Philippe Gautron, and Laurence Mosseri. Persistence and migration for C++ objects. In *European Conf. on Object-Oriented Programming (ECOOP)*, pp. 191–204, 1989.

21. Sun Microsystems Inc. *External Data Representation Standard:Protocol Specification*, March 1990.

22. J. E. White. *Mobile Agents*. MIT Press, 1996. To appear.

23. S. Zhou, S. Stumm, K. Li, and D. Wortman. Heterogeneous distributed shared memory. *IEEE Transactions on Parallel and Distributed Systems*, Vol. 3, No. 5, pp. 540–554, September 1992.

Protocol Classes for Designing Reliable Distributed Environments

Benoît Garbinato   Pascal Felber   Rachid Guerraoui

Laboratoire de Systèmes d'Exploitation
Département d'Informatique
Ecole Polytechnique Fédérale de Lausanne
Lausanne, Suisse
e-mail: *bast@lse.epfl.ch*

Abstract. In this paper, we present BAST, an extensible library of *protocol classes*. The latter is aimed at helping *system* programmers to build distributed programming environments. Protocol classes constitute the basic structuring components for higher-level programming models, such as the transactional model, and add flexibility to distributed environments. We focus on classes that implement a generic agreement protocol named *DTM* (Dynamic-Terminating-Multicast). To the programmer, the *DTM generic protocol* appears as a set of classes that can be specialized to solve agreement problems in distributed systems. In particular, we show how those classes can be derived to build *atomic commitment* and *reliable total order* protocols. An overview of the Smalltalk design and implementation of the BAST library is also presented.

1 Introduction

This paper describes BAST, an extensible class library of distributed protocols. BAST is aimed at assisting *system* programmers in building distributed programming abstractions for *application* programmers. It is more specifically intended to be used in the context of reliable (i.e., fault-tolerant) distributed environments design[1]. In this paper, we focus on protocol classes that involve solving the distributed consensus problem, since agreement is a central problem in many distributed algorithm that deal with failures.

1.1 Objects and distribution

Object concepts are emerging as a major trend in distributed systems, and current research in object-based distributed environment follow several directions. Those research directions can be grouped into three main streams: (1) the extension of object-based languages, (2) the design of reflexive architectures, and (3) the definition of basic abstractions.

---

[1] We use the term "distributed system" in a very general sense, whereas we use "distributed environment" when we want to refer to set of abstractions that support the programming of distributed applications.

Extension of object-based languages This research stream consists in adding new specialized abstractions to object-based languages, in order to support the programming of distributed applications. The CORBA standard object framework [11] belongs to this category. The aim of this approach is to facilitate the programming of distributed applications, using high-level languages.

Design of reflexive architectures Research in reflexive architectures [1, 30] consists in defining basic infrastructures for describing environment architectures, in an object-based language which is also used to describe applications. Approaches that provide limited reflexive facilities, such as GARF [9] and Composition-Filters [2], can also be considered to belong to this category. The aim of reflexive architectures is to provide ways of extending distributed environments with minimal impact on applications.

Definition of basic abstractions A third research stream consists in defining adequate abstractions that represent distributed systems, or specific parts of distributed systems. The idea here is to structure the architecture of distributed environments in the same way it is usually done for distributed applications. Expected benefits are modularity, extensibility, flexibility, and portability of the distributed environments on which applications are built.

The three research streams presented above are not competitive, but can be viewed as complementary ways to take benefits of object concepts in the context of distributed systems. For example, defining adequate abstractions is fundamental in order to take advantage of a reflexive architecture. This paper describes a research work which belongs to the third stream. We are concerned here with the design and implementation of a distributed environment as a set of objects. We focus on classes that are related to distributed agreement protocols, since the latter are fundamental to reliable distributed systems.

1.2 Reliability in distributed systems

"A distributed system is one that stops you from getting any work done when a machine you've never even heard of crashes." Leslie Lamport *in* [21].

A *reliable* distributed environment can be described as one that provides abstractions capable of hiding failures to its users (at least to some extent), and of preventing failures from putting it in a inconsistent state. In this context, two main paradigms for building reliable distributed applications have emerged over the years: the *transaction paradigm*, originated from the database community, and the *group paradigm*, originated from the distributed systems community. Each one of those two paradigms is tailored to solve a particular set of problems.

Transaction paradigm Many distributed environments provide the *transaction paradigm* [17] as the main building block for programming reliable applications. This concept has proven to be very useful for distributed database-like applications. However, the $ACID^2$ properties of the original transaction model are too strong for several applications. For example, the *Isolation* property is too strong for cooperative work applications, whereas the *All-or-nothing* property is too strong for applications dealing with replicated data. This is partly due to the fact that underlying agreement protocols are designed and implemented in an *ad hoc* manner and cannot be modified. The rigidity of the original transaction model has lead many authors to explore the design of more flexible transactional models, e.g., nested transactions, but the underlying agreement protocol still cannot be modified.

In designing the BAST class library, we have adopted an alternative approach, which consists in providing the basic abstractions required to implement various transaction models, rather than supporting one specific model. These abstractions implement support for reliable total order communications (allowing to build locking), atomic commitment, etc., and are aimed at being used by system programmers, not application programmers. As we shall see, those abstractions are based on agreement protocols.

Group paradigm Group-oriented environments like ISIS [4] or GARF [9] offer reliable communication primitives with various consistency levels, e.g., causal order multicast, total order multicast. These environments are based on the *group paradigm* as fundamental abstraction for reliable distributed programming. The group concept is very helpful to handle replication: a replicated entity (a process in ISIS or an object in GARF) is implemented as a group of replicas. It constitutes a convenient way of addressing replicated logical entities without having to explicitly designate each replica. When a failure occurs, members of a group are notified through a group membership protocol, and can act consequently. This is useful, for example, when implementing a primary-backup replication scheme: if the primary replica crashes, the backups replicas are notified through some membership protocol, and can then elect a new primary.

Membership protocols guarantee that all members of some group g agree on a totally ordered sequence of views $view_1(g)$, $view_2(g)$, ...; a view change occurs each time a member joins or leaves group g. Furthermore, multicasts to group g are guaranteed to be totally ordered *with respect to view changes*. Finer ordering criteria *within each view* are generally also available in environments such as ISIS or GARF, e.g., causal or total orderings. Membership protocols are normally based on agreement protocols. However, the strong coupling between the group concept and consistency leads to the inability to support reliable multicast that involve different replicated entities, i.e., several groups. This limitation makes group-oriented environments unable to seamlessly integrate transaction models. There again, underlying agreement protocols are hidden, and being not accessible they cannot be customized.

A major characteristic of the BAST class library is that it allows to decouple the group notion from consistency issues: groups are viewed merely as a *logical addressing capability*, while reliable multicast communications are supported by

<hr>

[2] *All-or-nothing, Consistency, Isolation,* and *Durability.*

adequate protocol classes. As a consequence, BAST naturally supports reliable multicasts involving different groups of replicas.

1.3 Protocols as structuring components

We believe that protocols should be basic structuring components of distributed environments. In the BAST class library, distributed protocols are manipulated as *classes of objects*. So, it is very easy to extend and/or customize high-level abstractions provided by distributed environments based on BAST.

What are protocol classes? A *protocol class* defines the behavior of objects capable of executing a particular distributed protocol. When the protocol is based on symmetric roles, only one class is necessary, while if it is based on asymmetric roles, there is the need for as many classes as they are roles involved in the protocol.

Protocol classes improve the reusability of complex algorithms, e.g., in BAST, the consensus protocol proposed by Chandra and Toueg [8] is implemented, once and for all, in reusable classes. So, customizations and optimizations are easily achieved through subclassing, and new protocols can be created and integrated to the environment with minimal efforts. This approach also provides a modular view of various distributed protocols, which helps to better understand the relationship between them. Making different protocols work together is then made easier. In BAST for example, transactions on replicated objects are achieved seamlessly because the atomic commitment protocol and the total order multicast protocol are implemented in well-defined classes, based on common *generic* protocol classes. We see the BAST library of protocol classes as our contribution to the definition of a well-structured framework for building reliable distributed environments.

DTM generic protocol Agreement plays a central role in many distributed algorithms that deal with failures. For this reason, classes that implement protocols solving the distributed consensus are of first importance in BAST. In the remainder of this paper, we present protocol classes that implement what we believe to be the common denominator of many reliable distributed algorithms: the *Dynamic-Terminating-Multicast* generic protocol (DTM). We also present how the corresponding protocol classes can be customized to solve the atomic commitment problem, which is central to transactional environments, and the total order multicast, which is central to group-oriented environments. Elsewhere [15], we have already proved that both a general atomic commitment and a total order multicast can be considered as instances of the DTM generic protocol.

1.4 About this paper

In next sections, we presents protocol classes that support the DTM generic protocol, and how those classes can be derived to build a total order multicast protocol and a general atomic commitment protocol. We also detail how

DTM classes have been implemented, and from which other protocol classes they inherit. More specifically, section 2 gives an overview of the BAST library of protocol classes, and presents its context and current status. Section 3 introduces the distributed system that we consider and the DTM generic protocol itself. Then, section 4 details the protocol classes that are given to system programmers wanting to use the DTM generic protocol; explanations on how to instantiate the generic dimensions of DTM are given here. Section 5 shows how we built a total order multicast and a general atomic commitment by subclassing DTM classes. For this section, we chose a language independent approach. The design of DTM generic protocol classes, in the context of our first Smalltalk prototype of the BAST class library, is presented in section 6. Section 7 compares the approach presented in this paper with other approaches described in the literature. Finally, section 8 summarizes what our approach, and the BAST class library that supports it, brings to reliable distributed programming, as well as the future research directions we are planning head to.

2 Overview of the BAST class library

The BAST library of protocol classes is implemented as the fundamental structuring component of the BASTET[3] *reliable distributed environment*. BASTET is aimed at providing a complete set of powerful abstractions, that support the design and implementation of reliable distributed applications. Figure 1 presents an overview of BASTET's architecture: apart from the operating system services (layer h), it is based on a fully object-oriented design and implementation. In the BASTET environment, various abstraction levels are provided, depending on the skills of programmers. At the highest level, all the complexity is hidden in ready-to-use components. This high-level layer of BASTET is an evolution of the GARF environment, which was aimed at supporting reliable distributed programming in a fairly automated way [9]. In BASTET, high-level abstractions are used to hide BAST's protocol classes to application programmers, while the BAST library is intended to be extended by system programmers.

2.1 BAST's protocol classes

The BAST library is based on an hierarchy of protocol classes, e.g., classes implementing objects capable of sending and receiving messages, classes implementing objects capable of detecting other objects' failures, etc. This approach allows to build protocols in an incremental way.

---

[3] You are probably wondering why we called our reliable distributed environment BASTET, and its protocol class library BAST. Well, *Bast*, also known as *Bastet*, was a cat-goddess in the Egyptian mythology, worshiped in the delta city of Bubastis. As you probably know, cats are said to have seven lives, which is quite a good replication rate to be fault-tolerant, isn't it! So, we thought the two names of the protectress of cats would be nice names for our reliable distributed environment and for our class library.

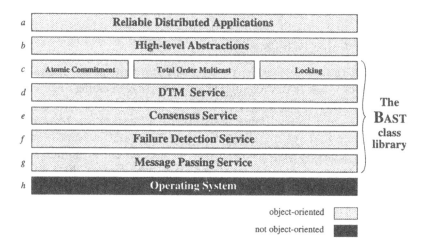

Fig. 1. Architecture of the BASTET reliable distributed environment

Since protocols can be manipulated as classes of objects in BAST, system programmers that have know-how in distributed systems can build new protocols, while less skilled programmers can simply use existing ones. The atomic commitment and the total order protocols, presented in section 5, are examples of such "ready-to-use" distributed protocols. New protocols can be built by expert programmers in distributed systems by instantiating generic protocols such as DTM, or by creating new ones using more basic components. Section 6 provides an overview of such lower-level components.

In the remainder of this paper, we first focus on layers c and d of the BAST class library. Those layers are the subjects of section 4 and section 5 respectively. Section 6 then presents layers e, f, and g, and how they are used to build the DTM generic protocol (layer d).

2.2 Current status of BAST

The BAST library of protocol classes, as well as the BASTET reliable distributed environment, are developed in the context of the *Phoenix* research project, at the Operating Systems Laboratory of the Swiss Federal Institute of Technology, Lausanne. The general objective of this on-going research project is to better understand what problems are implied by reliability in distributed systems, and how they can be solved through coherent and reusable tools.

At the moment, our first implementation of the BAST class library is coming to an end, and the BASTET environment is almost fully operational. This prototype is written in Smalltalk and will be used as reference version for further developments. We have already started to work on a C++ version of the BAST library, which will be used in the *Opendreams* project (ESPRIT n°29843). This project aims at designing a CORBA compliant platform for *reliable* (distributed) industrial applications.

3 DTM generic protocol

3.1 Distributed system model

The *distributed system* we consider is composed of a finite set of *distributed objects* $\Omega = \{o_1, o_2, \ldots, o_n\}$ that communicate by message passing. The *messages passing service* provides the means to designate distant objects through *remote object references*, and to send *messages* to them; a message can be any object. Communication primitives are reliable, i.e., a message sent by some object o_i to some object o_j is eventually received by o_j, if both o_i and o_j do not fail. This ensured by retransmitting messages if necessary. We suppose that objects fail only by crashing and that any network failure is eventually repaired.

Failure detectors In this paper, we make no assumption on the synchrony of our distributed system, i.e., we are not interested in knowing if communication delays are bounded or not. Instead, we use the notion of *failure detector*. Failure detectors encapsulate the properties of the underlying distributed system, by being abstractly characterized through reliability properties (namely completeness and accuracy [8]). Failure detectors are said to be *unreliable* if they can make mistakes in incorrectly suspecting objects to be faulty. The relationship between failure detectors and distributed systems can be expressed as follow: depending on the synchrony properties of the underlying distributed system, one can build failure detectors which differ from their reliability properties. Failure detectors have been classified according to their reliability properties in [8]. Some problems need reliable failure detectors to be solved, while others only need unreliable failure detectors.

3.2 Generic protocol

The DTM generic protocol enables an *initiator* object to multicast a message m to *Dst(m)*, a destination set of remote participant objects, and to reach agreement on *Reply(m)*, a set of replies $reply_k$ returned by each *participant$_k$* in response to m. Figure 2 presents an overview of the DTM generic protocol: arrows represent data exchanges, while numbers in circles show in what order data exchanges occur. The *initiator* object is on node A, while *participant$_i$* and *participant$_j$* are on node B and node C respectively; different nodes imply different address spaces. From now on, we consider that objects are *a priori* on different nodes. Since the interaction of the protocol with each participant is exactly the same, arrows are numbered for *participants$_i$* only.

Why is it generic? The DTM protocol is *generic* in the sense that the message m sent by the initiator, the set of participants *Dst(m)*, the response *reply$_k$* generated by each *participants$_k$*, and the interpretation of *Reply(m)*, the set of replies on which agreement is reached, are not defined *a priori*. One more generic dimension, the *validity condition*, allows to constrain *Reply(m)*; if that constraint

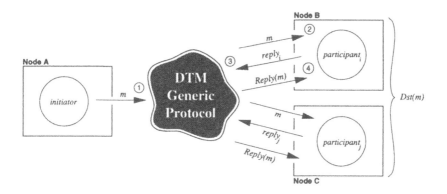

Fig. 2. DTM generic protocol

cannot be satisfied, the protocol will block. The reliability property of the DTM generic protocol lies in the fact that it will not *necessarily* block if one or more participants fail[4]: it depends on the chosen *validity condition*. The *Reply(m)* set received by all non-faulty participants might simply lack the replies of faulty participants. It is necessary to be able to express such a condition, since participants might fail and the *Reply(m)* set might have a contents that does not permit to take any satisfactory "decision" (e.g., *Reply(m)* could be trivially empty). An example of validity condition is the *majority condition*, that can be expressed as $|Reply(m)| > |Dst(m)|/2$, i.e., it requires a majority of non-faulty participants for the protocol not to block. Details on how those generic dimensions can be tailored to fit the needs of specific problems are given in sections 4 and 5.

4 DTM generic protocol classes

4.1 Classes Initiator and Participant

In BAST, system programmers wanting to use the DTM generic protocol have essentially to deal with two classes, the Initiator protocol class and the Participant abstract protocol class, which are subclassed when customizing the DTM generic protocol. Instances of those subclasses will play the role of the *initiator*, respectively the *participant*, as defined in section 3.2. According to our system model, initiators and participants objects are able to perform message passing (see section 3.1). Figure 3 presents what objects and operations are involved while the protocol is executing: fat arrows picture operation invocations on objects, bullet-arrows ($\leftarrow\bullet$) represent objects resulting from invocations, and numbers in circles show in what order invocations occur. Not surprisingly, figure 3 is very similar to figure 2.

---

[4] The DTM protocol is based on (possibly unreliable) failure detectors to determine if an object is faulty or not.

Objects executing the DTM protocol The protocol starts by the invocation of dtmcast() of an initiator object, passing it a message m, a set of remote participants objects $Dst(m)$ and a *validity condition*; this invocation results in a reliable multicast to the set of participants. When message m reaches some *participant$_k$*, the latter is invoked by the protocol through the receive() operation, taking m as argument. In turn, *participant$_k$* computes and returns its *reply$_k$*. Eventually, each non-faulty participant is invoked through the interpret() operation with the $Reply(m)$ set, on which consensus has been reached, as argument. So, as long as interpret() implements a deterministic algorithm, all participants will take the same "decision". Operations receive() and interpret() are invoked through callbacks by the DTM protocol.

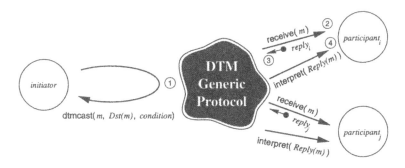

Fig. 3. Objects executing the DTM generic protocol

4.2 Generic dimensions

Since DTM is a generic protocol, one has to *instantiate*[5] it in order to solve some particular problem. To achieve this, one has to define the semantics of each *generic dimension* of the protocol. As we shall see, this can be done in many ways, depending on which dimension is considered, e.g., by deriving some class and redefining its operations, by creating an object of some class and passing it as argument to some operation involved in the protocol, etc. There are five generic dimensions to consider when instantiating the DTM generic protocol : (1) the semantics of message m, (2) the set $Dst(m)$ of participant objects to whom m is multicast, (3) the *validity condition*, (4) the semantics of *reply$_k$* generated by each participant, (5) the *interpretation* of the set of replies $Reply(m)$ on which objects in $Dst(m)$ agree.

We are now going to detail each of those generic dimensions and show how they can be used. Figure 4 presents the DTM protocol classes and their main operations, while figure 5 summarizes how generic dimensions are expressed using those classes.

---

[5] In this context, the verb "to instantiate" does not mean "to create an instance of some class", as in the object-oriented paradigm, but to "customize the DTM generic protocol".

Semantics of message m Class Initiator defines operation dtmcast(). The first argument of dtmcast() is an instance of some subclass of abstract class **Message**, which implements the generic message m. When instantiating DTM, one has typically to subclass the **Message** class to make it support the adequate semantics.

Set $Dst(m)$ of participants Generic dimension $Dst(m)$ (the set of participants) is implemented by the second parameter of operation dtmcast() and it is merely an instance of some **Set** class. This set contains remote object references, i.e., instances of class **MPObjectRef** provided by the *message passing service*. Those references are used in communications primitives to designate remote objects. Further details are given in section 6, which presents an overview of our first implementation, in particular by presenting the foundation classes of our message passing service. Neither **Set**, nor **MPObjectRef** are usually subclassed when instantiating DTM.

Validity condition The third parameter of dtmcast() is an instance of some subclass of abstract class **Condition**, which implements the generic *validity condition*. When subclassing **Condition**, one has to provide an implementation for its test() operation[6], which must yield true if the condition is satisfied and false otherwise. As for receive() and interpret(), operation test() is invoked by the protocol through a callback. This generic dimension is closely related to object failures and is at the heart of reliability issues. Its semantics and its use are detailed in section 4.3.

Semantics of $reply_k$ and interpretation of set $Reply(m)$ Class Participant is an abstract class which declares two unimplemented operations, receive() and interpret(); it is up to subclasses of Participant to provide their implementations. Operation receive() must return an instance of some subclass of abstract class Reply, which implements the semantics of the generic $reply_k$ each participant yields when invoked by the protocol. So, to instantiate generic dimension $reply_k$, one has to subclass Reply and to provide an implementation of receive() that yields an instance of that subclass. Operation interpret() must implement the generic *interpretation* of set $Reply(m)$. The latter set is passed by the DTM protocol to each participant as an object of some Set class, through the argument of interpret().

4.3 Validity conditions and object failures

The validity condition is tested while the DTM protocol is collecting participants' replies, and is at the heart of reliability issues. When invoked by the protocol, operation test() receives three sets as arguments: $Dst(m)$, $Reply(m)$ and $Suspect(m)$, a subset of $Dst(m)$. The latter contains objects of $Dst(m)$ that

---

[6] Operation test() is marked as *unimplemented* in class Condition.

Classes		Predefined Operations	
Initiator		dtmcast (m, $Dst(m)$, *condition*)	
Participant	*(abstract)*	receive (m) interpret ($Reply(m)$)	*(unimplemented)* *(unimplemented)*
Message	*(abstract)*	*none*	
Reply	*(abstract)*	*none*	
Condition	*(abstract)*	test ($Dst(m)$, $Reply(m)$, $Suspect(m)$)	*(unimplemented)*

Fig. 4. Classes implementing the DTM generic protocol

are *suspected* to be faulty. Set $Suspect(m)$ is necessary for instances of the DTM generic protocol where failures have to be considered in the agreement process, i.e., when the condition on $Reply(m)$ is expressed in terms of object failures.

Examples of validity conditions are given in sections 5.1 and 5.2, which present how DTM can be used to build an atomic commitment protocol and a reliable total order multicast protocol respectively. In the atomic commitment protocol presented there, the validity condition can be expressed as follow: $\forall object_k \in Dst(m) : reply_k \notin Reply(m) \Rightarrow object_k \in Suspect(m)$. That predicate expresses the fact that the atomic commitment can only terminate when the replies of all *non-suspected* participants are in $Reply(m)$.

Generic Dimensions	Instantiation done by ...
Semantics of m	subclassing class **Message** + passing an instance of **Message**'s subclass to operation **dtmcast()** of the **Initiator** subclass
Set $Dst(m)$	building a **Set** of **MPObjectRefs** + passing it to operation **dtmcast()** of the **Initiator** subclass
Semantics of $reply_k$	subclassing class **Reply** + implementing operation **receive()** of the **Participant** subclass + returning an instance of **Reply**'s subclass in operation **receive()**
Validity *condition*	subclassing class **Condition** + implementing its **test()** operation + passing an instance of **Condition**'s subclass to operation **dtmcast()** of the **Initiator** subclass
Interpretation of $Reply(m)$	implementing operation **interpret()** of the **Participant** subclass

Fig. 5. Instantiation of DTM generic dimensions

5 DTM generic protocol classes in action

We are now going to show how the generic protocol classes presented in section 4 can be customized to define higher-level abstractions for building reliable distributed environments. We will focus here on two elementary abstractions based on distributed protocols: the *reliable total order multicast* and the *atomic commitment*. As we show, both can be implemented as instances of the DTM generic protocol.

5.1 Atomic commitment

Overview of the problem The *atomic commitment problem* requires that participants in a transaction agree on *commit* or *abort* at the end of the transaction. If participants can fail and we still want all correct participants to agree, the problem is known as the *non-blocking* atomic commitment (NB-AC) [3]. In that case, the agreement should be commit if and only if all participants vote *yes* and if no participant fails. It has been proved that this problem cannot be solved in asynchronous systems with unreliable failure detectors [13]. This lead to specify a weaker problem: the non-blocking *weak* atomic commitment (NB-WAC), which requires merely that no participant is *ever suspected*. Because the DTM generic protocol makes no assumption on the properties of the failure detector it uses, both the NB-AC and the NB-WAC problems can be seen as instances of DTM, depending on the failure detector considered.

Protocol classes solving the atomic commitment To solve the atomic commitment problem using the DTM generic protocol, Initiator is subclassed into some Transaction class and Participant into some Manager class. Class Transaction defines two new operations: begin() and end(), while class Manager implements inherited operations receive() and interpret(). When a Transaction object is created, it is initialized with a set of MPObjectRef instances, which is stored into instance variable managerSet. Those remote object references designate the managers that will be accessed during the transaction. Operations begin() and end() initiate and terminate an atomic sequence of operations respectively; both operations are invoked by the client of the transaction.

When agreement on commit or abort is reached, each manager applies the decision to the data object under its responsibility; it does so by invoking operation apply() on itself. Data objects are held in instance variable dataObject, defined by class Manager. Each Manager object also has a currentManagerSet instance variable, which contains the manager set of the transaction to which that object currently belongs[7]. Figure 6 gives an overview of the atomic commitment protocol based on DTM; as in figure 3, arrows represent invocations on objects, while numbers in circles show in what order invocations occur. In figure 7, operations and variables defined by protocol classes Transaction and Manager are presented; we do not detail secondary classes there.

We now going to sketch how objects interact while the atomic commitment protocol is executing. Figure 8 presents the implementation main operations involved. The pseudo-code used there is very simple: statements are separated by symbol ";", variables are untyped and declared as in "|| voteReq ||", the assignment symbol is "←", and the value returned by an operation is preceded by symbol "↑".

---

[7] We are not interested in the problem of concurrently accessed managers here. However, for simplicity sakes class Manager defines only one currentManagerSet, so concurrency control has to be *pessimistic*, i.e., achieved by locking managers before starting a transaction. In order to avoid dead-locks, the locking phase could be based on the reliable total order multicast protocol presented in section 5.2 (see [14] for details).

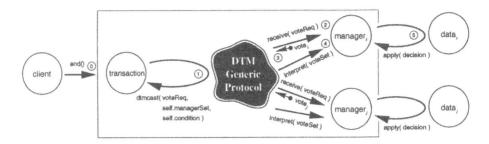

Fig. 6. Overview of the atomic commitment protocol with DTM

Class Transaction	Class Manager
public operations	*public operations*
begin (managerSet);	receive (voteReq);
end ();	interpret (voteSet);
instance variables	*private operation*
managerSet;	apply ();
condition;	*instance variables*
	dataObject;
	currentManagerSet;

Fig. 7. Protocol classes for the atomic commitment

On the initiator side When a client wants to terminate an atomic sequence of operations on distinct remote objects, it invokes the **end()** operation on the corresponding transaction object (see figure 8 (a)). Operation **end()** first creates a **VoteRequest** message, and stores it in a local variable **voteReq**. Class **VoteRequest** inherits from class **Message** and defines new instance variable **managerSet**. After operation **end()** has created message **voteReq**, it initializes member **voteReq.managerSet** with the transaction's manager set[8] (self.**managerSet**). Then, operation **end()** starts the atomic commitment protocol by invoking inherited operation dtmcast(). Generic set $Dst(m)$ and the generic *validity condition*, passed to dtmcast() as second and third arguments respectively, are Transaction's instance variables self.**managerSet** and self.**condition**. Variable self.**condition** contains an instance of a class **ACCondition**, derived from class **Condition**. Class **ACCondition** defines operation **test()** (see figure 8 (b)), which implements the validity condition for the atomic commitment problem. As mentioned in section 4.3, that condition is expressed in terms of manager failures. The same condition is suitable for the *NB-AC* problem and for the *NB-WAC* problem, since it all depends on the failure detector the DTM protocol is using. Predicate $\forall manager_k \in Dst(m) : reply_k \notin Reply(m) \Rightarrow manager_k \in Suspect(m)$, already discussed in section 4.3, is implemented by operation **test()**.

---

[8] That set was initialized through operation begin(), by the client of the transaction.

```
end ( )                                      receive ( voteReq )
  || voteReq ||                                || vote ||
  voteReq ← VoteRequest.new();                 self.currentManagerSet ← voteReq.managerSet;
  voteReq.managerSet ← self.managerSet;        vote ← self.vote ( voteReq );
  self.dtmcast( voteReq,                       ↑ vote;
             self.managerSet,                                                        (c)
             self.condition );                                                       (d)
                                         (a)  interpret ( voteSet )
                                         (b)    || decision ||
test ( managerSet, voteSet, suspectSet )         if  | voteSet | = | self.currentManagerSet |  then
  || predicate ||                                  decision ← commit ;
  predicate ← true ;                               foreach  vote ∈ voteSet  do
  foreach  manager_k ∈ managerSet  do                if  vote = no  then
    if  vote_k ∈ voteSet ∧ manager_k ∉ suspectSet  then    decision ← abort ;
      predicate ← false ;                          else
  ↑ predicate;                                       decision ← abort ;
                                                 self.apply ( decision );
```

Fig. 8. Implementation of the atomic commitment

On the participant side When message voteReq reaches a Manager object, operation receive() first puts voteReq.managerSet in its currentManagerSet instance variable (see figure 8 (c)); it then computes its vote (*yes* or *no*) and returns it to the DTM generic protocol. The vote is an instance of class Vote, which derives from class Reply and implements generic $reply_k$. The DTM protocol then collects the votes of all non-faulty managers and put them into voteSet, a set implementing the generic $Reply(m)$ set. During the collecting phase, the ACCondition object may be tested several times. Eventually, operation test() returns *true* and the DTM protocol invokes each (non-faulty) manager through operation interpret() and passes it voteSet, on which agreement has been reached. Operation interpret() then computes the final decision, which is *commit* only if all votes in voteSet are *yes* and if no manager was suspected (see figure 8 (d)). This last point is tested by Manager objects by comparing the size of voteSet with the size of their currentManagerSet; if both have the same size, it means that no manager was suspected by the DTM generic protocol. The decision is finally applied to the data object by invoking the apply() operation, which undertakes the appropriate actions.

5.2 Reliable total order multicast

Overview of the problem The *reliable total order multicast* problem can be specified by two primitives, *TO-multicast(m, Dst(m))* and *TO-deliver(m)*, and by a set of conditions on those primitives. Those conditions express that consistency and liveness must preserved despite object failures, and that if more than one object are in the intersection of several different $Dst(m)$ sets, they must all perform the corresponding *TO-deliver()* in the same order. Note that we are not talking of some broadcast primitive here: the *TO-multicast(m, Dst(m))* primitive requires the destination set $Dst(m)$ to be explicitly specified and that set can be different for each invocation[9]. This is why the order condition is expressed in terms of several $Dst(m)$ sets. A formal definition of the total order multicast problem can be found in [26]

The reliable total order multicast protocol that we present below has been described and proved elsewhere [26], without using the DTM generic protocol. To our knowledge, it is the first algorithm capable of solving total order multicast problem in a distributed system with *unreliable* failure detectors. Since it is quite a complex protocol, we first present it independently of its implementation as an instance of the DTM generic protocol.

Overview of the protocol The basic idea of the algorithm is to have each object in $Dst(m)$ to propose a time-stamp for message m, and to reach an agreement on the maximum of those time-stamps; the latter is then used as sequence number for message m, and messages are delivered according to their sequence numbers. Time-stamps are based on *Lamport's logical clocks* [16]. So, when object o receives message m, it sends its current logical clock value as proposed time-stamp to all other objects in $Dst(m)$. It then stores m in a queue of *pending messages*, i.e., all messages in that queue do not have their sequence number computed yet. When agreement is reached on m's sequence number, object o moves m from the queue of pending messages to a queue of *delivery messages*, i.e., all messages in that queue do have their associated sequence number but have not been delivered yet. Finally, object o performs $TO\text{-}deliver(m)$ for each message m in the delivery queue which sequence number is smaller than the proposed time-stamps of all messages in the pending queue.

Three additional conditions have to be fulfilled for the protocol to work: (1) *causal order* delivery must be ensured for all messages exchanged in the algorithm; (2) each logical object o in $Dst(m)$ has to be replicated and its replication rate must be such that there is always a majority of correct replicas of o in the system; (3) the sequence number has to be the maximum of the time-stamps that have been proposed by a *qualified majority* of replica objects in $Dst(m)$.

Condition (2) leads $Dst(m)$ to contain groups of objects (replicas) rather that individual objects, each group gathering the replicas of one logical object. The notion of group is used here merely as a *naming facility*, i.e., no group membership protocol (as in Isis [4]) is necessary for the algorithm to be correct[10]. The qualified majority of $Dst(m)$ is a set of objects that contains a majority of replicas of *every group* in $Dst(m)$. So, condition (3) can be expressed as the following predicate: $\forall g \in Dst(m) : |tsSet_g| > \frac{1}{2} \times |g|$, where $tsSet_g$ is the set of time-stamps proposed by replica objects in group g, when m's sequence number is computed. It is beyond the scope of this paper to explain why those additional conditions are necessary; details can be found in [26].

---

[9] In a broadcast primitive, the destination set is implicit and contains every object of the system, i.e., $Dst(m) = \Omega$.

[10] In this context, we interpret "*object $o \in Dst(m)$*" as "*object $o \in$ group $g \wedge$ group $g \in Dst(m)$*".

Protocol classes solving the reliable total order multicast To implement the total order multicast protocol presented above, using the DTM generic protocol, we subclass both the Initiator and Participant classes. Class MulticastService is a subclass of Initiator and its instances represent the *reliable multicast service* to client objects. This service offers several reliable multicast primitives, implementing various ordering semantics, e.g., fifo order, causal order, total order. Class MulticastService defines new operation toMcast(), which implements the total order multicast primitive *TO-multicast()* defined previously. Class Replica is a subclass of Participant and it implements new operation toDeliver(), as well as inherited operations receive() and interpret(). Operations toDeliver() implements the *TO-deliver()* primitive defined above. Instances of Replica represent object replicas to the multicast service: they are in charge of computing a sequence number for each received message and reordering messages accordingly. The actual replicated server object (to which messages are finally delivered) is held in instance variable serverObject, defined by class Replica. So, when a Replica object invokes operation toDeliver() on itself, the message passed as argument is delivered to the server object, with the guaranty that total order is satisfied. Figure 9 presents an overview of the total order multicast based on the DTM generic protocol; in that figure, objects replica$_i$ and replica$_j$ are *a priori* members of different groups.

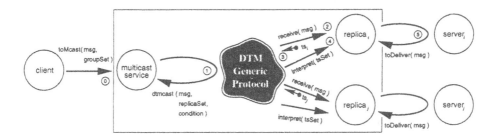

Fig. 9. Overview of the total order multicast protocol with DTM

We now going to sketch how objects interact while the total order multicast protocol is executing. Figure 11 presents the implementation main operations involved; the pseudo-code is the same as in figure 8

On the initiator side When a client object wants to issue a total order multicast to set of replicated logical objects, it first has to build a set of groups, each group containing the replicas' remote object references of one logical object. The client then invokes operation toMcast() on an instance of MulticastService, and passes it two arguments: msg, an instance of class TOMessage, and groupSet, the set of groups it just built. Operation toMcast() is implemented as follow (see figure 11 (a)): all groups of replicas are *merged* into replicaSet, a single set of remote object references; a validity condition is then created as an instance of class TOCondition; finally the invocation of dtmcast() is issued, with

```
Class MulticastService
    public operation
        toMcast ( msg, groupSet );
```

```
Class Replica
    public operations
        receive ( msg );
        interpret ( tsSet );
    private operations
        extractMsg ( tsSet );
        maxTimeStamp ( tsSet );
    instance variables
        lamportClock;
        serverObject;
        pendingQueue;
        deliveryQueue;
```

Fig. 10. Protocol classes for the reliable total order multicast

msg, replicaSet and condition as arguments. Class **TOMessage** is a subclass of Message and defines new instance variable ts; member msg.ts is used by each Replica object to hold its proposed time-stamp when msg is stored in the pending queue, and msg's sequence number when it is stored in the delivery queue. The pending queue and the delivery queue are held in Replica's instance variables pendingQueue and deliveryQueue respectively. Class TOCondition implements the validity condition of the total order multicast protocol, i.e., its test() operation evaluates the third condition presented earlier, based of the notion of qualified majority. In that condition, $Dst(m)$ contains groups of objects rather than individual objects. So, TOCondition's implementation of test() simply ignores the first argument passed to it by the DTM generic protocol[11] (see figure 11 (b)). Instance variable groupSet is used instead, which holds the set of groups that was passed to operation toMcast() by the client. Private operation select(), defined by class TOCondition, extracts from tsSet the proposed time-stamps of a particular group and puts them in a new set.

On the participant side When message msg reaches a Replica object, operation receive() updates its Lamport's clock, sets msg.ts to the updated logical time and stores msg in the pendingQueue (see figure 11 (c)). It then returns msg.ts to the DTM protocol. Member msg.ts contains an instance of class TimeStamp, which derives from class Reply and implements generic $reply_k$. The DTM protocol then collects time-stamps and put them into tsSet, a set implementing the generic $Reply(m)$. During the collecting phase, the TOCondition object may be tested several times. Eventually, operation test() returns *true* and the DTM protocol invokes each (non-faulty) replica through operation interpret() and passes it tsSet on which agreement has been reached. Operation interpret() then computes msg's sequence number, moves msg from the pendingQueue to the deliveryQueue, and performs toDeliver() for all messages that have been made *deliverable* by the newly computed sequence number (see figure 11 (d)). Operation interpret()

---

[11] First argument of test() contains the set of participants to the DTM generic protocol, i.e., Replica objects in that case, not groups.

```
toMcast ( msg, groupSet )                        receive ( msg )
   || replicaSet condition ||                        || ts ||
   replicaSet ← ⋃ group                              ts ← self.lamportClock.update( msg );
              group ∈ groupSet
   condition ← TOCondition.new();                     msg.ts ← ts;
   condition.groupSet ← groupSet;                      self.pendingQueue.add( msg );
   self.dtmcast( msg,                                  ↑ ts
              replicaSet,                                                              (c)
              condition );                                                             (d)
                                          (a)   interpret ( tsSet )
                                          (b)      || msg ||
test ( replicaSet, tsSet, suspectSet )             msg ← self.extractMsg( tsSet );
   || predicate ||                                  msg.ts ← self.maxTimeStamp( tsSet );
   predicate ← true ;                               self.pendingQueue.remove( msg );
   foreach group ∈ self.groupSet do                 self.deliveryQueue.add( msg );
      if | self.select( tsSet, group ) | ≤ ½ × | group| then   foreach m_d ∈ self.deliveryQueue do
         predicate ← false ;                             if ∀m_p ∈ self.pendingQueue : m_p.ts > m_d.ts  then
   ↑ predicate;                                             self.toDeliver( m_d );
                                                            self.deliveryQueue.remove( m_d );
```

Fig. 11. Implementation of the reliable total order multicast

relies on private operations extractMsg() and maxTimeStamp(), defined by class Replica. Those two operations allow to get the message associated to tsSet, and to compute the maximum time-stamp in tsSet respectively.

6 Design and implementation

6.1 Current prototype of the BAST class library

Our current prototype of the BAST library of protocol classes was implemented using the *Smalltalk* language and environment [10]. More specifically, we used VisualWorks, the commercial Smalltalk platform by ParcPlace Systems, Inc. The development took place on a network of Sun SPARCstations running the Solaris 2.4 operating system. Everything is an object in BAST, and Smalltalk was well-suited to support such an approach. As shown in figure 1, BAST is based on a *layered architecture* and provides various services, each of which corresponds to a particular protocol.

6.2 Inside the DTM generic protocol

In previous sections, we have presented the *public interfaces* of the DTM protocol classes, and how to use them. We are now going to "open" the DTM generic protocol, by presenting the "hidden face" of classes Initiator and Participant, i.e., how they implement DTM and on what other protocol classes they rely to do this.

The nature of the DTM protocol suggests that Participant objects have to be able to solve the *distributed consensus problem*, since they have to reach an agreement on the generic $Reply(m)$ (interpreted at the end of the protocol).

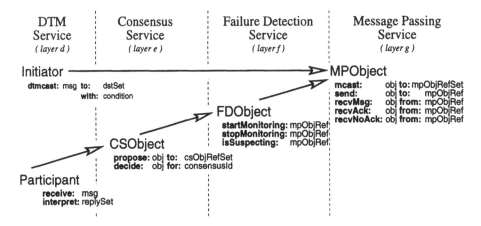

Fig. 12. BAST's protocol class hierarchy

Furthermore, if Participant objects were not able to detect (reliably or not) their faulty peers, the failure of a single participant would lead the protocol to block. This suggests that Participant objects must be able to monitor and to *suspect* each others. Finally, while the DTM generic protocol is executing, distant objects exchange messages, so Initiator and Participant objects should be capable of performing *message passing*.

Those considerations lead us to design the *class hierarchy* presented in figure 12, where arrows represent *"is subclass of"* relationships. In this hierarchy, classes are *protocol classes* as defined previously, that is, they implement objects that are capable of executing a particular protocol. Apart from DTM, all services of figure 12 are based on protocols with *symmetric roles*, so a single class is defined *per protocol*. In this figure, only *new* operations defined by each class are represented, e.g., class FDObject refines operation recvAck:from: but we only placed that operation under class MPObject. Private/secondary operations and classes are not represented. Each service in figure 12 corresponds to a layer in figure 1. Below, we detail classes that support the protocols corresponding to those services; the presentation order follows a bottom-up approach. Figures 13 and 14 present the interfaces of those protocol classes; for each class, we list newly defined operations, as well as inherited ones that are refined.

Message passing service Smalltalk does not provide support for distributed objects, so we implemented the foundation for distant objects to be able to send messages to each others: *the message passing service*. This service is the base of all other distributed protocols and defines two classes: MPObject and MPObjectRef. Instances of MPObject represent *remote objects* that are capable of executing *the message passing protocol*, i.e., they know how send (and receive) any object obj to (from) each others. Sending achieved by executing either operation send:to: or mcast:to:, while receiving in performed through a callback to recvMsg:from: by the message passing service. Because communications are *reliable*, callbacks to operations recvAck:from: and recvNoAck:from: are also per-

Class MPObject	Class FDObject	Class CSObject
instance operations	*instance operations*	*instance operations*
send:to:	startMonitoring:	propose:to:
mcast:to:	stopMonitoring:	decide:for:
recvMsg:from:	isSuspecting:	recvMsg:from:
recvAck:from:	recvMsg:from:	recvAck:from:
recvNoAck:from:	recvAck:from:	recvNoAck:from:
class operations	recvNoAck:from:	*class operations*
dispatchMsg:to:	*class operations*	dispatchMsg:to:
dispatchAck:to:	dispatchMsg:to:	*instance variable*
dispatchNoAck:to:	dispatchAck:to:	currentConsensusSet
	dispatchNoAck:to:	
	instance variable	
	suspectSet	

Fig. 13. Protocol classes MPObject, FDObject and CSObject

formed by the protocol when necessary; class **MPObject** implements those operations so they do nothing. Instances of **MPObjectRef** are used to designate remote objects and are passed as arguments to communication operations.

Reliable communications are implemented through *timeouts* and possible *retransmissions*. This task is managed by *private* class **MessagePassing**, which represent the message passing service on each node[12]; callbacks on **MPObject** are triggered by this class. To implement reliable communications, class **MessagePassing** relies on a low-level layer written in C: *the Reliable Communication Layer*[13] (*RCL*), developed in the context of the *Phoenix* project. This layer is built on top of the UDP protocol and adds reliability to it. This approach has the advantage to improve performance, since low-level message management, such as message packing and retransmitting, duplicated messages filtering, etc., is done in C. Furthermore, we are currently integrating RCL into Solaris 2.4 kernel, which should make the communication even faster.

On each node, class **MessagePassing** opens a UDP port used to send (and receive) messages to (from) others nodes. The mapping between local **MPObject** instances and the node where they can be found is managed by the **MessagePassing** class on that node. However, the dispatching of incoming messages is delegated by class **MessagePassing** to the class of the target object, e.g, if a message is addressed to some FDObject, then it is up to class FDObject to dispatch it. In order to do this, class **MPObject** defines *class operations* dispatchMsg:to:, dispatchAck:to: and dispatchNoAck:to:, which can be redefined by its subclasses. As we shall see in next paragraph, this mechanism is useful for example when common actions have to be undertaken for all instances of some subclass of **MPObject**, each time a message arrives on the node. Class **MessagePassing** is

---

[12] As said in section 3, different nodes imply different *address spaces*. In Smalltalk, this means that a node corresponds to an execution of the *Smalltalk virtual machine*.

[13] The VisualWorks environment provides powerful facilities that enable to *dynamically link* C libraries to the Smalltalk virtual machine, and then to call C functions from those libraries within Smalltalk code.

also responsible for marshaling and unmarshaling objects sent through RCL; this is done by using the *Binary Object Storage Service* (*BOSS*) provided by the VisualWorks environment.

Failure detection service In our approach, object failures are dealt with by *failure detectors*, and in BAST, this concept is supported by the *failure detection service*. This service is based on FDObject, a subclass of MPObject which implements the behavior of objects capable of executing *the failure detection protocol*. Each instance of FDObject manages suspectSet, a private set containing the MPObjectRef of every remote object it is currently suspecting. Class FDObject redefines operations recvMsg:from:, recvAck:from: and recvNoAck:from: so they adequately add or remove the MPObjectRef passed to them by the failure detection protocol. This class also implements new operations startMonitoring:, stopMonitoring: and isSuspecting:. The first two operations can be used to start and stop "pinging" a remote object respectively. Operation isSuspecting: returns true if the invoked FDObject is currently suspecting the remote object which reference is passed as argument.

In our first prototype of BAST, we made the assumption that objects on the same node do not fail *separately*, i.e., we only consider failures of Smalltalk virtual machines, not of individual objects. This is fairly reasonable, since we only consider *crash failures*: it makes little sense having one object to crash while others on the same node (i.e., on the same address space) don't. As a consequence, whenever a message is received on node A from a remote object located on node B, all objects on node A that are suspecting some object located on node B should stop doing so. Similarly, when an object on node B is no more reachable by some object on node A, all objects on node A that interested in some object located on node B should add it in their private suspectSet. The dispatching of suspicion additions and removals is performed by class FDObject, through its class operations dispatchMsg:to:, dispatchAck:to: and dispatchNoAck:to:.

Consensus service Agreement is a central problem of many reliable distributed protocols, in particular all those that can be viewed as instances of the DTM generic protocol. In BAST, support for solving the agreement problem is provided by *the consensus service*, which implements the $\diamond S$-consensus protocol proposed by Chandra and Toueg [8]. That protocol enables objects to reach agreement despite failures, in asynchronous systems augmented with *unreliable* failure detectors of class $\diamond S$ (see [8] for further details on the classification of failure detectors).

Our consensus service relies on CSObject, a subclass of FDObject which implements the behavior of objects that can execute the aforesaid consensus protocol. In the $\diamond S$-consensus protocol, objects executing the consensus protocol must be able to *suspect* each others; this is why a CSObject is also an FDObject. When a consensus protocol begins, each CSObject involved in it starts monitoring its peers, by calling operation startMonitoring: inherited from class FDObject.

A CSObject o_i stops monitoring another CSObject o_j, as soon as all executions of the consensus protocol involving both o_i and o_j terminate. This is done by invoking operation stopMonitoring:, inherited from class FDObject.

Instances of CSObject are capable of running more than one execution of the consensus protocol simultaneously, and they can propose *any* object as agreement value. Class CSObject defines new operations propose:to: and decide:for:. When a CSObject is invoked through operation propose:to:, a new execution of the consensus protocol starts for that object. As first argument, operation propose:to: takes *any* object and proposes it as its agreement value to all consensus objects referenced in its second argument, set csObjRefSet. Internally, a *unique* identifier is associated to that particular execution of the consensus. When an agreement is reached, class CSObject on each non-faulty node eventually receives the decision message and has to *dispatch* it to all local object(s) involved in that execution of the protocol. Instead of calling operation recvMsg:from: on the concerned object(s), operation dispatchMsg:to: performs a callback to decide:for: on them. First argument of decide:for: is the object on which agreement has been reached, while second argument is the identifier associated to that execution of the consensus protocol.

Class Initiator
    instance operation
        dtmcast:to:with:

Class Participant
    instance operations   *instance operations (continued)*
        dtmProtocolFor: collecReplies
        storeDstSetOf:as: stopCollecReplies
        getDstSetOf: waitForDecision
        storeCollectSetOf:as: dtmIdsConcernedBy:
        getCollectSetOf: recvMsg:from:
        storeValidityCondOf:as: recvAck:from:
        getValidityCondOf: recvNoAck:from:

Fig. 14. Protocol classes Initiator and Participant

DTM service We are now ready to look at the implementation of DTM protocol classes Initiator and Participant. Those classes mostly rely on inherited operations from their superclasses. Initiator and Participant's interfaces are summarized in figure 14, while figure 15 presents the Smalltalk code of the three main operations involved in the DTM generic protocol, i.e., dtmProtocolFor:, recvMsg:from:, and recvNoAck:from:. Those operations are defined by class Participant.

Class Initiator derives from MPObject, the class at the top of our hierarchy. Its implementation of operation dtmcast:to:with: directly relies on inherited operation mcast:to:. When invoked, operation dtmcast:to:with: initializes *private fields* of its first argument msg, an instance of a Message's subclass. It then multicasts msg to dstSet, the set of participants passed to it as second argument. Class

Message defines three private fields: dtmId, an identifier used to distinguish different execution of the DTM protocol, vCond, the validity condition, and dstSet, the set of participants to the protocol. Those informations are initialized using arguments passed to dtmcast:to:with:.

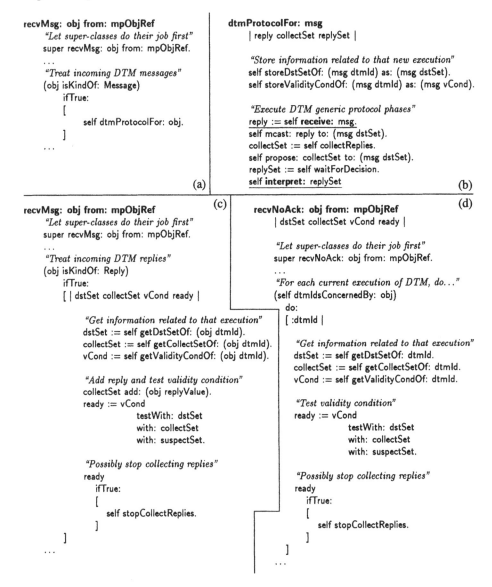

```
recvMsg: obj from: mpObjRef
    "Let super-classes do their job first"
    super recvMsg: obj from: mpObjRef.
    ...
    "Treat incoming DTM messages"
    (obj isKindOf: Message)
        ifTrue:
        [
            self dtmProtocolFor: obj.
        ]
    ...
                                                (a)
```

```
dtmProtocolFor: msg
    | reply collectSet replySet |

    "Store information related to that new execution"
    self storeDstSetOf: (msg dtmId) as: (msg dstSet).
    self storeValidityCondOf: (msg dtmId) as: (msg vCond).

    "Execute DTM generic protocol phases"
    reply := self receive: msg.
    self mcast: reply to: (msg dstSet).
    collectSet := self collectReplies.
    self propose: collectSet to: (msg dstSet).
    replySet := self waitForDecision.
    self interpret: replySet
                                                (b)
```

```
recvMsg: obj from: mpObjRef                     (c)
    "Let super-classes do their job first"
    super recvMsg: obj from: mpObjRef.
    ...
    "Treat incoming DTM replies"
    (obj isKindOf: Reply)
        ifTrue:
        [ | dstSet collectSet vCond ready |

            "Get information related to that execution"
            dstSet := self getDstSetOf: (obj dtmId).
            collectSet := self getCollectSetOf: (obj dtmId).
            vCond := self getValidityCondOf: (obj dtmId).

            "Add reply and test validity condition"
            collectSet add: (obj replyValue).
            ready := vCond
                        testWith: dstSet
                        with: collectSet
                        with: suspectSet.

            "Possibly stop collecting replies"
            ready
                ifTrue:
                [
                    self stopCollectReplies.
                ]
        ]
    ...
```

```
recvNoAck: obj from: mpObjRef                   (d)
    | dstSet collectSet vCond ready |

    "Let super-classes do their job first"
    super recvNoAck: obj from: mpObjRef.
    ...
    "For each current execution of DTM, do..."
    (self dtmIdsConcernedBy: obj)
        do:
        [ :dtmId |

            "Get information related to that execution"
            dstSet := self getDstSetOf: dtmId.
            collectSet := self getCollectSetOf: dtmId.
            vCond := self getValidityCondOf: dtmId.

            "Test validity condition"
            ready := vCond
                        testWith: dstSet
                        with: collectSet
                        with: suspectSet.

            "Possibly stop collecting replies"
            ready
                ifTrue:
                [
                    self stopCollectReplies.
                ]
        ]
    ...
```

Fig. 15. Smalltalk implementation of the DTM generic protocol

Since DTM involves the execution of the consensus protocol, **Participant** is a subclass of **CSObject**. When msg reaches a node, the local message passing service invokes the target participant through operation recvMsg:from:. The participant then invokes operation dtmProtocolFor: on itself, passing it msg (see figure 15 (a)). This call starts the DTM generic protocol, which has its various phases implemented through operation invocations in dtmProtocolFor: (see figure 15 (b)). The latter starts by storing informations related to that new execution of DTM and then invokes operation receive: with argument msg. Remember that operation receive: is implemented differently by each subclass of Participant, and that it returns reply, an instance of some Reply's subclass. Object reply is then sent to all objects referenced in msg's dstSet. Operation collectReplies is then invoked, and blocks until the validity condition associated to msg is satisfied. This condition is re-tested each time a *reply* or a *negative acknowledgment* (no ack) is received by the participant (see figures 15 (c) and (d)). There might be more than one execution of the DTM protocol that is concerned by an incoming *no ack*. Operation dtmIdsConcernedBy: returns a set containing the dtmId of each execution that should have its validity condition re-tested.

Eventually, the call to collectReplies returns and operation propose:to: is invoked with initSet, the set of collected replies, and msg's dstSet as arguments. The invocation of operation propose:to:, inherited from class CSObject, starts the $\diamond S$-consensus protocol; this call is non-blocking. By invoking waitForDecision, operation dtmProtocolFor: blocks until the consensus terminates. When operation waitForDecision returns, it yields replySet, the set of replies on which agreement has been reached. Finally, the protocol invokes operation interpret:, which implementation is delegated to subclasses of Participant, and passes it replySet as argument. This call concludes the execution of the DTM generic protocol. In figure 15 (b), we emphasized the two operations that enable to customize the DTM generic protocol, i.e., operations receive: and interpret:.

7 Related work

7.1 Distributed programming abstractions

Although not applied to the same research domain, our approach is similar to those of [18, 6, 7], in that the main objective is to define the basic generic abstractions for building a modular distributed environment. In the BAST library of protocol classes, we are concerned with building distributed agreement protocols, while [18] focuses on concurrent programming and [6, 7] focus on persistence storage and distributed object communication and execution.

O.L Madsen has presented in [18] a library of classes representing high-level abstractions for concurrent programming, such as *Rendez-Vous* and *Monitors*. Those abstractions are built on top of the lower level *Semaphore* abstraction. Following the same approach, BETA, described by S. Brandt and O.L Madsen in [6], is a set of "mandatory" abstractions to support distributed object execution, and remote object invocation. Among these abstractions are: *Ensemble*, representing a physical network node, *Shell*, representing a self-contained program module, and *NameServer*, providing a mapping between textual names and object references. CHOICES [7] is an example of a class library representing a distributed operating system. Traditional elements of operating systems, such as *Process*, *Domain* or *Disk*, are implemented as classes with well-defined interfaces. One can then customize the operating system, through inheritance, in order to match particular application needs.

7.2 Transactional libraries

D. McCue has presented a class library which enables to attach persistence and transactional features to application objects [19]. An interesting aspect of the library is the orthogonality of characteristics: (1) an object is persistent if its class inherits from class *Persistent*, (2) an object has a dedicated concurrency control if its class inherits from class *Concurrency-Controlled*, and (3) an object is recoverable if its class inherits from class *Recoverable* [29, 5]. These characteristics can be obtained separately but also together, through multiple inheritance. So, one can design objects with all transactional characteristics: serialisability, failure atomicity and permanence.

In [22, 24, 12], the transactional system itself is designed as a class library. This leads to a better modularity, and has enabled to change the underlying transactional protocols with minimal effects on the rest of the system. In [22], a (pessimistic) two-phases locking protocol can be customized for each class according to its semantics. In [24, 12], pessimistic concurrency control protocols are replaced by optimistic ones. All these changes are done with no effects on application objects.

However, none of the research mentioned above discuss the way transactional protocols, such as distributed locking and distributed atomic commitment, can be designed and implemented on top of lower level reusable components. With those approaches, protocols are assumed to exist and to be provided by the underlying distributed environment. Our work can be viewed as complementary to these research works. Our approach precisely aims at providing a generic way to design and implement protocols, particularly *agreement* protocols (e.g., for transactions), from more basic components, such as DTM protocol classes. The BAST class library neither addresses how to attach transactional features to application objects, nor is concerned with the way these protocols can be composed to build a transactional system.

7.3 Communication protocol libraries

Several authors have discussed the need for designing and implementing libraries of communication protocols. The STREAMS framework [25], a pioneer in the domain, and the *x*-Kernel [23], contain rich libraries of communication protocols, but they do not deal with reliability and agreement issues. More recently, both in the context of the HORUS [28] and the CONSUL [20] projects, libraries or reliable distributed protocols were provided. The proposed approaches consider however the *group abstraction* as the basic abstraction for reliable programming, and hence limit the scope of both environments. As we have discussed in section 1, transaction-oriented applications are very difficult to support on top of such group-oriented systems. D.C. Schmidt introduced the ASX framework [27], a set of C++ components that help building reusable communication infrastructures. Those components, also known as *wrappers*, are aimed at performing common communication-related tasks, e.g., connection establishment, routing, etc. However, there is no such thing as protocol classes in ASX, which can be seen as a toolbox of reusable components.

8 Concluding remarks

In this paper, we have introduced BAST, a library which offers a coherent hierarchy of *protocol classes*. Protocol classes are aimed at helping *system* programmers in building abstractions provided to *application* programmers. They can be used as the basic structuring components of distributed environments, and they significantly improve modularity. They also facilitate the customization and optimization of existing protocols, and enables to create new protocols very easily by subclassing.

In fault-tolerant distributed environments, protocol that enable to reach agreement despite failures play an essential role. The BAST library provides protocol classes that implement *DTM*, a generic protocol that can be customized to solve problems in distributed systems where failures can occur. We have presented how DTM generic protocol classes can be derived to solve the *atomic commitment problem*, and the *reliable total order problem*.

There are many research works on how to design distributed environments in terms of objects, but protocols are usually not modeled as classes. STREAMS [25] and x-Kernel [23] provide libraries of communication protocols but do not address fault-tolerance, while HORUS [28] and CONSUL [20] do. However, none of those systems view protocols as classes: protocols are dealt with as sets of functions. BAST is the only library of *protocol classes* we know of that addresses reliability issues. Furthermore, it provides protocol classes that support both the transaction paradigm and the group paradigm; this allows to smoothly integrate transactions on replicated objects. We see BAST as our contribution to the design of well-structured *fault-tolerant* distributed environments.

Our first prototype of the BAST class library is implemented in Smalltalk. We are currently implementing a C++ version of BAST, which will be used as base for other research projects. Future work will also consist in studying other protocols that are used to achieve fault-tolerance in distributed systems, and in seeing how they can fit into the BAST class hierarchy.

References

1. G. Agha, S. Frølund, R. Panwar, and D. Sturman. A linguistic framework for dynamic composition of dependability protocols. In *Dependable Computing for Critical Applications III Proceedings (DCCA-3)*, pages 197–207. IFIP Transactions, 1993. Elsevier.
2. M. Aksit, K. Wakita, J. Bosh, L. Bergmans, and A. Yonezawa. Abstracting object interactions using composition filters. In *Object-Based Distributed Programming*,

volume 791 of *Lecture Notes in Computer Science*, pages 152–184. Springer Verlag, 1993.

3. P.A. Bernstein, V. Hadzilacos, and N. Goodman. *Concurrency Control and Recovery in Database Systems*. Addison Wesley, 1987.

4. K. Birman and R. Van Renesse. *Reliable Distributed Computing with the Isis Toolkit*. IEEE Computer Society Press, 1993.

5. A. Black. Understanding transactions in the operating system context. *Operating Systems Review*, 25(28):73–77, January 1991.

6. S. Brandt and O.L Madsen. Object-oriented distributed programming in Beta. In *Object-Based Distributed Programming*, volume 791 of *Lecture Notes in Computer Science*, pages 185–212. Springer Verlag, 1993.

7. R. Campbell, N. Islam, D. Ralia, and P. Madany. Designing and implementing Choices: An object-oriented system in C++. *Communications of the ACM*, 36(9):117–126, September 1993.

8. T.D. Chandra and S. Toueg. Unreliable failure detectors for reliable distributed systems. Technical Report TR94-1458, Cornell University, Computer Science Department, October 1994. A preliminary version appears in PODC'91.

9. B. Garbinato, R. Guerraoui, and K.R. Mazouni. Implementation of the GARF replicated object plateform. *Distributed Systems Engineering Journal*, 2:14–27, 1995.

10. A.J. Goldberg and A.D. Robson. *SMALLTALK-80: The Language and its Implementation*. Addison Wesley, 1983.

11. Object Management Group and X/Open. *The Common Object Request Broker: Architecture and Specification*. Object Management Group, 1990. Document No. 91.12.1 (Revision 1.1).

12. R. Guerraoui. Modular atomic objects. *Theory and Practice of Object Systems*, 1(2):89–100, 1995.

13. R. Guerraoui. Revisiting the relationship between non-blocking atomic commitment and consensus. In J.-M. Hélary and M. Raynal, editors, *Distributed Algorithms - 9th International Workshop on Distributed Algorithms (WDAG'95)*, volume 972 of *Lecture Notes in Computer Science*, pages 87–100. Springer Verlag, September 1995.

14. R. Guerraoui and A. Schiper. A generic multicast primitive to support transactions on replicated objects in distributed systems. In *IEEE International Workshop on Future Trends in Distributed Computing Systems (FTDCS-95)*, August 1995. Korea.

15. R. Guerraoui and A. Schiper. Transaction model vs virtual synchrony model: Bridging the gap. In *Theory and Practice in Distributed Systems*, volume 938 of *Lecture Notes in Computer Science*, pages 121–132. Springer Verlag, 1995.

16. L. Lamport. Time, clocks, and the ordering of events in a distributed system. *Communications of the ACM*, 21(7):558–565, July 1978.

17. N. Lynch, M. Merrit, W. Weihl, and A. Fekete. *Atomic Transactions*. Morgan Koffmann, 1994.

18. O.L Madsen. Building abstractions for object-oriented programming. Technical report, University of Arhus, Computer Science Department, February 1993.

19. D. McCue. Developing a class hierarchy for object-oriented transaction processing. In *European Conference on Object-Oriented Programming Proceedings (ECOOP'92)*, volume 615 of *Lecture Notes in Computer Science*, pages 413–426, Utrecht (Netherland), June/July 1992. Springer Verlag.

20. S. Mishra, L. Peterson, and R. Schlichting. Experience with modularity in Consul. *Software-Practice and Experience*, 23(10):1053–1075, October 1993.

21. S. Mullender, editor. *Distributed Systems*. ACM Press, 1989.

22. G. Parrington and S. Schrivastava. Implementing concurrency control in reliable distributed object-oriented systems. In *European Conference on Object-Oriented Programming Proceedings (ECOOP'88)*, Norway, August 1988.

23. L. Peterson, N. Hutchinson, S. O'Malley, and M. Abott. Rpc in the x−Kernel: Evaluating new design techniques. *ACM Symposium on Operating Systems Principles*, 23(10):91–101, November 1989.

24. S. Popovitch, G. Kaiser, and S. Wu. An object-based approach to implementing distributed concurrency control. In *IEEE Conference on Distributed Computing Systems Proceedings*, pages 65–72, Arlington (Texas), May 1991.

25. D. Ritchie. A stream input-output system. *Bell Laboratories Technical Journal*, 63(8):1897–1910, 1984.

26. A. Schiper and R. Guerraoui. Faul-tolerant total order "multicast" with an unreliable failure detector. Technical report, Operating System Laboratory (Computer Science Department) of the Swiss Federal Institute of Technology, November 1995.

27. D.C. Schmidt. ASX: an object-oriented framework for developing distributed applications. In *Proceedings of the 6th USENIX C++ Technical Conference*. USENIX Association, April 1994.

28. R. van Renesse and K. Birman. Protocol composition in Horus. *ACM Principles of Distributed Computing*, 1995.

29. J. Wing. Decomposing and recomposing transaction concepts. In *Workshop OBDP93*, pages 111–122, 1994.

30. Y. Yokote. The Apertos reflective operating system: The concept and its implementation. In *Object-Oriented Programming Systems, Languages and Applications Conference Proceedings (OOPSLA'92)*, pages 414–434. ACM Press, October 1992. Special Issue of Sigplan Notices.

Dynamic Clustering in Object Databases Exploiting Effective Use of Relationships Between Objects

Frédérique BULLAT, Michel SCHNEIDER
Laboratoire d'Informatique
Université Blaise Pascal Clermont-Ferrand II
Complexe des Cézeaux, 63177 Aubière Cédex, FRANCE
E-mail: schneider@cicsun.univ-bpclermont.fr
Phone: (33) 73.40.74.35
Fax: (33) 73.40.74.44

Abstract

This paper concerns the problem of clustering objects onto units of secondary storage to minimise the number of I/O operations in database applications. We first investigate problems associated with most existing clustering schemes. We then propose STD, a Statistic-based Tunable and Dynamic clustering strategy which is able to overcome deficiencies of existing solutions. Our main contributions concern the dynamicity of the solution without adding high overhead and excessive volume of statistics. Reorganisations are performed only when the corresponding overhead is strictly justified. Clustering specifications are built from observation upon objects life, capturing any type of logical or structural inter-object links. Moreover, our clustering mechanism does not need any user or administrators hints, but remains user-controlled. A partial validation of STD has been made using Texas.

Keywords

Clustering, Buffering, Object-Oriented DataBase System, Performance.

1 Introduction

Clustering is an effective mechanism for improving object-oriented DBMS. Various inter-object links allow navigation through the database and retrieval of complex objects. For an object-oriented system, it is very important to traverse the object graphs structure efficiently. Clustering of related objects on disk minimises the number of pages accessed during a transaction and has thus a great impact on the overall performance of the system. It reduces client-server communication and disk I/O costs but also the number of locks to manage as well as the number of writes to store in journals. It improves paging performance and client buffer memory usage. So, 'intelligent' physical placement of objects is a central issue for performance requirements.

Several characteristics can commonly be identified in existing clustering strategies [3]. First, they are mainly static. Objects are grouped at creation and are not reclustered afterward at run time when use of data evolve. Moreover, systems do not generally offer any measuring and reorganisation tools. Second, clustering is rarely self-driven and user's hints or explicit placement schema are used at object creation time. Third, existing schemes are designed to cluster objects by considering structural relationships among classes inside the database schema. They commonly don't consider logical[1] relationships, neither IS-A relationships nor multiple relationships among objects. Moreover, clustering schemes are all based on a common policy for every objects of a given class. This does not allow any individual object behavior. Finally, most clustering policies use disk pages as clustering unit. Hence, they do not consider performance issued by the physical dispositions of accessed pages. Clustering among several pages may be really efficient especially if coupled with an appropriate buffering policy. Besides, related objects placed in consecutive pages on disk can be accessed avoiding expensive moving of disk heads.

This paper introduces a new clustering scheme that may be convenient for any object-oriented DBMS. Its main objectives are autonomy, flexibility, dynamicity and of course efficiency. It tries to reach the best physical placement regarding the database use. STD clustering specifications are based on operations performed on individual objects in order to meet the requirements of different access patterns. We try to determine how objects are actually used together, regardless the type of relationships. For the reclustering problem, we propose a dynamic scheme that may reorganise the storage space when placement of objects becomes obsolete (i.e. when objects are not used by applications as they usually were). This can occur for many reasons: schema evolution, changing of parent objects, added or removed structural or logical links. A cost model is introduced to assist reorganisation decisions. A great effort is made, first, to reduce the number of statistics to a minimal representative set; then, to correctly estimate the benefit of reclustering before doing any change; and finally, to wait for the appropriate moment, in order to avoid penalising applications when reclustering. Clustering units are chunks (sets of contiguous disk pages) instead of individual pages. Moreover, the clustering proposal is improved by a specific buffering scheme, including appropriate prefetching and replacement policies. The entire solution is self-driven but remains user-controlled through tuning parameters.

The remainder of this paper is organised as follows. Section 2 addresses the problems associated with most of existing clustering schemes. Section 3 stresses out our motivations and presents the principles of the STD clustering scheme. Section 4 presents the underlying machinery existing behind this solution from an implementation point of view. Section 5 proposes a partial validation of STD

---

[1] We mean by 'logical' relationship all links that are not described in the DB schema but that may be constructed at any time by applications in order to manipulate logically related objects. Examples of such relationships can be: extensions of classes containing objects having the same values for some attributes (in order to run database requests), or collections of neighboured objects often accessed together when displaying geographical cards. This kind of relationship is expressed of course with physical pointers but differs from classical structural links.

through an implementation with Texas and some experiments to situate the efficiency of the clustering. Finally, section 6 concludes this paper and discusses costs, feasibility and perspectives for this work.

2 Related Work

This section presents the main characteristics of most existing clustering schemes and points out several associated problems. One can refer to [3] for more details on object clustering strategies. First, in most operational OODBMS, clustering depends on user hand-activation (made through application code, as in ObjectStore [15], ONTOS [16], and GemStone [17] or by means of online commands, as in ORION [14] or with a clustering procedure, as in Cactis [13]). We think that placement of objects should be considered at any time by the system. It may of course need user hints, but should not depends on hypothetical external activations. O_2 seems to be the only operational system to propose a systematic clustering solution integrated to the DBMS [1] (this clustering strategy will be operational for the next version). Other solutions [5, 8, 11] have been suggested but never implemented.

Another common characteristic is the lack of dynamicity. Many suggestions have been made to get reclustering of objects [6, 8]. But these solutions are not really dynamic[2]. In fact, they only control placement of objects when objects are modified. We think that, for many reasons, an object may become misclustered even if it has not been modified (when clustering specifications evolve, for example). We have only found one proposal [11] that can be really considered as 'dynamic'. Based on a garbage collection process, it is very attractive because it adds only small overhead to the existing process. However, disk garbage collection is itself a very expensive process, and, for this reason, is rarely implemented in existing DBMS, except in GemStone [17]. Moreover, we think that dynamicity is at the same time, absolutely necessary but also very dangerous since disk space organisation may never stabilise and prove costly. Before reclustering, costs and benefits must be precisely estimated.

Besides, we consider that, in most cases, the importance of user hints is too high. Often, for example in ONTOS [16], ObjectStore [15] and ORION [14], users state precisely how to cluster some objects by indicating in what target segment or near what object y an object x must be stored (within applications code or by means of online commands). Sometimes, systems accept user hints related to the DB schema. In ENCORE [12] and EOS [11], users affect priorities to structural links between classes. O_2 proposes to define a specific placement schema, by means of placement trees [1] created by the DB Administrator. None of these solutions are really convenient because programmers, administrators and even users may have no correct idea on the way objects will be used together. This is the reason why in Cactis [13], for example, no user hint is required. The system tries to determine itself a good clustering.

---

[2] We qualify by 'dynamic' any solution able to detect and replace every object that becomes misclustered for any reason.

The most critical point of a clustering strategy is, of course, the pertinence of the clustering specifications. There are two major kinds of specifications: (i) those based on structural links between classes (depicted in the DB schema), (ii) those built with observation upon objects life. For the first kind (i), solutions differ essentially on the nature of the considered links. In most cases, systems base their clustering policy on structural links (defined in the DB schema). [7] and [8] propose to cluster upon other kinds of relationships, as equivalence relationships and version relationships. Generally, one type of relationship is considered at a time. [8] suggests a multi-level strategy to order different weighted links in a same clustering sequence. Moreover, IS-A relationships[3] and logical relationships are never considered. Concerning the second kind (ii), many papers propose to base clustering on access probabilities deduced from statistics [13, 19, 20, 21]. Defaults of many published works in this domain are the lack of precise information concerning: (j) the way to collect, store and handle statistics, (jj) the generated costs, (jjj) what to do while there are not enough statistics, (jjjj) the necessity of braking and balancing system reactions when confronted to continuous statistics changes. In the two kinds of strategies (i) (ii), clustering specifications are generalised at the class-level. So that, all objects of a given class are clustered in the same way, denying any individual behavior. Lastly, few systems handle the problem of shared objects in a deterministic way. If an object x is linked through the same type of relationship to several other objects, there are several clustering solutions. Some systems, as ENCORE [12], allow replication of object x, so that each replicated object is stored near its parent. Other systems, as EOS [11], rely on user hints. The others are self-electing systems: i.e. they either place randomly x close to one of the objects, or use statistics to take decisions [13, 19].

We can also note a lack of control and tuning tools. O_2 proposes a cost model [2] based on analysis of objects methods, but it has not been implemented. [6] suggests to control clustering efficiency within the buffering module. But nothing is said about the way to do it. Finally, clustering efficiency is generally reduced by the lack of adapted buffering schemes, and especially by the lack of adapted replacement policies [9]. Traditional LRU replacement policies, for example, do not consider relationships existing between objects of different pages when electing pages for replacement. As a result, some likely-to-be-used objects may be swapped out because the buffer manager does not take into consideration that these objects are strongly related to currently-used objects. The I/O gain introduced by clustering is then decreased by traditional buffering. [6] has suggested a context-sensitive replacement policy which would take care of inter-object relationships to set relevant priorities on pages. However, the proposed solution does not take advantage of a cluster-based policy. It has not yet been implemented but it seems that the corresponding overhead may prove costly.

---

[3] Clustering objects upon the inheritance graph is pertinent only in the case of DBMS having a vertical distribution storage model (inherited attributes and member attributes are not physically stored in the same object).

3 The STD Clustering Strategy

3.1 Motivations

This section addresses the main objectives of our policy. They consist in the following points:

Clustering specifications pertinency
Considering pertinent clustering specifications is the primary point of an effective strategy. First, we opt for clustering objects upon observations, rather than upon user estimations. We think that schema analysis is not completely appropriate to deduce clustering specifications. Then, we consider that different objects of a given class may have different behaviors. So, efforts will be made to avoid clustering on classes links basis. Finally, we want to capture any type of inter-object relationship. We are only interested in the frequency of simultaneous accesses to objects. Our objective is to obtain a distance between two objects on disk proportional to their attractive force, whatever the reason for their simultaneous uses. It includes many kinds of relationships: (i) structural links depicted in DB schema (composite links, references, IS-A relationships), (ii) logical links which lead applications to construct data structures incorporating objects identifiers, (iii) physical fragmentation of objects due to the storage model of object managers (to store variable-length attributes or inherited attributes, for example). Also, we would like to be able to solve shared objects conflicts, thanks to the managed statistics.

Space organisation pertinency
First, clustering must be an integral part of object management fonctionalities. It must be a constant preoccupation of the system, and its activation must not depend on users. Second, we consider that clustering among several pages is an important issue for efficient clustering. So, we will introduce an adapted type of storage unit. Finally, we think that dynamicity of the solution must be closely controlled. This means that: (i) storage costs (statistics storage costs and cluster storage costs) must be reduced, (ii) reorganisation pertinency must be measured. Reclustering must occur only if estimated gains exceed reorganisation costs. It must take into account the transactional rate in order to minimise concurrency problems and user transaction penalisation during reclustering operations. Reactions must be balanced and braked up, when confronted to continuous statistics changes. Besides, reclustering of an object necessitates to consider the whole set of related objects. We must avoid bringing two objects closer, without looking at the other related objects which also have an attractive force to respect.

Buffering policy
Introducing a buffering policy adapted to STD clustering is also one of our preoccupation, in order to benefit of clustering among several pages. This includes prefetching and cluster-based replacement policies. Prefetching will be closely controlled and replacement algorithm will not be more expensive than LRU-like policies.

Control and tuning tool
The last objective is to integrate tuning capabilities, in order to control system reactivity and statistics pertinency, for example.

3.2 About Statistics and Dynamicity

Clustering objects upon observation of objects life means statistics management.

This choice supposes that if, in the recent past, objects were often used together, they are likely-to-be-together-used in the near future. Statistics on the use of databases allow estimations of access probabilities. Besides, a dynamic clustering scheme must recluster scattered related pages when access costs become too high. However, if the corresponding overhead is not justified, reclustering may actually degrade performance. Modifying placement of a set of objects o_i is justified only if reorganisation overhead (T_{reorg}) plus the total time of future accesses (T_{clus}) to the clustered o_i is smaller than the total time of current accesses to the scattered o_i (T_{scat}) [8].

$$T_{reorg} + T_{clus} < T_{scat}$$

If n is the number of future accesses (read or write) to the individual o_i, we have: $T_{scat} = n * t_{scat}$ and $T_{clus} = n * t_{clus}$ where t_{scat} and t_{clus} are elementary access times. So, have we :

$$T_{reorg} < (n*t_{scat}) - (n*t_{clus})$$
$$n > \frac{T_{reorg}}{t_{scat} - t_{clus}}$$

This formula can be paraphrased as follows: the higher the overhead is, the larger the number of future accesses; the higher the clustering benefit is, the smaller the future access rate.

Ideally, we may manage a complete set of statistics in order to keep trace of: (i) any simultaneous access between two objects, (ii) access frequencies of any accessed object. Then, we could evaluate reclustering benefits. Certainly, it is not interesting to recluster when access frequencies are too small, even if objects are strongly related. But according to implementation considerations, it is impossible to manage the whole set of statistics for every objects, and during the whole objects life. The way of managing STD statistics solves this kind of problem.

3.3 The STD policy
Preliminaries
Our solution proposes to place strongly related objects as close as possible to each other. We consider that valuated links can be determined only during objects life. Weights of links are of course unknown at object creation time. We then propose to have a default placement of objects, using classical DB schema clustering specifications (priorities on structural links, as in EOS [11], for example). Modification of this initial placement will be considered as soon as estimated weights of links will become really significant.

The concept of inter-object link
As we said in section 3.1, we want to capture any type of inter-object relationships (structural, logical, inheritance, version, equivalence, etc...). This includes the relationships defined explicitly through the DB schema (aggregation, references, inheritance), as well as those defined by programmers (for example to retrieve some logically related objects), and those introduced by the system (for example, to retrieve all attributes of fragmented objects). All these links are materialised in the database by pointers using OID. So, detecting and valuating links necessitates following each dereferencement of persistent pointers made by the system during database life. This explains why we propose to characterise any inter-object link, leading to simultaneous use of objects, by the following definition.

<u>Definition</u>: There is a *link* (o_i, o_j) between two objects o_i and o_j when o_j is accessed from o_i during a transaction. Each dereferencement of a persistent pointer is considered as a link between the initial object and the referenced object.

Statistics collecting

Statistics are collected within transactions, during an *Observation Period P*. During P, each transaction T_i memorises links detected between objects. At commit time, an asynchronous process p_i is created to analyse each T_i observation results and to compute: (i) the number of times a link has been detected during T_i between each pair of related objects, (ii) the number of accesses to each object accessed during T_i. Observation results computed by each process p_i are stored in two transient data structures: observations (i) are stored in an Observation Matrix called MO, observations (ii) are stored in an Observation Vector called VO[4]. MO and VO are concurrently updated after commit time by processes p_i. MO(i,j) represents the number of times the link (o_i, o_j) has been detected during P, from o_i to o_j, by all transactions. MO is a sparse matrix where entries are identifiers (OID) of the referenced objects. Its size is incremented by one each time a new entry is added. Since a maximal size n is a priori assigned to MO, the length of P varies according to the DB access rate.

Elementary linking factors

In order to weight a link between two objects o_i and o_j, we propose the following indicator computed from the statistics:

$$\frac{MO(i, j)}{VO(i)} + \frac{MO(j, i)}{VO(j)}$$

It constitutes an estimation of the probability $p(o_i/o_j)$ of accessing o_j when accessing o_i plus the probability $p(o_j/o_i)$ of accessing o_i when accessing o_j. Of course, this estimation is very rough since it comes from a limited observation period. However, we are not at all interested in a fine estimation of this probability since the use of objects dating from a distant period is no longer relevant of the current use. So, in the following definition, we speak about a factor instead of an effective probability.

<u>Definition</u>: The *elementary linking factor fe_{ij}* used to weight attractive force between objects o_i and o_j is deduced from observations within period P and computed, as indicated by Figure 1.

The two thresholds T_{fe} and T_{fa} are used to validate links observed during P. T_{fe} is the value under which a computed linking factor is not considered as significant, since the frequencies of accessing o_i from o_j and o_j from o_i during P were too small. T_{fa} is the value under which the number of accesses to individual objects is too small to justify the reclustering overhead (see section 3.2).

---

[4] From an implementation point of vue, such structures may not be stored as matrices and vectors. Hash tables, for example, may be used to keep and retrieve efficiently STD transient and persistent statistics.

```
for i --> 2 to n, for j --> 1 to n-1,    // Every link belonging to MO is processed
do
  if MO(i,j) ≠ 0
  then
      if (VO(i) >= Tfa) or (VO(j) >= Tfa)
          // Access frequencies to objects must be high enough to
          // consider the corresponding linking factor as significant
      then
```

$$fe_{ij} = ME(i,j) = \frac{MO(i,j)}{VO(i)} + \frac{MO(j,i)}{VO(j)}$$

```
          if fcij < Tfe then feij = 0
          // The linking factor is considered as not significant
          // and set to null if its value is under the Tfe threshold
      endif
  endif
enddo
```

Fig. 1. Computing of elementary linking factors

The *elementary linking factor matrix ME* is constructed at the end of the period P. It is sparse and triangular (fe_{ij} values are the same as fe_{ji} values since they represent the frequency of having objects oi and oj accessed simultaneously, regardless the link orientation). It defines a *graph of elementary inter-object links* (Figure 2). This is a non-oriented weighted graph in which nodes represent objects and arcs represent weighted relationships among objects.

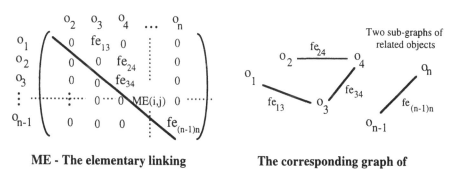

ME - The elementary linking   The corresponding graph of
factor matrix   elementary links

Fig. 2. Elementary inter-object links

Consolidated linking factors
Significance of elementary linking factors is limited to the context of a period P. They are used to compute consolidated linking factors.

<u>Definition</u>: The *consolidated linking factors fc_{ij}* are persistent values updated at the end of period P, as follows:

$$fc_{ij(new)} = w*fc_{ij(old)} + (1-w)*fe_{ij}$$

where w is a weighting coefficient introduced to respect the different levels of significance (factors computed during a period P are much less significant than factors consolidated by several periods results).

Consolidated factors are stored in the persistent *consolidated linking factors matrix MC*. As ME, matrix MC is a triangular sparse matrix. Each cell $MC(i,j)$ is a composite structure containing: (i) the consolidated linking factor fc_{ij} for the link (o_i,o_j), (ii) the date $udate_{ij}$[5], of the last updating of fc_{ij}, (iii) a flag $cflag_{ij}$ indicating if o_i and o_j have already been clustered together, this flag is managed by the reclustering procedure (see section 4.1.2 for details).

Elimination of obsolete consolidated factors
Updates of consolidated linking factors are dated in order to periodically eliminate links that have not been detected for a long time.

```
for i --> 2 to n, for j --> 1 to n-1,
do
  if fe_ij ≠ 0
  then
        fc_ij(new) = w*fc_ij(old) + (1 - w)*fe_ij
        udate_ij=Pcurrent
        if (fc_ij > T_fc and cflag_ij = 0)
        then
            n_d= n_d+ 1
            clusdemand(n_d)=(o_i,o_j)
        endif
  endif
enddo
```

Fig. 3. Consolidation phase

<u>Definition</u>: Consolidated linking factors fc_{ij} are considered as obsolete after a time T_v following the last link (o_i,o_j) detection. Periodically, consolidated links are eliminated as follows:

$$fc_{ij} = 0 \text{ if } P_{current} - udate_{ij} > n_p \text{ (modulo p)},$$

where $P_{current}$ is the current period P number, n_p is the number of periods P included

---

[5] The date is stored as a period number (modulo p). It is equal to the number of the last period in which a significant link has been detected between o_i and o_j.

in T_v, and p is the modulo value used to increment $P_{current}$.

Elimination of consolidated linking factors does not imply the reclustering of o_i and o_j. It only means that o_i and o_j have not been used together for a long time. So, if they were already clustered, they are now considered as free to be moved later closed to other objects, if it becomes necessary.

Determination and memorisation of reclustering demands
Consolidated linking factors are considered as pertinent indicators for clustering. Figure 3 presents how reorganisation demands are registered, in the *consolidation phase*, after computation of elementary factors at the end of each period P.

Definition: The weight of a consolidated linking factor fc_{ij} is high enough to justify clustering of o_i and o_j, as soon as: $fc_{ij} > T_{fc}$, where T_{fc} is the threshold value under which clustering benefit do not exceed reclustering overhead.

Determination of the T_{fc} value is essential (see section 4.2). It directly influences the DB stability but also the storage space organisation pertinency.

Triggered reclustering works
At the end of a period P, n_d reclustering demands are registered. These demands are grouped in reclustering units in order to distribute reclustering on separate work-times. As soon as the transactional rate is low enough (the I/O rate is periodically scanned), one reclustering unit is processed at a time (details are given in section 4.1).

Buffering
The purpose of buffering is to cache likely-to-be-used objects in main memory in order to avoid I/O operation every time an object is required. Buffering schemes cover two different issues: (i) page replacement policies, (ii) buffer allocation [10]. We are only interested in the first point, which is closely linked to clustering policies. LRU-like policies are usually recognised as good policies because they are simple and efficient. However, when buffers are full, such replacement schemes evict the least-recently-used page, without regarding if contained objects are related or not with currently-used objects. So, some likely-to-be-used objects may be swapped on disk.

We said earlier that having grouping units larger than individual pages is an important issue for clustering. We think that clustering among several pages is improved by: (i) loading partial or entire clusters in memory, (ii) keeping all pages of likely-to-be-used clusters in memory. So, the buffering solution included in the STD clustering proposal consists in: (j) having the possibility of running DB applications in a 'smart'[6] prefetching mode; entire clusters or moving cluster-windows are prefetched in advance, (jj) modifying LRU-like policies, in order to date cluster (or cluster-window) uses instead of page uses, (jjj) electing for replacement the least-recently-used cluster (or the least-recently-used cluster-window) instead of the least-recently-used page. This buffering scheme may be named LRUc (Least-Recently-used cluster).

The 'smart' STD prefetching policy is based on the moving cluster-window concept presented in the following definition and described in Figure 4.

---

[6] 'smart' means that depth of prefetching is closely controlled. Aggressive prefetching policies may not be truly effective since they may prefetch objects not actually needed.

Definition: A *moving cluster-window* is a limited view of the physical stored cluster (composed of s pages), that may be the unit of prefetching. It is a sub-graph of the object graph stored in the cluster, centered to the initial required object. Instead of loading the individual page containing the accessed object o_i, the most strongly related objects, stored around o_i in the cluster, will be prefetched.

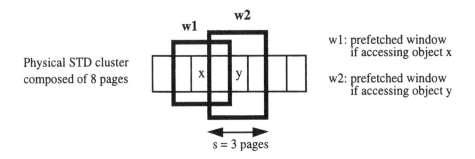

Physical STD cluster composed of 8 pages

w1: prefetched window if accessing object x

w2: prefetched window if accessing object y

s = 3 pages

Fig. 4. The concept of moving cluster-window.

4 Algorithmic Details

4.1 Reclustering Technique

We have seen how our statistic-based model allows detection of strong inter-object links, weighted by their access frequencies. Definition and computation of linking factors allows determination of sub-graphs G_k containing strongly related objects.

Definition: *Clusters* are variable-length chunks of storage space, containing strongly related objects o_i. Each cluster is a set of contiguous disk pages, large enough to receive the related o_i and having a unique identifier (clusterID). The system knows at any time the cluster to which any object o_i belongs.

Objective: To have each sub-graph G_k stored within a cluster. Inside each cluster, the distance on disk between two objects will be proportional to the importance of the corresponding linking factor.

Construction of Reclustering Units

Among the n_d reclustering demands registered at the end of period P (each concerning two objects o_i and o_j to cluster), several records may be related to one another, by having one of objects o_i or o_j in common. Related records must be processed at the same time, since all of the concerned objects will be stored in the same cluster.

Definition: A reclustering unit U_k is a sub-graph of related objects, for which reclustering demand(s) have been recorded and which have to be stored in a same cluster. The set of reclustering units is constructed from the reclustering file after the consolidation phase. All objects of a reclustering unit will be processed at a same time. Figure 5 gives an example of the construction of reclustering units.

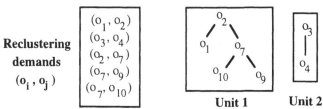

Reclustering demands

(o_i, o_j)

(o_1, o_2)
(o_3, o_4)
(o_2, o_7)
(o_7, o_9)
(o_7, o_{10})

Unit 1   Unit 2

Fig. 5.   Construction of reclustering units.

Reclustering Procedure

A reclustering unit U_k is a graph of related objects (minimum two objects), corresponding to new significant attractive forces. Processing a given unit consists in the following phases:

(i) Determining in the MC matrix all objects connected to graph U_k, in order to determine the new graph G_k of consolidated links corresponding to the current reclustering unit.

(ii) Creating the object clustering sequence corresponding to graph G_k, by means of the algorithm presented in section 4.1.3.

(iii) Distributing the obtained object sequence among one or several pages.

(iv) Storing the object sequence into a new cluster (another allocated disk space composed of contiguous pages).

(v) Freeing places occupied previously by moved objects.

(vi) Memorising the new belonging cluster for each reclustered object and updating in the MC matrix flags indicating whether two objects belong to the same cluster or not.

Figure 6 presents an example of such processing, considering: (a) database space organisation before clustering, (b) the current value of consolidated factors in MC, (c) the T_{fc} threshold value, and (d) the unit to process: Unit 2 of Figure 5. (e) and (f) presents how this unit is processed through phases (i) to (v).

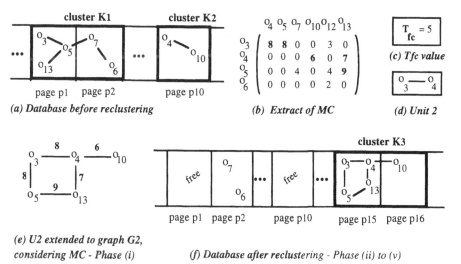

(a) Database before reclustering

(b) Extract of MC

(c) Tfc value

(d) Unit 2

(e) U2 extended to graph G2, considering MC - Phase (i)

(f) Database after reclustering - Phase (ii) to (v)

Fig. 6.   Processing of a reclustering unit

We can see on the example processed in Figure 6 that if links become obsolete (set to null, as the link (o6, o7)) or no longer pertinent (under the T_{fc} value, as the link (o5,o7)), they are not considered in the new cluster construction. Then, some objects (o6 and o7 in Figure 6) may remain in the same page, but no longer belong to any cluster.

Determination of the Stored Object Sequence

The algorithm used to order the object sequence is inspired by the Kruskal algorithm (construction of a minimum-cost spanning tree from a general graph) and by the solution proposed in [8] to suggest a multi-level strategy able to order at the same time different types of relationships between objects. Of course, we do not adapt this algorithm for the same purpose, since we are not interested in distinguishing the different types of links. Besides, we are not interested in directed links as in [8]. Contrary to the Kruskal algorithm, our proposed scheme must of course consider maximum-costs in order to obtain distance on disk between two related objects proportional to their attractive force. The idea of super-node introduced in [8] is kept but has been slightly modified.

Definition: A *super-node* in an object graph is a set of related objects, constructed progressively, by grouping objects related by the most relevant arc, relatively to the following rules.

Rule R1: The list of objects in a super-node S (for example S= {o2, o5, o4, o9}), can only be considered in the direct order (o2, o5, o4, o9) or in the reverse order (o9, o4, o5, o2), so that the distance between objects remains continuously unchanged.

---

while graph G_k is not reduced to a single super-node
do
  Identify the most relevant weight W among every weighted arcs
  Construct list L containing arcs weighted by W
  for each arc a_i belonging to L
    do
      Group and arrange in a same super-node nodes related by arc a_i
  enddo
  for each super-node S connected to the same node by several arcs
  do
    Determine and keep only the most weighted arc.
  enddo
enddo
The clustering sequence is given by the final super-node.

Fig. 7.   Ordering the related objects.

Rule R2: When two super-nodes S1, S2 are grouped in a super-node S, we must identify, in the initial graph, which arc (o_i,o_j) is responsible for the grouping. Then, in order to minimise the distance between o_i and o_j (in the super-node S and finally on disk), we may have: (i) S constructed either with {S1, S2} or with {S2, S1}, (ii) objects inside S1 and S2 maintained in the same order or reversed.

<u>Rule 3</u>: When constructing a super-node S, any arc (weighted to w) existing previously between an object of S and another node (simple-node or super-node) N_i, becomes an arc between S and N_i (weighted to w).

Figure 7 presents our proposed ordering scheme. An example is processed in Figure 8.

For each object o_i in the obtained clustering sequence, the distance on disk between o_i and each of its related object is proportional to the weight of the corresponding link. The clustering sequence obtained in the example processed in Figure 8 is: {o_5, o_1, o_4, o_3, o_7, o_8, o_{10}, o_2, o_{18}}.

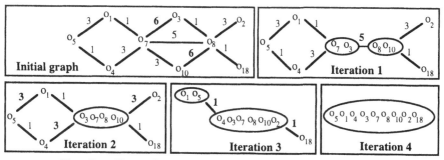

Fig. 8.   Example of an obtained clustering sequence.

The problem resulting from shared objects in other clustering strategies is solved here in a deterministic way, since we choose systematically the most weighted link.

4.2 Tuning Capabilities

A set of tuning parameters, described in Figure 9, has been introduced in order to control mainly system reactivity and statistics pertinency. Until now, their determination is under the DB administrator responsibility but we are currently processing extensive experiments in order to fix some of the proposed parameters to optimal values or range of values. In particular, determination of the thresholds value is essential since they directly influence the DB stability as well as the storage space organisation pertinency.

Activation/deactivation options (Figure 10) are proposed to take into consideration particular behaviors of specific databases or transactions. For example, for a special transaction used one time in a year and using intensively the database in a specific way, programmers may choose intentionally not to update STD statistics. Besides, for particular databases inside which objects life are very short, the DB administrator may choose intentionally to keep initial default placement of objects (NoRecluster and NoStatDB options).

n   Maximum entries in the Observation Matrix MO during a period P.

n_p Number of observation periods after which a consolidated factor fc_{ij} is obsolete if the link (oi, oj) has not been detected.

p   The number of the current observation period is computed modulo p.

T_{fa} Threshold value (in number of object accesses during a period P) under which the number of accesses to individual objects is too small to be considered in elementary linking factors computation

T_{fe} Threshold value under which elementary linking factors are not considered to update consolidated factors.

T_{fc} Threshold value under which a consolidated linking factor is not considered as significant (toactivate reclustering or to be considered in new cluster construction). Reclustering under this value, would be globally negative.

w   Weighting coefficient introduced to minimise significance of elementary observations relative to consolidated observations.

s   Size of the current moving cluster-window
(number of pages prefetched in case of accessing a clustered object).

Fig. 9.   Tuning parameters.

For each database:
- *Prefetching* NoPrefetchDB/ PrefetchClusterDB / PrefetchWindowDB
- *Dynamicity*   NoRecluster / Recluster
- *Statistics*   NoStatDB / StatDB

For each transaction:
- *Prefetching* NoPrefetch / PrefetchCluster / PrefetchWindow
- *Statistics*   NoStat / Stat

Fig. 10.   STD options.

5 Tests with Texas

5.1 Main Characteristics of Texas

Texas is a persistent storage system for C++, designed and developed at the University of Texas, Austin [18]. Our choice of Texas for testing STD technique comes essentially from the fact that the source is free available and can be easily modified. Texas runs under Unix and is a virtual memory mapped system. The source is coded in C++ and the data formats in memory are those of C++. Persistent objects are stored on disk pages in the same format as they are in memory. Texas uses physical OID coded on four octets. When a disk page is loaded in memory, all the disk adresses toward referenced objects must be converted to memory adresses. The conversion, usually called swizzling, is made in Texas by reserving a memory page for each referenced disk page. But a referenced disk page is effectively loaded in memory only the first time it is needed (when a fault page is detected).

During an execution, a database is represented by an object called Pstore. This object is used to memorize the main information concerning the management of the database and more particularly: (i) a pointer to the zone containing the root objects (each root object can be accessed through a name), (ii) a pointer to the zone of available pages, (iii) a pointer to the swizzling table containing the links beetween each disk page and its corresponding memory page.

5.2 Implementation of the STD Technique Through Texas

The implementation has necessitated a complete comprehension of the internal working of the system and of the code organization. It has been made thanks to many sollicitations of the authors via e-mail. It is not possible to describe here in details the modifications and the adjunctions made on the source. We only give the main principles. Implementation is achieved by tying data structures as attributed of the Pstore object and algorithms as methods.

The new attributes added to Pstore are the following:

- *observation* for the implementation of the observation matrices

- *consolidation* for the implementation of the consolidation matrice

- *clustering* for the implementation of the clustering

- *objectlist* for the implementation of the temporary access sequence to objects during a transaction.

The construction of a cluster unit is made according to the following stages:

i) Each OID of the unit is used to load the referenced page and to capture the size of the corresponding object database.

ii) The cluster is created at the end of the file. The objects of the unit are copied in the order of the cluster sequence. The size of each object is used to control that the current page is not full. Otherwise a new page is allocated to the cluster. A list, called *movedobjectlist*, is used to store the old and the new OID for each object.

iii) To upade pointers to moved objects, each page is loaded in memory. Each time an adress contains an old OID in the *movedobjectlist*, it is replaced by the new one. The replacement is made by the swizzling module of Texas which has been modified to take into account the *movedobjectlist*.

5.3 The Benchmark

We have adapted the well known OO1 Catell benchmark [4] to test STD technique. It is based on (i) a database schema containing two types of objects (ii) recommandations to generate an instance of a database and (iii) several typical manipulations.

The database schema is given on figure 11. The size of the two attributes X,Y of the type *Part* can be modified if necessary to vary the tests. Each *Part* object is connected to three other *Part* objects. Connections are represented through the type *Connection* : there exists one *Connection* object for each pair of connected *Part* objects.

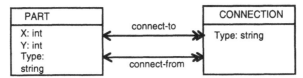

Fig. 11. The database schema for the benchmark

An instance of a database is generated with a number of *Part* objects equal to *partnb*. 90% of the connections are randomly established by respecting a principle of locality. More precisely a *Part* object is randomly connected with three *Part* objects having indices in the interval max(i-refzone*partnb) and min(i+refzone*partnb) where refzone is a ratio fixing the amplitude of the locality (max and min are used to impose the interval to be included in [1, partnb]). The other 10% of the connections are established with any object in the database.

Among the different manipulations suggested by the benchmark, we will use only the traversal. It consists in exploring the different objects which can be reached through the connections from a root object generated with the database. Since cycles are always possible, the traversal is not a finite procedure and must be stopped at a predetermined level from the root. The number of visited objects is a simple function of the level. A traversal with 4 levels reads 160 objects. A same object can be found many times during the traversal. This situation does not induce any problem for STD technique which consists in following the effective use of objects.

5.4 Tests and Results

STD technique has been designed to take into account different applications on the database and it is important to simulate the concept of application. In our tests an application is charaterized by

-a traversal (i.e. a root and a level)

-the number of times *trnb* the traversal is made.

Different roots have been generated with the database to simulate three different applications numbered 1 to 3. The efficiency of STD is measured by the number of page faults, before the clustering and after the clustering.

We now give the most significant results we have obtained.

The first experiment (figure 12) concerns the influence of the refzone parameter with a unique application. The clustering power of STD is very effective even for narrow localities (for his benchmark, Cattel considers that a value of 0.01 for refzone is realistic).

partnb	5000
Tfa	1
Tfc	1

refzone	before	after	ratio
0.001	17	4	4.2
0.01	38	5	7.6
0.05	55	5	11.0
0.1	57	5	11.4
0.2	66	5	14.2

Fig. 12. Number of page faults before and after reclustering
depending on refzone

The second experiment (figure 13) has the objective to situate the influence of the T_{fa} parameter with three different applications. The average ratio has been obtained by weighting the individual ratios with the weight of each application. The efficiency of STD is maximal for $T_{fa}=4$. For $T_{fa}=4$, application 3 has no longer any influence on the clustering. For $T_{fa}=8$, only application 1 influences the clustering. When $T_{fa}=16$, a unique cluster of seven objects is constructed (this cluster results from cycles in the connections between *Part* objects). This run ensures that T_{fa} has really the expected effect. These different threshold values for T_{fa} depend directly on the values of *trnb* (traversal number) for the three applications. *trnb* represents approximately the average number of object uses for an application.

partnb	5000	application			before	after				
		#	trnb	level		Tfa=1	Tfa=4	Tfa=8	Tfa=12	Tfa=16
refzone	0.01	1	15	4	38	7	6	5	5	38
		2	5	4	29	7	6	30	30	30
Tfc	1	3	2	4	40	7	36	40	40	41
		average ratio				5.0	4.1	2.6	2.6	1.0

Fig. 13. Number of page faults before and after reclustering
depending on T_{fa}

For this experiment, the three applications share the use of many objects. Other experiments have shown that the number of shared objects have little influence on the results. We can say that STD technique clusters the objects in the best way, independantly the existence of shared objects.

The third experiment (figure 14) situates the influence of the T_{fc} parameter in similar conditions. The efficiency of clustering is maximal for $T_{fc}=1$ and diminishes slightly when T_{fc} varies from 1 to 50. The diminution becomes very important when T_{fc} reaches number 50. When T_{fc} is greater than 50 we observe a degradation due to the fact that only a few objects are clustered in supplementary pages at the end of the file. The database remains strictly unchanged when $T_{fc}=100$.

partnb	5000	application			before	after			
		#	trnb	level		Tfc=1	Tfc=30	Tfc=35	Tfc=51
refzone	0.01	1	15	4	38	7	8	9	40
		2	5	4	29	7	7	7	31
Tfa	1	3	2	4	40	7	7	9	43
		average ratio				5.0	4.7	4.2	0.9

Fig. 14. Number of page faults before and after reclustering
depending on T_{fc}

The last experiment reported here (figure 15), concerns some measures about the execution time (i) for the traversal before and after the clustering, (ii) for the consolidation phase and (iii) for the clustering. The conditions are those of figure 13. The before traversal includes the observation time which is very small (a fraction of a second) compared with the traversal time. First we can observe that the ratio between the traversal times before and after has not exactly the same value as the ratio between the number of page faults before and after. This comes from the fact that I/O operations resulting from a page fault have variable execution time. When T_{fa} increases, the execution times for the consolidation phase and for the clustering decrease since the collecting activity diminishes and the number of clustered object becomes lower.

		Execution time in seconds	Tfa=1	Tfa=4	Tfa=8	Tfa=16
partnb	5000					
		Before traversal	10	9	9	9
refzone	0.01	After traversal	3	4	5	8
		Consolidation phase	4	3	2	1
Tfc	1	Cluster construction	13	10	9	6
		Number of objects in clusters	364	274	176	65

Fig. 15. Some execution times for different values of T_{fa}

(runs on SUN SPARC/ELC under SUN OS V4.3.1)

The conclusion that we can draw from these results can be reasonably optimistic. First, it appears that T_{fa} and T_{fc} control effectively the strategy and are not difficult to adjust. Second, the balance between the gain and the overhead of STD technique when $T_{fa}=1$ and $T_{fc}=1$ can be established as follows. Including the consolidation time, there remains an excess of 10-(3+4)=3 seconds between the time before and after. Thus, after only five runs of the three applications, the total excess overcomes the clustering time and the reclustering technique becomes globally beneficial. In fact, the consolidation time is relatively smaller than the value taken here since it must be considered on a total period. So, for this benchmark, the balance is really much more favorable. Hovever, this benchmark does not integrate all the aspects of the STD technique and this preliminary conclusion must be confirmed by more extensive tests.

6. Conclusion

The STD strategy described in this paper is an attempt to incorporate in a unique framework several proposals able to improve performance in object database systems. The main idea is to take advantage of effective use of inter-object relationships to manage clustering of objects on disk and cluster-based buffering. We first have investigated problems associated with most existing clustering schemes in order to justify our precise motivations. Several points are rather innovating in the STD clustering proposal: (i) Clustering specifications are not made at a class level, so that distinct objects of a same class may be clustered in a different way. (ii) Clustering is made upon observation of effective use of links between objects rather than on a priori user hints or DB schema analysis. (iii) Considering that any relationship, leading to simultaneous use of objects, is expressed in databases by physical pointer traversals, the STD concept of link allows detection of any type of relationships (structural relationships defined in the schema, but also implicit links installed by programmers or by the DBMS itself). Clustering sequences take into consideration the different types of link, but do not have to distinguish them. Distance between related objects on disk only respects attractive force between objects. (iv) Automatic dynamic reclustering, free of user activations, is proposed. It deals implicitly with modifications of programs code and with database schema evolution. (v) Even if the solution is based on statistics management, efforts have been made to reduce storage costs, to filter and keep only pertinent information, and to brake-up reorganisations when confronted to continuous statistics changes. A strict control of reclustering avoids continuous reorganisations and excessive overhead. (vi) STD clustering scheme allows a deterministic solution to the problem of shared objects. (vii) Another idea is to accept large clusters among several contiguous disk pages. This permits to minimise disk head moves when large sets of related objects are accessed. Besides, the buffering policy has been adapted to take advantage of such clusters. In particular, we proposed a 'smart' prefetching policy and suggested to replace LRU policies by cluster-based replacement policies. Our approach remains efficient thanks to the idea of moving cluster-window centered on the page of the accessed object. (viii) The clustering mechanism does not require any user or administrator hints but remains user-controlled, with the presence of tuning parameters and activation/deactivation options.

A partial implementation of the STD technique has been made using Texas. It permits to experiment the clustering efficiency with a benchmark adapted from OO1. It appears that in nominal conditions, the number of fault pages is divided by five after reclustering. Overhead of STD technique is balanced by gain in access time only after five uses of the application.

This strategy may be convenient for any OODBMS, but requires some attention for its implementation. It is necessary to add an observation module inside the object manager in order to follow the dereferencements of persistent pointers. Besides, it implies management of different data structures (matrices, graphs) to store observations and determine the clusters. Many solutions do exist. Adaptations can be made to minimise occupied memory space and processing overhead. Besides, implementing dynamic reclustering in systems having physical object identifiers requires specific solutions. Problems encountered are the same as those encountered with DB schema evolution. Physical OID implies specific techniques to maintain DB integrity when moving objects (forwarding pointers, as in O_2, for example). Moreover, the STD clustering scheme implies specific solutions for storage space management. In particular, technical solutions must be developed inside DBMS running on Unix systems, to be able to allocate contiguous disk pages. The object manager must also be able to manage and reuse free disk space and to store instances of different classes in a same disk page.

We think that the STD proposal relies on pertinent motivations, considering the limited solutions available today in existing systems and the lack of advanced implemented proposals. However, if this approach constitutes an issue to enhance the performance of object systems, we know that its great tuning capabilities have to be reduced to a minimum set of relevant parameters. Experiments on Texas permit us to evaluate the behavior of T_{fa} and T_{fc}. They confirm our intuitive expectations. We think that these parameters must be fixed at values depending on the use of the database. For example, a good compromise is to fix T_{fa} at the value of the average number of object uses. We lead actually other experiments to validate the dynamical aspect of STD and to determine plausible value for T_{fe}.

Bibliography

1. V. Benzaken, C. Delobel, *"Enhancing performance in a persistent object store: clustering strategies in O_2"*, 4th International Workshop on Persistent Object Systems, September 1990, pp. 403-412.

2. V. Benzaken, *"An evaluation model for clustering strategies in the O_2 Object-Oriented Database System"*, Third International Conference on Database Theory, December 1990, pp. 126-140.

3. F. Bullat, "Regroupement physique d'objets dans les bases de données", to appear in the I.S.I. Journal, 'Ingénierie des Systèmes d'Information', Vol. 2, no. 4, September 1995.

4. R.G.G. Catell, *"An Engineering Database Benchmark"*, in 'The Benchmark Handbook for Database and Transaction Processing Systems", Morgan Kaufman Publishers, 1991, pp. 247-281.

5. E.E. Chang, *"Effective Clustering and Buffering in an Object-Oriented DBMS"*, Ph.D. Dissertation in Computer Science, Report no. UCB/CSD 89/515, University of California, Berkely, June 1989.

6. E.E. Chang, R.H. Katz, *"Exploiting Inheritance and Structure Semantics for Effective Clustering and Buffering in an Object-Oriented DBMS"*, ACM SIGMOD Conference, New York, 1989, pp. 348-357.

7. E.E. Chang, R.H. Katz, *"Inheritance in Computer-Aided Design Databases: Semantics and Implementation Issues"*, CAD, Vol. 22, no. 8, October 1990, pp. 489-499.

8. J.B. Cheng, A.R. Hurson, *"Effective Clustering of Complex Objects in Object-Oriented Databases"*, ACM SIGMOD Conference, New York, 1991, pp. 22-31.

9. J.B. Cheng, A.R. Hurson, *"On the Performance Issues of Object-Based Buffering"*, ACM SIGMOD Conference, New York, 1991, pp. 22-31.

10. W. Effelsberg, T. Haerder, *"Principles of Database Buffer Management"*, ACM Transactions on Database Systems, Vol. 9, no. 4, December 1984, pp. 560-595.

11. O. Gruber, L.Amsaleg, *"Object grouping in EOS"*, Workshop on Distributed Object Management, University of Alberta, August 1992, pp. 117-131.

12. M. Hornick, S. Zdonick, *"A shared Segmented Memory System for an Object-Oriented Database"*, ACM Transactions on Office Information Systems, Vol. 5, no. 1, January 1987, pp. 70-95.

13. S.E. Hudson, R. King, *"Cactis: A Self-Adaptive, Concurrent Implementation of an Object-Oriented Database Management System"*, ACM Transactions on Database Systems, Vol. 14, no. 3, September 1989, pp. 291-321.

14. W. Kim, J. Banerjee, H-T. Chou, J. F. Garza and D. Woelk, *"Composite Object Support in an Object-Oriented Database System"*, International Conference on OOPSLA, Orlando (Florida), October 4-8 1987, In proceedings of ACM SIGMOD Conference, 1987, pp. 118-125.

15. C. Lamb, G. Landis, J. Orenstein and D. Weinreb *"The ObjectStore Database System"*, Communications of the ACM, Vol. 34, no. 10, October 1991, pp. 50-63.

16. ONTOLOGIC Cie, *"ONTOS Client Library Reference Manual"*, December 1990.

17. Servio Corporation, *"GemStone V. 3.2 Reference Manual"*, 1992.

18. V. Singhal, S.V. Kakkad, P.R. Wilson, *"Texas: An Efficient, Portable Persistent Store"*, 5th International Workshop on Persistent Object Systems, San Miniato, Italy, September 1992.

19. J.W. Stamos, *"Static Grouping of small objects to Enhance Performance of a Paged Virtual Memory"*, ACM Transactions on Computer Systems, Vol. 2, no. 2, May 1984, pp. 155-180.

20. E.M. Tsangaris, J.F. Naughton, *"A Stochastic Approach for Clustering in Object Bases"*, ACM SIGMOD Conference, Denver, May 1991, pp. 12-21.

21. E.M. Tsangaris, *"Principles of Static Clustering for Object-oriented Databases"*, Technical Report no. 1104, University of Wisconsin-Madison, August 1992.

Acknowledgements: The authors wish to express their deep gratitude to S. V. KAKKAD (OOPS Research Group of Computer Science Deparment, University of Texas) for its collaboration through e-mail about Texas.

Conceptual Design of Active Object-Oriented Database Applications Using Multi-level Diagrams

Mauricio J. V. Silva [*]   C. Robert Carlson

Department of Computer Science
Illinois Institute of Technology
10 West 31st Street, Chicago, IL 60616
email: silvmau@charlie.acc.iit.edu, cscarlson@minna.iit.edu

Abstract

Several active object-oriented database systems have been developed to address the needs of applications with complex requirements and time execution constraints (e.g. computer integrated manufacturing). However, no comprehensive and integrated modeling approach has been described for conceptually modeling active object-oriented database applications.

This paper deals with these issues by extending the research of object-oriented methods with an integrated approach, called A/OODBMT (Active Object-Oriented Database Modeling Technique), which integrates and extends the Object Modeling Technique (OMT) method for conceptually designing active object-oriented database applications.

A/OODBMT models database applications by defining and integrating four new types of models, namely the nested object model (NOM), the behavior model (BM), the nested rule model (NRM), and the nested event model (NEM). The nested object model extends the OMT object model by adding nesting capabilities, and by providing a better abstraction mechanism for developing database applications in multi-level diagrams. Moreover, the nested object model adds rules to classes to specify their active behavior. The behavior model combines the dynamic and the functional modeling techniques proposed in the OMT method. In addition, the behavioral model represents database transactions through transaction diagrams. The nested rule model supports a comprehensive set of rules and visually defines the rules and their interactions using multi-level diagrams. The nested event model supports a comprehensive set of events and visually represents them in the context of rules.

1 Introduction

One of the major problems with the development of new and emerging database applications (e.g. computer integrated manufacturing) is that rules describing the policy of an organization are hard coded and dispersed all over different programs. This approach leads to applications that are harder to validate and difficult to maintain [Tsal91, Rasm95]. Moreover, as part of their semantics these applications need to be

---

* Supported by the Brazilian Government Agency - CAPES

active, i.e, continually monitoring changes to the database state and reacting by executing an appropriate action without user or application intervention[Chak93].

Active Object-Oriented Database Systems (AOODBSs) [Daya88, Geha91, Buch92, Gatz92, Anwa93, Kapp94] try to solve these problems by providing event driven behavior necessary for implementing time critical reactions, and by integrating rules with the database. A rule is composed of three components: an event, a condition and an action. The rule monitors the database, which only executes the action of the rule when the event occurs and the condition is evaluated to "true" [Carl83, Daya88]. Rules are used to declaratively specify all the control aspects of an application and are easy to manage because of their explicit specification.

While there has been considerable research and development of AOODBs [Kapp95, Buch95], little attention has been paid to defining an integrated modeling technique for conceptually modeling AOODBs applications.

Object-Oriented methods and modeling techniques [Mona92, Hutt94] can be useful for modeling the object-oriented schema of an active object-oriented database application. However, missing from these approaches is an integration of their models with rules and the capability to model database related features such as database transactions.

This paper adds to the research on object-oriented methods by developing an integrated approach, called A/OODBMT (Active Object-Oriented Database Modeling Technique), which integrates and extends the Object Modeling Technique (OMT) method [Rumb91] for conceptually designing active object-oriented database applications.

We chose to integrate and extend the OMT method because it is one of the most popular methods for analysis and design of object-oriented software development, and was developed specifically for modeling and reasoning about complex applications [Rumb91, Thur94]. Moreover, because OMT uses object-oriented models, it is capable of modeling the real world of interest more naturally than other models which do not consider the behavior of the application[Rumb91, Mart95].

A/OODBMT models database applications by defining and integrating four new types of models, namely the nested object model (NOM), the behavior model (BM), the nested rule model (NRM), and the nested event model (NEM). The nested object model extends the object model originally proposed in [Rumb91] by adding nesting capabilities proposed in [Carl89], and by providing a better abstraction mechanism for developing database applications in multi-level diagrams. Moreover, the nested object model adds rules to classes to specify their active behavior. The behavior model combines the dynamic model and the functional model originally proposed in [Rumb91]. In addition, the behavioral model represents database transactions through transaction diagrams. The nested rule model supports a comprehensive set of rules, and visually define rules and their interactions in multi-level diagrams. The nested event model supports a comprehensive set of events, and visually represents them using multi-level diagrams.

In A/OODBMT, each model describes one aspect of the system but contains references to the other models(see Figure 1). The nested object model contains descriptions of the classes and objects in the system that the behavioral model operates on.

The operations in the nested object model are described in the behavior model. The behavior model also uses operation events defined in the nested event model to describe the control aspects of the objects. Rules referenced in the nested object model are defined in nested rule model, and are executed in the context of the database transactions defined in the behavioral model. Rules specified in the nested rule model are triggered by events defined in nested event model.

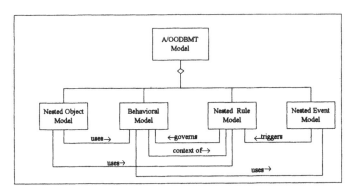

Fig. 1. Relationships among A/OODBMT Models

The remainder of this paper is organized as follows. Section 2 describes previous research and compares it to this approach. Section 3 describes the steps followed during conceptual design of active database applications using A/OODBMT models, and illustrates the application of these steps by modeling a library database system. Finally, Section 4 concludes the paper.

2 Related Work

The purpose of this section is to compare existing approaches to our approach. We analyze these approaches in the context of five modeling issues involved in the development of active object-oriented database applications. These include modeling objects, modeling passive object behavior (operations), modeling transactions, modeling rules (active behavior), and modeling events.

Current object-oriented methods have been used to model the objects of a system. However, their representation of objects employs "flat-diagrams", which can lead to very complicated diagrams if the objects have many associations [Carl89]. The Nested Object Model in A/OODBMT has been defined to deal with this problem. It provides a multi-level representation approach to the definition of the objects in a system, including their attributes, methods and rules.

In the object-oriented paradigm, the functionality of a system is achieved by the interaction and execution of object methods. Most object-oriented methods have used state diagrams to model object operations[Shal92, Jaco92, Rumb91]. In particular, [Rumb91] has used Harel state diagrams [Hare88], since it models the operations in multi-level diagrams. Moreover, [Rumb91] has used data-flow diagrams to model the functionality of the whole database application. From the data-flow diagram, object operations are extracted. Like [Rumb91], we use Harel state diagrams with data-flow diagrams. The difference is that instead of representing the data flow diagram for the whole system, we create a data-flow diagram for each operation and its activities.

The interaction of the objects in a system defines a transaction. Moreover, the active behavior of the systems (i.e. rules) is only executed within the context of a transaction. Although current object oriented methods (e.g. [Rumb91, Jaco92, Booc94, Cole94]) model the interaction of objects in a system, they do not model database transactions. Missing from their representation are the database commands(e.g. transaction begin, abort, commit) used to define transactions and subtransactions. Our approach is to extend the modeling of object interactions with database transaction commands.

Existing visual approaches to rule specification include [Bich94, Mart95, Tsal91, Shen92, Grah94, Pras94]. All of these approaches support event /condition /action (ECA) rules. [Shen92], [Grah94], [Pras94], and [Mart95] specify production rules, pre/ post condition of operations. However, only a few approaches (e.g., [Tsal91, Pras94]), support exception, and contingency rules. Only [Grah94] provides support for grouping rules, by allowing a rule to be defined as the disjunction of simple rules. But, none of the approaches support the grouping of exclusive rules representing one abstract rule. None of the approaches define the semantics for rule overriding. Only petri-net like approaches [Tsal91, Pras94] show the interconnection of rules in "flat diagrams", which can lead to highly connected diagrams that are almost impossible to comprehend. Our approach is to integrate previous approaches and extend them by visually representing a comprehensive set of rules and their interactions including composite rules in a multi-level model, called the nested rule model. We also provide the semantics for overriding rules and support a wealth of coupling modes for rule execution [Bran93].

The modeling of events is crucial to active object-oriented database systems, since they determine when rules will be evaluated. Existing active object-oriented database systems model events textually, which is not an appropriate level for designing applications. Moreover, existing visual approaches (e.g. [Mart95, Bich94, Gatz94]) do not support a comprehensive set of both simple and composite events. Further, existing approaches do not represent events at multiple levels of abstraction using multi-level diagramming techniques. Our approach deals with these problems by supporting a comprehensive set of events and by providing a high-level graphical representation of events in multi-level diagrams.

3 Active Database Conceptual Design using A/OODBMT Models

In this section, we give the steps followed during conceptual design for the modeling of an active database application. We illustrate the application of these steps by modeling a library database system. The requirements of the library database system are described in Figure 2. From these requirements, we build the A/OODBMT models and show their integration. Only the essential points of the A/OODBMT models will be discussed in the forthcoming subsections. The detailed description of the application of A/OODBMT can be found in [Silv95a].

The steps defined for conceptual database design in A/OODBMT are:

(i)   Design the static structure of object/classes using the nested object model.

(ii)   Design the passive behavior (methods) of object/classes and the database transactions using the behavior model.

(iii) Design the active behavior (rules) of object/classes using the nested rule model.

(iv)   Design the events that appear in rules using the nested event model.

Note that, although we describe the steps above in a sequential order, the actual process of modeling an application is iterative. For instance, after building the behavioral model and identifying the operations of a class, we may have to go back and add them to the nested object model. Further, rules identified in the nested rule model for a specific object/class, have their name added to the rule part of the corresponding object/class in the nested object model.

In the following subsections we describe the nested object model, the behavioral model, the nested rule model, and the nested event model in turn.

3.1 Nested Object Modeling

The nested object model (NOM) is used to represent the static aspects of applications and is based on the object model [Rumb91] enhanced with nesting capabilities [Carl89] and rules. The major concepts found in NOM include class, object, relationships, attributes, operations, rules, and complex objects. A detailed description of NOM can be found in [Silv95a].

NOM enhances the object model by allowing objects/classes and associations to be abstracted as either simple or complex. Complex classes and associations can be expanded into sub-diagrams, where a more detailed specification is provided. This allows one to describe the static aspects of the application in multi-level diagrams, which facilitate the comprehension of the model. Without nesting the diagrams, very large object models resemble circuit diagrams rather than comprehensible structures [Carl89]. Further, NOM adds rules to the definition of a class and its instances (objects) to specify their declarative behavior. Only the names of the rules are placed inside an object/class as the actual definition of the rule is shown in the nested rule model.

The nested object model is built in several steps described below. We illustrate each step by applying it to the library database system example. The complete nested object model of the library database example is described in Figure 3. Note that in

Figure 3, we have also included the method and the rule part of the classes which will be discussed later in this article.

---

(1) The library system is composed of books and members.

(2) The library is opened from 10 a.m. - 10 p.m. (Mondays to Fridays) and from 10 a.m. - 6p.m. in the weekends.

(3) A member is a person and is characterized by a name, a ss# and an address. There are two types of members: students, and faculty.

(4) A book is characterized by a title, an author, a date of publishing and a publisher.

(5) A person may check out books only if he/she is a member of the library, otherwise an invalid checkout request message is sent to the person. Only available books can be checked out.

(6) All members may check out books for 2 weeks.

(7) When a person checks out a book, he/she must provide the title of the book and his/her ss#.

(8) When a book is checked out, a due date for returning the book is set.

(9) Books are expected to be returned by the due date. If the book is returned after the due date, it is considered to be overdue.

(10) When a person returns a book , if it is overdue a fine of 10 cents per day is charged to the member for each book not returned on time. A faculty member will receive only warnings for the first 5 overdue books. After that, the faculty member will start paying fines for overdue books.

(11) A notice is mailed to a member if he/she has a book that has been overdue for seven consecutive days .

Fig. 2. Library Database System Example

(i) Identifying the Classes and Attributes in the System

A class is a description of a group of related objects with similar behavior, semantics, and relationships [Rumb91]. In NOM, a class is composed of three parts: attributes, operations, and rules. It is depicted as a four part box, with the name of the class on the top part, a list of attributes with optional types on the second part, a list of operations with optional arguments and return value types on the third part, and a list of rule names on the fourth part. The attribute, operation, and rule sections of the class box can be omitted to reduce the detail of a visual specification.

From the library database requirements, we identify six major classes: *Person*, *Member, Student Member, Faculty Member, Library*, and *Book*. From line (3) we

372

define a class *Person* with attributes name, *ss#* and *address*. From (10), we define a class *Member* with an attribute *fine*. From line (4) and (9) we define a class *Book* with attributes *title, author, type, date of publishing, publisher, duedate, and status.*

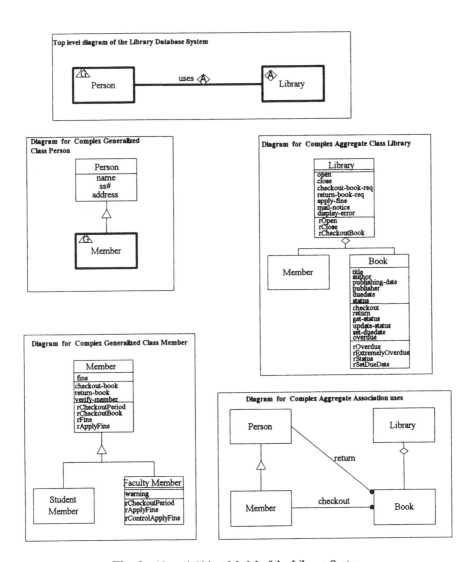

Fig. 3. Nested Object Model of the Library System

(ii) Identifying the Relationships in the System

A relationship is a characteristic that specifies a mapping from one object to another [Hutt94]. In NOM, there are three types of relationships, namely association, aggregation and generalization [Rumb91].

From line (1) of the library database example, we identify that class *Library* is an aggregation of classes *Member* and *Book*. From line (3), we identify that class *Person* is a generalization of class *Member* and that class *Member* is a generalization of classes *Student Member, and Faculty Member*. From line (5), we identify a *check-out* association from class *Member* and *Book*. From line (10), we identify an association *return* from class *Person* to class *Book*.

(iii) Identifying Complex Classes

A complex class is a virtual class. It is used to visually improve the understanding of NOM. Expanding a complex class yields a lower level diagram, which defines the elements of the complex class.

There are two types of complex classes, namely complex aggregate classes and complex generalized classes. A complex aggregate class is always related to a class, which has an aggregate relationship (e.g. class *Library* in Figure 3). A complex aggregate class represents a higher abstraction of the related aggregate class. It has the same name as the related aggregate class and is depicted as a bold class box with a diamond with the letter A (aggregation) inside, placed on the upper left corner of the box. Expanding a complex aggregate class yields a subdiagram showing the aggregation relationship of the related aggregate class and its components. A complex generalized class is always related to a class which has a generalization relationship referred to as a general class (e.g. class *Person* in Figure 3). A complex generalized class represents a higher abstraction of the general class. It has the same name as the related general class and is depicted as a bold class box with a triangle with the letter G (generalization) inside, placed on the upper left corner of the box. Expanding a complex generalized class yields a lower level diagram, showing the generalization relationship of the related general class and its components.

By using the aggregation and generalization relationships derived from step (ii), we identify that class *Person* and *Member* are complex generalized classes and that class *Library* is a complex aggregate class.

(iv) Identifying Complex Associations

A complex association is a visual construct to improve the understanding of NOM. The purpose of a complex association is to consolidate all the associations related to the pairs of classes or their subclasses and/or subcomponents. Expanding a complex association between two classes yields a lower level diagram, defining all the associations between the classes and their subcomponents .

There are two types of complex associations in NOM, namely complex aggregate associations and complex generalized associations. A complex aggregate association is formed from a "serial" path between the participating classes. It is depicted by a bold line connecting the related classes with the name of the association followed by a diamond with the letter A (aggregation) inside. A complex generalized association is formed from a set of "parallel" associations between two classes. It is depicted by a bold line connecting the related classes with a name of the association followed by a triangle with the letter G (generalization) inside.

By using the associations derived from step (ii), we identify a complex aggregate association *uses* from class *Person* to class *Library*. The complex aggregate association *uses* is composed of the associations *checkout* and *return*.

3.2 Behavioral Modeling

The behavioral model represents the temporal and transformational aspects of a system. It combines and integrates the dynamic (state diagrams) and functional model (data-flow diagrams) originally proposed in [Rumb91], adding database transaction capabilities. Thus, the behavioral model is composed of three diagrams: state diagrams, data-flow diagrams and transaction diagrams.

State diagrams are used to describe the life history of objects of a particular class. It specifies and implements the control of objects, identifying object operations and activities. Data-flow diagrams are used to describe the operations of an object/class. Transaction diagrams define the database transactions of the system, describing the sequence of communications between objects.

The behavioral model is built in several steps described below. We analyze the library database requirements and build the state diagram, data-flow diagram and transaction diagram for some of the classes identified in the nested object model.

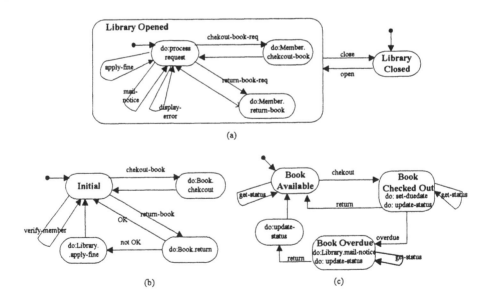

Fig. 4. State Diagrams for the Library System

(i) Building State Diagrams

In the behavioral model, each class will have a state diagram. A state diagram represents the life history of objects in a class and shows the sequence of operations that takes objects into several different states. It is a graph whose nodes are states of an object and whose arcs are transitions between states caused by events applicable to that object. The graphical notation used for a state diagram is the Harel statecharts [Hare88].

The state diagrams derived from the library system are described in Figure 4. We define state diagrams only for the main classes of the library system, namely *Library*, *Member, and Book*. Class *Library* will have the following operations: *open, close, checkout-book-req, return-book-req, apply-fine, mail-notice, and display-error* (see Figure 4(a)). Class *Member* will have the following operation: *checkout-book, return-book, and verify-member* (see Figure 4(b)). Class *Book* will have the following operations: *checkout, return, overdue, set-duedate, get-status, and update-status* (see Figure 4(c)).

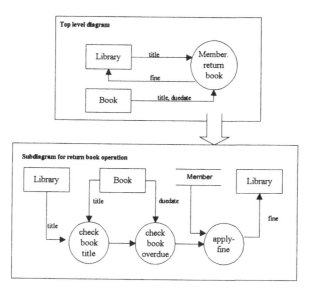

Fig. 5. Data-flow Diagram for return-book Operation

(ii) Building Data-flow Diagrams

In the behavioral model, a data-flow diagram (DFD) is used to describe the operation of an object/class identified in the state diagram. It is represented as a graph whose nodes are processes (transform data), actors (produce and consume data) and datastores (store data), and whose arcs are data-flows (move data) and control-flows (control process evaluation). The graphical notation used for a DFD is based on the notation proposed by [Dema79].

The level 0 of a DFD represents the operation of a class as a single process. Each operation has a set of activities described in a lower level diagram and are also represented as a process. Some activities may need to access the state of the class, which is represented as a dataflow from the datastore with the name of the class to the activity process. Moreover, some activities may use operations defined in other classes. In this case, these other classes are represented as actors with a dataflow connecting the activity process.

Since the operations derived from the state diagram of the library database example are very simple, we only show for illustrative purposes the data-flow diagram for the *return-book* operation in class Member (see Figure 5).

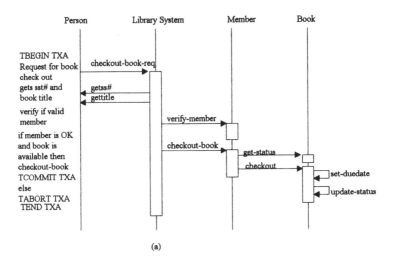

(a)

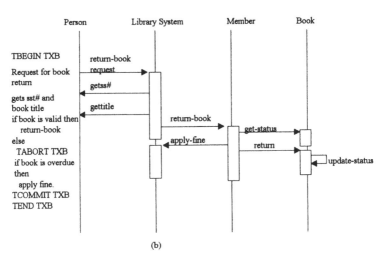

(b)

Fig. 6. Describing the Checkout and Return Book Transactions

(iii) Building Database Transactions

In the behavioral model, database transactions are described by transaction diagrams. Transaction diagrams extend interaction diagrams [Jaco92], with transaction commands, i.e. TBEGIN, TEND, TABORT, TCOMMIT. Each transaction defined has a name and represents a unit of work describing the interaction between the objects in the system.

In the transaction diagram, each object/class participating in the transaction is represented by a column drawn as a vertical line. The interactions between the objects are shown as operation invocations. Each operation of a class involved in the transaction is shown as a rectangle in its class column. The object originating the transaction is represented as the left most column and is called an "external object" to the system. To the left of the external object column we describe the transaction in natural language (pseudocode). The pseudocode describes what is happening in a particular part of the transaction (class operations).

From the library database example, we identify two major transactions in the system. The first one checks out books from the library and is described in Figure 6(a). The second returns books to the library and is described in Figure 6(b).

3.3 Nested Rule Modeling

The nested rule model (NRM) is a high-level graphical approach for conceptually designing rules in active object-oriented databases. NRM models a comprehensive set of rules, using two types of diagrams - nested rule diagrams (NRDs) and rule interaction diagrams (RIDs).

In NRD, a rule is depicted by an ellipse and has a name and a type (simple or composite), which is represented inside the rule icon separated by a line (see Figure 7). NRDs visually represent both simple and composite rules by using two types of abstraction techniques, embedding and nesting. Simple rules may be used to constrain the structure of objects and may also govern the object's behavior through dynamic rules, such as event-condition action or exception rules. Composite rules enable the designer to express complex object behavior by applying a set of constructors to simple rules and previously defined composite rules. Further, NRDs define the semantics of rule inheritance and overriding, and describe how the coupling mode of rules can be specified.

RIDs visually represent the interactions between rules, using multi-level diagrams. Multi-level diagrams are used to avoid the complexity of flat diagrams, where complex interconnection of rules may become impossible to comprehend because of the number of connecting lines. Both diagrams (NRD and RID) may be used together, so that the database designer can have a multi-level view of the rules defined for an object and at the same time visualize their interactions.

Below, we describe the steps used to build the NRM of an application. We use the library database example to illustrate the application of each step.

(i) **Identifying Static Simple Rules**

Static rules define constraints on the structure of a class that must always hold. These constraints are specified in terms of classes, objects, attributes and associations. Since static rules are always true and are defined in the context of an object/class, they are represented by placing an invariant condition within the context object/class all embedded within the rule icon (see Figure 7).

In NRD, static rules can be classified into the following constraint rules: attribute constraints, attribute domain constraints, mandatory/optional attribute constraints, attribute cardinality constraints, population type constraints, association cardinality constraints, existence dependence constraints, relational constraints, and uniqueness constraints. Below we describe each of the static rule types. Examples of constraint rules not illustrated in this paper can be found in [Silv95a].

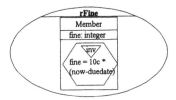

Fig. 7.   Attribute Constraint for Class Member

a) Attribute Constraint: It is a constraint imposed on the attributes of a class or an object. An attribute constraint can also represent constraints that span multiple classes/objects. In this case, we attach the attribute constraint to a control object/class.

From the library example line (10) - "When a person returns a book , if it is overdue a fine of 10 cents per day is charged to the member for each book not returned on time.", we derive an invariant attribute constraint rule *rFine* in class *Member* (see Figure 7) .

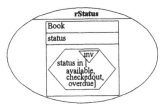

Fig. 8.   Domain Constraint for Class Book

b) Attribute Domain Constraint: It is a constraint imposed on the domain of object/classes attributes. It is described by an enumeration if the domain is restricted to a list of discrete elements, or it is described by an interval in the case of well ordered domains. In NRD, domain constraints are represented in a textual form placed inside an invariant condition icon. The internal BNF syntax for the definition of a domain constraint is: *[(<class_name>|<object_name>).]<attribute_name> in [<list_of_elements>| <interval>]*

Based on the library example, a book can be in states available, checkedout or overdue. To model these different states, we define a domain constraint rule *rStatus* in class *Book* (see Figure 8) . *rStatus* is specified with attribute *status* restricted to a list of elements *(available, checkedout, and overdue)*.

c) Mandatory/Optional Attribute Constraint: It is a constraint that specifies that the attributes of a class or object must always have a value (mandatory) or may not have a value (optional).

d) Attribute Cardinality Constraint: It is a constraint that specifies the minimum and maximum occurrences of a multivalued attribute.

e) Population Type Constraint: It is a constraint that limits the number of objects in a class.

f) Association Cardinality Constraint: It is a constraint that limits the number of associations between two objects/classes.

g) Existence Dependent Constraint: It is a constraint that an object cannot exist without being associated with another object.

h) Relational Constraint: It is a constraint that an object must maintain correspondence (inverse) with another object. That is, if an object is updated, the related inverse object must also be updated.

i) Uniqueness Constraint: It is a constraint that determines that every object of a class has a unique value for an attribute.

(ii) Identifying Dynamic Simple Rules in NRD

Dynamic rules monitor the way an object's processes may execute and relate to one another and how objects respond to specific events and exceptions. In NRD, dynamic rules include event-condition-action rules, exception rules, contingency rules, precondition rules, postcondition rules, and production rules. In this article, only the dynamic rules related to the library database example will be illustrated. Examples of the dynamic rules not illustrated in this paper can be found in [Silv95a].

a) Event-Condition-Action Rule: The Event-Condition-Action (ECA) rule defined by [Daya88] was originally used by [Carl83] to extend relational databases with active capabilities. The ECA rule enables the database to monitor a situation represented by an event and one or more conditions and execute the corresponding actions when the event occurs and the conditions are evaluated to true. In NRD, a named event is only referenced in the rule using an event icon (a parallelogram). The actual description of the event is represented using the nested event diagram, which is described in the next section. A condition determines if an action can be executed and is represented by a condition icon (a hexagon). A condition that is always "true", can be omitted. An action is always represented as a process which is applicable to a specific object. An action is implemented as a method in the object and can actually trigger the execution of other rules. In addition, the action part can be used to control the reasoning of production rules. The complete ECA rule is depicted by an event icon connected with an arrow to the condition icon and which in turn is connected to the action icon with an arrow. Below we show examples of ECA rules for the classes *Library, Member, and Book*. ECA rules of class *Member* that are overridden by class *Faculty Member* are described later in this article.

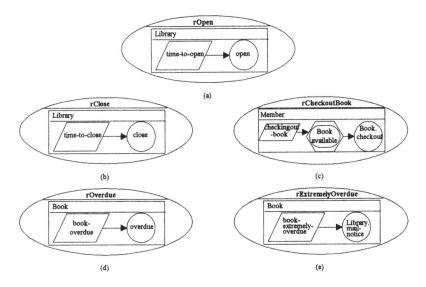

Fig. 9. ECA Rules for the Library System

- ECA rules for class Library: From line(2) we identify rules *rOpen and rClose* for opening and closing the library. *rOpen* has an event *time-to-open* and an action which is the operation *open* (see Figure 9(a)). *rClose* has an event *time-to-close* and an action which is the operation *close* (see Figure 9(b)).

- ECA rules for class Member: From line(5) we identify a rule *rCheckoutBook* for checking out a book. *rCheckoutBook* has an event *checkingout-book,* a condition testing if the book is in state *available*, and an action *checkout* applied to the book (see Figure 9(c)).

- ECA rules for class Book: From line(9) we identify a rule *rOverdue* for returning an overdue book. *rOverdue* has an event *book-overdue*, which determines when the operation *overdue* is executed (see Figure 9(d)). From line (11), we identify a rule *rExtremelyOverdue* for a person who keeps an overdue book more than seven consecutive days. *rExtremelyOverdue* has an event *book-extremely-overdue*, and an action which is the operation *mail-notice* in class *Library* (see Figure 9(e)).

b) Exception Rule: An exception rule is a special case of an ECA rule. It specifies an event, a condition, a main action and a series of exception actions. However, only one action will be executed when the event occurs and the condition is evaluated. Each action will have a triggering value attached to the end of the incoming arrow from the condition. An action is executed if its triggering value matches the value returned by the condition evaluation. If no match is found, the main action is executed. The main action is defined by a straight arrow from the condition. Each exception action is represented as a branch of the straight arrow. Below we show an example of an exception action in which a condition returns two values: TRUE (T) or FALSE (F).

From the library example line (5) - "A person may check out books only if it is a member of the library, otherwise an invalid checkout request message is sent to the person.", we define an exception rule *rCheckoutBook* in the context of the class *Library* (see Figure 10). *rCheckoutBook* has an event *checkout-book-requested*, a condition using the *verify-member* method to check if the person is a member, a main action which is an operation *checkout-book* in class Member with a triggering value *T* (TRUE), and an exception action *display-error* with a triggering value *F* (FALSE).

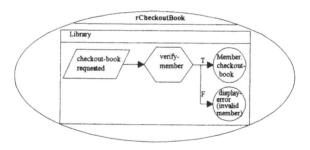

Fig. 10. Exception Rule for class Library

c) Contingency Rule: Contingency rules are specified for actions that are time-constrained. If these actions cannot be carried out within a pre-specified time, alternative actions need to be executed. In NRD, contingency rules are represented by modifying an ECA rule by defining an action to be constrained by a condition that specifies its timing constraints.

d) Operation Precondition Rule: An operation precondition rule expresses those constraints under which an operation will be allowed to be performed.

e) Operation Postcondition Rule: Operation Postcondition rules are constraints that guarantee the results of an operation. From the library database example, we define a postcondition rule named *rSetDueDate (duedate = now + 2 weeks)* in class *Book*, which must hold after executing the operation *set-duedate* (see Figure 11).

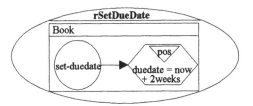

Fig. 11. Postcondition rule rSetDueDate

f) Production Rule: A production rule specifies the policies or conditions for inferring or computing facts from other facts. It is composed of a condition and an action and can be used for representing heuristic knowledge. Production rules are controlled by ECA rules, i.e. production rules will only be evaluated when triggered by an ECA rule.

(iii) Identifying Composite Rules in NRD

Composite rules enable the database designer to structurally abstract rules. They are particularly useful when the number of rules becomes very large and very difficult to comprehend. In this case, the rules are divided and grouped into related rules (components) represented by a composite rule.

There are two possible ways to represent a composite rule. The first approach, called nesting, is to define the composite rule and its components at different levels of abstraction through multi-level rule diagrams. The composite rule is represented in a diagram at level i, and can be expanded to a subdiagram at level i + 1, where its components are represented. At the higher level diagram, a composite rule is drawn as a bold ellipse with the composite rule name and a keyword representing the composite rule type within an upside down triangle (see Figure 12(a)). The keyword is used to inform the type of subdiagram that will be shown to the designer, once the composite rule is expanded. The second approach, called embedding, is to define all the component rules at the same level of abstraction, by enclosing all the component rules inside the rule icon (see Figure 12(b)). By placing component rules within the composite rule, we avoid using edges to describe the composite rule, which reduces the complexity of the diagram.

Both approaches may be used by the designer to represent different composite rules. When there are too many subdiagrams for a composite rule one should use the second approach (embedding), and when there are too many levels of embedded icons one should use the first approach (nesting). It is up to the designer to decide how to combine the two approaches.

In NRD, composite rules are classified into the following rules: disjunction rules and exclusive rules. A disjunction rule represents a set of rules, called member rules, which may be applicable to an object/class. A disjunction rule is successfully applied to an object, when one of its member rules has been successfully executed (i.e. committed). An exclusive rule R represents a set of rules, which cannot be applicable to an object/class at the same time. An exclusive rule is successfully applied to an object, when only one of its rules has successfully executed (i.e. committed), but the other rules have failed (i.e. aborted or deactivated).

For example, let us consider that we change the requirements of the library system to allow a faculty member to checkout books for a period of one month if he/she has no books overdue, but reduce the checkout period to three weeks after the fifth overdue book.

To model this example, we assume that rules *rCheckout1Month* (representing a checkout period of one month), and *rCheckout3Weeks* (representing a checkout period of three weeks) have already been defined. Then, we define a more general rule *rCheckoutPeriod* in class Faculty Member as a composite exclusive rule of *rCheckout1Month* and *rCheckout3Weeks* (see Figure 12).

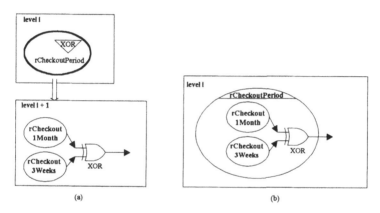

Fig. 12. Composite Exclusive Rule rCheckoutPeriod

(iv) Identifying the Coupling Mode of Rules in NRD

In AOODBSs, rules are triggered within a database transaction (i.e., triggering transaction) and are executed according to their coupling modes to the transaction. The coupling modes of a rule determine at what point in the triggering transaction the rule will be evaluated and determine whether the rule will be executed as a separate top level transaction or will be executed as a subtransaction of the triggering transaction.

In NRD, we support the comprehensive collection of coupling modes defined in [Bran93]. These coupling modes include immediate, deferred, separate, parallel causally dependent, sequential causally dependent, and exclusive causally dependent. Coupling modes are represented by keywords identifying the coupling mode type and are depicted by attaching the keyword to the connections between an event and a condition as well as a condition and an action. ECA rules without an explicit representation of their coupling modes are assumed to have an immediate mode. Below, for each coupling we list its name, its keyword name within parenthesis, and give a full description of its meaning.

- Immediate (*imm*): The rule is evaluated immediately after its event is detected and is executed as a subtransaction of the triggering transaction.

- Deferred (*def*): The rule is evaluated immediately before the triggering transaction commits and is executed as a subtransaction of the triggering transaction.

- Separated (*sep*): The rule is evaluated immediately after its event is detected and is executed as a separate top level transaction independent of the triggering transaction.

- Parallel Causally Dependent (*pcd*): The rule is evaluated immediately after its event is detected and is executed as a separate top level transaction with commit and abort dependency with the triggering transaction. That is, the rule may execute in parallel to the triggering transaction as a top level transaction, but may not commit until the triggering transaction commits and must abort if the triggering transaction aborts.

- Sequential Causally Dependent (*scd*): The rule is evaluated immediately after its event is detected and is executed as a separate top level transaction only after the triggering transaction has committed.

- Exclusive Causally Dependent (*ecd*): The rule is evaluated immediately after its event is detected and is executed as a separate top level transaction in parallel with the triggering transaction, but it only commits if the triggering transaction has aborted. This type of coupling mode is used for contingency rules.

Figure 13 shows a rule *rExtremelyOverdue* in class *Book*, where the rule is evaluated *immediately*, but the action of *mailing a notice* is executed as a *separate* transaction.

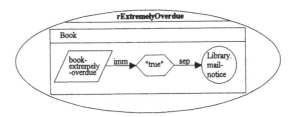

Fig. 13. Rule with an Immediate/Detached Coupling Mode

(v) Identifying the Inheritance and Overriding of Rules in NRD

Rules attached to a class are automatically inherited by each subclass. Like methods, rules can be overridden. Overriding a rule means that the subclass has attached to it a modification or a refinement of the rule. There are two main reasons the designer may want to override a rule: to specify a rule that is the same as the inherited rule, except it adds some behavior usually affecting new attributes of the subclass, or to tighten the specification of a rule by tightening the type of the arguments used in the expressions.

In NRD, a rule can only be overridden by another rule of the same type and the same name. Below we give the definition of the semantics for overriding rules in the context of a class A and a subclass B.

Static Rules:

A static rule R1 with an invariant condition C1 in class A is overridden by a rule in subclass B, if and only if the rule has the same name R1, but a different invariant condition.

Dynamic Rules:

a) ECA Rule Overriding: An ECA rule R1 with an event E1, a condition C1, and action A1 in class A is overridden by a rule in subclass B, if and only if the rule has the same name R1, the same event E1 but either a different condition or action.

b) Exception Rule Overriding: An exception rule R1 with an event E1, a condition C1, an action A1 and an exception action A2 is overridden by a rule in subclass B, if and only if the rule has the same name R1, the same event E1 but with either a different condition, action, or exception action.

c) Contingency Rule Overriding: A contingency rule R1 with an event E1, a condition C1, an action A1, a pre-specified execution time T1 and an alternate action A2 is overridden by a rule in subclass B, if and only if the rule has the same name R1, the same event E1 but either a different condition, action, pre-specified time, or alternate action.

d) Operation Precondition Rule Overriding: An operation precondition rule R1 with precondition P1 and action A1 is overridden by a rule in subclass B, if and only if the rule has the same name R1 with a different precondition, but the same action A1.

e) Operation Postcondition Rule Overriding: An operation postcondition rule R1 with an action A1 and postcondition P1 is overridden by a rule in subclass B, if and only if the rule has the same name R1 with the same action A1, but different postcondition.

f) Production Rule Overriding: A production rule R1 with condition C1 and action A1 is overridden by a rule in subclass B, if and only if the rule has the same name R1 with the same condition C1 but different action.

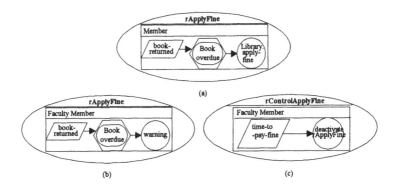

Fig 14. Rule Inheritance and Overriding for classes Member and Faculty Member

Not all inherited rules may be suitable for a subclass [Dill93, Kapp94]. To model this case in NRD, we override a rule that is not suitable for the subclass and falsify its condition and nullify its actions. Thus, a rule will still be propagated to the subclasses, but it will never be executed, unless it is overridden again.

Moreover, there are situations where the database designer wants to deactivate a rule, stopping the inheritance of a rule. This is particularly useful for experimenting with "what-if" scenarios, analyzing the impact of different rules on the system behavior [Buch95, Kapp94, Dill93]. In NRD, the activation/ deactivation of a rule is represented by an action using the keywords *activate/deactivate* followed by the name of the rule. A deactivated rule is represented with a gray background. Below we illustrate the overriding of rules in the library database system.

- Example of Rule Overriding: From the library example line(10) - "When a person returns a book , if it is overdue a fine of 10 cents per day is charged to the member for each book not returned on time. A faculty member will receive only warnings for the first 5 overdue books. After that, the faculty member will start paying fines for overdue books.", we define a rule *rApplyFine*, which is first defined in class *Member*, and then redefined in class *Faculty Member*. In class *Member*, *rApplyFine* is defined with an event *book-returned*, a condition that the book is *overdue*, and an action which is the operation *apply-fine* in class *Library* (see Figure 14(a)). In class *Faculty Member*, *rApplyFine* overrides the rule in class *Member* with a different action, which is an operation *warning* (see Figure 14(b)). Also, in order to deactivate the overriding of rule *rApplyFine*, we define another rule *rControlApplyFine*, which is executed after the *Faculty Member* has received *five warnings*. *rControlApplyFine* has an event *time-to-pay-fine*, and an action *deactivate rApplyFine* (see Figure 14(c)).

(vi) Identifying the Interconnection of Rules in RID

Rule interaction diagrams (RIDs) visually show the interdependence between rules. It is a very useful diagram to show the database designer, the cascading of rules, and how they relate to each other. The interdependence between rules is based on the action of each rule. If the action of a rule R1, causes an event which triggers the evaluation of another rule R2, then R1 is a triggering rule for R2.

In a tightly coupled environment where rules are highly interdependent, any flat diagram representing the interconnection of these rules is likely to be highly connected. In the case of many connected rules, a flat diagram can become almost impossible to comprehend. An effective solution to this problem is to use multi-level diagrams [Carl89] to represent the interconnection of rules.

RID uses multi-level diagrams to show the interdependence of rules. To support the definition of multi-level diagrams, RID defines a new type of rule object, called a rule connector. A rule connector is an object in the RID which contains the same name of a rule defined in the NRD. It is depicted by a dotted ellipse with the related rule name inside (see Figure 15) and it is used to depict the triggering rules of a rule.

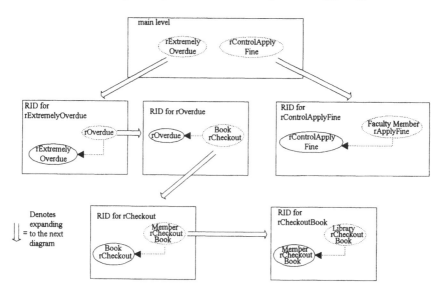

Fig. 15. Rule Interaction Diagrams for the Library System

RIDs are organized hierarchically. At the main level (diagram level zero) all the rules that do not trigger the execution of another rule are represented as rule connector objects. Moreover, each rule will have a diagram and will be referred to as the "main rule". The main rule will be represented with an ellipse, if simple, and a bold ellipse, if composite, with its name inside. All the triggering rules of the main rule will be represented in the diagram as rule connector objects and will be linked to the main rule with dotted arrows. The navigation between rule interaction diagrams is done by expanding a rule connector.

In NRM, RIDs and NRDs are used in an integrated way. The integration between these diagrams is achieved by allowing the main rules in RID to be expanded into NRDs. This allows a multi-level view of the rules defined for an object, showing at different levels of abstraction the visual definition and interaction of rules.

From selected rules defined in the library database system, we derive the following interactions described in Figure 15. Rule *rExtremelyOverdue* in class Book is triggered by rule *rOverdue*, which is in turn triggered by rule *rCheckout*. Rule *rCheckout* is triggered by rule *rCheckoutBook* in class Member, which is in turn triggered by rule *rCheckoutBook* in class Library. Rule *rControlApplyFine* is triggered by rule *rApplyFine* in class *Faculty Member*.

3.4 Nested Event Modeling

The Nested Event Model (NEM) visually models the events referenced in rules using a multi-level diagram, called the Nested Event Diagram (NED). NED models a comprehensive set of events, integrating the event types present in existing active object-oriented database systems. NED is composed of primitive (simple) and composite (complex) events. Primitive events correspond to elementary occurrences, and composite events correspond to events that are formed by applying a set of constructors to primitive and composite events. Below we use the nested event model to describe the events used in the rules defined for classes *Library, Member, Faculty Member and Book*. Event types not illustrated in this article can be found in [Silv95a].

(i) Identifying Primitive Events

A primitive event describes a point in time specified by an occurrence in the database (method execution events, and transaction events), temporal events, and explicit events.

a) Method Execution Event: In AOODBs, methods implement an operation for a specific class. The method executes when an object receives a message with the name of the method. The execution of a method gives rise to two events: an event which occurs immediately before the method is executed and an event immediately after it has executed [Geha92]. The parameters of a method can be later used in conditions specified in rules.

In NED, a method execution event is related to a particular class or to a particular object, only if a particular class name or object name is given. The BNF syntax for a method event is: *(before|after) [(<class_name>|<object_name>).]<method_name>*

Note that the class name can be omitted when specifying a method execution event. Below we represent the method execution events used by the rules in the library database example.

- Events for class Library: The event *checkout-book-requested* was referenced in rule *rCheckoutBook* (see Figure 10) and occurs after a request for checking out a book is made. It is modeled as a method execution event which occurs *after* operation *checkout-book-req* is executed (see Figure 16(a)).

- Events for class Member: The event *book-returned* was referenced in rule *rApplyFine* (see Figure 14(a)) and occurs after a book is returned. It is modeled as a method execution event which occurs *after* the operation *return-book* is executed (see Figure 16(b)). The event *checkingout-book* was referenced in rule *rCheckoutBook* (see Figure 9(c)) and occurs before a book is checked out. It is modeled as a method execution event which occurs *before* the operation *checkout-book* is executed (see Figure 16(c)).

(a)   (b)   (c)

Fig. 16. Method Execution Events for classes Library and Member

b) Transaction Event: We treat transaction events as a special case of a method execution event. Transaction events are defined after or before transaction operations are executed (e.g. after tCommit). A transaction operation can be considered as a method applied to each object involved in the transaction.

c) Temporal Event: Temporal events are defined as an explicit point in time. They can be divided into two categories: absolute temporal events, and periodic temporal events.

Absolute Temporal Event: An absolute temporal event is specified with an absolute value of time [Daya88]. It is depicted by showing the year, month, week, day and time within a box inside an event icon.

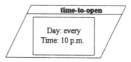

Fig. 17. Representation of Event "time-to-open"

Periodic Temporal Event: A periodic temporal event is an event that periodically reappear in time [Daya88]. Periodic temporal events are defined like absolute temporal events where some of the data fields can be omitted, meaning that the omitted data field matches *any* valid value for that field. In addition, the data field which represents the periodicity has the keyword *every* attached to it. The temporal event occurs periodically at every point in time that matches the partial specification. From the library database example, we represent the event *time-to-open*, referenced in rule *rOpen* (see Figure 9(a)) as a periodic event which occurs every day at 10 a.m. (see Figure 17).

d) Explicit Event: An explicit (also called external or abstract) event is defined by the database designer and is explicitly signaled inside applications of the database system [Chak93]. This event may have parameters which are supplied at the time it is signaled to the AOODBS. An explicit event is depicted inside of an event icon with the following BNF syntax: *EXPLICIT <event_name> [(<parameters>)]*

(ii) Identifying Composite Events

The primitive events defined above are only able to represent elementary events. However, there are many applications that need to model composite (complex) events, which are composed of primitive and also previously defined complex events. Composite events are defined by applying event constructors to previously defined events, called component events, and occurs at the point of occurrence of the last event that was needed to make it happen [Geha92]. Like NRM, NEM uses two types of abstraction techniques, nesting (see Figure 20(a)) and embedding (see Figure 20(b)), to visually represent composite events. It is up to the designer to decide how to combine the two approaches.

In NED, composite events are classified into the following events: conjunction event, disjunction event, monitoring interval event, relative temporal event, closure event, history event, every-nth event, negative event, and sequence event.

a) Conjunction Event: The conjunction of events E1 and E2 occurs when both E1 and E2 have occurred, regardless of order[Gatz92].

b) Disjunction Event: The disjunction of two events E1 and E2, occurs when E1 occurs or E2 occurs [Gatz92]. Figure 18 represents the disjunction of two monitoring events *close-weekdays* and *close-weekends.*

c) Monitoring Interval Event: A monitoring interval event occurs when an event E happens anytime in an interval I and some condition C holds during the interval [Gatz92].

An interval I is specified by a starting and ending point in time and is depicted by a bar. The starting point and ending point of an interval can be defined by the occurrences of two events. A condition C is always associated with an interval. It is depicted within the bar interval. If there are no conditions related to the interval we do not represent the condition icon. An arrow with a flash below the time interval denotes the point in time of the occurrence of the monitoring interval event.

If an interval has a starting or ending point defined by an absolute or periodic temporal event, the interval is represented with the textual description of the date and time of the temporal event placed below its left and right end. Below we show a monitoring interval events in the library database example.

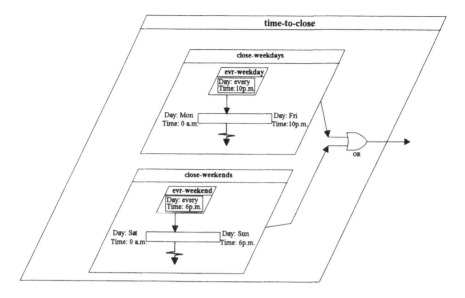

Fig. 18. Representation of Event "time-to-close"

• Events for class Library: The event *time-to-close* was referenced in rule *rClose* (see Figure 9(b)) and occurs every weekday at 10 p.m., or Saturdays and Sundays at 6 p.m. It is modeled as a composite event, which represents the disjunction of two monitoring events, called *close-weekdays* and *close-weekends* (see Figure 18). The monitoring temporal event *close-weekdays* occurs only if a periodic event *evr-weekday* occurs at 10 p.m. between Monday and Friday. The monitoring temporal event *close-weekend* occurs only if a periodic event *evr-weekend* occurs at 6 p.m. between Saturday and Sunday.

d) Relative Temporal Event: A relative temporal event [Daya88] is a special case of a monitoring interval event. It corresponds to a specific point in time in relation to a triggering event E. A relative temporal event occurs after a triggering event E has occurred and a time interval I has elapsed. The triggering event E can be any event specified in NED.

• Events for Class Book: The event *book-overdue* was referenced in rule *rOverdue* (see Figure 9(d)) and occurs at the book's duedate after it had been checked out. It is modeled as a relative temporal event caused after the execution of the operation *checkout*, with an interval defined by the *book's duedate* (see Figure 19(a)). The event *book-extremely-overdue* was referenced in rule *rExtremelyOverdue* (see Figure 9(e)) and occurs when a book has been overdue for seven days. It is modeled as a relative temporal event caused after the execution of the operation *overdue*, with an interval of *seven days*, subject to a constraint that the book is in state *overdue*(see Figure 19(b)).

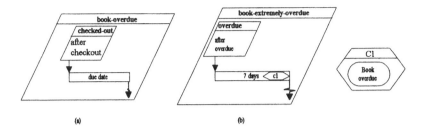

Fig. 19. Representation of Events "book-overdue" and "book-extremely-overdue"

e) Closure Event: A closure event signals only the first occurrence of an event E, even if the event E continues to occur [Gatz92]. The closure event is denoted by placing an '*' to the "out arrow" of the event (e.g. see event *checked-out* in Figure 20).

f) History Event: In some applications an event may repeatedly occur. In such a case, a history event designates a specific occurrence as the triggering event [Gatz92]. The history event is denoted by placing an occurrence identifier to the "out arrow" of the event (e.g. see event *warning* in Figure 20).

g) Every-nth Event: A Every-nth event is used to describe events that occur periodically [Geha92]. It is defined similarly to a history event by placing the keyword *every* before the occurrence number.

h) Negative Event: A negative event is specified by applying an negative constructor to an event. A negative constructor applied to an event E occurs only if event E did not occur [Gatz92]. The non-occurrence of an event is depicted by a cross over the event icon.

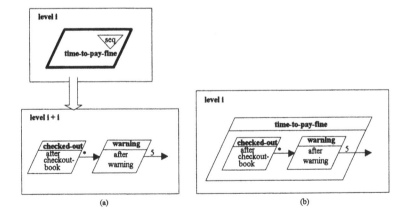

Fig. 20. Sequence Event "time-to-pay-fine" in class Faculty Member

i) Sequence Event: A sequence of two events E1 and E2, occurs when E2 occurs, provided E1 has already occurred [Geha92]. The time of occurrence of E1 is guaranteed to be less than E2.

• Events for class Faculty Member: The event *time-to-pay-fine* was referenced in rule *rControlApplyFine* (see Figure 14(c)). It is modeled as a sequence event which occurs after the method *warning* has been executed five times, since the first time a book had been *checked-out*. In Figure 20, we show the two possible ways (nesting, and embedding) to depict the sequence event *time-to-pay-fine*.

4 Conclusion

In this paper we proposed an integrated approach to active object-oriented database conceptual design, called A/OODBMT, based on several modeling techniques namely, the nested object model (NOM), the behavioral model (BM), the nested rule model (NRM), and the nested event model (NEM).

The nested object model is based on the object model originally defined in [Rumb91]. It extends the object model with nesting capabilities[Carl89], and provides abstraction mechanisms for developing database applications using multi-level diagrams. Moreover, it extends the object model to include rules to the definition of objects to specify the active behavior of objects. The behavioral model is based on the dynamic and functional models proposed in [Rumb91]. It integrates and extends these models to define the operations of objects. Moreover, the behavioral model enhances interaction diagrams [Jaco92] to describe the database transactions of the system. The nested rule model is based on a comprehensive survey [Silv95a] of rule specification approaches. It integrates and extends these approaches by supporting a comprehensive set of rules and by visually representing the rules and their interactions using multi-level diagrams. The nested event model is based on a comprehensive survey [Silv95a] of event specification approaches. It integrates and extends these approaches by supporting a comprehensive set of events and by visually representing events using multi-level diagrams in the context of rules.

The conceptual design of active object-oriented database applications is defined by integrating   all the A/OODBMT models. Therefore, the significance of A/OODBMT is that:

(1)   It provides a multi-level representation approach to the definition of the objects in a system, including their attributes, operations and rules, based on a new object model, called nested object model.

(2)   It describes rules to be encapsulated within objects, localizing the modification of rules.

(3)   It provides the modeling of database transactions in a conceptual level, so that the context of rule evaluation is understood.

(4) It provides a high-level graphical representation of active behavior through the specification of rules using multi-level diagrams. A very comprehensive set of rules is supported, and the modeling of the their coupling modes, inheritance, overriding and interactions is described.

(5) It provides a high-level graphical representation of active behavior through the modeling of events using multi-level diagrams. A very comprehensive set of events is supported and events are defined in the context of rules .

(6) It provides a complete description of how the different models used to represent the database application are integrated at higher-levels of abstraction in multi-level diagrams.

Therefore, we believe the presented approach is well suited for the design of active object-oriented database application, because of its semantic richness and the ability to deal with the complexity of many object/classes, rules and their interaction, and events. We are currently developing a CASE tool that will, not only support the graphical notation proposed in this paper, but also support the automatic code generation of the active object-oriented database schema.

References

[Anwa93] Anwar, E., Mangis, L., and Chakravarthy, S., "A New Perspective On Rule Support For Object-Oriented Databases" In *Proc. of the 1993 ACM SIGMOD Int'l Conference on Management of Data*, June 1993, pp. 99-108.

[Bich94] Bichler, P., and Schrefl, M., "Active Object-Oriented Database Design Using Active Object/Behavior Diagrams," In *Proceedings of the Fourth International Workshop on Research Issues in Data Engineering*, IEEE Comp. Soc. Press, Los Alamitos, CA, USA, 1994.

[Booc94] Booch, G., *Object-Oriented Analysis and Design with Applications*, Benjamin/Cummings, 1994.

[Bran93] Branding, H., Buchmann, A. P., Kudrass, T., and Zimmermann, J., "Rules in an Open System: The REACH rule system," In Paton, N., and Williams, M. (eds.), *Rules in Database Systems*, Workshops in Computing, Springer-Verlag, 1993, pp. 111-126.

[Buch92] Buchmann, A. P., Branding, H., Kudrass, T., and Zimmermann, J. "REACH: a REal-time, ACtive and Heterogeneous mediator systems," In *IEEE Bulletin of the Technical Committee on Data Engineering*, Vol. 15, No. (1-4), December 1992.

[Buch95] Buchmann, A. P., A., Zimmermann, Blakeley, J. A., and Wells, D. L., "Building an Integrated Active OODBMS: Requirements, Architecture, and Design Decisions," In *Proceedings of the 11th International Conference on Data Engineering*, 1995.

[Carl83] Carlson, C. R. and Arora, A. K., "UPM: A Formal Tool for Expressing Database Update Semantics", In *Proceedings of the Third International Conference on Entity-Relationship*, North Holland, NY, 1983, 517-526.

[Carl89] Carlson, C. R., and Ji, W., " The Nested Entity-Relationship Model," *In the 8th International Conference on Entity-Relationship Approach*, October 1989.

[Chak93] Chakravarthy, S. and Mishra, D., "Snoop: An expressive event specification language for active databases," Technical-Report UF-CIS-TR-93-007, University of Florida, March 1993.

[Cole94] Coleman, D., Arnold, P., Bodoff, S., Dollin, C., Gilchrist, H., Hayes, F., Jeremaes, P., *Object-Oriented Development: the Fusion Method*, Prentice Hall, 1994.

[Daya88] Dayal, U., "Active Database Management Systems," In *Proceedings 3rd International Conference on Data Knowledge Bases*, Jerusalem, Israel, June 1988.

[Dema79] DeMarco, T., *Structured Analysis and System Specification*, Prentice Hall, 1979.

[Dill93] Dillon, T., and Tan, P. L., *Object-Oriented Conceptual Modeling*, Prentice Hall, 1993.

[Gatz92] Gatziu, S., and Dittrich, K., "SAMOS: An active object-oriented database system," In *IEEE Bulletin of the Technical Committee on Data Engineering*, Vol. 15, No. (1-4), December 1992.

[Gatz94] Gatziu, S. and Dittrich, K., "Detecting composite events in active database systems using Petri nets," In *Proceedings of the Fourth International Workshop on Research Issues in Data Engineering*, IEEE Comp. Soc. Press, Los Alamitos, CA, USA, 1994.

[Geha91] Gehani, N. H., and Jagadish, H. V., "Ode as an Active Database: Constraints and Triggers," In *Proceedings of the 17th International Conference on Very Large Databases*, Barcelona, September 1991.

[Geha92]   Gehani, N. H., Jagadish, H. V., and Shmueli, O., "Event Specification in an Active Object-Oriented Database," In   *Proc. of the 1992 ACM SIGMOD Int'l Conf. on Management of Data*,   CA, June 1992, pp. 81-90.

[Grah94]   Graham, I., *Migrating to Object Technology*, Addison-Wesley, 1994.

[Hare88]   Harel, D., "On Visual Formalisms," *Communications of the ACM*, Vol. 31, No. 5, May 1988, pp. 514-530.

[Hutt94]   Hutt, Andrew. T. F., "Object Analysis and Design: comparison of methods," John Wiley & Sons Inc., 1994.

[Jaco92]   Jacobson, I., Christerson, M., Jonsson, P., and Overgaard, G., *Object-Oriented Software Engineering: A Use Case Driven Approach*, Addison-Wesley, 1992.

[Kapp94]   Kappel, G., Rausch-Schott, S., Retschitzegger, W., and Vieweg, S., "TriGS: Making a passive object-oriented database system active," *Journal of Object-Oriented Programming*, June/July 1994, pp. 40-51.

[Kapp95]   Kappel, G., Rausch-Schott, S., Retschitzegger, W., Tjoa, A., Vieweg, S., and Wagner, R., "Active Object-Oriented Database Systems for CIM Applications," In Marik, V. (ed.), *CIM-Textbook (TEMPUS-Project)*, Springer LNCS, (in print), 1995.

[Mart95]   Martin, J., and Odell, J., *Object-Oriented Methods: a foundation*, Prentice Hall, Englewood Cliffs, NJ, 1995.

[Mona92]   Monarchi, D. E., and Puhr, G. I., "A Research Typology for Object-Oriented Analysis and Design," *Communications of the ACM*, Vol. 35, No. 9, September 1992, pp. 35-47.

[Pras94]   Prasad, B., Perraju, T., Uma, G., and Umarani, P., "An Expert System Shell for Aerospace Applications," *IEEE Expert*, August 1994, pp. 56-64.

[Rasm95]   Rasmus, D. W., "Ruling classes: The heart of knowledge-based systems," In *Journal of Object-Oriented Programming*,   Vol. 5, No. 4, July/August 1995, pp. 41-43.

[Rumb91]   Rumbaugh, J., Blaha, M., Premerlani, W., Eddy, F., and Lorensen, W., *Object-oriented modeling and design*, Prentice Hall,   EngleWood Cliffs, 1991.

[Shla92]   Shlaer, S. and Mellor, S. J., *Object Lifecycles : modeling the World in States*, Prentice Hall, 1992.

[Shen92] Sheng, O. R. L., and Wei, C., "Object-Oriented Modeling and Design of Coupled Knowledge-base/ Database Systems," *IEEE 8th International Conference on Data Engineering*, 1992, pp. 98-105.

[Silv95a] Silva, M. J. V., *A/OODBMT, an Active Object-Oriented Database Modeling Technique*, Ph.D. Thesis, Illinois Institute of Technology, 1995.

[Silv95b] Silva, M. J. V., and Carlson, C. R., "MOODD, a Method for Object-Oriented Database Design," *Data & Knowledge Engineering Journal*, Elsevier Science Publishers, Vol. 17, No. 2, November 1995.

[Thur94] Thuraisingham, B. and Schafer, A., "RT-OMT: A Real-Time Object-Modeling Technique for Designing Real-Time Database Applications," In *Proceedings of the IEEE Workshop on Real-Time Applications*, IEEE Comp. Soc. Press, Los Alamitos, CA, USA, 1994.

[Tsal91] Tsalgatidou, A., and Loucopoulos, P., "An Object-Oriented Rule-Based Approach to the Dynamic Modelling of Information Systems," In Sol, H. G., and Van , K. M. H. (eds.), *Dynamic Modelling of Information Systems*, North-Holland, Elsevier-Publications, 1991., pp. 165-188.

Bridging the Gap between C++ and Relational Databases

Uwe Hohenstein

Corporate Research and Development, Siemens AG, ZFE T SE 4, D-81730 München
(GERMANY)
E-mail: Uwe.Hohenstein@zfe.siemens.de

Abstract. This work presents a new approach to access existing relational databases from C++ programs in an easy and natural way. The coupling of both worlds makes use of data reverse engineering techniques. Semantics that is inherent to relational data is made explicit by using object-oriented concepts extensively. Relationships and subtypes are expressed directly in order to take great benefit of them. C++ application programs are thus given the ability to handle relational data as if they were C++ objects.

The key to our approach is a powerful specification language that allows for defining object-oriented views, i.e., describing how object types, relationships between them, and subtype hierarchies are derived from relational tables. Even complex relational situations can be remodelled in an intuitive and concise manner.

Given a concrete specification, a C++ database interface is generated preserving the object-oriented view for accessing relational data. Access methods are automatically implemented on top of the relational system.

1 Introduction

Nowadays, it is widely accepted that the object-oriented paradigm reduces the difficulty of developing and evolving complex software systems. Object-oriented programming languages encompass useful constructs such as inheritance and encapsulation that can be used to define complex objects and behavioural properties of objects. These pleasant characteristics make them more desirable for handling many kinds of new applications than conventional programming languages.

Applications written in object-oriented programming languages naturally want to store objects in a database and retrieve them. In fact, object-oriented DBSs (database systems) pick up this point and enhance object-oriented languages to support database capabilities like persistence, transactions, and queries in a homogeneous manner so that the programmer gets the illusion of just one language.

But on the other hand, enterprises are just advanced to gain confidence in relational DBSs since robustness and reliablity are gradually accepted. Storing data in relational databases, lots of applications have been developed on top of such systems recently. This data is a necessary input to many decision making processes. New emerging applications will *still* need to access this relational data. Consequently, many companies will *not* replace their legacy system with object-oriented ones for the forseeable future [IEEE95, PeH95].

In fact, there is no principle problem to make relational data accessible from object-oriented programming languages. Database applications can be written using embedded SQL statements. But this approach suffers from the need to manage two languages with absolutely different paradigms and to interface them with extra programming effort (*"impedance mismatch"*). Furthermore, the *"semantic gap"* is coming to light: The application maintains complexly structured objects, while the relational DBS provides simple tuples. Retrieved tuples must be converted to objects, and objects must be broken down to tuples. The handling is cumbersome and makes application programs difficult to write and hard to read.

In this paper, we accomodate ourselves to the significance of legacy data existing in relational DBSs and the programming language C++ [Str91]. The main contribution consists of proposing a flexible and homogeneous coupling of both worlds, solving the problems of impedance mismatch and semantic gap in an elegant way. The impedance mismatch is avoided by staying completely in C++. Database features are encapsulated in predefined C++ classes and methods, thus hiding the specific coupling mechanisms of relational systems.

We bridge the gap between C++ and relational databases by translating the relational definitions of data to equivalent object-oriented class definitions. Principally, tables can be represented by C++ classes that get the same attributes. In spite of being able to conceal the cursor concept by means of methods, the application still handles tuples instead of objects. Tuples can be manipulated in a C++ way, but tuples are isolated, as there are no relationships. Our solution to the semantic gap is *semantic enrichment*. The semantics of tables, being hidden in foreign keys etc., is made explicit. Relationships, subtypes, and embedded structures are expressed explicitly in object-oriented terms. By using the C++ type system extensively, applications are able to benefit directly from the support for inheritance and polymorphism already available in C++.

In sum, C++ application developers see an object-oriented representation of relational data. Passing on the modelling power of C++ to the operational level retains the higher degree of abstraction. Manipulating and accessing data is completely done on a more abstract level in terms of object-oriented concepts, handling objects and relationships. In addition to features for navigating through the database, powerful associative queries are supported in an object-oriented way. Software development productivity is increased by eliminating the need for programmers to code the mapping between the data structures of the programming language and the database.

There are some commercial C++ class libraries such as RogueWave's DBtools that attempt to ease the access of relational databases for C++ applications. They only encapsulate database functionality and essentially hide the embedding of SQL in a programming language. The handling of relational databases gets a *C++-like appearing*, but the real concepts of object-orientation like inheritance are not applicable. Other work such as [HoO93] addressed some but not all of the SQL/C++ issues. They proceed in a *bottom-up* manner and store C++ classes in relational databases by breaking down objects into tuples. To use existing relational databases, this implicit mapping must be inverted in order to find a schema that maps onto the existing tables. Some other tools such as Persistence and UniSQL [Kim92] behave similarly. Closer to our work comes the approach of O-R-Gateway [AlT92]. Generating a C++ view of relational data *automatically,* their approach suffers from not treating all relational situations correctly. The interface provides only a rudimentary object-oriented view. Other proposals like [ABV92] make things easier as they do not rely on C++ and existing databases, but design an *object-oriented database programming language* from scratch.

In the following, we present our approach. Section 2 is concerned with the database interface for C++. The interface we provide is that defined by ODMG-93 [Cat94], the future *standard* for object-oriented DBSs. ODMG-93 proposes an object-oriented data manipulation facility that corresponds to the C++ type system and provides a C++ conforming way to handle data. Most vendors of object-oriented DBSs are committed to support this standard soon.

Afterwards, we present the basis for semantic enrichment, a logic-based specification language (Section 3). This language allows for remodelling tables in the ODMG-93 object model. Object-oriented views are specified in an intuitive and easy to understand way. The semantics of tables is made explicit, it is "re-engineered" in object-oriented terms in the sense of data reverse engineering [HTJC93, CACM94, CBS94, PrB94, PeH95].

The specification of semantic enrichment must be done manually, but the C++ database interface is provided automatically due to a *generative* approach. Given a specification, a generator produces the C++ interface. This interface implements an ODMG-compliant access to the relational database. Section 4 presents the overall architecture of the generative approach and elucidates the most important parts of the implementation.

The work we present here is part of a project called "Flexible Integration of Heterogeneous Database Systems" (FIHD) which is concerned with database interoperability. Section 5 outlines some further aspects of FIHD. The overall goal is to provide applications with one single ODMG-compliant interface to operate on several database systems. The generative approach builds the first step to incorporate relational systems in such an interoperability approach.

2   The ODMG-93 Database Standard

2.1   Object Model and Object Definition Language

The database standard ODMG-93 is principally independent of programming languages. An object model provides concepts to define objects in a neutral form. We briefly summarize the essential terms and concepts used throughout the paper. Figure 1 presents a simple example modelling a company database.

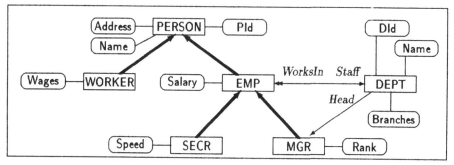

Fig. 1. Sample ODMG Schema

There are *object types* (in the sense of C++ classes) like PERSON and DEPT (department) that possess *attributes*. Every person (of type PERSON) has a number (PId), a Name, and an Address. Attributes are associated with a domain, which may be primitive like Long and Float or predefined like Date, Time and String. Object types are also valid domains. For instance, attribute Address may be of domain ADDRESS, which is an object type structured as ZIP code, City, Street, and Houseno. However, this does not represent a relationship between PERSON and ADDRESS; a person's address is embedded in PERSON, it is not an object and cannot be referenced from other objects. Furthermore, there are predefined templates for Set's, Bag's, List's, and Varray's which can be applied to domains, e.g., Set<String>. Bags are multisets, which retain duplicates. Lists possess an order so that the i-th element can directly be accessed by its position number.

ODMG-93 provides an explicit *relationship* concept. WorksIn is a *single-valued* relationship, it points to exactly one object of type DEPT. In contrast, Staff is *multi-valued* (denoted as a double-headed arrow), referring to a collection (set or list) of objects. WorksIn and Staff specify different directions of the same semantic relationship. Such a relationship is called *bidirectional*. Referential integrity is automatically guaranteed, there is no danger of 'dangling pointers'. Furthermore, both directions are kept consistent in contrast to simple pointers. If a relationship between two objects is newly established, then it is visible from both sides. Relationships can be *unidirectional*, too: The relationship Head is directed, from one object type to another. The direction is important for access. Referential integrity is not controlled and must be maintained manually.

Object types can be organized in *subtype hierarchies*. Object type PERSON has two subtypes, (blue-collar) WORKER and EMPloyee, and EMP in turn has subtypes SECRetary and MGR (manager), graphically indicated by broad arrows. As in C++, each subtype inherits all the properties of its supertype(s), attributes as well as methods and relationships. Multiple inheritance is possible and especially useful to express non-disjoint subtypes.

As usual, methods can be defined and attached to object types in order to define the behaviour of objects.

An Object Definition Language (ODL) reflects the concepts of the object model and allows for the specification of types and relationships among them in a syntactic form. The ODL is still independent of language-specific concerns.

2.2 Object Manipulation and Querying in the C++ Binding

ODL specifications can be transformed into C++ and Smalltalk, obtaining equivalent class representations. Corresponding *C++* and *Smalltalk binding* define their appearings. In case of C++, every object type is transformed into a C++ class. Attributes and relationships are mapped to data members of corresponding C++ domains or predefined classes. Indeed, relationships result in pointer-like shapes. All those C++ classes are used by programs to invoke database functionality. They do not reflect only the structure of object types, but also provide generic methods for manipulating data in C++ by means of an Object Manipulation Language (OML). Each object type possesses predefined methods like a new operator to create new objects, a delete_object method to delete an object, methods for navigating along relationships, for transaction management, querying, etc. These C++ methods enable application programs to access databases. The following piece of code presents a short C++ application program.

```
Database db;    db.open( "myDB" );
Transaction t;  t.start();
Ref<EMP>    e = new(db) EMP  (3, "Lucky Luke", 3000);
Ref<DEPT>   d = new(db) DEPT (10, "Cowboys" );
e->WorksIn = d;   cout << e->WorksIn->Name << endl;
...
d->Staff.delete_element(e);
Set<Ref<EMP>> empSet = d->Staff;
t.commit();
db.close();
```

Database and Transaction are predefined classes that manage database and transaction handling. After opening a database "myDB", a transaction is started. The basis for handling objects are so-called *references* given by a Ref template. They behave like C++ pointers in a certain sense, however, they are able to refer to transient *and* persistent objects. Particularly, attribute access and method invocation is done via '->'. Here, an object of type EMP with a PId 3, a name "Lucky Luke" and a salary of 3000 is created by applying operator new (provided a corresponding constructor exists for EMP). The operator new is overloaded as it requires a parameter db, the database the object is to be stored in. Similarly, a department "Cowboys" is created. The employee e is hired by this department: d is assigned to the WorksIn relationship. Since the WorksIn/Staff relationship is bidirectional, the employee is implicitly inserted into the staff of department d. This can explicitly be done by d->Staff.insert_element(e), too. The employee is fired by d->Staff.delete_element(e). Additional methods are available to process the staff as a set of employees (Set<REF<EMP>>), e.g., iterators can be created to handle a collection element by element. All modifications to data are temporary, until a commit is made to the transaction. Any changes to objects and relationships are then stored persistently in the database.

All these methods are predefined for performing database operations. It is important to note that *user-defined* methods can be defined in C++ and attached to classes in order to provide object behaviour. These methods can of course invoke database functionality by using those predefined functions.

A special method oql(result, predicate) allows invoking associative queries. The parameter predicate of type char* contains a string that defines the query specified in an Object Query Language (OQL); result obtains the query result. For example, the query "select d.Name from d in Depts where d.Head.Name = 'Lucky Luke' " computes the names of those departments d (in the extent Depts) that are headed by 'Lucky Luke'. OQL is an object-oriented extension of SQL designed to work on the constructs of the object model. It enhances SQL in an orthogonal manner with object-oriented features like inheritance and traversal along relationships. Due to space limitations, the reader is referred to [Cat94] for further details about the OQL.

3 Specification Language

In order to bridge the semantic gap between C++ and relational databases, the basic principle of our approach consists of remodelling relational schemas in the ODMG model in a semantic enrichment process [CaS91, MaM90, NNJ93, HoK95]. Applications are given "real" object-oriented views of the relational data including relationships and subtype hierarchies. It is just now that applications reap the full benefits of object-orientation, as they are no longer responsible for managing relationships and inheritance by their own.

It is very important that semantic enrichment is obliged to make explicit the correct and precise semantics because object-oriented operations will get a wrong semantics otherwise. There is the necessity of expressing any kind of semantics in relational data. Hence, our approach stresses *expressiveness*. The price we pay for comprehensive remodelling capabilities is a *manual* specification of enrichment. We consider this matter not so bad due to the following reasons:

- The information in demand is often available in form of (object-oriented) design documents, which provide a good basis for semantic enrichment.

- There has been a flurry of activities in the field of data reverse engineering to propose algorithms, methodologies, and heuristics [HTJC93, CBS94, PrB94]. This work as well as knowledge acquisition approaches [CaS91, MaM90], which analyze the contents of databases in order to detect semantics, do a valuable job. Hence, our approach is complementary and can benefit from this work already done.

- Automatic types of reverse engineering and knowledge detection do not always produce satisfactory results. For example, earlier approaches simply do not attempt to rebuild subtypes, or are only able to rebuild subtypes created by just one strategy (e.g., [CaS91, AlT92, YaL92]). Multi-level subtype hierarchies are rarely managed properly.

We propose an approach that is capable of remodelling any relational situations in object-oriented terms by extensively using all the concepts of the ODMG-93 object model. In particular, the general case of of multi-level hierarchies can be handled. A powerful *specification language* is used to this end, taking into account several enrichment concepts in an orthogonal manner. This language allows one to precisely describe how tables in the relational database schema can be combined to object types. Nevertheless, we do not want to overshoot the mark. We do put emphasis on powerful mechanisms to derive object types form tables in various ways. But we have to avoid problems with *view updates*. This is important because we automatically generate object-oriented operations (see later) the effect of which must be unambiguous when operating on tables. Hence, no schematic discrepancies [SCG92], which restructure table and attribute names to attribute *values*, are expressible. Such aspects are a matter of taste how to see data, and consequently less necessary to express real semantics.

The syntax of the specification language bridles the horse from the back. It is specified what object types are the outcome and how they correspond to tables. This is advantageous because an object type is generally made up of several tables. The syntax remains intuitive and easily understandable, and the object types are immediately visible. The language adopts the ODL of ODMG-93 and introduces some amendments in order to express connections between object-oriented and relational schemas.

We are now discussing the specification language in more detail. The discussion is based on some relational representations of the schema in Figure 1. The examples will give a feeling about the underlying principles, i.e., how to cluster several tables into one object type, how to rebuild relationships, and how to regain complete subtype hierarchies.

3.1 Deriving Object Types and Relationships from Tables

We consider the relational schema given in Figure 2. Table M represents managers (MGR), while table D contains departments (DEPT). The branches of departments are stored in table B (Dld, Loc, No) the tuples of which contain the branches for each department Dld value by value; each branch receives a number enumerating the branches of a department. The headquarter is located in AA (No=1), BB is the second place, and so on. The Mgr column in table D is a foreign key, it refers to the manager in M who is the *Head* of that department.

The enrichment specification in Figure 2 combines the tables D and B to one object type DEPT with a multi-valued attribute Branches. Object types are defined as interface declarations as in ODL. The extent clause defines a variable to access the objects of a type: Depts is necessary to constitute an entry point in DEPT for querying data; only then can objects of a type be queried in an associative manner. The key-clause contains (object-oriented) key attributes that care for uniqueness. For example, the Dld-values of departments are requested to be unique. The part in curly brackets specifies attributes and relationships. This is the usual way to define object types in the ODL.

Those interface declarations form the basis for logic-based extensions that express connections between object-oriented and relational schemas. The clause from relation relates the specified object type to a table. It specifies in what table the objects of a type are found. DEPT from relation D[Dld] means that type DEPT is directly built from table D. Dld is the relational key of D. Each tuple, which is uniquely identified by its key value, refers to one object. We presuppose a key for each table, because it is necessary to constitute object identifiers in the runtime system (see later on). Composite keys are possible and denoted as $(a_1,a_2,a_3,...)$.

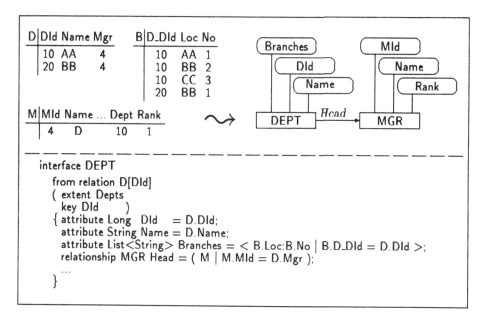

Fig. 2. Sample Enrichment

Equations '=' occurring behind the attributes relate object type attributes to relational attributes. The simplest form is Long DId = D.DId and directly connects an object type attribute DId with domain Long to a relational attribute DId. Attributes are renamed by specifying different names on the left hand side of the equations. Renaming is useful to choose intuitive and self-explanatory names.

The list-valued attribute Branches is made explicit in DEPT by using a list constructor <...> in Branches = < B.Loc:B.No | B.D_DId = D.DId >: Compute the Loc values for each tuple in B that possesses a D_DId equal to the DId of the department. In this case, the attribute No is used to determine the order in the list. Similarly, a set constructor could have been applied to build a *set* of branches: Branches = { B.Loc | ... }. In the same way, the effect of normalization can be inverted. It is possible to 'cluster' any tables related by attributes to one object type [YaL92].

Similarly, relationships can be expressed. The Head of a department (represented by a foreign key Mgr) is made explicit in a specification by relationship MGR Head = (M | M.MId = D.Mgr): The head consists of that tuple in M (identified by the respective key) that possesses an MId equal to the Mgr-value of the department. Round brackets convert a tuple in M into a corresponding object of type MGR.

If the relationship Head were represented by a table H(DId,MId), containing the Id's of the participating tables, then the specification would look like relationship MGR Head = (M | M.MId = H.MId, H.DId = D.DId) .

In both cases, composite attributes for expressing the relationships can also be handled and specified.

3.2 Subtype Hierarchies

Remodelling subtype hierarchies requires advanced concepts, since several relational representations exist. Some approaches to semantic enrichment [MaM90, CaS91, YaL92] are able to make subtype relationships explicit. However, they generally take into account only one strategy (the vertical one below) and lack the handling of multi-level subtype hierarchies. But it is just the "implementation" of subtypes offers a wide spectrum of possibilities. It is important to detect them correctly, even if they have been applied in a mixed manner.

We refer to the subtype hierarchy given in Figure 1, however, we disregard relationships for a moment. Let us assume in the following that PId 1 is a real person, 2 an employee, 3 a secretary, 4 a manager, and 5 and 6 are workers.

Vertical Partitioning. Possibly the most common way of representing subtype hierarchies is a *vertical* partitioning. Let us organize the tables P, E, M, S, and W in Figure 3 into a subtype hierarchy. Each table refers to one object type in the hierarchy, as usual, and contains all the *elements* of the corresponding type, i.e., the instances of the type and all its subtypes. Only the specific attributes of the type are found in the table; attributes inherited from supertypes are available in the tables associated with that supertype. The following inclusions then hold between supertype and subtype tables: $P.Id \supseteq W.WId$, $P.Id \supseteq E.EId$, $E.EId \supseteq S.SId$, and $E.EId \supseteq M.MId$. To access the attributes of supertypes, tables must be joined over the Id attributes: Take the MId-value of a manager and look in E and P for tuples that have the same value as EId and Id, resp., to get the properties inherited from PERSON and EMP. Please note that those Id attributes do not need to be keys, but they must guarantee uniqueness of attribute values.

P	Id	Name	Addr
	1	A	A_town
	2	B	B_city
	3	C	C_village
	4	D	D_village
	5	E	E_city
	6	F	F_town

E	EId	Salary
	2	2000
	3	3000
	4	4000

S	SId	Speed
	3	133

M	MId	Rank
	4	1

W	WId	Wages
	5	555
	6	666

```
interface PERSON from relation P[Id]
    { attribute PId = P.Id;
      attribute Name = P.Name;
      ... }
interface EMP        : PERSON from relation E [EId =P.Id]   ...
interface WORKER : PERSON from relation W[WId=P.Id]   ...
interface SECR      : EMP      from relation S [SId =E.EId] ...
interface MGR       : EMP      from relation M[MId=E.EId] ...
```

Fig. 3. Vertical Partitioning of Subtypes

The enrichment specification in Figure 3 should be understood as follows.

The elements of PERSON are found in table P, as usual (from relation), elements of subtype EMP in E, and so on. Since each table contains only the specific attributes of that object type, the connection to the supertype table must be established. This is done by EMP : PERSON from relation E[EId = P.Id]: Tables E and P are related by attributes EId (of relation E) and Id (of P): A person is an employee if its Id occurs in E as EId. Composite attributes are again possible.

Horizontal Partitioning. Horizontal partitioning of types into tables is another subtype representation. As shown in Figure 4, one table again holds the information of one object type in the hierarchy. The structure of each table comprises the specific information of its corresponding type and, unlike vertical partitioning, the attributes of supertypes, too. Hence, the attributes inherited from supertypes are directly available in each table. But each table contains only the *instances* of the type itself. Hence, a manager is stored in M only, however, including the EMP and PERSON information. On instance level, exclusion conditions are fulfilled between super-and subtype tables: $P.Id \cap E.EId = \emptyset$, $P.Id \cap W.WId = \emptyset$, $E.EId \cap S.SId = \emptyset$, and $E.EId \cap M.MId = \emptyset$.

P	Id	Name	Addr			
	1	A	A_town			

E	EId	Name	Addr	Salary	
	2	B	B_city	2000	

W	WId	Name	Addr	Wages
	5	E	E_city	555
	6	F	F_town	666

S	SId	Name	Addr	Salary	Speed
	3	C	C_village	3000	133

M	MId	Name	Addr	Salary	Rank
	4	D	D_village	4000	1

interface PERSON from relation P[Id] + W[WId] + E[EId] + S[SId] + M[MId]
{ attribute Long PId = P.Id + W.WId + E.EId + S.SId + M.MId;
   attribute String Name = P.Name + W.Name + E.Name + S.Name + M.Name; ... }

interface EMP : PERSON from relation E[EId] + S[SId] + M[MId]
{ attribute Float Salary = E.Salary + S.Salary + M.Salary; }

interface WORKER : PERSON from relation W[WId]
{ attribute Float Wages = W.Wages; }

interface MGR : EMP from relation M[MId]   interface SECR : EMP from relation S[SId]
{ attribute Long Rank = M.Rank; }   { attribute Long Speed = S.Speed; }

Fig. 4. Horizontal Partitioning of Subtypes

Figure 4 demonstrates how to rebuild the subtype hierarchy. Each from relation clause defines how to compute all the elements of a type. The elements of PERSON, spread over the tables P, W, E, S and M, are obtained by computing the union ('+') of tuples. As objects are made of tuples of different tables, the key values of those tuples must be used to build object identifiers. The parts [...] indicate the corresponding key attributes. Attribute correspondences are specified in the same way: Id = P.Id + W.WId + E.EId + S.SId + M.MId identifies semantically equivalent attributes in tables; the Ids of persons are stored in all of those tables, however, in differently named columns!

Flag Approach. In contrast to the first strategies, one single table can represent the whole hierarchy as well. One table P contains all the information about all the object types. Flags like Emp?, etc. determine the specific subtype. Flags can denote elements or instances. They represent elements in Figure 5: Tuples having Emp?=true correspond to elements of EMP. Naturally, only sensible flag combinations must occur. For example, Emp?=false and Secr?=true is not valid, a secretary must also be an employee. Furthermore, non-applicable attributes must be NULL so that Emp?=false implies Salary=NULL.

P	Id	Name	Addr	Emp?	Salary	Mgr?	Rank	Secr?	Speed	Worker?	Wages
	1	A	A_town	false	NULL	false	NULL	false	NULL	false	NULL
	2	B	B_city	true	2000	false	NULL	false	NULL	false	NULL
	3	C	C_village	true	3000	false	NULL	true	133	false	NULL
	4	D	D_village	true	4000	true	1	false	NULL	false	NULL
	5	E	E_city	false	NULL	false	NULL	false	NULL	true	555
	6	F	F_town	false	NULL	false	NULL	false	NULL	true	666

interface PERSON from relation P[Id] ...

interface EMP : PERSON from relation P[Emp? = true]
   { attribute Float Salary = P.Salary; }

interface WORKER : PERSON from relation P[Worker? = true] ...

interface SECR : EMP from relation P[Secr? = true] ...

interface MGR : EMP from relation P[Mgr? = true] ...

Fig. 5. Flag Approach

If flags denote instances instead, then Emp?=true holds for real instances of EMP only. SECR instances still have Secr?=true, but now Emp?=false. Then, at most one flag can be true for each tuple in P.

Some variants of the flag approach are conceivable. In place of flags, an enumeration type type of domain { Emp, Secr, Mgr, Worker } can serve the same purpose. For example, the instances of EMP get a type-value Emp. The subtype specification can also be done by condition, e.g., Salary!=NULL could detect EMP instances. Even more general expressions could be used. However, there will be no possibility to distinguish between "value is unknown" and "value is inapplicable (no subtype attribute)", because both are represented by NULL.

Flag approaches can again be handled in the from relation clause. As usual, the part in [...] defines how to compute elements. The specification given in Figure 5 defines that any tuple in table P with Emp? = true refers to an object of type EMP. These objects are identified by PId, as arranged in PERSON.

Other flag approaches are handled by different forms of conditions. For example, if flags denote instances, the conditions look like

interface EMP : PERSON from relation P[Emp? = true or Secr? = true or Mgr? = true]

Those tuples of P are elements of EMP which have one of the (exclusive) flags Emp?, Secr? or Mgr? true. Naturally, this discriminant form allows for arbitrary conditions like [Salary!=NULL] and [type=Emp], too.

Complete Materialization. Another relational representation uses the schemas of horizontal, but the instances of vertical partitioning. For example, type EMP is represented by a table E(EId, Name, Addr, Salary) and contains three tuples with EIds 2, 3 and 4. This leads to redundancy, as the table P(Id, Name, Addr) contains the Name and Addr information for all tuples. Consequently, the name 'B' of Id 2 is stored in P and E. Since each table contains the whole information of a type, all the elements and all the attributes, we call it *complete materialization*. Rebuilding the hierarchy from these tables is done in the following way:

interface EMP : PERSON from relation E[EId =P.Id]
attribute Float Salary = E.Salary = S.Salary = M.Salary;

The form of from relation is similar to vertical partitioning, as each table contains elements. Hence, the correlation to supertype tables is expressed by EId=P.Id. But in contrast to vertical partitioning, redundancies must be reflected for the attributes: Employees' Salaries are stored in E, M and S.

3.3 Multiple Inheritance

Subtypes are disjoint w.r.t. instances in C++ and the ODMG object model. On the other hand, this is not true for tables, since they can contain tuples with the same Id. For instance in Figure 6, an employee with EId 3 occurs in S and E, (s)he is a secretary and a manager at the same time.

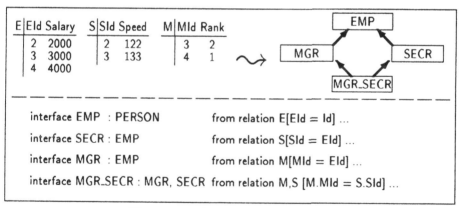

Fig. 6. Non-disjoint Subtype Tables

Non-disjoint types can be modelled by means of multiple inheritance. An artificial subtype MGR_SECR represents the intersection of MGR and SECR. MGR_SECR is necessary to be able to insert objects like 3 that are both manager and secretary. The attributes inherited from EMP via MGR and SECR are virtual and occur only once in MGR_SECR. The type EMP enables accessing all the elements, no matter whether managers, secretaries, or both. Please be conscious of telling apart elements and instances: 2 and 3 are elements of SECR, however, 2 is the only instance, as 3 has become an instance of SECR_MGR.

Multiple inheritance is denoted as in C++, specifying several supertypes behind a colon: MGR_SECR : MGR, SECR. According to the semantics of from relation, elements of MGR_SECR are characterized: The set of elements is computed by intersecting tables M and S by a condition M.MId = S.SId.

3.4 Additional Concepts

Additional forms are available to handle further aspects which are important for building object-oriented views of tables. We briefly summarize them.

Multivalued attributes like Branches are sometimes available as a constant number of relational attributes, if the collection has a fixed size or an upper bound. This is particularly useful for small collections. Hence table D may look like D (DId, Name, Branch1, Branch2, Branch3), if there will be at most 3 branches in a department. In order to handle this, constant sets can be built over columns: Set<String> Branches = { Branch1, Branch2, Branch3 } .

Several relational attributes may correspond to a predefined ODMG data type such as Time and Date. For example, three Long-valued attributes Day, Month, and Year, assume that they occurred in table D, could be combined to form a date of foundation. A corresponding attribute equation then makes use of a tuple constructor (...) and looks like Date Foundation = (D.Day, D.Month, D.Year) .

Sometimes it is useful to structure several relational attributes in a similar manner, even if no predefined domains are applicable. Relational attributes ZIP, City, Street, and Houseno obviously represent addresses. It is useful to define an embedded structure Address that contains these components. The address of a person could be made explicit by defining an embedded type address that is used as domain for Address. A corresponding equation is similar to above.

New object types may be introduced, e.g., to concentrate common attributes into a *generalized* object type. Suppose tables A (AId, a, c, d) and B (BId, b, c, d) are given. Both tables can be generalized to a newly defined supertype C that receives c and d. Supertype C does typically not contain instances of its own. Indeed, creating instances, it is not clear in which table to put them.

Owing to *optimization* reasons, tables are often merged after design, in order to avoid costly join operations. Combined with previously discussed concepts, the specification language allows for splitting up tables into several object types.

One important point has been neglected so far. Relational DBSs possess modelling constructs such as not null that are provided neither in C++ nor in ODL. In order to reflect the relational semantics entirely, we introduced corresponding restrictions. Keywords like not null can be specified for attributes (in the relational sense), and relationships can be defined as mandatory: Any object must participate in a relationship of that type.

3.5 Complex Example

In order to demonstrate the power of the specification language, we are now presenting a complex relational schema that comprehends several of the concepts discussed previously in combination. Particularly, we use a relational representation of Figure 1 that incorporates different subtype strategies within one hierarchy. Sometimes, it is quite useful to having applied different strategies. Reasons for that might be to speed up access for specific applications, which have different preferences for each level of the hierarchy. We apply a vertical strategy to PERSON–EMP and EMP–SECR, a horizontal one to EMP–MGR, and a flag approach to PERSON–WORKER. We obtain the tables given in Figure 7.

P	Id	Name	Addr	Worker?	Wages
	1	A	A_town	false	NULL
	2	B	B_city	false	NULL
	3	C	C_village	false	NULL
	5	E	E_city	true	555
	6	F	F_town	true	666

E	EId	Salary	Dept
	2	2000	10
	3	3000	20

S	SId	Speed
	3	133

M	MId	Name	Addr	Salary	Dept	Rank
	4	D	D_village	4000	10	1

D	DId	Name	Mgr
	10	AA	4
	20	BB	4

B	D_DId	Loc
	10	AA
	10	BB
	10	CC
	20	BB

```
interface PERSON    // no supertype
  from relation P[Id] + M[MId]
  ( extent Persons
    key PersId    )
  { attribute Long PersId = P.Id+M.MId;
    attribute String Name = P.Name+M.Name;
    attribute String Address = P.Addr+M.Addr;
  }

interface EMP : PERSON
  from relation E[EId=P.Id][EId]+M[MId];
  ( extent Emps )
  { attribute Float Salary = E.Salary+M.Salary;
    relationship DEPT WorksIn inverse Staff
    = (D | D.DId = E.Dept+M.Dept); }


interface MGR : EMP
  from relation M[MId]
  { attribute Long Rank = M.Rank;
  }
```

```
interface DEPT    // no supertype
  from relation D[DId]
  ( extent Depts
    key DId    )
  { attribute Long DId = D.DId;
    attribute String Name = D.Name;
    attribute String Address = D.Addr;
    attribute Set<String> Branches =
      { B.Loc | B.D_DId = D.DId }
  relationship MGR Head =
    (M | MId = D.DId);
  relationship Set<EMP> Staff
    inverse WorksIn =
      { E+M | E.Dept+M.Dept=D.DId };
  }

interface SECR : EMP          // vertical
  from relation S[SId=E.EId]
  { attribute Long Speed = S.Speed; }

interface WORKER : PERSON    // flag
  from relation P[Worker?=true]
  { attribute Float Wages = P.Wages; }
```

Fig. 7. Complex Specification of Semantic Enrichment

The tables reflect the characteristic inclusions $E.EId \subseteq P.Id$ and $S.SId \subseteq E.EId$ of vertical partitioning. According to horizontal partitioning, an exclusion condition $E.EId \cap M.MId = \emptyset$ holds. M contains additional employees who possess different Ids and have the complete PERSON and EMP attributes. Workers, finally, do not have a table of their own, but are part of P with a discriminant flag Worker?.

The WorksIn and Head relationships are represented by foreign keys Dept and Mgr, respectively. The Dept column in E refers to the department's DId, the employee works in, and similar for Mgr. Please note that horizontal subtypes receive all the properties of their supertypes. Hence, M also has an attribute Dept, since EMP's relationship to DEPT is valid for managers, too. Even the attributes of indirect supertypes are repeated. M obtains the attributes of P, although it is not a direct horizontal subtype of P. This is necessary, because M cannot "inherit" the attributes of PERSON otherwise by means of joins!

Figure 7 presents a specification that regains the schema given in Figure 1. PERSON from relation P[Id] + M[MId] specifies a horizontal strategy. The elements of PERSON are obtained by computing the union ('+') of tuples in P and M. Horizontal strategy is reflected in attribute equations: Name = P.Name + M.Name specifies that people's names occur in P and M.

The form EMP : PERSON from relation E[EId = P.Id][EId] + M[MId] represents a vertical strategy first of all: E[EId = P.Id] means that E is a vertical subtype of P. The tables E and P are related by attributes EId (of table E) and Id (of P). E[...][EId] + M[MId] specifies that EMP objects are stored in the tables E and M due to horizontal partitioning. Please note that different attributes could have been used for vertical and horizontal strategy!

WORKER : PERSON from relation P[Worker? = true] indicates a flag approach: The type WORKER is subtype of PERSON represented by a flag Worker? in table P.

Set<EMP> Staff = { E + M | E.Dept + M.Dept = D.DId } expresses a set-valued relationship to EMP for interface DEPT. Staff consists of those tuples in E and M (identified by respective keys) that have the department's DId as value of Dept. Keyword inverse marks a relationship as bidirectional, thus relating WorksIn of EMP to Staff of DEPT. The inverse relationship WorksIn is analogously computed by (D | D.DId = E.Dept + M.Dept). Head and Branches are specified as in Figure 2.

4 Generative Approach

4.1 Principle

The specification of object-oriented views is done manually by means of a specification language. Nevertheless, the database interface is produced automatically due to a generative principle: Given as input any specification of semantic enrichment, a generator produces a pile of C++ classes according to the language-specific ODMG C++ binding (cf. Subsection 2.2). The generated output provides a C++ database interface implemented on top of the relational system. Each interface declaration results in exactly one C++ class that defines generic methods for manipulation and navigation according to the ODMG standard. User-defined methods are added to these classes. C++ applications that want to access the relational database need only compile and link these classes into application programs. Figure 8 illustrates the process of generation. Software components are represented by boxes and require input data and produce output, both shown as parallelograms. Closed lines denote data flow, while broken lines define function calls.

Let us discuss the information flow between the basic components. Starting point is a *specification* defining semantic enrichment for a relational database.

A *Parser* first takes the name of a relational database and then reads the information about the database *schema*: Table and attribute names are found in the dictionary of the relational system. This information is stored in a meta database and forms the relational part of *meta-information*. Parsing the enrichment specification, information about the derived object-oriented schema and its connection to relational tables is added to the meta information.

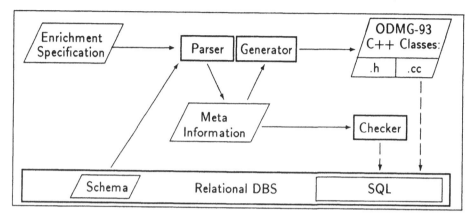

Fig. 8. Generative Approach

The implementation of the parser uses a comfortable compiler-compiler. The syntax of the specification language is defined in a yacc-like format, and semantic actions such as filling the meta database are implemented in C++. In addition to that, a lot of *context-sensitive syntax rules* are supervised. For example, all table and attribute names occuring in a specification must exist in the relational schema, and attributes must belong to the tables. The various constructs to remodel subtype hierarchies and relationships have additional demands.

A *Generator* takes the meta information as input and generates the ODMG-93 conforming classes. The output consists of C++ header files (".h"), which contain the C++ class definitions including the signatures of methods, and implementation files (".cc") implementing those methods. Naturally, the implementation of methods must call SQL in order to access the database.

As mentioned before, the meta database comprises the information about the relational schema, the outcoming object-oriented schema, and interrelations between them. Figure 9 gives a simplified view of the meta information. The left side consists of the relational part: R_TABLE contains the table names of a given schema; a table consists of several R_COLUMNs, and each R_COLUMN possesses a relational R_DOMAIN. One or more columns build the *key* of a table. Analogously, the right side contains the object-oriented counterpart, O_TYPEs with several O_ATTRibutes and associated O_DOMAINs. Relationships between object types are kept in O_RELSHIP; each relationship has a *source* type and a *destination*. Subtype hierarchies are reflected by *subtypes/supertypes* relationships. In the middle, information about semantic enrichment is placed. Each O_TYPE is related to several tables depending on the subtype strategy. In general, one table is the *base* table of an object type. Consequently, each O_TYPE refers to an ENRICHMENT object (via *enriches*) that determines the *base* table and its *key* columns. Subtype strategies are reflected by special subtypes of ENRICHMENT. For instance, HORIZONTAL keeps a list of pairs (R_TABLE, R_COLUMN) according to the '+' (plus) form of from relation. Similarly, attribute and relationship equations are handled by ATTR_ENRICHMENT and R_ENRICHMENT. This simplified view illustrates that all the information about a specification is stored.

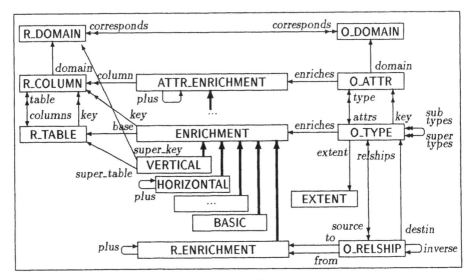

Fig. 9. Meta-Schema

Specifying semantic enrichment explicitly, obviously, not every enrichment specification makes sense. In principle, the user *supposes* that the database comprises the semantics specified, but the database does not know what semantics it has to satisfy. An *Integrity Checker* has the task to prevent users from specifying nonsense by checking the relational data against a specification. Subsection 4.3 discusses this point in more detail.

4.2 Architecture of the Runtime System

The output produced by the generator is an object-oriented runtime system that provides an ODMG-93 conforming access to relational data. C++ classes represent the relational data, however, in a less simple form than just tables. Moreover, methods define means for manipulation. These methods work on objects and are automatically implemented on relational SQL. In fact, the implementation is done in direct correspondence to the semantic enrichment. For example, referring to Figure 7, we consider the case of creating a new employee:

$$\text{Ref<EMP> emp = new(db) EMP (3, "Lucky Luke", 3000);} \qquad (1)$$
$$\text{emp->WorksIn = d;} \qquad (2)$$

The first C++ statement implies an SQL insert into tables E and P due to a vertical subtype strategy: Employees are stored in both tables. Assigning a department to the employee requires an update of the foreign key attribute Dept in E (Dept represents the WorksIn relationship).

Let us discuss the architecture of the generated runtime system. The implementation files (.cc) do not directly use the relational database system due to portability, efficiency, and reduced amount of generated code. Hence, the runtime system is layered in order to bridge the gap between the ODMG interface and relational operations. Figure 10 gives a brief survey about the layering.

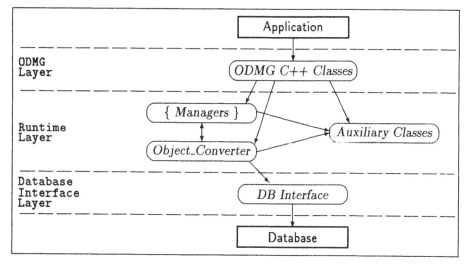

Fig. 10. Runtime System

The upper **ODMG Layer** consists of ODMG-93 conforming C++ classes that provides database access. Some classes like Transaction, Database and templates like Iterator<T>, Ref<T> and Set<T> are independent of the enrichment specification. Others indeed are dependent, in particular those classes that represent interface definitions.

The ODMG layer classes use functionality supplied by a **Runtime Layer**. This layer consists of several forms of *Managers*, a Transaction_Manager, Database_Manager, Extent_Manager, Object_Manager, and Query_Manager. The *Query_Manager* handles OQL queries, by translating them into relational SQL queries [Hoh95]. An *Object_Manager* manages all the objects at runtime in a cache. All modifications to objects are first made in the cache. When a commit occurs, all changes are made persistent in the database, i.e., objects are taken from the cache and put into the relational database. Figure 11 illustrates the principle of the Object_Manager.

Ref objects, the substitutes for pointers, refer to temporary identifiers, socalled *tids*, in the cache. This is advantageous because several references e1, e2 can point to the same object, e.g., if this object is fetched several times into different references. Tids avoid synchronizing modifications via different references, as just one physical instance of the object exists:

The internal structure of the Object_Manager can be understood as a collection of triples (tid, key, object pointer). Key and Tid are *Auxiliary Classes*. Key maintains the key values of any tuple. Keys are used to build object identifiers in the runtime system.

We discuss the connection between the ODMG Layer and the Object_Manager by listing the actions for creating a new object emp in OML (cf. (1) above). Operator new is overloaded as it now yields a reference instead of a pointer. The implementation of new creates the storage for an EMP object; attributes remain unset firstly. Then a tid entry is requested from the Object_Manager. An entry in the cache is made, relating tid and object pointer.

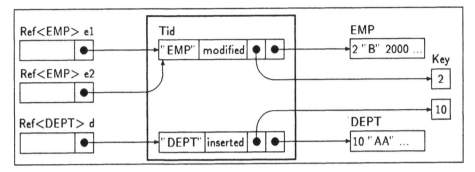

Fig. 11. Object_Manager

The implementation of the constructor EMP::EMP(Long k, ...), being implicitly invoked afterwards, reserves the key k in the relational database. If the key already exists, an error is returned. Furthermore, a Key instance is created from k. Tid and key are then associated in the cache. The Key instance serves as an object identifier: The pair (EMP, 3) uniquely identifies an object in the database, since 3 is unique in type EMP. The assignment emp = ... finally lets the reference of the newly created employee point to the entry in the cache.

The methods to allocate storage and to associate Key's, Tid's, and object pointers are part of the Object_Manager. Additional methods are available to look up objects by means of keys or tid's. The internal state of objects, i.e., whether they are deleted, inserted, or modified, is maintained and can be asked and set by corresponding methods. Any modifications are made in the cache, making topical the objects' states. Only if a commit is invoked at the ODMG layer, changes are made persistent. Indeed, the implementation of this method scans the cache and calls operations according to the objects' states, i.e., delete, insert, or update them. These basic operations are provided by the beneath Object_Converter.

The *Object_Converter* consists of several classes; each interface has a corresponding Object_Converter of its own. They support basic operations

- to load_objects into cache for a given key or tid,
- to load_extent (elements) and load_instance sets in order to materialize whole object types,
- to load_relationships of objects given by tid, and
- to store, modify, and delete objects.

The implementation of these methods is dependent on the specification of semantic enrichment as the effect varies from type to type due to specific mappings onto tables and columns. For example, inserting an object of type EMP has an impact on table E and P; both contain information about employees. But storing a department is only done in D.

The Object_Converters incorporate several strategies to load objects from the database into the cache. Their goal is to find a good compromise between efficient access, main memory occupation, and necessity of information. In any case, if an object is demanded (calling load_object), all the information directly available in the corresponding base table is fetched into cache. Materializing an EMP object thus picks up all the information stored in E, i.e., EId, Salary, and Dept; the Dept-value is converted into a relationship WorksIn, but the related department is not always loaded. State information in the Object_Manager maintains what parts of an object have been fetched, what attributes, relationships, attributes of supertypes, and so on. Consequently, it is known what is available and what has to be fetched on demand. Sometimes, further information can be easily computed by joins in advance. For example, the department of an employee, which is referred by column Dept in E and M, can be materialized when fetching an employee by joining D, E, and M. Similarly attributes of supertypes can be pre-fetched by joins, e.g., a join between E and P to make available attributes inherited from PERSON. Nevertheless, too many joins in one SQL statement are rather inefficient. Global parameters like a maximal number of joins to be performed, maximal amount of storage for one object, total cache size, etc. can be tuned in order to control materialization. In a simple case, just a "lazy fetching", picking up elementary properties of an object, is possible.

The Object_Converters could in principle access the relational database directly. However, we put a **Database Interface Layer** in between due to portability; each relational DBS has its own call level interface. Exchanging the underlying relational DBS thus requires few modifications in only this layer.

4.3 Constraints Checking

Specifying semantic enrichment manually, there must be a monitor checking whether an enrichment specification makes sense, i.e., whether the database contains the semantics specified by a user. Comprising this semantics means for relational systems that certain conditions are satisfied by the relational data. Those integrity constraints are monitored by an integrity checker.

Given an enrichment specification, many constraints are derived by the generator automatically. For example, DEPT from relation D[DId] requires that DId is a candidate key for relation D: DId is obliged to uniquely identify tuples. The below SQL query Q_1 yields all tuples that violate this constraint:

```
select *              select * from S s          select *
from  D               where not exists (select *  from  E e , M m
group by DId              from  E e               where m.MId = e.EId
having cnt(DId) > 1       where e.EId = s.SId )
```

$< Query\ Q_1 >$ $\qquad\qquad$ $< Query\ Q_2 >$ $\qquad\qquad$ $< Query\ Q_3 >$

Typical constraints claim for inclusion and exclusion conditions. Hence, as SECR is vertical subtype of EMP in Figure 7, the inclusion S.SId $\subseteq$ E.EId must hold; Q_2 detects violation. Horizontal strategy demands exclusive key values in tables, e.g., $\mathsf{E}.\mathsf{EId} \cap \mathsf{M}.\mathsf{MId} = \emptyset$, respectively Q_3. Combining strategies produces constraints that are even more complex like $\mathsf{E}.\mathsf{EId} \subseteq \sigma_{\mathsf{Worker?=false}}(\mathsf{P}.\mathsf{Id})$.

These SQL queries are automatically generated and must yield an empty result; the constraints are violated otherwise, and the specified enrichment is not sensible. However, the queries supervise correctness only at the time of monitoring; constraints might not hold later on so that periodic checking is necessary. In fact, those queries are also useful in the reverse engineering process to indicate, e.g., subtype relationships. This is taken into account by the process described in [HoK95].

5   Conclusions

In this paper, we described an approach to interfacing existing relational databases from C++ programs. Handling the database is completely done in C++. In contrast to some commercial tools that encapsulate database access in special classes, we take a step further and eliminate the semantic gap between relational tuples and C++ objects. Our solution to this problem is *semantic enrichment* [MaM90, CaS91, HoK95]. Powerful object-oriented view of tables can be built by taking full benefit of object-oriented concepts. Hence, relational data is manipulated in an object-oriented manner, i.e., real objects are handled instead of tuples. Relationships can be traversed like pointers, and inheritance is applicable.

Our approach consists of specifying how tables are combined to object types by using a powerful *specification language*. This is advantageous because the approach is capable of remodelling complex relational situations as classes. Having defined a specification of semantic enrichment, a generator produces a corresponding object-oriented database interface. The methods, as well as their implementations on top of a relational system, are generated automatically. The overall result behaves like an object-oriented DBS. Nevertheless the goodies of relational systems, i.e., powerful query capabilities in the sense of SQL are still available, now in an object-oriented fashion. Deficiencies of querying, often recognized in object-oriented systems, are thus eliminated.

The generated interface complies with the future *standard* ODMG-93 [Cat94] for object-oriented DBSs. Hence, our approach facilitates replacing relational systems with object-oriented ones without affecting applications. Similarly, data can easily be migrated from relational to object-oriented systems, since migration programs can read objects from existing relational databases and then store them in an object-oriented DBS by handling just one interface. This is a first contribution to handle the hard problem of *legacy data* [IEEE95]. We are just extending our tool to ease the process of enrichment. [HoK95] presents a graphical approach to interactively design semantic enrichment.

The presented approach has been implemented on SUN workstations in AT&T C++ on top of the relational system INFORMIX. The implementation makes use of a compiler-compiler to produce the generator. The generative principle is designed to provide flexibility. Hence it is easily possible to exchange the underlying DBS.

Motivation for our work comes from a project concerned with database interoperability [HNS92]. A global interface, relying again on ODMG-93, should provide database access to several kinds of database systems, relational, object-oriented ones, and others. Object-orientation provides a good basis for integrating heterogeneous systems [Har92, BNPS94]. The essential idea is to first translate schemas of component DBSs, expressed in the native data model of the system, into the ODMG-93 model. This leads to a *homogenization* of schemas. Thus, syntactic heterogeneity resulting from different data models and access interfaces of the component systems is eliminated. Our generator supports the homogenization of relational systems in an effective way, as it expresses implicit semantics directly in the ODMG object model and provides an ODMG database interface. Using ODMG-93 plays an important role: Soon or later, object-oriented DBSs will support this standard database interface. Then, no real homogenization will be necessary for them.

The main concern of the successive integration step is identifying conflicts between several homogenized schemas, to resolve them and to merge the schemas into global schema(s). Global schemas give a user the illusion of a homogeneous "database system", with a unified, database spanning, and transparent access to all the integrated data.

Future work will be directed to that integration step. We carry on applying our generative principle. Object classes that represent global schemas are automatically generated. They now provide an integrated database interface for all databases. An integration specification language is used to dissolve semantic heterogeneity between schemas. Syntactic constructs are necessary to handle typical problems of schema integration like different units of measurement ($ vs. £) and homonyms and synonyms. Means to give schemas a new structure are useful to overcome structural differences [ScN88], e.g., if some unit is modelled by an attribute in one schema, but as an object type elsewhere [SpP91, SCG92]. Generalization is an important concept to bring together objects of the same type, but from different databases [KDN90]. Vertical fragmentation has an orthogonal effect: Objects are built by "joining" objects from different databases. Hence logical links between thus far disjoint databases must be newly specified.

Up to now, a prototype that integrates INFORMIX and the object-oriented database systems Objectivity/DB and VERSANT has been implemented, but a lot of work is still necessary.

References

[ABV92]   M. Aksit, L. Bergmans, S. Vural: *An Object-Oriented Language-Database Integration Model: The Composition-Filters Approach.* In [Mad92]

[AlT92]   A. Alashqur, C. Thompson: *O-R Gateway: A System for Connecting C++ Application Programs and Relational Databases.* In: C++ Conference, Portland 1992, USENIX Association, Berkeley

[BNPS94]   E. Bertino, M. Negri, G. Pelagatti, L. Sbattella: *Applications of Object-Oriented Technology to the Integration of Heterogeneous Database Systems.* In: Distributed and Parallel Databases 1994, Vol. 2

[CACM94]   *Reverse Engineering.* Special Issue of Comm. of the ACM 37(5), 1994

[CaS91]   M. Castellanos, F. Saltor: *Semantic Enrichment of Database Schemas: An Object-Oriented Approach.* In: Proc. of 1st Int. Workshop on *Interoperability in Multidatabase Systems* Kyoto (Japan), 1991

[Cat94]   R. Cattell (ed.): *The ODMG-93 Standard for Object Databases.* 2nd edition, Morgan-Kaufmann Publishers, San Mateo (CA) 1994

[CBS94]   R. Chiang, T. Barron, V. Storey: *Reverse Engineering of Relational Databases: Extraction of an EER model from a Relational Database.* Data&Knowledge Engineering 12, 1994

[ERA93]   Proc. 12th Int. Conf. on *Entity-Relationship Approach.* Karlsruhe 1993

[Har92]   M. Härtig: *An Object-Oriented Integration Framework for Building Heterogeneous Database Systems.* In [HNS92]

[HNS92]   D.K. Hsia, E.J. Neuhold, R. Sacks-Davis (eds.): Proc. of the 5th IFIP WG 2.6 Database Semantics Conference (DS-5) on *Interoperable Database Systems,* Lorne (Australia), 1992

[Hoh95]   U. Hohenstein: *Query Processing in Semantically Enriched Relational Databases.* In: Basque Int. Workshop on Information Technology (BIWIT'95) "Data Management Systems", San Sebastian (Spain), 1995

[HoK95]   U. Hohenstein, C. Körner: *A Graphical Tool for Specifying Semantic Enrichment of Relational Databases.* In: 6th IFIP WG 2.6 Work. Group on Data Semantics (DS-6) "Semantics of Database Applications" 1995

[HoO93]   U. Hohenstein, E. Odberg: *A C++ Database Interface Based upon the Entity-Relationship Approach.* In: Proc. of 11th British National Conf. on Database Systems (BNCOD11), Keele (England) 1993

[HTJC93]   J.-L. Hainault, C. Tonneau, M. Joris, M. Chandelon: *Schema Transformation Techniques for Database Reverse Engineering.* In [ERA93]

[IEEE95]   *Legacy Systems.* Special Issue of IEEE Software 12(1), 1995

[Kim92]   W. Kim: *On Unifying Relational and Object-Oriented Database Systems.* In [Mad92]

[KDN90]   M. Kaul, K. Drosten, E. Neuhold: *ViewSystem: Integrating Heterogeneous Information Bases by Object-Oriented Views.* In: Proc. 6th Int. Conf. on Data Engineering, Los Angeles 1990

[Mad92]   O.L. Madsen (ed.): European Conf. on Object-Oriented Programming (ECOOP92), Utrecht 1992

[MaM90]   V. Markowitz, J. Makowsky: *Identifying Extended ER Object Structures in Relational Schemas.* IEEE Trans. on Software Engineering 16(8), 1990

[NNJ93]   B. Narasimhan, S. Navathe, S. Jayaraman: *On Mapping ER and Relational Models into OO Schemas.* In [ERA93]

[PeH95]   G. Pernul, H. Hasenauer: *Combining Reverse with Forward Engineering - A Step forward to Solve the Legacy System Problem.* In: Int. Conf. on Database and Expert Systems Applications, 1995

[PrB94]   W. Premerlani, M. Blaha: *An Approach for Reverse Engineering of Relational Databases.* Communications of the ACM 37(5), May 1994

[SCG92]   F. Saltor, M. Castellanos, M. Garcia-Solaco: *Overcoming Schematic Discrepancies in Interoperable Databases.* In [HNS92]

[ScN88]   M. Schrefl, E. Neuhold: *A Knowledged-Based Approach to Overcome Structural Differences in Object-Oriented Database Integration.* In: The Role of Artifical Intelligence in Database & Information Systems. IFIP Working Conf., Canton (China) 1988

[SpP91]   S. Spaccapietra, C. Parent: *Conflicts and Correspondence Assertions in Interoperable Databases.* ACM SIGMOD-RECORD 1991, 20(4)

[Str91]   B. Stroustrup: *The C++ Programming Language.* 2nd edition, Addison-Wesley 1991

[YaL92]   L.-L. Yan, T.-W. Ling: *Translating Relational Schema With Constraints Into OODB Schema.* In [HNS92]

Generalising the BETA Type System

Søren Brandt and Jørgen Lindskov Knudsen

Department of Computer Science
University of Aarhus
DK-8000 Aarhus C, Denmark
Email: {sbrandt,jlknudsen}@daimi.aau.dk

Abstract. The type system of object-oriented programming languages should enable the description of models that originate from object-oriented analysis and design. In this paper, the BETA type system is generalised, resulting in direct language support for a number of new modelling aspects. The increased expressive power is obtained from a synergy between general block structure and the generalised type hierarchy, and not from syntactic additions to the language.

The type hierarchy described in this paper is a superset of the class hierarchy. In order to regain an orthogonal and internally consistent language, we investigate the impact of the new type hierarchy on other parts of the language. The resulting increase in expressive power serves to further narrow the gap between statically and dynamically typed languages, adding among other things more general generics, immutable references, and attributes with types not known until runtime.

Keywords: language design, type systems, object-oriented modelling, constraints, BETA.

1 Introduction

The type system of an object-oriented language should enable the description of important aspects of models that originate from object-oriented analysis and design. For example, an object-oriented model may describe issues like "the manufacturer of my car" and "the wheel of a car". "The manufacturer of my car" is an immutable reference from "my car" to the actual manufacturer, implying that 1) the manufacturer is not a part of the car, 2) the manufacturer existed before the car, and 3) the reference can never change in the entire lifetime of the car. Here, both "the manufacturer" and "my car" are concrete objects.

Another example is "the wheel of a car", that refers to a part object ("the wheel") of some other object ("a car"), but without determining the concrete car object. The type "the wheel of a car" is therefore a concrete type only relative to a concrete car object, but includes enough information to imply that this specific type does not describe the wheel of a truck.

A common understanding of types in object-oriented languages is as predicates on classes. For example, in BETA [Madsen et al. 93b], C++ [Stroustrup 93], and Eiffel [Meyer 92], a type is the name of a class C. Interpreted as a type, the class name C is a predicate that evaluates to true on the set of subclasses of C.

Other languages, such as Sather [Omohundro 93] and Emerald [Black et al. 87], separate the type and class hierarchies, but still interpret types as predicates on classes: The predicate evaluates to true for classes that *conform* to the type. In any case, a typed reference can only refer to instances of classes on which the type predicate evaluates to true.

Even though the BETA type system is very expressive as compared to most statically typed OO languages, it is at times found to be more restrictive than necessary. The quest for flexible yet static type systems is a search for good compromises between the ultimate freedom of expression in a dynamically typed language, and the safe but constraining rigidity of completely static type systems. The generalisation of the BETA type system presented in this paper is an attempt to gain more flexibility without sacrificing the level of static type checking supported, and to allow expression of a number of models arising in object-oriented analysis and design.

The BETA type system is generalised in two directions: Firstly, by allowing type expressions that do not uniquely name a class, but instead denote a closely related set of classes. Secondly, by allowing types that cannot be interpreted as predicates on classes, but must be more generally interpreted as predicates on objects. We then investigate the impact this generalisation has on other parts of the language. The result is a large increase in expressive power.

The type system described in this paper originates from the development of MetaBETA [Brandt & Schmidt 96], a reflective extension of BETA, featuring a dynamic meta-level interface accessible to programs at runtime. The challenge of adding a dynamic meta-level interface to a statically typed language without circumventing the type system lead to the generalisation of the BETA type system described in this paper. It is a major ingredient in the MetaBETA approach, allowing dynamic reflection in a statically typed language.

This paper assumes some basic knowledge of the BETA language. For readers not familiar with the language, a short BETA primer is included in Appendix A. Section 2 describes current BETA type checking, Section 3 generalises the BETA type system, and Section 4 investigates the effect of the generalised type system on object creation operators. Section 5 shows some examples of the expressive power gained from the generalisations, Section refpatvarextension generalises the BETA concept of dynamic pattern references, and Section 7 describes the semantics of generalised attribute declarations. Finally, Section 8 describes some limitations on the generalised type system, and Sections 9 and 10 point to future work and presents our conclusions.

2 BETA type checking

The type checking rules of BETA are heavily influenced by BETA's general support for localisation in the form of pattern (class) nesting. Simula [Dahl et al. 84] originally introduced this property, inspired by the general block structure in the Algol languages. However, class nesting in Simula is more restricted than in

BETA. This section describes aspects of the BETA type system needed for the purposes of this paper. Other aspects are described in [Madsen et al. 93a].

2.1 Terminology

BETA is a block structured language allowing general pattern nesting: Objects are instances of patterns and have attributes that are references to either other objects or patterns. These references may be either dynamic of static.

Dynamic object references may refer to different objects at different points in time. However, dynamic object references cannot refer to arbitrary objects: They are subject to *qualification* constraints[1]. Likewise, dynamic pattern references may, subject to qualifications, refer to different patterns at different points in time. The BETA declaration:

```
aCircle: ^Circle;
```

declares aCircle as a dynamic object reference (^) qualified by Circle, i.e., it is only allowed to refer to instances of Circle or instances of subpatterns of Circle. Statically it can only be assumed that attributes defined for the Circle pattern are available in the object referred to by aCircle. At runtime, the actual object referred to by aCircle may have several other attributes (since it might be an instance of a subpattern of Circle), but these cannot be accessed through the aCircle reference, since they are not statically known. An unconstrained declaration can be made using Object as qualification:

```
o: ^Object;
```

o can refer to any object, but only operations defined for all object types are allowed on object references qualified by Object.

Most BETA type checking is done at compile time. However, by allowing attributes to have a virtual type that can be specialised in subpatterns, BETA supports covariant[2] pattern hierarchies, and runtime type checks can therefore not be completely avoided in the general case[3]. To enforce strong typing, BETA therefore in some cases reverts to runtime type checking on destructive assignments that cannot be statically accepted or rejected.

For example, writing o[]->aCircle[], the value of the Object reference o may be assigned to the Circle reference aCircle. The compiler is unable to accept or reject this assignment, since it cannot statically deduce whether the assignment is type correct: It knows nothing of the actual type of the object

---

[1] The *qualification* of a BETA dynamic reference corresponds to the *type* of an Eiffel reference or a C++ pointer.

[2] Covariance means that a subpattern may specialise inherited attributes. Hence, the pattern and its attributes are simultaneously specialised — they are covariant. For an interesting discussion on covariance, see [Shang 95].

[3] Usually, static typing of hierarchical type systems is ensured by enforcing contravariant or nonvariant relationships between super/sub-types in a type hierarchy [Black et al. 87, Omohundro 93].

referred to by o. To handle this problem, the compiler inserts a runtime type check.

In summary, type checking in BETA is based on qualified (typed) attribute declarations. A qualification limits the possible values of a dynamic reference, and is usually the name of a pattern. A qualified reference can only refer to instances of the qualification or instances of subpatterns of the qualification. Hence, the qualification tells the compiler what operations are applicable to any object that can potentially be referred.

2.2 Formal Notation

In BETA, the term "attribute" encompasses all variables and procedures in a BETA program. To describe the qualification constraints on attributes, this section introduces some formal notation. The aim of this notation is to enable precise description of the semantics of the different kinds of attributes in a BETA program:

```
dor:  ^Circle;          (* Dynamic Object Reference  *)
sor:  @Circle;          (* Static Object Reference   *)
dpr:  ##Circle;         (* Dynamic Pattern Reference *)
pd:   Circle(# ... #);  (* Pattern Declaration       *)
so:   @Circle(# ... #); (* Singular Object           *)
```

The notation is summarised in Figure 1, where attr and q are path expressions, o is an object, and p_{sub} and p_{super} are patterns. The details of the notation are described in the following.

attr:	The attribute denoted by the path expression attr.
object(attr:)	The object referred to by the object reference attr:.
location(attr:)	The object of which attr: is an attribute
pattern(attr:)	The pattern referred to by the pattern reference attr:.
q##	The path expression q interpreted as a qualification.
qual(attr:)	The qualification of the attribute attr:.
pattern-of(o)	The pattern of which the object o is an instance
extension(q##)	The extension of the qualification q##.
$p_{sub} \leq p_{super}$	p_{sub} is a sub-pattern of p_{super}.

Fig. 1. Formal notation used in this paper.

Adding a trailing colon to a path expression is used to reflect that we are talking about the attribute itself, and not its value. For example, to denote the aCircle attribute itself, we shall write aCircle:.

The **object**() function returns the object referred to by an object reference attribute. For example, **object**(aCircle:) is the object currently referred to by the attribute aCircle:.

location(attr:) returns the object that contains the attr: attribute. For example, **location**(aCalc2.clear:) is **object**(aCalc2:) in Figure 9 of Appendix A.

The **pattern**() function returns the pattern referred to by a pattern reference attribute. For example, **pattern**(dpr:) denotes the pattern currently referred to by dpr:.

To avoid ambiguities, we shall use a.b.c## to denote the qualification interpretation of a path expression a.b.c. If, for example, a.b.c denotes a pattern, the expression a.b.c could be taken to mean "the result of creating and executing a new instance of **pattern**(a.b.c:)". Likewise, in a later section we will allow qualification expressions denoting object reference attributes, and in that case the BETA expression a.b.c would mean "evaluate the do-part of **object**(a.b.c:)". The a.b.c## notation avoids these ambiguities.

The **qual**() function returns the qualification of an attribute, and is defined for all kinds of BETA attributes: For the dor:, sor:, and dpr: attributes, **qual**() returns the qualification expression to the right of, respectively, ^, @, or ##. Hence, **qual**(dor:) = **qual**(sor:) = **qual**(dpr:) = Circle##. Pattern declarations such as pd are fixed points for **qual**(), and **qual**(pd:) therefore returns the pd pattern itself. For singular object declarations such as **object**(so:), **qual**() returns the otherwise anonymous pattern of which **object**(so:) is the only instance. Exactly what constitutes a pattern will be described in Section 2.3.

The **pattern-of**() function returns the pattern of which an object is an instance. For example, after evaluating:

```
      myCircle: Circle (# ... #); (* Circle subpattern *)
      aCircle: ^Circle;
   do &myCircle[]->aCircle[];     (* Object instantiation *)
```

pattern-of(**object**(aCircle:)) is the myCircle pattern.

The notation $p_{sub} \leq p_{super}$ means that the pattern p_{sub} is a subpattern of p_{super}. Hence, used as a qualification, all objects that qualify to p_{sub} also qualify to p_{super}. The set of objects qualifying to a pattern p is denoted **extension**(p). Hence, we shall define the $\leq$ relation on patterns by:

$$p_{sub} \leq p_{super} \overset{def}{\Leftrightarrow} \mathbf{extension}(p_{sub}) \subseteq \mathbf{extension}(p_{super}) \tag{1}$$

The meaning of **extension**(p) will be defined in Section 2.3. For example, myCircle $\leq$ Circle, since all instances of myCircle are in the extension of Circle.

With the notation introduced, we may now formally express the general qualification constraints on dynamic object and pattern references. Consider the declarations:

```
dor: ^Q;
dpr: ##Q;
```

The qualification constraint on the dynamic object reference dor: is:

$$\textbf{pattern-of(object(dor:))} \leq \textbf{qual(dor:)} \tag{2}$$

meaning that the object referred to by dor: must at all times be an instance of a subpattern of the qualification of dor:, in this case Q##.
The qualification constraint on the dynamic pattern reference dpr: is:

$$\textbf{pattern(dpr:)} \leq \textbf{qual(dpr:)} \tag{3}$$

meaning that the pattern referred to by dpr: must at all times be a subpattern of the qualification of dpr:, in this case Q##.

2.3 The Impact of Block Structure

BETA is a block structured language allowing general pattern nesting: Objects are instances of patterns and have attributes that may themselves be patterns. This influences the type system since the apparently "same" pattern attribute of different objects in fact denotes different patterns. This is illustrated by the example in Figure 2, which declares a pattern Window with the nested (class) pattern Line and the nested (method) pattern drawline. Furthermore, two instances of Window, w1 and w2, are declared.

The patterns w1.Line and w2.Line are different, since the draw method in instances of each of these patterns draws a line in separate windows. This has consequences also when using w1.Line and w2.Line as qualifications, as illustrated in Figure 2: References qualified by w1.Line cannot refer to instances of w2.Line and vice versa.

```
Window:                              w1,w2: @Window;
  (# drawline:                       l1: ^w1.Line; l2: ^w2.Line;
     (# p1,p2: @Point;            do &w1.Line[]->l1[];  (* OK *)
        enter (p1,p2) do ...         &w2.Line[]->l2[];  (* OK *)
     #);                             l1[]->l2[];      (* ERROR *)
  Line:                              l2[]->l1[];      (* ERROR *)
     (# p1,p2: @Point;
        draw: (# do (p1,p2)->drawline #);
     #);
  #);
```

Fig. 2. Nested pattern example

Two important concepts in understanding the BETA type system and its relation to block structure, is patterns and object descriptors. An object descriptor, as shown in Figure 3, is a source code entity, whereas a pattern is a corresponding runtime entity.

In the BETA grammar, the syntactic category <ObjectDescriptor> matches source code of the form shown in Figure 3. Every occurrence of the syntactic

```
Super
(# Decl1; Decl2; ... Decln (* attribute-part *)
enter In                    (* enter-part *)
do Imp1; Imp2; ... Impm      (* do-part *)
exit Out                    (* exit-part *)
#)
```

Fig. 3. Syntactic category <ObjectDescriptor>

category <ObjectDescriptor> in a program source uniquely defines an object descriptor. In addition to being the meat of pattern declarations, (see Figure 7 in Appendix A), object descriptors occur in singular object declarations, as well as nested directly in the do-part of other object descriptors (as exemplified by Figure ?? in Appendix A).

General block structure allows pattern nesting to an arbitrary level, and a nested BETA pattern is therefore a closure defined by a a unique object descriptor and an *origin* object. The origin of a pattern is significant for two purposes: Firstly, instances of the pattern may need access to attributes of the origin object [4]. Secondly, the origin affects the set of objects qualifying to a pattern when used as a variable qualification, and is therefore significant for type checking purposes. A pattern p is uniquely identified by the pair:

$$(\mathbf{origin}(p), \mathbf{descriptor}(p))$$

where **origin**(p) is the object of which p is an attribute, and **descriptor**(p) is the object descriptor for p. Due to inheritance, a pattern may have a super pattern, **super**(p), uniquely identified by the pair:

$$(\mathbf{origin}(\mathbf{super}(p)), \mathbf{descriptor}(\mathbf{super}(p)))$$

leading to a chain of patterns starting in p and terminating with the Object pattern. For patterns declared at the outermost block-level, no origin reference is needed, since there is no surrounding object.

---

[4] The *static link* between activation records of languages, such as Pascal, where procedures may be declared local to other procedures is a special case of the BETA origin reference.

Direct pattern instances An object is a *direct instance* of a pattern iff the object was created as an instance of that pattern. A direct instance of a pattern p contains a reference to **descriptor(p)** and also a reference to each of the origin objects found in the pattern chain starting in p. For example, the w1.Line pattern corresponds to the pair (**object**(w1:), Window.Line). As illustrated in Figure 4, the l1 instance of w1.Line therefore has a reference to the object descriptor corresponding to Window.Line, and an origin reference to the w1 object. The Window instance w1 has a reference to the object descriptor for Windows, but no origin reference, since the Window pattern is declared at the outermost block-level. That objects l1 and l2 are instances of different patterns follows from their origin references pointing to different objects, although l1 and l2 share the descriptor of Window.Line objects.

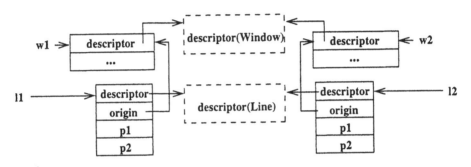

Fig. 4. Lines have an origin reference to the Window instance in which their pattern is nested.

The extension of a pattern Finally, we may now define the extension of a pattern as follows: An object o that is a direct instance of a pattern p is in the extension of a pattern q, i.e., o ∈ **extension**(q), iff q can be found in the chain of patterns starting in p.

3 A Generalised Qualification Concept

In this section, we introduce a generalised qualification concept. The BETA type system is generalised by 1) allowing type expressions that do not uniquely name a class, and 2) by allowing types that are interpreted as predicates on objects. The generalisation is obtained without adding new syntax to the language.

In most situations, current BETA *only* allows qualification expressions that uniquely name a pattern. But logically there is no reason why a qualification should always be equivalent to a specific pattern. In fact, current BETA does allow one special kind of qualification that does not uniquely name a pattern: Recall that at runtime, a BETA pattern p is a closure defined by an origin object and an object descriptor. By naming the object descriptor but leaving the origin unspecified, a qualification that corresponds to a *set* of patterns results. In current BETA, this is allowed in the case of dynamic object references, as exemplified by aShape below:

```
Window: (# Shape: (# ... #)#); aShape: ^Window.Shape;
```

Seen as a predicate on patterns, the Window.Shape qualification evaluates to true on any pattern Shape nested inside *some* Window object w, and subpatterns of these.

Figure 5 illustrates the process of pattern specialisation as a stepwise narrowing of the pattern extension. But no matter the degree of specialisation, the

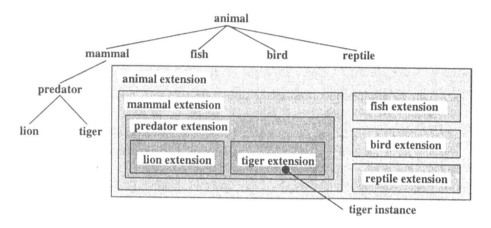

Fig. 5. Classification hierarchy and corresponding extension sets

extension of a pattern continues being unlimited, since any pattern has an unlimited number of instances. Hence BETA, like all other OO languages, only allows the expression of qualifications with unlimited extensions.

In principle we can imagine qualification extensions of any size, finite or unlimited. By explicitly listing a number of object names, any qualification with finite extension can be specified. As a tentative syntax for such qualifications, consider w: ^[w1,w2,w3] ;, with the intended meaning that the dynamic object reference w is allowed to refer to any of the objects w1, w2, or w3. However, not wanting to change the syntax of BETA, we restrict our attention to lists of length one, i.e., allowing the use of a single object name in place of a qualification.

3.1 Taxonomy of Generalised Qualifications

The previous section introduced the idea of generalising the set of qualifications allowed. This section divides qualifications into 8 main categories along three binary axes.

Syntactically, a BETA qualification expression is a path expression, i.e., a dot-separated list of names: A qualification q is generally of the syntactic form $n_1.n_2....n_m$, where each n_i is a name that denotes either a pattern attribute or an object reference attribute. Qualification expressions appear in several situations:

– As qualifications in variable declarations:

```
dor: ^q;  (* dynamic object reference *)
dpr: ##q; (* dynamic pattern reference *)
```

– As values assigned to dynamic pattern references: `do q##->dpr##`
– As pattern specification in part object declarations: `sor: @q;`
– As super specification in pattern declarations:

```
p: q(# ... #);    (* pattern declaration *)
pv:< q(# ... #);  (* virtual pattern declaration *)
```

– As super specification in singular object declarations and method executions:

```
sor: @q(# ... #); (* singular object *)
do q(# ... #)        (* method execution *)
```

The first axis along which we classify qualification expressions q distinguishes *pattern qualifications* and *object qualifications*: If n_m is the name of a pattern reference attribute, q is called a pattern qualification. If n_m is the name of an object reference attribute, q is called an *object qualification*.

The second axis distinguishes *full qualifications* and *partial qualifications*: If all n_i, $i < m$, are names of object reference attributes, q is called a full qualification. If some n_i, $i < m$ is the name of a pattern attribute, q is called a partial qualification. Partial qualifications do not uniquely identify an object attribute.

These two axes result in four qualification categories as depicted in Figure 6.

	$n_1....n_{m-1}$: only objects	$n_1....n_{m-1}$: at least one pattern
n_m: object	full object qualification	partial object qualification
n_m: pattern	full pattern qualification	partial pattern qualification

Fig. 6. Qualification categories for $q=n_1.n_2....n_m$

The third and last axis distinguishes *static qualifications* from *dynamic qualifications*: If all n_i are names of static pattern attributes or static object reference attributes, q is called a *static qualification*. Otherwise, q is called a *dynamic qualification*. A static qualification has a static extension, whereas the extension of a dynamic qualification depends on the time of evaluation.

Note that the classification of qualification expressions only depends on the statically known kind of the attributes named in the expression, and can therefore easily be known by the compiler.

Example 1. Full pattern qualifications such as `Window` and `aWindow.Shape` uniquely name a pattern. Partial pattern qualifications such as `Window.Shape` correspond to sets of related patterns. Full object qualifications such as `aWindow` or `aShape` correspond to qualifications with a single element extension, i.e., they name an object. Finally, for an example of a partial object qualification consider the following code:

```
Person: (# name: @Text #);
aPersonName: ^Person.name;
```

`aPersonName` is here constrained by a static partial object qualification to refer to the name of *some* person, but without restricting the specific person.   □

3.2   Qualification Hierarchies

Inheritance is the basis for building pattern hierarchies such as the one shown in Figure 5. BETA pattern hierarchies is a generalisation of class hierarchies in languages such as Eiffel and C++. With the introduction of generalised qualifications, another hierarchy has emerged: The qualification hierarchy.

A pattern name is a special case of qualification (the full pattern qualification), and the set of patterns is thus a subset of the set of qualifications. The inheritance relation equips the set of patterns with a partial order as defined by Equation 1 in Section 2.2. Likewise, the qualification hierarchy is partially ordered: For full pattern qualifications, the partial order corresponds to the inheritance relation. In general, we shall define the partial order on qualifications by means of their extension. This is a straightforward generalisation of Equation 1:

$$q \leq q' \overset{def}{\Leftrightarrow} \text{extension}(q) \subseteq \text{extension}(q')$$

where q and q' are both qualification expressions. For example, the extension of a full object qualification o is a single-element set:

$$
\begin{aligned}
&o \leq q \\
\overset{def}{\Leftrightarrow}\ & \text{extension}(o) \subseteq \text{extension}(q) \\
\Leftrightarrow\ & \{o\} \subseteq \text{extension}(q) \\
\Leftrightarrow\ & o \in \text{extension}(q)
\end{aligned}
$$

The special value NONE[5] means *no object*. By definition, NONE qualifies to any
qualification, and is therefore the bottom ($\perp$) of the qualification hierarchy:

$$\forall q : \text{NONE} \leq q$$

In current BETA, the pattern hierarchy is the basis for type checking. In
generalised BETA, the qualification hierarchy takes over, and hence allows more
general qualifications.

We have introduced a qualification hierarchy which is different from the pattern hierarchy. However, as opposed to the type and class hierarchies of, e.g.,
Emerald, the qualification and pattern hierarchies are not separate, since the
pattern hierarchy is embedded in the qualification hierarchy. Another difference
from the Emerald type hierarchy is that our qualification hierarchy contains
qualifications that uniquely identify single objects.

4 Generalised Semantics for Object Creation Operators

The BETA operators & and @ are used to create new objects, i.e., new instances
of BETA patterns: & is used for dynamic object creation in imperative code, and
@ is used in declarations to denote the creation of static part objects as part of
their location:

```
Person: (# left_arm, right_arm: @arm #);
aPerson: ^Person;
do &Person[]->aPerson[];
```

Here, a new person object is created using the & operator. A reference to the
new person object is then assigned to the dynamic object reference aPerson.
Along with the new Person object, a number of static part objects, the limbs,
are created. Creation of the limbs happens automatically, since they are declared
using the @ operator, which also binds the newly created limbs to the identifiers
left_arm and right_arm.

The & operator takes a single qualification parameter q. The @ operator takes
two parameters: A qualification parameter q, and an identifier parameter id.
Current BETA requires that the q parameter given to & and @ denotes a pattern,
i.e., q must be a full pattern qualification. Given a qualification q, the semantics
of both operators is to create a new instance of the pattern denoted by q. In
addition, @ binds the newly created object to the identifier parameter id.

To what extent can these semantics be generalised to allow other kinds of
qualification parameters to & and @? Given a qualification with a finite extension,
the "create a new object" semantics do not apply anymore, since all objects
contained in a finite extension are by definition already there, and any new
object would therefore not be part of that extension. We therefore generalise the

---
[5] NONE corresponds to the null pointer in C++, and the special value Void in Eiffel.

semantics of **&** from "create new object" into:

$$\&(q) = \begin{cases} \text{new } q & \text{if } q \text{ is a full pattern qualification} \\ o & \text{if } q \text{ is a full object qualification and } \textbf{extension}(q) = \{o\} \ (4) \\ error & \text{otherwise} \end{cases}$$

That is, applying **&** to a qualification q always returns an object that qualifies to q. But in case of q being a full object qualification, the returned object is no longer new[6].

The object creation operator, **&**, is evaluated each time the statement of which it is part is executed. The static object reference operator, **@**, is evaluated once, namely at creation time of its location. The result of evaluating @(id, q) is to bind the value &(q)[] to the identifier id. Afterwards, the binding of id is not allowed to change.

5 Examples

Before considering all possible declarations in more detail, we show some examples of the expressive power gained from the introduction of generalised qualifications and object creation operators.

Example 2. The following code demonstrates one way of binding an immutable reference to an already existing object:

```
aWindow: ^Window;
Foo: (# sor: @aWindow #);
aFoo: ^Foo;
do &Foo[]->aFoo[];
```

When an instance of Foo is created, the static object reference sor: is bound to the value &(aWindow##)[], where aWindow is a dynamic full object qualification. According to Equation 4, this means that aFoo.sor: is bound to refer the object referred to by aWindow: at the time when aFoo is created. I.e., aFoo.sor: becomes an immutable reference to **object**(aWindow:). □

Generalised qualifications allow us to think of full object qualifications as specialisations of qualifications with unlimited extensions. This results in virtual patterns that can be specialised into full object qualifications.

Example 3. Consider the relation between a child and each of its parents. These relations are immutable references bound when the child comes into existence. In generalised BETA, we can express this as follows:

---

[6] The decision to disallow partial qualifications as parameter to **&** is more or less arbitrary. It could be argued that a better choice would be to create a new object along with the objects necessary to provide the environment of the new object. For example, &Window.Shape[], could create a new Window object w, followed by the creation of an instance of w.Shape.

```
Person:
  (# FatherBinding:< Person; father: @FatherBinding;
     MotherBinding:< Person; mother: @MotherBinding;
  #);
makeChild:
  (# newfather, newmother: ^Person
  enter (newfather[], newmother[])
  exit &Person
          (# FatherBinding:: newfather;
             MotherBinding:: newmother;
          #)[]
  #);
```

Here, a `Person` is defined to have an immutable reference to each parent. Due to `Person` having `Person` part objects, `Person` is an abstract pattern of which it is impossible to create direct instances. However, by further binding `FatherBinding` and `MotherBinding` into full object qualifications, it becomes possible to create a `Person`, and at the same time bind the parent references. Current BETA forces us to describe the parent references by dynamic references, which is unfortunate since people do not tend to change biological parents. Conversely, generalised BETA is able to directly model that parent references are immutable and that the parents existed before the child. To solve the chicken-and-egg problem of creating the very first `Person` instance, we can create a person with no parents:

```
do (NONE,NONE)->makeChild->adam[];
```

□

To be used as super specification in a pattern declaration, a qualification expression must be a full pattern qualification: A partial qualification would be ambiguous, and a full object qualification would correspond to the action of specialising an object. Likewise, in a part object declaration, the pattern specification must eventually evaluate to a full qualification for the part object to be unambiguously defined. Notice however, that an abstract pattern may declare part objects of only partially known type, as long as concrete subpatterns specify a full qualification for the part.

Example 4. Consider an abstract `CodeDisplay` pattern:

```
Grammar: (# PrettyPrinter:< (# ... #); ... #);
CodeDisplay:
  (# PrettyPrinter:< Grammar.PrettyPrinter;
     pp: @PrettyPrinter;
  #);
```

A `CodeDisplay` uses a prettyprinter to actually display the code, but the exact type of the pretty-printer depends on the type of `Grammar` being used. `CodeDisplay` is an abstract pattern, because the type of the `pp` part object is ambiguous. However, on creation of a `CodeDisplay`, the actual grammar used is known, and can be used to disambiguate the type of `pp`:

```
aGrammar: @Grammar;
aCodeDisplay: @CodeDisplay
  (# PrettyPrinter:: aGrammar.PrettyPrinter #);
```

□

We may also make good use of partial pattern qualifications in expressing generics: In BETA, the type parameter of a generic class is expressed by a nested virtual class [Madsen & Møller-Pedersen 89].

Example 5. Consider the declaration of a generic list pattern:

```
List:
  (# Element:< Object; (* Element type *)
     insert: (* Insert element *)
       (# new: ^Element
       enter new[] do ...
       #);
  #);
```

To create a list of persons, the generic `List` class is specialised by final binding the `Element` virtual:

```
aPersonList: @List(# Element:: Person #);
```

But to create a generic `Shape` list, we must use a partial pattern qualification:

```
ShapeList: List (# Element::< Window.Shape #)
```

which is illegal in current BETA, since the `Element` virtual in `ShapeList` does not uniquely name a pattern. In generalised BETA, however, the example is perfectly legal. Further specialising `ShapeList`, we can now create lists that can contain shapes from specific windows only, or use `ShapeList` directly to create a list of all shapes, regardless of the window to which they belong:

```
w1,w2: @Window;
w1shapes: @ShapeList(# Element:: w1.Shape #);
w2shapes: @ShapeList(# Element:: w2.Shape #);
allShapes: @ShapeList;
```

In current BETA, a list containing all `Shape` objects can only be declared as a list that can contain any object, thereby losing all static information on the type of objects in the list.

□

Example 6. Consider the declaration of a dynamic text reference: `aText: ^Text;` One might be interested in declaring a dynamic text reference that is only allowed to refer to text objects that are actually person names:

```
Person: (# name: @Text; ... #);
aPersonName: ^Person.name;
```

Clearly, `aPersonName` can only refer to text objects, but the type system now also expresses and enforces that the text referred is the name of a person.   □

6   Generalised Dynamic Pattern References

Dynamic pattern references were originally introduced in BETA to support patterns as first-class values [Agesen et al. 89], e.g., allowing patterns as method parameters. In practice, dynamic pattern references are used in several ways:

- As function and method pointers.
- As dynamic class references.
- As qualification references, allowing explicit runtime type checks.

In Section 3 we argued that patterns are a special case of the more general qualification concept. It is therefore natural to introduce a corresponding generalisation of dynamic pattern references, turning them into dynamic *qualification references*. However, to avoid introducing new terminology, we retain the term dynamic pattern reference.

In current BETA, a dynamic pattern reference value is obtained by appending the **##** operator to object names or pattern names: The expression o## returns **pattern-of(**o**)**, i.e., a reference to the pattern of which the object o is an instance. Likewise, the value of the expression p## is a reference to the pattern p. In both cases, a reference to a full pattern qualification is obtained. These semantics give rise to the following irregularities:

1. If **object(**so:**)** is a singular object, the BETA expression so## returns a reference to the otherwise anonymous pattern **pattern-of(object(**so:**))** of which **object(**so:**)** is the only instance. This breaks the anonymity of **pattern-of(object(**so:**))**, and using so##, it is then possible to create new instances of the pattern. This would destroy the singularity of **object(**so:**)**, and singularity can therefore not be guaranteed by the compiler.

2. There is currently no way to obtain a reference to qualifications other than full pattern qualifications. For example, partial qualifications are currently not first-class values, and can therefore not be passed as method parameters. Consider the copy method below, intended to copy an object unless it is of a specific type:

```
copy:
  (# o,ocopy: ^Object; dont_copy: ##Object;
  enter (o[],dont_copy##)
  do (if not (o##<=dont_copy##) then
          o[]->performCopy->ocopy[];
     if);
  exit ocopy[]
  #);
do (anObject[],Window.Shape##)->copy->aCopy[];
```

As illustrated, a desired use of copy might be to copy all objects that do not qualify to Window.Shape##. Unfortunately, Window.Shape## is a partial pattern qualification, and the example is therefore illegal, since only references to full pattern qualifications are currently allowed.

To remove these irregularities, we change and generalise the ## operator into:

The value of the expression $n_1.n_2....n_m$## is the qualification denoted by the path expression $n_1.n_2....n_m$ at evaluation time.

Note that for dynamic qualification expressions, each evaluation of the expression may result in a new qualification. For full object qualifications o, the above definition changes the value of o## from **pattern-of(object(o:))**, to the full object qualification with extension {**object(o:)**}. The expression &(o##)[] thus becomes equivalent to o[], and the singular object irregularity has disappeared. Likewise, the copy example is now fully legal.

7   Attribute Declaration Semantics

Previous sections generalised the notions of qualifications and object creation operators. In this section, we list the semantics for all attribute types in light of the new qualification concept. As will be seen, very few surface changes have been made to the semantics of attribute declarations. The real changes stem from generalisations to the qualification hierarchy, and the resulting changes to the object creation operators. To describe the semantics of attribute declarations, we consider the following attribute properties:

- Is destructive assignment allowed?
- Initial value.
- Possible values.

BETA supports four attribute kinds, described in turn below.

Static Object References: sor: @q

The only interesting property of a static object reference is its initial value, since destructive assignment is not allowed. We use the notation **crt(sor:,expr)** to denote the value of expr at the time when **location(sor:)** is created.

The initial value of sor: is given by

$$\mathbf{object}(sor:) = \mathbf{crt}(sor:,\&qual(sor:)[])$$

with the value of &qual(sor:)[] defined by Equation 4 in Section 4. The above equation is the same as in current BETA, with the new possibilities resulting from Equation 4.

Static Pattern References: spr:q or spr: q(# ... #)
    In current BETA, static pattern references always declare new patterns. This is consistent with the declaration of static object references, that always create new objects. However, we have generalised static object references to allow them to be bound to already existing objects, and generalised dynamic pattern references to be able to refer to any kind of qualification. As a combination, static pattern references can be bound to any kind of qualification, including existing ones.
    Again, the behaviour of static pattern reference spr: is essentially captured in a single equation:

$$\mathbf{pattern}(spr:) = \mathbf{crt}(spr:,qual(spr:))$$

We may split static pattern reference declarations into two cases:

  − spr: q(# ... #), declaring the pattern (**location**(spr:), q(# ... #)).
  − spr: q, where spr: gets bound to **crt**(spr:,q##).

The last case is new, and allows static pattern references to be bound to existing qualifications. For example, this allows a dynamic qualification to be evaluated and then bound to a static pattern reference, leading to attributes whose qualification is not known until runtime. As will be demonstrated later, the result is a great flexibility while retaining the need to do runtime type checks only on potentially dangerous assignments, as opposed to the need in dynamically typed languages to do an implicit type-check (method lookup) on each message send.

Dynamic Object References: dor: ^q;
    The initial value of **object**(dor:) is NONE, with possible values given by a generalisation of Equation 2 in Section 2.2:

$$\mathbf{object}(dor:) \le qual(dor:)$$

Dynamic Pattern References: dpr: ##q
    The initial value of **pattern**(dpr:) is NONE, with possible values given by Equation 3 from Section 2.2:

$$\mathbf{pattern}(dpr:) \le qual(dpr:)$$

8   Restrictions on Qualifications

We have described a generalised concept of qualified, (typed), attributes, adding considerably to the expressive power of the BETA language. However, not all the described qualifications on dynamic references can be efficiently enforced.

As described in Section 2, the BETA type system is not completely statically checkable, and therefore needs a minimal number of runtime type checks. Generalising the type system should not make it inherently more difficult to check. For this reason, we choose to allow only qualifications that can be enforced by a combination of compile time checking and occasional (constant-time) runtime checks on potentially dangerous assignments.

In general, we only allow a qualification q on a dynamic reference dr:, if it is checkable by only monitoring assignments to dr:. If the qualification itself is dynamic, (as explained in Section 3.1), not only the attribute itself must be monitored, but also its qualification, resulting in complex relationships between the allowed values of dynamic attributes. Although it is possible to implement a runtime system that maintains constraint graphs in order to enforce dynamic qualifications, we choose to disallow dynamic qualifications to avoid severe unpredictable runtime overheads. Thus, if the declaration of a dynamic reference attribute results in a qualification equation, (see Section 7), with a dynamic right-hand side, the declaration will be declared illegal, and rejected by the compiler.

Example 7. Consider the declaration of a dynamic object reference attribute aShape with a dynamic qualification:

```
Window: (# Shape: (# ... #) #);
aWindow: ^Window;
aShape: ^aWindow.Shape;
```

Here, the qualification constraint object(aShape:) $\leq$ aWindow.Shape## must be enforced, which requires that we monitor the value of object(aShape:) *and* the value of object(aWindow:), since extension(aWindow.Shape) changes if object(aWindow:) changes. In the general case, knowing where to do runtime checking therefore requires either global information at compile time, or the maintenance of a constraint graph at runtime. We do not find any of these options acceptable, and hence choose to disallow this kind of qualification.   □

In fact, the current Mjølner BETA compiler does allow the above kind of dynamic full pattern qualification. However, the dynamic full pattern qualification aWindow.Shape is interpreted as the static partial pattern qualification Window.Shape. and therefore only the less restrictive object(aShape:) $\leq$ Window.Shape constraint is enforced. The following scenario is thus accepted without compile time or runtime errors:

```
    do &Window[]->aWindow[];
       &aWindow.Shape[]->aShape[]; (* OK *)
       &Window[]->aWindow[]; (* object(aShape:) illegal!! *)
```

Fortunately we can disallow this type of dynamic full pattern declaration with virtually no loss of expressive power, since we can convert the dynamic qualification into a static qualification:

```
    aDynWin: ^Window;
    do &Window[]->aDynWin[];
       (# aStatWin: @aDynWin;
          aShape: ^aStatWin.Shape;
       do &aStatWin.Shape[]->aShape[]; (* OK *)
          &Window[]->aDynWin[];        (* OK *)
          &Window[]->aStatWin[]; (* compile time error *)
       #)
```

Note that aStatWin.Shape is a static qualification whose extension cannot change, and therefore does not need to be monitored at runtime: Assignment to aDynWin does not change the extension of aStatWin.Shape, and assignment to aStatWin is a compile-time error.

However, if we were content with the knowledge that **object**(aShape:) qualifies to the Shape pattern of *some* window, and do not care about the exact window, we should have used a partial pattern qualification:

```
    aDynWin: ^Window;
    aShape: ^Window.Shape;
    do &Window[]->aDynWin[];
       &aDynWin.Shape[]->aShape[]; (* OK *)
       &Window[]->aDynWin[];       (* OK *)
```

Example 8. Another illegal example is the declaration of object references with dynamic partial object qualifications:

```
    Vehicle: (# owner: ^Person #);
    aVehicleOwner: ^Vehicle.owner;
```

Again, the problem is that the qualification itself is dynamic: In this case, a Vehicle changing owner may result in the breaking of the qualification constraint on aVehicleOwner, since the previous owner may thereby stop being the owner of any vehicle. □

Static Binding of Dynamic Qualifications The decision to disallow dynamic qualifications for dynamic references is not a real limitation. In general, if we wish to specify something like:

```
    anObject: ^dynqual
  do o[]->anObject[]; ...
```

where **dynqual** is some dynamic qualification expression, we can transform it into:

```
  o[]->(# statqual: dynqual; anObject: ^statqual;
        enter anObject[] do ...
        #)
```

which enforces a static qualification on the **anObject** reference. This technique is called *static binding of dynamic qualification* and can be used to resolve all dynamic qualifications.

Example 9. As a more complete example of using this technique, consider a **List** pattern, where the qualification of the types of objects in the **List** can be controlled dynamically:

```
    List:
      (# elementType: ##Object;
         insert:
           (# elmType: elementType; new: ^elmType;
           enter new[] do ...
           #);
         changeElementType:
           (# newElementType: ##Object;
           enter newElementType##
           do scan
             (#
             do (if not (current##<=newElementType##) then
                   current[]->delete
                 if)
             #);
             newElementType##->elementType##
           #);
      #);
```

We may now create a List object to contain Window.Shape objects:

```
      winShapeList: @List;
  do Window.Shape##->winShapeList.changeElementType;
     &aWindow.Shape[]->winShapeList.insert;
```

If we later choose to restrict the same List object to contain only **aWindow Shapes**, we can dynamically choose to do so by:

```
do aWindow.Shape##->winShapeList.changeElementType;
```

causing all Shapes that do not qualify to aWindow.Shape## to be removed from
the list. At all times during the lifetime of winShapeList, the elements in the
list will automatically conform to the qualification, given by the elementType
attribute.

We can also create a List that can only contain instances of a pattern unknown until runtime, for example because it is loaded dynamically:

```
aList: @List;
aPattern: ##Object;
do 'aPatternName'->loadPattern->aPattern##;
aPattern##->aList.changeElementType;
&aPattern[]->aList.insert;
```

It should be noted that runtime type checks are clearly still needed to enforce the typing in these examples, but considering the dynamic nature of the
examples, avoiding runtime checking would also be a surprising achievement.
However, the example does ensure that the element type is enforced, although
it is not known until runtime.   □

The generalisation of BETA qualifications has resulted in a type-system with
an increased expressive power. Several of the new possibilities are easy to implement, and add considerably to the expressive power of the BETA language,
without adding new syntax.

Static attributes do not require continuous monitoring, since they are bound
to a value that is acceptable at creation time, and afterward are not allowed
to change. Therefore, any qualification expression is acceptable as the type of a
static attribute.

For dynamic references, we have chosen to disallow attribute declarations
with dynamic qualifications, since their enforcement requires either global compile-
time knowledge, or the maintenance of a constraint-graph at runtime. Neither of
these options are acceptable in a language with support for separate compilation
and efficient execution.

9 Future Work

Static type systems are continuously under attack from dynamic type systems.
Dynamic type systems play an important role in early software development
such as prototyping and explorative programming. Conversely, static type systems show their strength in industrial software production. This tension has
resulted in an almost religious war amongst language designers for at least
the last decade, but it seems that it is now time to join forces: The last few
years have seen much research in type inference of dynamic type systems, extracting type information from a given program. The information may then be

utilised as an aid to the programmer, giving him a better understanding of the types implicitly specified in the program, but also as a help to the compiler and runtime system in order to optimise the runtime efficiency of the program [Chambers & Ungar 90, Oxhøj et al. 92, Plevyak & Chien 95, Agesen 95].

The work reported in this paper only deals with this tension in a limited way, by allowing more flexible type declarations without compromising the level of static type-checking already supported. However, industrial strength type systems must look for better ways to support early software development. One way to go is to investigate the possibilities for introducing dynamic typing components into static type systems.

10 Conclusion

This paper examined the current BETA type system and proposed generalisations that can be introduced without extensive runtime overhead, and without changing the language syntax. The paper investigated the impact of these generalisations on other parts of the language, in order to regain an orthogonal and internally consistent language.

We have investigated the tension between BETA block structure and the type system, giving rise to the introduction of the concepts of full and partial pattern qualifications. Partial pattern qualifications are types that do not uniquely relate to a single pattern, resulting in increased flexibility in expressing dynamic references and generics.

Analysis of BETA qualification expressions revealed that any conceivable path expression can be given a perfectly logical type-interpretation, giving rise to increased expressive power without changing the language syntax. We have examined the generalised qualifications, finding that the BETA language has been augmented with several new and powerful mechanisms, including creation-time bound immutable object references, creation-time bound immutable pattern references, virtual object binding, and more general generics.

Finally, we have examined the runtime overhead of the new facilities, revealing that a particular kind of qualifications, the dynamic qualifications, impose severe runtime overhead. Albeit dynamic qualifications are very powerful, we have excluded them from this proposal due to their runtime overhead. Further investigations into these qualifications are needed in order to fully understand the ramifications. Fortunately, in most cases where dynamic qualifications seem the obvious choice, it is found that the type constraints needed can be specified by either using the newly introduced partial qualifications, or by re-binding dynamic qualifications to static pattern references.

In general terms, we have extended the flexibility of the BETA type system without imposing any additional runtime overhead. Object relations that naturally arise in object-oriented analysis and design have been given direct language language support, without adding new language concepts or syntax. The flexibility has been gained from a more general interpretation of existing concepts.

11 Acknowledgements

The authors would like to thank Erik Ernst, René Wenzel Schmidt, and the anonymous ECOOP referees who read earlier drafts of this paper and provided many valuable comments.

References

[Agesen 95] O. Agesen. The Cartesian Product Algorithm: Simple and Precise Type Inference of Parametric Polymorphism. In *Proceedings of the Ninth European Conference on Object-Oriented Programming (ECOOP'95)*, Aarhus, Denmark, August 1995.

[Agesen et al. 89] O. Agesen, S. Frølund, and M. Olsen. Persistent and Shared Objects in BETA. Master's thesis, Department of Computer Science, University of Aarhus, April 1989.

[Black et al. 87] A. Black, N. Hutchinson, E. Jul, H. Levy, and L. Carter. Distribution and Abstract Types in Emerald. *IEEE Transactions on Software Engineering*, 13(1), January 1987.

[Brandt & Schmidt 96] S. Brandt and R. W. Schmidt. The Design of a Meta-Level Architecture for the BETA Language. In C. Zimmermann, editor, *Advances in Object-Oriented Metalevel Architectures and Reflection*. CRC Press Inc, Boca Raton, Florida, 1996.

[Chambers & Ungar 90] C. Chambers and D. Ungar. Iterative Type Analysis and Extended Message Splitting: Optimizing Dynamically-Typed Object-Oriented Programs. In *Proceedings of the SIGPLAN'90 Conference on Programming Language Design and Implementation*, White Plains, NY, June 1990.

[Dahl et al. 84] O. Dahl, B. Myrhaug, and K. Nygaard. Simula 67 Common Base Language. Pub. 725, Norwegian Computing Center, Oslo, 1984.

[Madsen & Møller-Pedersen 89] O. L. Madsen and B. Møller-Pedersen. Virtual Classes – A Powerful Mechanism in Object-Oriented Programming. In *Proceedings of the Fourth Conference on Object-Oriented Programming Systems, Languages and Applications (OOPSLA'89)*, volume 24 of *Sigplan Notices*, October 1989.

[Madsen et al. 93a] O. Madsen, B.Magnusson, and B. Pedersen. Strong typing of Object-Oriented Languages Revisited. In J. Knudsen, O. Madsen, B. Magnusson, and M. Löfgren, editors, *Object-Oriented Environments*. Prentice Hall, September 1993.

[Madsen et al. 93b] O. L. Madsen, B. Møller-Pedersen, and K. Nygaard. *Object-Oriented Programming in the BETA Programming Language*. Addison Wesley, Reading, MA, June 1993.

[Meyer 92] B. Meyer. *Eiffel, The Language*. Prentice Hall, 1992.

[Omohundro 93] S. Omohundro. The Sather Programming Language. *Doctor Dobb's Journal*, pages 42 – 48, October 1993.

[Oxhøj et al. 92] N. Oxhøj, J. Palsberg, and M. I. Schwartzbach. Making type inference practical. In *Proceedings of the Sixth European Conference on Object-Oriented Programming (ECOOP'92)*, Utrecht, The Netherlands, June 1992.

[Plevyak & Chien 95] J. B. Plevyak and A. A. Chien. Precise Concrete Type Inference for Object-Oriented Languages. In *Proceedings of the Ninth Conference on*

445

Object-Oriented Programming Systems, Languages and Applications (OOP-SLA'94), Portland, OR, October 1995.

[Shang 95] D. L. Shang. Covariant Deep Subtyping Reconsidered. *ACM SIGPLAN Notices*, 30(5):21 – 28, May 1995.

[Stroustrup 93] B. Stroustrup. *The C++ Programming Language*. Addison Wesley, 1993.

A A BETA Primer

This section briefly introduces the BETA language, and may be skipped by readers familiar with BETA. For a comprehensive description of the language, readers are referred to [Madsen et al. 93b].

A.1 Patterns

A BETA program execution consists of a collection of objects. An object is an instance of a pattern. The pattern construct unifies programming language concepts such as class, generic class, method, process, coroutine, and exception. This results in a syntactically small language, but is also a point of confusion for programmers with background in more traditional languages because classes and methods in BETA have the same syntax. In this paper, we use the convention that patterns with names beginning with an upper-case letter correspond to classes, whereas patterns with names beginning with a lower-case letter correspond to methods[7].

A pattern declaration has the form shown in Figure 7, where P is the name

```
P: Super
    (# Decl1; Decl2; ... Decln      (* attribute-part *)
    enter In                        (* enter-part *)
    do Imp1; Imp2; ... Impm         (* do-part *)
    exit Out                        (* exit-part *)
    #)
```

Fig. 7. Structure of a pattern declaration

of the pattern and Super is an optional superpattern for P. The attribute-part is a list of declarations of reference attributes, part objects, and nested patterns. The most important forms taken by Decli are the following:

– R1: ^Q where Q is a pattern, declares R1 as a *dynamic reference* to instances of (subpatterns of) Q. R1 is similar to a pointer in C++, and may thus refer

---

[7] Occasionally, the same pattern is used as both a method and a class, although such cases do not occur in this paper.

to different objects at different points in time. The value of R1 is changed through destructive assignments of the form `newvalue[]->R1[]`.

– R2: `@Q` where Q is a pattern, declares R2 as a *static reference* to an instance of the pattern Q. R2 is also called a *static part object*. "Static" means that R2 is an immutable reference that cannot be changed by destructive assignment. It is bound to a new instance of Q when the object containing the R2 attribute is created.

– R3: `Q (# ... #)`. R3 declares and names a nested pattern R3 with super pattern Q. R3 can be used as a nested class or as a method pattern.

– R4: `< Q`. Declares R4 as a new *virtual* pattern that can be specialised in sub-patterns of P. The operators `::<` and `::` are used to specialise a virtual pattern.

– R5: `##Q`. Declares R5 as a *dynamic pattern reference*, allowed to refer to the pattern Q, or any subpattern of Q. Dynamic pattern references are in practice used as dynamic method and function references, class references, and dynamic qualification references (described later).

The enter-part, In, describes input parameters to instances of P (formal parameters), the do-part describes the actions performed by executing instances of P, and the exit-part, Out, describes the output parameters (return values).

```
Calc:
    (# add:                       (* add is non-virtual *)
        (# a,b,c: @Integer;
        enter (a,b)
        do a+b->c; c->display;
        exit c
        #);
    clear:<                       (* clear is virtual    *)
        (#
        do 0->display; INNER; (* INNER used for specialisation *)
        #);
    display: @                    (* display is a part object *)
        (# value: @Integer;
        enter value
        do value->screen.putint;
        #);
    #);
```

Fig. 8. An example BETA pattern.

Figure 8 shows a BETA fragment defining a simple calculator. The `Calc` pattern is used as a class. The `add` pattern is a non-virtual pattern, serving as a method for instances of the surrounding `Calc` pattern. The `clear` pattern is a virtual pattern, serving as a virtual method which can be specialised in subpatterns of Calc. Finally, display is a static part object modelling the display of the calculator. Creation of a Calc instance and invocation of its add method is done by:

```
aCalc: ^Calc; value: @Integer;
do &Calc[]->aCalc[]; (1,2)->&aCalc.add->value;
```

First, an instance of Calc is instantiated, using the object creation operator &. Object expressions followed by the box ([]) operator means "object reference". Thus, evaluation of &Calc[] creates a new calculator object and returns an object reference which is assigned to the dynamic object reference aCalc. &aCalc.add creates an instance of the add pattern and executes its do-part. The arrow (->) exiting (1,2) assigns the actual parameter list (1,2) to the formal enter list (a,b) of the method object, while the arrow exiting &aCalc.add assigns the formal exit list (c) to the actual exit list, in this case one-element list (value). Syntactic sugar allows the & sign to be omitted in the case of method executions. Thus, we may instead write:

```
aCalc: ^Calc; value: @Integer;
do &Calc[]->aCalc[]; (1,2)->aCalc.add->value;
```

For readability, we shall use the syntactically sugared method call syntax.

A.2 Specialisation

In BETA, a virtual pattern can be *specialised* in a subpattern, not overridden. Execution of an object always begins at the top of the inheritance hierarchy, and control is transfered down the specialisation chain at each INNER imperative. The INNER imperative has no effect in the most specific pattern.

For example, the virtual pattern, Calc.clear, may be extended in subpatterns of Calc:

```
Calc2: Calc                    (* subpattern of Calc *)
   (# clear::<                 (* further binding *)
         (# do INNER; 'Clear'->screen.putline #);
   #);
   aCalc2: @Calc2;
do aCalc2.clear;
```

Calc2 inherits from Calc, and extends (::<) the clear virtual pattern to report whenever the screen is cleared. The execution of aCalc2.clear begins at the do-part of Calc.clear (in Figure 8), and then, at the INNER imperative, control is transferred to the do-part of Calc2.clear. The INNER imperative in Calc2.clear has no effect, since clear has not been further extended. When the do-part of Calc2.clear terminates, control returns to the do-part of Calc.clear which returns directly to the caller of aCalc2.clear. Thus, execution of aCalc2.clear first clears the display, and then writes Clear to the terminal screen.

Specialisation of virtual patterns using ::< is called *further binding*. After further binding, the clear pattern is still virtual, and can be further extended in subpatterns of Calc2. Using a *final binding* (::) the pattern is extended and at the same time converted to a non-virtual pattern which cannot be further extended.

It is possible to specialise a method without creating a new pattern: Firstly, assuming that aCalc2 is the only instance of Calc2 we need, aCalc2 could be declared as a *singular object*, as shown in Figure 9a.

```
aCalc2: @Calc                            do aCalc2.clear
   (# clear:: (* final binding *)           (#
       (#                                    do 'Very '->screen.puttext
       do INNER;                             #);
          'Clear'->screen.putline;
       #);
   #);
do aCalc2.clear;
```

Fig. 9. (a) Singular object declaration. (b) Call-spot specialisation.

This ensures that aCalc2 will be the only object of its kind, and avoids name space pollution with the superfluous Calc2 name. The example demonstrates that instance creation and specialisation may happen simultaneously. Secondly, specialisation and execution can happen simultaneously. For example, the method aCalc2.clear can be specialised directly at the call-spot, as shown in Figure 9b, where the display is cleared, and **Very Clear** is written to the terminal screen.

A.3 Dynamic Pattern References

An example usage of the *dynamic pattern reference* attribute kind is shown below:

```
calcP: ##Calc; aCalc: ^Calc;
do Calc2##->calcP##; &calcP[]->aCalc[];
```

The dynamic pattern reference calcP is allowed to refer to the Calc pattern or subpatterns of Calc. Above, the Calc2 pattern is assigned to calcP, and then an instance of the Calc2 pattern now referred to by calcP is created and assigned to aCalc. Dynamic pattern references may be compared using relational operators <=, >=, and =, in order to check inheritance relationships.

Metaphoric Polymorphism: Taking Code Reuse One Step Further

Ran Rinat[1] and Menachem Magidor[2]

[1] Institute of Computer Science, Hebrew University, Jerusalem 91904, Israel
E-mail: rinat@cs.huji.ac.il
[2] Institute of Mathematics, Hebrew University, Jerusalem 91904, Israel
E-mail: menachem@sunset.huji.ac.il

Abstract. We propose two new constructs for object oriented programming that significantly increase polymorphism. Consequently, code may be reused in ways unaccounted for by existing machinery. These constructs of *type correspondence* and *partial inheritance* are motivated from *metaphors* of natural language and thought. They establish correspondences between types non of which is (necessarily) a subtype of the other. As a result, methods may operate on objects - and may receive arguments - of types different than the ones originally intended for. The semantics of the proposed constructs generalizes that of ordinary inheritance, thereby establishing the latter as a special case. We show that the incorporation of these constructs in programming supports the process of natural software evolution and contributes to a better conceptual organization of the type system.

1 Introduction

One important benefit of object oriented programming is the ability to reflect conceptual structure in software: the class hierarchy of an object oriented system represents to a large extent the categorical hierarchy of the real-life domain in which it operates. Some of the most important constructs of object oriented programming are counterparts of mechanisms that exist in human cognitive activity. For example, inheritance reflects the **is-a** relationship between concepts ([2], [15], [14]), and genericity represents what may be called "parameterized concepts".

Imitating cognitive mechanisms leads to a better organization of software, resulting in a higher degree of *code reuse*. In particular, because classes are organized in an inheritance hierarchy, a single piece of code may apply to a whole sub-hierarchy of classes. With genericity, types that have common properties and behavior may be derived from a single generic class, allowing them to share the code for that class. This can also be conceived as a sort of organization method, imitating human conceptual capabilities.

The (human) conceptual system, however, has a much more complex structure than what is captured by existing object oriented constructs. This structure is analyzed by George Lakoff in his book [6]. One factor that is singled out there as being central in human categorization is that of *metaphors*. In an earlier book by the same author and by Mark Johnson ([7]), which is wholly dedicated to the issue of metaphors, it is argued that "the human conceptual system is metaphorically structured and defined". The authors demonstrate through numerous examples, that metaphors are not (just) elements of poetry, but are constantly used in everyday speech, affecting the way in which people perceive, think and act. Quoting from [7], "The essence of metaphor is understanding and experiencing one thing in terms of another". We bring their first example to illustrate what is meant by that: consider the metaphor ARGUMENT IS WAR. This metaphor is reflected in everyday language by many expressions:

- Your claims are *indefensible*.
- She *attacked every weak point* in my argument.
- His criticisms were *right on target*.
- If you use that *strategy*, he'll *wipe you out*.
- I've never *won* an argument with her.

As seen by this example, notions from the realm of war are applied to arguments. However, an argument is not *really* a war, in the sense that only *part* of what constitutes the concept *war* is applicable to arguments. Put it another way, there is a *partial mapping* from the building blocks of *war* to those of *argument*.

Looking at this argumentation, and considering the benefit that has been gained from incorporating conceptual oriented constructs into programming, it seems reasonable that metaphors could motivate some useful programming constructs.

We propose two new constructs for object oriented programming: *type correspondences* and *partial inheritance*. Both of them are based on the observation that a piece of code, originally written to work with certain types, can actually work with other ones, which are not necessarily subtype compatible. The idea, motivated by metaphors, is to *partially* relate two types in a useful way.

To illustrate, assume we have a class *INTEGER* with methods *multiply* (n:*INTEGER*): *INTEGER* and *power* (n:*INTEGER*): *INTEGER*. The first returns the result of multiplying the receiving object by n, and the second returns the result of raising it to the power of n. We also have a class *MATRIX* of square matrices of a given fixed size, equipped with a method *matrix_multiply (some_matrix:MATRIX): MATRIX* which returns the result of multiplying the target object by *some_matrix*. Our goal is to make use of the fact that the power function on matrices relates to matrix multiplication just as the power function on integers relates to integer multiplication, in order to be able to apply *power* to matrices. This is what metaphors do: they use similarities between concepts to apply notions of one to the other.

To account for that we define a *type correspondence* that relates the types *INTEGER* and *MATRIX*, mapping *multiply* of *INTEGER* to *matrix_multiply* of *MATRIX*. Having done that, and assuming that *power* is implemented using *multiply* (but not in any specific manner), we may now apply *power* to objects of type *MATRIX*. That is, we may issue a call matrix.*power*(n), where matrix is a (variable of type) *MATRIX* and n is an integer. It will work, because whenever *multiply* is mentioned in *power*'s text, *matrix_multiply* will be invoked instead, since *multiply* has been mapped to it in the type correspondence. Thus, the code for *power*, originally written for integers, has been reused for *MATRIX*, which is not a subtype of *INTEGER*[3]. Note that *INTEGER* may have other attributes and methods not mapped to *MATRIX*, such as *prime:BOOLEAN*, and so the mapping is partial in that sense. The proposed syntax for type correspondences, that also declares *power* as applied to *MATRIX*, is given in Sect. 2.1.

In this examples, a new working method has been added to the type *MATRIX*. But the main point is not so much this enrichment of *MATRIX*'s set of methods, as it is the use of a certain piece of code (that of *power*) with argument types not originally intended for. *power* actually has two arguments: **self** and n, both *intended* to be integers. Our type correspondence makes the text of *power* meaningful when the first argument (**self**) is a matrix and the second still an integer. That *power* is also added to the list of methods supported by *MATRIX* so as to legalize calls such as matrix.*power*(n) is another separate feature offered by the construct of type correspondence. This becomes clearer if we take *power* to be a free-standing function rather than a method of *INTEGER*. In this case *power(k,m : INTEGER) : INTEGER* receives two (intended) integers k and m and returns k^n. Given the type correspondence relating *INTEGER* to *MATRIX*, we could supply a matrix argument for k, yielding a matrix result.

The second construct we propose is *partial inheritance*. It is conceptually the same as type correspondences, only it establishes the (partial) correspondence while actually creating one of the classes.

The *INTEGER-MATRIX* case is a toy example that involves only one type correspondence. However, in realistic cases, a set of type correspondences will be needed in favor of a single reuse task, involving a collection of collaborating classes. In fact, when partial inheritance is also employed, we conjecture that frameworks, that is libraries of collaborating classes, could be reused in new and unanticipated ways. Although we do not show a framework example in this paper, a complicated enough scenario is outlined in Sect. 3.2, which we believe testifies to that effect.

The semantics of the proposed constructs is defined in a way that generalizes ordinary inheritance and allows a uniform treatment of type correspondences, partial inheritance and ordinary inheritance altogether. We argue that this semantics also leads to a type system with a richer semantic structure, a fact that manifests itself in higher potentials for code reuse. This structure reflects the conceptual organization of the problem domain, and supports the process of natural *software evolution* (Sect. 4.1).

Type correspondences and partial inheritance increase polymorphism, because they allow a given piece of code to be interpreted in new ways - in *metaphoric* ways. Following the terminology of *subtype* and *parametric* polymorphism employed in the context of inheritance and genericity respectively, we term the phenomena resulting from the inclusion of these constructs in programming *metaphoric polymorphism*.

---

[3] We assume that *power* receives a *positive* integer as argument.

As can be seen by the *INTEGER-MATRIX* example, metaphoric polymorphism raises some fundamental issues regarding type correctness. To start with, functions (methods of some type or free-standing) are supposed to accept arguments which are not subtype-compatible with the declared signature. These issues are briefly discussed in Sect. 4.2, and a full analysis is deferred to another paper.

Section 2 introduces type correspondences (2.1), and defines their semantics (2.2). Section 3 introduces partial inheritance (3.1), and outlines a real-life scenario that we believe testifies to the scaling up potential of the proposed constructs (3.2). Section 4 shows how these constructs support natural software evolution and structure (4.1), and discusses the new kind of polymorphism suggested here along with its implications on type correctness (4.2). Section 5 compares our approach to previous work. Section 6 concludes with suggestions for further research.

2 Type Correspondences

In this section we introduce the construct of *type correspondence* that enables programmers to take advantage of similarities between *existing types*. It establishes a partial mapping between two types, allowing appropriate pieces of code, originally expecting one, to work with the other. This construct is defined in 2.1, where it is informally described through some examples. The title *metaphoric polymorphism* is also explained in 2.1. A semantics treating type correspondences and inheritance uniformly is given in 2.2.

2.1 Construct Definition

A *type correspondence* is a programming construct that establishes a *partial* mapping between the attributes and methods of one type, called the *source* of the correspondence, to those of another, called the *target*. It may also specify some of the source's methods as being applied to the target. This will have the effect of legalizing calls, invoking methods listed in the **apply** part (along with their original implementations) on objects of the target's type, although that type does not have these methods listed in its definition, nor did it inherit them from an ancestor.

While executing the implementations for these applied methods on objects of the target type, references to attributes and methods of the source type will be interpreted in the target type according to the **map** part of the correspondence. In general, the mapping defined in the correspondence will be used whenever there is a need to interpret (on run time) a reference *exp.f* to a method or attribute, where the *intended* type of *exp* is the source type and the object at hand is of the target type. Such interpretations will very likely be needed while executing the applied methods, but they are also likely to be needed while executing any routine for which an object of the target type has been supplied while one of the source type was expected. This will be exemplified in a moment.

```
relate source_type to target_type
    [map source_att_or_method to target_att_or_method
         source_att_or_method to target_att_or_method
         .
         .
         . ]
    [apply source_method [as name_in_target ]
           source_method [as name_in_target ]
           .
           .
           . ]
end;
```

Fig. 1. A proposed syntax for the construct of type correspondence

Figure 1 shows a possible syntax for a type correspondence. As an example recall the case from the introduction, involving a class *INTEGER* with methods *multiply* (n:*INTEGER*): *INTEGER* and *power* (n:*INTEGER*): *INTEGER*, and another one *MATRIX* with a method *matrix_multiply* (some_matrix: *MATRIX*): *MATRIX*. Here is the type correspondence that allows the application of *power* to *MATRIX*, as discussed in Sect. 1:

```
relate INTEGER to MATRIX
    map multiply to matrix_multiply
    apply power as matrix_power
end;
```

Given this type correspondence, and assuming that *power* of *MATRIX* is implemented using *multiply*, the following call will be valid, where matrix1 and matrix2 are of type *MATRIX*[4]:

matrix1 := matrix2.*matrix_power*(5);

When the statement in the example arrives at execution, matrix2 is bound to some object of type *MATRIX*. Now, this type does not originally have a method called *matrix_power*, but in the type correspondence, *power* of *INTEGER* is applied to *MATRIX* as *matrix_power*. Therefore, the code for *power* will be executed. While executing, calls to *multiply* will be encountered, which will be interpreted as calls to *matrix_multiply*, because of the mapping of *multiply* to *matrix_multiply* in the type correspondence. We have thus added a new working method to the class *MATRIX* without having to implement it. In other words, the code for *power* of *INTEGER* has been reused in a new context, which is not a class inheriting from *INTEGER*.

---

[4] We assume that *power* receives a *positive* integer as argument.

The **apply** and **map** parts of a type correspondence have different roles. In fact, they could be separated to yield two different constructs. The mapping is the more essential part, enabling the use of certain pieces of code (that of *power* in this example) with types not originally intended for. *power* actually has two arguments: **self** and n, both *intended* to be integers. The type correspondence makes the text of *power* meaningful when the first argument (**self**) is a matrix and the second still an integer. The **apply** part makes *matrix_power* available as a new method of the type *MATRIX*, while establishing the code of *INTEGER*'s *power* as the one to be executed when it is called. Applying a method also maps it implicitly to the newly added one in the target. Thus, our type correspondence maps *power* of *INTEGER* to *matrix_multiply* of *MATRIX* although it is not explicitly specified.

The mapping established by a type correspondence in the **map** part may be useful regardless of the methods it applies, if any. For example, if *power* were a free-standing function expecting two integer arguments n and k, and returning n^k, then our type correspondence would enable calling it with a matrix as first argument, with no need for an **apply** part. As another example, consider a free standing-function *three_multiply* (n,m,k: *INTEGER*): *INTEGER*, which returns n×m×k. In the presence of the type correspondence relating *INTEGER* to *MATRIX*, *three_multiply* may be invoked with matrices as arguments:

matrix1 := *three_multiply* (matrix2, matrix3,matrix4);

three_multiply could of course be a method of some unrelated type, not just a free-standing function.

Note that the mapping is partial: *INTEGER* may have other attributes and methods which are not mapped to *MATRIX*, e.g. a method *prime:BOOLEAN*. Also note that in order for this to work, all that is required is for *power* to be implemented using *multiply*, but not in any specific way. For example, n^m may be computed by multiplying n $m-1$ times by itself, or it may proceed by computing n^2, then multiplying it by itself to yield n^4, and so on in $O(log(m))$ steps. Thus, type correspondences somewhat trade the principle of encapsulation for code reuse, but only to the extent, that in order to apply a method, one must know what other methods and attributes it refers to, not (exactly) how it works[5].

Back to the discussion of type correspondences in general, mapping a source's attribute or method f to h in the **map** part means that references to f directed at (= sent to) objects whose intended type is the source, but whose actual type is the target, will be interpreted as references to h. We shall have more to say on *intended types* in 2.2 .

In the **apply** part, it is possible, but not necessary, to give the applicable source's methods new names in the target's context. This is done using the **as** keyword. If f appears in the **apply** part of some type correspondence with target T, we say that f *is applied to* T (by that type correspondence). This means that it is possible to invoke f on objects of type T, even though f is not listed nor

---

[5] What exactly needs to be known and how to express it is an issue for further research. See Sect. 6.

inherited in T's definition. If f is applied to T without renaming, or some g is applied to T and is renamed as f, we say that f is *added* to T (by that type correspondence).

Here are some points and restrictions concerning the definition of type correspondences:

- Each source_attr_or_method is either an attribute (instance variable) of the source, a method of the source, or a method added to the source by some type correspondence (a method or attribute is *of* a type if it is defined there directly or it is inherited from some ancestor).

- Each target_attr_or_method is either an attribute of the target, a method of the target, or a method added to the target by some type correspondence.

- Attributes are mapped to attributes and methods are mapped to methods[6]. If method f_1 is mapped to method f_2 then f_1 and f_2 must have declared signatures of the same arity, that is they must have the same number of arguments, and either both are functions or both are procedures. There are no restrictions regarding relationships between argument types.

- Only methods may be applied, and all those that are applied must be of the source, or added to it by some type correspondence.

Clearly, it is not the case that a matrix argument to a routine may be supplied whenever an integer is required, as it is not the case that any method of *INTEGER* may be successfully applied to *MATRIX*. For instance, the method *prime:BOOLEAN* of *INTEGER* could not be applied to *MATRIX* because integer division has no counterpart in matrices (in the specific type correspondence of the example and also in principle). Similarly, a call matrix1.*matrix_power* (matrix2) would be illegal because there is no counterpart to the successor function in matrices. These limitations stem from the fact that type correspondences are *partial* mappings between types. The question of what is valid and what is not is an issue of type correctness, and is briefly discussed in Sect. 4.2. We note here that type correctness in the presence of type correspondences can be well defined and algorithmically verified. These results will be reported elsewhere.

The essential contribution made by type correspondences is the ability to *interpret* a given piece of code in new ways. The mechanisms of inheritance and genericity also give rise to a similar phenomena. With respect to these mechanisms, this ability is referred to as *subtype polymorphism* (for inheritance) and *parametric polymorphism* (for genericity). Following this terminology, we term the phenomena resulting from the inclusion of type correspondences (as well as *partial inheritance* introduced in Sect. 3) in programs *metaphoric polymorphism*.

The *INTEGER-MATRIX* example consisted of a single type correspondence. However, in the general case, a set of type correspondences may be combined for the purpose of a single reuse task. This is the case when the *pattern* to be

---

[6] In languages that also treat attributes as functions without arguments, such as EIF-FEL, methods may be mapped to attributes (but not vice versa).

reused consists not only of a single class, but of a set of collaborating classes. For instance, if one class is part of another one, then partially relating the containing class could also require relating the contained one.

The following example illustrates this on a toy case. A more realistic example, that also includes partial inheritance, is given in 3.2. Consider a type *INTEGER_LIST* having a method *first*, which positions the cursor (some sort of pointer) on the first element of the list, a method *next:INTEGER*, that returns the element at the cursor's position and advances it one further, and a method *min_list:INTEGER*, which returns the minimal element of the list. Suppose also that we have a type *COURSE* with a method *first_student* that sets some pointer to the first student in the course according to the alphabetical order, and a method *next_student:STUDENT* that returns the student at the current position and advances to the next according to the alphabetical order.

We now wish to apply the *min_list* method of *INTEGER_LIST* to *COURSE* in order to find the student with the minimal grade. To do that, it is necessary to get down to the building blocks of *INTEGER_LIST* and of *COURSE*, that is to the level of integers and students. Suppose further that the type *INTEGER* has a method *less_than(INTEGER):BOOLEAN*, and that the type *STUDENT* has a method *has_lower_grade(STUDENT):BOOLEAN*. Now, assuming that the method *min_list* is implemented using the methods *first*, *next* and *less_than*, the following type correspondence will allow the desired application:

relate *INTEGER_LIST* **to** *COURSE*
    map *first* **to** *first_student*
        next **to** *next_student*
    apply *min_list* **as** *worst_student:STUDENT*
end;
relate *INTEGER* **to** *STUDENT*
    map *less_than* **to** *has_lower_grade*
end;

The observation that a complex structure, consisting of several type correspondences, can be used to relate two sets of collaborating classes in favor of some reuse task suggests that *frameworks* may be used in new ways when type correspondences are allowed for. This point becomes more prominent when *partial inheritance*, presented in Sect. 3, is brought into the scene.

Type correspondences may also be useful in combination with with *constrained genericity* as implemented in EIFFEL ([8]) and with *class substitutions* ([12], [11]). We cannot elaborate on that due to lack of space.

2.2 Semantics: Dispatch in the Presence of Type Correspondences

As discussed above, type correspondences allow functions (methods or freestanding) to be invoked with arguments different from the intended ones. This means that when a call $exp.f(exp_1, ..., exp_n)$ invoking the method f on exp arrives at execution, it is no longer guaranteed that exp is bound to an object of type S, where S is the *intended type* of exp. Intuitively, the intended type of an expression is the type of exp as anticipated by the programmer who wrote it. If exp is a local variable, an attribute, or a formal argument, then its intended type is its declared type. If it is, however, a compound expression involving function invocations, then determining the intended type is a more subtle task. For example, the intended type of the expression *three_multiply*(n,m,k) is $INTEGER$, but the intended type of *three_multiply*(matrix1,matrix2,matrix3) is $MATRIX$. The latter is true despite the fact that *three_multiply*'s signature declares the resultant type as $INTEGER$. We do not give a precise definition of the intended type of a general expression in this paper but only state that this notion can be well defined. For the current presentation, an intuitive understanding will suffice. Alternatively, the reader may think of exp as being a simple expression (i.e. one identifier), in which case its intended type is its declared type.

Continuing the discussion, the problem is that f is (supposedly) a method of exp's intended type, not of o's type, o being the object actually attached to exp when $exp.f(exp_1, ..., exp_n)$ arrives at execution[7]. The handling of this situation proceeds in two steps (T denotes o's type):

1. Identify which method of T (if any) is referred to by f. In the $INTEGER$-$MATRIX$ example, when *power*'s text is executed on a matrix, a call n.*multiply* (m) might be encountered, where n is intended to be an integer but is in fact a matrix. Given the mapping defined by the type correspondence, *matrix_multiply* is identified as $MATRIX$'s method referred to by *multiply*.

2. Determine the implementation, i.e. the actual code, to be invoked. With *matrix_multiply* there is nothing special here: just use its implementation as defined in the class $MATRIX$. However, type correspondences contribute to this step too, when it comes to finding an implementation of an applied method. For example, when a call matrix.*matrix_power*(n) is encountered, it is the implementation of $INTEGER$'s *power* that should be invoked.

Before defining how these steps are carried out, let us point out that they conceptually exist even without type correspondences. To see that, consider the inheritance structure shown in Fig. 2, which assumes a language that supports attribute and method *renaming*, such as EIFFEL. Part (a) of that figure shows a directed graph whose nodes are types, representing an ordinary inheritance hierarchy between $PERSON$, $EMPLOYEE$ and $STUDENT$. In part (b) the nodes are elements of the form $S.f$ where S is a type and f is a method or an attribute of S. There is an edge $T.h \rightarrow S.f$ iff T (directly) inherits S and $h = f$ or f is renamed h in T. Thus, for example, $STUDENT$ inherits $PERSON$ while renaming *income* as *scholarship* and leaving *age* as is. Now, if a call person.*income*() arrives at execution[8], where person is a variable of type $PERSON$ bound to an

---

[7] Moreover, even if o's type has a method named f, it is not a-priori clear that it is this method that we want to invoke.

[8] We assume *income*, *salary* and *scholarship* to be functions with no arguments.

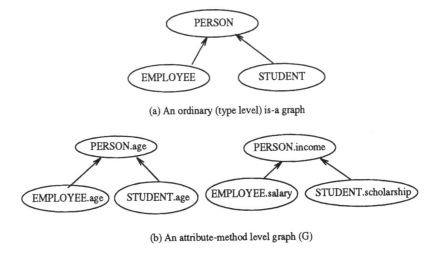

(a) An ordinary (type level) is-a graph

(b) An attribute-method level graph (G)

Fig. 2. Bringing the inheritance graph to the attribute-method level

object of type $STUDENT$ (which is a subtype of $PERSON$), then $scholarship$ is identified as $STUDENT$'s method referred to by $income$. This is because there is a path in the graph from $STUDENT.scholarship$ to $PERSON.income$, $PERSON$ being the intended type and $STUDENT$ being the actual type.

The same attribute-method level graph may also serve for the second step - that of finding the implementation. This is done by conducting a search starting at the identified method ($STUDENT.scholarship$ in the example) looking for a closet implementation[9].

We now extend this analysis to handle type correspondences as well. For the first step, i.e. that of identifying the actual type's method referred to, construct a graph $G_{identify}$ whose nodes are elements of the form $S.f$ where S is a type and f is a method or an attribute of S or a method added to S by some type correspondence[10]. Add an edge $T.h \rightarrow S.f$ to $G_{identify}$ when either of the following holds:

1. T inherits S in its definition and either f is not renamed and $f = h$, or f is renamed as h.
2. There is a type correspondence with source S and target T, in which f is mapped to h (in the **map** part).
3. There is a type correspondence with source S and target T, in which f is applied as h.
4. There is a type correspondence with source S and target T, in which f is applied without renaming and $f = h$.

---

[9] In the presence of multiple inheritance, either all inherited methods and attributes should have different names, perhaps after renaming (as in EIFFEL), or some linearization strategy should be employed during the search.

[10] Note that if T inherits S and f was added to S by some type correspondence then f will also be a method of T, and there will be a node $T.f$ in $G_{identify}$.

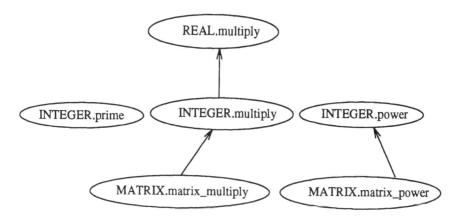

Fig. 3. $G_{identify}$ for the *INTEGER-MATRIX* example

The last two items reflect the fact mentioned in 2.1, that applying implicitly implies mapping. Figure 3 shows the graph for the *INTEGER-MATRIX* example. In that figure, one node for the type *REAL*, from which *INTEGER* inherits, is also included in order to show that type correspondences join the inheritance relation to yield one graph.

Given $G_{identify}$, we say that *T.h corresponds* to *S.f* if there is a path (of length 0 or more) from *T.h* to *S.f*. Thus, the graph defines a reflexive binary *correspondence relation* between attributes and methods of types. $G_{identify}$ is required to be *unambiguous*, that is for any types S and T and any method or attribute f of S there should be at most one h such that *T.h* corresponds to *S.f*. Ambiguity is also a potential problem without type correspondences. For example, in Eiffel such ambiguities must be resolved using the SELECT keyword.

For the second step, i.e. that of finding an implementation, we need a slightly different graph when type correspondences are in effect. Let G_{impl} be a graph similar to $G_{identify}$, only without the edges added due to **map** parts, that is without item 2 in the definition of $G_{identify}$.

With these graphs at hand, dispatching in the presence of type correspondences proceeds as in Fig. 4.

The correspondence relation between methods and attributes of types represented by $G_{identify}$ generalizes the ordinary inheritance relation between types. It contains all information present in the latter plus what is given by type correspondences. Given $G_{identify}$, we no longer care whether this or that edge is there because of inheritance or because of some type correspondence. Thus, the correspondence relation abstracts over the reasons that justified its construction. It directly represents a type system possessing a certain structure, and it can express a richer semantic structure than what can be expressed with an ordinary type-level inheritance relation. This richer structure results in higher potentials for code reuse.

Note, however, that the same *amount of code sharing* allowed for by a given type correspondence could be simulated using inheritance. For instance, in the

Let $exp.f(exp_1, ..., exp_n)$ be a statement invoking the method f on exp, where the intended type of exp is S. Suppose that when this statement arrives at execution, exp is bound to an object o of type T (because there are type correspondences, T is not necessarily a subtype of S). Let $G_{identify}$ and G_{impl} be obtained from the inheritance relation and the type correspondences altogether as described. To find the code to be executed proceed as follows:

1. *Identify which method of T is referred to by f:* search for a method h such that $T.h$ corresponds to $S.f$, that is, there is a path (of length 0 or more) in $G_{identify}$ from $T.h$ to $S.f$ (because $G_{identify}$ is unambiguous, there can be at most one such h). If the search is unsuccessful, terminate and return a "no such method" run time error (an appropriate type checking strategy should aim at detecting this at compile time). Otherwise, proceed to the next step.

2. *Search for an implementation:* perform a search on G_{impl} starting at $T.h$, looking for a closest node (to $T.h$) containing an implementation.

Fig. 4. Method dispatch in the presence of type correspondences.

INTEGER - MATRIX example, one could introduce an abstract class *MULTI-PLIABLE* having methods *multiply* and *power*, the first of which is virtual (deferred). Then, letting *INTEGER* and *MATRIX* inherit from *MULTIPLIABLE*, each implementing *multiply* appropriately, will have achieved the same amount of code sharing. The main reasons why this observation does not render type correspondences superfluous are that they support the process of natural software evolution, and that they spare unnatural abstractions. See Sect. 4.1 for a full discussion.

Some object-oriented experts may object to the late addition of methods to classes, resulting from the **apply** part of type correspondences. The potential criticism is that in OOP all methods of a class should be defined in one place. However, what the **apply** does is no different from what ordinary inheritance does. With inheritance too, a class possesses methods not visible in its declaration. To overcome this, the environment may provide a *class flattener* ([8]), that gives a description of a class along with all its inherited attributes and methods. Such a tool may, and in fact should, bring in methods applied through type correspondences as well. This is also in line with our semantics that treats both constructs uniformly.

Finally, there are other statements and expressions besides those of the form $exp.f(exp_1, ..., exp_n)$ that need be analyzed when type correspondences are present. Among them are references to attributes and unqualified method calls. We cannot treat them here due to lack of space, but they do not introduce more difficulties than those discussed.

3 Partial Inheritance

A type correspondence partially relates types that exist independently of it, and in fact might have been defined long before the correspondence was identified and recognized as beneficial. However, after realizing that the main point is the association of attributes and methods, rather than full types, to one another, it is only natural to provide a mechanism that derives one class from another while only taking *part* of its methods and attributes.

We propose *partial inheritance* for this purpose. There is nothing conceptually new here with respect to type correspondences: partial inheritance also gives rise to metaphoric polymorphism, that is the ability to metaphorically interpret a given piece of code. The only difference is that it establishes the (partial) correspondence while actually creating one of the classes. The new derived class is not (necessarily) a subtype of the one from which it is derived. Partial inheritance suggests itself as a natural generalization of (full) inheritance, and its semantics is also merged into the framework introduced in the previous section.

Suppression of attributes and methods in inheritance has been proposed before, and there are also experimental languages that support it. But in these languages, this is only conceived as a technical feature, not as a way of establishing a partial relation between types. It is in order to emphasize this point that we have chosen to present type correspondences first.

Combining partial inheritance and type correspondences provides a manner of reusing sets of collaborating classes in new ways. After defining the construct of partial inheritance in 3.1 below, we lay out in 3.2 an example that illustrates how a large software consisting of classes working together can be significantly expanded on the basis of reuse. If such an expansion were carried out without partial inheritance and type correspondences, then either the class hierarchy would need to be reorganized, or the new classes would need to be written directly without reusing existing components. Although that example regards a specific software, it strongly suggests that whole patterns could be reused from frameworks in new and unanticipated ways when constructs giving rise to metaphoric polymorphism are allowed for.

3.1 Construct Definition and Semantics

Figure 5 specifies an EIFFEL-like syntax for partial inheritance. Here is an explanation of the clauses mentioned in the figure:

- The **take** clause specifies those attributes of the inherited class that will become part of the inheriting class. The keyword **all** may be used to specify full inheritance.

- In the **rename** clause, some of the attributes and methods specified in the **take** clause may be given new names in the inheriting class.

- The **redefine** clause lists all methods whose implementations are redefined in the inheriting class. The methods listed here must appear among those defined in the inheriting class for the first time, where their new implementations are given.

```
class inheriting_class_name inherit inherited_class_name
     take
          (att_or_method,att_or_method,...,att_or_method) | all
     rename
          att_or_method as new_name
          att_or_method as new_name
          .
          .
          .
     redefine
          att_or_method,att_or_method,...,att_or_method
```

Rest of the class definition

```
end class_name;
```

Fig. 5. A proposed syntax for partial inheritance

As a simple example, consider again the types *INTEGER* and *MATRIX*, but this time suppose that only *INTEGER* existed in the environment and we wished to derive *MATRIX*, including the method *matrix_power*, from it. Figure 6 shows how this is done using partial inheritance. Note that by this derivation *MATRIX* does not become a subtype of *INTEGER*. The latter has other methods such as *prime*.

```
class MATRIX inherit  INTEGER
     take
          multiply, power
     rename
          multiply as  matrix_multiply
          power as  matrix_power
     redefine matrix_multiply
```

New implementation for *matrix_multiply*

Rest of the class definition

```
end MATRIX;
```

Fig. 6. Using partial inheritance to derive *MATRIX* from *INTEGER*

The semantics of partial inheritance is naturally described within the framework of Sect. 2.2: whenever C_1 partially inherits C_2, extend both $G_{identify}$ and G_{impl} as follows:

– Add nodes $C_2.f$, where f is an attribute or method taken from C_1 (if f is renamed as h, then add $C_2.h$ instead).

– Add edges $C_2.h \rightarrow C_1.f$ whenever f is taken and renamed as h, or it is taken without renaming and $f = h$.

– Add nodes $C_2.f$ for every new attribute or method f first introduced in C_2.

Having extended the graphs as described, dispatching in the presence of partial inheritance (and type correspondences, and full inheritance) proceeds as in Fig. 4 of Sect. 2.2.

3.2 An Example

The real-life scenario of this subsection involves partial inheritance and type correspondences that join in favor of a single reuse task. A real software would surely include many more classes, and those listed here are understood as forming only a partial picture. However, it should be clear from the example that a real software of this kind could be expanded in the same spirit.

Consider an airline company which has been in the air travel business for some time, during which a large object oriented software supporting its activities has been constructed for it. Among the classes of this software, there is one called *FLIGHT* that has attributes like *number, date, origin, destination, departure_time, arrival_time, passengers, carrier* and more. *carrier* holds an object of type *AIRCRAFT*, the one carrying out the flight. *passengers* holds a list of type *AIR_PASSENGER*.

The class *FLIGHT* also has several methods, one of which is *register_seats* (passenger_list: *LIST[AIR_PASSENGER]*, class: *AIR_CLASS*[11], smokers_flag : *BOOLEAN*) . This method operates by first invoking a method *get_seats* on the flight's carrier, and then distributing the seats returned by the aircraft among the passengers listed in *passenger_list*. The distribution proceeds by invoking the method *set_seat*(seat: *AIR_SIT*) on each passenger of the list. The result of the method *register_seats* will thus be reflected in the attribute *passengers* of the flight object (i.e. some of them, namely those included in *passenger_list*, will have seats). *get_seats*, a method of the type *AIRCRAFT*, has the following signature: *get_seats*(number : *INTEGER*, class: *AIR_CLASS*, smokers_flag: *BOOLEAN*): *LIST(AIR_SIT)*. It returns a list of available seats according to the desired number, class, and smokers/non-smokers preference.

Suppose that at a certain point, this company decides to expand its business to include railway traffic as well. It decides to treat train journeys much the same as flights. Naturally, the supporting software must be modified to handle this expansion. It would be of great efficiency if existing code could be reused without change and without harming what already works. We show how to use partial

---

[11] Do not confuse this with classes of OOP. Here we mean first class, business class and tourist class.

```
class TRAIN_JOURNEY inherit FLIGHT
    take
            number, date, origin, destination, departure_time, arrival_time,
            passengers, carrier, register_seats
```

Rest of the class definition

```
end TRAIN_JOURNEY;

relate AIRCRAFT to TRAIN
    map get_seats to get_seats
end;

relate AIR_PASSENGER to TRAIN_PASSENGER
    map passenger_name to passenger_name
    map sitting_place to sitting_place
    map set_seat to set_seat
end;
```

Fig. 7. Deriving *TRAIN_JOURNEY* from *FLIGHT*

inheritance to derive a new class *TRAIN_JOURNEY* from the class *FLIGHT* with the help of some type correspondences.

Suppose a class *TRAIN* has been somehow defined (it could be derived from *AIRCRAFT* through partial inheritance, but we shall assume it was not). *TRAIN* also has a method *get_seats*(number: *INTEGER*, class: *TRAIN_CLASS*, smokers_flag: *BOOLEAN*): *LIST(TRAIN_SIT)* with signature and semantics similar to that of *AIRCRAFT*. Note, however, that instead of *AIR_CLASS* we here have *TRAIN_CLASS*. Also, the way *get_seats* operate in each type is different. For example, trains have wagons, and so looking for available seats is different. For that reason, a list of *TRAIN_SIT* is returned rather than a list of *AIR_SIT*. We also assume that these new types (*TRAIN_CLASS* and *TRAIN_SIT*) have been defined separately. Finally, we assume that a class *TRAIN_PASSENGER* have been defined, differing from *AIR_PASSENGER* only in keeping train seats instead of air seats, and, subsequently, in having the method *set_seat*(seat: *TRAIN_SIT*) with this different signature[12].

Figure 7 shows the derivation of *TRAIN_JOURNEY* from *FLIGHT* using partial inheritance and the type correspondences needed for it. Note that quite a number of methods and attributes have been inherited by *TRAIN_JOURNEY*, and there could probably be many more if the example were complete. Also note that there may be other attributes and methods of *FLIGHT* not inherited by

---

[12] *TRAIN_PASSENGER* could certainly be derived from *AIR_PASSENGER* through generalized inheritance.

TRAIN_JOURNEY such as *maximum_weight_allowed, free_meal_menu* etc. This is no wonder since *TRAIN_JOURNEY* is not a subtype of *FLIGHT*.

4 Discussion of Metaphoric Polymorphism

4.1 Support for Natural Software Evolution and Structure

In Sect. 2.2, we have remarked that the same amount of code sharing achieved by type correspondences can be simulated via (full) inheritance. To simulate a type correspondence relating T to S, define a new class encapsulating those attributes and methods of T which are mapped or applied to S, and let T and S inherit from this new class, redefining implementations as needed. The same technique may be applied to simulate partial inheritance via full inheritance. However, this is only a technical simulation that in many cases does not fit well into the *development process*. Consider the following points:

- If one or both of the two types related via a type correspondence existed before the correspondence was identified and recognized as beneficial, then this simulation requires to *reorganize* the class hierarchy, so that the existing type(s) will inherit from the new abstract class. This means touching a working code - a fine potential for problems. This argument applies equally to partial inheritance, in case the inherited class already existed as a functioning component. Even if the language supports a *generalization* mechanism as proposed in [13], then using our proposed constructs will still be more appropriate in many cases: see the next two points, the rest of this subsection and the comparison to related work in Sect. 5.

- Partial inheritance along with type correspondences may be the only way to adapt *supplied* components or frameworks, as it is unreasonable to let imported components inherit user defined classes.

- The new abstract class might turn out to be an ad-hoc class, not representing any natural abstraction. One should aim at minimizing the number of such classes present in the system.

Let us back-up these arguments by a deeper rationale. As we have been emphasizing, the proposed constructs are motivated from metaphors. In many cases, metaphors of thought precede abstractions, and in that sense they are more basic. For example, it is unlikely that the notion of *vehicle* was conceived just after the invention of the first vehicle. Rather, there probably was some sort of vehicle, say a carriage. Then another sort emerged, say a train, and terms from one were applied to the other. For example, the notions *driver* and *passenger* were applied from carriages to trains. Then perhaps a new sort of vehicle came about, and some of these notions were applied to it as well. After some time, enough concepts shared enough terms to *justify* the encapsulation of these common terms into the new abstraction of *vehicle*. From that time on, carriages, trains, cars etc. were considered vehicles.

Now, the key word is *justify*: not all metaphors end up as abstractions, and if they do, it is after some time. One might say that there is a trade off in the conceptual network: we can have fewer concepts related by metaphors, or we can pay the price of reorganizing the network, ending up with simple taxonomic (sub-concept) relationships, but with more concepts.

In view of this discussion, we propose the following principle argumentation for the inclusion of type correspondences and partial inheritance in object oriented languages:

1. **The underlying rationale.** Metaphors that partially relate concepts are first class citizens of language and thought. It therefore makes sense to incorporate appropriate counterparts in programming to yield a more elaborate organization of the type system, reflecting conceptual structure, and resulting in higher potentials for code reuse.

2. **Support for natural software evolution and structure.** The conceptual network often evolves through metaphors. Partial inheritance and type correspondences can be used to reflect this *evolution* in software. This means that functionality can be added to software in a manner that parallels its discovery. In practice, it means that components may be reused, without change and without adding any unnecessary abstractions, in ways unanticipated by their developers. Abstraction can take place at a later stage, if and when it is justified. In this development paradigm, software evolves along with its designers' way of thinking. As is the case in the conceptual level, the question of justification involves a trade off: either leave things as they are, or pay the price of reorganization to gain a simpler structure, but with more types.

3. **Adaption of supplied components.** Since frameworks or supplied classes cannot be made to inherit user defined classes, partial inheritance and type correspondences may be the only way to adapt them to a given application. As noted in Sect. 3, we conjecture that these constructs open a new range of possibilities for the exploitation of frameworks.

Finally, we note that the process by which a type correspondence or a partial inheritance clause is replaced by a new abstraction can be automated. This suggests once again, that abstracting should be delayed until it is justified, whence it can be done automatically, requiring the user only to supply a meaningful name - a task that can be carried out properly just when the abstraction is indeed meaningful.

4.2 Polymorphism Based on Semantic Correspondences

Most typed object-oriented languages support subtype polymorphism and dynamic method dispatch. This means that an identifier may be bound on run time to objects of any type which is a subtype of its declared type, and that a method invocation on that identifier will be dynamically dispatched according to the type of the object to which it is bound.

This sort of polymorphism is entirely based on the subtype relation between types. Indeed, the *definition* of what it means for one type to be a subtype of another was engineered to suit subtype polymorphism. Such a definition may be found in [1]. It implies that T_1 is a subtype of T_2 iff objects of type T_1 may appear wherever objects of type T_2 are expected. In [3] it was shown that inheritance and subtyping are distinct, and that identifying them may lead to insecure type systems. This is because inheritance does not imply subtyping, on which safe substitutability must be based. EIFFEL is singled out there (and previously in [4]) as possessing this problem.

Nevertheless, substitutability must be based on subtyping only in as much as one insists on a type checking strategy that never looks back on anything but a class' declared interface once it has been successfully compiled. Although such strategy is surely desirable for obvious reasons, one's adherence to it should be weighted against the benefit that might be gained from constructs that render it inappropriate. Of course, some other strategy should be suggested to handle such constructs[13].

Throughout this paper we have demonstrated the advantages of basing poly-morphism on *semantic correspondences* between types, not (just) on subtyping. $MATRIX$ is not a subtype of $INTEGER$, but because the programmer seman-tically related them via a type correspondence, the former may be beneficially substituted for the latter in *appropriate contexts*. But to enjoy this flexibility, one must abandon the conception that T_1 is allowed to be substituted for T_2 only if it can be substituted for it in *any* context, that is only if T_1 is a subtype of T_2. It is enough that the substitution be valid in the *given* context, represented by the program or class library at hand. That is to say, a program is quit safe if it issues a call *three_multiply* (matrix1,matrix2,matrix3) but does not issue calls such as *three_multiply* (matrix1,n,m) or matrix1.*matrix_power*(matrix2).

The type safety of programs or class libraries allowing such polymorphism can be well defined and algorithmically verified through an appropriate type checking procedure. Such a procedure cannot exclusively rely on a class' declared interface once it has been compiled, but it does not necessarily have to involve analyzing a class' text more than once. Roughly speaking, the compiler can generate appropriate constraints while compiling a class, listing the conditions that must be met by arguments supplied to methods of that class. For a given method, these constraints may be thought of as a "generalized signature". Then, only this information, not the class' text, will be re-consulted on need.

Note that the declared signature of routines no longer restrict arguments to the specified types. Nevertheless, user type annotations do not loose their mean-ing: they serve to interpret routines by providing the *intended types* of identifiers and (indirectly) of compound expressions. A routine's text is interpreted with respect to these intended types given the correspondence relation and the actual

---

[13] The *system level validity* originally intended for EIFFEL ([8]) was a strategy meant to resolve its type checking problems, that resulted from the (justified) desire not to restrict substitutability to subtypes. Recently, however, Meyer declared his intention to adopt a new rule ([9]) which will actually restrict polymorphism to subtypes.

provided types. But still, when one looks at a given routine's text, one need not be bothered with the possibility of this text being interpreted metaphorically: for all he or she is concerned, the text is understood, maintained, assessed for quality etc. as if the types handled by the routine are those actually declared. Later on, someone may take this routine and apply it - or supply arguments - other than the ones for which it was originally written. Deciding whether or not such use will be valid is the job of the type checking procedure. Thus, user type annotations still keep their most important advantage of *readability*, because when one *reads* a routine, she or he need not concern themselves with its possible metaphoric interpretations.

Finally, we note that the definition of type correctness should preserve the *context independence* of subtype substitutability, that is it should imply the unconditional safety of providing arguments to a routine which are subtype compatible with its declared signature. This will ensure that no extra work will be done by the compiler for subtype polymorphism relative to the situation in existing languages. Results to that effect will be reported elsewhere.

5 Related Work

This section discusses some related work and compares it to ours.

The as-a relationship. In [10] Mitchell et al. propose a relationship between classes, called **as-a**, that is meant to support code reuse. They argue (as others did previously) that people do not always use inheritance in ways that reflect **is-a** relationships between heirs and ancestors, but they often tend to use it for reasons of convenience, in order to reuse some implementations. As they say, "...programmers do use inheritance to reuse code from one class into another, with no intention of substituting objects of one class for objects of the other via dynamic binding and with no intention of explaining or legitimating the use of inheritance in terms of an is-a relationship in the modeling domain".

The authors of [10] propose not to fight this tendency, but to support it in a way that will ensure safe usage of such implementation inheritance. To account for this, they propose to allow what we called here partial inheritance, and to support its correct usage by an **as-a** relationship. This relation actually involves three parameters: a class C_1 **as-a** C_2 **for** some operation o. The idea is that if this holds then o may be safely inherited from C_2 to C_1. **As-a** relationships are established in a formal system that uses equations relating attributes in both classes, to prove certain implications between the post and pre-conditions of the operation at hand.

There is an important fundamental difference between their approach and ours. The authors of [10] stress that the problem they address is that of implementation inheritance, that is the apparent desire of programmers to inherit without any conceptual basis. This is exemplified in the quotation given above. Consequently, they devise a tool that enables one to establish that it is indeed correct to inherit in such circumstances (when it is correct). But they are not interested at all in the relationship that is permanently established via such (partial) inheritance between the two types[14].

Our approach, on the other hand, is entirely based on the observation that one should allow types to be partially related because it reflects *conceptual metaphors*. Partial inheritance is conceived as just one way of achieving this. Contrary to Mitchell et al. we consider such relationships to be a strong basis for substitutability, that is for semantic (or metaphoric) polymorphism. Indeed, that is the main point that we wish to convey (see Sect. 4.2). In our approach, a matrix **is-a**[15] integer as far as it concerns *appropriate contexts*. This approach also led us to (first) introduce the construct of type correspondence that may relate two existing types, while they talk only of inheritance. There are many other essential and technical differences between these two approaches that we could not discuss due to lack of space.

Generalization. In [13] Pedersen proposes a construct that generalizes over a set of classes to yield one parent class. The set of methods of the new class is the intersection of the sets of methods of all classes generalized over (minus some methods explicitly removed). This construct indeed offers a way of reusing an existing class from which, in our terms, we would like to *partially* inherit. This proceeds by first abstracting over the existing one while removing unnecessary methods, and then inheriting. While such a construct should be useful, there are cases in which it forces the inclusion of unnecessary abstractions in the class hierarchy, and others in which it is not applicable (see Sect. 4.1). We believe that this construct should co-exist with ours to provide maximum flexibility. As argued in 4.1, however, type correspondences and partial inheritance will usually better suit the natural evolution of software. Moreover, given these constructs, generalization at a later stage can be automated.

Fine-grain inheritance. This notion was proposed by Johnson and Rees in [5]. It is a strategy according to which classes should be as minimal as possible (feature-wise), so as to make them fully inheritable. They urge designers to define many small classes, representing "small concepts". Without starting a discussion on what makes up a concept, it seems inevitable that followers of such strategy will end up defining many ad-hoc, perhaps conceptually unclear, classes. We believe that the problem addressed by [5], that of reusing a library in ways not predicted by its authors, should find its solution through a paradigm that accounts for elaborate relationships between real and obviously justified concepts. We hope to have made a contribution in this direction.

Ada-style genericity. In Ada, it is possible to write generic packages that are parameterized not only by types, but also by operations on these types. It should therefore be possible to write one generic package that implements *power* while parameterizing on its first argument's type and on the multiplication operation. Apparently, there is no need to abstract over *INTEGER* and *MATRIX* for this package (i.e. there is no need to define a type *MULTIPLIABLE*), which is similar

---

[14] And maybe for that reason they speak of *classes*, not *types*.

[15] There is no mistake here - we did not mean as-a.

to our case. But the resemblance is only apparent, since the abstraction is there anyway: it is this generic package that constitutes the abstraction. Whoever writes it thinks of multipliables, that is (abstract) types that have a multiplication operation. Our approach genuinely avoids the abstraction. It makes it possible to use *power*, written exclusively for *INTEGER* and even as part of it, for matrices. In that sense, our approach offers an alternative to generic programming because there is *really* no need to abstract in order to reuse. Of course, genericity is very useful when the abstraction is justified and made on time.

6 Conclusion and Further Research

We have proposed the constructs of *type correspondence* and *partial inheritance* for object oriented programming, both of which are motivated by metaphors of natural language and thought. They have been shown to introduce a new kind polymorphism into programming, called *metaphoric polymorphism*, which results in previously unavailable code reuse potentials. The semantics of these constructs was defined as a generalization of ordinary inheritance, and was shown to yield a type system with a richer semantic structure. These constructs were shown to support natural software evolution and structure.

A first and most important issue for further research is type correctness in the presence of metaphoric polymorphism, as discussed in 4.2. We shall report results to that effect in future works.

Because **is-a** relationships play a central role in knowledge representation, and in *semantic nets* in particular, it may prove beneficial to examine the applications of the proposed semantics, involving a correspondence relation in a level lower than types (concepts), to this field.

Another issue is that of *method specification*. In order for one to *consider* applying a method in a type correspondence, one must know something about the methods and attributes referred by that method's implementation and how they are inter-related[16]. A similar knowledge is required in order to consider providing routine arguments which are not subtypes of the required ones. What that "something" is, and how it may be expressed, is a matter for further research. Algebraic specifications are a possible direction, but less formal methods could also be considered. Recently, Stata and Guttag ([16]) proposed to provide *specialization specifications* to programmers that adapt classes by inheritance, which are different from the specifications given to other programmers, who just use them as black box components. Their specialization specifications divide the methods of a class into independent groups of cooperating methods. Then, only entire groups can be overridden in inheritance. Their approach may prove beneficial for our case.

We have conjectured in this paper that metaphoric polymorphism opens new opportunities to use *frameworks*. Finding some large scale examples to that effect is one more research option.

---

[16] Whether or not the application is in fact correct will be determined by the type checking procedure.

While presenting the metaphor motivated constructs, we have advocated the stance that reflecting conceptual structures and mechanisms in programming is practically beneficial. We believe that many more contributions can be made to programming on these grounds.

Acknowledgments

We thank Yossi Gil and Ari Rappoport for their comments on earlier versions of this paper. We also thank the referees for their comments, especially the one who provided a long and detailed list of valuable suggestions.

References

1. R.M. Amadio and L. Cardelli. Subtyping recursive types. *ACM Transactions on Programming Languages and Systems*, 15(4), 1993.
2. G. Booch. *Object-Oriented Analysis and Design with Applications*. The Benjamin/Cummings Publishing Company, Inc, 1994.
3. E.R. Cook, W.L Hill, and P.S. Canning. Inheritance is not subtyping. In C.A. Gunter and J.C Mitchell, editors, *Theoretical Aspects of Object-Oriented Programming*. The MIT Press, 1994.
4. W.R. Cook. A proposal for making eiffel type-safe. *The Computer Journal*, 32(4), 1989.
5. P. Johnson and C. Rees. Reusability through fine-grain inheritance. *Software-Pratice and Experience*, 22(12), December 1992.
6. G. Lakoff. *Women, Fire and Dangerous Things: What Categories Reveal About the Mind*. The University of Chicago Press, 1987.
7. G. Lakoff and M. Johnson. *Metaphors We Live By*. The University of Chicago Press, 1980.
8. B. Meyer. *Eiffel, the Language*. Prentice Hall, 1992.
9. B. Meyer. Beware of polymorphic catcalls. Personal research note, http://www.eiffel.com/doc/manuals/technology/typing/cat.html, 1995.
10. R. Mitchell, J. Howse, and I. Maung. As-a: a relationship to support code reuse. *Journal of Object-Oriented Programming*, 8(4), July/August 1995.
11. J. Palsberg and M.I. Schwartzbach. *Object-Oriented Type Systems*. John Wiley & Sons, 1994.
12. J. Palsberg and M.I. Schwartzbach. Type substitution for object oriented programming. In *OOPSLA/ECOOP '90 conference proceedings, ACM SIGPLAN Notices, Volume 25, Number 10*, October 1990.
13. H. Pedersen. Extending ordinary inheritance schemes to include generalization. In *OOPSLA '89 conference proceedings, ACM SIGPLAN Notices*, 1989.
14. J. Rumbaugh. Dishinerited! examples of misuse of inheritance. *Journal of Object-Oriented Programming*, 5, February 1993.
15. J. Rumbaugh, M. Blaha, W. Premerlani, F. Eddy, and W. Lorenson. *Object-Oriented Modeling and Design*. Prentice Hall, 1991.
16. R. Stata and J. Guttag. Modular reasoning in th presence of subclassing. In *OOPSLA '95 conference proceedings, ACM SIGPLAN Notices, Volume 30, Number 10*, October 1995.

Activities: Abstractions for Collective Behavior *

Bent Bruun Kristensen[1] and Daniel C. M. May[2]

[1] Institute for Electronic Systems, Aalborg University
Fredrik Bajers Vej 7, DK-9220 Aalborg Ø, Denmark
e-mail: bbkristensen@iesd.auc.dk
[2] Department of Information Systems, Monash University
Caulfield East, Victoria 3145, Australia
e-mail: dmay@ponderosa.is.monash.edu.au

Abstract. Conventional object-oriented modeling lacks support for representing the interaction between objects in a conceptually intuitive way – often dispersing the logic/control of interplay throughout the objects. We introduce the concept of an *activity* as an abstraction mechanism to model the interplay between objects.
Activities model how our human cognition organizes interaction into units of collective behavior. They are described as classes, allowing interaction to be modeled by such abstraction processes as generalization and aggregation.
At the analysis and design level activities are presented as a general modeling tool for describing the collective behavior of systems of objects. We also discuss how activities can be supported at the implementation level by extending existing language constructs in relation to object-oriented programming languages.

1 Introduction

Objects are a powerful means of modeling entities that exist. But what of the interaction between them? We need effective modeling approaches that will allow us to describe the way objects work together – this need is especially acute in systems where the number and organization of objects becomes increasingly complicated. Where interaction is widely dispersed, discerning the purpose achieved by such interaction becomes difficult.

An abstraction may be used as a tool to help us understand the nature of a problem, as well as describing a possible design solution. Moreover, an abstraction should aid in understanding the purpose which a system accomplishes through the interaction of its sum parts.

Most of all, we need abstractions that are intuitive to our comprehension of problems – offering a modeling approach that is closer to our understanding of how things are organized in the real world.

This paper presents the *activity abstraction mechanism*, that seeks to capture the interplay between groups of objects throughout at different points in

---

* This research was supported in part by the Danish Natural Science Research Council, No. 9400911.

time. The activity is a modeling and language mechanism that may be used to create *abstractions* relating other objects together – describing not merely their participation in the relationship, but their interplay.

Modeling with Activities. As an illustrating example, we examine the activity of reviewing papers for an upcoming conference – this can be referred to as a `paper_review`. This activity requires a certain degree of interaction/interplay between those who are involved in it. For instance, an `author` will submit a paper for review, while the `chairman` will distribute papers to each `reviewer` who must report back.

There will usually be some sort of specification that describes how the activity should be carried out. For instance, with the `paper_review`, the specification might be carried out in three distinct portions:

(a) `author submits paper to chairman`
   `chairman distributes papers to reviewers`
   `reviewers submit referee reports to chairman`
(b) `paper_selection`
(c) `chairman informs authors about result`

Figure 1 illustrates `paper_review`, its participants and specification (directive).

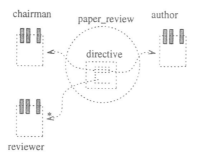

Fig. 1. Graphical illustration of `paper_review`

We should first note that `paper_review` is only one type of `review` that can take place. For example, a `periodical_review` is the review of a submitted article that takes place for a periodical; it is somewhat similar but involves an `editor` rather than a `chairman` and its selection process is different. Both `paper_review` and `periodical_review` are specialized types of `review`.

The directive that specifies how `paper_review` should be carried out may also be seen as a specialization of a more general `review` directive, namely the following:

```
prepare_review_process
carry_out_review_process
complete_review_process
```

Each of these portions correspond to (a), (b) and (c) above (which are more specialized). The participants of these activities may also be similarly classified. For instance, all `review` activities involve a `coordinator` and an `author`. Thus, in a `paper_review`, we can refine a `coordinator` to be a `chairman` – in a `periodical_review`, we can specialize a `coordinator` to become an `editor`.

These different types of `review` activity might have similar methods. For example, producing a `status_report` (produce a listing of the current status of the ongoing reviewing process) is something that each `review` activity must do – a `paper_review` will produce a specialized type of `status_report`, as will a `periodical_review`.

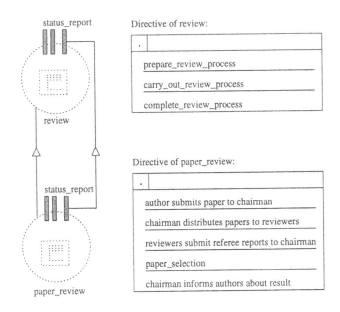

Fig. 2. `paper_review` is a specialization of `review`

Figure 2 illustrates how `paper_review` is specialized from `review`. The directive of `review` is refined in `paper_review`. The figure also notes that the method `status_report` of `paper_review` is a refinement of the same method of `review`.

Finally, it is important to realise that an activity may be constituted from smaller sets of activities (part-activities). For example, within the `paper_review` activity, there is a `paper_selection` activity to choose acceptable papers.

Thus, there are important characteristics of activities that we can note.

Their behavior is *collective*; that is, they can be contained into some logical unit (such as `paper_review`). Activities may be *composed* of smaller activities (e.g. `paper_selection`). Principles of generalization/specialization may apply to activities (`review`) and their participants (`coordinator`). An activity may also have methods (behaviour) that may be specialized (e.g. produce `status_report`) – such methods may access and control the state of the ongoing process modelled by the activity. It is worthwhile noting that an activity can have a set of properties or state (e.g. which reviews have been returned?, is the review process complete?).

And there are the entities that will participate in an activity (e.g. `author`, `chairman`, `reviewers`), while a set of directions specifies how the activity will be carried out.

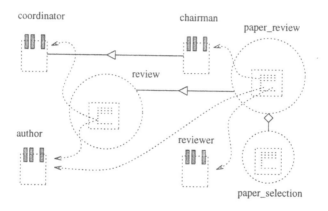

Fig. 3. Relationships in `paper_review`

Figure 3 shows the specialization and aggregation relationships between activities and participants in the `paper_review` example.

Collective Behavior is Objectified. An activity can be defined as an interplay between entities over a given time – intuitively, this corresponds to a general everyday understanding of an 'activity'. It is normal to describe our participation in an activity as a coherent unit; we engage in an activity as a single module and describe it to others in the same way (e.g. "They reviewed the papers, then they ate lunch"). The significant feature of viewing activities as units of collective operation is a reduction in complexity.

The activity abstraction mechanism depicts the relationships that links interacting objects. It is more than a mere gathering objects – applying the object-oriented paradigm, this parcel of collective behavior is objectified, resulting in an object that represents a contiguous unit of process. Activities will then possess properties similar to those of regular objects: they may be aggregated, special-ized, recursively defined, etc. Thereby, it is possible to describe the functionality of a system by combining the behavior of different types of activities – in the same way, these activities may be described in terms of the interplay between their participants.

The interplay between the participants, which is described collectively, is quite different to an object- or participant-centric view (refer Fig. 4). Rather than specifying "what is done to whom", a collective description states "who is doing what to whom". In an object-centric description, the 'who' is implicit, whereas the collective description makes it explicit. Therefore, the atomic elements of an activity's directive will usually comprise three things: subject (who), object (whom) and verb (what is done). There is more clarity in such a description – participants are more clearly identified, and the nature of their interplay can be more quickly discerned.

The notion of *time* has been implicit thus far in our discussion of the activity abstraction. It is a key characteristic of activities that they are *temporal* in nature; an activity such as `paper_review` has inception, execution and termination phases. We emphasize that this is similar to the everyday activities that we encounter which possess a finite lifetime.

The primary benefit of characterizing the behavior of a software system as comprising activities is that it models our human approach to reducing com-plexity in how we handle everyday tasks – in the same way that our cognition clusters information to enhance comprehension, the activity abstraction seeks to resolve complexity by clustering the interplay between objects.

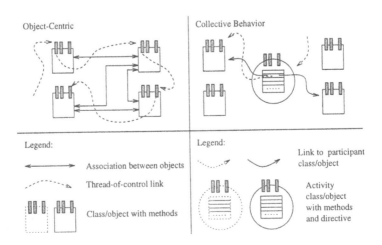

Fig. 4. Object-Centric and Collective Behavior

In Fig. 4, we illustrate two alternative forms of execution sequence – the usual object-centric method invocation where a method of one object invokes a method of another, etc (a recursive sequence of method invocations); and an alternative scheme employing collective behavior, where the activity prescribes a sequence of interplays each including a caller and a method call for the (called) object.

Of course, there is a functional flavour to activities. It is critical to note that while purely functional modelling is insufficient to cope with describing systems, its style of examining process and functionality appeals to us on an intuitive level. Instead of advocating a binary 'either/or' approach to modelling, it is possible to combine the functional perspective with object-oriented concepts. This may result in a way of looking at the world that is more natural and powerful than either individual perspective affords.

Paper Organization. In Sect. 2 we discuss the use of activities for modeling in the analysis design processes. We use "card games" as a concrete example, and we discuss the fundamental characteristics of activities in general terms. In Sect. 3 we discuss the implementation of activities. We discuss various proposals for special language constructs for both direct support and simulation of activities in object-oriented programming languages. In Sect. 4 we review theoretical and practical experiments with activities. In Sect. 5 we summarize the proposals and the results of the paper, compare them with related work (frameworks/design patterns in software architecture and notation/language mechanisms in object-oriented analysis, design, and implementation), and discuss further challenges.

2 Designing with Activities

We shall use a card game as a concrete example to illustrate the use of activities in analysis and design. Through this example, we demonstrate and discuss the fundamental characteristics of activities. Activities as abstractions in object-oriented analysis and design is originally introduced in (Kristensen 93a).

Card Game Example. Our intuitive understanding of a card game is that it is a human activity – it involves a specific kind of interplay between people that exists over a duration of time. More importantly, like other activities we engage in, a card game comprises recurring patterns of interplay that form its totality. As such, the card game is an intuitive example that allows us to identify a commonly understood activity, and explicitly abstract and model its aspects.

Figure 5 illustrates the structure for a bidding process of a game, consisting of an activity the_bidding and the participating objects Peter, Mary, John, and Jane. the_bidding models an actual bidding activity at some specific point in time. Activities are abstractions over the interplay between entities, – here exemplified by the card game example. We have abstracted and classified that specific activity as a bidding activity (to be described later) and each of the persons as a player in the card game.

The particular example that serves as our model is the card game of Five Hundred. The object of the game is to score 500 points before the other players.

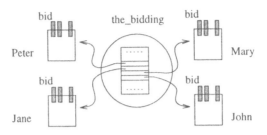

Fig. 5. The Card Game Example

Each game comprises one or more rounds; players are dealt cards and play against one another in each round. A player wins (or loses) points at the end of each round depending on how well he/she plays.

We distinguish between part-activities and sub-activities. Descendant activities – activities specialized from another (super)activity – are called *sub-activities* or just activities. Activities that can be aggregated to form larger activities (whole-activities) are called *part-activities*.

Part-Activities. At the highest level of organization, we can create a `cardGame` activity that represents the totality of interplay in the game. This activity actually comprises several subordinate phases: a `gameOpening` phase (where initialization and set-up take place), a `gameRounds` phase (in which one or more rounds are played), and a `gameClosing` phase (where clean-up procedures take place). We consider the activity `cardGame` to be composed of the part-activities `gameOpening`, `gameRounds` and `gameClosing` executed in sequence.

As most of the significant interplay takes place during each round, we shall further decompose the `gameRounds` part-activity. This phase of the game comprises one or more rounds – each of which is a part-activity. Like the `cardGame`, a `gameRounds` part-activity consists of an opening phase (`roundOpening`), a central execution phase (`roundPlay`) and a closing phase (`roundClosing`).

Figure 6 illustrates the hierarchical class organization of the `cardGame`: a part-whole hierarchy (where `gameOpening`, `gameRound` and `gameClosing` are part-activities of `cardGame`).

Activity Directive. In our normal understanding, the `gameRound` part-activity is where most of the card playing takes place. Each round has three distinct stages:

1. `dealing`: Cards are dealt to each player.
2. `bidding`: Each player is successively asked to make a bid – the players bid against each other, until the highest bidder is found. The player with the winning bid starts the game.
3. `trickTaking`: After bidding, the players engage in taking tricks. A trick involves each player putting down a card; the player whose card beats the

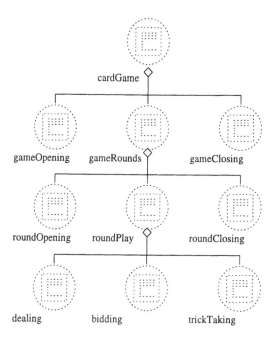

Fig. 6. Card Game: Part-Activities

others is said to have taken the trick. For 4 players, the trick-taking phase of each round involves the playing of 10 tricks.

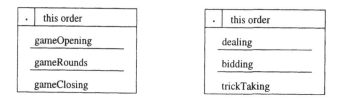

.	this order
	gameOpening
	gameRounds
	gameClosing

.	this order
	dealing
	bidding
	trickTaking

Fig. 7. Directives for `cardGame` and `roundPlay`

In Fig. 7, we illustrate the use of special diagrams for describing the structure of the directives of the `cardGame` and `roundPlay` activities. The notation '.' represents sequential action according to a given specification (e.g. deal cards according to rules).

Each activity/part-activity is responsible for managing its associated interplay. For instance, the `bidding` part-activity has to control the sequence of bids performed by the players – as each player makes a bid, the part-activity will ensure that certain constraints are in force: Is the present bid legal? Who is the next bidder? When is the bidding process over and who is the winner?

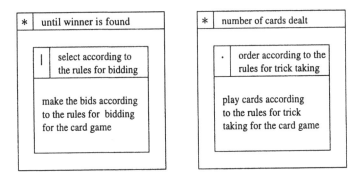

Fig. 8. Directives for `bidding` and `trickTaking`

In Fig. 8, we describe the structure of the directives of the `bidding` and `trickTaking` activities. The notation '*' indicates iterative execution – for example, continue execution performing these actions "until a winner is found". The notation '|' indicates that a selection action will take place, matching a given condition (e.g. perform bidding actions, then select the highest bidder).

Sub-Activities. The game of Five Hundred is only one example of a card game; we may consider Bridge as another example. Therefore, activities may be specialized – `cardGame` may be specialized to the sub-activities `fiveHundred` and `bridge`. Most of the part-activities of `cardGame` may be specialized similarly.

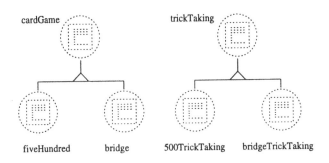

Fig. 9. Card Game: Sub-Activities

Figure 9 illustrates the hierarchical organizations of the `cardGame`: two generalization hierarchies where `fiveHundred` and `bridge` are sub-activities of `cardGame` and `500TrickTaking` and `bridgeTrickTaking` are sub-activities of `trickTaking`.

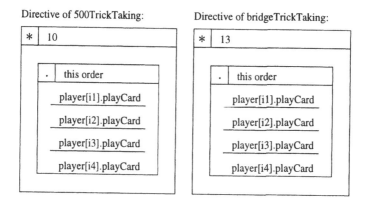

Fig. 10. `500TrickTaking` and `bridgeTrickTaking`

In Fig. 10, we describe the structure of the directives of the `500TrickTaking` and `bridgeTrickTaking` activities as specializations of the directive of the `trickTaking` directive (Fig. 8).

Properties of Activities. We have briefly mentioned how activities may have properties. The `roundPlay` activity has information about which cards have been played (`cards_played`) during the round and which tricks have so far been taken by the players (`tricks_taken`). The properties `cards_played` and `tricks_taken` of `roundPlay` are examples of *emergent properties* because they only emerge through the interplay of the part-activities of `roundPlay`. In other words, these properties do not exist independently of the part-activities.

The `bidding` activity has a property `bidding_steps` that details how each bidding step takes place, while the property `legal_bid` ensures that the next bid made by some player is a legal step (in relation to `bidding_steps`). The properties `bidding_steps` and `legal_bid` are examples of sub-activity properties for `500bidding` and `bridgeBidding`, that are refined (inherited) from the super-activity `bidding`. Thus, in the sub-activities, the checking of a bid's legality is specialized according to the rules of the particular card game.

In Fig. 11, the properties `cards_played` and `tricks_taken` for `roundPlay` and `bidding_steps` and `legal_bid` for `bidding` are shown in relation to the part-whole and generalization hierarchies.

Summary: Designing with Collective Activities. Activities are abstraction mechanisms over the interplay between entities, as exemplified by the card game ex-

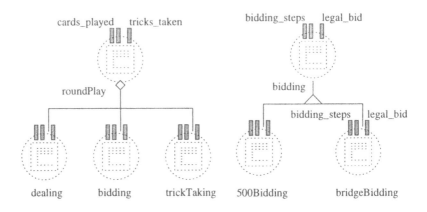

Fig. 11. Properties for `roundPlay` and `bidding`

ample. In the card game, the players are the entities; they are seen to *participate* in the game. For simplicity, we assume that the number and roles of players is fixed. During the game, the players will take turn either bidding, playing a card, etc – according to the rules of the card game (be it Five Hundred or Bridge). This sequence of behavior forms the card game activity. The legal sequence (and control) of possible behavior taken by the participating players is an abstraction over the possible games to be played in the specific type of card game.

The term *collective activity* denotes the abstraction of the actual sequence of behavior (in terms of the activity phenomenon) taken by the *participants* – on instantiation, the collective activity is *in progress*. The *directive* is the behavior description part of the collective activity. The term *collective structure* denotes the totality of the activity phenomenon and the participating phenomena – on instantiation, a collective structure is said to be *performing*.

Figure 12 illustrates the fundamental components of activities: the collective structure consisting of a collective activity (with directive) and a number of participants.

As the card game example indicates, the principles of aggregation and specialization may be applied to collective activities. In relation to aggregation, we have seen that it is possible to form whole-activities using subordinate part-activities. Elaborating on this, we can say that participants involved in these part-activities are seen as participants of the whole-activity. An activity's directive is also subject to aggregation. The directives of part-activities form the whole-activity's functionality – specifying the whole-activity's directive.

With respect to specialization, general activities and their participants (`review` and `coordinator`) may be refined (`paper_review` and `chairman`), and additional participants may be included. It is also possible to apply specialization to the directive of a general activity. This is possible by specializing the directives of an activity's part-activities (for example using virtual part-activities) or by explicitly adding to an activity's directive (for example via an `inner`-like mechanism).

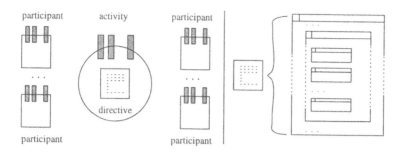

Fig. 12. Collective Structure, and Directive

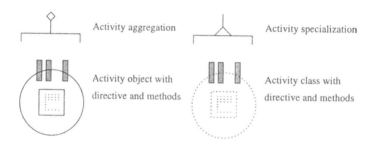

Fig. 13. Abstraction Diagrams

Figure 13 summarizes the class/object notation proposed for the activity as an abstraction mechanism. A general description of abstraction for activities in the form of classification, specialization and aggregation is given in (Kristensen 93b).

We have proposed a special notation for expressing the sequencing of an activity's directive. In (Kristensen & May 96) a more complete description of the diagrams is given. The diagrams employ the fundamental imperative sequencing forms (*sequence, selection, iteration*) , and are inspired from other diagrammatic notations (Nassi & Shneiderman 73).

3 Implementation of Activities

The following sections focus on the mapping from design with activities onto object-oriented language constructs. We discuss language constructs which, when added to existing object-oriented programming languages will directly support the activity as a language mechanism. Such constructs are seen as an extension to these languages rather than a radical shift in programming perspective. In the uni-sequential execution the implementation of activities may be supported by a set of abstract classes.

3.1 Integrating Activity and Participant

Fundamentally, we see activities as relations between entities. At the same time, participants will belong to an activity. Our language constructs to support such properties of collective behavior.

Activities as Relations. The activity is described by a *relation-class*. The participants are temporarily related through their participation in the activity.

Activities can be seen as a type of relation between domains (which represent the participants). Therefore, we may define an activity class A acting as a relation between participant classes B, C and D:

```
CLASS B ( ... )
CLASS C ( ... )
CLASS D ( ... )

CLASS A [B, C, D] ( ... )
```

Such a declaration may be further extended. In the following example, objects of class B, C, D may be accessed from the names rB, rC, rD. Given "rB : B", rB is a reference to an object of class B – while "rC :* C" means that rC may refer to an arbitrary number of C objects (one-to-many cardinality).

```
CLASS A [rB : B, rC :* C, rD : D] ( ... )
```

Figure 14 illustrates the relation A with domains B, C and D.

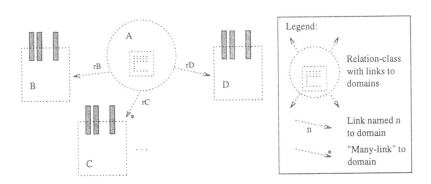

Fig. 14. Activity as a Relation

Figure 15 describes the `paper_review` activity in relation to its participants `chairman`, `reviewer`, and `author`, named respectively `the_chairman`, `reviewers`, and `an_author`:

```
CLASS chairman ( ... )
CLASS reviewer ( ... )
CLASS author ( ... )

CLASS paper_review
  [ the_chairman : chairman,
    reviewers :* reviewer,
    an_author : author ]
  ( ... )
```

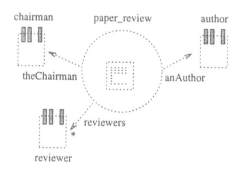

Fig. 15. `paper_review` as a Relation

The relations-class may be extended to include optional domains in order to describe the dynamically varying situation, where participant are coming and going during the activity. We shall not describe the use of activity objects for access of the participants etc, but refer to general descriptions of relation classes and objects in (Rumbaugh 87).

Participation using Roles. Often, participants in an activity have no logical existence when the collective structure is not performing. A person may take part in a `paper_review` activity several times during a year: the `reviewer` aspect of this person is only existent when he/she participates in the `paper_review`. Additionally, a participant may take part in several activities during some period of time, either in the same or different kinds of activities. Hence, different aspects of the participants may be relevant for different kinds of activities.

For example, a person taking part in a `paper_review` activity may be simultaneously writing a paper with some colleagues. In the `paper_writing` activity the person is an `author` whereas in the `paper_review` activity, he is a `reviewer`.

He/she may still take part in several paper_review and paper_writing activities during the same period. Language and modelling constructs should be able to give force to such design models.

Throughout the course of his/her lifetime, a person will take on roles *in addition* to his/her own functionality – at some point, a person will also act in the added capacity of a reviewer and as an author. To support these dynamic role changes, we introduce the concept of *role* (Kristensen & Østerbye 96) and *subject* (Harrison & Ossher 93). The concepts of role and subject allow different perspectives to be dynamically added to an object (for a given period of time), augmenting its integral properties. It is should be noted that this is distinct from dynamic class mutation as well as view of some existing object with its properties given.

In general, an entity may assume a number of roles at a given time. These roles may be allocated and deallocated dynamically. Roles are described as *role-classes*. A role-class is defined to be role for some class or other role-class. In the use of roles here, we define activities as relation-classes with role-classes as their domains. An object will play the roles given as a domain of the relation-class when the object takes part in an activity of the relation-class. This is then a means of describing the dynamic participation of entities in activities, as well as participation in several activities simultaneously.

R1 and R2 are role-classes for class C. The relation-classes A1 and A2 have the role-classes respectively R1 and R2 as one of their domain classes.

```
CLASS C ( ... )

CLASS R1 ROLE C ( ... )
CLASS R2 ROLE C ( ... )

CLASS A1 [... , R1, ...] ( ... )
CLASS A2 [... , R2, ...] ( ... )
```

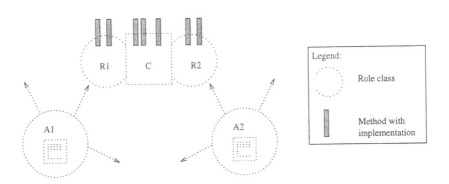

Fig. 16. participants as Role-Classes

Figure 16 illustrates a class C with role-classes R1 and R2 associated. An object of class C can acquire role-objects form R1 and R2 during its life cycle. The diagram shows that a role of role-class R1 (R2) is acquired for the activity A1 (A2).

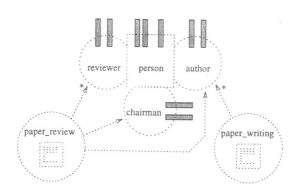

Fig. 17. Roles in `paper_review` and `paper_writing`

In Fig. 17, we illustrate how roles may be organized in the conference example. The diagram describes how `reviewer` is a role-class to `person` when a `person` is engaged in a `paper_review` activity. The same `person` may may engaged in a paper writing activity, `paper_writing`, where he/she plays the role of an `author`. A `person` object can have role-objects from these role-classes allocated and deallocated during its life-cycle.

```
CLASS person ( ... )

CLASS reviewer ROLE person ( ... )
CLASS author ROLE person ( ... )
CLASS chairman ROLE person ( ... )

CLASS paper_review
  [ the_chairman : chairman,
    the_reviewers :* reviewer,
    an_author : author ]
  ( ... )

CLASS paper_writing
  [ the_authors :* author ]
  ( ... )
```

3.2 Simulation of Activities

In uni-sequential execution (a single thread at one time), we need to integrate the participant's behavior with the progress of the corresponding activity. Either the activity or one of its participants is executing. To model how the participants are taking part in the activity, execution control has to switch between a participant and the activity to secure coordination. In the support of activities in the uni-sequential case we distinguish between *initiating* activities, where the activity is in charge and the participants are invoked from the activity in order to contribute to the process, and *reactive* activities, where the participants take initiative and the activity is 'awakened' to control and guide the process.

Initiating Activities. Participants may be seen as passive objects controlled and activated by the collective activity – the initiating activity. In this scenario, the activity will have the initiative towards the participants – invoking methods of the participants, in order to make them contribute to the progress of the activity. A participant may then (acting on its internal logic or by asking the user for direction) invoke one of the activity's methods. The activity is seen to be continuously guiding the participants, controlling their behavior through its method invocations.

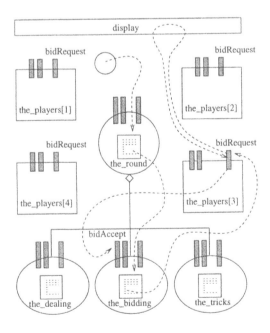

Fig. 18. Card Game: Initiating round

The following simplified version of the card game illustrates initiating activities – a single round of a Five Hundred game is modeled. An activity object the_round, will sequentially invoke three part-activities: the_dealing, the_bidding and the_tricks. Each of these part-activities respectively model the dealing, bidding and trick-taking phases of a round. The four players (the_players[4]) are the participants in the_round. Each player has a number of operations which model the various requests he/she can make during the game. The life-cycle of bidding is to repeatedly find and ask the next player to bid until the bidding is complete (according to the rules of the game). In the example, we have the operation bidRequest which asks a player to make a bid. The actual bid is registered by invoking the bidAccept method of the part-activity the_bidding. The bidding class has an operation bidAccept available to the players for placing their bids. In Fig. 18, we illustrate activities, part-activities, participants and a calling sequence in the example.

Reactive Activities. Alternatively, participants may be seen as active – actively executing or having some interface to 'active' users who will invoke the participants' methods. The main point to note is that participants will have the initiative towards the collective activity – the reactive activity, calling methods of the activity. In turn, these calls may provide feedback to the participants to direct what kind of 'input' is required next. The role of the collective activity is to police the behavior of the participants (rather than actively controlling), in some cases prohibiting a participant from performing certain actions.

In the simplified version of the card game, the life-cycle of the_bidding object is lie dormant until activated. When 'awakened' by a player, the_bidding object verifies the player's bid. This life-cycle continues until bidding is complete. For example, we have a player who makes a bid by invoking the operation bidRequest. The actual bid is registered by invoking the bidAccept method of the part-activity the_bidding. Once activated, the directive of the_bidding checks the legality of this bid. Also note that in this design, the whole-activity the_round lies dormant until the part-activity the_bidding wakes it from its waiting state. In Fig. 19, we illustrate activities, part-activities, participants and a calling sequence in the example.

Simulation by Abstract Classes. In the case of uni-sequential execution an alternative to extensions to existing language constructs is a set of abstract classes to support the use of activities. In (Kristensen & May 94) the implementation of both initiating and reactive activities in C++ (Stroustrup 91) is presented. In (Kristensen & May 96) the classes are expressed in an abstract, general object-oriented programming language – which may be translated into an existing language. Only initiating activities are simulated in detail. In the simulation it is assumed that classes can have action clauses, virtual references/methods, and inheritance for methods (action clauses and methods are extended by means of the inner mechanism originally introduced in SIMULA (Dahl et al. 84).

In these approaches we *simulate* activities in some existing object-oriented programming language, and we rely on the mechanisms available in the language.

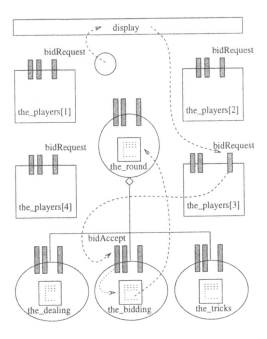

Fig. 19. Card Game: Reacting round

These mechanisms support – and restrict – our expressive freedom in describing the aggregation and specialization of participants and activity directives.

3.3 Concurrent Execution in Activities

In general, objects may execute concurrently (or multi-sequentially with interleaved execution, with only one active object at a time). We need special communication and synchronization constructs to properly describe the interplay between active (concurrently executing) objects, – in the form of activities and participants.

Active Objects. We introduce briefly a simple model with active objects. The ACTION clause illustrates that objects like oC may have an individual action part – on instantiation, an object will immediately execute its action part and is inherently active.

```
CLASS C
(
  METHOD M   ( ... )
  METHOD M'' ( ... )
  OBJECT R : C'
```

```
ACTION:
   ...
   M''
   ...
   R.MM
)
```

```
OBJECT oC : C
```

The description of the action part may involve the activation of methods in class C and methods for other objects than oC. Because the objects are active, the interaction between objects is usually coordinated by means of various forms of language mechanisms[3] available for the synchronization of the execution of the life cycle of the object and method activation requests from other objects. In the model we assume that when the object oC attempts a method request to R by R.MM, then oC must wait until R explicitly accepts this invocation. When the invocation is accepted the objects are synchronized and the invocation can take place.

Multi-Sequential Execution. The action part of an activity object describes the interaction of the activity with other entities (activities/participants). The collective activity is seen as a supplementary part of the life cycle of its participating entities – the life cycle of such an entity is described both in its own action part *and* in the various collective activities in which it is participating.

Given activity A and participant rC, some form of communication will take place between these two objects during execution. If rC is executing and A attempts a method execution rC.M, then A must wait until rC explicitly accepts this invocation. To avoid the additional synchronization arising from such a scheme, we specify that a participating entity may execute its action part *interleaved* with that of the method being invoked from an activity in which the entity takes part. For example, if rC is executing its action part and A calls rC.M, both method M and rC's action part may execute in interleaved fashion.

The following schematic example illustrates the mechanisms introduced:

```
CLASS A [rB : B, rC : C]
( ...
```

```
ACTION:
   ...   rC::M   ...   rB::rC.M   ...
)
```

```
OBJECT oA : A
```

The activity object oA is of activity class A. The object rC is a participant of class C – we assume that rC denotes the object oC. The construct rC::M means

---

[3] According to (Chin & Chanson 91) this is an *active object model*; the model is *static* with exactly one thread per object and the thread is controlled by the description in the action part.

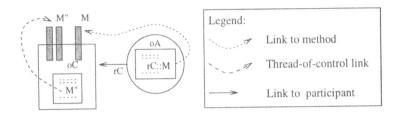

Fig. 20. Execution of `rC::M`

that the object `rC` is requested to execute its method `M` (Fig. 20) – because it is requested by an activity `oA` it is as if object `rC` itself requested the execution of `M`. This corresponds to the object `rC` invoking one of its own methods – the only difference is that the description is given outside `oC`. At the time of this request, the object `oC` may be executing its action part (e.g. executing `M''`). Here, the method `M` and the action part of `oC` are executed interleaved: at certain (language defined) locations, `oC` will switch between the execution of `M` and its action part.

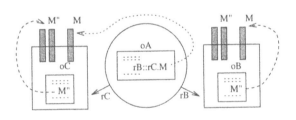

Fig. 21. Execution of `rB::rC.M`

The construct `rC::M` is only one example of the mechanisms that may be employed in collective activities and participants. The other example is `rB::rC.M`, where the participant `rB` requests `rC` to execute its method `M` (Fig. 21). In this case the activity specifies both the invoking participant `rB`, the invoked participant `rC` and the method `M`. Because this situation is as if the object `rB` itself requested the method execution `rC.M` a synchronization may be involved between `rC` and `rB` (as a case of ordinary communication between the active objects `rB` and `rC`).

In the `paper_review` example, `the_chairman` and `the_reviewers` may be actively performing other actions than those in connection with the `paper_review` (such as research, teaching, writing). It would be natural to describe such tasks in the life cycle of these objects (in the action part). Furthermore, `the_chairman` and `the_reviewers` may be engaged in other collective activities concurrently (e.g. participating in a selection committee, writing a paper) – possibly in different roles.

```
CLASS reviewer
( ...
  METHOD remind : ( ... )
  METHOD submit : ( ... )
  METHOD is_busy : ( ... )
)


CLASS author
( ...
  METHOD submit_paper : ( ... )
)


CLASS chairman
( ...
  METHOD distribute : ( ... )
)


CLASS paper_review
  [ the_chairman : chairman,
    the_reviewers :* reviewer,
    an_Author : author ]
( ...

ACTION:
  ...
  the_author::submit_paper
  the_chairman::distribute
  ...
  if the_reviewers[i]::is_busy then
     the_chairman::the_reviewers[i].remind
  ...
)


OBJECT a_paper_review : paper_review
```

The situation could arise where one of the_reviewers did not supply a referee report within the specified time. Here, it is possible for the paper_review activity to monitor the overall progress of the activity, checking for such an occurrence – the activity may then send a reminder to one of these the_reviewers on behalf of the_chairman.

Figure 22 demonstrates how a paper_review activity may request participants (here the_reviewers[i]) to invoke methods while they are performing their own sequence of execution. The directive shows how the activity may communicate on behalf of the participants (here the_chairman).

In general, activities may be performed simultaneously – interleaved or concurrent (e.g. paper_review and paper_writing activities). Nested execution is supported by the sequential execution of part-activities. Additionally, overlapping execution of part-activities (either interleaved or concurrent) may also be supported (the prepare_review_process and the carry_out_review_process may over-

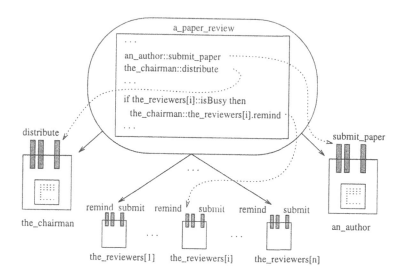

Fig. 22. Requests sent by `paper_review`

lap without problems to speed up the process).

The refinement of the directive of an activity in the multi-sequential case – by means of a multiple **inner** mechanism (Kristensen 93b) – is motivated by two principles. Firstly, it should be possible to describe additional sequences of action which must be executed simultaneously (interleaved or concurrent) with sequences of the existing directive. Secondly, it should be possible to ensure that parts of the existing directive of an activity are refined, allowing the part of the existing directive *and* the refined part to execute together as a unit. These two principles may be applied in a mixed sequence in the refinement of the directive.

4 Experiments

In this section we review some practical and theoretical experiments based on the notion of activities; we classify activities in the dichotomy of software abstraction; we summarize the experience from a project focused on the construction of a framework for card games; and we compare implementations based on design patterns and the activity abstraction.

Where should activities be classified in the dichotomy of software abstraction? Activities are distinct from frameworks and design patterns. A framework (Johnson & Foote 88) is a software architecture, including an abstract program. In essence, it provides a reusable design solution for a specific class of software – the design decisions that are common to the framework's domain are captured. Frameworks are specialized to become applications in the domain.

A design pattern can be seen as an organizational idiom, comprising an

abstract code component. A pattern represents the core of a solution to similar recurring problems, comprising a general arrangement of classes/objects (Gamma et al. 94). Design patterns are more abstract design elements than frameworks (they may be applied in the construction and design of a framework) and their architectural granularity is finer.

The activity is a modelling and programming mechanism that may be used to describe a wide variety of programs and program fragments, abstract or concrete. It is an abstraction mechanism, able to be used to create abstractions of varying definition – from the more abstract/general (design patterns) to the more concrete (frameworks). This abstraction mechanism enables us to have another basic component in the design vocabulary we use when creating such abstractions.

Frameworks, design patterns and abstraction mechanisms are also used differently in the program development process. The universe of frameworks and design patterns is not, by nature, finite. Therefore, it will be necessary to search for and identify appropriate frameworks/design patterns that may be applicable to the problem. In the case of a framework, you will need to understand its functionality and how to customize it. With design patterns, it is necessary to recognize the context in which a pattern could be applied and how it should be realized in a concrete design.

An abstraction mechanism forms part of the language. It is therefore *fundamental* in its influence on how we conceive the world around us, how we initially form our understanding, and then later in expressing it. Such mechanisms give us a basic lexicon with which we can describe higher-level, structured abstractions – like frameworks and design patterns.

Card Games and C++. The activity abstraction was investigated in a project described in (May 94). The objective of the project was to explore issues related to the design and construction of object-oriented frameworks – the C++ language was used to build software artifacts through the course of the project.

The problem domain on which the study concentrated was that of card games, namely, designing a framework for writing card game applications. Several pieces of software were produced: a Blackjack game (to gain experience in the problem area), a card game framework, and a Five Hundred game.

We explored the activity abstraction to address the issue of representing more complicated sequences of interplay yet simplifying their complexity. A framework for activities was created, which later became the basis for a card game framework. This was eventually used to create the Five Hundred game.

Limitations were encountered using C++. In its 'standard' form, the language lacks multi-sequential and concurrent mechanisms – it is not possible to properly represent multiple executing active objects or reactive activities. Further, there is no support for locality.

Overall, the project indicated that most mainstream object-oriented languages had little support for the facilities required to accurately simulate activities. While activities could be implemented in such languages, the absence of such support will result in an implementation solution that does not properly

match the design solution – and is less intuitive. Languages should provide more flexible constructs (e.g. sub-method inheritance, locality, roles) to enable the design model to be implemented *and communicated* in a far more natural way.

Conference Organizing and the Mediator. The activity abstraction was compared to design patterns, especially the Mediator (Gamma et al. 94), in an implementation project. Descriptions of a subset of a conference organizing system was developed and compared.

The intent of the Mediator pattern is to "Define an object that encapsulates how a set of objects interact. Mediator promotes loose coupling by keeping objects from referring to each other explicitly, and it lets you vary their interaction independently".

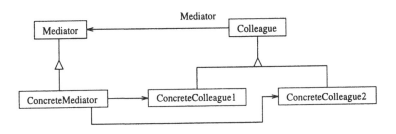

Fig. 23. Structure of the Mediator Pattern

In Fig. 23 the structure of the Mediator pattern is reproduced. The `Mediator` class corresponds to an activity and the `Colleague` classes to participants. The `ConcreteMediator` class implements cooperative behaviour by coordinating `Colleague` objects, and knows and maintains its colleagues. Each `Colleague` class knows its `Mediator` object, and each `Colleague` class communicates with its mediator whenever it would have otherwise communicated with another colleague.

From our description in the experiment, the Mediator pattern appears to be similar to how we characterise the collective behavior of activities. Indeed, there is centralisation of control into an object – which manages the interaction between other objects. But while the overall architectural techniques are similar, motivation and focus for collective behavior is different.

At its heart, the design pattern aims to provide an abstract, general design solution to a set of problems. It is structured to be less well-defined and more informal. In short, it is an abstraction that is not supposed to be set in concrete: its malleability and generality is its strength.

On the other hand, our approach has been at a more elemental and atomic level. The purpose of our research was to inquire into the nature of interaction – first, our intuitive understanding, then mapping into an object-oriented domain. We have therefore characterised and defined how we picture activities: the ways in which object-oriented concepts may be applied to them, and how they relate to each other and their participants.

The activity is an abstraction mechanism – a type of brick that can be used to build abstractions. In the same way that a *class* is used to create abstractions (like design patterns), the *activity* is used as well-defined component in constructing abstractions. In short, the activity is a mechanism that is supposed to be capable of extension, but well-defined and less vague.

Similar to the class, it is used 'as is' rather than requiring a mapping into specific domains (like design patterns). Therefore, it is possible to envisage building libraries of components that have been constructed using activities (and other mechanisms). The nature of this abstraction mechanism covers the ambit of modelling and programming languages. Thus, we can use activities as building mechanisms in creating modelling abstractions then isomorphically map into a concrete language.

Furthermore, the emphasis of the Mediator pattern is to promote loose coupling and encapsulate object interaction. The activity abstraction mechanism also seeks to give force to these goals; of themselves, they are useful and worthwhile objectives. But the emphasis of our inquiry was to represent and give force to the properties of interaction – collective and otherwise.

We also investigated beyond the generalised object arrangement scheme embodied by the Mediator. The present paper looks at a dichotomy of how activities can be classified into initiating and reactive forms, how they may exploit the power of object-oriented properties in a natural fashion, and supporting the characteristics of activities using concepts such as *relations* and *roles*. This clearly exceeds the scope and definition of the Mediator pattern.

In essence, activities are used to build abstractions – solutions.

5 Summary

The underlying assumption in this paper is that in existing object-oriented methodologies and languages, objects appear as isolated elements with an implicit and poor description of the interplay structure between them. However, as human beings we identify such interplay structures as another kind of phenomena – usually known as activities – and inspired of this kind of phenomena we introduce an abstraction mechanism, which may be used to model the interplay structures. This language mechanism – the activity – is expressive and powerful for the modeling of organization and interplay of usual objects, – the collective behavior of objects.

Related Work. While not discussed explicitly, collective activities are within the ambit of Booch's description of an object (Booch 94): "tangible and/or visible thing; something capable of intellectual apprehension; and something toward which thought or action is directed". Most pointedly, "an object models some part of reality and is therefore something that exists in time and space".

In OMT (Rumbaugh et al. 91) the dynamic model is a collection of state diagrams that interact via shared events. A *state diagram* describes the life cycle of a class of objects – but only from a local perspective. State diagrams are also related to the object structure: the aggregation of objects implies the aggregation of the state diagrams of these objects, resulting in composite states; the specialization of classes implies that a subclass inherits the state diagram of its superclass and together with the state diagram added it works as a composite of concurrent state diagrams.

Responsibilities, collaborations, and *contracts* from (Wirfs-Brock et al. 90) define the dependencies between objects and subsystems. However, these are only concerned with the static dependencies, and there is no support for the description of the dynamic interplay between them.

Use cases from (Jacobson et al. 92) models system functionality. Use cases – with actors of various kinds – are abstractions of the user's interaction with a system. The actor and system in dialogue is a sequence of transactions each initiated by some stimulus from the actor. An actor may be involved in a number of use cases. A user is seen as an instantiation of an actor, and an actual execution of an interaction session with a user is seen as an instantiation of a use case. This instantiation yields an object. A use case is described by a state transition graph, and user stimuli imply state changes. The description of a use case is organized as a basic course and several alternative courses. A use case may be seen as a special case of a collective activity, which is restricted to the system functionality; it is an abstraction, but no generalization and aggregation hierarchies are discussed for use cases, only the distinction between abstract/concrete use cases, as well as the insertion of a "part" use case into another by means of *extends*.

BETA (Madsen et al. 93) has active objects in the form described here but no mechanisms for supporting the combined execution of the directive of an activity-object and the life cycles of its participants. The aggregation and specialization as presented here can (with a few exceptions) be seen as an adaptation of corresponding mechanisms of BETA. Relations and roles – as described here – are not supported.

Contracts (Helm et al. 90) are specifications of behavioral dependencies between cooperating objects. Contracts are object-external abstractions and include invariants to be maintained by the cooperating objects. The inter-object dependencies are made explicit by means of supporting language mechanisms. The result is that the actions – i.e. the reactions of an object to changes – are removed from the object and described explicitly in the contracts: the objects are turned into reactive objects, whereas the reaction-patterns for an object in its various relations with other objects are described in the corresponding contracts. The intention of the contract mechanism is not the modeling of real world phenomena and their interdependencies – rather, it is to have a mathematical, centralized description that supports provable properties. In (Holland 92) a further development of contracts is presented. Contracts are used for representing and reusing algorithmic programming clichés.

According to (Gamma et al. 94) the *Mediator design pattern* has the following benefits and drawbacks: It limits subclassing. It decouples colleagues. It simplifies object protocols. It abstracts how objects cooperate. It centralizes control. These qualities are also valid for the activity abstraction. In contrast, the description of the Mediator pattern does not include any considerations about multi-sequential execution of participants and activities. A straightforward use of the Mediator pattern the multi-sequential case will certainly lead to a lot of unnecessary synchronization. Furthermore, we have presented a notation/language constructs for activities for use both in the design phase and in the implementation phase. Most design patterns, including the Mediator pattern, can be used in both these phases too. The activity is defined differently for these phases, in order to support the informal, intuitive description during design, as well as the formal, though still high level description in terms of relations, roles etc at the implementation level.

There are well-known, existing abstraction mechanisms that are commonly used to construct *control abstractions* (Tennent 81). Such examples include the procedure, coroutine, and various process mechanisms. Similarly, the activity mechanism supports abstraction of control. However, in the same way that the class is not merely equivalent to a record or structure, the activity mechanism integrates concepts of functional behavior with object-oriented modelling capabilities. Activities can be used to coordinate/control objects – not merely stating an order or sequence of action, but explicitly stating the nature of the interplay: the participants, their relationships, and the actions that take place between activities and participants.

In (Aksit et al. 94) *Abstract Communication Types* (ACTs) are classes/objects in the object-oriented language Sina. The purpose of ACTs is to structure, abstract and reuse object interactions. The *composition filters* model is applied to abstract communications among objects by introducing *input* and *output composition filters* that affect the received and sent messages. Using an input filter a message can be accepted or rejected and, for example, initiate the execution of a method. Inheritance is not directly expressed by a language construct but is simulated by the input filter by delegating a message to the methods supported by *internal* objects. Several primitive filters are available in Sina, e.g. *Dispatch*, *Meta*, *Error*, *Wait*, and *RealTime*. In ACTs the Meta filter is used to accept a received message and to reify this as an object of class *Message*. The requirements for ACTs include large scale synchronization and reflection upon messages; the ACT concept is used as an object-oriented modeling technique in analysis and design. ACTs appear to be a technical, very comprehensive concept that – according to (Aksit et al. 94) – supports a wide variety of object interaction kinds including action abstraction, distributed algorithms, coordinated behavior, inter-object constraints, etc.

Results. The main results are summarized as:

– Intuitive and general understanding of the fundamentals of activities as abstractions for collective behavior. Activities support the modeling of the organization of and interplay between objects in object-oriented analysis, design, and implementation.

- Activities support modeling that is more similar and intuitive to our human understanding – in our clustering of information and abstracting of detail (particularly of processes): A notation to support the modeling with activities in analysis and design.
- In the implementation activities offer an orthogonal solution to expressing and manipulating collective behavior of objects:
  (1) Abstract classes for the support of implementation of activities.
  (2) Language features for direct support of activities as an abstraction mechanism in object-oriented programming languages.

Challenges. There exist numerous issues with activities that remain to be investigated and/or resolved:

Dynamic participation: An activity relates the interplay between various participating entities. The actual entities participating may change during the activity – entities may join or leave the activity. This has been achieved to a certain degree by allowing participants to assume additional roles during the life cycle of an activity. However, this is a participant-centric view of dynamic participation. From the activity's point of view, it is not possible to tell which participants are involved in the activity. (This is a general problem in programming languages – to be able to "know" which objects are associated in a given relationship.)

Part-whole activity state access: It is an open question as to the degree of state access enjoyed between part-activities and their whole-activities. Should a part-activity have state access to its enclosing whole-activity? Part-activities will not generally execute in isolation or ignorance of their whole-activities' properties – however, a relatively high degree of encapsulation should be enforced between activity classes. Conversely, it is a question as to whether a whole-activity has automatic access to the state of its part-activities.

References

Aksit, M., Wakita, K., Bosch, J., Bergmans, L., Yonezawa, A.: Abstracting Object Interactions Using Composition Filters. Proceedings of the ECOOP '93 Workshop on Object-based Distributed Processing, Guerraoui, R., Nierstrasz, O., Riveill, M. (Eds.), LNCS 791, Springer-Verlag, 1994.

Booch, G.: Object Oriented Analysis and Design with Applications. Benjamin/Cummings, 1994.

Chin, R. S., Chanson, S. T.: Distributed Object-Based Programming Systems. ACM Computing Surveys, Vol. 23, No. 1, 1991.

Dahl, O. J., Myhrhaug, B., Nygaard, K.: SIMULA 67 Common Base Language. Norwegian Computing Center, edition February 1984.

Gamma, E., Helm, R., Johnson, R., Vlissides, J.: Design Patterns: Elements of Reusable Object-Oriented Software. Addison Wesley, 1994.

Harrison, W., Ossher, H.: Subject-Oriented Programming (A Critique of Pure Objects). Proceedings of the Object-Oriented Programming Systems, Languages and Applications Conference, 1993.

Helm, R., Holland, I. M., Gangopadhyay, D.: Contracts: Specifying Behavioral Compositions in Object-oriented Systems. Proceedings of the European Conference on Object-Oriented Programming / Object-Oriented Programming Systems, Languages and Applications Conference, 1990.

Holland, I. M.: Specifying Reusable Components Using Contracts. Proceedings of the European Conference on Object-Oriented Programming, 1992.

Jacobson, I., Christerson, M., Jonsson, P., Overgaard, G.: Object-Oriented Software Engineering, A Use Case Driven Approach. Addison Wesley, 1992.

Johnson, R. E., Foote, B.: Designing Reusable Classes. Journal of Object-Oriented Programming, 1988.

Kristensen, B. B.: Transverse Classes & Objects in Object-Oriented Analysis, Design, and Implementation. Journal of Object-Oriented Programming, 1993.

Kristensen, B. B.: Transverse Activities: Abstractions in Object-Oriented Programming. Proceedings of International Symposium on Object Technologies for Advanced Software (ISOTAS'93), 1993.

Kristensen, B. B., May, D. C. M.: Modeling Activities in C++. Proceedings of International Conference on Technology of Object-Oriented Languages and Systems, 1994.

Kristensen, B. B., May, D. C. M.: Modeling with Activities: Abstractions for Collective Behavior. R 96-2001, IES, Aalborg University, 1996.

Kristensen, B. B., K. Østerbye: Roles: Conceptual Abstraction Theory & Practical Language Issues. Accepted for publication in a Special Issue of Theory and Practice of Object Systems (TAPOS) on Subjectivity in Object-Oriented Systems, 1996.

Madsen, O. L., Møller-Pedersen, B., Nygaard, K.: Object Oriented Programming in the Beta Programming Language. Addison Wesley 1993.

May, D. C. M.: Frameworks: An Excursion into Metalevel Design and Other Discourses. Department of Computer Science, Monash University, 1994.

Nassi, I., Shneiderman, B.: Flowchart Techniques for Structured Programming. Sigplan Notices, 8 (8), 1973.

Rumbaugh, J.: Relations as Semantic Constructs in an Object–Oriented Language. Proceedings of the Object–Oriented Programming Systems, Languages and Applications Conference, 1987.

Rumbaugh, J., Blaha, M., Premerlani, W., Eddy, F., Lorensen, W.: Object-Oriented Modeling and Design. Prentice-Hall 1991.

Stroustrup, B.: The C++ Programming Language. 2/E, Addison-Wesley 1991.

Tennent, R. D.: Principles of Programming Languages. Prentice Hall, 1981.

Wirfs-Brock, R., Wilkerson, B., Wiener, L.: Designing Object-Oriented Software. Prentice Hall, 1990.

Author index

Lecture Notes in Computer Science

For information about Vols. 1–1026

please contact your bookseller or Springer-Verlag